Research Anthology on Usage and Development of Open Source Software

Information Resources Management Association
USA

Volume II

Published in the United States of America by
IGI Global
Engineering Science Reference (an imprint of IGI Global)
701 E. Chocolate Avenue
Hershey PA, USA 17033
Tel: 717-533-8845
Fax: 717-533-8661
E-mail: cust@igi-global.com
Web site: http://www.igi-global.com

Library of Congress Cataloging-in-Publication Data

Names: Information Resources Management Association, editor.
Title: Research anthology on usage and development of open source software
  / Information Resources Management Association, editor.
Description: Hershey, PA : Engineering Science Reference, [2021] | Includes
  bibliographical references and index. | Summary: "This comprehensive
  reference book covers the latest and most emerging research, concepts,
  and theories for those working with open source software with the goal
  of demonstrating various ways of its tremendous potential with room for
  improvement and advancement, though it has faced challenges and issues
  throughout the years"-- Provided by publisher.
Identifiers: LCCN 2021030071 (print) | LCCN 2021030072 (ebook) | ISBN
  9781799891581 (hardcover) | ISBN 9781799891598 (ebook)
Subjects: LCSH: Shareware (Computer software) | Open source software. |
  Computer software--Development.
Classification: LCC QA76.76.S46 R47 2021 (print) | LCC QA76.76.S46
  (ebook) | DDC 005.3--dc23
LC record available at https://lccn.loc.gov/2021030071
LC ebook record available at https://lccn.loc.gov/2021030072

British Cataloguing in Publication Data
A Cataloguing in Publication record for this book is available from the British Library.

For electronic access to this publication, please contact: eresources@igi-global.com.

Editor-in-Chief

Mehdi Khosrow-Pour, DBA
Information Resources Management Association, USA

Associate Editors

Steve Clarke, *University of Hull, UK*
Murray E. Jennex, *San Diego State University, USA*
Ari-Veikko Anttiroiko, *University of Tampere, Finland*

Editorial Advisory Board

Sherif Kamel, *American University in Cairo, Egypt*
In Lee, *Western Illinois University, USA*
Jerzy Kisielnicki, *Warsaw University, Poland*
Amar Gupta, *Arizona University, USA*
Craig van Slyke, *University of Central Florida, USA*
John Wang, *Montclair State University, USA*
Vishanth Weerakkody, *Brunel University, UK*

List of Contributors

Table of Contents

Section 2
Multi-Industry Applications

Section 3
Prediction Models, Big Data, and Statistics

Preface

Great emphasis has recently been placed on the accessibility of all research. From the Open Access movement that is driving authors to ensure that their research is openly available without purchase to the open collaboration ideals of open source software, it is clear that researchers recognize the importance that openly available content has on the advancement and innovation of society. Open source software is growing as the world increasingly implements new technology into all aspects of life; open source software is one of many innovations that has become more popular as it continues to grow and offers benefits in a wide range of areas. Allowing users to use, study, change, and distribute the software and its source code, open source software has allowed for the improvement and efficiency of systems in a variety of industries, including education, finance, waste reduction, and more.

Thus, the *Research Anthology on Usage and Development of Open Source Software* seeks to fill the void for an all-encompassing and comprehensive reference book covering the latest and emerging research, concepts, and theories for those working with open source software. This two-volume reference collection of reprinted IGI Global book chapters and journal articles that have been handpicked by the editor and editorial team of this research anthology on this topic will empower computer scientists, programmers, developers, systems engineers, designers, industry professionals, teachers, academicians, researchers, and students with an advanced understanding of critical issues and advancements of opensource software.

The *Research Anthology on Usage and Development of Open Source Software* is organized into three sections that provide comprehensive coverage of important topics. The sections are:

1. Development, Standards, and User Expectations;
2. Multi-Industry Applications; and
3. Prediction Models, Big Data, and Statistics.

The following paragraphs provide a summary of what to expect from this invaluable reference tool.

Section 1, "Development, Standards, and User Expectations," provides investigations on the development and design of open source software, challenges to its standardization, and what users expect from adopting open source software into their systems. The first chapter of this section, "A Systematic Review of Attributes and Techniques for Open Source Software Evolution Analysis," by Profs. Munish Saini and Kuljit Kaur Chahal of Guru Nanak Dev University, India, uses various techniques for understanding the OSS evolution process from different perspectives and reports a meta-data analysis of the systematic literature review on the topic in order to understand its current state and to identify opportunities for the future. The following chapter, "Exploratory Analysis of Free and Open Source Software Ecology," by Prof. K.G. Srinivasa of Chaudhary Brahm Prakash Government Engineering College, India and Profs.

Ganesh Chandra Deka and Krishnaraj P.M. from M. S. Ramaiah Institute of Technology, India, confirms the existence of power law in Sourceforge.net and reveals that there is a separate core and are periphery groups of developers in Sourceforge.net, as well as in other forges like Freecode and Rubyforge. The next chapter, "Open Source Software Development Challenges: A Systematic Literature Review on GitHub," by Profs. Abdulkadir Seker and Halil Arslan of Sivas Cumhuriyet University, Turkey and Profs. Banu Diri and Mehmet Fatih Amasyalı from Yıldız Technical University, Turkey, conducts a literature review on studies that used GitHub data based on a GitHub dataset source study instead of a keyword-based search in digital libraries. Another chapter in this section, "On Challenges for Implementing ISO Standards in Software: Can Both Open and Closed Standards Be Implemented in Open Source Software?" by Profs. Björn Lundell and Jonas Gamalielsson of the University of Skövde, Sweden and Prof. Andrew Katz of the University of Skövde, Sweden and Moorcrofts LLP, UK, elaborates on the implications and suggests ways of addressing the challenges of implementing standards in software. Another chapter in this section, "Analysis of Free and Open Source Software (FOSS) Product in Web Based Client-Server Architecture," by Prof. Pushpa Singh of Accurate Institute of Management and Technology, Greater Noida, India and Prof. Narendra Singh from G. L. Bajaj Institute of Management and Research, Greater Noida, India, studies FOSS products used in web-based client server architecture and provides information about FOSS product such as FireFox (web browser), Apache (web server), and MySQL (RDBMS). An additional chapter, "Strategy of Good Software Governance: FLOSS in the State of Turkey," by Prof. Hüseyin Tolu of Recep Tayyip Erdogan University, Turkey, discusses in what matters and for what reasons software governance of Turkey has locked into the ecosystems of PCSS; considers causes, effects, and potential outcomes of not utilizing FLOSS in the state of Turkey; and argues that Turkey has taken a pragmatic decision-making process of software in the emerging cybernetics that leads and contributes to techno-social externality of PCSS hegemonic stability. Following this chapter is "On Solving the Multi-Objective Software Package Upgradability Problem" by Profs. Noureddine Aribi and Yahia Lebbah of Lab. LITIO, University of Oran 1, Oran, Algeria, which proposes a Leximax approach based on mixed integer linear programming (MILP) to tackle the upgradability problem while ensuring efficiency and fairness requirements between the objective functions. The next chapter, "Finding Influential Nodes in Sourceforge.net Using Social Network Analysis," by Prof. K.G. Srinivasa of Chaudhary Brahm Prakash Government Engineering College, India and Profs. Ganesh Chandra Deka and Krishnaraj P.M. from M. S. Ramaiah Institute of Technology, India, studies the contribution of volunteers in the development of Free and Open Source Software in Sourceforge.net and discovers the small set of developers who can maximize the information flow in the network. An additional chapter in this section, "The Cultural and Institutional Barrier of Knowledge Exchanges in the Development of Open Source Software," by Prof. Ikbal Maulana of Indonesian Institute of Sciences, Indonesia, discusses the diffusion and development of OSS in Indonesia after the government took "Indonesia, Go Open Source" (IGOS) initiative, which initiative united government organizations, communities, R&D institutions, and universities. A concluding chapter, "Understanding Users' Contributions in Open Source Software Communities: A Social Influence Perspective," by Prof. Tao Zhou of Hangzhou Dianzi University, China, examines user contributions in OSS communities and indicates that contribution intention is significantly affected by social identity, which includes cognitive, affective and evaluative identity, as well as that the subjective norm has a negative effect on contribution intention. The next chapter, "Trust in Open Source Software Development Communities: A Comprehensive Analysis," by Prof. Amitpal Singh Sohal of IKG Punjab Technical University, Kapurthala, Punjab, India; Prof. Sunil Kumar Gupta from Beant College of Engineering and Technology, Gurdaspur, Punjab, India; and Prof. Hardeep Singh of Guru

Nanak Dev University, Amritsar, Punjab, India, presents the significance of trust for the formation of an Open Source Software Development (OSSD) community and offers an overview of various existing trust models, which aids in the development of a trust evaluation framework for OSSD communities. Another concluding chapter, "The Impact of Project Initiators on Open Source Software Project Success: Evidence From Emerging Hosting Platform Gitee," by Prof. Ling Wang of China University of Political Science and Law (CUPL), Beijing, China and Prof. Jinxiao Wang from Tsinghua University, Beijing, China, focuses on studying the role of open source software project initiator in affecting the OSS project success from the perspective of individual and collective behaviors. The next chapter, "Does an Open Source Development Environment Facilitate Conventional Project Management Approaches and Collaborative Work?" by Prof. Richard Garling of American Military University, USA, focuses on how an open source development environment facilitates conventional Waterfall project management approaches and how an open source development environment facilitates Agile project collaborative work. The final chapter in this section, "Prospects of Open Source Software for Maximizing the User Expectations in Heterogeneous Network," by Prof. Pushpa Singh of Accurate Institute of Management and Technology, Greater Noida, India and Prof. Rajeev Agrawal from G.L. Bajaj Institute of Technology and Management, Greater Noida, India, focuses on the prospects of open source software and tools for maximizing the user expectations in heterogeneous networks.

Section 2, "Multi-Industry Applications," considers the various uses and benefits of applying open source software in different fields from education to banking. The opening chapter in this section, "Open Source Software Usage in Education and Research: Network Traffic Analysis as an Example," by Profs. Vladimir V. Syuzev, Ark M. Andreev, and Samih M. Jammoul of Bauman Moscow State Technical University, Russia, presents the trend of using open source software in higher education, discusses pros and cons of using open source software in engineering education, presents network traffic analysis as an example of recent effective research topics, and provides a set of open source tools to perform the research's practical steps. Another opening chapter in this section, "Open Sourcing the Pedagogy to Activate the Learning Process," by Prof. Alan Rea of Western Michigan University, Kalamazoo, USA and Prof. Nick Yeates from UMBC, Baltimore, USA, describes how 19 undergraduates in a web development and design course at a Midwest university worked collaboratively with leading open source software provider, Red Hat, to revamp the Teaching Open Source website. Another chapter, "Optimization Scenarios for Open Source Software Used in E-Learning Activities," by Prof. Utku Köse of Suleyman Demirel University, Turkey, discusses some possible applications of artificial intelligence to include optimization processes within open source software systems used in e-learning activities, focuses on using swarm intelligence and machine learning techniques for this aim, and expresses some theoretical views for improving the effectiveness of such software for a better e-learning experience. The following chapter, "DuBot: An Open-Source, Low-Cost Robot for STEM and Educational Robotics," by Profs. Michail Kalogiannakis and Stamatios Papadakis of the University of Crete, Greece; Profs. Avraam Chatzopoulos and Michail Papoutsidakis of the University of West Attica, Greece; Prof. Sarantos Psycharis of the School of Pedagogical and Technological Education, Greece; and Dethe Elza from Richmond Public Library, Canada, presents the design and development of an open source, low-cost robot for K12 students, suitable for use in educational robotics and science, technology, engineering, mathematics (STEM). The next chapter, "Open Source Online Learning in Rural Communities," by Prof. Gary L. Ackerman of Windsor (Vermont) School, USA, focuses on three cases in which open source technology was installed to support teaching and learning in three rural communities by detailing the projects, assessing the method of technology planning, and addressing unanswered questions. Another chapter,

"Open Source Software Virtual Learning Environment (OSS-VLEs) in Library Science Schools," by Prof. Rosy Jan of the University of Kashmir, India, discusses some of the most used OSS VLEs, determines the suitability of a VLE for higher education, and explores and identifies the recent contributions to the concept by analyzing ongoing virtual learning initiatives and projects by different organizations and information centres to stimulate future Research and development trend in the field. The next chapter, "A Multi-Step Process Towards Integrating Free and Open Source Software in Engineering Education," by Prof. K.G. Srinivasa of Chaudhary Brahm Prakash Government Engineering College, India and Profs. Ganesh Chandra Deka and Krishnaraj P.M. from M. S. Ramaiah Institute of Technology, India, presents a three-stage process which can be adopted by teachers and institutes to utilize the benefits of FOSS to the fullest. An additional chapter, "Development of Assessment Criteria for Various Open Sources GIS Software Packages," by Prof. Shahriar Shams of Institut Teknologi Brunei, Brunei, focuses on the assessment criteria enabling developers, researchers, and GIS users to select suitable OGIS software to meet their requirements for analysis and design of geospatial application in multidisciplinary fields, and highlights the importance of assessment criteria, followed by an explanation of each criteria and their significance with examples from existing OGIS software. Another chapter, "Transmission Line Routing Using Open Source Software Q-GIS," by Prof. Sandeep Chakravorty of Indus University, Ahmedabad, India; Prof. Amitava Ray from Jalpaiguri Government Engineering College, Jalpaiguri, India; and Profs. Shabbir Uddin and Karma Sonam Sherpa of Sikkim Manipal Institute of Technology, Sikkim Manipal University, Rangpo, India, contends that planning for power systems is essentially a projection of how the system should grow over a specific period of time, given certain assumptions and judgments about the future load and the size of investment in generating capacity additions, transmission facilities expansion, and reinforcements. Another chapter in this section, "An Open Source Software: Q-GIS Based Analysis for Solar Potential of Sikkim (India)," by Profs. Dipanjan Ghose, Sreejita Naskar, Shabbiruddin, and Amit Kumar Roy of Sikkim Manipal Institute of Technology, Sikkim Manipal University, East Sikkim, India, investigates the land suitability for medium-scale solar power installations in Sikkim by using open source software Quantum-Geographic Information System (Q-GIS) combined with multi-criteria decision making (MCDM) techniques. The next chapter, "Role of Free and Open Source GIS in River Rejuvenation," by Profs. Smart Kundassery and Babu C. A. of Cochin University of Science and Technology, India, focuses on the possibilities emerging out of integration of free and open source GIS that can eventually succeed in bringing forth a ray of hope to the forlorn riverine ecosystem. The following chapter, "Designing a Framework of Ethnomedicinal Plant Knowledge Integration Using OSS," by Prof. Piyali Das of MUC Women's College, Burdwan, India, provides a framework for design an information retrieval system for ethnomedicine or knowledge on medicinal plants that are used to manage human ailments. Another chapter, "Critical Barriers to Business Intelligence Open Source Software Adoption," by Prof. Placide Poba-Nzaou of the University of Quebec in Montreal, Montreal, Canada; Prof. Sylvestre Uwizeyemungu from the University of Quebec in Trois-Rivières, Trois-Rivières, Canada; and Mariem Saada of DiCentral, Montreal, Canada, proposes a framework that categorizes and structures 23 barriers to OSBI adoption by organizations including 4 that were identified by BI Experts but not explicitly found in the literature and contributes to OSS and Information Systems (IS) research literature on BI adoption in general, as well as provides specific insights to practitioners. Another chapter, "Open Source Software in Financial Auditing," by Prof. Tânia Correia of Instituto Politécnico de Coimbra, Portugal; Prof. Isabel Pedrosa from Instituto Politécnico de Coimbra, Portugal & Instituto Universitário de Lisboa, Portugal; and Prof. Carlos J. Costa of the Universidade de Lisboa, Portugal, focuses on which factors affect open source software adoption by carrying out a survey aimed at financial auditors. The following chapter in this section, "Application of Quality in Use Model to Evaluate the User Experience of Online Banking Software," by Profs. Manar Abu Talib, Areej Alsaafin, and Selma Manel Medjden of the University of Sharjah, Sharjah, UAE, compares two pieces of banking software that show the great potential of OSS, especially in the banking field: one open source and one closed source. One of the final chapters in this section, "Challenges and Trends in Home Automation: Addressing the Interoperability Problem With the Open-Source Platform OpenHAB," by Profs. Cristina Portalés and Sergio Casas of the University of Valencia, Spain and Dr. Kai Kreuzer of openHAB Foundation e.V., Germany, analyzes current trends and challenges in HA and proposes a way to deal with the interoperability problem by means of the open source platform openHAB. Another concluding chapter, "Enhancing Information Retrieval System Using Change-Prone Classes," by Prof. Deepa Bura of Manav Rachna International Institute of Research and Studies, India and Prof. Amit Choudhary from Maharaja Surajmal Institute, India, aims to find the association between changes and object-oriented metrics using different versions of open source software using execution time, frequency, run time information, popularity, and class dependency in prediction of change-prone classes. The final chapter in this section, "Optimized Test Case Generation for Object Oriented Systems Using Weka Open Source Software," by Profs. Rajvir Singh and Anita Singhrova of Deenbandhu Chhotu Ram University of Science and Technology, Haryana, India and Prof. Rajesh Bhatia of PEC University of Technology, Chandigarh, India, presents a novel technique for an optimized test case generation for ant-1.7 open source software.

Section 3, "Prediction Models, Big Data, and Statistics," investigates prediction models including fault prediction in open source software, as well as its connection to Big Data. The opening chapter of this section, "Demography of Open Source Software Prediction Models and Techniques," by Profs. Kaniz Fatema and M. M. Mahbubul Syeed of American International University, Bangladesh and Prof. Imed Hammouda of South Mediterranean University, Tunisia, reports on a systematic literature survey aimed at the identification and structuring of research that offers prediction models and techniques in analyzing OSS projects and provides insight into what constitutes the main contributions of the field, identifies gaps and opportunities, and distils several important future research directions. Another opening chapter, "Predicting Change Prone Classes in Open Source Software," by Prof. Amit Choudhary of Maharaja Surajmal Institute, Delhi, India and Profs. Deepa Godara and Rakesh Kumar Singh from Uttarakhand Technical University, Sudhowala, India, focuses on the association between changes and object-oriented metrics using different versions of open source software. The next chapter, "Predicting the Severity of Open Source Bug Reports Using Unsupervised and Supervised Techniques," by Profs. Pushpalatha M. N. and Mrunalini M. of Ramaiah Institute of Technology, Bengaluru, India, uses unsupervised and supervised learning algorithms to automate the prediction of bug report severity. The next chapter, "Ensemble Techniques-Based Software Fault Prediction in an Open-Source Project," by Prof. Wasiur Rhmann of Babasaheb Bhimrao Ambedkar University, Amethi, India and Prof. Gufran Ahmad Ansari from B. S. Abdur Rehman Crescent Institute of Science and Technology, India, uses ensemble models for software fault prediction, collects change metrics-based data for an open source android project from GIT repository, obatins code-based metrics data from PROMISE data repository, and uses datasets kc1, kc2, cm1, and pc1 for experimental purposes. Another chapter, "Generalized Multi-Release Framework for Fault Prediction in Open Source Software," by Profs. Shozab Khurshid and Javaid Iqbal of the University of Kashmir, Srinagar, India and Prof. A.K. Shrivastava of International Management Institute, Kolkata, West Bengal, India, presents a general framework for multi-release OSS modeling incorporating imperfect debugging and change points. The following chapter in this section, "Logging

Analysis and Prediction in Open Source Java Project," by Profs. Sangeeta Lal and Neetu Sardana of Jaypee Institute of Information Technology, India and Prof. Ashish Sureka of Ashoka University, India, performs an in-depth, focused, and large-scale analysis of logging code constructs at two levels: the file level and catch-blocks level and answers several research questions related to statistical and content analysis. The next chapter, "Using Design of Experiments to Analyze Open Source Software Metrics for Change Impact Estimation," by Profs. Miloud Dahane and Mustapha Kamel Abdi of the Université Oran 1, Oran, Algeria; Profs. Mourad Bouneffa and Henri Basson of the Université du Littoral Côte d'Opale, Dunkirk, France; and Dr. Adeel Ahmad from Laboratoire d'Informatique Signal et Image de la Côte d'Opale, Calais, France, describes the use of the design of experiments method to evaluate the influence of variations of software metrics on the change impact in developed software. Another chapter, "Introduction to the Popular Open Source Statistical Software (OSSS)," by Prof. Gao Niu of Bryant University, USA; Prof. Zhijian Wu from New York University, USA; and Prof. Zichen Zhao of Yale University, USA, introduces the two most popular Open Source Statistical Software (OSSS), R, and Python, along with their integrated development environment (IDE) and graphical user interface (GUI). A concluding chapter, "What Is Open Source Software (OSS) and What Is Big Data?" by Prof. Richard S. Segall of Arkansas State University, USA, discusses what Open Source Software is and its relationship to Big Data and how it differs from other types of software and its software development cycle. One of the final chapters in this section, "Open Source Software (OSS) for Big Data," by Prof. Richard S. Segall of Arkansas State University, USA, discusses Open Source Software and associated technologies for the processing of Big Data. The final chapter in this section, "Role of Open Source Software in Big Data Storage," by Profs. Rupali Ahuja, Jigyasa Malik, Ronak Tyagi, and R. Brinda of the University of Delhi, India, discusses the role of open source software in big data storage and how various organizations have benefitted from its use and provides an overview of popular open source big data storage technologies existing today.

Although the primary organization of the contents in this work is based on its three sections offering a progression of coverage of the important concepts, methodologies, technologies, applications, social issues, and emerging trends, the reader can also identify specific contents by utilizing the extensive indexing system listed at the end. As a comprehensive collection of research on the latest findings related to open source software, the *Research Anthology on Usage and Development of Open Source Software* provides computer scientists, programmers, developers, teachers, academicians, researchers, students, and all audiences with a complete understanding of the challenges that face those working with open source software. Given the need for a comprehensive guide on the latest issues, challenges, advancements, and overall history of open source software, this extensive book presents the latest research to address the challenges and provide further opportunities for improvement.

Chapter 25
Role of Free and Open Source GIS in River Rejuvenation

Smart Kundassery
Cochin University of Science and Technology, India

Babu C. A.
Cochin University of Science and Technology, India

ABSTRACT

Rivers represent one of the sources of freshwater. The existence and survival of humanity is intricately connected with the availability of freshwater resources. It is valuable to provide comprehensive information of all water resources through online geo-visual interfaces. Specific web slices can be of use, such as the illustration of headwater sources along with details of streams of various orders and tributaries up to the point of merging with the sea downstream. Since the local self-government departments, Grama Panchayat, can play a crucial role, they too are eager to know the details of the drainage network flowing within each administration unit. The possibilities emerging out of integration of free and open source GIS is enormous and can eventually succeed in bringing forth a ray of hope to the forlorn riverine ecosystem.

INTRODUCTION

The water resources perform a pivotal role in sustaining life on the Planet Earth. Myriad forms of flora and fauna flourish and nourish through the intake of water. Human race too is not an exception. For the humanity to sustain and thrive on the Planet Earth, the indispensable prerequisite is the availability of freshwater. All cross-sections of the society, primitive and present, have depended on freshwater for subsistence. In the terrestrial landscape, the major sources of freshwater are the rivers. Ample supply of freshwater from the rivers well ensured and nurtured the initial vibes of the civilizations to sprout along the valleys of rivers, be it the Tigris-Euphrates river valley (4400 B.C.-2000 B.C.) along the Tigris and Euphrates rivers in Mesopotamia (Jason, 2010), Harappan civilization (2300 B.C.-1700 B.C.) along the Indus river valley (Fairservis, 1967), Nile river valley (3000 B.C.-30 B.C.) along the Nile river in Egypt and Yellow river valley (2100 B.C.-1 A.D.) along the Yellow river in China (Gernet, 1996). These civili-

DOI: 10.4018/978-1-7998-9158-1.ch025

zations are hence aptly known ever since as the river valley civilizations. Manifold ecological functions are infused by the rivers and extended numerous invaluable services to the ecosystem as well. The river continuum is thus regarded not just a flow of water over terrestrial landscapes but a flux of energy and matter of immense ecological concern.

Ever since the dawn of the civilizations, the rivers have espoused a momentous role in many religious ceremonies too. Most of the rivers of India are depicted as the avatars of Goddesses. Consequently, the rivers upheld a divine status and waters hold significant role in the holy rituals. The largest of the certain massive human congregation (Figure 1) occur alternately in the banks of the rivers, viz. the Ganges at Haridwar; the confluence of the Ganges and the Yamuna and the mythical Saraswati at Allahabad; the Godawari at Nashik; and the Shipra at Ujjain. On reminiscence, the rivers are thus indeed a living and sacred entity in holistic insights and not just a commercial commodity awaiting exploitation. In recognition of the many facets rivers enrich human life and endeavour, United Nations General Assembly has declared 2003 as the 'International Year of Freshwater [55/196]'; 2005-2015 as the International Decade for action, with the focal theme "Water for Life" (United Nations, 2004). The year 2013 is observed as the 'International Year of Water Cooperation', United Nations, 2011). 'World Rivers Day' is being celebrated on the last Sunday of September. Apart from these, annually, March 14 is observed as the 'International Day of Action for Rivers'. 'World Water Day' is observed on March 22 every year.

In quintessence, the vitality and vibrancy of the Nature is exalted by numerous rivers gushing across the planetary terrain. However, world over, the rivers are facing interferences from various natural as well as human induced processes. The natural processes are often related with the variations associated with the global warming and climatic changes. The human induced processes have multifarious roots. For long, the creation of dams and reservoirs were a compelling necessity for the prevention of recurring floods, generation of electricity and irrigating large tracts of lands. Later, in the process, the structures caused physical alterations to the river flow, caused irrecoverable damage and disturbance to the riverine system and even blocked the migration routes (Marmulla, 2001) of fishes (Figure 2). Eventually, the dams fragmented the natural floodplains of rivers to the utmost destructive extent (Figure 3/4). Unabated deforestation in the catchment area enhances the risk of catastrophic floods to a considerable extent. The natural forests are highly efficient in storing the precipitation and reduce the direct runoff. The loss of the forests, wetlands, grasslands and floodplains exasperated the flood risk factor. The best illustration of this intricately correlated scenario is the summer floods in the Yangtze River in China during 1998 (Zhou, et al., 2002). Excessive water abstraction for agricultural irrigation, urban consumption, industrial use and pollution cause immense threat to the riverine system. Threats to rivers are on the rise.

Consequently, the rivers are undergoing a fast-paced shrinkage of the headwater sources. The emerging scenario of the scarcity of water trends the water resources as a precarious entity. Globally, critical scenarios have already evolved to adopt fair water usage. The incurring compulsion calls for the effective management of the available freshwater resources. All the freshwater resources with dim prospects have to be identified for revival and rejuvenation. The free and Open Source Geographical Information System (GIS) has a significant role in aiding river revival and rejuvenation processes.

WATER RESOURCES ON THE PLANET EARTH

In the Solar System, the human race resides in a habitat known as the Planet Earth. The Planet Earth is one among eight planets in the Solar System. As of now, these eight planets together are endowed with

178 natural satellites. Remarkably, nine among these natural satellites have already expounded clear evidences for the presence of water bodies. These water bodies are now known as 'planetary oceans'. The ocean on the Earth, which we all are familiar, harbours on a planet. Curiously, the newly discovered abodes of oceans are found to exist in some of the natural satellites of the planets of the Solar System! These planetary objects are the natural satellites of the planets viz., the Jupiter, the Saturn, the Uranus and the Neptune. Presently, subsurface oceans exist on the Europa, the Ganymede, the Callisto; the Mimas, the Dione; the Ariel; and the Triton. A subsurface ocean means the water body lies sandwiched between an icy crust and a rocky interior. In contrast, on the Enceladus, an open ocean; and on the Titan, instead of a globe encircling ocean, numerous random and unrelated seas are found to dot the northern hemisphere (Kundassery and Babu, 2015).

All these pristine environments favour air-sea interaction processes and do contribute toward the modulation of the planetary climatology. These planetary objects are also regarded as the ideal environments where the hope and probability of finding signatures of alien life does exist. In essence, the Solar System abounds with remarkable deposits of water. Still incredible is the scenario that among these diverse planetary and satellite landscapes, the Planet Earth is the one and only one habitat where life as we sense does exist. Thus, the Earth holds a unique and distinct position in the spatial and temporal perspectives of the Solar System. The uniqueness relies in the presence of a congenial environment ardently supporting the evolution of life. The elixir nurturing the evolution, sustenance, nourishing and flourishing of life is nothing but the ubiquitous presence of water resources.

The formation scenario of water on the surface of the Earth is noteworthy at this moment. It is now widely accepted that the Planet Earth was formed around 4.54 billion years ago (Tera, 1980). Recent scientific evidences (Sarafian et al., 2014) ascertain that the water (H_2O) appeared primitively on the surface of the Earth during the formation of the planet itself. On the Planet Earth, ~70.900% of the surface area is covered with the water (H_2O). The compositions of the planetary oceans' elsewhere are as diverse and varied as ethane (C_2H_6) and methane (CH_4). Over the terrestrial landscape, water occurs naturally in ice caps, glaciers, snow and permafrost and as soil moisture. Much of the surface water is contained in rivers and lakes; while beneath the surface as groundwater. The solar irradiance causes evaporation of the molecules from the ocean. The molecules, on condensation, form clouds and subsequently fall as rain or snow and ultimately reach back to the ocean. Thus, the main source of water over the terrestrial landscapes is the ocean.

Of the water (H_2O) content available on the Planet Earth, the oceans, seas and bays hold 96.540% of the total water content. The water composition of the oceans, seas and bays in the terrestrial landscape is inherently saline. Saline groundwater holds 0.930% and saline lakes holds 0.006%. The freshwater resources on the Planet Earth thus hold a meagre 2.524%. The gist is, of all the water repository on the Planet Earth, saline water makes up about 97.476% and only 2.524% is fresh water! Of the total freshwater content of the Planet Earth, about 68.600% exists as ice caps, glaciers and permanent snow. 30.100% of the freshwater resides as groundwater content. The surface water and other freshwater sources hold the remaining 1.200%.

We have every reason to be more concerned and conscious about the remaining 1.200% of the surface and other freshwater resources. Because, within this 1.200%, ice caps, glaciers and permanent snow hold 68.600%. Freshwater lakes hold 0.260%, fresh groundwater holds 30.100% and swamps hold 0.030%. Soil moisture holds 0.050%. The atmosphere contains 0.040%, whereas biological water holds 0.003%. The rest of the fresh water is contained in rivers. Interestingly, rivers thus hold just 0.006% of the total freshwater content (Shiklomanov, 1993) of the Planet Earth! In other words, the critical scenario slowly unveiling and clearly emerging is that the fresh water available for the human consumption from rivers is just 0.0002% of the total water contained in the Planet Earth (Figure 5)!

WATER ECONOMY OF INDIA

The statistics enumerated through the recent 15th census of India during 2011 (http://censusindia.gov. in) reveals a total population of 1,210,569,573 people (over 1.2 billion) inhabiting India's geographical area of 329 million hectares. Agrarian economy, sanitation requirements, moreover, survival of the ever exploding population of the nation is rigorously met from the precipitation process. On an average, the geographical extent of India receives about 3840 Billion Cubic Meters (BCM) of precipitation (UNICEF, FAO and SaciWATERs, 2013), rainfall and snowfall together, every year. However, this precipitation too is not uniformly distributed over the entire land area. It varies from less than 100 millimetres in Rajasthan to more than 3,000 millimetres in Kerala and over 11,000 millimetres in Meghalaya. Moreover, the precipitation is seasonal. Precipitation is thus uneven in distribution over space and time. Of all the rain that falls on the terrestrial landscape, some evaporates back in to the atmosphere, some percolates in the ground and some is used by the forests. The remaining flows into the rivers.

The total surface water resource runoff potential of the country is estimated as 1,869.37 BCM (Billion Cubic Meters). Another 431.42 BCM can be used from the ground water recharge potential of the country. Thus, the available water potential of the nation is 2300.79 BCM. However, out of the available surface water resource runoff potential, the estimated utilisable freshwater potential to support ever exploding population of India is just 654 BCM (FAO UINICEF, 2013). An alarming situation arising in due course is the fact that the current water usage of the nation is marked as 634 BCM (FAO UINICEF, 2013). With a population of over 1.2 billion, the 'average per capita water availability' of the nation during 2011 was 1545 m³/year, and projected towards 2050 is 1140 m³/year. Almost 29% of the rural population and 23% of the urban population would still lack access to adequate safe, sustainable and potable water. A per capita availability of less than 1700 m³ is termed as a 'water-stressed' condition while per capita availability below 1000 m³ is termed as a 'water-scarcity' condition (Chaturvedi, 2012). In gist, the nation is marching towards a water-stressed condition (Figure 6). Under the spell of all these complex environmental aspects, the need of the hour is the implementation of a clear 'River Literacy' programme.

Necessity for the Implementation of River Literacy

In the regional scenario, Kerala, the southernmost state in the west coast of India, is endowed with 44 rivers. Most of them originate from the Western Ghats and drains into the Arabian Sea. Among these, there are 3 rivers, viz., Kabbini, Bhavani and Pambar which also originate from the Western Ghats, but they flow eastwards into the neighbouring States of Karnataka and Tamil Nadu. The societal requirements for livelihood are met from these water resources. During the past few years, most of the riverine ecosystems in Kerala, as elsewhere, have been heading towards a continuous degradation stage. Kerala is already included in moderate category of desertification process (Chouhan, 2005). Alarmingly, the signs of the desertification are observed in the region under the bounty of River Bharathapuzha, the second longest river in the state. Almost 175 villages are dependent on the River Bharathapuzha for subsistence. As elsewhere, the climatic factors, deforestation, clay mining, illicit human activities such as river sand mining, among a plethora of other factors, have contributed and played a cumulative role to aggravate the riverine degradation processes (Figure 7). According to the Planning Commission (2007), Government of India, in the national scenario, non-availability of potable water is posed to be a major crisis in terms of spread and severity. In the global context also, mighty rivers too are drying up at an alarming rate. Worldwide, the emerging situations have serious consequences not only for humankind, but also for the flora and fauna and on the future of the Planet Earth. The existence and survival of human race is thus intricately connected with the presence of freshwater resources, better within the immediate reach.

In this context, 'River Literacy' is defined as the 'ability to appreciate the manifold functions lotic ecosystems bestow on inhabitants of Planet Earth so as to initiate and embark on a prolonged process of river conservation, restoration, revival and rejuvenation process in volition' (Kundassery & Babu, 2013). Implementation of 'River Literacy' is envisaged to enhance community perception and awareness of the diverse and crucial aspects water resources behold to nurture and sustain life on Planet Earth. It is envisaged that 'River Literacy' will eventually lead to adopt optimum conservation, management and utilization principles of water resources to ensure prolonged access to freshwater resources. Moments when potable water dips almost to the level of being scarce, it is commendable and valuable to provide comprehensive information of the detailed status of all freshwater resources through online geo-visual Interfaces. The availability of the pertinent critical information at the fingertips will invoke participation of the enlightened mass in the conservation, revival and rejuvenation of the freshwater resources. RiverineGiS, a geo-visual illustration showcasing the rivers of a southern state along the west coast of India, is envisaged and implemented in this perspective.

RiverineGiS Geo-Visuals

Geo-visual illustrations of water resources herald manifold purposes. As explained elsewhere, down through the millennium, all drainage networks are under continuous mode of adapting itself to the climatic and natural changes in the terrestrial landscapes. As the world progressively heads to the 21st century, the Indus in Asia, the Nile in north-eastern Africa, the Colorado in United States, notable among several others, now struggles to merge with the water mass. There are instances of tributaries of rivers, such as Noyyal (Figure 8) of River Kaveri, in Tamil Nadu, completely dried up beyond interventions for probable rejuvenation. Rivers such as Uthrapalli, in Southern Kerala, is just extinct beyond revival even almost a century ago. Requirements for the water abstraction always arise still many more rivers are constantly under peril arising out of unwarranted human intentions and interventions. The perspectives emerging from the scrutiny of trends is very clear. Do preserve, conserve, inherit and adapt technologies for the optimum conservation and utilization of the natural resources and all sources of potable water for posterity too to live amicably on planet Earth! However, in the process of river revival, rejuvenation, moreover, in the restoration processes, few scenarios emerge at the global front as well as at grassroots. The foremost is the realization that various schemes envisaged so far, for river conservation does not bring the desired results. The schemes implemented for river restoration too could not bring anticipated results and fail miserably at grassroots.

A poignant point is becoming increasingly evident. Many well-documented resources of natural and environmental resources do exist. However, the realistic scenario existing at the micro-level, for the community working at the grassroots, is that utter scarcity of information pertaining to the natural drainage resources still do exist. It is the nearby community who knew the river health pulses well and not the occasional onlookers! The local community need to be enlightened, thoroughly lit with river literacy snippets, well-illustrated and included in all river restoration process to reap the envisaged benefits of river rejuvenation programs. Harsh reality of non-accessibility of crucial pertinent information can hamper constructive intervention of activists. Unless we address these crucial instances of relevant information retrieval at the grassroots, blown up to the full extent of severity, at later decades, the situation could seriously hamper the national progress outlined through various indicators of societal well-being. A paradigm shift is imminent and now proceeding with fast pace to include all stakeholders especially the inspired and motivated near the riverbanks in the rejuvenation process, be it the mighty Ganges or the River Bharathapuzha.

Rejuvenating a river requires participation of activists of different capacity from a wide spectrum of society, from policy makers, administrators and workers in the grassroots. All these inter-dependent work forces require detailed drainage maps. A public domain map, apart from the traditional paper-based maps, too is essential because there should not be a situation where lack of information derails the initiatives to conserve every rivers of the Planet Earth. The technologies available today are apt and mature enough to develop such an Interface in public domain. Wikimapia, Google Earth and Bhuvan have leapfrogged technology in this regard. However, region-specific, especially of the water resources of Kerala, is so far absent in public domain (Kundassery & Babu, 2013).

From the laymen perspectives, this scenario happens because some of the information is laid in documents having restricted access for content. Moreover, most of the literature remains inside bound volumes but not as geo-spatial digitized content, even if it exists, it is only in the closed camp of relevant professionals. Comprehensive aspects concerning the rivers in an easily accessible digital form are still less available. For example, scientific literature suggests River Periyar originates from the Sivagiri group of hills. River Periyar is the longest river in the state. However, it is very difficult to locate Sivagiri hills from existing web mapping domains. The situation is not much different, be it Google Maps (http://maps.google.co.in), (Wikimapia (http://wikimapia.org), or even ISRO Bhuvan (http://bhuvan.nrsc.gov.in). To know the geo-spatial locations of tributaries Mullayar and Periyar of River Mullaperiyar need much exercise; situations are not much different for other rivers elsewhere. In the process, there exist a few probable hurdles to overcome to initiate community participation in the conservation, revival and rejuvenation of the freshwater resources at the grass roots. Foremost is to mitigate the lack of digital access even to basic information pertaining to the riverine environment!

The community participation in the protection, conservation, revival, rejuvenation and management of the freshwater resources has to be ensured to make the programs viable. Therefore, the first step in this regard is the need and presence of a medium to present and access basic riverine information. Equally, the medium could also be conceptualized as a Web-GIS Interface to collate and present the riverine database. This Interface can then be designed as a dynamic user Interface through appropriate web technologies as a portal to deliver crucial scientific elements for societal empowerment through easily perceptual knowledge snippets. Recent technological advancements in web based GIS make it possible that the relevant riverine literature content can now be made available to larger cross sections of the society including student community, research scholars, planners and elite public alike. This will also be helpful for river activists. Being available, all relevant riverine information in public domain will increase rapid availability as well as accessibility to evoke a much wider movement and participation. Alternatively, enthusiasts have all the relevant knowledge at fingertips to initiate congress for river restoration process.

Ultimately, the success of river restoration process is intricately connected with the amalgamation of committed brave heart's spanning the entire ecosystem. There are serious researchers who do analysis of the changes in the land use pattern in different spatial and temporal scales and influencing parameters on its evolution. Science communication activists bring the results of hard-core scientists to grassroots in order to enlighten the masses and make them understand the relevance to appreciate subtleties of Grandma Nature. In addition, there are activists who need geo-spatial information at fingertips and appropriate technologies to initiate new vibes of restoration of the ecosystem. The utmost essential requirement for this to ensue in a constructive way is the availability of geo-spatial data framed with appropriate modes of information technology. Thus, it seems essential and meaningful for an attempt to generate a GIS based geo-visual framework of the water resources.

The deficit of sufficient regional information in the public domain motivated the proposition of RiverineGiS. RiverineGiS is the Web-GIS illustration of the water resources of Kerala. The Interface is conceived, developed and implemented for supporting the river literacy campaigns at the grass roots. Through RiverineGiS, geo-visuals of rivers and snippets of the critical problems faced by the riverine environment are presented to stress the need for immediate implementation of a comprehensive river conservation movement. The conservation and optimum usage of natural resources can occur only when community perception through river literacy is enhanced to ensure community participation. Free and Open Source Software are used to develop RiverineGiS.

FREE AND OPEN SOURCE WEB-GIS

Traditionally, map and atlas were used to illustrate geographical information. In print media, a map could be as simple as displaying the glimpses of a geographical area. Because of the static nature of these maps, the information portrayed had limited accessibility of content. Whoever possesses and procures only could use the map and atlas for the intended purposes. The emergence of geo-spatial techniques has resulted in a radical visual enrichment in the representation and analysis of the terrestrial landscapes. At the core of this enhanced functionality is geographically referenced data. Geographically referenced data outlines the criteria to help identify its location in the real world through geo-referenced coordinates such as latitude and longitude.

Web GIS refers to a variety of internet-based applications that rely on geographically referenced data. Web GIS is essentially a stripped Geographic Information System but distributed over a network using HTML protocols as its core mode of communication. Indeed the resources are generated through a Desktop GIS, which is then served through an online Web GIS application. In fact, the transformation from a Desktop GIS into a Web-based GIS has specific motivation. From the localhost restriction, Web GIS provides online connectivity and access of geographic information through various protocols to wider audience geographically apart.

The design and deliverance of geographically referenced data through a Web GIS application assumes a few indispensable features. Foremost, the focus is on what spatial data is intended to distribute through the geo-spatial application. The specific datasets and parameters are subsequently formulated to fulfil the user engagement and interaction to the portal. Later, based on the theme of the application, the spatial database is distinctively configured as base maps and overlays. This is achieved through generation and gathering of spatial data that can be shared and having implications for societal benefit. There could be one or more base maps, while there are certain restrictions in the number of operational layers rendered online. For example, OpenLayers, a front-end library, impose a restriction for 100 layers. Both raster and vector datasets are possible to serve through the application.

For individuals working at the grassroots for river rejuvenation, the most appropriate entity to intervene in this process is the access to appropriate geo-spatial software. Free and Open Source GIS software has their niche in this regard. As is well demonstrated, all proprietary software needs massive and periodical financial investment. For the activists working in the grassroots as well as for most Non-governmental Organizations (NGO), recurring software expenditure is a major hindrance. For wider acceptance and mass deployment, the natural implementation choices of Web-GIS stacks are preferably Free and Open Source Software (FOSS) than proprietary. Free and Open-source Software (FOSS) is the comprehensive term which embraces both domains of the free software and open-source software philosophies (Miller, et al., 2010). Apart from the financial liberation for prolong and continuous usage, free and open source also advocate the liberty to re-use and modify the source code according to the personal requirements of the individual and re-distribution of the improved content.

RiverineGiS: Geo-Visual Slices of Water Resources of Kerala

Nature has bestowed a bountiful of 44 rivers, most belonging to the category of medium rivers according to the national norms. Rivers has certain sources and flows down slopes carving a course until its end at the mouth. Beyond these generalizations, if somebody wants to know the geographical locations from where each of these rivers arises, then, matter gets worse. Well, the details are inside paperbacks, but not as interactive and geo-spatial content in the public domain. RiverineGiS depict selected natural resources and environmental parameters for the geo-visualization of the water resources of Kerala. The RiverineGiS Interface presents the entire drainage network draped over the Digital Elevation Model (DEM) of the terrain for the natural realization of the panorama. Initially, the water resource of Kerala, a southern state along the west coast of India is portrayed through RiverineGiS. Through the RiverineGiS Interface, each of the 44 rivers of Kerala and their tributaries are illustrated from headwater sources along with details of streams of various orders and tributaries up to the river mouth.

The critical aspects which makes imperative to make available online the relevant geo-spatial content are as follows. Analysed in minute details, an activist is confronted with certain critical circumstances. River Periyar, the longest river in the state of Kerala, has 283 tributaries. Being fed and enriched by the monsoon rains not all tributaries can be identified throughout the year. However, there exist perennial streams and tributaries of the river system. It is hard to figure out the names of those numerous tributaries as well. Neither Google Earth, Google Maps, Wikimapia nor ISRO Bhuvan fails miserably in providing the details. They do provide but of the datasets, they are of custodian and accumulated over time. Unless we identify and take constructive steps to conserve those precious rivulets in terms of the long-term sustenance oriented process, humanity will be slowly aiding the depletion of finite natural resources one after another.

In the system of public governance, there exist different entities entitled to perform specific function. Since the local self-government departments (LSGD) and grama panchayat can play a crucial role in the river rejuvenation process, they too are eager to know the details of the drainage network flowing within the capacity of each administration unit. A local community too exists who knew well the pulses of the ecosystem. Using Open Source GIS, they can contribute the local and traditional knowledge for the societal well-being. It is the apt tool to illustrate the burning problems in the neighbourhood. For those enthusiastic activists, the best way to unleash their creativity for aiding national progress is nothing but Open Source Geographical Information System. The Web GIS Interface can then be used to educate as well as to illustrate where lies and the extent of the imminent geographical problem. That thread is enough to lay spark for more people to contribute to the Interface and will eventually led to a conglomeration of expertise in the revival and rejuvenation process. Of course, wonders have happened even without the application of geo-spatial technologies as in Rajasthan. Nevertheless, the possibilities emerging out of integration of free and open source GIS is enormous and can eventually succeed in bringing forth a ray of hope to the forlorn riverine ecosystem.

Illustration of RiverineGiS Geo-Visual Interface

Through the RiverineGiS Interface (Figure 9), clients can pan, zoom and browse for information related to the water resources of Kerala. This effort has increased rapid availability as well as accessibility to evoke a much wider awareness and participation in the conservation efforts of rivers in the state. The interface can be understood through three options. 'Select a River' combo box allows easy auto panning to the originating geographical extent of each River. This tool is significant in understanding the drainage course of a single River, from origin up to the river mouth. 'Pan and Zoom' toolbar embedded within the map window allows flexible panning and viewing of random geographical extents. Different base layers are provided to tag streams, tributaries and rivers to different administration entities.

Geo-Visual Concepts

Geo-informatics is defined as "Science and Technology dealing with the structure and character of spatial information, its capture, its classification and qualification, its storage, processing, portrayal and dissemination, including the infrastructure necessary to secure optimal use of this information" (Raju, 2003). Geographic Information System (GIS) is one of the branches of Geo-informatics. GIS enables stacking of layers of information from varied sources into a unified software domain to analyse the relationships, if any, and correlate the physical and environmental entities within the geographical context to derive an optimum deduction. The database thus generated can be organized to distribute and enabled to access over a local or wide area network. The database can also be hosted in a server for easier access in public domain.

Data Sources

The RiverineGiS Interface is composed of raster and vector data. Raster data is the base layer; GEBCO (www.gebco.net) is used to depict bathymetry, and the data from the Shuttle Radar Topographic Mission (SRTM) for topography. In the present dataset, depth varies up to 8698 m, whereas elevation up to 2536 m and the variations are depicted through a colour index. Topographical sheets of entire Kerala from Survey of India at 1: 50,000 scale (http://www.surveyofindia.gov.in) are used to generate vector layers except administrative boundaries, airports, KSRTC and railway stations, mud banks and sand mining kadavu in Palakkad District. Administrative boundaries are generated from GADM Database of Global Administrative Areas (www.gadm.org). Airports, KSRTC and railway stations are generated from Google Maps. Mud banks and sand-mining Kadavu in Palakkad District (CESS, 2004) are generated from various scientific publications corroborated through field surveys. Kerala State Gazetteer (Ramachandran, 1986) and Water Resources of Kerala: A Compendium of Advance Report (Vaidyanathan, 1958) provided basic literature for rivers of Kerala.

Software

Free and Open Source Software is used in development. Geographic Resources Analysis Support System (GRASS GIS) and Quantum GIS Version 1.7.1 through 2.10.1 was used for basic GIS operations and for the generation of Vector layers and its attributes. OGC compliant Web Map Servers, viz., MapServer and Geoserver are used to develop the mapping application. MapServer is hosted in Apache Server whereas Geoserver requires either an Apache Tomcat or Jetty Server; we used Apache Tomcat. PostgreSQL together with PostGIS 1.5 is used to generate the vector database. The database is then fed into Geoserver (2.1.3), and front-end is developed using OpenLayers 2.13. Geoserver map script was generated using java script. RiverineGiS MapServer Interface was generated using MapScript.

Thematic Layers

The following themes were generated: drainage of 44 rivers of Kerala along with ocean boundaries, maritime boundary, and bathymetry and administration units consisting of district, panchayat, and village and watershed boundary. Connectivity, viz., national highway, state highway, railway, airport, port and harbour, railway and KSRTC stations, place names, mountains and reserved forests, beaches, light houses, mud banks along Kerala coast, sand mining kadavu in Palakkad are also incorporated into the RiverineGiS Interface.

Applications of RiverineGiS Interface

The RiverineGiS Interface also demonstrates usefulness of the RiverineGiS geo-visuals as an innovative tool for interactive academic and scientific research under the backdrop of natural landscapes. The highlights of the RiverineGiS Interface are as follows. Through the RiverineGiS Interface, the geo-visual information pertaining to the entire rivers of Kerala is delivered into public domain. Through the Interface, clients can pan, zoom and browse for information related to the water resources of Kerala in the backdrop of natural landscapes (Figure 10). The clients can pan right from the headwater sources, each of the tributaries through river mouth and beyond the coastal oceans.

The ecologically sensitive areas in Western Ghats lies within the 500 m contour above M.S.L. (Gadgil, 2011). The significance of this zone is illustrated through the theme 'Ecologically Sensitive Areas' in the Western Ghats (Kerala). Out of the 44 rivers of Kerala, 34 rivers originate from the Western Ghats. Out of these 34 rivers, 17 rivers originate from ecologically sensitive villages in Western Ghats (Kerala). These 17 rivers have 33 origin locations spread across the 'Ecologically Sensitive Areas' in the Western Ghats (Kerala). These aspects alone vouch for the significance of the implementation of the RiverineGiS Interface. We cannot demarcate that a river should flow along a particular direction favouring population needs, rather we should constrain a zone ecologically favouring riverine environment, which then sustains population in its cradle.

Critical aspects of the riverine environment that require immediate attention, viz. illicit river sand mining are highlighted. Illegal sand mining poses serious environmental issues. Sand mining persists in almost all the rivers of Kerala. It is more rampant in Bharathapuzha (Figure 11). It is estimated that the sand extraction from River Bharathapuzha is 1652 truckloads per day (TLPD); whereas in River Bhavani, it is 40 TLPD, (CESS, 2004). We have also developed a database through which it is easier to identify the kadavu, panchayat and village details and are part of 'RiverineGiS'. The Interface presents the geographical locations where rampant illegal sand mining persists. The locations are identified and mapped. The Interface also supplements scientific literature explaining the environmental impacts of sand mining along with visual narratives from the riverbanks by various channels for enhanced awareness of the socio-economic impacts. Science communication and awareness information explaining the adverse impacts imposed is also provided.

The OpenWeatherMap (http://openweathermap.org) service provides free weather data and forecast API suitable for any cartographic services like web and smartphone applications. Weather data is received from global meteorological broadcast services. The service use data from two weather services - NOAA that use GFS model, and Environment Canada. Both models are global, and determine the total atmospheric dynamics on the planet as a whole; with a grid size of about 50 km and longer ranged forecast of 5-7 days. RiverineGiS Interface is over layered with OpenWeather WMS to yield weather conditions persisting in river basins. Currently, in the weather mashup (Figure 12), meteorological parameters such as clouds and precipitation forecasts, pressure, temperature and wind magnitude are supported. Mashup enables forecasting of meteorological conditions prevailing in the catchment areas of a river basin. This allows the possibility of monitoring formation of severe weather phenomena to take appropriate safety measures to avert human and property loss. Thus, RiverineGiS can be used simultaneously for educational and planning purposes. Inclusion of appropriate themes allows supplementing on-going river rejuvenation efforts of various user groups.

CONCLUSION

Rivers as a source of freshwater are the lifeline of societies and arteries of the habitable Planet Earth. Without drainage system, what waits is a barren desert. A dewdrop or a raindrop, each droplet beholds and nurture life on Planet Earth. We have to save and preserve it for posterity to survive and continue habitat on Planet Earth. RiverineGiS is the first step towards achieving this end.

ACKNOWLEDGMENT

The motivation for the development of the RiverineGiS Web-GIS Interface was inspired through numerous chance encounters with the community who ardently hoped to revive River Bharathapuzha. Heartfelt thanks to the grass root community for imparting traditional knowledge of the riverine habitat. The assistance extended by Mr. Praveen Balakrishnan and Mrs. Sajna Ansari, ORGIN, during various stages of the project is duly acknowledged.

REFERENCES

CESS. (2004). *Bharathapuzha and Its Problems with Special Preference to Sand Mining from the River Stretch between Chamravattom and Thirunavaya*. Trivandrum: Centre for Earth Science Studies.

Chaturvedi, M. C. (2010). *India's Waters: Advances in Development and Management*. CRC Press.

Chouhan, T. S. (2005). *Degree, Extent and Treatment of Desertification Hazards in India. Sociedade & Natureza, 1*(1), 901–919.

Fairservis, W. A. (1967). The origin, character, and decline of an early civilization. *American Museum Novitates, 2302.*

Gernet, J. (1996). *A History of Chinese Civilization.* Cambridge University Press.

Kundassery & Babu. (2013). RiverineGIS-A Geo-visual Framework for enhancing River Literacy. *Indian Cartographer, 33,* 453–458.

Kundassery & Babu. (2015). An Oceanographic Exploration of the Solar System. *PLANEX,* 7-11.

Madhav Gadgil Commission. (2011). *Report of the Western Ghats Ecology Expert Panel.* The Ministry of Environment and Forests, Government of India.

Marmulla, G. (Ed.). (2001). *Dams, fish and fisheries-Opportunities, challenges and conflict resolution. FAO Fisheries Technial Paper, Issue 419.* Food and Agriculture Organization of the United Nations.

Miller, K. W., Voas, J., & Costello, T. (2010). Free and Open Source Software. *IT Professional, 12*(6), 14–16. doi:10.1109/MITP.2010.147

Planning Commission. (2007). *Report of the Steering Committee on Water Resources for Eleventh Five Year Plan (2007-2012).* Government of India.

Raju, P. L. N. (2003). Fundamentals of Geographic Information System. *Proc. of the Training Workshop, held at Dehra Dun,* 103-120.

Ramachandran Nair, K. K. (1986). *Kerala State Gazetteer* (Vol. 1). Thiruvananthapuram, Kerala: Kerala Council for Historical Research.

Sarafian, A. R., Nielsen, S. G., Marschall, H. R., McCubbin, F. M., & Monteleone, B. D. (2014). Early accretion of water in the inner solar system from a carbonaceous chondrite-like source. *Science, 346*(6209), 623–626. doi:10.1126cience.1256717 PMID:25359971

Shiklomanov, I. (1993). World fresh water resources. In Water in Crisis: A Guide to the World's Fresh Water Resources. Oxford University Press.

Tera, F. (1980). Reassessment of the Age of the Earth. *Carnegie Institution of Washington Year Book, 79,* 524–531.

UNICEF, FAO, & SaciWATERs. (2013). *Water in India: Situation and Prospects.* Author.

United Nations General Assembly Resolution. (2004). *A/RES/58/217, International Decade for Action, "Water for Life", 2005-2015.* Author.

United Nations General Assembly Resolution. (2011). *A/RES/65/154, International Year of Water Co-operation, 2011.* Author.

Ur, J. A. (2010). Cycles of Civilization in Northern Mesopotamia, 4400–2000 BC. *Journal of Archaeological Research, 18*(4), 387–431. doi:10.100710814-010-9041-y

Vaidyanathan, P. H. (1985). Water Resources of Kerala: A Compendium of Advance Report. Kerala, India: Public Works Department, Govt. of Kerala, Trivandrum.

Zhou, X., Lin, D., Yang, H., Chen, H., Sun, L., Yang, G., ... Brown, L. (2002). Use of landsat TM satellite surveillance data to measure the impact of the 1998 flood on snail intermediate host dispersal in the lower Yangtze River Basin. *Acta Tropica, 82*(2), 199–205. doi:10.1016/S0001-706X(02)00011-6 PMID:12020893

APPENDIX

Figure 1. Pilgrims of Kumbh Mela gather to take bath in the Ganges
(© 2010, Coupdoeil / Philipp Eyer. Distributed under a CC BY-SA 3.0 license).

Figure 2. Reduced flow downstream of dams affects fish abundance
(© 2008, Smart Kundassery).

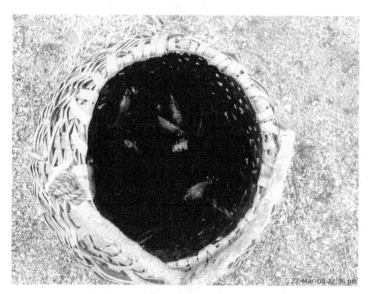

Figure 3. Where is the river here?
(© 2013, Smart Kundassery).

Figure 4. Full reservoir level in the alternate side of dam
(© 2013, Smart Kundassery).

Figure 5. River bed is dry except these few drops!
(© 2008, Smart Kundassery).

Figure 6. Other side of 'Digital India'
(© 2015, Smart Kundassery.).

Figure 7. View of second largest river, Bharathapuzha, in Kerala
(© 2008, Smart Kundassery).

Figure 8. River Noyyal in Tamil Nadu
(©2013, Smart Kundassery).

Figure 9. RiverineGiS interface
(© 2015, Smart Kundassery).

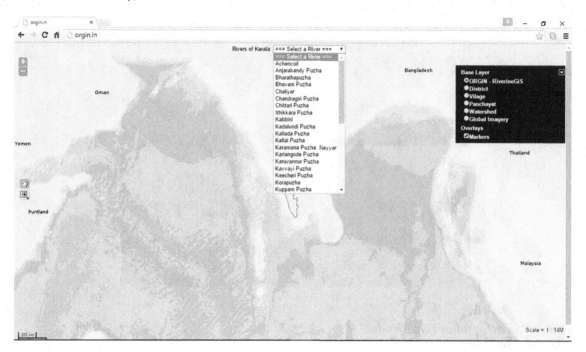

Figure 10. Geo-visuals of rivers
(©2015, Smart Kundassery).

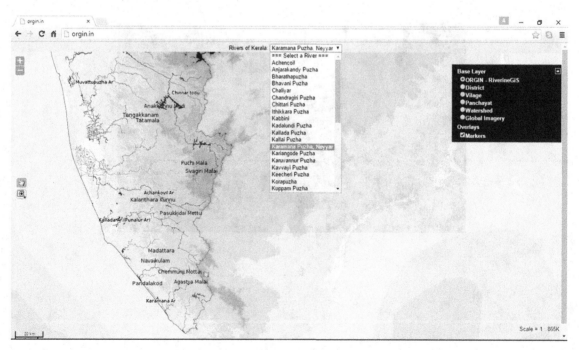

Figure 11. River sand mining
(©2013, Smart Kundassery).

Figure 12. RiverineGiS weather mashup
(©2015, Smart Kundassery).

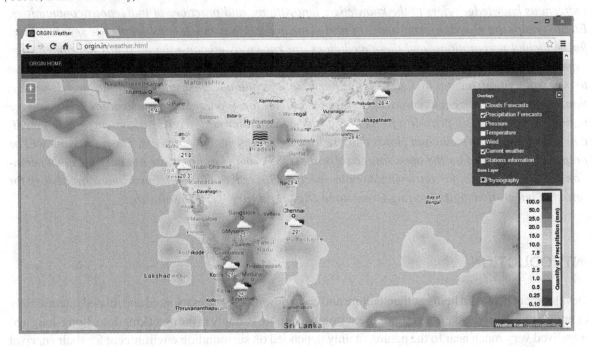

Chapter 26
Designing a Framework of Ethnomedicinal Plant Knowledge Integration Using OSS

Piyali Das
MUC Women's College, Burdwan, India

ABSTRACT

Indigenous knowledge refers to the knowledge, innovations, and practices of indigenous communities. Ethnic groups are repository knowledge of herbal medicine. Many indigenous people use several plants for medicinal preparations, and these medicines are known as ethnomedicine. It has developed from experience gained over centuries. Species of ethnomedicinal plants are threatened in most of nations due to overexploitation, habitat loss, destructive harvesting techniques, unsustainable trade, and deforestation. Documented indigenous knowledge on ethnomedicine forms part of the documentary heritage of the nation. The chapter will provide a framework for design an information retrieval system for ethnomedicine or knowledge on medicinal plants that are used to manage human ailments. The framework will be prepared, established on the open source software (OSS), and is appropriate not only for documentation but also beneficial for retrieving domain-specific knowledge. The model provides a framework for resource integration digitally using Greenstone Digital Library (GSDL) software.

INTRODUCTION

Development of human being as their culture and civilization has been associated and related intentionally or unintentionally with their surrounding environment, more strongly to the plant kingdom. Long-long ago man lived very much near to the nature, mainly depended on surrounding environment for their survival which becomes an integral part of lives of indigenous communities surviving in and depending on them. From the very beginning of human civilization dependency on nature, made them knowledgeable about various economic and medicinal properties of nature and natural resources by trial and error process. The

DOI: 10.4018/978-1-7998-9158-1.ch026

history of medicine indicates that almost every major civilization and culture has developed their own system for curing diseases. This acquired, undocumented, unique knowledge which are very useful for their livelihood is known as Indigenous knowledge and the people associated with are called Indigenous people. Ethnomedicine is a good example of indigenous knowledge (IK) which has affected the lives of both the indigenous community as well as the global community also. Accordingly, indigenous people in India, has a rich culture of traditional medicine, well known as "tribal" or "Adivasi", become the repository of information and knowledge, which is exclusively belongs to a specific culture or society and basically tacit knowledge that is confined in human mind and not written elsewhere. They enrich through generations and transferred on from one generation to other, without any written documents. An efficient documented information system in any discipline is very important for its development and also useful to other people who are wish to depend on their cultural believe for healthiness, Ethnomedicine is not an exception. In view of this, it becomes effective to design an information retrieval system to accumulate traditional knowledge on different plants, helpful to controlling disease and wellness, under single umbrella, through which information will reach to the hands of their potential users.

ETHNOMEDICINE CONCEPT

Regardless of the advancement of synthetic chemistry and biotechnology, tribal knowledge and their use for mankind are still useful for community healthcare and drug development in the present and future era as well as for integration of cultural heritage and biodiversity. World Health Organization (WHO), stated that demand of ethnomedicine has increased in all provinces of the developing and less developed world and its use is rapidly expanding in the industrialized countries also. Today nearby 80% of the world's populace has faith in primarily on plants and plant extracts for healthcare (Modern Ghana, 2013).

Ethnomedicine, in general, the communal medicine which is concerned with the treatment and prevention of health diseases and ailment that are generally consider for play a beneficial role in health care. Ethnomedicine refers to the study of traditional medical practice which is concerned with the health, diseases and illness and also addresses the healthcare seeking process and healing practices (Krippner, 2003). Medical beliefs and practice of indigenous community is called Ethnomedicine. Indigenous community means peoples inhabitant of a specific territory or geographical region having a historical continuity belief in a specific culture that developed on their territories, consider themselves distinct from other sectors of the societies now existing on those territories (Indigenous Peoples at the UN, n.d.). They form at present non-dominant sectors of society and are determined to preserve, develop and transmit to future generations their ancestral territories, and their ethnic identity, as the basis of their continued existence as peoples, in accordance with their own cultural patterns, social institutions and legal system. The sum-total of innovation, talent and observation based on the theories, way of life and experiences of indigenous community to different cultures, where explainable or not, used in the anticipation, identification, enhancement or treatment of substantial and overall health may called ethnomedicine. Ethnomedical practitioners generally receive their education through a long apprenticeship, and may administer the therapy in a ritual and evoke the help of a deity. Ethnic medical practice is waning in cultures influenced or colonized by Western civilization.

The term ethnomedicine appears in academic literature is somewhat in a different meaning. In the American anthropological literature the medicine in ethnomedicine usually refers to knowledge and ideas about health and healthcare. In European and biological literature the medicine tends to refer to medication or treatment practice (Singer and Erickson., 2014). Ethnomedicine is a practice or believe of the traditional practitioner of various ethnic groups, and especially by indigenous communities. The word ethnomedicine is also every so often used as a synonymous term for traditional medicine. ("American Journal of Ethnomedicine", n.d.)

IMPORTANCE OF ETHNOMEDICINAL KNOWLEDGE INTEGRATION

At the early stage of civilization, human livelihood was mainly going in nearby environment; they used plants for food, shelter, medicines etc. Using that knowledge, many of the modern drugs today have been derived from plant sources. The root of ethnomedicine is ancient conventional written source, of course, along with awareness and experience that has been passed away orally over the centuries (Stoller., 1984).

Designing a framework for integration of traditionally developed ethnomedicinal knowledge by the tribal regarding the use of medicinal plants in digital environment has its communal importance. To implement effective mechanisms for Ethnomedicinal knowledge, the present framework or outline, facilitates to use it as a platform for the preservation and management of the knowledge of ethnomedicine digitally and this, in turn, will integrate the knowledge of ethnomedicine into the existing knowledge systems for the benefit of society. The web-based digital resource integration on the selected domain, ethnomedicine, has various advantages over traditional resource integration service and few have been listed below:

- Providing full-text searching, i.e., general information about each plant species and their region of occurrence etc. is available in a single window;
- Global access to medicinal use of specific plant species in real time by remote users may make available through database;
- Browsing facility through various fields, e.g., plant name, disease name, made available as per potential user requirements;
- Instant access over the web through a common user interface;
- Up-to-the-minute updated access to newly added data;
- Dynamic updating of the digitized collection from any location;

ETHNOMEDICINAL KNOWLEDGE INTEGRATION: USING OPEN SOURCE SOFTWARE

Framework is used to draw possible courses of action or to present a preferred approach to an idea or thought. It is stated as a set of reference which is widely accepted enough to serve as the guiding principles of research within a particular discipline. The present framework for integration of ethnomedicinal knowledge is important as it designs for understanding of different phases of tasks associated with the documentation of ethnomedicine in digital environment. It provides structures approach to the organization of information on one or other aspects of ethnomedicine.

A reference framework is designed here to incorporate Ethnomedicinal resource that has been developed by using Green Stone Digital Library (GSDL) software which is a free Open Source Software (OSS). It provides autonomy & advantage to collection building within multilingual & multimedia information.

It is cost effective also. This software creates beautiful ways to integrate and distribute document digitally. It supports to publish digital collections on the Internet or on CD-ROM of Ethnomedicinal objects. This, in turn, enables one to build full-text search indexes and browsing classifiers for any collection of Ethnomedicinal objects. It describes or works to present an idea or thought to build a greenstone digital library software comprehensive, open source system for construction and maintain digital collection.

To build up this collection first of all data on various medicinal plants, their use by the traditional healer for treated various disease, are collected with the help of Data Collection Schedule, interview and observation methods. Domain specific comprehensive data are collected through Data collection schedule on two broad groups: *(I)Domain specific comprehensive data relating to Ethnomedicinal plants* (Generic Information, Availability of Plant, Perspective of Plant Use, Remedial Perspective, Mode of Administration) and *(II)Data on the use of medicinal plants on the tribal populace* (data on name, age, sex, level of education, occupation, ethnicity, source of experience, Experience period, diseases treated). Information related to 60 medicinal plant species has been collected on the basis of observation and interview of 22 informants or traditional healer which are arrange systematically. On the basis of this collected information we design a digital collection with the help GSDL software.

STEPS FOR COLLECTION BUILDING WITH THE HELP OF GSDL SOFTWARE

Step 1: Installation of Software

Greenstone Digital Library (GSDL) is accessible for different operating system (e.g., Windows, Linux), for the present work GSDL is installed in Windows XP operating system.

Steps for install GSDL are as follows:

- One can download GSDL and its associate software from http://www.greenstone.org/ *or* http://greenstonesupport.limk.ac.in/. People mostly download windows operation system from http://www.greenstone.org, they provide the latest version of software.
- As a pre-requisite to run GSDL we need JAVA to download which can be download from http://java.sun.com.
- Select the language to installation (we select English as language). GSDL 2.86 software is installed in computer by choosing the Local Library mode and just chooses the default options in the installation wizard.
- To work with collection of image we need "Imagemagick" which can download from http://www.imagemagick.org, which is required software for building ethnomedicinal collection.

After the finalization of installation process, check whether it is done properly by Click on Start → Programme → Greenstone Digital Library → Greenstone librarian interface. We get two interfaces of GSDL, one is librarian interface and another one user interface.

Step 2: Incorporation of Metadata into Software

In GSDL to incorporate newly created metadata (e.g., scientific name, use of plant, disease treated, etc.) open *Metadata Set Editor (GEMS)* and follow the steps.

Start → all programme → Greenstone digital library → Metadata Set Editor (GEMS) → File → New

Step 3: Collection Building

The easiest way to start a new digital library collection we have to use *Greenstone's Librarian Interface*. To start a new collection, file → new ... Our intention is to create digital integration of ethnomedicine, 60 records have prepared and build separately, at first in Microsoft word format and then converted those into HTML web page documents format. Each record describes each Ethnomedicinal plants and related information and must gather them in a single named file which will constitute the collection.

To build up a fresh collection after opening *Greenstone's Librarian Interface (GLI)* require to perform the following steps (Mukhopadhyay, 2005) one by one:

1. **Gather:** Gather information on the topic for construct the collection
2. **Enrich:** Each object should be encoded by using own-developed schema
3. **Design:** Construct the information, as per its appearance, requirement and the access facilities of the end user
4. **Format:** Customization the manifestation of user interface for searching and browsing
5. **Create:** Collection building on ethnomedicine

Step 3.1. Collection Building on Ethnomedicine Using GSDL

To create a digital library collection on ethnomedicine is to use *Greenstone's Librarian Interface (GLI)*, a component of Greenstone Digital Library software (Open the GLI from the Start → Programme → Greenstone Digital Library → Greenstone Librarian Interface).

Figure 1. New collection screen

Now click on GSDL Administrator → File → New pop-up window appear and Put the name of the collection against *collection title* (e.g., Ethnomedicine) and a brief description about the collection against *description of content* (e.g., Integration of Ethnomedicine). Now choose New Collection on the *Base this collection on* dialogue box and click "Ok". Now the collection is ready by a name which can be changed, modified time to time.

Figure 2. Creation of new collection in GSDL

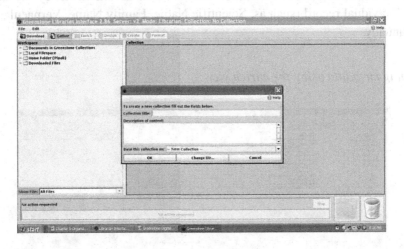

Step 3.2. Gather

Now in the "gather" panel navigate to the folder in local file space that contains the file(s) we want to use and it consent to the user to gather the require information by exploring the entire computer. After that, select the directory appear in left hand panel (e.g., Records on Ethnomedicine) → Select the files (e.g., record1, record2, record3, etc.) → Drug and drop the collection into right hand panel from left hand panel (drug the information either individually or as set of information from folders or subfolders).

Figure 3. Gathering document by exploring the computer

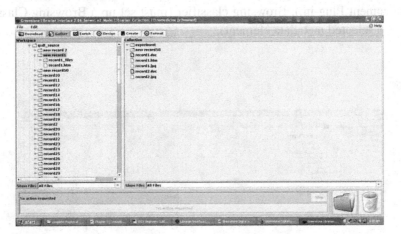

Step 3.3. Enrich

After gathering all document (related to Ethnomedicine) then next step is to enrich each documents through addition of metadata. Click on 'Enrich' tab and it will bring up a panel. Left side of the panel under Collection tab shows the files. Here selects the individual document one by one and add metadata to each selected individual record (such as, Scientific Name, Family Name, Vernacular Name, disease treated, etc.,) manually.

Figure 4. Assigning metadata using the enrich view

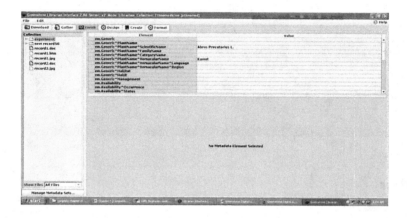

Step 3.4. Design

Now design the entire collection by choosing the desired features specified in the Design menu. In the collection design menu there are so many facets which are given in the left hand side panel, such as, Document Plug-ins (All plug-ins, required for manage common documents, at the time of installation by default they are loaded in a specific way), Create Search Indexes (for creating *Search Indexes,* appear just below the Document Plug-in,), Browsing classifier (must set up a Browsing Classifier because it helps to browse by a selected metadata element).

Figure 5. Plug ins

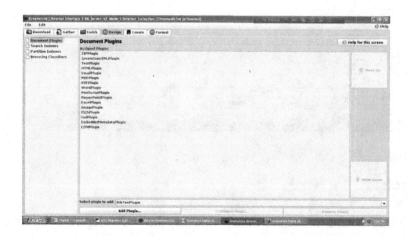

Figure 6. Adding indexes

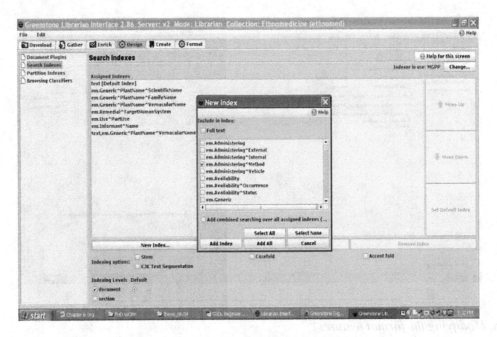

To insert the necessary Plug-ins wanted to convert the document into the given document format (greenstone archive format), click on Document Plug-ins, essential for Greenstone. All plug-ins, needed for handling common documents, will be loaded by default at the time of installation. Search Indexes indicate that whether the search is restricted within to paragraph or the entire text or to the chapter of the entire document. To create *Search Indexes,* click on the Search Indexes, given just under the Document Plug-in button. Default indexes can be removed through selecting the index description under *Assigned Indexes* and then click on the Remove Index button. By the same technique we can add new index, through clicking on new index button.

Step 3.5. Format

Format Features allow unlimited choices in adapting the appearance of the entire collection. The page-display of the collected works including the display-page of the collection or the main menu page that comes after clicking on the browsing classifiers button or on making a search, are created by the features provided under the Format tab.

To make available general information about the collection we have to select "*general*" in the format tab. If you wish to introduce a logo or icon of the collection in the homepage, select a picture and click on "*about page*" and "*home page*", then click *browse* button. After select the picture, the full path of the picture will appear in the address box lying against the Browse button.

Format feature helps one to change or edit any format by choosing the suitable feature from the *Choose Feature* option. One can also able to add new format string in the *Format Features* by click on the *Add Format* button.

.Figure 7. Designing the collection: general information

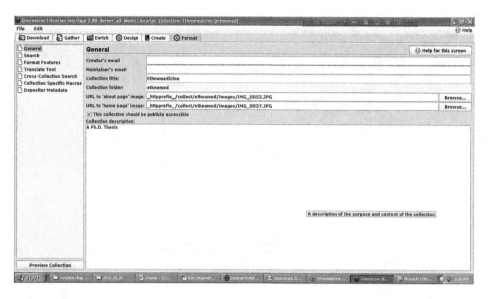

Figure 8. Modifying the format features

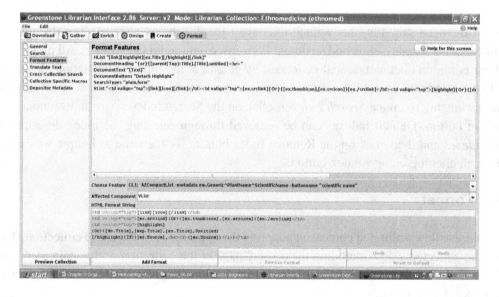

Format feature → Choose feature → Put the HTML Format string value. (Choose feature according to browsing classifier).

Step 3.6: Create

In *Create* panel, click on the *build collection* button and the progress in building the collection will shown by progress bar. To view the buildup collection, after the completion of the building process, click on the *Preview Collection* button.

Figure 9. Building a collection

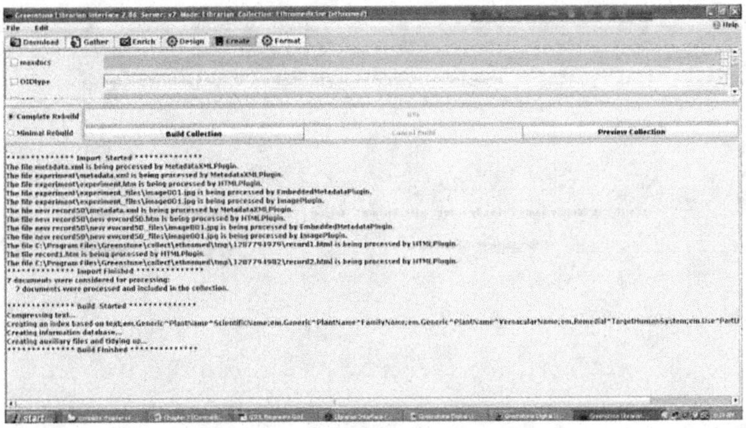

Step 4: Collection Make Available on CD-Rom

The Greenstone Digital Library Software can be used to available the whole collections over the WWW. GSDL software has a beautiful feature that if one wishes to transfer Greenstone application into an installable CD-ROM for sharing in the middle of large number of audience it allows to do that. The CD-ROMs work under every versions of the windows operating system. It requires the zip file which is to be extracted from C:\Program Files\gsdl\bin\windows. Now to make available the collection into a CD-ROM gives a name to the CD-ROM, tick the check box pertaining to the collection to be exported and click '*Write CD/DVD image*' button and at the end click *close* button. Now write the content of the folder (C:\ProgramFiles\Greenstone\ tmp\ "Ethnomedicine") into a blank CD-ROM to create self-installing windows CD-ROM.

SEARCH AND BROWSING

To prepare a accessible and searchable search engine on Ethnomedicine by using GSDL, the methods and mechanism which are describe previously step by step is applied.

The GSDL make available search and browsing facilities both simple and in advance manner search methods. Users '*select the collection*' from homepage to go into the user interface. From there user can select any searching keywords like, Local name, part use, and browse by click on button.

At the same way we can decrease the recall value with the help of advanced search mode. If one desires to search medicinal species name whose 'leaves' is used as medicine or remedy in 'Fever', a list of plants appeared as search result:

In case of browse by required field can be accessed by clicking the required field button. This brings up a list on documents stored in alphabetical order. If one wishes to know plants available in newly created digital library by browsing with field "Scientific name" it is displayed as bellow:

In same way we can browse by other parameters such as family name, part use, target human system, region and Informants.

Figure 10. Main user interface

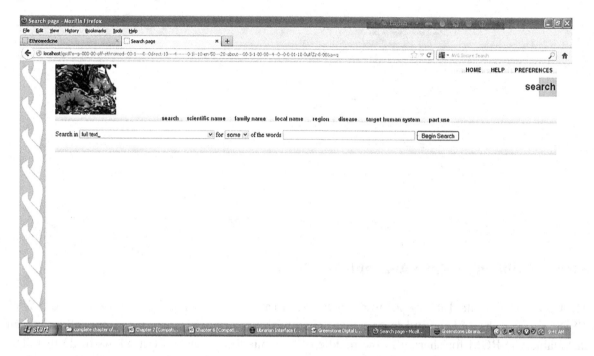

Figure 11. Search the collection

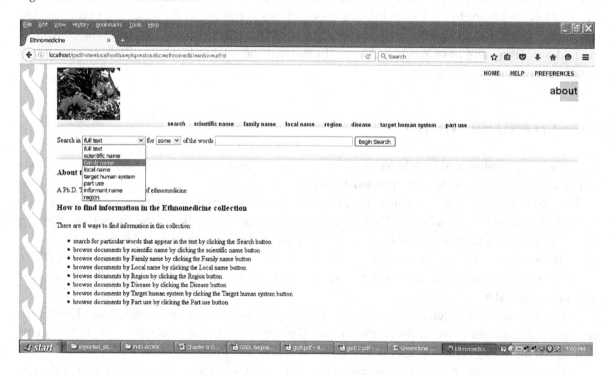

Figure 12. Display of advance search: 'leaves' is used as medicine in 'fever'

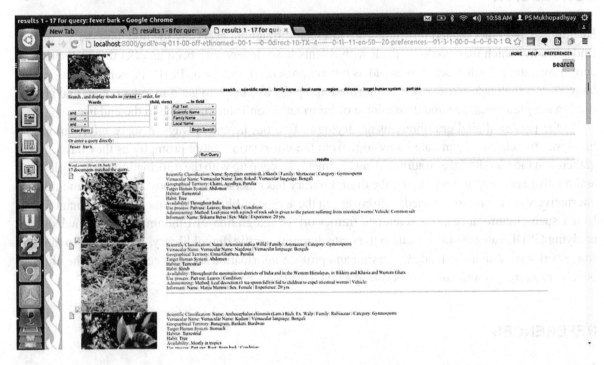

Figure 13. Display the result browses by 'scientific name'

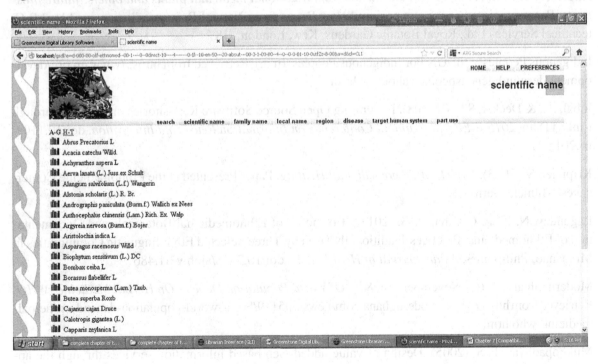

CONCLUSION

Healthiness and other related infirmities are foreseen throughout everyday life and have driven man to find ways by which they could be dealt with. Plants have dependably been an effective wellspring of cure from nature. Such practice is as old as human presence (Andersen, 1991). Present collection may be work as a replica to retrieve desire information rapidly and helps to get it in few minutes and also be used to integrate, organize and disseminate of information on Ethnomedicine to the end user.

At the present digital era librarians are trying to find out inventive ways to serve information in a lucid way to help users generate knowledge from the information, more promptly as they have always gathered in the non-digital or traditional environment. To cope up with the information needs with speed and relative accuracy and reliability, the digital library has emerged as the most pro active and reliable alternative source, and so knowledge discovery in these type of libraries becomes a predominant factor. Under such circumstances, this reference framework of integration of Ethnomedicinal knowledge by applying GSDL can provide a solution to create domain specific digital library. We hopeful to that this framework may well are extended to design and provide information services accessible to the ultimate beneficiary through web and also as datasets on CDROM.

REFERENCES

About Greenstone. (n.d.). Retrieved from http://www.greenstone.org/

Andersen, F. L. E. (1991). *Pharmaceuticals from traditional medicinal plants and others: future prospects.* Paper presented at the symposium "New Drugs from Natural Resources" sponsored by I.B.C. technical Services Ltd., Royal Botanic Gardens, Kew, London, UK.

Indigenous Peoples at the UN For Indigenous Peoples. (n.d.). Retrieved from https://www.un.org/development/desa/indigenouspeoples/about-us.html

Iqbal, A., & Decker, S. (2015, 08). Integrating Open Source Software Repositories on the Web through Linked Data. *2015 IEEE International Conference on Information Reuse and Integration.* doi:10.1109/iri.2015.27

Krippner, S. (2003). *Models of Ethnomedicinal Healing.* Paper Presented at the Ethnomedicine Conferences, Munich, Germany.

Lagunday, N. E., & Cabana, V. G. (2013). Taxonomy of Ethnomedicinal Botanicals and Documentation of Ethnomedicinal Practices Traditionally Used by Three Selected Ethnolinguistic Communities in Mindanao, Philippines. *Asian Journal of Health, 3*(1). doi:10.7828/ajoh.v3i1.486

Modern Ghana. (2013, November 26). *80% Of World Population Depend On Herbal Medicine -WHO.* Retrieved from https://www.modernghana.com/news/505179/80-of-world-population-depend-on-herbal-medicine-who.html

Mukhopadhyay, P. S. (2005). Design of value-added web based information services through the application of open source software. 182-201. In Automation and networking of the college libraries. Maulana Azad College.

Singer, M., & Erickson, P. I. (2014). *A companion to medical anthropology*. Wiley-Blackwell.

Stoller, P. (1984). Medicinal Plants and Traditional Medicine in Africa. Abayomi Sofowara.; Medicinal Plants of North Africa. *Loufty Boulos. Medical Anthropology Newsletter*, *15*(2), 54–54. doi:10.1525/maq.1984.15.2.02a00220

Tilburt, J. (2008). Herbal medicine research and global health: An ethical analysis. *Bulletin of the World Health Organization*, *86*(8), 594–599. doi:10.2471/BLT.07.042820 PMID:18797616

Witten, I. H., & Bainbridge, D. (2005). Building digital library collections with greenstone *Proceedings of the 5th ACM/IEEE-CS Joint Conference on Digital Libraries - JCDL '05* 10.1145/1065385.1065530

ADDITIONAL READING

Abera, B. (2014). Medicinal plants used in traditional medicine by Oromo people, Ghimbi District, Southwest Ethiopia. *Journal of Ethnobiology and Ethnomedicine*, *10*(1), 40. doi:10.1186/1746-4269-10-40 PMID:24885586

Hussain, A. (2008). *Ethnomedicine: Indian perspectives and practices*. Icfai University Press.

Maheshwari, J. K. (1996). *Ethnobotany in South Asia*. Scientific.

Pan, I., & Das, S. K. (2012). *Digital library: Pragmatic approach, GSDL 2.71 version*. Prova Prakashani.

Saha, N. C., & Suman, D. (2015). Development of Digital Library by Using GSDL in Library 2.0 Environment: A Practical Approach. *Library Herald*, *53*(3), 245. doi:10.5958/0976-2469.2015.00028.7

WIPO and the traditional knowledge conundrum. (2017). *Protecting Traditional Knowledge*, 317-324. doi:10.4324/9781315666358-20

This research was previously published in the Handbook of Research on Emerging Trends and Technologies in Library and Information Science; pages 332-345, copyright year 2020 by Information Science Reference (an imprint of IGI Global).

Chapter 27
Critical Barriers to Business Intelligence Open Source Software Adoption

Placide Poba-Nzaou
ⓘ https://orcid.org/0000-0002-7007-764X
University of Quebec in Montreal, Montreal, Canada

Sylvestre Uwizeyemungu
University of Quebec in Trois-Rivières, Trois-Rivières, Canada

Mariem Saada
DiCentral, Montreal, Canada

ABSTRACT

Over the past few years, managers have been hard pressed to become more data-driven, and one of the prerequisites in doing so is through the adoption of Business Intelligence (BI) tools. However (1) the adoption of BI tools remains relatively low (2) the acquisition costs of proprietary BI tools are relatively high and (3) the level of satisfaction with these BI tools remain low. Given the potential of open source BI (OSBI) tools, there is a need for analyzing barriers that prevent organizations from adopting OSBI. Drawing a systematic review and a Qualitative Survey of BI Experts, this study proposes a framework that categorizes and structures 23 barriers to OSBI adoption by organizations including 4 that were identified by BI Experts but not explicitly found in the literature. This paper contributes to OSS and Information Systems (IS) research literature on BI adoption in general and provides specific insights to practitioners.

INTRODUCTION

Over the past two decades or so, business intelligence (BI) and analytics have grown into a more and more important phenomenon for both academic and business communities (Chen, Chiang, & Storey, 2012). For instance, a special issue on BI published by the last authors in the journal *Management Information*

DOI: 10.4018/978-1-7998-9158-1.ch027

Systems Quarterly (MISQ) highlights the increasing importance of BI research in academia. Based on an 11-year survey (from 2004 to 2014) of senior IT executives from 2552 organizations located all over the world, Luftman et al. (2015) reported that, from a business perspective, analytics/business intelligence ranks first among the five most influential technologies. Another survey of over 4000 IT professionals from 93 countries and 25 industries identified business analytics as one of the four major technology trends in the 2010s (IBM, 2011). In fact, managers are hard pressed to become more data-driven (Kiron, Prentice, & Ferguson, 2014) while many scholars have underscored a broader new phenomenon qualified as "data-driven economy" (Mandel, 2012) or "analytics paradigm" (Delen & Zolbanin, 2018). In this context, the adoption and use of BI tools are considered one of the first prerequisite for organizational competitiveness that includes but is not limited to data-driven decision-making culture (McAfee, Brynjolfsson, Davenport, Patil, & Barton, 2012). In fact, apart from the fundamental data processing and analytical technologies included in BI and associated tools, they "include business-centric practices and methodologies that can be applied to various high-impact applications such as e-commerce, market intelligence, e-government, healthcare, and security" (Chen et al., 2012, p. 2).

However, despite the recognition of the importance of BI tools, their high potential in generating business value at both operational and strategic levels (Fink, Yogev, & Even, 2017), the rate of their adoption remains low. It is estimated that only 30% of all employees are using BI tools (Gartner, 2017a), and that penetration levels would increase to over 50% percent only "if cost, technology and other institutional challenges were not barriers to increase use" (Datamation, 2013, p. 1). The high costs associated with BI tool licenses and maintenance are echoed by Sallam, Richardson, Hagerty, and Hostmann (2011) who, in addition, underscore the complexity and low ease of use of proprietary BI tools. Another fact worth mentioning is the low level of satisfaction with BI tools and initiatives experience (Advaiya, 2017; Sallam et al., 2011).

Although most organizations have adopted proprietary BI tools that dominate the BI market, Sallam et al. (2011) reported an increasing interest in low-cost options, including open source BI tools as credible alternative solutions. A survey by Clutch revealed that 83% of business users and 88% of data scientists are likely to use open source software —as opposed to paid, proprietary solutions—in the future (Peacock, 2017).

In summary, considering (1) the struggles faced by organizations with their proprietary BI tools (Advaiya, 2017; Sallam et al., 2011) (2) the low adoption rate of BI tools (Datamation, 2013; Gartner, 2017a) (3) with the recognition of OSBI as a credible alternative to proprietary BI tools as well as the availability of OSBI tools with capabilities comparable to that of proprietary tools (Thomsen & Pedersen, 2009), there is a need to better understand the most critical barriers that prevent organizations from adopting OSBI tools.

Furthermore, a systematic review of BI studies included in this study reveals three major weaknesses in the current literature. First, the majority of studies are normative and lack empirical or theoretical foundations. Second, none of the studies focus on the perspective of BI experts. Third, as for the literature on business value creation from BI (Trieu, 2017), the body of knowledge on barriers associated with the adoption of BI tools is fragmented, thus it's lacking an all-encompassed, integrated framework. Such a framework is important, as it will facilitate knowledge accumulation (Hammersley, 2007), as well as evidence-based practices.

This study addresses the above-mentioned gaps in the literature by first providing a framework derived from a systematic review that identifies barriers to the adoption of BI tools by organizations. Building on the framework, this research – using a Qualitative Survey design – compares the barriers extracted from the academic literature with the most critical barriers elicited by open source BI experts in answering the following question: "What are the most critical barriers that prevent organizations from adopting open source BI tools?" Here barriers are defined as any factors preventing or discouraging the adoption of OSBI by organizations.

Following the introduction, the conceptual background is presented. Then the research methodology is described. The subsequent section is devoted to the presentation and discussion of the research results. Lastly, the article concludes with implications for research and practice as well as directions for future research.

BACKGROUND

Defining Business Intelligence

There is no consensus on the definition of Business Intelligence (BI). Based on Davies (2002, p. 313) the definition of intelligence is "the acquisition, interpretation, collation, assessment, and exploitation of information". Following the last author, Chung, Chen, and Nunamaker (2003, p. 1) suggest to define BI as "the acquisition, interpretation, collation, assessment, and exploitation of information in the business domain." According to the Garner IT Glossary (2018, p. 1) Business Intelligence can be defined as "an umbrella term that includes the applications, infrastructure and tools, and the best practices that enable access to and analysis of information to improve and optimize decision making and performance". The Gartner report written by Sallam et al. (2011) identified 13 essential capabilities that define a BI platform. These capabilities are organized along three functional dimensions: integration, information delivery, and analysis: *Integration* – BI infrastructure, metadata management, development tools, and collaboration – *Information Delivery* – reporting, dashboards, ad hoc query, search based BI, and productivity suite integration – *Analysis* – OLAP, interactive visualization, scorecards, predictive modeling and data mining. Park, El Sawy, and Fiss (2017) identified seven key functionalities of BI tools: providing access to multiple data sources, rule-based exception handling, alerting managers about business events, accessing the enterprise-wide consistent database, supporting what-if analysis, presenting data visually, and extracting patterns from data. Adopting an architectural view, Chaudhuri, Dayal, and Narasayya (2011) suggest five components that define BI: data sources, data movement, streaming engines, data warehouse servers, mid-tier servers, and front-end applications.

Broadly speaking, there are three main alternatives for an organization wishing to adopt BI tools. Each one can be deployed on premises or through a cloud-based service: proprietary, custom, or open source. As indicated by Table 1, each alternative has different ratings with regard to two main differentiating characteristics of IT innovation (Wang, 2009); that is, their characteristics related to their "conceptual form" or "material form".

A survey on Business Intelligence Data Analytics conducted by Clutch (2016) revealed that the market is dominated by proprietary BI solutions. According to Apps Run The World (2011), in 2016, the top 10 analytics and BI software vendors accounted for nearly 60% of the global analytics and BI applications market, with the top five being SAP (11% of the market share) followed by SAS Institute, IBM, Oracle and Tableau. However, for the past several few years, open source business intelligence has been gaining "credence", "as more companies adopt BI and large vendors partner with open source players in an evolving BI ecosystem" (D'Souza, 2011, p. 1). The importance of the open source BI segment is illustrated by the high popularity of Hadoop (Stackowiak, Licht, Mantha, & Nagode, 2015), and a number of key takeovers such as the acquisition of Jaspersoft by TIBCO in April 2014 (TIBCO, 2014) and the acquisition of Pentaho by Hitachi Vantara in June 2015 (Hitachi, 2015).

Table 1. BI alternatives and associated ranking

BI solution alternative BI attribute	Proprietary software	Custom development	Open source software
Conceptual form			
Governance metaphor	Chapel	Cathedral	Bazaar
Ability to access and modify the source code (Olsen & Saetre, 2007)	–	+	+
Ability to try out the software at a very low cost (Dedrick & West, 2004)	–	–	+
Independence (Olsen & Saetre, 2007)	–	+	+
High level of maintainability (Bonaccorsi, Piscitello, Merito, & Rossi, 2006)	–	+	+
Low acquisition and possession costs (Olsen & Saetre, 2007)	–	+/–	+
Sharing of development costs (Sledgianowski, Tafti, & Kierstead, 2008)	–	+/–	+
Material form			
Property of source code (Olsen & Saetre, 2007)	–	+	+
Rare need to invest in specific servers (Sledgianowski et al., 2008)	–	+	+
Based on most recognized software standards, middleware or languages such as XML and JBoss (Smets-Solanes, 2003)	+/–	+	+
+ the BI solution alternative is highly rated on the BI attribute - the BI solution alternative is lowly rated on the BI attribute +/- the BI solution alternative is moderately rated on the BI attribute Adapted from Poba-Nzaou, Raymond, and Fabi (2014, p. 483)			

Adoption of Open Source Business Intelligence Tools by Organizations

According to Gartner (2017b), open source is now an essential part of the modern IT industry, and they call for every CIO to secure the most developed strategies so as to manage specific risk, as well as rewards in order to take the maximum advantage from this powerful phenomenon. In fact, started decades ago within the infrastructure software in horizontal domains, the open source phenomenon has expanded beyond IS business applications in vertical domains (Fitzgerald, 2006), and has since reached the domain of mission-critical and strategic packaged application software, such as enterprise resource planning (ERP), Electronic Health Record (HER), and BI software. According to Thomsen & Pedersen (2009), although open source business intelligence tools are popular in some industries, their adoption by organizations is still limited. The author underscores that there are available mature OSBI tools when considering capabilities related to Extraction-Transfer-Load (ETL) tools, as well as Database Management Systems (DBMs) and On-Line Analytical Processing (OLAP) servers, and OLAP clients. Thus, there is a need to understand the barriers that prevent organizations from adopting OSBI tools.

A first systematic review was performed on a research published prior and up to July 5th 2017 in five major research databases: ABI inform Global, Springerlink, Business source Complete, Emerald and Scopus. At this stage, it is important to remember that the inclusion of systematic review in the research theoretical background has been done in previous research (e.g. Poba-Nzaou, Lemieux, Beaupré, and Uwizeyemungu (2016)).

To be eligible for the systematic review, studies had to fulfill two inclusion criteria: (1) be a peer-reviewed article published in English (2) report on barriers to the adoption of open source BI tools. This first research used combinations of three key words: "Business intelligence" and "Open source", combined with one of the following key words: obstacle, barrier, challenge. The research led to the identification of 137 articles, among which 107 were excluded after the reading of the abstracts, leading to 30 articles to be read in full. However, after reading all the articles in full, none was relevant to the themes of the study: 12 were not about open source, 10 were not about adoption and 4 did not mention any barrier or obstacle or challenge.

Given that the first systematic review was unsuccessful, the second systematic review was performed in three major research databases with a broader scope; that is, not restricted to BI but extended to open source in general: ABI/INFORM Global, Business Source Complete and Scopus. To be eligible, studies had to fulfill two inclusion criteria: (1) be a peer-reviewed article published in English (2) report on the adoption of open source software. Given that research on open source business intelligence is relatively young, the research team decided to extend the search to articles published in international peer-reviewed conferences. An additional search was thus performed in the Association for Information Systems' (AIS) digital library, which is the major central repository for research papers, including conference proceedings and journal articles related to information systems. Starting with 441 articles, 24 were excluded because of redundancy. The remaining 417 articles were processed as indicated by the flow chart (see figure 1).

Figure 1. Flow chart of study selection process

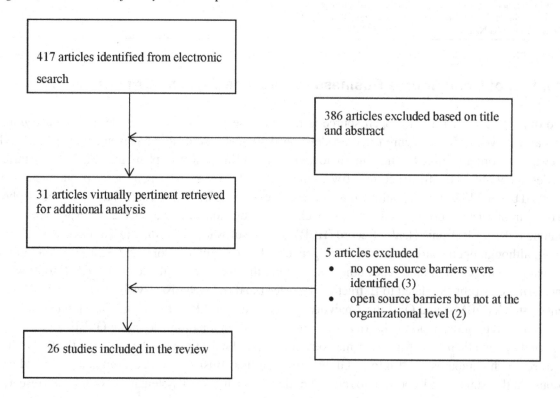

The previous research on information systems suggests that the adoption and implementation of technological innovation are influenced by technological, organizational, and environmental factors (e.g. Poba-Nzaou and Raymond (2011); Poba-Nzaou et al. (2016)). This research uses the technology-organization-environmental (TOE) framework (Depietro, Wiarda, & Fleischer, 1990) which is one of the most widely used frameworks for studying the adoption of technological innovation (Venkatesh & Bala, 2012). Through the scheme of TOE, the technological context describes internal as well as external technologies that are relevant to the organization. It comprises of factors such as availability of current and new technological innovations. Organizational context covers the characteristics of the organization, for instance, firm size, and the extent of resources available within the organization. Alongside other resources, *slack resources* designate resources that are in surplus in comparison to the regular operating of the organization. Environmental context represents the industry or in a broad sense, the "field" in which the firm operates (DiMaggio & Powell, 1983). Table 2 presents the synthesis of the 23 barriers found in the 26 studies of the systematic review; the barriers are organized according to the TOE framework.

Broadly speaking, the systematic review reveals that: (1) the majority of studies are normative and lack empirical or theoretical foundations (2) none of the studies focus on the perspective of BI experts (3) the related body of knowledge is scattered; thus, it is lacking an all-encompassed, integrated framework. It is important to remember that the last observation is consistent with the results of a recent review of research on "getting value from BI" conducted by Trieu (2017, p. 1).

Research Design - Qualitative Survey

According to Jansen (2010, p. 1), whereas "the statistical survey analyzes frequencies in member characteristics in a population the qualitative survey analyzes the diversity of member characteristics within a population. The diversity of member characteristics may either be predefined or developed in open coding". Fink (2003) recommended the use of qualitative survey analysis for researches aimed at exploring meanings and experiences which is the case for the current study. Other previous studies have adopted the Qualitative Survey method to elicit experts' knowledge (e.g. Felix, Rauschnabel, & Hinsch, 2017).

Data Collection and Analysis

As for most qualitative studies, we adopted a purposeful sampling strategy combined with a snowball sampling strategy (Patton, 1990). Experts' selection was based on five criteria: (1) occupy a position in information technology and communication (ICT) domain within an organization (2) have a minimum of five years of professional experience in ICT (3) have a minimum of three years of experience with open source technologies (4) have a minimum of five years of professional experience with enterprise systems (e.g. ERP, CRM, SCM), and (5) show a strong interest in BI technologies. Initially 52 potential respondents were identified from three sources: (1) researchers' professional networks (2) a professional social network and (3) internet searches. All the profiles were recorded in a database. After a screening of the profiles, only 20 met the inclusion criteria, but the research team was not able to identify the correct email address or telephone of seven of them. Thus, a formal invitation to participate in the study was sent by email to 13 respondents, along with a brief description of the research project and the expected commitment, as well as a request to recommend potential respondents. Overall, 8 experts agreed to participate; five were unable to commit to the study due to time constraints. Of note is the fact that an additional set of six experts were recommended by those contacted directly by the research team. However, three were not able to actually commit to the study due to time constraints, and among them, two suggested interview appointments beyond the deadline set by the researchers. At that stage, it is important to underscore that it was initially decided to start the interviews with the selected 11 experts, while remaining ready to recruit new experts if theoretical saturation was not reached (Lincoln & Guba, 1985). Theoretical saturation is the point at which the qualitative analyst does not see new information in the data related to the codes or themes (Guest, Bunce, & Johnson, 2006). However, the point of saturation was reached after nine interviews were conducted.

Table 2. Barriers to the Adoption of BI Tools

TOE dimensions	Barrier description	Support in the literature
Technological OSS specific	Fear, Uncertainty and Doubt (FUD) with regard to open source product characteristics (sustainability, reliability, quality, variability, functionalities, usability, security, privacy, maturity, interoperability, intellectual property, etc.)	(Côté & Egelstaff, 2007; Gallego, Luna, & Bueno, 2008a; Nagy, Yassin, & Bhattacherjee, 2010; Palanisamy & Mukerji, 2012; Poba-Nzaou & Uwizeyemungu, 2013; Safadi, Chan, Dawes, Roper, & Faraj, 2015; Stol, Babar, Avgeriou, & Fitzgerald, 2011; Williams van Rooij, 2007)
	Fear, Uncertainty and Doubt (FUD) with regard to open source service provider characteristics (longevity, service quality, etc.) and services availability.	(Poba-Nzaou & Uwizeyemungu, 2013)
	Fear, Uncertainty and Doubt (FUD) with regard to open source product governance (e.g. strategy on intellectual property, development community organization, relationship with users, release schedules and speed)	(Gallego et al., 2008a; Gallego, Luna, & Bueno, 2008b; Goode, 2014; Gwebu & Wang, 2010; Palanisamy & Mukerji, 2012; Paré, Wybo, & Delannoy, 2009; Poba-Nzaou & Uwizeyemungu, 2013; Safadi et al., 2015; Vanmeulebrouk, Rivett, Ricketts, & Loudon, 2008; Weilbach & Byrne, 2013)
	Complexity of the open source software ecosystem (e.g. high number of license types, high number of fork projects, etc.)	(Palanisamy & Mukerji, 2012; Stol et al., 2011)
	Complexity of open source products (e.g. long learning curve, complex configuration, etc.)	(Crowston & Wade, 2010; Foll & Foil, 2008; Gallego et al., 2008a; Hauge, Ayala, & Conradi, 2010; Macredie & Mijinyawa, 2011; Paré et al., 2009; Poba-Nzaou & Uwizeyemungu, 2013; Stol et al., 2011)
	Low level of integrability (functional, technical) and interoperability with existing organizations' legacy information systems	(Gallego et al., 2008a; Harris et al., 2016; Mutula & Kalaote, 2010; Nagy et al., 2010; Safadi et al., 2015; Stol et al., 2011)
	Lack of training courses and reliable information or documentation on open source products in the market	(Buchan, 2011; Buchana & Naicker, 2014; Côté & Egelstaff, 2007; Grodzinsky, Miller, & Wolf, 2003; Hauge et al., 2010; Palanisamy & Mukerji, 2012; Paré et al., 2009; Stol et al., 2011)
	Lack of responsible third party engagement	(Paré et al., 2009; Poba-Nzaou & Uwizeyemungu, 2013)
	Hidden costs	(Buchan, 2011; Gallego et al., 2008a; Gwebu & Wang, 2010; Hauge et al., 2010; Mutula & Kalaote, 2010; Nagy et al., 2010; Palanisamy & Mukerji, 2012; Paré et al., 2009; Safadi et al., 2015; Stol et al., 2011)
	Insufficient visibility in the market and lack of marketing actions	(Poba-Nzaou & Uwizeyemungu, 2013)
	Shortage of enterprises providing integrated services including support, training, installation, maintenance, etc.	(Côté & Egelstaff, 2007; Foll & Foil, 2008; Grodzinsky et al., 2003; Gwebu & Wang, 2010; Mutula & Kalaote, 2010; Palanisamy & Mukerji, 2012; Safadi et al., 2015; Stol et al., 2011; Williams van Rooij, 2007; H. Wu & Cao, 2009; J. Wu, Goh, Li, Luo, & Zheng, 2016)

continues on following page

Table 2. Continued

TOE dimensions	Barrier description	Support in the literature
Organizational	Stereotype, prejudice, misunderstanding over open source business models	(Grodzinsky et al., 2003; Palanisamy & Mukerji, 2012; Poba-Nzaou & Uwizeyemungu, 2013)
	Internal inertia (political pressure, conservative attitudes and practices of IT managers and executives, etc.)	(Gallego et al., 2008a; Paré et al., 2009; Poba-Nzaou & Uwizeyemungu, 2013)
	Cultural and structural obstacles (e.g. disadvantageous tender/procurement processes vis-à-vis open source solution, unfavorable quality assessment approach, etc.)	(Gallego et al., 2008a; Paré et al., 2009; Poba-Nzaou & Uwizeyemungu, 2013)
	Lack or insufficiency of internal resources (technical and functional skills, knowledge, infrastructure, guiding policies, etc.)	(Foll & Foil, 2008; Gallego et al., 2008a; Hauge et al., 2010; Mutula & Kalaote, 2010; Nagy et al., 2010; Palanisamy & Mukerji, 2012; Paré et al., 2009; Tomazin & Gradišar, 2007; Vanmeulebrouk et al., 2008; Weilbach & Byrne, 2013)
	Fear of users' resistance or rejection	(Côté & Egelstaff, 2007; Gallego et al., 2008a; Kim, Chan, & Lee, 2014; Safadi et al., 2015)
	Strong dependence on proprietary software and providers (lock-in)	(Mutula & Kalaote, 2010)
Environmental	Lack of government and policy makers' awareness and support	(Macredie & Mijinyawa, 2011; Mutula & Kalaote, 2010; Poba-Nzaou & Uwizeyemungu, 2013)
	External political pressure	(Paré et al., 2009; Poba-Nzaou & Uwizeyemungu, 2013; Safadi et al., 2015)
	Effect of fashion phenomenon trends in the market	(Gallego et al., 2008a)
	Insufficient visibility and legitimacy in the market	(Gallego et al., 2008a; Poba-Nzaou & Uwizeyemungu, 2013)
	Insufficient dissemination of knowledge concerning open source software in higher education institutions	(Poba-Nzaou & Uwizeyemungu, 2013)
	Shortage of skilled labor with OS expertise including combination of technical and functional competencies on open source products	(Poba-Nzaou & Uwizeyemungu, 2013)

Table 3 presents the demographic profile of the study panel of 11 Canadian BI experts.

To achieve an appropriate level of internal validity, two sources of evidences were used, semi-structured interviews, and field notes. The interviews lasted one hour and thirty minutes on average, using the same interview guide for all respondents in order to facilitate comparative analysis (Miles & Huberman, 1994). The content of the interview guide was based on the TOE framework that was also used to classify the barriers extracted from the literature. It contained initial information gathering on the respondent characteristics including education, position, and professional experience. Critical barriers that may impede the adoption of open source BI were then discussed. Based on the framework, specific questions were asked about the identification of the most critical barriers related to open source BI specific characteristics, those related to the characteristics of the adopting organizations, those related to the characteristics of the environment in which the adopting organization operates. Then, respondents were asked to identify barriers that don't match any of the three categories. All interviews were tape-recorded and transcribed verbatim for a total of 50 pages.

Table 3. Demographic profile of respondents

Gender	Male	82%
	Female	18%
Age(years)	50-59	18%
	40-49	45%
	30-39	27%
	<59	9%
Highest education degree	High school diploma	9%
	Bachelor or other undergraduate degree	18%
	M.Sc.	27%
	Doctorate	45%
Professional experience with BI (years)	<10	82%
	>=10	18%
Role	Expert	45%
	Vice-president	9%
	Director	36%
	Researcher	9%
Industry sector	Public sector administration	9%
	Media industry	9%
	Consulting services	55%
	Transportation	9%
	Higher education	18%
Size of organization	Large (>=500)	27%
	Medium (100-499)	36%
	Small (<=100)	9%
Annual revenue (Million $ CAN)	0.15-1	9%
	<1.6 - 5	18%
	6 - 15	27%
	250-450	18%
	Undisclosed	27%
Use of BI tools	Yes	91%
	No	9%

The data analysis began immediately after the first interview and it essentially followed the principles of interpretative research suggested by Klein and Myers (1999). In the same manner as Poba-Nzaou et al. (2016, p. 4013), first, "one of the research team members' read and reread the verbatim transcript starting in run-of-river mode, to develop a deep understanding of the material". Then the researcher performed a semantic analysis of the transcript following three steps (Tanner & Stone, 1998). During the first step, statements were extracted from each interview's transcript and copied in different rows on a table. Thereafter, statements conveying the same meaning were combined. By doing so, the researcher created categories. Lastly, a label was assigned to each set of statements. Afterwards, relying on TOE framework dimensions as vehicles, the researcher derived abstraction and connected experts' statements with theoretical categories in accordance with the "principle of abstraction and generalization" by moving back and forth within and between experts' statements and the TOE framework dimensions, following the "hermeneutic circle principle" (Klein & Myers, 1999). The processes ended up with a final list of 18 barriers after eliminating duplicates and combining all statements that conveyed the same meaning. A researcher familiar with BI literature critically reviewed the combined list of barriers for clarity in regard to the statements extracted from the verbatim transcript. Based on this review, minor adjustments were made to the list of barriers in order to enhance the clarity of the categories that were created. Table 4 shows the revised framework based on the results of the Qualitative Survey.

Table 4. Revised framework based on the results of the Qualitative Survey

TOE dimensions	Challenge description	SRL	QLS	Rank
Technological OSS specific	Fear, Uncertainty and Doubt (FUD) with regard to open source product characteristics (durability, reliability, quality, variability, functionalities, usability, security, privacy, maturity, etc.)	✓	✓	4
	Fear, Uncertainty and Doubt (FUD) with regard to open source service provider characteristics (longevity, service quality, etc.) and services availability	✓	✓	3
	Fear, Uncertainty and Doubt (FUD) with regard to open source product governance (e.g. strategy on intellectual property, release schedules)	✓	✓	5
	Fear, Uncertainty and Doubt (FUD) with regard to open source business models	NL	✓	6
	Complexity of the open source software ecosystem (e.g. high number of license types, high number of fork projects, etc.)	✓	✓	5
	Complexity of open source products (e.g. long learning curve, complex configuration, etc.)	✓	NE	NA
	Low level of integrability (functional, technical) and interoperability with existing organizations' legacy information systems	✓	✓	4
	Lack of training courses and reliable information or documentation on open source products in the market	✓	✓	4
	Lack of third party engagement for technical support and maintenance services	✓	NE	NA
	Hidden costs	✓	✓	5
	Insufficient visibility in the market and lack of marketing actions	✓	✓	6
	Shortage of enterprises providing integrated services including support, training, installation, maintenance, etc.	✓	NE	NA
	Obligation to share own specific source code customization and associated consequences	NL	✓	5
Organizational	Stereotype, prejudice, misunderstanding over open source business models	✓	✓	2
	Internal inertia (political pressure, conservative attitudes and practices of IT managers and executives, etc.)	✓	✓	1
	Cultural and structural obstacles (e.g. disadvantageous tender/procurement processes vis-à-vis open source solution, unfavorable quality assessment approach, etc.)	✓	NE	NA
	Monopolization of BI initiatives by IS departments	NL	✓	6
	Lack or insufficiency of internal resources (technical and functional skills, knowledge, guiding policies, etc.)	✓	✓	2
	Fear of users' rejection	✓	NE	NA
	Strong dependence on proprietary software and providers (lock-in)	✓	NE	NA
	Risk aversion of IT managers	NL	✓	5

continues on following page

Table 4. Continued

TOE dimensions	Challenge description	SRL	QLS	Rank
Environmental	Lack of government and policy makers' awareness and support	✓	✓	NA
	External political pressure	✓	✓	3
	Effect of fashion phenomenon trends in the market	✓	NE	NA
	Insufficient legitimacy in the market	✓	NE	NA
	Insufficient dissemination of knowledge concerning open source software in higher education institutions	✓	NE	NA
	Shortage of skilled labor with OS expertise including combination of technical and functional competencies on open source products	✓	✓	6

SRL: systematic review of the literature
QLS: qualitative survey
NL: not explicitly found in the systematic review of the literature
NE: not mentioned by experts
NA: not applicable
Rank: based on frequency of mention by experts

RESULTS AND DISCUSSION

Noteworthy is the fact that the list on Table 4 consists of barriers associated with each of the three dimensions of the Technology-Organization-Environment (TOE) framework. However, 4 out of the 18 barriers identified by the experts cannot be related to those derived from the systematic review of the academic literature. In the same manner, 9 out of the 23 barriers identified from the systematic review cannot be related to those mentioned by the panel of experts. It seems important to remember that understanding these gaps is important for advancing both research and practice (Avolio, 2017).

The next section follows a discussion of the four barriers mentioned by the experts but not explicitly identified in the academic literature on the adoption of open source software. The section is closed by discussing the barriers that were found from the systematic review but were not mentioned by our panel of experts.

Barriers Identified by Experts but Not Explicitly Identified in the Academic Literature

Among the four barriers mentioned by the panel of experts but not found explicitly in the literature, two are related to the characteristic of the technology, and the other two are related to the characteristics of the adopting organization. We will first discuss the two barriers related to the characteristics of the technology: obligation to share one's own specific customization and associated consequences; and fear, uncertainty and doubt (FUD) with regard to open source product business models. Then we will discuss those related to the characteristics of the adopting organization: monopolization of BI initiatives by IS departments; and risk aversion of IS managers.

Obligation to Share One's Own Specific Source Code Customization and Associated Consequences

Although seen as intriguing, several scholars stress that "source code sharing" is rooted in the history and spirit of open source software (e.g. Hauge et al., 2010; Hecker, 1999; Lerner & Tirole, 2005). The obligation of sharing the source code generally arises from the clauses defined in the licenses. Following Lerner and Tirole (2005), we consider three classes of licenses: highly restrictive (general public license (GPL)), restrictive (e.g., lesser general public license (LGPL)), and unrestrictive (e.g., the Berkeley Software Definition (BSD)-type license). Two attributes characterize GPL license: (1) the fact that "any derivative work remained subject to the same license" and (2) the prescription of "the mixing of open and closed source software in any distributed works" (Lerner & Tirole, 2005, p. 23). Among OSS licenses, GPL is the most widely used (Bonaccorsi et al., 2006; Lerner & Tirole, 2005). Compared to GPL, LGPL (lesser GPL) concedes a greater flexibility concerning the "mixing" requirement, as with this license "programs are allowed to link with (or employ) other programs or routines that are not themselves available under an open source license" (Lerner & Tirole, 2005, p. 23). The BSD-type licenses allow a greater flexibility to users. These licenses authorize the free use of the OSS and the capacity to modify the software. In addition, the BSD-type licenses allow the use of source code in proprietary software, whether modified or not. Additionally, source code created under these licenses, or derived from such code, can get "closed" and be commercialized by anyone (not just by the original developers) (Onetti & Capobianco, 2005).

Nonetheless, analyzing the implications of "source code sharing" from the perspective of the adopting organization reveals at least one tension between "companies' need for control of intellectual assets and programmers' relations to communities outside the firm." (Rolandsson, Bergquist, & Ljungberg, 2011, p. 581). Consequently, these characteristics may constitute a critical barrier for the adoption of OSBI by organizations. This is particularly true in cases where the technology allows for the generation of a business value associated with a competitive advantage.

FUD with Regard to Open Source Business Models

FUD stands for Fear, Uncertainty and Doubt, and was coined by Gene Amdahl, an ex-IBM executive who founded Amdahl Corporation in 1970 (Pfaffenberger, 2000). "FUD is a marketing strategy or technique that has been used by market-dominant firms in the computer industry to weaken competitors" (Irwin, 1998, p. 1). Generally, a FUD operation makes use of a variety of approaches, including cautioning customers about the risks of moving to an unreliable new product, as well as a storm of press releases aimed at confusing customers as regards to the merits of the new product, and biased benchmark tests (Pfaffenberger, 2000). According to Nagy et al. (2010, p. 149) "it is widely believed that proprietary software vendors often use fear, uncertainty and doubt to undermine and cut the market potential of their open source competitors".

Following (Björkdahl, 2009, p. 1470), a business model is defined as "the logic and the activities that create and appropriate economic value, and the link between them". Operationally speaking, a business model provides a heuristic logic that helps to link technical or functional potential of a technological tool with the realization of economic value (Chesbrough & Rosenbloom, 2002). According to West (2007), the business model of such an innovation as open source project has two main functions: creating value for customers and capturing value for the open source project actors. For their part, Helander and Rissanen (2005) stressed that the business model of open source project is difficult to apprehend because the value created in open source projects can often not be "owned" by a single organization, and thus the business models cannot be studied in the same way as for proprietary software. The authors maintain that the value of open source projects is created for the network, not for individual organizations or other entities or individuals. In this context, it is worth remembering that the network in question is generally composed of entities of various sizes, roles and levels of commitment, including large and well-known for-profit organizations (e.g. IBM, Google, RedHat, etc.), not-for-profit organizations (e.g. Linux foundation, Free software foundation, Universities, Government agencies, etc.), and numerous SMEs and individuals. Thus, a deep understanding of the business models of the companies involved in open source software projects requires linking them to the business models of the other network stakeholders and perhaps including some other components outside of the network (Helander & Rissanen, 2005).

In fact, in most open source business models, software is usually available free of charge, with or without conditions; and in most cases revenues are realized through the sale of complementary services, such as consulting, implementation, documentation, and maintenance (Hecker, 1999). For their part, based on two dimensions, that is, OSS production and OSS distribution, Watson, Boudreau, York, Greiner, and Wynn Jr (2008) identified four different business models: open community, corporate distribution, sponsored OSS, and second-generation OSS. Open community is the most well-known business model of OSS. This model relies mainly on volunteers for the development and support of the software with limited commercial interests. In contrast, with the corporate distribution model, a corporation takes advantage of an OSS product of good quality that is developed by open community model. More specifically, a corporation gets involved in the project with the aim of improving distribution methods for the OSS product, as well as providing complimentary services for adopting organizations (Watson et al., 2008). The corporate model therefore depends on the community model. RedHat and SpikeSource are two examples of such OSS model. Compared to the previous two examples, the Sponsored Open Source model portrays OSS projects that are directly sponsored by corporations or foundations or by both. Apache Web Server and Eclipse are two examples of sponsored OSS by Apache Foundation and IBM respectively. The last business model labeled Second-generation or professional open source, brings together OSS projects that are controlled by a firm whose business model is considered hybrid, in the sense that it fits between a corporate distribution business model and a sponsored business model. One of the characteristics of this model is the control of the source code that allows the controlling firm to exploit their intimate knowledge of the code to provide higher-quality service that has the potential to compete with other service providers (Watson et al., 2008). Examples of such open source projects include MySQL and JBoss. Although other authors identified several business models of open source projects, Widenius and Nyman (2014) indicated that they can be classified in two main categories: those that require complete (or at least partial) ownership of the code by the open source project or a representative entity, and those that do not. One fact is worth mentioning here: The ownership of the source code is defined by the license, and there is a "proliferation" of OSS licenses. "Proliferation refers to the scores of open source licenses that are now in use, with more being created all the time" (Gomulkiewicz, 2009, p. 263). Indeed, there are currently 83 OSS licenses approved by the Open Source Initiative (OSI, 2008). Thus, it seems that in reality OSS business model is a complex concept that needs to be classified in a continuum from closed to open. As a result, the business model can at times not only be easily subject to FUD, but might also act as a critical barrier to OSS adoption.

At the same time, the finding of open source business model as a critical barrier is surprising. In fact, a 2008 survey by IDC of OSS vendors covering their experience in selling OSS in 2007, concluded by declaring open-source software business model as viable, on the ground that the majority of revenue from OSS (59 percent on average) was from subscriptions (Rosenberg, 2008). And since that time, the open source phenomenon has continued to be debated while OSS has continued to grow in the software industry, and now many private as well as public organizations rely on OSS applications or code (Ghapanchi, 2015).

Monopolization of BI Initiatives by IS Departments

Traditionally, the Information Systems (IS) specialists within the IS department were the only ones responsible for organizations' IS investments (Bassellier, Benbasat, & Reich, 2003; Devece, 2013). The authors maintained that since the acknowledgement of the strategic nature of IS tools, researchers and managers agree on the fact that the responsibility of Information Systems should be shared between IS and business professionals. According to Poba-Nzaou, Uwizeyemungu, and Clarke (2018, p. 2), the need for shared responsibility was later "accentuated by the popularity of Enterprise Systems (e.g. Enterprise Resource Planning (ERPs)) that are configured at the organizational level by business professionals with the help of integrators. The last authors underscored that in this regard, IS competencies held by business professionals such as finance or human resource or production managers turn into one of the prerequisites for creating business value from IS.

In this context, it is surprising that IS departments tend to monopolize BI initiatives instead of sharing the responsibility with non-IS professionals. At least one explanation and one implication can be drawn from this barrier. Given that the tendency by IS departments to monopolize IS initiatives has been observed in the past at the early stage of diffusion of major enterprise systems such as ERP, we contend that this attitude is likely to stem from the novelty of BI technologies and it may soon change. Concerning the implication, we contend that this situation may explain partially why early surveys revealed a low level of user satisfaction with BI initiatives, products and experiences. For instance, a survey conducted by LogiXML, reveals that about half of non-Technical BI users are dissatisfied with their IS departments' ability to deliver (Logi Analytics, 2011). In the same vein, Advaiya (2017) indicates that nearly two-third (67%) of the respondents are not satisfied with the BI tools that they use.

Risk Aversion of IT Managers

At an individual level, risk aversion is defined "as a preference for a sure outcome over a prospect with an equal or greater expected value" (Tversky & Fox, 1995, p. 269). Basically, it has been recognized that risk aversion of managers is one of the main barriers that impedes organizations from adopting technological innovation (Czerkawski, 2010).

It is important to remember that many organizations still view OSS as much riskier, with little or no assurance that the software will be supported in the present and in the future (Benlian & Hess, 2011). In particular, organizations tend to associate higher risk to OSS because they are attracted by the following characteristics of proprietary software (Bonaccorsi et al., 2006, p. 1086):

Licensed software is usually packaged according to industrial standard in terms of documentation, maintenance, product updating, and product responsibility clauses. These are highly appreciated by final customers, because they greatly reduce the perceived risk. … The perceived customers' risk of buying from small new entrants offering open standards is significantly higher.

In addition, managing OS BI risk can be quite different from proprietary BI. In fact, contrary to proprietary software, in the case of OSS, a client organization has no means to transfer accountability to a third party, hence it has to bear the full risk (Morgan & Finnegan, 2010). Thus, in light of the above discussion, it seems probable that IS managers with a determined risk aversion attitude may have an incentive to avoid selecting OS BI tools. It is thus not surprising that IS managers risk aversion emerges as a critical barrier to OS BI adoption by organization.

Barriers Identified from the Systematic Review of the Literature but not Mentioned by the Panel of Experts

As stated earlier, amid the 23 barriers found from the systematic review, 9 were not mentioned by our panel of experts. Among them, three are related to each one of the three dimensions of the TOE framework. The three technological barriers are: Complexity of open source products (e.g. long learning curve, complex configuration, etc.); Shortage of enterprises providing integrated services including support, training, installation, maintenance, etc.; Lack of third party engagement for technical support and maintenance services. The three organizational barriers are: Structural obstacles (e.g. disadvantageous tender/procurement processes vis-à-vis open source solution; unfavorable quality assessment approach, etc.); Fear of users' rejection; Strong dependence on proprietary software and providers (lock-in). The three environmental barriers are: Effect of fashion phenomenon trends in the market; Insufficient legitimacy in the market; Insufficient dissemination of knowledge concerning open source software in higher education institutions.

In this situation, a natural question arises: Why do none of the BI experts of our panel mention those barriers? Without pretending to provide a definitive answer to this question, a few elements are worth mentioning. At first glance, it may be argued that there were too few experts. However, given that (1) the study sample is appropriate that is, it is composed of participants who "have knowledge of the research topic" (Morse, Barrett, Mayan, Olson, & Spiers, 2002, p. 18) (2) data was saturated after nine interviews and "by definition, saturating data ensures replication in categories; replication verifies, and ensures comprehension and completeness" (Morse, Barrett, Mayan, Olson, & Spiers, 2002, p. 18) a second explanation is considered: those barriers were not mentioned by the panel of experts because none of them are perceived as being part of "critical" barriers that may impede organizations from adopting open source BI tools. A third plausible explanation is rooted in Rousseau and Fried (2001, p. 1) call for incorporating context into the research process, including interpretation and reporting. They stressed that contextualization is "more important in contemporary organizational behavior research than it has been in the past". In fact, our panel is made of Canadian BI experts from the province of Quebec. Within the province, the open-source community is well organized and enjoys a relatively high visibility. For instance, in 2009, the Quebec government clearly stated its advocacy for the use of open source software whenever it's the best choice. It also explained it will ensure that the Quebec administration will have the support they need to adopt, implement and use open source software (Gouvernement du Québec, 2009). In 2013, the government created a center of expertise dedicated to open source software (Blanchet, 2015). Furthermore, in 2015 it created a new open-source license named "Licence Libre du Québec (LiLiQ)" that was tailored to meet the needs of the administration; LiLiQ was approved by OSI in January 2016 (Gouvernement du Québec, 2018). On the business side, in 2011, in the province of Quebec, there were about 30 enterprises specializing in OSS related services, and about 10 that can be categorized as OSS vendors (L'Association professionnelle des entreprises en logiciels libres - APELL, 2011). Of note is the fact that several governments all over the word have adopted guidelines or laws that encourage the adoption of open source software (Qu, Yang, & Wang, 2011).

Lastly, additional insights are generated by comparing these barriers with those found by Poba-Nzaou and Uwizeyemungu (2013). In fact, 5 out of 9 barriers not mentioned by the current study panel were among the 10 most important barriers to the adoption of open source mission critical application by organizations in the province of Quebec, found by Poba-Nzaou and Uwizeyemungu (2013). This finding seems to indicate that the open source phenomenon has evolved to the point where those barriers are no longer considered "critical" to the adoption of open source BI in the context of Quebec, Canada. This means that, in summary, the open source BI phenomenon may have reached a certain level of maturity, at least in Quebec.

RESEARCH CONTRIBUTIONS AND LIMITATIONS

It is important to remember that, from a business executive's perspective, business intelligence (BI) emerges as one of the most promising technologies in recent years in terms of business value creation (Kappelman, McLean, Luftman, & Johnson, 2013). However, the study of the adoption of open source BI by organizations is in its infancy (Trieu, 2017), despite the empirical evidence of their growing presence in the business environment in firms worldwide. This research focuses on the identification of critical barriers that may inhibit organizations from adopting open source business intelligence tools, and which may also prevent them from developing needed capabilities required for securing strategic organizational outcomes. This exploratory study is an initial step toward a deeper understanding of factors that inhibit organizations from adopting open source business intelligence tools.

A systematic review of the literature resulted in the identification of 23 barriers. To understand these barriers in the context of organizational settings, their classification was done according to three categories derived from TOE framework (Technology-Organization-Environment)(Depietro et al., 1990). This was subsequently compared with a list of 18 barriers derived from a qualitative survey of 11 Canadian BI experts.

This study contributes to the nascent body of knowledge on the adoption of BI tools in general, and to open source BI tools in particular in two ways. First, it provides an initial foundation for understanding these barriers from BI experts' perspectives. Findings from the systematic review by the authors of this study reveal that this is one of the first endeavors to focus on barriers associated with the adoption of BI tools, from the perspectives of BI experts and the first investigation of Canadian BI experts' views on open source BI adoption.

From a practical standpoint, this research provides IS managers, as well as open source BI providers and consultants with an initial structured lens to better understand the most important barriers that prevent organizations from adopting open source BI tools. These barriers require further consideration by all stakeholders interested in the adoption or deployment of open source BI.

From a methodological standpoint, following Poba-Nzaou et al. (2016), this research provides one main contribution that is a rigorous analysis of Qualitative Survey data, based on two principles of interpretive research (Klein & Myers, 1999): the fundamental principle of Hermeneutic Circle, and the principle of Abstraction and Generalization.

To conclude, the authors acknowledge some areas of limitations, and call for further studies of open source business intelligence to be conducted. First, though it is adequate for a qualitative survey and methodologically sufficient, the size of the panel was small. Second, it could be interesting to compare these barriers with those preventing organizations from adopting open source software in areas where they are very popular (such as web server, operating systems, etc.). Third, since this exploratory study focuses on BI experts in only one country, Canada, the authors also recommend future studies investigating the views of BI experts in other countries and involving other BI stakeholders (e.g. users, executives, etc.), as such studies can increase the validity of the findings from this study. Fourth, as this initial study focuses solely on barriers, the authors also recommend that future studies, including the identification of strategies that may be initiated by relevant stakeholders in dealing with the identified barriers. Lastly, future researches may benefit from adopting other research methods as well, such as case study, surveys or experiments, as they may provide richer insights than the qualitative survey adopted in this study.

REFERENCES

Advaiya. (2017). *BI and Analytics Adoption and Usage Report*. Retrieved from https://www.advaiya.com/thanks-bi-adoption-report/

Apps Run The World. (2011). *Human Capital Management. Enterprise Applications Market Report 2010-2015*. Retrieved from https://www.appsruntheworld.com/wp-content/uploads/2015/09/Human-Capital-Management-Applications-Market-2010-2015.pdf

Avolio, B. J. (2017). The practice and science connection: Let's not obsess over minding the gap. *Industrial and Organizational Psychology: Perspectives on Science and Practice*, *10*(4), 558–569. doi:10.1017/iop.2017.56

Bassellier, G., Benbasat, I., & Reich, B. H. (2003). The influence of business managers' IT competence on championing IT. *Information Systems Research*, *14*(4), 317–336. doi:10.1287/isre.14.4.317.24899

Benlian, A., & Hess, T. (2011). Opportunities and risks of software-as-a-service: Findings from a survey of IT executives. *Decision Support Systems*, *52*(1), 232–246. doi:10.1016/j.dss.2011.07.007

Björkdahl, J. (2009). Technology cross-fertilization and the business model: The case of integrating ICTs in mechanical engineering products. *Research Policy*, *38*(9), 1468–1477. doi:10.1016/j.respol.2009.07.006

Blanchet, J.N. (2015). Le centre du libre éclate. Retrieved from http://www.journaldemontreal.com/2015/10/16/le-centre-du-libre-eclate

Bonaccorsi, A., Piscitello, L., Merito, M., & Rossi, C. (2006) How is it possible to profit from innovation in the absence of any appropriability? In IFIP International Federation for Information Processing (pp. 333-334).

Buchan, J. (2011). Developing a dynamic and responsive online learning environment: A case study of a large Australian university. In Free and Open Source Software for E-Learning: Issues, Successes and Challenges (pp. 92-109). Hershey, PA: IGI Global.

Buchana, Y., & Naicker, V. (2014). The effect of mobile BI on organisational managerial decision-making. *Journal of Applied Business Research*, *30*(4), 1003–1018. doi:10.19030/jabr.v30i4.8649

Chaudhuri, S., Dayal, U., & Narasayya, V. (2011). An overview of business intelligence technology. *Communications of the ACM*, *54*(8), 88–98. doi:10.1145/1978542.1978562

Chen, H., Chiang, R. H., & Storey, V. C. (2012). Business intelligence and analytics: From big data to big impact. *Management Information Systems Quarterly*, *36*(4), 1165–1188. doi:10.2307/41703503

Chesbrough, H., & Rosenbloom, R. S. (2002). The role of the business model in capturing value from innovation: Evidence from Xerox Corporation's technology spin-off companies. *Industrial and Corporate Change*, *11*(3), 529–555. doi:10.1093/icc/11.3.529

Chung, W., Chen, H., & Nunamaker, J. F. (2003). Business intelligence explorer: a knowledge map framework for discovering business intelligence on the Web. *Paper presented at the 36th Annual Hawaii International Conference on System Sciences.*

Clutch. (2016). 2016 Business Intelligence Data Analytics Survey. Retrieved from https://clutch.co/analytics#survey

Côté, J., & Egelstaff, J. (2007). Supporting Not-For-Profits. *The Open Source Business Resource*, 11.

Crowston, K., & Wade, M. (2010). Introduction to JAIS special issue on empirical research on free/libre open source software. *Journal of the Association for Information Systems*, *11*(11), I–V. doi:10.17705/1jais.00246

Czerkawski, B. Ö. (2010). Free and Open Source Software for E-Learning: Issues, Successes and Challenges: Issues, Successes and Challenges. Hershey, PA: IGI Global.

D'Souza, S. (2011). Open source business intelligence: The next big thing? Retrieved from https://www.computerweekly.com/news/2240035963/Open-source-business-intelligence-The-next-big-thing

Datamation. (2013). Business Intelligence Adoption: Gaining Ground. Retrieved from https://www.datamation.com/applications/business-intelligence-adoption-gaining-ground.html

Davies, P. H. (2002). Intelligence, information technology, and information warfare. *Annual Review of Information Science & Technology*, *36*(1), 312–352. doi:10.1002/aris.1440360108

Dedrick, J., & West, J. (2004). An exploratory study into open source platform adoption. *Paper presented at the 37th Annual Hawaii International Conference on System Sciences.* 10.1109/HICSS.2004.1265633

Delen, D., & Zolbanin, H. M. (2018). The analytics paradigm in business research. *Journal of Business Research*, *90*, 186–195. doi:10.1016/j.jbusres.2018.05.013

Depietro, R., Wiarda, E., & Fleischer, M. (1990). The context for change: organization, technology and environment. In T. LG & F. M (Eds.), The Processes of Technological Innovation (pp. 151-175). Lexington, MA: Lexington Books.

Devece, C. (2013). The value of business managers' 'Information Technology' competence. *Service Industries Journal*, *33*(7-8), 720–733. doi:10.1080/02642069.2013.740463

DiMaggio, P., & Powell, W. W. (1983). The iron cage revisited: Collective rationality and institutional isomorphism in organizational fields. *American Sociological Review, 48*(2), 147–160. doi:10.2307/2095101

Felix, R., Rauschnabel, P. A., & Hinsch, C. (2017). Elements of strategic social media marketing: A holistic framework. *Journal of Business Research, 70*, 118–126. doi:10.1016/j.jbusres.2016.05.001

Fink, A. (2003). *The survey handbook* (Vol. 1). Sage. doi:10.4135/9781412986328

Fink, L., Yogev, N., & Even, A. (2017). Business intelligence and organizational learning: An empirical investigation of value creation processes. *Information & Management, 54*(1), 38–56. doi:10.1016/j.im.2016.03.009

Fitzgerald, B. (2006). The transformation of open source software. *Management Information Systems Quarterly, 30*(3), 587–598. doi:10.2307/25148740

Foll, D. L., & Foil, F. A. (2008). Open source software in telcosa gentle tsunami. *Journal of the Institute of Telecommunications Professionals, 2*(2), 7–11.

Gallego, M. D., Luna, P., & Bueno, S. (2008a). Designing a forecasting analysis to understand the diffusion of open source software in the year 2010. *Technological Forecasting and Social Change, 75*(5), 672–686. doi:10.1016/j.techfore.2007.02.002

Gallego, M. D., Luna, P., & Bueno, S. (2008b). User acceptance model of open source software. *Computers in Human Behavior, 24*(5), 2199–2216. doi:10.1016/j.chb.2007.10.006

Gartner. (2017a). Survey Analysis: Why BI and Analytics Adoption Remains Low and How to Expand Its Reach. Retrieved from https://www.gartner.com/doc/3753469/survey-analysis-bi-analytics

Gartner. (2017b). *What Every CIO Must Know About Open-Source Software*. Retrieved from https://www.gartner.com/doc/3660617/cio-know-opensource-software

Gartner. (2018). IT Glossary. Retrieved from https://www.gartner.com/it-glossary/

Ghapanchi, A. H. (2015). Predicting software future sustainability: A longitudinal perspective. *Information Systems, 49*, 40–51. doi:10.1016/j.is.2014.10.005

Gomulkiewicz, R. W. (2009). Open source license proliferation: Helpful diversity or hopeless confusion. *Wash. UJL & Pol'y, 30*, 261.

Goode, S. (2014). Exploring organizational information sharing in adopters and non-adopters of open source software: Evidence from six case studies. *Knowledge and Process Management, 21*(1), 78–89. doi:10.1002/kpm.1430

Gouvernement du Québec. (2009). Les logiciels libres. Retrieved from https://www.tresor.gouv.qc.ca/ressources-informationnelles/logiciels-libres/

Gouvernement du Québec. (2018). Forge gouvernementale. Retrieved from https://forge.gouv.qc.ca/licence/

Grodzinsky, F. S., Miller, K., & Wolf, M. J. (2003). Ethical issues in open source software. *Journal of Information. Communication and Ethics in Society, 1*(4), 193–205. doi:10.1108/14779960380000235

Guest, G., Bunce, A., & Johnson, L. (2006). How many interviews are enough? An experiment with data saturation and variability. *Field Methods*, *18*(1), 59–82. doi:10.1177/1525822X05279903

Gwebu, K. L., & Wang, J. (2010). Seeing eye to eye? An exploratory study of free open source software users' perceptions. *Journal of Systems and Software*, *83*(11), 2287–2296. doi:10.1016/j.jss.2010.07.011

Hammersley, M. (2007). The issue of quality in qualitative research. *International Journal of Research & Method in Education*, *30*(3), 287–305. doi:10.1080/17437270701614782

Harris, N. L., Cock, P. J. A., Lapp, H., Chapman, B., Davey, R., Fields, C., ... Munoz-Torres, M. (2016). The 2015 Bioinformatics Open Source Conference (BOSC 2015). *PLoS Computational Biology*, *12*(2). doi:10.1371/journal.pcbi.1004691

Hauge, Ø., Ayala, C., & Conradi, R. (2010). Adoption of open source software in software-intensive organizations–A systematic literature review. *Information and Software Technology*, *52*(11), 1133–1154. doi:10.1016/j.infsof.2010.05.008

Hecker, F. (1999). Setting up shop: The business of open-source software. *IEEE Software*, *16*(1), 45–51. doi:10.1109/52.744568

Helander, N., & Rissanen, T. (2005). Value-creating networks approach to open source software business models. *Frontiers of E-Business Research*, *2005*, 840–854.

Hitachi. (2015). Hitachi Data Systems Completes Pentaho Acquisition. Retrieved from https://www.hitachivantara.com/en-us/news-resources/press-releases/2015/gl150604.html

IBM. (2011). 2011 IBM Tech Trends Report. Retrieved from https://www.ibm.com/developerworks/community/blogs/ff67b471-79df-4bef-9593-4802def4013d/entry/2011_ibm_tech_trends_report_the_clouds_are_rolling_in_is_your_business_ready5?lang=en

Irwin. (1998). What is FUD? Retrieved from http://www.cavcomp.demon.co.uk/halloween/fuddef.html

Jansen, H. (2010). The logic of qualitative survey research and its position in the field of social research methods. *Paper presented at the Forum Qualitative Sozialforschung/Forum: Qualitative Social Research*.

Kappelman, L., McLean, E., Luftman, J., & Johnson, V. (2013). Key Issues of IT Organizations and Their Leadership: The 2013 SIM IT Trends Study. *MIS Quarterly Executive*, *12*(4).

Kim, H. W., Chan, H. C., & Lee, S. H. (2014). User resistance to software migration: The case on Linux. *Journal of Database Management*, *25*(1), 59–79. doi:10.4018/jdm.2014010103

Kiron, D., Prentice, P. K., & Ferguson, R. B. (2014). The analytics mandate. *MIT Sloan Management Review*, *55*(4), 1.

Klein, H. K., & Myers, M. D. (1999). A set of principles for conducting and evaluating interpretive field studies in information systems. *Management Information Systems Quarterly*, *23*(1), 67–93. doi:10.2307/249410

L'Association professionnelle des entreprises en logiciels libres - APELL. (2011). *L'industrie du logiciel libre québécoise*. Retrieved from www.agirs.org

Lerner, J., & Tirole, J. (2005). The scope of open source licensing. *Journal of Law Economics and Organization, 21*(1), 20–56. doi:10.1093/jleo/ewi002

Lincoln, Y., & Guba, E. (1985). *Naturalistic inquiry. Newburry Park*. Newbury Park, CA: Sage.

Logi Analytics. (2011). Half of Non-Technical Business Intelligence Users Dissatisfied with IT's Ability to Deliver, Survey Shows. Retrieved from https://www.logianalytics.com/news/half-of-non-technical-business-intelligence-users-dissatisfied-with-its-ability-to-deliver-survey-shows/

Luftman, J., Derksen, B., Dwivedi, R., Santana, M., Zadeh, H. S., & Rigoni, E. (2015). Influential IT management trends: An international study. *Journal of Information Technology, 30*(3), 293–305. doi:10.1057/jit.2015.18

Macredie, R., & Mijinyawa, K. (2011). A theory-grounded framework of Open Source Software adoption in SMEs. *European Journal of Information Systems, 20*(2), 237–250. doi:10.1057/ejis.2010.60

Mandel, M. (2012). Beyond goods and services: The (unmeasured) rise of the data-driven economy. Progressive Policy Institute.

McAfee, A., Brynjolfsson, E., Davenport, T. H., Patil, D., & Barton, D. (2012). Big data: The management revolution. *Harvard Business Review, 90*(10), 60–68. PMID:23074865

Miles, M. B., & Huberman, A. M. (1994). *Qualitative data analysis: An expanded sourcebook*: sage.

Morgan, L., & Finnegan, P. (2010). Open Innovation in Secondary Software Firms: An Exploration of Managers' Perceptions of Open Source Software. *The Data Base for Advances in Information Systems, 41*(1), 76–95. doi:10.1145/1719051.1719056

Morse, J. M., Barrett, M., Mayan, M., Olson, K., & Spiers, J. (2002). Verification strategies for establishing reliability and validity in qualitative research. *International Journal of Qualitative Methods, 1*(2), 13–22. doi:10.1177/160940690200100202

Mutula, S., & Kalaote, T. (2010). Open source software deployment in the public sector: A review of Botswana and South Africa. *Library Hi Tech, 28*(1), 63–80. doi:10.1108/07378831011026698

Nagy, D., Yassin, A. M., & Bhattacherjee, A. (2010). Organizational adoption of open source software: Barriers and remedies. *Communications of the ACM, 53*(3), 148–151. doi:10.1145/1666420.1666457

Olsen, K. A., & Saetre, P. (2007). IT for niche companies: Is an ERP system the solution? *Information Systems Journal, 17*(1), 37–58. doi:10.1111/j.1365-2575.2006.00229.x

Onetti, A., & Capobianco, F. (2005). Open source and business model innovation. the funambol case. *Paper presented at the first International Conference on Open source Systems.*

OSI. (2008). Licenses by Name. Retrieved from https://opensource.org/licenses/alphabetical

Palanisamy, R., & Mukerji, B. (2012). Adoption Of Open Source Software For Enhancing Customer Satisfaction: A Case Study From Canadian Educational Sector. *Journal of Services Research, 12*(2).

Paré, G., Wybo, M. D., & Delannoy, C. (2009). Barriers to open source software adoption in Quebec's health care organizations. *Journal of Medical Systems*, *33*(1), 1–7. doi:10.100710916-008-9158-4 PMID:19238891

Park, Y., El Sawy, O. A., & Fiss, P. C. (2017). The Role of Business Intelligence and Communication Technologies in Organizational Agility: A Configurational Approach. *Journal of the Association for Information Systems*, *18*(9), 648–686. doi:10.17705/1jais.00001

Patton, M. Q. (1990). *Qualitative evaluation and research methods*. Newbury Park, CA: SAGE Publications, inc.

Peacock, A. (2017). Business Intelligence Survey 2017: Mobility and Access. Retrieved from https://clutch.co/analytics/resources/business-intelligence-survey-mobility-access

Pfaffenberger, B. (2000). The rhetoric of dread: Fear, uncertainty, and doubt (FUD) in information technology marketing. *Knowledge, Technology & Policy*, *13*(3), 78–92. doi:10.100712130-000-1022-x

Poba-Nzaou, P., Lemieux, N., Beaupré, D., & Uwizeyemungu, S. (2016). Critical challenges associated with the adoption of social media: A Delphi of a panel of Canadian human resources managers. *Journal of Business Research*, *69*(10), 4011–4019. doi:10.1016/j.jbusres.2016.06.006

Poba-Nzaou, P., & Raymond, L. (2011). Managing ERP system risk in SMEs: A multiple case study. *Journal of Information Technology*, *26*(3), 170–192. doi:10.1057/jit.2010.34

Poba-Nzaou, P., Raymond, L., & Fabi, B. (2014). Risk of adopting mission-critical OSS applications: An interpretive case study. *International Journal of Operations & Production Management*, *34*(4), 477–512. doi:10.1108/IJOPM-03-2012-0117

Poba-Nzaou, P., & Uwizeyemungu, S. (2013). Barriers to Mission-Critical Open Source Software Adoption by Organizations: A Provider Perspective. *Paper presented at the the 19th Americas conference on information systems (AMCIS 2013)*, Chicago, IL.

Poba-Nzaou, P., Uwizeyemungu, S., & Clarke, C. (2018). Patterns underlying required HR and IT competencies: A content and cluster analysis of advertisements of HR manager positions. *International Journal of Human Resource Management*, 1–24. doi:10.1080/09585192.2018.1424019

Qu, W. G., Yang, Z., & Wang, Z. (2011). Multi-level framework of open source software adoption. *Journal of Business Research*, *64*(9), 997–1003. doi:10.1016/j.jbusres.2010.11.023

Rolandsson, B., Bergquist, M., & Ljungberg, J. (2011). Open source in the firm: Opening up professional practices of software development. *Research Policy*, *40*(4), 576–587. doi:10.1016/j.respol.2010.11.003

Rosenberg, D. (2008). IDC survey proves opensource software as viable business model. Retrieved from https://www.cnet.com/news/idc-survey-proves-open-source-software-as-viable-business-model/

Rousseau, D. M., & Fried, Y. (2001). Location, location, location: Contextualizing organizational research. *Journal of Organizational Behavior: The International Journal of Industrial. Occupational and Organizational Psychology and Behavior*, *22*(1), 1–13. doi:10.1002/job.78

Safadi, H., Chan, D., Dawes, M., Roper, M., & Faraj, S. (2015). Open-source health information technology: A case study of electronic medical records. *Health Policy and Technology, 4*(1), 14–28. doi:10.1016/j.hlpt.2014.10.011

Sallam, R. L., Richardson, J., Hagerty, J., & Hostmann, B. (2011). *Magic quadrant for business intelligence platforms*. Stamford, CT: Gartner Group.

Sledgianowski, D., Tafti, M. H., & Kierstead, J. (2008). SME ERP system sourcing strategies: A case study. *Industrial Management & Data Systems, 108*(4), 421–436. doi:10.1108/02635570810868317

Smets-Solanes, J.-P., & de Carvalho, R. A. (2003). ERP5: A next-generation, open-source ERP architecture. *IT Professional, 5*(4), 38–44. doi:10.1109/MITP.2003.1216231

Stackowiak, R., Licht, A., Mantha, V., & Nagode, L. (2015). *Big Data and the Internet of Things: Enterprise Information Architecture for a New Age*. Apress. doi:10.1007/978-1-4842-0986-8

Stol, K.-J., Babar, M. A., Avgeriou, P., & Fitzgerald, B. (2011). A comparative study of challenges in integrating Open Source Software and Inner Source Software. *Information and Software Technology, 53*(12), 1319–1336. doi:10.1016/j.infsof.2011.06.007

Tanner, C. K., & Stone, C. D. (1998). School Improvement Policy--Site-Based Management. *education policy analysis archives, 6*, 6.

Thomsen, C., & Pedersen, T. B. (2009). A survey of open source tools for business intelligence. *International Journal of Data Warehousing and Mining, 5*(3), 56–75. doi:10.4018/jdwm.2009070103

TIBCO. (2014). TIBCO Software Acquires Jaspersoft. Retrieved from https://www.tibco.com/press-releases/2014/tibco-software-acquires-jaspersoft

Tomazin, M., & Gradišar, M. (2007). Introducing open source software into Slovenian primary and secondary schools. *Informatica, 31*(1).

Trieu, V. H. (2017). Getting value from Business Intelligence systems: A review and research agenda. *Decision Support Systems, 93*, 111–124. doi:10.1016/j.dss.2016.09.019

Tversky, A., & Fox, C. R. (1995). Weighing risk and uncertainty. *Psychological Review, 102*(2), 269–283. doi:10.1037/0033-295X.102.2.269

Vanmeulebrouk, B., Rivett, U., Ricketts, A., & Loudon, M. (2008). Open source GIS for HIV/AIDS management. *International Journal of Health Geographics, 7*(1), 53. doi:10.1186/1476-072X-7-53 PMID:18945338

Venkatesh, V., & Bala, H. (2012). Adoption and impacts of interorganizational business process standards: Role of partnering synergy. *Information Systems Research, 23*(4), 1131–1157. doi:10.1287/isre.1110.0404

Wang, P. (2009). Popular concepts beyond organizations: Exploring new dimensions of information technology innovations. *Journal of the Association for Information Systems, 10*(1), 2. doi:10.17705/1jais.00182

Watson, R. T., Boudreau, M.-C., York, P. T., Greiner, M. E., & Wynn, D. Jr. (2008). The business of open source. *Communications of the ACM, 51*(4), 41–46. doi:10.1145/1330311.1330321

Weilbach, L., & Byrne, E. (2013). Implementing open source software to conform to national policy. *Journal of Systems and Information Technology, 15*(1), 78–96. doi:10.1108/13287261311322594

West, J. (2007). Value capture and value networks in open source vendor strategies. *Paper presented at the 40th Annual Hawaii International Conference on System Sciences HICSS 2007.*

Widenius, M. M., & Nyman, L. (2014). The business of open source software: A primer. *Technology Innovation Management Review, 4*(1), 4. doi:10.22215/timreview/756

Williams van Rooij, S. (2007). Perceptions of open source versus commercial software: Is higher education still on the fence? *Journal of Research on Technology in Education, 39*(4), 433–453. doi:10.1080/15391523.2007.10782491

Wu, H., & Cao, L. (2009). Community collaboration for ERP implementation. *IEEE Software, 26*(6), 48–55. doi:10.1109/MS.2009.171

Wu, J., Goh, K. Y., Li, H., Luo, C., & Zheng, H. (2016). The effects of communication patterns on the success of open source software projects: An empirical analysis from social network perspectives. *Journal of Global Information Management, 24*(4), 22–44. doi:10.4018/JGIM.2016100102

This research was previously published in the International Journal of Business Intelligence Research (IJBIR), 10(1); pages 59-79, copyright year 2019 by IGI Publishing (an imprint of IGI Global).

Chapter 28
Open Source Software in Financial Auditing

Tânia Correia
Instituto Politécnico de Coimbra, Portugal

Isabel Pedrosa
Instituto Politécnico de Coimbra, Portugal & Instituto Universitário de Lisboa, Portugal

Carlos J. Costa
Universidade de Lisboa, Portugal

ABSTRACT

The auditing software is an essential tool to the auditor, being a mechanism that helps to achieve auditing goals to obtain efficiency, quality, and to increase reliability on data analysis and evidence collection. The auditing software can be proprietary software or free and open source software. The purpose of this chapter is to understand which factors affect open source software adoption. To achieve these goals, a survey aimed at financial auditors was carried through, and 64 complete answers were collected. Results indicate that the most used software is the proprietary software and that 43% of the respondents belong to the first stage of open source software assimilation. Additionally, it was verified that the external environment is the macro factor, which positively affects the adoption of open source software in auditing.

INTRODUCTION

The use of audit software is relevant support for auditing, by helping the auditor achieve auditing objectives, increase efficiency, quality and reliability in data analysis and on evidence collection. Regarding software adoption, in recent years, several companies worldwide have been gradually making use of part or all the systems in the form of Copyleft. Among them are several large private and public groups, such as Lufthansa, Walmart, Dow Jones, Amazon.com. Also state bodies and institutions such as NASA and the Pentagon, also use free and open source software.

DOI: 10.4018/978-1-7998-9158-1.ch028

As long as free and open source software is considered reliable by the most demanding organizations in the world, it is relevant to analyse if it is used in the context of financial auditing. This chapter's objective is to answer the following questions: 1) Which computer tools are the most used by financial auditors? 2) Are auditors using Free and Open Source Software (FOSS) as a tool to accomplish their tasks? 3) What are the predictive factors that can significantly influence the adoption or rejection in the use of the FOSS for auditing purposes? 4) What are the facilitating and inhibiting factors in the assimilation of FOSS for auditing?

The main contribution of this is to increase the knowledge on the most utilized tools on auditors' daily work, and, mainly, on the free and open source tools for auditing purposes. In addition, authors intend to contribute to a better awareness of the process of adoption and migration to free and open source software for auditing.

The present chapter is composed of this first section, introduction, a section about the Background, then the objectives and methodological approach. The last parts of the chapter are results, solutions, and recommendations, future directions and conclusions.

BACKGROUND

In this section, the main aspect related to free and open source adoption and auditing software are analysed. This section starts with a comparison between free software, open source software and proprietary software. Then, it describes the evolution of free and open source software, the advantages and inhibitors of free and open source software. Then, it analyses the computer-assisted audit Tools/Software for auditing purposes and open source software adoption. The level of assimilation of open source software is also subject of study.

Free Software vs. Open Source Software vs. Proprietary Software

According to the definition of the Free Software Foundation's website - FSF (FSF, 2017), coined by Richard Stallman, Free Software means that users comply with the four freedoms in software usage.

The freedom to run the program as you wish, for any purpose (freedom 0).

The freedom to study how the program works and change it, so it does your computing as you wish (freedom 1). Access to the source code is a precondition for this.

The freedom to redistribute copies so you can help others (freedom 2).

The freedom to distribute copies of your modified versions to others (freedom 3). (FSF, 2017)

When users complain with these four freedoms, the whole community/society has the opportunity to benefit from undertaken changes. Access to the source code is a precondition for this.

Software that complies with these four principles is referred to as Free Software. Copyleft is added to the four freedoms referred to above. And according to the FSF website (FSF, 2017), it is a method that requires all modified versions and extensions of free software to remain free.

According to the Open Source Initiative (OSI), the Open source does not just mean access to the source code (Laurent, 2004). The distribution terms of open-source software must comply with several following criteria. It is expected to free redistribution and supply the source code. Derived works must be distributed according to the same license, and the integrity of the author's source code should be protected. The license must not discriminate against people, groups or endeavour. In what concerns license, it must not be specific to a product, nor restrict other software and must be technology-neutral. While free software emphasizes freedom, Open Source is an approach that more emphasis on software quality. (Raymond, 1999). These two concepts have much in common and are sometimes confused. However, the difference lies fundamentally in the will of the creator for the distribution and redistribution over the characteristics referred to above.

In contrast to the concepts above, proprietary software is software that is made available upon payment of a use license. The creator owns the rights to the software, not allowing the client to sell, query, modify or redistribute the software. This concept is associated with the Copyright that intends to keep the intellectual property private. Throughout this article, when mentioning open source software, free software, and open source software, it is assumed that they will all have the same meaning.

Evolution of Free and Open Source Software

Over time, this theme has been developed, according to its historical milestones presented below. Where its historical landmarks are presented (MUST always put an introductory text linking the various topics that will include in this). There are some associations in the U.S. In 1969, the first version of Unix was created by Ken Thompson, a researcher at Bell Labs. In universities, large computers used this operating system for some time. Universities and research centres distributed free Unix with their open source code. In 1971, Richard Stallman of the Massachusetts Institute of Technology (MIT) inaugurated the Open Source movement, producing several open source programs at the MIT Artificial Intelligence Lab. In 1983, Richard Stallman started the GNU Project and later the Free Software Foundation (Laurent, 2004). In 1991, Linus Torvalds made the Linux source code available via the internet and requested collaboration from other developers to develop it. Cooperation was positive, and in less than two years, Linux had already become a reasonably stable system. In 1999, Raymond published "The Cathedral & the Bazaar: Musings on Linux and open source by an accidental revolutionary," comparing open source development with the owner (Raymond, 1999).

In the Portuguese context, the Linux Caixa Mágica (Trezentos et al., 2007), was a distribution made for schools until the end of high school, giving support from 2000-2010. Ansol (ANSOL, 2018) represents the Portuguese Association for the free and libre software, defending and promoting the four liberties of free software. Free software is named after the four freedom rules, rather than the cost of its license. ESOP (ESOP, 2018) on the other hand is the association of companies open source software; this association has the mission of guaranteeing service quality of the Portuguese open source companies.

The use of free and open source software is essential in some sectors as the public administration in Portugal. Some important decisions were taken, especially in 2011 and 2012. According to the Law 36/2011 of 21 of June, is established the use of open standards in the computer systems of the government. In the 14th November of 2011, the Portuguese Government through the Council of Ministers Resolution no. 46/2011 deliberated the setting up of the "Project Group for Information and Communication Technologies" (PGICT) to rationalize and reduce costs in Public Administration (PA), regarding the management and use of Information Communication and Technology (ICT) Costs ICT . To reach those goals, the PGICT drew the "Global Strategic Plan for Rationalization of ICT in Public Administration (PGETIC)." This strategic plan was organized around five central action axis: (i) Improve governance mechanism; (ii) Cost reduction; (iii) Use ICT to enhance administrative change and modernization; (iv) implementing common ICT solutions and (v) stimulating economic growth. In the context of Axis V, related to economic growth it is proposed the measure 21, called "Open Source Software". The measure 21 Open Source Software has as its main purpose to promote open source software (OSS) in the Public sector. Its purpose is to make available the best OSS practices and solutions. The software contracting should be preceded by technical and economic viability study, using TCO (the total cost of ownership) and compared with FOSS solutions. This measure has as the main purpose increasing the usage of open source. However, it also allows negotiating with software's vendor better conditions for the public organizations.

Advantages and Inhibitors of Free and Open Source Software Usage

The use of open source software has various implications on microeconomics (Aparicio & Costa, 2012), such as cost savings for open source software adopters; increase profits per sale in the market; pricing advantages; flexibility for vendors; rise of the total market size; companies become more independent of the software houses in the long run. Open source software also may have a good impact on the macroeconomic level (Aparicio & Costa, 2012) regarding the balance of payments (BoP) it can improve the imbalances, because of the software licenses and royalties paid to the exterior. Regarding the labour market, it also gives the opportunity to create more employment in the country specialized in open source. According to the literature (e.g., (Aparicio & Costa, 2012; Costa & Aparicio, 2006; Kavanagh, 2004), there are several advantages related to the use of the free and open software. The social cost is low. FOSS increase independence from the suppliers. Initial disbursement tends to be close to zero. Hardware obsolescence is reduced than in proprietary software. FOSS tends to be more robust and safe. FOSS increases the ability to tailor applications and redistribute a modified version. There is abundant and free support from the community. FOSS tends to be very configurable systems and applications.

Literature (Aparicio & Costa, 2012; Kavanagh, 2004) also refers to the inhibitors related to the use of free software. For example, the user interface is not uniform in applications. Installation and configuration may be hard and difficult. Development and support labour may be scarce and difficult to train.

Kavanagh (2004) point out other advantages such as the possibility of sharing the source code and adapt the software to users' needs and software with higher quality when compared to other types, as it has more users. Therefore, software is tested, and errors are found faster and easily. As referred by (Kavanagh, 2004)some people indicate inhibitors in addition to those already mentioned as lack of guarantees and support since free software generally exempts the author from any liability and quality, reputation, and image are viewed there is not a well-known organization behind the software.

Garcia, Santos, Pereira, and Rossi (2010) carried out research with computer specialists, about the use of free software comparing it with the use of proprietary software. They point out that the main advantages are: reducing costs, ease of use, customization, safety and quality, less dependence on third parties, support and maintenance of software. However, they point out that the main unfavourable aspects are the support and maintenance of the programs and emphasized that social category was also low, revealing that the main issue on how users usually try to solve problems with software and try to know it better was not assured.

Aparicio & Costa (2012) mentioned that additional reasons to use Open Source Software are the availability of Open Source Software to individuals, companies and organizations, and the Government and the options to language customization.

Researchers also developed a study focused on local public administration to determine if FOSS is being adopted by the central government (Godinho, 2012) and also local government (Fernandes, 2011) . In what concerns local municipalities Fernandes (2011) concluded that they were used to support the most critical computer systems and to reveal the determining factors to the adoption or rejection of such technology. Fernandes (2011) concluded that 54% of the respondents were already using FOSS and three factors were particularly relevant to predicting the adoption of FOSS: Awareness of success exemplars, Existence of stable infrastructure and Availability of human resources in OSS (Fernandes, 2011).

Among management software as ERP, Enterprise Resource Planning software, despite the number of researchers working on the topic and the use of OSS at Academia, Open Source ERPs still have a low number of organizational users (Costa & Aparicio, 2006, Costa, 2007). Recently, there was an effort to translate and localize ERP software (e.g., (Batista, Costa, & Aparicio, 2013; Lopes & Costa, 2008) and to improve usability (Costa, 2010). Nevertheless, in Portugal, the invoicing system must be certified by the requirements of Decree n° 363/2010 and this new Decree n° 340/2013. This situation creates barriers to the diffusion of open source software in the context of the corporate finance system.

Computer-Assisted Audit Tools/Software for Auditing Purposes

Computer-assisted Audit Tools, CAATs, are instruments that the auditor possesses to achieve its objectives, as they were defined previously in audit planning. CAATs are essential for streamlining the auditing process through process automation; complex calculations result in analysis and report creation (Pedrosa & Costa, 2012a).

Hunton (2003) state that there are two concepts of computer-assisted audit software: Computer Assisted Audit Tools and Techniques (CAATT) and Computer Assisted Audit Techniques (CAAT). Computer Assisted Audit Tools and Techniques (CAATT) is a concept that encompasses two categories, "Tools" that are software used to improve auditor productivity and data extraction and analysis, and the "Techniques" that adds greater efficiency and effectiveness to audit procedures. Computer Assisted Audit Techniques (CAAT) is a concept that brings together greater efficiency and effectiveness in auditing procedures.

The various regulatory bodies that group audit-related professions (as The Institute of Internal Auditors - IIA, The International Federation of Accountants - IFAC, ISACA and The American Institute of Certified Public Accountants - AICPA) advocate the use of information technologies for auditing. They point a positive contribution of Computer-assisted Audit Techniques to the effectiveness and efficiency of audit procedures (Pedrosa, Costa, & Laureano, 2015). Pedrosa, Costa, & Laureano (2015) define CAATs as *"any mechanized tool for auditing, such as general-purpose auditing applications, auditing support software, utility audit programs, and computer-aided audit techniques."* Their research also points out that several International Standards for Auditing (ISA) recommend the use of CAATs, namely: ISA 230, ISA 240, ISA 320, ISA 330, ISA 505, ISA 520 and ISA 570.

There are three categories of software for the audit process, according to Lanza (1998): 1) Data Extraction and Analysis Programs, 2) Audit management programs and 3) Instrumental utilities.

Data Extraction and Analysis Programs are intended to investigate the contents of tables in databases and generate comparative reports. In this category, it is included in the following software: Active Data, ACL Data Analysis, CaseWare IDEA Analytics, TeamMate Analytics, and SE Audit.

Audit management programs incorporate specific audit functions, such as risk analysis and evaluation, control of procedures and checks, the creation of automated internal control lists and questionnaires to follow up the audit. In this group, the following software may be included: ACL Workpaper Management, MetricStream Audit Management, MKInsight Audit Management, MyWorkpapers, SAP Audit Management, TeamMate Audit Management, Thomson Reuters AutoAudit, SIPTA - Audit Work Papers System, SIAUDI - Internal Audit and IDEAGen Pentana.

Instrumental utilities include all generic, non-audit-specific programs that have the potential to be used in auditing, such as word processors, spreadsheets, and data extractors based on SQL-Structured Query Language. In this category, we highlight the following software: Microsoft Word, Microsoft Excel, Libre Office, and Apache OpenOffice.

Kim, Mannino, & Nieschwietz (2009) proposed a classification on CAATs based on features, as Database queries, Ratio Analysis, Audit Sampling, Digital Analysis, Data Mining: regression/ANOVA, Data Mining: Classification. Pedrosa & Costa (2012b) included a new feature: Working Papers, to group all the software utilized to support and document auditors' procedures.

Open Source Software Adoption

Glynn, Fitzgerald, & Exton (2005)] conducted a study on one of the most important models of open source organizational adoption derived from the theory of innovation adoption. Adoption of open source software that is, identifying the factors that influenced organizations to adopt this risky project and the factors that prevented them from adopting it.

The model comprises four macro factors that are the (1) external environment, (2) organizational context, (3) technological context and, (4) individual factors.

According to Tornatzky, Fleischer, & Chakrabarti (1990), the external environment represents the space where the organization carries out its activity, referring to industry, its competitors, market regulations and relations with governments. Glynn, Fitzgerald, & Exton. (2005) state that open source software is a paradigm shift in software in an organization's business environment, and for this reason, the authors argue for the need to focus on the outside of the organization. It includes factors such as attitude towards risk in the activity sector; the existence of success stories in the adoption of open source software; government or institutional support; the need for transparency, effective management of public funds, security and the existence of purchase agreements with representatives of proprietary software.

The authors of the model identify the organizational context as a factor that describes the characteristics of an organization. This factor has been referred in some studies on adoption of innovation, as, is by Tornatzky, Fleischer, & Chakrabarti (1990) and Fichman (1992) on the need to increase focus beyond an individual level. The following factors are included in this context: size of the organization, the degree of centralization, support from the administration and the availability of resources (such as limited financial resources or the existence of human resources with open source software experience).

Technological context is related to the technologies that the organization has at its disposal. In this component, Glynn, Fitzgerald, & Exton (2005) add factors such as: technological benefits of open source software, the possibility of superior software quality, possible advantages of having access to source code, dissatisfaction with existing software, the ability of open source software to run on old hardware and the existence of a stable and coherent information technology infrastructure backed by proprietary software.

Individual factors Glynn, Fitzgerald, & Exton (2005) also include in their model the individual factors, based on the adoption of open source software implicitly has a strong ideological motivation, which occurs at the individual level. The charisma and leadership of an "OSS Champion" (someone in the organization with wide experience and motivation in the use of open source software, someone that may assist its pears in any difficulty) are factors that may also have a significant influence on the adoption of open source software.

These factors were researched in a large-scale context of the adoption of open source software at Beaumont Hospital, Dublin, Ireland. The factors that make up the model are presented in Figure 1, where factors that assume an increase in the degree of adoption of open source software are referenced with (+), and factors that are contrary (acting as inhibitors) to the adoption of open source software are referenced with (-). They concluded that the major influences in the external environment are the network externality effects and the fact that other organizations were adopting OSS. Concerning organizational factors, the fact that the OSS is free is seen as important and the existence of an OSS Champion.

Figure 1. Framework to investigate OSS adoption.
Source: Glynn, Fitzgerald, & Exton (2005, p. 226)

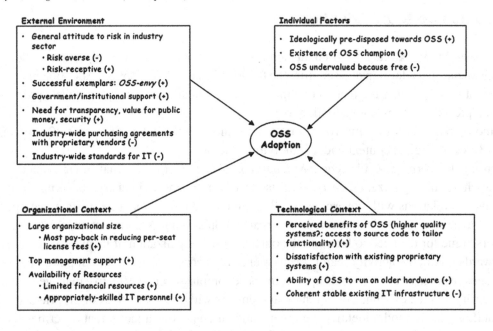

Level of Assimilation of the Open Source Software

A relevant issue in the context of FOSS's use is the level/stage of OSS Assimilation. The assimilation stage may be viewed as a combined measure of the earliness of initiation of assimilation activities (awareness, interest, evaluation/trial, commitment, limited deployment, and general deployment), and an absence of rejection, stalling, or discontinuance (Meyer & Goes, 1988). Glynn, Fitzgerald, & Exton (2005, p. 230) run their research with the stages and criteria defined by Fichman & Kemerer (1997): Stage 1 – Awareness, Stage 2 – Interest, Stage 4 – Commitment, Stage 5 - Limited Deployment and Stage 6 - General Deployment.

At stage 1 (Awareness), Key decision makers are aware of FOSS. At stage 2 (Interest), the organization is actively committed to learning more about FOSS. At stage 3 (Evaluation and Trial), the organization has acquired specific FOSS products and has initiated an evaluation or trial. At stage 4 (Commitment), the organization has committed to using a specific FOSS product in a significant way or for a production project. At stage 5 (Limited Deployment), the organization has established a program of regular but limited use of the FOSS product. Finally, at stage 6 (General Deployment) the organization is using FOSS product for at least one large and mission-critical system

The stages of assimilation are ordered, from the lower ("1 - Awareness") to the higher ("6 - General Deployment").

OBJECTIVES AND METHODOLOGICAL APPROACH

Research Question and Objectives

Free and Open source software is being used by the most demanding organizations, like American military forces or governments all over the world. Governments, and specifically the Portuguese government issued laws encouraging the usage of open source. But on the other hand, there are also some restrictions resulting from invoice software certification, that creates important barriers to free and open source software diffusion in the context of finance software (invoicing, billing, accounting). On the other hand, while billing, invoicing and accountancy are the first software systems to be implemented in companies, the use of software tools in the context of auditing is far from being an easy task. What happens in the context of financial auditing?

This study's objective is to answer the following questions:

- Which computer tools are the most used by financial auditors?
- Are auditors using Free and Open Source Software as a tool to accomplish their tasks?
- What are the facilitating and inhibiting factors in the assimilation of Free and Open Source Software for auditing?
- What are the predictive factors that can significantly influence the adoption or rejection in the use of the Free and Open Source Software for auditing?

The main contribution of this research is on the knowledge about the most utilized tools on auditors' daily work, and, mainly, on the free and open source tools for auditing purposes. In addition, the authors intend to contribute to a better awareness of the process of adoption and migration to open source software for auditing.

Methodological Approach

To comply with the proposed objectives, it was adopted a positivist and quantitative approach. Supported in the literature was created a questionnaire, focusing the main dimensions related to free and open source adoption.

The questionnaire includes a brief introduction to the research topic, 18 questions, and includes a final space for comments and observations. The respondents have an expected response time of 10 minutes.

Respondents were assured that all responses would be confidential, and the results obtained would only be used in the context of this research and publication.

The questionnaire encompasses five areas of information, the characterization of the organization, the set of macro factors previously described (external environment, organizational context, technological context, and individual factors), the level of assimilation of open source software, knowledge and use of audit software.

The data was collected through the previous questionnaire in the online application LimeSurvey. The questionnaire was administered with the collaboration of IPAI, the Portuguese Institute of Internal Audit.

RESULTS, SOLUTIONS, AND RECOMMENDATIONS

In this chapter, the results obtained in the questionnaire will be presented, regarding the characterization of the sample, knowledge, and use of the respondents alluding to software for audit, macro factors influencing the adoption of open source software, and the level of assimilation of open source software that characterizes the organization,

Characterization of the Sample

From the 64 respondents to the questionnaire, 66% are male, with an average age of 38.56 years and the district with the most respondents is Lisbon. Regarding the academic formation, 69% of the respondents are graduates, and 31% are masters. Respondents main currently area of work is accounting (19%), auditing (15%), banking (14%), and government. They predominantly perform functions as internal auditor, external auditor, and auditing director. Their age at present function is, on average, 8.65 years and the average contact time with open source software has been 5.8 years.

Regarding the organizational characterization, which is based on the number of employees employed by the organization and the number of employees directly involved in the audit department, they present high values in the standard deviation, which shows a disparity of values. However, the most common number of employees is 10, with one employee directly involved in the auditing area, which indicates that mostly respondents belong to small organizations.

Knowledge and Use of Respondents Alluding to Audit Software

Based on literature review, respondents were asked if they knew several tools (despite they have never utilized it) and, then, if they use it or not: ActiveData for Excel; ACL Workpaper Management; ACL Data Analytics; CaseWare IDEA Analytics; IDEAGen Pentana; MetricStream Audit Management; Microsoft Excel; MKInsight Audit Management; MyWorkpapers; SAP Audit Management; TeamMate Analytics; TeamMate Audit Management; Thomson Reuters AutoAudit; SIPTA; SiAudit; Libre Office; SE Audit, and OpenOffice. Previous questions were relevant to answer the first objective of this chapter, "*Which computer tools are the most used by financial auditors?*".

Regarding audit software, it was concluded that the best-known software among respondents is Microsoft Excel (87.5%) followed by Caseware IDEA Analytics (45.3%), SAP Audit Management (40.6%), ACL Data Analytics (39.1%), and Open Office (31.3%). Respondents pointed new items as ACD Auditor,

Rstudio, SharePoint, MyClient, Caseware Working Papers, and DRAI10. However, there was only one answer to each one of the new listed tools.

Regarding usage, 59 respondents answered the question using a Likert Scale (from 1-Strongly disagree to 7- Strongly agree). Taking the ones who stated that they "Somewhat agree," "Agree" or "Strongly agree," the software that is the most commonly used is Microsoft Excel (86.4%), followed by SAP Audit Management (18.6%) and Caseware IDEA Analytics (16.9%). Concerning Open Source Software, Open Office has 10.2% of respondents saying that they use it on a daily basis. Mostly professionals in the audit area use spreadsheets as the main tool. They often use the proprietary name (Excel) as synonymous of the spreadsheet. But even though, it seems that the proprietary software, like Microsoft Excel which was already mentioned in previous research for financial auditors: there is evidence that Microsoft Excel has about twice the number of users than its competitors ACL, Caseware IDEA, Access (Pedrosa, Laureano, & Costa, 2015).

Macro Influencing Factors in the Adoption of the Open Source Software

In the analysis of the factors influencing the adoption of open source software, the macro factors "external environment" and "technological context" stand out, as they present the most consensual answers, considering that they may significantly influence the adoption of open source software adoption.

In the external environment, it is observed - with the great agreement - that the change from proprietary software to open source software can be problematic due to the absence of maintenance contracts and the lack of knowledge of success stories. These factors are inhibitors of the adoption of open source software, not giving security in this type of applications, because the open source software does not offer the legal comforts that the proprietary software usually grants. The knowledge of other organizations have already opted for this type of software, would contribute to the increase of confidence with this type of solutions, as reported by Glynn, Fitzgerald, & Exton (2005). This Chapter's conclusions on macro influencing factors are listed in Figure 2.

In the technological context, there was greater agreement that the audit department was stabilized and based on proprietary software. In an organization where there are favourable agreements with proprietary software vendors, the implementation of open source software may be more difficult to initiate, resulting in an inhibitor for the adoption of open source software, as mentioned by Glynn, Fitzgerald, & Exton (2005).

Level of Assimilation of Free and Open Source Software That Characterizes the Organization of Respondents

The results obtained from the questionnaire revealed that 43.1% of the respondents defined the level of assimilation of open source software in the organization where they work as "Awareness" assuming that management is aware of the existence of open source software. With roughly 29.3% characterizing their organization with the level of assimilation of open source software of "Interest," attributing that the organization is committed to learning more about open source software. The maximum level of assimilation of open source software "Limited Deployment" and "General Deployment" is 6.9% of the respondents. These results translate the need to try to understand the reasons for auditing professionals not to break the barrier of adopting this type of solution and stay on the first and second stages: awareness and interest.

Figure 2. Conclusions on macro factors on OSS adoption

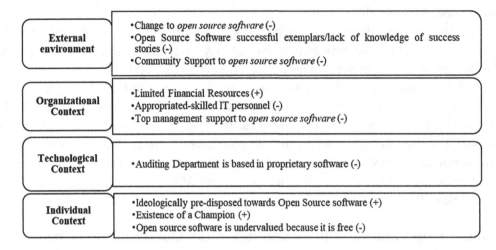

FUTURE RESEARCH DIRECTIONS

A limitation of the research reported here is the small number of answers. Only 64 respondents answered the questionnaire. A new approach to disseminate the questionnaires to accomplish a higher number of respondents will help to understand if the low numbers related to the use of Free and Open Source Software was connected to the number of internal auditors or if the present conclusions could be generalized to all auditors. In addition, it would be important to understand if the conclusions are coherent to other countries. New research should focus on countries that defined strategies to Free and Open Source Software's use and, then, understand if, among their auditors, the use of Free and Open Source Software is higher than the present ones. It would also be opportune to repeat this study as soon as Millennials are in the labour market: their profile is seen as very distant from the generation that is now in the organizations so, it would be interesting to understand if that also affects their choices between proprietary and open source software. In what concerns Portuguese governments there is an incoherent approach related to the usage of free and open source software. The government issued some measures to increase usage of free and open source software (like the previously referred PGETIC), but on the other hand, the certification of invoicing software almost killed the possibility of disseminating software related to finance. Some challenges, like the impact of Article 13 of the EU directive on copyright may be subject of study in a future research.

CONCLUSION

The main objective of this chapter is to identify which tools are the most used by professionals in the financial auditing area and whether they are using free and open source software as a tool to perform their tasks. In addition, knowing the level of assimilation of free and open source software in the context of auditing, another objective was to recognize the factors that could influence the adoption or rejection of the use of open source software for auditing.

The results were obtained through an online questionnaire and its analysis allowed identifying that the most used software by auditing professionals are spreadsheets software. In this context, the most used is proprietary software Microsoft Excel. There is even the confusion between Excel and spreadsheet. The respondents demonstrated that they also know software such as Caseware IDEA Analytics, SAP Audit Management, ACL Data Analytics, and Open Office. In what concerns open source systems, just a small number of auditors indicated Open Office Si Audit and open Office. It may suggest that these professionals are aware of the existence of open source software as Libre Office, SiAudit and OpenOffice but they chose not to use it.

The level of assimilation of open source software confirms the previous tendency: the respondents characterize the use of Open Source software in the organization where they are working by using the stages of "awareness" and "interest." This demonstrates that the management has knowledge of open source software, and the organization is actively engaged in learning more about this type of application, but they are not yet using it. Moreover, they do not go beyond the "interest" barrier and do not transpose into "experimentation".

From this study, another of this chapter's conclusion is that the macro factors that can influence the use of open source auditing tools by the organizations are the external environment factor and the technological context factor. These factors are related to the lack of knowledge of success cases at the level of assimilation of this type of application, the problem of changing the proprietary software to open source and the audit department is stabilized with proprietary software.

ACKNOWLEDGMENT

We gratefully acknowledge financial support from FCT- Fundação para a Ciencia e Tecnologia (Portugal), national funding through research grant UID/SOC/04521/2013.

The Instituto Português de Auditoria Interna supported this research by disseminating the questionnaires among its members.

REFERENCES

ANSOL. (2018). *ANSOL - Associação Nacional para o Software Livre*. Retrieved June 16, 2018, from https://ansol.org/

Aparicio, M., & Costa, C. J. (2012). Macroeconomics Leverage Trough Open Source. In *Proceedings of the Workshop on Open Source and Design of Communication* (pp. 19–24). Academic Press. 10.1145/2316936.2316941

Batista, M., Costa, C. J., & Aparicio, M. (2013). ERP OS Localization Framework. In *Proceedings of the Workshop on Open Source and Design of Communication* (pp. 1–8). New York: ACM. 10.1145/2503848.2503849

Costa, C. (2007). In C. J. Costa (Ed.), *"ERP Open Source," in Information Technology, Organizations and Teams* (pp. 159–170)., press.itml.org

Costa, C. J. (2010). Testing Usability of ERP Open Source Systems. In *Proceedings of the Workshop on Open Source and Design of Communication* (pp. 25–30). New York: ACM. 10.1145/1936755.1936763

Costa, C. J., & Aparicio, M. (2006). Organizational Tools in the Web: ERP Open Source. In *Proceedings of the IADIS International Conference on WWW/Internet* (pp. 401–408). Academic Press.

ESOP. (2018). *ESOP - Associação de Empresas de Software Open Source Portuguesas*. Retrieved June 1, 2018, from http://www.esop.pt/

Fernandes, N. (2011). *O software open source como suporte à infra-estrutura de TI na administração pública local portuguesa: Factores determinantes na sua adopção - Mestrado em Gestão de Sistemas de informação*. ISCTE-IUL.

Fichman, R. G. (1992). *Information Technology Diffusion: A Review of Empirical Research*. MIT Sloan School of Management.

Fichman, R. G., & Kemerer, C. F. (1997). The Assimilation of Software Process Innovations: An Organizational Learning Perspective. *Management Science*, *43*(10), 1345–1363. doi:10.1287/mnsc.43.10.1345

FSF. (2017). *Free software is a matter of liberty, not price — Free Software Foundation — working together for free software*. Retrieved January 21, 2017, from http://www.fsf.org

Garcia, M. N., dos Santos, S., Pereira, R. da S., & Rossi, G. B. (2010). Software livre em relação ao software proprietário: Aspectos favoráveis e desfavoráveis percebidos por especialistas. *Gestão & Regionalidade*, *26*(78), 106–120.

Glynn, E., Fitzgerald, B., & Exton, C. (2005). Commercial Adoption of Open Source Software : An Empirical Study. In *2005 International Symposium on Empirical Software Engineering*, *2005* (pp. 225–234). Academic Press. 10.1109/ISESE.2005.1541831

Godinho, R. (2012). *O Open Source Software na Administração Pública Central Portuguesa*. ISCTE-IUL.

Hunton, J. E. (2003). Core Concepts of Information Systems Auditing. John Wiley & Sons.

Kavanagh, P. (2004). Open source software: implementation and management. Elsevier.

Kim, H.-J., Mannino, M., & Nieschwietz, R. J. (2009). Information technology acceptance in the internal audit profession: Impact of technology features and complexity. *International Journal of Accounting Information Systems*, *10*(4), 214–228. doi:10.1016/j.accinf.2009.09.001

Lanza, P. (1998). La informática en el trabajo de auditoria. *Auditoria Publica*, *13*, 93–98.

Laurent, A. M. S. (2004). *Understanding open source and free software licensing: guide to navigating licensing issues in existing & new software*. O'Reilly Media.

Lopes, N. G., & Costa, C. J. (2008). ERP Localization: Exploratory Study in Translation: European and Brazilian Portuguese. In *Proceedings of the 26th Annual ACM International Conference on Design of Communication* (pp. 93–98). New York: ACM. 10.1145/1456536.1456555

Meyer, A., & Goes, J. (1988). Organizational Assimilation of Innovations: A multilevel Contextual Analysis. *Academy of Management Journal*, *31*(4), 897–924.

Pedrosa, I., & Costa, C. J. (2012a). Computer Assisted Audit Tools and Techniques in Real World: CAATT's Applications and Approaches in Context. *International Journal of Computer Information Systems and Industrial Management Applications*, *4*, 161–168.

Pedrosa, I., & Costa, C. J. (2012b). Financial Auditing and Surveys : how are financial auditors using information technology? An approach using Expert Interviews. In *ISDOC '12 Proceedings of the Workshop on Information Systems and Design of Communication, June 11, 2012, Lisbon, Portugal* (pp. 37–43). Academic Press.

Pedrosa, I., Costa, C. J., & Laureano, R. M. S. (2015). Motivations and limitations on the use of Information Technology on statutory auditors' work: an exploratory study. In CISTI 2015 Proceedings, 2015 (pp. 1132–1137). Aveiro, Portugal: Academic Press.

Pedrosa, I., Laureano, R. M. S., & Costa, C. J. (2015). Motivações dos auditores para o uso das Tecnologias da Informação na sua profissão: aplicação aos Revisores Oficiais de Contas. *Revista Ibérica de Sistemas E Tecologias de Informação, 15*, 101–118.

Raymond, E. S. (1999). *The Cathedral & the Bazaar: Musings on linux and open source by an accidental revolutionary*. O'Reilly Media. doi:10.100712130-999-1026-0

Tornatzky, L. G., Fleischer, M., & Chakrabarti, A. K. (1990). *The processes of technological innovation*. Lexington Books.

Trezentos, P., Dicosmo, R., Laurière, S., Morgado, M., Abecasis, J., Mancinelli, F., & Oliveira, A. (2007). New Generation of Linux Meta-installers. In Research Track of FOSDEM (pp. 1–8). Academic Press.

ADDITIONAL READING

Ahmi, A. (2012). *Adoption of Generalised Audit Software (GAS) by External Auditors in the UK*. London: Brunel University.

Ahmi, A., Saidin, S. Z., & Abdullah, A. (2014). IT Adoption by Internal Auditors in Public Sector: A Conceptual Study. *Procedia: Social and Behavioral Sciences*, *164*(August), 591–599. doi:10.1016/j.sbspro.2014.11.151

Aksulu, A., & Wade, M. (2010). A comprehensive review and synthesis of open source research. *Journal of the Association for Information Systems*, *11*(11), 576–656. doi:10.17705/1jais.00245

Almeida, N. V., & Pedrosa, I. (2011). Open source data mining tools for audit purposes. In *Proceedings of the 2011 Workshop on Open Source and Design of Communication - OSDOC '11* (pp. 33–34). New York, New York, USA: ACM Press. 10.1145/2016716.2016724

Chau, P., & Tam, K. (1997). Factors Affecting the Adoption of Open Systems: An Exploratory Study. *MIS Quarterly: Management Information Systems*, *21*(1), 1–24. doi:10.2307/249740

Holton, C. (2009). Identifying disgruntled employee systems fraud risk through text mining: A simple solution for a multi-billion dollar problem. *Decision Support Systems*, *46*(4), 853–864. doi:10.1016/j. dss.2008.11.013

ISACA. (2011). *IT Control Objectives for Cloud Computing: controls and assurance in the cloud*. ISACA.

Laureano, R. M. S., & Pedrosa, I. (2016). A Utilização de Ferramentas Informáticas para a Realização de Tarefas de Verificação: implementação no Microsoft Excel e no CaseWare IDEA. *In CISTI 2016 Proceedings - 11th Iberian Conference on Information Systems and Technologies*, jun 15-18.

Le Grand, C. H. (2013). IT Auditing for Modern Technology Management. *Edpacs*, *47*(6), 1–14. doi:1 0.1080/07366981.2013.795047

Mahzan, N., & Lymer, A. (2014). Examining the adoption of computer-assisted audit tools and techniques: Cases of generalized audit software use by internal auditors. *Managerial Auditing Journal*, *29*(4), 327–349. doi:10.1108/MAJ-05-2013-0877

Pedrosa, I. (2015). *Computer-assisted audit tools and techniques use: determinants for individual acceptance*. ISCTE-IUL.

Pedrosa, I., & Costa, C. J. (2014). New trends on CAATTs: what are the Chartered Accountants' new challenges? *In ISDOC '14 Proceedings of the International Conference on Information Systems and Design of Communication*, May 16–17, 2014, Lisbon, Portugal (pp. 138–142).

Pedrosa, I., Costa, C. J., & Laureano, R. M. S. (2015). Use of Information Technology on Statutory auditors' work: new profiles beyond Spreadsheets' users. In CISTI 2015 Proceedings, 2015 (pp. 774–779). Aveiro, Portugal.

Rechtman, Y. (2004). Open-source software implications to CPAs. *The CPA Journal*, (January): 66–69.

KEY TERMS AND DEFINITIONS

Computer-Assisted Audit Tools (CAATs): Any mechanized tool for auditing, such as general-purpose auditing applications, auditing support software, utility audit programs, and computer-aided audit techniques.

Open Source Software: Like in free software, open source software should comply to the four freedoms. But, while free software emphasizes freedom, Open Source is an approach that more emphasis on software quality.

This research was previously published in Organizational Auditing and Assurance in the Digital Age; pages 188-202, copyright year 2019 by Business Science Reference (an imprint of IGI Global).

Chapter 29
Application of Quality in Use Model to Evaluate the User Experience of Online Banking Software

Manar Abu Talib
University of Sharjah, Sharjah, UAE

Areej Alsaafin
University of Sharjah, Sharjah, UAE

Selma Manel Medjden
https://orcid.org/0000-0003-1926-8886
University of Sharjah, Sharjah, UAE

ABSTRACT

Open source software (OSS) has recently become very important due to the rapid expansion of the software industry. In order to determine whether the quality of the software can achieve the intended purposes, the components of OSS need to be assessed as they are in closed source (conventional) software. Several quality in-use models have been introduced to evaluate software quality in various fields. The banking sector is one of the most critical sectors, as it deals with highly sensitive data; it therefore requires an accurate and effective assessment of software quality. In this article, two pieces of banking software are compared: one open source and one closed source. A new quality in use model, inspired by ISO/IEC 25010, is used to ensure concise results in the comparison. The results obtained show the great potential of OSS, especially in the banking field.

DOI: 10.4018/978-1-7998-9158-1.ch029

INTRODUCTION

The impact of open source resources on business has been noted in many sectors, especially with recent gains in various open source technologies from OSS to open source libraries (Hecht & Clark, 2018, Official Statistics of Finland, 2011). Banking is one of these sectors. Bearing in mind the sensitivity of the data managed by banks, banking software has to meet stringent criteria in terms of security and efficiency (Popp, 2015). In order to assess the suitability of software from this perspective, some quality standards must be defined.

Computer software is a term that includes all the parts of a computer system that handle data. Software can be a computer program, a library or any set of instructions that manage data. Open Source Software (OSS) is software that allows users to access and modify the source code, while closed source software provides users with functionality that can only be accessed through its unalterable user interface.

One advantage of OSS is its low cost. Since OSS source code is licensed to be freely accessible, only implementation, maintenance and training charges are necessary to start using an OSS product. However, if any support is needed, OSS users must rely on online communities, while closed source products generally offer after-sale support services. Another important advantage is the flexibility that OSS products provide. Indeed, as the source code of OSS is accessible, users can make any necessary changes in the product. On the other hand, closed source products require users to adapt to the environment provided, without any possibility of making changes.

In all fields, the software components need to be assessed to determine whether the software quality is sufficient for the intended purposes. Recently, a large number of quality models have been introduced to help organizations determine if a given software can perform the required tasks adequately and effectively. These quality models also ensure that the widest range of people can use the software, as they improve accessibility and acceptance, increase efficiency, reduce errors and training requirements, and improve productivity (Bevan, 2001).

The quality of a software product plays a significant role in the success of a business, as it reflects the level of customer satisfaction. Every quality model measures software quality based on a number of characteristics. The first quality model, introduced by Jim McCall (1977), assessed quality factors to evaluate user satisfaction and guide developer priorities. The second quality model was a hierarchical model introduced by Boehm, Brown, Kaspar, Lipow, McLeod, and Merritt (1978). It consisted of primitive characteristics, intermediate level characteristics and high-level characteristics. Finally, a more recent quality model proposed by Geoff (1995) addresses the relationship between quality attributes and sub-attributes.

In this paper, the authors apply Alnanih's new quality in use model (Alnanih, 2015), inspired by ISO/IEC 25010 (ISO/IEC 25010:2011), to assess two online banking software products: an open source product called Cyclos, (Social TRade Organisation, 1970), and a closed source product called E-pay Suite (Canopus Innovative Technologies, 1992). The qualitative approach has four phases: pre-experiment, data gathering, data analysis and evaluation. The aim of this study is to assess whether or not the open source product is capable of performance similar to that of the closed source product.

The rest of this paper is structured as follows: first, we present a comprehensive set of quality in use models for assessing OSS, followed by an explanation of the methodology used to assess the two banking software products—one open source and one closed source. We then provide a description of the experiments conducted and a discussion of the results. Finally, our conclusions are provided, along with some practical applications for the future.

BACKGROUND

Over the past years, a wide range of open source evaluation tools have been used in different fields. In this section, the authors give an overview of the quality models available in the literature and discuss their applicability to OSS.

Open Source Maturity Model (OSMM)

In 2003, the open source maturity model (OSMM) was developed by Capgemini (Duijnhouwer & Widdows, 2003). The OSMM uses product maturity for the purpose of comparing various software products, with the aim of selecting the product that best fits the organization's objectives. While OSMM is a non-free software, authorized distribution is permitted. This model has two categories of indicator: product and application. The product indicator has four sub-categories: product, integration, use and acceptance. The application indicator considers several environmental, current, and future user requirements (Duijnhouwer & Widdows, 2003). The categories and subcategories of OSMM are illustrated in Figure 1. It is clear from the figure that OSMM considers of all the characteristics of product quality available in ISO/IEC 25010 (ISO/IEC 25010:2011), however, it only assesses the usability in the quality in use category.

Figure 1. Open Source Maturity Model (OSMM) (Duijnhouwer & Widdows, 2003)

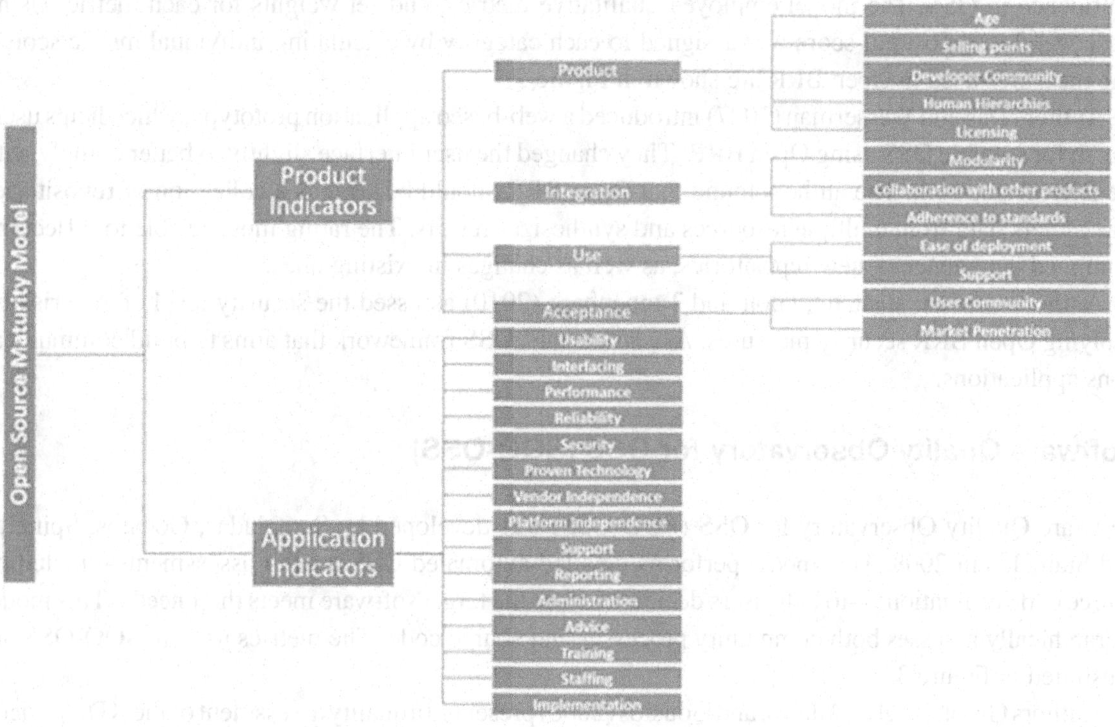

In 2015, a survey of 200 Moroccan Small and Medium Enterprises (SMEs) was conducted by Houaich and Belaissaoui in order to identify their needs, knowledge and ability to adopt open source technology

(Houaich & Belaissaoui, 2015). The authors matched the SMEs with suitable open source technology by designing a new assessment model, E-OSSEM, using the OSMM product category. This model allowed the authors to choose the most suitable open source technology for each SME. Another research work by Akbari and Peikar (2014) analyzed Free/Open Source (FOSS) GIS tools in web mapping and spatial databases. The authors compared different WebGIS FOSS tools analytically using OSMM. These tools included UMN MapServer, MapGuide OS and FOSS spatial databases such as PostGIS. This work concluded that UMN MapServer is a completely mature OSS, and that its functionality and quality is comparable to other conventional (closed source) software products. In addition, it demonstrates that PostGIS is a highly competitive closed source software, especially with regard to its 3D functionality.

Open Business Readiness Rating (Open BRR)

In 2007, the Carnegie Mellon West Center sponsored the Open Business Readiness Rating (Open BRR) for SpikeSource, Open Source Investigation, Intel, and CodeZoo (Wasserman, Pal & Chan, 2006). The aim of this model design was to enable institutions to choose open source software that best suited their needs. It was found to improve the time required to evaluate an OSS by using a systematic approach consisting of four phases. In the first phase, a quick assessment was performed to create a shortlist of potential candidates. In the second phase, various metrics were ordered according to their importance. In the third phase, data was gathered and analyzed. Finally, in the fourth phase, the data was translated into a Business Readiness Rating to enhance the decision-making process and increase potential user confidence in OSS. The model employed qualitative metrics, and set weights for each metric. Using these weights, an overall score was assigned to each category by calculating individual metric scores. The measures used in Open BRR are shown in Figure 2.

Authors Das and Wasserman (2007) introduced a web-based application prototype, which helps users search for suitable OSS using Open BRR. They changed the user interface slightly to better comply with the BRR framework. The authors found that Open BRR should be seen as a collection of repositories that gathers data from multiple resources and synthesizes results. The rating must be able to reflect the continued emergence of new repositories, as well as changes in existing ones.

Authors Groven, Haaland, Glott and Tannenberg (2010) assessed the security level of Asterisk by applying Open BRR security measures. Asterisk is a FLOSS framework that aims to build communications applications.

Software Quality Observatory for OSS (SQO-OSS)

Software Quality Observatory for OSS (SQO-OSS) was developed by Samoladas, Gousios, Spinellis and Stamelos in 2008. This model performs detailed automated OSS quality assessments—including source code evaluations—to help users decide whether the target software meets their needs. This model hierarchically assesses both community processes and source code. The metrics used in SQO-OSS are illustrated in Figure 3.

Authors Groot, Kügler, Adams, and Gousios (2006) presented a quality assessment of the KDE project, which aimed to enable engineers to identify modifications needed to enhance the original product. The study found that the SQO-OSS model helps OSS developers write better software, while simultaneously helping potential users make better-informed choices.

Figure 2. Open Business Readiness Rating (Open BRR) (Wasserman et al., 2006)

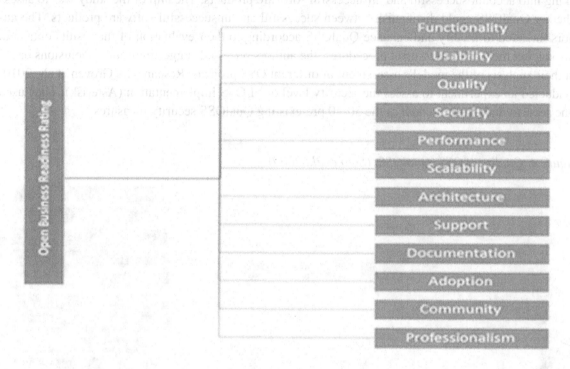

Figure 3. Software Quality Observatory for OSS (SQO-OSS) (Samoladas et al., 2008)

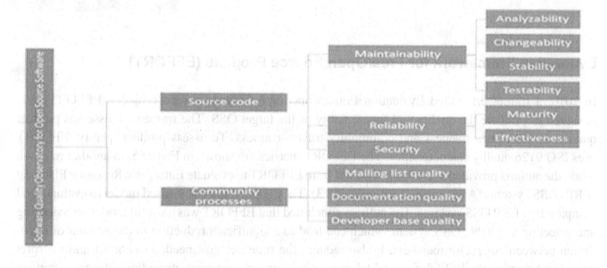

Quality of OSS (QualOSS)

In 2009, Soto and Ciolkowski developed the Quality of OSS (QualOSS) model, which focuses on OSS robustness and evolvability. This model has two main categories of quality characteristics: product-related and community-related (shown in Figure 4). However, QualOSS does not include characteristics from any of the quality in use categories. Soto et al. (2009) applied QualOSS to twenty FLOSS programs, taking into account successful and unsuccessful software products. The aim of the study was to assess whether QualOSS could distinguish between successful and unsuccessful software products. The authors intended to modify and enhance QualOSS according to their evaluation of the results obtained. Introducing their own assessment procedures, the authors provided suggestions and conclusions based on their analysis of the model's assessment of different OSS projects. Researchers Groven et al. (2010) conducted an experiment to assess the security level of FLOSS implementation (Asterisk). They used nine security indicators, as well as the 30-40 pre-existing QualOSS security measures.

Figure 4. Quality of OSS (QualOSS) (Soto et al., 2009)

Evaluation Framework for Free/Open Source Projects (EFFORT)

In 2010, a framework called Evaluation Framework for Free/Open source projects (EFFORT) was designed to evaluate the quality and functionality of the target OSS. The framework assesses product quality, product attractiveness and community trustworthiness. To assess product quality, EFFORT uses ISO 9126 quality characteristics. The EFFORT metrics are shown in Figure 5. In another research work, the authors provided a customized model from EFFORT to evaluate Enterprise Resource Planning (ERP) OSS systems (Aversano & Tortorella, 2013). They applied the customized model to evaluate and compare five ERP OSS systems. The authors concluded that EFFORT was a useful model for assessing and selecting a suitable OSS system, which can lead to a significant reduction in the amount of negotiation between enterprise members. It also reduces the time and cost needed to collect and interpret data. Furthermore, the EFFORT model takes user opinions into account, providing relevance markers linked to metrics and questions during the process of data collection. In their research, Aversano and Tortorella (2011) used the same approach and customized EFFORT to design Free OSS (FOSS) for Customer Relationship Management (CRM) systems. They applied the customized model to four of the most common CRM systems. This led to good results for product quality and attractiveness; however, the results were less viable for community trustworthiness.

Figure 5. Evaluation Framework for Free/Open Source Projects (EFFORT) (Aversano & Tortorella, 2010)

ISO/IEC 25010

In 2011, the ISO/IEC 25010 model was developed to determine the quality characteristics that should be considered when assessing a software product (ISO/IEC 25010:2011). System quality is the degree to which the system meets the stated and implicit needs of different stakeholders, therefore providing value. The needs of these stakeholders are fairly representative of the quality model, which defines the quality in use model and the product quality model. The quality in use model consists of five characteristics, illustrated in Table 1, related to the consequence of the interaction when the software product is used in a particular way. This system model applies to the complete human-computer system, which includes the computer systems and software products in use. The product quality model consists of eight characteristics, illustrated in Table 1, related to the software's static properties and the dynamic properties of the computer system. The model applies to both software products and computer systems. The characteristics specified in both models relate to all software products and computer systems. The characteristics and sub-characteristics provide consistent terminology to identify, measure and evaluate the quality of the system and the software product. They also offer a range of quality characteristics to which declared quality requirements can be compared for completeness. Although the product quality model is designed to assess software and computer systems, many of the characteristics can also be applied to broader systems and services.

The following table presents the model characteristics discussed in this section as compared to the ISO/IEC 25010 (ISO/IEC 25010:2011) features. There is clearly a lack of quality in use evaluation for this type of software in the literature.

Table 1. Comparison between ISO/IEC 25010 and OSMM, Open BRR, QualOSS, SQO-OSS, and EFFORT

ISO 25010	Quality Characteristics	OSMM	Open BRR	Qual OOS	SQO-OSS	EFFORT Model
Product Quality	Functional Suitability	👍	👍	👍		👍
	Reliability	👍		👍	👍	👍
	Performance Efficiency	👍	👍	👍		👍
	Operability	👍	👍	👍		
	Security	👍	👍	👍	👍	
	Compatibility	👍		👍		
	Maintainability	👍	👍	👍	👍	👍
	Transferability	👍		👍		👍
Quality in Use	Effectiveness				👍	
	Efficiency					
	Satisfaction					
	Safety					
	Usability	👍	👍			👍

METHODOLOGY

According to Creswell, there are five qualitative methods: narrative research, grounded theory research, phenomenological research, ethnographic research and case study research. This paper uses case study research, which is concerned with using real-life research methods as well as observations, interviews and reports. It is similar to social sciences research methods used in psychology, medicine and law. Case study research can fall into three categories: single instrumental, collective and intrinsic case study. Case selection can be challenging (Creswell, 2013).

In this paper, the authors apply Alnanih's new quality in use model (Alnanih, 2015), inspired by ISO/IEC 25010 (ISO/IEC 25010:2011), to assess two online banking software products: one open source and one closed source. First, the two software applications to be compared were selected: the OSS chosen was Cyclos and the closed source software was E-pay Suite. The goal of this work is to assess whether the open source product is capable of a similar quality of performance as that of the closed source product. ISO/25010 is an extension of the ISO/9126 standard, which forms the basis for most of the above models (Figure 6).

The qualitative approach will have four phases to be described in detail later in this section: pre-experiment, data gathering, data analysis and evaluation. We identify the tasks and the participants, prepare the spreadsheets and questionnaires and set the hypothesis in Phase One. In Phase Two, we gather data by recording the performance of each user and requiring them to complete the questionnaire. We analyze the data in Phase Three, calculating the quality in use metrics and testing the hypothesis. Finally, we evaluate the results of the computed metrics and evaluate user satisfaction in Phase Four.

Figure 6. ISO/IEC 25010 (ISO/IEC 25010:2011)

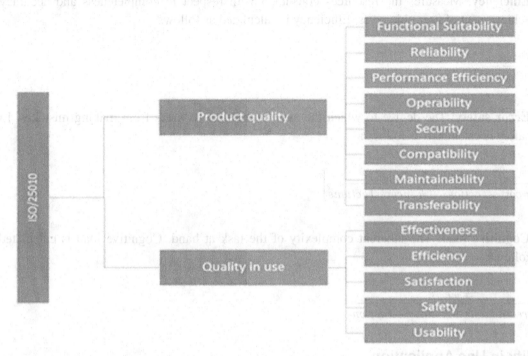

Proposed Quality in Use Approach

ISO/IEC 25010 (ISO/IEC 25010:2011) addresses two types of OSS product quality characteristics; namely, quality in use and product quality. This section discusses quality in use characteristics, as the evaluation of these characteristics in OSS is lacking in the literature.

Quality in use is defined as the degree to which a product or system can be used by specific users to meet their needs to achieve specific goals with efficiency, effectiveness, freedom from risk, and satisfaction in specific contexts of use (ISO/IEC 25010:2011)

In this work, Alnanih's new quality in use model is used (Alnanih, 2015). This model consists of the following quality in use characteristics (Figure 7):

- **Effectiveness**: Completeness and accuracy for users in terms of achieving specified goals. Effectiveness is calculated as follows:

$$\frac{Min \ \# \ correct \ actions}{\# \ correct \ actions + \# \ incorrect \ actions}$$

- **Productivity**: The ratio of the functional value of the software produced to the labor and expense of producing it. Productivity is calculated as follows:

$$\frac{Min \ \# \ correct \ actions}{Time \ Period}$$

- **Efficiency**: Measures the resources consumed with respect to completeness and accuracy of achievement of user objectives. Efficiency is calculated as follows:

$$\frac{Effectiveness}{Time\,Period}$$

- **Error safety**: The degree to which the system prevents its users from making mistakes. Error safety is calculated as follows:

$$1 - \left(\frac{\#\,incorrect\,actions}{\#\,correct\,actions + \#\,incorect\,actions} \right)$$

- **Cognitive load**: The inherent complexity of the task at hand. Cognitive load is calculated as follows:

$$\frac{\#\,views}{\#\,correct\,actions + \#\,incorrect\,actions}$$

Quality in Use Application

This case study aims to assess whether the OSS Cyclos (Social TRade Organisation, 1970) can be as effective as the closed source software E-pay Suite (Canopus Innovative Technologies, 1992). The authors therefore conducted an experimental assessment to compare the two software products on the basis of the stages shown in Figure 8.

Phase One: Pre-Experiment

In this phase, the authors organized the various parts of the experiment to achieve accurate results. For the aim of this work, the authors selected 10 tasks of different types that were available in both software products. Some tasks were purely related to banking, while others allowed users to customize their accounts. In addition, some tasks were designed to provide the user with a sense of security. The selected tasks were the following:

Step 1: Access personal information.
Step 2: Check previous transactions.
Step 3: Search for transactions occurring during the last month.
Step 4: Transfer $100 to any user.
Step 5: Change the language.
Step 6: Check the account balance.
Step 7: Save an account statement.
Step 8: Print an account statement.
Step 9: Check the details of the last login.
Step 10: Check messages.

Figure 7. Alnanih New Quality-in-Use Model (Alnanih, 2015)

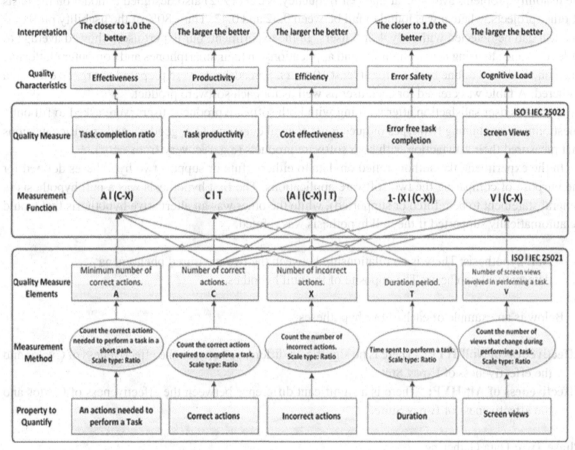

Figure 8. Proposed quality in use methodology

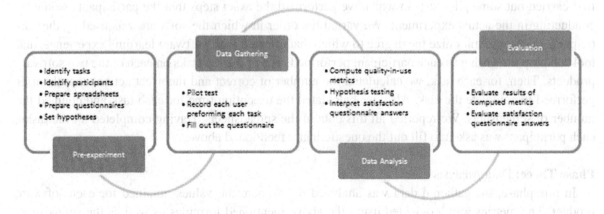

These tasks were performed by ten professional participants who were expert users, which means that they were already familiar with online banking tasks (the group was mainly composed of PhD holders). A test on usability conducted by the authors in 1993 (see also Nielsen, 2012) obtained an average of $p=0.31$ for a number of studied projects. Therefore, 5 participants would be enough to detect 85% of the usability problems available at that test frequency. Virzi (1992) also designed a model on the basis of other projects, where p was found to fall between 0.32 and 0.42. Thus, 80% of the usability problems in a test can be detected with only 4 or 5 users. In the experiment, our expert users showed average to little resistance to using new technology and applications on their smartphones and computer platforms. Each one had used online banking for at least 10 years. Spreadsheets were prepared to organize the data gathered. A table was created for each user as well as for each software product.

To assess user satisfaction after working with both software products, users were asked to fill out a questionnaire containing two types of questions: general questions (e.g. gender), and specific questions that measured their satisfaction with both software products (e.g. recovery from error).

In the experiment, the authors relied on data to either refute or support two hypotheses defined for the purpose of comparing the two software applications. The first hypothesis was a null hypothesis (a general statement to be refuted or supported), while the other was an alternative hypothesis that would be automatically supported if the null hypothesis was refuted.

a.   Null hypothesis: There is no relationship between the two measured phenomena.
b.   Alternative hypothesis: The opposite of the null hypothesis.

Below is an example of each of our hypotheses:

Effectiveness of Null-HYP: "There is no significant difference between the effectiveness of Cyclos and the effectiveness of E-pay Suite."
Effectiveness of Alt-HYP: "There is a significant difference between the effectiveness of Cyclos and the effectiveness of E-pay Suite."

Phase Two: Data Gathering

This phase constitutes the first transfer phase of the actual experiment, in which we gathered the data used to compare the two software. To ensure that we were ready to conduct the experiment, we first carried out some pilot tests in which we performed the exact steps that the participants would be conducting in the actual experiment. We varied the order in which the software was used by the participants in order to minimize the degree to which that affected their software learning experience, and took a laptop screenshot as each participant performed each of the ten tasks on each of the two software products. Then, for each task, we calculated the number of correct and incorrect actions that the user performed to complete the task. Also, we calculated the execution time for each task and counted the number of screenshots. We reported all this data in the spreadsheets. Having completed all the tasks, each participant was asked to fill out the questionnaire mentioned above.

Phase Three: Data Analysis

In this phase, the gathered data was analyzed to compare the values obtained for each software product. The metrics were computed using the above-mentioned formulas as well as the spreadsheet data. We used an Excel tool to calculate the value of the t-Test, which would be useful for comparing two groups of mean values. The average of all tasks was computed for each user, metric and software product. Then, the t-Test value was calculated using the average calculated for each software product. To interpret the results obtained from the questionnaires, a different type of analysis was used for each of the two types of questions. For the general assessment questions, the authors counted the answers, while for the questions related to ease of use, they set an objective scoring method that would not favor either software product. The two scoring scales are shown in Figure 9.

Figure 9. Scoring method

Very Easy	Easy	Neutral	Difficult	Very Difficult
+2	+1	0	-1	-2

(a) Scores for ease of use

Strongly Agree	Agree	Neutral	Disagree	Strongly Disagree
+2	+1	0	-1	-2

(b) Scores for general assessment of the software

Phase Four: Evaluation

According to hypothesis testing convention, if the p-value obtained from the t-Test results is greater than alpha (i.e. 0.05), then the null hypothesis cannot be refuted for that factor. If the p-value is less than alpha, then the alternative hypothesis is supported, and the mean value should be used for the comparison between the two software products.

To evaluate the participants' answers, the authors compared the values obtained in the results. In this comparison, the focus was on noticeable differences (greater than 2).

EXPERIMENT RESULTS

To represent the findings, the authors computed the mean value of all averages in each metric for both software products. The results are shown in Figure 10.

Figure 10. Overall comparison of Cyclos and E-pay Suite

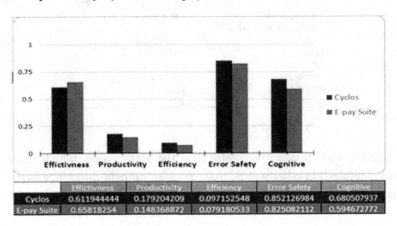

	Effictivness	Productivity	Efficiency	Error Safety	Cognitive
Cyclos	0.611944444	0.179204209	0.097152548	0.852126984	0.680507937
E-pay Suite	0.65818254	0.148368872	0.079180533	0.825082112	0.594672772

Below, the obtained results are explained to indicate whether the hypotheses are supported or not.

- **Effectiveness:** The obtained p-value is greater than the alpha value, which means that Effectiveness Null-HYP is not refuted. In other words, there is no significant difference between the effectiveness of Cyclos and that of E-pay Suite. The effectiveness results of the t-Test are shown in Figure 11.

Figure 11. t-Test results for Effectiveness

t-Test: Paired Two Sample for Means

	Average	*Average*
Mean	0.6119444444	0.6581825397
Variance	0.00915827555	0.00553028253
Observations	10	10
Pearson Correlation	-0.2170261896	
Hypothesized Mean Difference	0	
df	9	
t Stat	-1.09663845	
P(T<=t) one-tail	0.1506368538	
t Critical one-tail	1.833112933	
P(T<=t) two-tail	0.3012737077	
t Critical two-tail	2.262157163	

- **Productivity:** The obtained p-value is smaller than the alpha value, which means that Productivity Null-HYP is refuted and the mean value is used to compare the two software products. The mean value of the productivity of Cyclos is greater than the mean value of the productivity of E-pay Suite, as shown in Figure 12. In other words, the productivity of Cyclos is significantly superior to that of E-pay Suite. The productivity results of the t-Test are shown in Figure 12.

Figure 12. t-Test results for Productivity

t-Test: Paired Two Sample for Means

	Average	*Average*
Mean	0.1792042085	0.1483688722
Variance	0.00101063116	0.0019701382
Observations	10	10
Pearson Correlation	0.8238883847	
Hypothesized Mean Difference	0	
df	9	
t Stat	3.808103986	
P(T<=t) one-tail	0.0020820612	
t Critical one-tail	1.833112933	
P(T<=t) two-tail	0.0041652247	
t Critical two-tail	2.262157163	

- **Efficiency:** The obtained p-value is greater than the alpha value, which means that Efficiency Null-HYP is not refuted. In other words, there is no significant difference between the efficiency of Cyclos and that of E-pay Suite. The efficiency results of the t-Test are shown in Figure 13.

Figure 13. t-Test results for Efficiency

t-Test: Paired Two Sample for Means		
	Average	Average
Mean	0.09715254779	0.07918053314
Variance	0.0009328052056	0.0007717564736
Observations	10	10
Pearson Correlation	-0.6930225103	
Hypothesized Mean Difference	0	
df	9	
t Stat	1.058905061	
P(T<=t) one-tail	0.1586169814	
t Critical one-tail	1.833112933	
P(T<=t) two-tail	0.3172339628	
t Critical two-tail	2.262157163	

- **Error Safety:** The obtained p-value is greater than the alpha value, which means that Error Safety Null-HYP is not refuted. In other words, there is no significant difference between the error safety of Cyclos and that of E-pay Suite. The error safety results of the t-Test are shown in Figure 14.

Figure 14. t-Test results For Error Safety

t-Test: Paired Two Sample for Means		
	Average	Average
Mean	0.8521269841	0.8250821123
Variance	0.003273963215	0.007427386358
Observations	10	10
Pearson Correlation	0.2112001848	
Hypothesized Mean Difference	0	
df	9	
t Stat	0.9212376031	
P(T<=t) one-tail	0.1904787965	
t Critical one-tail	1.833112933	
P(T<=t) two-tail	0.3809575931	
t Critical two-tail	2.262157163	

- **Cognitive Load:** The recorded p-value is smaller than the alpha value, which means that Cognitive Load Null-HYP is not refuted and the mean is used to compare the two software products. The mean value of the cognitive load of Cyclos is greater than that of E-pay Suite, as shown in Figure 15. In other words, Cyclos has a significantly higher cognitive load than E-pay Suite. The cognitive load results of the t-Test are shown in Figure 15.

The results clearly show that Cyclos and E-pay Suite have similar performance in terms of efficiency, effectiveness and error safety. However, Cyclos outperforms E-pay Suite slightly when it comes to productivity and cognitive load.

The questionnaire results revealed that the majority of participants were male and that most of them were educated at a PhD level. Most of them had experience with online banking, having used online banking services frequently for more than two years. In terms of user satisfaction, the questionnaire results showed that, in general, the participants were equally satisfied with both software products. However, they found it easier to navigate through E-pay Suite's interface. Nevertheless, the overwhelming majority of the participants would prefer to use Cyclos over E-pay Suite.

Figure 15. t-Test results for Cognitive Load

t-Test: Paired Two Sample for Means

	Average	Average
Mean	0.6805079365	0.5946727717
Variance	0.004224886201	0.003930528865
Observations	10	10
Pearson Correlation	0.1058091405	
Hypothesized Mean Difference	0	
df	9	
t Stat	3.178413203	
P(T<=t) one-tail	0.005606666055	
t Critical one-tail	1.833112933	
P(T<=t) two-tail	0.01121333211	
t Critical two-tail	2.262157163	

DISCUSSION

During the experiment, the authors observed that the participants faced some difficulties while performing tasks in both Cyclos and E-pay Suite. In this section, these difficulties are discussed in order to highlight weaknesses in the two software products. In addition, positive feedback from the participants about both products is noted.

The user interface of E-pay Suite displays menus and submenus on the left side of the window. At the center of the window, the content of each submenu is presented. Figure 16 shows the E-pay Suite interface layout.

Figure 16. Graphical User Interface of E-pay Suite

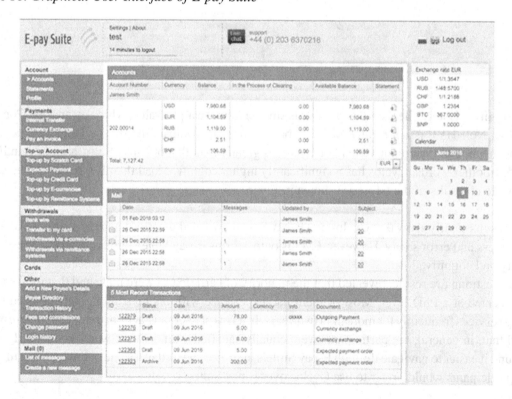

Some participants noted that personal information is not organized logically, and some found it challenging to understand the meaning of the language icons in E-pay Suite, which they felt should be accompanied by suitable abbreviations. In addition, participants were confused about which button to click on to complete a money transfer: "Save" or "Sign". The terms "Submit", "Confirm'', or "Transfer" seemed to them to be more appropriate than "Sign" to describe this task. In addition, a list of frequent recipients is not provided for the user when entering the recipient's name. While it is easy to reach an account statement by clicking on a button in the account menu in E-pay Suite, the list of transactions is displayed in ascending order, whereas some of the participants would prefer to have them listed in descending order. Finally, in order to access the functions available in E-pay Suite, the user is required to click on the text describing a side menu item (i.e. the item's name), instead of clicking anywhere in the region of the item. Participants found this frustrating since this step requires precise clicking.

In contrast, the user interface of Cyclos offers two ways to access the functions provided, either from the menu bar or via dashboard icons. Each menu item or icon has a side menu (submenu) that provides related functions. The layout of the Cyclos user interface is shown in Figure 17.

Figure 17. Graphical User Interface of Cyclos

On the Cyclos user interface, displaying the icons on the dashboard simplifies access to various functions; however, participants found that this made the home page appear crowded. Moreover, they found it difficult to remember how to access specific functions, given that there are two ways to access them. This is not an issue in E-pay Suite since all functions are displayed on the side of the window. In Cyclos, the names of menu items are not always clear (e.g. the terms "Personal" and "Information" were easily confused by participants when they requested access to their personal information). The participants struggled to save or print an account statement since the combined Save/Print button is quite small. These buttons are separate in E-pay Suite and easy to find. The Cyclos interface allows the user to change the language of the page via icons with the name of the language displayed, a feature that is not provided on the E-pay Suite interface. Even so, most of the participants were unable to find the language settings easily in Cyclos, since they are outside the window range. Another issue with Cyclos—a key one—was that the software does not allow the user to transfer a particular amount ($100 is the minimum amount that can be transferred). However, Cyclos displays search results for specific transactions immediately, as expected by the participants, while E-pay Suite does not.

CONCLUSION AND FUTURE WORK

The banking sector is a critical sector that deals with highly sensitive data. The accuracy and effectiveness of the software used in the sector are therefore critical issues. In this paper, a comprehensive set of available quality models and their application to OSS was proposed. The authors applied a new quality in use model (Alnanih, 2015), inspired by ISO/IEC 25010 (ISO/IEC 25010:2011), through a series of phases that were designed to assess two online banking software applications: Cyclos (open source) and E-pay Suite (closed source). These phases included data gathering, data analysis and interpretation/evaluation of results. The results prove that the performance of Cyclos is comparable to that of E-pay Suite, based on a recent quality in use model. At the end of the experiment, the authors were able to conclude that Cyclos is not only as efficient and effective as E-pay Suite, but that it is more productive. Moreover, the results of the questionnaires filled out by the participants showed that, from a user standpoint, Cyclos works well, although the participants favored E-pay Suite for ease of navigation of its user interface. However, Cyclos is open source software, which means that its user interface is fully customizable and can easily be improved.

Proving that OSS products have the capabilities to perform as well as if not better than closed source software competitors indicates that there is great potential in open source technology. In the future, the authors plan to evaluate OSS from different fields and compare the results with those obtained from the banking sector. This will bring to light the reliability of open source technology. Another possible direction is to design a new quality in use model that fits the characteristics of both closed and open source software.

REFERENCES

Akbari, M., & Peikar, S. R. H. (2014). Evaluation of free/open source software using osmm model case study: Webgis and spatial database. *Advances in Computer Science: an International Journal, 3*(5), 34–43.

Alnanih, R. (2015). *CON-INFO: A Context-based Methodology for Designing and Assessing the Quality of Adaptable MUIs in Healthcare Applications* [Doctoral dissertation]. Concordia University.

Aversano, L., & Tortorella, M. (2010, June). Evaluating the quality of free/Open source systems: A case study. *Proceedings of the International Conference on Enterprise Information Systems* (pp. 119-134). Springer.

Aversano, L., & Tortorella, M. (2011, June). Applying EFFORT for evaluating CRM open source systems. *Proceedings of the International Conference on Product Focused Software Process Improvement* (pp. 202-216). Springer. doi:10.1007/978-3-642-21843-9_17

Aversano, L., & Tortorella, M. (2013). Quality evaluation of floss projects: Application to ERP systems. *Information and Software Technology*, 55(7), 1260–1276. doi:10.1016/j.infsof.2013.01.007

Bevan, N. (2001). Quality in use for all. In C. Stephanidis (Ed.), *User Interfaces for All: methods, concepts and tools* (pp. 353–368). CRC Press.

Boehm, B. W., Brown, J. R., Kaspar, H., Lipow, M., McLeod, G., & Merritt, M. (1978). *Characteristics of software quality*. TRW Series of Software Technology.

Canopus Innovative Technologies. (1992). E-pay Suite. Retrieved from http://epaysuite.com/

Creswell, J. W. (2013). *Qualitative Inquiry & Research Design: Choosing Among Five Approaches* (3rd ed.). Thousand Oaks, CA: SAGE Publications, Inc.

De Groot, A., Kügler, S., Adams, P. J., & Gousios, G. (2006, June). Call for quality: Open source software quality observation. *Proceedings of the IFIP International Conference on Open Source Systems* (pp. 57-62). Springer. doi:10.1007/0-387-34226-5_6

Dromey, R. G. (1995). A model for software product quality. *IEEE Transactions on Software Engineering*, *21*(2), 146–162.

Duijnhouwer, F. and Widdows, C. (2003). Open source maturity model.

Groven, A. K., Haaland, K., Glott, R., & Tannenberg, A. (2010, August). Security measurements within the framework of quality assessment models for free/libre open source software. In *Proceedings of the fourth european conference on software architecture: Companion volume* (pp. 229-235). ACM.

Hecht, L., & Clark, L. (2018). *Survey: Open Source Programs Are a Best Practice Among Large Companies*. The New Stack.

Houaich, Y. A., & Belaissaoui, M. (2015, February). Measuring the maturity of open source software. *Proceedings of the 2015 6th International Conference on Information Systems and Economic Intelligence (SIIE)* (pp. 133-140). IEEE. doi:10.1109/ISEI.2015.7358735

ISO. (2011). ISO/IEC 25010:2011 Systems and software engineering – Systems and software Quality Requirements and Evaluation (SQuaRE) – System and software quality models. Retrieved from https://www.iso.org/obp/ui/#iso:std:iso-iec:25010:en

McCall, J. A. (1977). *Factors in software quality. General Electric*. National Technical Information Service.

Nielsen, J. (2012). Usability 101: Introduction to usability. NN Group. Retrieved from http://www.nngroup.com/articles/usability-101-introduction-to-usability/

Nielsen, J., & Landauer, T. K. (1993) A Mathematical Model of the Finding of Usability Problems. *Proceedings of INTERCHI '93*. Academic Press.

Official Statistics of Finland (OSF). (2011) Use of information technology in enterprises. Retrieved from http://www.stat.fi/til/icte/2011/icte_2011_2011-11-24_tie_001_en.html

Popp, K. M. (Ed.). (2015). *Best Practices for commercial use of open source software: Business models, processes and tools for managing open source software.* BoD–Books on Demand.

Samoladas, I., Gousios, G., Spinellis, D., & Stamelos, I. (2008, September). The SQO-OSS quality model: measurement based open source software evaluation. *Proceedings of the IFIP International Conference on Open Source Systems* (pp. 237-248). Springer. doi:10.1007/978-0-387-09684-1_19

Social TRade Organisations. (1970). Cyclos. Retrieved from https://www.cyclos.org/

Soto, M., & Ciolkowski, M. (2009, October). The QualOSS open source assessment model measuring the performance of open source communities. *Proceedings of the 3rd International Symposium on Empirical Software Engineering and Measurement ESEM 2009* (pp. 498-501). IEEE. doi:10.1109/ESEM.2009.5314237

Soto, M., & Ciolkowski, M. (2009, September). The QualOSS Process Evaluation: Initial Experiences with Assessing Open Source Processes. *Proceedings of the European Conference on Software Process Improvement* (pp. 105-116). Springer. doi:10.1007/978-3-642-04133-4_9

Virzi, R. A. (1992). Refining the test phase of usability evaluation: How many subjects is enough? *Human Factors, 34*(4), 457–468. doi:10.1177/001872089203400407

Wasserman, A. I., Pal, M., & Chan, C. (2006). Business readiness rating for open source. *Proceedings of the EFOSS Workshop*, Como, Italy. Academic Press.

Wasserman, T., & Das, A. (2007). Using FLOSSmole data in determining business readiness ratings.

This research was previously published in the Journal of Cases on Information Technology (JCIT), 22(2); pages 34-51, copyright year 2020 by IGI Publishing (an imprint of IGI Global).

Chapter 30
Challenges and Trends in Home Automation:
Addressing the Interoperability Problem With the Open–Source Platform OpenHAB

Cristina Portalés

ⓘ https://orcid.org/0000-0002-4520-2250

University of Valencia, Spain

Sergio Casas

ⓘ https://orcid.org/0000-0002-0396-4628

University of Valencia, Spain

Kai Kreuzer

openHAB Foundation e.V., Germany

ABSTRACT

Home automation (HA) systems can be considered as an implementation of the internet of everything (IoE) where many devices are linked by intelligent connections in order to improve the quality of life at home. This chapter is dedicated to analyzing current trends and challenges in HA. Energy management, safer homes, and improved control over the house are some of the benefits of HA. However, privacy, security, social disruption, installation/maintenance issues, economic costs, market fragmentation, and low interoperability represent real problems of these IoE solutions. In this regard, the latest proposals in HA try to answer some of these needs with low-cost DIY solutions, wireless solutions, and IP-based HA systems. This chapter proposes a way to deal with the interoperability problem by means of the open-source platform openHAB. It is based on the concept of a home automation bus, an idea that enables the separation of the physical and the functional view of any device, allowing to create a technology-agnostic environment, which is perfect for addressing the interoperability problem.

DOI: 10.4018/978-1-7998-9158-1.ch030

INTRODUCTION

The vision of a smart home that takes advantage of the latest advances in digital and information technologies - being able to anticipate our actions and satisfy our needs through intelligent or automatic actions - has been around for decades. The idea of bringing computers to our background in a *ubiquitous computing* paradigm was forecasted in 1991 by Weiser (Weiser, 1991), so that computers would increasingly enable the integration of simple objects, such as clothing labels, key fobs, light bulbs, etc. in an unobtrusive way in the user's life (Toschi, Campos, & Cugnasca, 2017). This vision is indeed very appealing and seductive, since it has an enormous potential in improving our daily life, saving time, money and energy, improving home comfort, safety, security, health care, weather-awareness and many other aspects.

With homes implementing Internet of Things (IoT) scenarios, this smart home vision is closer to reality than ever. The IoT is envisioned as a network that allows everyone and everyday objects to be connected anytime and anyplace. Smart homes can be seen as an interactive people-centric application of IoT, which is aimed at improving the quality of life (Feng, Setoodeh, & Haykin, 2017). The decrease in electronic hardware production costs is causing the number of IoT-capable devices to grow at astonishing rates. In fact, the number of IoT devices has already well exceeded the number of human beings living in our planet (Swan, 2012). Therefore, home automation is expected to benefit from this new digital revolution. Although not all smart home technologies provide direct communication between their devices and the Internet - gateways are needed in most systems -, smart home networks are considered IoT applications.

However, a smart home is much more than a building with connected digital components. Since many devices are connected together for a common purpose, in an orchestrated, convergent way, this smart home vision clearly represents an example of the Internet of Everything (IoE) paradigm, where individual devices are meaningful only in the context of the intelligent network in which they work, connecting data, processes, things and people.

There is not a standard or fixed definition of the term *smart home*. In fact the concept of *home* has many different connotations and meanings, as opposed to house/building (Gram-Hanssen & Darby, 2018). Nevertheless, it is widely accepted that a smart home is one (leaving aside the sociological connotations about the word home) that incorporates automation systems to provide its inhabitants with remote control and sophisticated monitoring over the building. A possible definition is "a dwelling incorporating a communications network that connects the key electrical appliances and services, and allows them to be remotely controlled, monitored or accessed."(Ye & Huang, 2011). This definition does not include an intelligent/smart behavior or even automations, but it is understood that a smart home is able to perform automatic programmable actions on behalf of their inhabitants and without human intervention. This ability is known as *home automation* (HA) and opens the possibility to treat the house as a digital system where all computer science paradigms can be applied, including artificial intelligence, machine learning, data mining, automatic reasoning or even big data. Although home automation and smart home do not refer to the exact same thing, they are often considered as synonyms (Stojkoska & Trivodaliev, 2017).

History on HA can be traced back to the final decades of the 19th century. Although no digital technology was involved, the comfort increase provided by the introduction of electricity at home in the late 1800s was significant. Of course, the concept of highly-automated digital home available for a mass market that we identify today as a smart home came only in the final quarter of the 20th century (Gram-Hanssen & Darby, 2018).

Despite the appealing futuristic visions of smart homes, the truth is that HA technologies have not been massively adopted (Brush et al., 2011). Although prospective users apparently have rather positive views about HA, (Hargreaves & Wilson, 2017) and a few systems have experimented some market success lately, worries about loss of independency, privacy, cost, interoperability and some other socio-technical risks (Wilson, Hargreaves, & Hauxwell-Baldwin, 2017) represent barriers that hinder the evolution and adoption of this technology. This shows the necessity of performing further research in the smart home field.

This chapter is dedicated to analyzing the current situation of the HA field, identifying strengths, weaknesses, opportunities, threats, trends and the many challenges this technology faces. One of these challenges is how to deal with the problem of interoperability in a fragmented market. We propose a way to overcome this issue by using the open-source software platform openHAB.

The chapter is structured as follows. Section 1 has already introduced the topic. Section 2 reviews the different features, technologies and applications of home automation. Section 3 deals with the strengths, weakness, challenges, opportunities and trends in home automation. Section 4 is dedicated to explain the openHAB platform. Section 5 explains how to use this software platform to deal with the interoperability problem. Finally, section 6 draws the conclusions and outlines possible future research lines.

SMART HOMES: FEATURES, APPLICATIONS AND TECHNOLOGIES

Different types of devices can be identified in home automation solutions: sensors, actuators, controllers, network-support devices, gateways and user interfaces. These devices are usually arranged in a network with different topologies (bus, ring, mesh, etc.) and different communication protocols, in order for the devices to communicate information between them and with the outside world. The communication networks used in smart home devices are called Home Area Networks (HANs). Of course, particular devices could act simultaneously as different types of devices. As consumer electronics can be in most cases miniaturized, it is not unusual that sensors and actuators act also as network-support devices, especially in wireless HANs (WHANs). There are also sensors that can play the role of actuators, and controllers that have gateway functionalities.

Sensors are used to collect information about the environment (both inside and outside home). Temperature, light, humidity, presence, motion, smoke, water, carbon monoxide, wind, atmospheric pressure, rain, sound, acceleration or vibration are some of the physical variables that can be measured used in a smart homes. Battery state, signal range, connection status can also be measured to perform self-diagnostics of the HAN.

Actuators allow to modify the environment in which the home inhabitants live. Relays, switches, dimmers, roller shutters, blinds, heaters, air conditioners, ventilation systems, garage doors, water/gas supply valves or irrigation systems are examples of actuators that can be remotely and automatically controlled by smart homes.

Controllers are special devices meant to manage, command and supervise the devices of the HAN, so they can be added to and removed from the network, setup and create intelligent and automatic actions based on their information. In most home automation systems, there is a single controller, or at least a single controller per network, if several HANs are simultaneously used.

Network-support devices are elements that allow a HAN to work properly or enhance their reliability. Depending on the network type, topology and physical communication technology employed, these devices could be signal repeaters, transducers, multiplexers, data routers, hubs, etc.

Gateways are devices that allow a HAN to receive and send information to other networks that do not use the same communication protocol. The foreign network could also be a HAN, or may be a different kind of network, like Ethernet or a mobile-phone network. Gateways to the Internet are especially important in IoT/IoE scenarios.

Finally, *user interfaces* are devices or means that are used to communicate information to and from the user, so that they can control the operation of the smart home and monitor its status. User interfaces can be tangible or intangible. Examples of tangible interfaces include tablets, smart phones, buttons, panels, rocker switches, contact breakers or key fobs. Intangible interfaces represent more natural interaction paradigms, like voice, gestures, looks, or body motion.

IoT devices can be applied for home automation in several different ways and for many different applications: light control, ventilation and air conditioning, security (door/window sensing, security cameras), safety (water/gas/carbon monoxide leak detection), entertainment (TV, music, games), presence and motion detection, economy (appliance control, electric metering), energy management, irrigation systems and gardening, comfort (roller shutters, heating), health care (children monitoring, elderly or disabled support), cleaning (vacuum cleaning, connection with home appliances), weather awareness, etc. Almost any application of digital and information technologies to the home environment can be considered home automation.

HA systems are based on different technologies. Although wired solutions are much more secure, reliable, robust and efficient, wireless home automation networks are becoming increasingly common, due to the difficulty or reluctance of wiring an existing home. New buildings are easier to adapt to wired HANs. However, a wireless HAN is easier to install, replace or update. For this reason, given the pace and the uncertainty at which home automation technology evolves, wired solutions represent a higher risk than wireless solutions and most homeowners choose WHANs. In addition, some technologies are able to operate through different physical mediums like Konnex (KNX), X10, LonWorks or Insteon (Stojkoska & Trivodaliev, 2017; Toschi et al., 2017; Withanage, Ashok, Yuen, & Otto, 2014) providing great flexibility.

Examples of wired technologies are KNX (twisted pair, power line and Ethernet), X10 (power line), Insteon (power line), LonWorks (twisted pair, optical fiber and power line) and HomePlug (power line). Examples of wireless home automation technologies are ZigBee, Z-Wave (Figure 1), Bluetooth, Wi-Fi, 6LoWPAN, EnOcean, UWB, Wavenis (Rathnayaka, Potdar, & Kuruppu, 2011) and also the radio-frequency versions of wired systems: KNX-RF, X10-RF, Insteon-RF and LonWorks-RF.

SMART HOMES: CHALLENGES AND TRENDS

Strengths and opportunities in HA are almost countless. With an increasing population demanding more and more energy - with its corresponding carbon footprint and contribution to global warming - an effective use of energy is crucial for the survival of our planet. Home automation should play a vital role in creating energy-efficient and energy-aware environments.

Figure 1. Some Z-Wave devices. From left to right, top to bottom: a door/window sensor, a Z-Wave controller, a dimmer, a flood sensor, a motion sensor, a smoke sensor, a temperature chip and a relay switch (Fibar Group S.A., 2018)

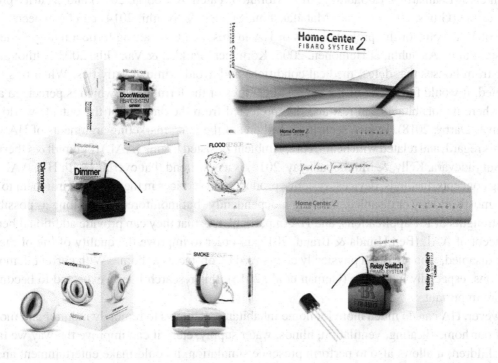

The concept of IoE has the potential to transform residential houses and offices making them more ecologically friendly. In fact, prospective users see energy management as the main purpose and benefit of HA (Wilson et al., 2017). However, IT solutions do indeed need energy to operate and there are sometimes "hidden energy costs" (Hargreaves, Wilson, & Hauxwell-Baldwin, 2018). Energy savings by means of HA is explored through a well-established research line (Friedli, Kaufmann, Paganini, & Kyburz, 2016; Jahn et al., 2010; Louis, Caló, Leiviskä, & Pongrácz, 2015; Mehdi & Roshchin, 2015), which connects with the widely studied topic of smart grids (Lobaccaro, Carlucci, & Löfström, 2016; Zhou et al., 2016). One of the conclusions of this research body is that, although, smart homes could be energy-aware environments and are expected to reduce energy consumption, HA could also create a demand for previously unwanted products and services, causing an increase in energy consumption and environmental damage (Darby, 2018). Therefore, it is important that the HA system needs less energy to operate than it saves (Hargreaves et al., 2018). In this regard, home automation systems based on energetically efficient exploitation of resources represent the most promising trend in HA technology. EnOcean (Ploennigs, Ryssel, & Kabitzsch, 2010), an energy-harvesting HA solution is an example of how the IoE paradigm could be used in a sustainable way. Its energy-aware design has an impact in performance and throughput (Ploennigs et al., 2010). Nevertheless, this paradigm represents what a smart home should really be, and the authors hope this kind of solutions become a trend in the near future, although we are aware that market is driven by many factors and energy is just one of them.

Safer homes, both in terms of safety against accidents (A. Jose & Malekian, 2017; Lee & Lee, 2004) - such as fire, gas leaks, water leaks and especially the deadly and silent carbon monoxide poisoning -, health care (Laamarti & El Saddik, 2017; Moraitou, Pateli, & Fotiou, 2017) and security/protection against crime (Gibbs, 2016; Prasad, Mahalakshmi, Sunder, & Swathi, 2014) can be expected through the use of HA. Some of the projected uses of HA in this area are starting to be a reality (Friedewald, Da Costa, Punie, Alahuhta, & Heinonen, 2005; Korhonen, Parkka, & Van Gils, 2003), although we are still far from houses that detect medical conditions and avoid criminal activities. When this vision is completed, it would fulfill one of the expected features of the term home, which is perceived as a safe haven where its inhabitants can rest and live protected from the dangers of the outside world (Gram-Hanssen & Darby, 2018). In fact, security is still one of the main marketing arguments of HA vendors.

In this regard, and related with health care, Ambient Assisted Living (AAL) (Schmidt & Obermaisser, 2017; Suryadevara, Kelly, & Mukhopadhyay, 2014) is a new trend that overlaps with HA. AAL focuses on using concepts, methods, devices, systems, products and services in the home environment to support people, mostly elderly or disabled, in living independently (but monitored) for as long as possible. One of the strengths of IoT applications, and HA in particular, is that they can provide additional benefits to the concept of AAL (Ben Hmida & Braun, 2017) in order to improve the quality of life of the elderly and the disabled, who are often physically challenged by obstacles at home. With current demographic projections, especially in Europe (Geman et al., 2015), this research line is expected to become more and more important.

However, HA can do much more for home inhabitants. It allows to remotely monitor and modify the state of our home (heating, ventilation, blinds, water supply, etc.), it can improve the way we take care of our children, it allows also to perform presence simulation, it could make entertainment and multi-media devices easier to interconnect and it can provide our home with weather-awareness, allowing, for instance, to anticipate actions in reaction to weather changes (increase heating power before a winter storm starts, close windows and roller shutters on windy days, etc.).

Despite the incredible potential of the application of IoE to the smart home field, this application area still faces many challenges and problems. Security risks (A. C. Jose & Malekian, 2015) are one of the most worrisome problems of HA technologies. Some HA solutions have proven to be vulnerable to hacker attacks (Sivaraman, Chan, Earl, & Boreli, 2016) (Jacobsson, Boldt, & Carlsson, 2016). This is especially true in wireless networks (Knight, 2006) where information is not confined within a cable. In addition, privacy concerns are one of the most challenging problems that this technology should over-come to convince some hesitant users. As IoE devices are able to communicate with almost any other device, there is the risk that our private information be shared and monetized. As devices are designed to be very easy to use, obscuring almost everything that goes on at the 'back end' (Burgess, Mitchell, & Highfield, 2018), we cannot be sure that our intimacy is not being compromised.

Unlike traditional security concerns by traditional burglars, digital criminals can attack a home from almost any place in the world and they can do it whenever they like. Moreover, their attacks could remain unnoticed or cause severe damage, not only physical damage but also financial, emotional or reputational damage. Security in smart homes have many peculiar connotations that make good solutions especially harder to implement (A. C. Jose & Malekian, 2015). First, almost all data stored at home is completely personal. Thus, it could be particularly attractive for criminals. Second, HA systems usually consist of devices from different manufacturers. Each one comes with different features, problems and vulnerabilities. Third, HANs do not typically have a dedicated network administrator. Fourth, HANs are typically constantly changing, with the addition or removal of devices. From an engineer perspective, it is a nightmare to provide security to a network whose topology and content is unknown. Last, but not least, home automation environments are meant to be easily used. Security always introduces a degree of complication. Therefore, security procedures that reduce the convenience of using the HA may be rejected by users.

In this regard, social disruption represents a very important problem in smart homes. Technology is meant to make life easier. Home automation solutions that are too hard to understand, too complicated, too difficult to maintain or make users change their lifestyle may be rejected by them. It is important that machines fit the human environment instead of forcing humans to enter theirs. As Weiser cleverly pointed out "the most profound technologies are those that disappear. They weave themselves into the fabric of everyday life until they are indistinguishable from them" (Weiser, 1991). Seamless integration is therefore crucial to avoid social disruption.

However, the research community seems to have paid little attention to the evaluation of smart home initiatives in terms of real end-users' acceptability. Indeed, there is a striking contrast between the many research papers that deal with network technologies and estimate potential benefits of smart homes by means of simulations, compared to the relatively few works that report on measured efficiency and acceptability in real conditions (Darby, 2018). The authors believe this situation should change and this research direction should become a trend in home automation.

Another important social aspect is the impact of installing an HA ecosystem at home. Wired systems are often too invasive and sometimes require architectural or building changes in the house. Wireless devices are easier to install but suffer from the problems of interference, signal range and battery life. A system in which devices fail due to poor signal or in which the user needs to constantly change batteries, would be inacceptable if a true IoE paradigm is used with tens or hundreds of devices at home. The increasing complexity of HA solutions due to the large number of devices that may be installed, makes maintenance a problem that should not be overlooked.

The economic cost is also a problem. Some of the home automation solutions are expensive. Thus, they need to prove that this money is worth spending, saving energy bills, or providing a level of comfort that users feel important to pay for. IoE devices should not be expensive, since mass production is causing a reduction in production costs. Nevertheless, as home automation is usually linked to upper-class householders, prices are typically high. We believe market will find a way to solve this problem without any scientific or technological input.

Market fragmentation is also a big problem. Due to protocol incompatibility and lack of standardization, customers can find themselves locked in a vertical solution, where vendors claim to provide the whole chain of products from sensors and actuators to gateways and servers (Jacobsson et al., 2016), but do not offer customers the possibility and freedom of choosing products from different vendors when theirs do no offer the features users want. In such cases, potential users may feel disoriented and may refuse to enter the home automation market. This market fragmentation generates one of the main problems of smart home technologies: interoperability, which will be addressed later.

New trends are trying to offer answers to these problems. In response to the high price of some home automation technologies, low cost Do-It-Yourself (DIY) solutions are being proposed in recent years. This is an interesting trend in home automation, with many scientific works proposing DIY HA solutions, especially in newly industrialized and developing countries. Raspberry Pi (Chavan, Patil, & Naik, 2017; Kulkarni, Joshi, Jadhav, & Dhamange, 2017; Pampattiwar, Lakhani, Marar, & Menon, 2017; A. Patil, Shaikh, Ghorpade, Pawar, & Memane, 2017; S. A. Patil & Pinki, 2017; Prasad et al., 2014; Younis, Ijaz, Randhawa, & Ijaz, 2018), Arduino boards (Bolaji, Kamaldeen, Samson, Abdullahi, & Abubakar, 2017; Chandramohan et al., 2017; ElShafee & Hamed, 2012; Kannapiran & Chakrapani, 2017; More,

Gai, Sardar, Rupareliya, & Talole, 2017; Piyare & Tazil, 2011; Soliman, Dwairi, Sulayman, & Almalki, 2017) and many others (Patel & Kanawade, 2017; Vikram et al., 2017) have been used to propose low-cost DIY HA systems. Most of these solutions have been proposed in the last three years, reflecting the fact that this idea is a clear trend in HA.

The problem with these solutions is that they are typically not interoperable with other DIY solutions, unless a common software is used, increasing market fragmentation. In addition, in most cases they are usually not compliant with an easy installation and maintenance. Nevertheless, some of the proposed systems provide functions and services similar to those of market products. Therefore DIY HA solutions are important to show that home automation is not necessarily an expensive business.

In response to market fragmentation, IP-based home automation is also starting to be explored. Although the Internet Protocol (IP) was not specially designed for home automation, IP-based home automation solutions are being proposed lately, despite the initial skepticism of scientists and researchers (Mainetti, Patrono, & Vilei, 2011). They are an emerging and promising trend in HA since IP-based solutions have the advantage that IP is a very common protocol with many services and protocols already implemented. In fact, many protocols used in other related areas, such as Modbus, have also IP versions of the protocols, in order to make them widely available. In addition, IP allows identifying devices with a unique worldwide accessible address for each device and it is the "language" of the Internet. This represents the ideal case for the IoT/IoE paradigm, since non-IP-based HANs need gateways to allow their nodes to be addressable and accessible to the outside world (see Figure 2). IP-based HANs could dramatically increase the capillarity of the Internet (Gomez & Paradells, 2010). However, this could come at a cost, since having several devices connected to the Internet, from different vendors (with different security policies and possibly connecting to private corporate cloud systems), increases the vulnerability of your home. In addition, these devices could jeopardize privacy as they could store private data in remote locations. Solutions are needed for these problems (Kreuzer, 2014).

IP-based HA can be provided by using 802.11.x (Wi-Fi) networks (ElShafee & Hamed, 2012; Jakovljev, Subotić, & Papp, 2017), which is not particularly efficient in terms of energy consumption, or by the recently proposed IPv6 over Low-Power Wireless Personal Area Networks (6LoWPAN), which was specifically designed for home automation and IoT scenarios (Arndt, Krause, Wunderlich, & Heinen, 2017; Dorge & Scheffler, 2011; Huang & Yuan, 2015; Tudose et al., 2011).

Wi-Fi solutions have the advantage that Wi-Fi infrastructure is present in almost every home (surely in houses that want to be "smart" by using HA), most of them using Wi-Fi routers giving direct access to the Internet. However, previous standards of the 802.11 family (802.11.a/b/g/n/ac) were not designed for home automation and the complexity, efficiency, power consumption and latency of Wi-Fi solutions are not in line with the needs of HA. For instance, both Z-Wave and ZigBee are by definition mesh networks, while Wi-Fi has a star topology. Only very recently, Wi-Fi Mesh (802.11s specification) has become available and might solve range issues of Wi-Fi for HA. The rest of the problems are also expected to change with the arrival of the 802.11.ah protocol (known as *HaLow*), which is designed for the IoT (Ahmed, Rahman, & Hussain, 2016; Banos, Afaqui, Lopez, & Garcia, 2017; Del Carpio et al., 2016).

The 6LoWPAN concept is based on the idea that "the Internet Protocol could and should be applied to even the smallest of devices" (Mulligan, 2007). This vision is fully compliant with IoT/IoE scenarios. 6LoWPAN allows IPv6 packets to be sent over IEEE 802.15.4 networks. 6LoWPAN shares the same physical and MAC layer with ZigBee, but upper layers make them incompatible (as seen in Figure 2). A tough battle between 6LoWPAN, 802.11.ah, Z-Wave, ZigBee and even Bluetooth LE can be expected in the following years (Del Carpio, Di Marco, Skillermark, Chirikov, & Lagergren, 2017).

Figure 2. Interoperability problems in WHANs. Solid lines represent feasible connections. Dashed lines represent unfeasible direct communication.

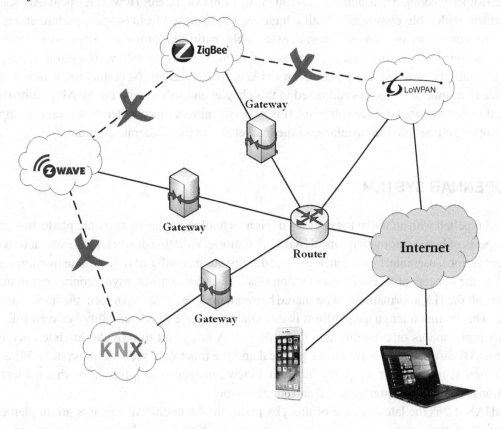

In this regard, WHANs are gaining importance in the HA sector, with respect to wired solutions. As soon as battery-problems are solved, the authors expect that wired technologies will be reserved for offices and new buildings whereas wireless solutions are going to be the preferred choice for mainstream residential customers. This tendency is already starting to take root.

Different IT companies compete to provide smart home capabilities. The result is a fragmented field with many different smart home ecosystems: Apple HomeKit, Google Home, Fibaro, EnOcean, Amazon Echo-Alexa, Nest, etc. Most of these ecosystems are not interoperable, although in some cases they share the same underlying physical technology. The vision of IoE is very appealing, since hundreds of devices in our homes have the ability to communicate creating a common intelligent ecosystem. However, if devices do not share a common language, this vision could be completely ruined. Users face a difficult decision: bet all their money on a single technology, with the risk of betting on the wrong product line, or just refuse to enter the home automation environment.

This challenge represents also an opportunity to create standard mechanisms in order to make the different solutions interoperable. We believe that interoperability is one of the most important requirements that the HA industry should fulfill in the near future.

This chapter deals with the interoperability problem in HANs - arguably the most important problem in HA - by proposing a way to make different smart home technologies work together through the use of the open-source platform openHAB. Several open-source home-automation platforms have been proposed in recent years, such as Home Assistant, Calaos, OpenMotics, MisterHouse, Domoticz, ioBroker, OpenNetHome, Jeedom, Smarthomatic, EventGhost, LinuxMCE, etc. However, openHAB stands out as a platform with a big community, with a huge list of supported technologies, mature enough to be used in complex scenarios, vendor-agnostic, extendable, multi-platform and fairly easy to learn. In the next sections this home automation platform is explained. We will show how to use it in order to solve the interoperability problem and make several HANs work together. Nevertheless, it is important to emphasize that some of the issues addressed in this chapter and solved with openHAB platform may be addressed with other open-source solutions. It is not in the aim of this chapter, however, to compare the different open-source solutions available in the market and in the academic community.

THE OPENHAB SYSTEM

openHAB (spelled with an initial lower case "o") is a technology-agnostic software platform that covers all the aspects of home automation (openHAB Foundation e.V., 2018) devices, protocols, automatic and intelligent actions, user interfaces, data logging, administration, configuration, remote monitoring, etc. It is based on the concept of a "Home Automation Bus", a vendor-agnostic asynchronous communication bus where all the HA information can be shared between the IoE devices that form the home automation network. This common language/platform is essential to provide interoperability between IoE devices from different vendors or even different technologies. A key point to provide this interoperability is that openHAB distinguishes between the physical and the functional view of the system. Whereas the physical view is required for setup, the functional view represents the information that matters to HA applications, such as user interfaces and automation logic.

openHAB 2.2 is the latest release of this HA platform. All openHAB releases are implemented in Java. Therefore, they can be run on almost any computer architecture and operating system (anyone that is able to run the Java Virtual Machine) such as Windows, Linux or macOS. Much effort has been done to provide support for low-cost computers, such as *openHABian*, a Linux distribution for ARM single-board computers like the Raspberry Pi and the PINE64, with all the bundles and packages necessary to run openHAB already pre-installed. For this reason, DIY implementations can be implemented with openHAB at a very small cost.

openHAB 2 uses Apache Karaf and Eclipse Equinox for a modular OSGi runtime environment (OSGi Alliance, 2018). Each component in openHAB is therefore an OSGi bundle. Jetty is used as an HTTP server, so that a REST service is provided to access and set-up the system, and web-based user interfaces can provide remote control and supervision of the home.

In addition, the former openHAB 1.x architecture has served as the base upon which the *Eclipse SmartHome* (ESH) framework (Smirek, Zimmermann, & Beigl, 2016) has been built, which in turn became the core component of openHAB 2. Both openHAB and ESH are open-source platforms available under the terms of the Eclipse Public License.

Five fundamental concepts are used in openHAB: things, channels, items, events and links. A *thing* is an entity that is able to provide HA capabilities. Although things are often associated with physical devices like sensors or actuators, a thing can also represent a web service or any other source/recipient of information that could be meaningful for the HA system. Things can potentially provide many smart home functionalities at once by means of one or several channels. A *channel* represents the information and functionality that things can provide to the system. In this regard, channels are passive and can be seen as just a declaration of what a thing can offer. Although a thing could provide many channels, users can choose which channels are effectively used by their openHAB instance. Channels are activated by linking them to items. An *item* represents the exact functionality that can be used by applications. There are several types of items: Switch, Dimmer, Contact, Number, Color, DateTime, Location, Rollershutter, Image, Player, String and Group. Each type represents one particular smart home functionality. Depending on the type, items can have different states, which can be read, sent or modified through the openHAB bus by means of *events*. Events in openHAB are significant occurrences that represent either changes or commands in the home. Events are sent through the openHAB bus and are typically associated with items. The state of items is kept in a data structure called the *item repository*. The item repository is updated when state changes are received from the event bus and can be queried by automation logic, persistence services and user interfaces. Things and items are bound by means of links. A *link* is an association between one channel and one item. Channels can be linked to multiple items and items can be linked to multiple channels. From a user perspective, things need to be set-up before the system is used, and channels should be linked to items so that their functionality becomes available. openHAB offers also a special type of thing called bridge. A *bridge* is a thing that provides openHAB with access to other things, like a gateway or an authentication server.

In order to separate the physical view and the functional view of devices and services, a thing represents the physical view, whereas items represent the functional view. The whole openHAB system is built around this idea. Items represent a virtual HA layer that encapsulates the functionality used by applications, hiding the physical details, so that interoperability between different technologies is possible. However, items do not necessarily refer to physical actions performed by devices. Items that represent parameters of the system or any other information whose value is not obtained from things, can be defined too (see Figure 3). The values of these items can be modified directly by the user via user interfaces or can be used as flags or system variables updated and modified by openHAB by means of rules. An example of this is an item that enables or disables an alarm system. This item would be either directly controlled by the user or set to on and off by the system by means of automatic rules.

It is important to emphasize that openHAB is not designed to be executed by the hardware devices that form the HAN. Instead, openHAB serves as an integration hub between different devices and acts as a broker between different protocols and services. Therefore, an openHAB installation is typically composed of a single instance of this software platform running on a single computer, which acts, in turn, as a global home automation controller.

Another important advantage of openHAB is that it is completely modular thanks to its OSGi-based architecture. There is a base functionality that implements the core concepts and data-types necessary to make the home automation bus work, but the particular capabilities that depend on specific technologies are offered by *add-ons*. Add-ons provide openHAB with different functionalities: bindings, user interfaces, persistence, actions, transformation services, voice services and third party integration (see Figure 4).

Bindings connect different device types and technologies to the openHAB system. By adding a particular binding to the system, openHAB is able to translate the signals from that particular protocol/ service/technology to openHAB. More specifically, bindings translate event bus events to and from external devices, services or systems. The fact that bindings communicate information through the event bus ensures that software coupling remains low. A binding can implement one direction or both. Therefore, bindings can be classified as "In-", "Out-" or "InOut-Bindings". There are more than 150 bindings, which allow to interconnect technologies and services like KNX, Z-Wave, ZigBee, DMX, EnOcean, Philips Hue, Homematic, NTP, Yahoo Weather, Wake-on-LAN, Belkin WeMo, Samsung TV, LG TV,

Nest, Modbus, and many others. The number of bindings is expected to increase since openHAB is not just a software platform. It is also a home automation open-source community devoted to improving the smart home experience and building an ecosystem around it.

Figure 3. Physical and virtual layers in openHAB

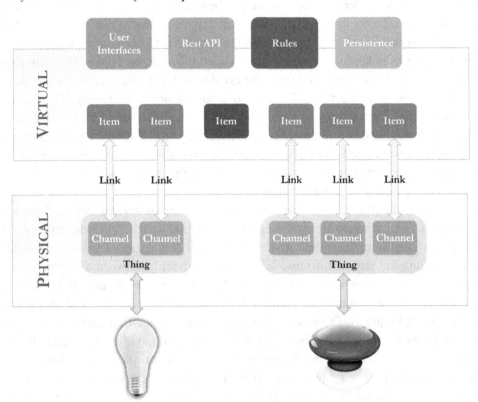

User interfaces offer a front-end for user remote control, configuration and complex monitoring of home automation systems. System administration is performed through a web dashboard called *Paper UI*. Remote control and monitoring can be performed by several web interfaces or by smartphones apps (Android, iOS and Windows 10 versions are available). Two predefined user interfaces are provided with openHAB: *Basic UI* and *Classic UI*, both being web front-ends.

Persistence add-ons offer the possibility of storing time-series of states for items. Persistence services are necessary to build graphs showing the evolution of the items of a HA system. They can also be used to create automatic rules based on historic states, to achieve a better use of energy (avoiding repeated queries to the status of different sensors), to calculate average values and to recover the status of an item when a physical problem occurs. Multiple persistence services with different technologies are provided through several add-ons: MySQL, rrd4j, MQTT, JDBC, mapDB, Java Persistence API and InfluxDB. Many others can be added.

Actions are predefined operations that can be executed when a custom rule is defined in order to implement some kind of automatic behavior. openHAB offers a set of core actions that are always available, and a set of actions that can be installed through add-ons. The set of core actions available in openHAB include the modification/update of the state of an item (by sending the new state through the event bus), actions related with the audio system (change volume, play a sound or even say a given text through a text-to-speech engine), logging actions, timers or HTTP requests. Installable actions include: e-mail sending (through SMTP), Twitter integration, Telegram notifications, iOS and Android notifications, XMPP messages, KODI integration and many others.

Transformation services are used to translate raw information from sensors and devices to human-readable messages, by means of predefined JSON, XSLT, regular expressions and many other processes.

Voice services provide text-to-speech (TTS) and speech-to-text (STT) features. Several APIs and web services are available for that purpose.

Third party integration is performed to support the integration of technologies and ecosystems to which openHAB must be made available as a sub-system. openHAB has support for Apple HomeKit, Amazon Echo/Alexa, Google Calendar, Dropbox and many others.

Figure 4. openHAB 2 architecture

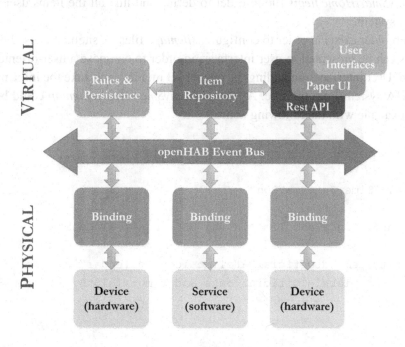

openHAB is set-up by a series of configuration files. In openHAB 2 there is also the possibility of performing most of the set-up actions by means of the intuitive web interface *Paper UI*, so that the steps can be completed by users without much technological background. There are five main elements to configure in order to create a HA system with openHAB: things, items, sitemaps, persistence and rules. Each of these aspects is configured within a folder called *conf* in the openHAB installation.

The *things* subfolder (within the *conf* folder) is used for the configuration of things. Any thing that is used in openHAB is configured by means of a file with *.things* extension. For instance, to configure an NTP service, a file called *ntp.things* can be added to that folder. The following example represents a possible content for this file, so that a thing called *TimeUK* is defined from an NTP service, implemented in the NTP binding, to get the official time in the UK:

```
Thing ntp:ntp:TimeUK [hostname="uk.pool.ntp", refreshInterval=60, re-
freshNtp=30]
```

It is important to point out and emphasize that the *.things* file contains physical details for this element to work (in the example, an Internet host name).

An *items* subfolder is reserved for defining items. Although many item files can be created, a single file could be used to list and define all the items used by our system. Let us assume we name it *mySmartHome.items*. Following the NTP example, an item can be defined in this file to account for the date and time provided by the NTP server configured in the *ntp.things* file. This line would serve for that purpose:

```
DateTime dtOfficialDateTime {channel="ntp:ntp:TimeUK:dateTime"}
```

Note that this links the *dateTime* channel of the *TimeUK* thing with an item called *dtOfficialDate-Time* of type *DateTime*. *dateTime* is one of the channels provided by the NTP binding. More lines can be added to the *mySmartHome.items* file in order to define and link all the items users need for their home automation system.

A *sitemaps* subfolder exists in order to configure *.sitemaps* files. A sitemap is used by openHAB to select what items can be presented in user interfaces in order to compose a user-oriented presentation of the HA system. User interfaces, including the openHAB mobile apps, take the information about the structure of the HA system from this file. A file called *mySmartHome.sitemap* could be setup for our previous simple example with the following content:

```
sitemap mySmartHome label="My openHAB Smart Home"
{
    Frame label="Time Information"
    {
        Text label="Date and Time in the UK" icon="calendar"
        {
            Text item= dtOfficialDateTime icon="calendar"
                    label="Official date and time: [%1$tA, %1$td.%1$tm.%1$tY]"
        }
    }
}
```

Similarly, persistence services are configured by *.persist* files in a *persistence* subfolder. These files describe what items need to be persisted, configuring also the frequency and some other properties. An example of a *mySmartHome.persist* file that configures openHAB to persist the *dtDateTime* item once in an hour, restoring also its value on start-up, could be like this:

```
Items
{
    dtOfficialDateTime: strategy = everyHour, restoreOnStartup
}
```

Last but definitely not least, openHAB offers the possibility to create predefined scripts that can be executed whenever a particular event occurs or a condition is met. These scripts are known as rules and are configured through *.rules* files in a *rules* folder. They are programmed in Xtend language, which is a dialect of Java. Existing Java library and code can be used seamlessly, and Java programmers should have no difficulties in creating rules with this programming language. In addition, simple rules can be defined from the openHAB 2 web administration front-end, so that less experienced users can also benefit from the possibility of creating custom rules.

An example of a *.rules* file with two rules, one for sending an e-mail when the system starts and one for sending a Telegram message when the main door is open, is presented next. For the second rule, it is assumed that three items exist in the system: *ctMainDoor*, representing a door contact sensor, *swAlarmEnabled*, representing a way to enable or disable the alarm of the house and *swAlarmSound*, which represents a siren actuator that emits a loud sound whenever it is turned on. For a detailed explanation of the rules syntax and other technical details, readers should refer to (openHAB Foundation e.V., 2018).

```
rule Start
when
    System started
then
    sendMail("myAccount@gmail.com", "openHAB message", "openHAB is starting")
end
rule DoorIsOpen
when
    Item ctMainDoor changed to OPEN
then
    sendTelegram("myTelegramId", "Main door is open!")
    if (swAlarmEnabled.state == ON)
        swAlarmSound.sendCommand(ON)
end
```

There are other elements that can be configured in openHAB, like icons, transformation services and actions. In addition, most of the add-ons that are part of openHAB can be configured by *.cfg* files in a *services* subfolder. Each add-on, like mail action, Twitter and Telegram actions, Apple HomeKit integration, KNX binding, smart TV bindings, etc. have their own *.cfg* so that particular hardware elements can be set-up.

ADDRESSING THE INTEROPERABILITY PROBLEM WITH OPENHAB

openHAB can be used to address the interoperability problem. In fact, openHAB has been successfully used in several projects at different scales. openHAB modular and technology-agnostic architecture makes it perfect for a variety of scenarios (Guimarães, Henriques, Pereira, & da Silva Silveira, 2018; Heimgaertner, Hettich, Kohlbacher, & Menth, 2017) and it can be used for almost any IoT/IoE application.

Solving the interoperability problem with openHAB is actually very simple. These are roughly the steps needed to integrate different services, products, protocols or devices and make them work together with openHAB. First, of course it is necessary to download, install and set-up openHAB. Next, search for the appropriate bindings that provide the functionality of the technologies you want to use, and setup the bindings with the right configurations. This step depends on the technologies you are using, but the process requires typically to setup a *.cfg* file for each binding. Next, add and configure things representing the devices/services you want to use, create items that represent the functionality you need from these devices, and link the items with the devices/services by means of links. With the *Paper UI* interface these steps are quite simple and can be performed with a visual front-end. (openHAB Foundation e.V., 2018). Optionally you may want to create rules to perform automatic actions (based on the defined items) or even store information by means of persistence services.

This procedure is better explained by showing an example. As a use case, we will show how to use openHAB to integrate four different technologies and ecosystems: KNX, Z-Wave, NTP and Samsung TV. Let us imagine that we have the following elements:

- 1 personal computer and a router providing LAN and Internet connection.
- 1 heating system controlled by a water boiler fueled by gas, with no thermostat.
- 1 KNX power supply.
- 1 KNX 8-channel actuator. One channel is connected to the water boiler and it is used to switch the gas burner on/off. The rest of the channels are used for lighting.
- 1 KNX-IP gateway connected to the router.
- 1 Z-Wave USB controller, connected to the PC.
- 1 Z-Wave 3-in-1 sensor, able to monitor motion (presence), temperature and light.
- 1 Samsung smart TV, connected to the router.
- 1 mobile phone (either iPhone, Android or Windows 10) with access to the router (either locally or via Internet) and the openHAB app installed.

Let us assume that we want to use the Z-Wave temperature sensor to serve as thermostat for the heating system and the motion and light sensor to turn the lights off when there is no human presence or there is enough natural light (more than 100 lumens). Let us also assume that we want to automatically turn off the TV at midnight and that the KNX device can also perform automatic actions on the lights and the heater based on the time of day. To do so, it needs a clock input, which we want to get from an NTP server in Spain.

For this simple but multi-technology scenario, we need to install the following openHAB bindings: KNX, Z-Wave, NTP and Samsung TV. Let us assume that the KNX endpoint for the clock input is 1/0/1, the KNX endpoint of the channel controlling the water boiler is 1/0/2, the KNX endpoint for the lights we want to control is 1/0/3, the local IP address of the KNX gateway is 192.168.1.2, the IP address of the PC is 192.168.1.3, the IP address of the smart TV is 192.168.1.4 and the device id for the Z-Wave sensor is 5f923bca:node2. With these requirements, we only need to create the following items:

```
DateTime dtDateTime   {channel="ntp:ntp:TimeES:dateTime", knx="1/0/1"}
Number nbSetPointTemp   "Desired Temperature"
Contact ctMotion   "Motion"   {channel="zwave:device: 5f923bca:node2:sensor_
binary"}
Number nbTemp   "Temp."   {channel="zwave:device:5f923bca:node2:sensor_ tem-
perature "}
```

```
Number nbLight    "Light"    {channel="zwave:device: 5f923bca:node2:sensor_ lu-
minance "}
Switch swHeater    {knx="1/0/2"}
Switch swLights    {knx="1/0/3"}
Switch swTvPower    "Television On/Off"    {channel="samsungtv:tv:myTv:power"}
Switch swTvMute    "Television Mute"    {channel="samsungtv:tv:myTv:mute"}
```

We assume that we have a thing called *TimeES*, which provides us with the time in peninsular Spain and a thing called *myTV* representing the Samsung smart TV (see Appendix).

The *dtDateTime* item will receive the time from the NTP service and feed the KNX input so that KNX knows the correct time of day. This way, both technologies become interoperable. As simple as that! Note that the syntax of the KNX binding does not use channels, since it is a legacy openHAB 1.x binding.

The item *nbSetPointTemp* is not linked to any channel. It will be included in a sitemap so that the user decides the target temperature for the room. Using any of the available user interfaces, the user will be able to control the heating system and many other aspects of this home with his/her phone, by means of the openHAB mobile app.

The items *ctMotion*, *nbTemp* and *nbLight* represent the information about motion (presence), temperature and light, provided by the Z-Wave sensor.

The item *swHeater* is linked to the KNX channel of the heater. It allows to switch it on/off from the KNX network. To perform the thermostat operation, we will need to create a very simple rule to toggle this item depending on the values of *nbSetPointTemp* and *nbTemp*.

The items *swTvPower* and *swTvMute* allow to monitor and control the state of the smart TV. With *swTvPower* we can switch it on/off, and with *swTvMute* we can mute/unmute the TV. To switch it off at midnight, we will need to create a rule in order to send an OFF command whenever the clock reaches midnight.

The Appendix shows the rules (*example.rules*) and some other configuration files needed to understand this example. It is important to note that this is a very simple example, yet much more impressing features could be added to this simple system without needing additional hardware: Apple HomeKit integration, presence simulation, notifications, etc.

As it can be seen, the open-source technology-agnostic philosophy of openHAB is perfect for HAN interoperability, and it is actually very simple to make different devices from different vendors, technologies and protocols work together. Although we have explained how to setup the most important configuration files, the example previously shown can also be configured with *Paper UI* instead. There is hence no need to be a technician to setup openHAB and most bindings are very easy to use. Nevertheless, there are potential security risks that should be taken into account when using bindings from untrusted sources. Due to its open and modular architecture, it is feasible to design a binding to expose system protected data over the REST interface (Ramljak, 2017). To solve this problem, openHAB 2 offers a repository binding where trustworthy bindings – supervised by the openHAB community - are uploaded.

CONCLUSION

The interconnection of computing elements have evolved very rapidly in the last 30 years. At first, when computers were tools used only for engineers and scientists, computers were interconnected to share data and processing power. This was the era of the *Internet of Computers* (Moser, Harder, & Koo, 2014). Later, computers became familiar objects used also for leisure and social interaction and almost every person owned a computer. When people started to use computers and Internet to access social media (Twitter, Facebook, etc.) the era of the *Internet of People* began. At the same time, computing elements different than desktop or laptop computers (mobile phones, tablets, sensors, single-board computers etc.), started to be very common. With all these devices connected, the idea of the *Internet of Things* was fulfilled. Now, researchers are focused on finding ways to create intelligent networks in which the elements are not just connected but serve a common meaningful purpose. This is the *Internet of Everything*.

Home automation is a perfect example of an IoE scenario. The goal is to create a network of interconnected elements at home, designed and placed to serve a common purpose: improve the quality of life. Therefore, its potential benefits are enormous. Smart energy consumption, safety, security, health-care, assisted living, entertainment, and a boost in home comfort are some of the few strengths and opportunities to apply HA. Nevertheless, as a human-centric technology, smart homes have to deal also with many challenges and problems such as digital security, social disruption, market fragmentation, economic, installation and maintenance costs.

Several trends have emerged to address some of these problems. AAL, low-cost DIY solutions, IP-based and wireless HA systems are some of the current trends in the smart home sector.

Market fragmentation has caused a really serious interoperability problem in smart homes. With several HA technologies and ecosystems, it is necessary to find a way to avoid any kind of vendor lock-in and make the different HA services and networks interoperable. This chapter proposes to use openHAB, an open-source vendor-agnostic software platform, to address this problem. openHAB has been specifically designed to separate the physical and the functional views of HA devices. Therefore, interoperability in HA could be easily handled by using openHAB, as it is explained in the chapter, until a standardized smart home protocol is proposed and accepted by the industry, the research community and of course, smart home users. IP-based HANs seem a natural solution for both reaching a standardized solution and also fully exploiting the benefits of IoE by means of worldwide addressable home devices.

As a people-centric IoE application, HA should be completely dedicated to fulfill the user needs. More frequently than would be desired, technology-focused HA systems have been designed, forgetting about what users really demand. One important question that HA engineers should ask is: What is a smart home? In the authors' opinions, home automation is whatever their smart home users want it to be!

REFERENCES

Ahmed, N., Rahman, H., & Hussain, M. I. (2016). A comparison of 802.11 AH and 802.15. 4 for IoT. *ICT Express*, *2*(3), 100–102. doi:10.1016/j.icte.2016.07.003

Arndt, J., Krause, F., Wunderlich, R., & Heinen, S. (2017). *Development of a 6LoWPAN sensor node for IoT based home automation networks*. Paper presented at the Research and Education in Mechatronics (REM), 2017 International Conference on. 10.1109/REM.2017.8075226

Banos, V., Afaqui, M. S., Lopez, E., & Garcia, E. (2017). Throughput and Range Characterization of IEEE 802.11 ah. *IEEE Latin America Transactions*, *15*(9), 1621–1628. doi:10.1109/TLA.2017.8015044

Ben Hmida, H., & Braun, A. (2017). Enabling an Internet of Things Framework for Ambient Assisted Living. In R. Wichert & B. Mand (Eds.), *Ambient Assisted Living: 9. AAL-Kongress, Frankfurt/M, Germany, April 20 - 21, 2016* (pp. 181-196). Cham: Springer International Publishing. 10.1007/978-3-319-52322-4_13

Bolaji, A. Q., Kamaldeen, R. A., Samson, O. F., Abdullahi, A. T., & Abubakar, S. K. (2017). A Digitalized Smart Mobile Home Automation and Security System via Bluetooth/Wi-Fi Using Android Platform. *International Journal of Information and Communication Sciences*, 2(6), 93. doi:10.11648/j.ijics.20170206.11

Brush, A., Lee, B., Mahajan, R., Agarwal, S., Saroiu, S., & Dixon, C. (2011). Home automation in the wild: challenges and opportunities. *Proceedings of the SIGCHI Conference on Human Factors in Computing Systems*. 10.1145/1978942.1979249

Burgess, J., Mitchell, P., & Highfield, T. (2018). Automating the digital everyday: An introduction. *Media International Australia*, 166(1), 6–10. doi:10.1177/1329878X17739020

Chandramohan, J., Nagarajan, R., Satheeshkumar, K., Ajithkumar, N., Gopinath, P., & Ranjithkumar, S. (2017). Intelligent Smart Home Automation and Security System Using Arduino and Wi-fi. *International Journal of Engineering And Computer Science*, 6(3), 20694–20698.

Chavan, J., Patil, P., & Naik, P. (2017). Advanced Control Web Based Home Automation with Raspberry Pi. *International Journal of Advance Research. Ideas and Innovations in Technology*, 3(2), 221–223.

Darby, S. J. (2018). Smart technology in the home: Time for more clarity. *Building Research and Information*, 46(1), 140–147. doi:10.1080/09613218.2017.1301707

Del Carpio, L. F., Di Marco, P., Skillermark, P., Chirikov, R., & Lagergren, K. (2017). Comparison of 802.11ah, BLE and 802.15.4 for a Home Automation Use Case. *International Journal of Wireless Information Networks*, 24(3), 243–253. doi:10.100710776-017-0355-2

Del Carpio, L. F., Di Marco, P., Skillermark, P., Chirikov, R., Lagergren, K., & Amin, P. (2016). *Comparison of 802.11 ah and BLE for a home automation use case*. Paper presented at the Personal, Indoor, and Mobile Radio Communications (PIMRC), 2016 IEEE 27th Annual International Symposium on.

Dorge, B. M., & Scheffler, T. (2011). *Using IPv6 and 6LoWPAN for home automation networks*. Paper presented at the Consumer Electronics-Berlin (ICCE-Berlin), 2011 IEEE International Conference on.

ElShafee, A., & Hamed, K. A. (2012). Design and implementation of a WIFI based home automation system. *World Academy of Science, Engineering and Technology*, 68, 2177–2180.

Feng, S., Setoodeh, P., & Haykin, S. (2017). Smart Home: Cognitive Interactive People-Centric Internet of Things. *IEEE Communications Magazine*, 55(2), 34–39. doi:10.1109/MCOM.2017.1600682CM

Fibar Group S.A. (2018). *Fibaro*. Retrieved 02/03/2018, 2018, from http://www.fibaro.com

Friedewald, M., Da Costa, O., Punie, Y., Alahuhta, P., & Heinonen, S. (2005). Perspectives of ambient intelligence in the home environment. *Telematics and Informatics*, 22(3), 221–238. doi:10.1016/j.tele.2004.11.001

Friedli, M., Kaufmann, L., Paganini, F., & Kyburz, R. (2016). *Energy efficiency of the Internet of Things. Technology and Energy Assessment Report prepared for IEA 4E EDNA*. Lucerne University of Applied Sciences.

Geman, O., Sanei, S., Costin, H.-N., Eftaxias, K., Vyšata, O., Procházka, A., & Lhotská, L. (2015). *Challenges and trends in Ambient Assisted Living and intelligent tools for disabled and elderly people*. Paper presented at the Computational Intelligence for Multimedia Understanding (IWCIM), 2015 International Workshop on. 10.1109/IWCIM.2015.7347088

Gibbs, W. W. (2016). DIY Home Security. Deter Intruders with an Extra Loud Alarm. *IEEE Spectrum*, 20–21.

Gomez, C., & Paradells, J. (2010). Wireless home automation networks: A survey of architectures and technologies. *IEEE Communications Magazine*, *48*(6), 92–101. doi:10.1109/MCOM.2010.5473869

Gram-Hanssen, K., & Darby, S. J. (2018). "Home is where the smart is"? Evaluating smart home research and approaches against the concept of home. *Energy Research & Social Science*, *37*, 94–101. doi:10.1016/j.erss.2017.09.037

Guimarães, C. S. S., Henriques, R. V. B., Pereira, C. E., & da Silva Silveira, W. (2018). *Proposal IoT Architecture for Macro and Microscale Applied in Assistive Technology. In Online Engineering & Internet of Things* (pp. 36–43). Springer.

Hargreaves, T., & Wilson, C. (2017). *Perceived Benefits and Risks of Smart Home Technologies. In Smart Homes and Their Users* (pp. 35–53). Springer. doi:10.1007/978-3-319-68018-7_3

Hargreaves, T., Wilson, C., & Hauxwell-Baldwin, R. (2018). Learning to live in a smart home. *Building Research and Information*, *46*(1), 127–139. doi:10.1080/09613218.2017.1286882

Heimgaertner, F., Hettich, S., Kohlbacher, O., & Menth, M. (2017). *Scaling home automation to public buildings: A distributed multiuser setup for OpenHAB 2*. Paper presented at the Global Internet of Things Summit (GIoTS). 10.1109/GIOTS.2017.8016235

Huang, Z., & Yuan, F. (2015). Implementation of 6LoWPAN and its application in smart lighting. *Journal of Computer and Communications*, *3*(03), 80–85. doi:10.4236/jcc.2015.33014

Jacobsson, A., Boldt, M., & Carlsson, B. (2016). A risk analysis of a smart home automation system. *Future Generation Computer Systems*, *56*, 719–733. doi:10.1016/j.future.2015.09.003

Jahn, M., Jentsch, M., Prause, C. R., Pramudianto, F., Al-Akkad, A., & Reiners, R. (2010). *The energy aware smart home*. Paper presented at the Future Information Technology (FutureTech), 2010 5th International Conference on. 10.1109/FUTURETECH.2010.5482712

Jakovljev, S., Subotić, M., & Papp, I. (2017). *Realisation of a Smart Plug device based on Wi-Fi technology for use in home automation systems*. Paper presented at the Consumer Electronics (ICCE), 2017 IEEE International Conference on. 10.1109/ICCE.2017.7889340

Jose, A., & Malekian, R. (2017). Improving Smart Home Security; Integrating Logical Sensing into Smart Home. *IEEE Sensors Journal*, *17*(13), 4269–4286. doi:10.1109/JSEN.2017.2705045

Jose, A. C., & Malekian, R. (2015). Smart home automation security. *SmartCR, 5*(4), 269–285.

Kannapiran, S., & Chakrapani, A. (2017). A Novel Home Automation System using Bluetooth and Arduino. *International Journal of Advances in Computer and Electronics Engineering, 2*(2), 41–44.

Knight, M. (2006). How safe is Z-Wave? *Computing and Control Engineering, 17*(6), 18–23. doi:10.1049/cce:20060601

Korhonen, I., Parkka, J., & Van Gils, M. (2003). Health monitoring in the home of the future. *IEEE Engineering in Medicine and Biology Magazine, 22*(3), 66–73. doi:10.1109/MEMB.2003.1213628 PMID:12845821

Kreuzer, K. (2014). *Privacy in the Smart Home - Why we need an Intranet of Things*. Retrieved 02/03/2018, from http://www.kaikreuzer.de/2014/02/10/privacy-in-smart-home-why-we-need/

Kulkarni, B. P., Joshi, A. V., Jadhav, V. V., & Dhamange, A. T. (2017). IoT Based Home Automation Using Raspberry PI. *International Journal of Innovative Studies in Sciences and Engineering Technology, 3*(4), 13–16.

Laamarti, F., & El Saddik, A. (2017). *Home automation serving a healthier lifestyle*. Paper presented at the Medical Measurements and Applications (MeMeA), 2017 IEEE International Symposium on. 10.1109/MeMeA.2017.7985846

Lee, K. C., & Lee, H.-H. (2004). Network-based fire-detection system via controller area network for smart home automation. *IEEE Transactions on Consumer Electronics, 50*(4), 1093–1100. doi:10.1109/TCE.2004.1362504

Lobaccaro, G., Carlucci, S., & Löfström, E. (2016). A review of systems and technologies for smart homes and smart grids. *Energies, 9*(5), 348. doi:10.3390/en9050348

Louis, J.-N., Caló, A., Leiviskä, K., & Pongrácz, E. (2015). Environmental impacts and benefits of smart home automation: Life cycle assessment of home energy management system. *IFAC-PapersOnLine, 48*(1), 880–885. doi:10.1016/j.ifacol.2015.05.158

Mainetti, L., Patrono, L., & Vilei, A. (2011). *Evolution of wireless sensor networks towards the internet of things: A survey*. Paper presented at the Software, Telecommunications and Computer Networks (SoftCOM), 2011 19th International Conference on.

Mehdi, G., & Roshchin, M. (2015). Electricity consumption constraints for smart-home automation: An overview of models and applications. *Energy Procedia, 83*, 60–68. doi:10.1016/j.egypro.2015.12.196

Moraitou, M., Pateli, A., & Fotiou, S. (2017). Smart Health Caring Home: A Systematic Review of Smart Home Care for Elders and Chronic Disease Patients. In P. Vlamos (Ed.), *GeNeDis 2016: Geriatrics* (pp. 255–264). Cham: Springer International Publishing. doi:10.1007/978-3-319-57348-9_22

More, S. S., Gai, A. A., Sardar, V. S., Rupareliya, C. S., & Talole, P. T. (2017). Home Automation on Android Using Arduino. *Journal of Android and IOS Applications and Testing, 2*(1).

Moser, K., Harder, J., & Koo, S. G. (2014). *Internet of things in home automation and energy efficient smart home technologies.* Paper presented at the Systems, Man and Cybernetics (SMC), 2014 IEEE International Conference on. 10.1109/SMC.2014.6974087

Mulligan, G. (2007). The 6LoWPAN architecture. *Proceedings of the 4th workshop on Embedded networked sensors.* 10.1145/1278972.1278992

openHAB Foundation e.V. (2018). openHAB - a Vendor and Technology Agnostic Open Source Automation Software for Your Home. Retrieved 02/03/2018, 2018, from https://www.openhab.org

OSGi Alliance. (2018). *OSGi -The Dynamic Module System for Java.* Retrieved 02/03/2018, 2018, from www.osgi.org

Pampattiwar, K., Lakhani, M., Marar, R., & Menon, R. (2017). Home Automation using Raspberry Pi controlled via an Android Application. *International Journal of Current Engineering and Technology, 7*(3), 962–967.

Patel, S. M., & Kanawade, S. Y. (2017). Internet of Things Based Smart Home with Intel Edison. *Proceedings of International Conference on Communication and Networks.* 10.1007/978-981-10-2750-5_40

Patil, A., Shaikh, I. S., Ghorpade, V. P., Pawar, V. D., & Memane, P. S. (2017). Home Automation using Raspberry Pi & Windows 10 IOT. *Imperial Journal of Interdisciplinary Research, 3*(3).

Patil, S. A., & Pinki, V. (2017). Home Automation Using Single Board Computing as an Internet of Things Application. *Proceedings of International Conference on Communication and Networks.* 10.1007/978-981-10-2750-5_26

Piyare, R., & Tazil, M. (2011). *Bluetooth based home automation system using cell phone.* Paper presented at the Consumer Electronics (ISCE), 2011 IEEE 15th International Symposium on. 10.1109/ISCE.2011.5973811

Ploennigs, J., Ryssel, U., & Kabitzsch, K. (2010). *Performance analysis of the EnOcean wireless sensor network protocol.* Paper presented at the Emerging Technologies and Factory Automation (ETFA), 2010 IEEE Conference on. 10.1109/ETFA.2010.5641313

Prasad, S., Mahalakshmi, P., Sunder, A. J. C., & Swathi, R. (2014). Smart Surveillance Monitoring System Using Raspberry PI and PIR Sensor. *Int. J. Comput. Sci. Inf. Technol, 5*(6), 7107–7109.

Ramljak, M. (2017). *Security analysis of Open Home Automation Bus system.* Paper presented at the Information and Communication Technology, Electronics and Microelectronics (MIPRO), 2017 40th International Convention on. 10.23919/MIPRO.2017.7973614

Rathnayaka, A. D., Potdar, V. M., & Kuruppu, S. J. (2011). Evaluation of wireless home automation technologies. *Digital Ecosystems and Technologies Conference (DEST), 2011 Proceedings of the 5th IEEE International Conference on.* 10.1109/DEST.2011.5936601

Schmidt, M., & Obermaisser, R. (2017). Adaptive and technology-independent architecture for fault-tolerant distributed AAL solutions. *Computers in Biology and Medicine.* doi:10.1016/j.compbiomed.2017.11.002 PMID:29157726

Sivaraman, V., Chan, D., Earl, D., & Boreli, R. (2016). Smart-phones attacking smart-homes. *Proceedings of the 9th ACM Conference on Security & Privacy in Wireless and Mobile Networks*. 10.1145/2939918.2939925

Smirek, L., Zimmermann, G., & Beigl, M. (2016). Just a Smart Home or Your Smart Home–A Framework for Personalized User Interfaces Based on Eclipse Smart Home and Universal Remote Console. *Procedia Computer Science, 98*, 107–116. doi:10.1016/j.procs.2016.09.018

Soliman, M. S., Dwairi, M. O., Sulayman, I. I. A., & Almalki, S. H. (2017). Towards the Design and Implementation a Smart Home Automation System Based on Internet of Things Approach. *International Journal of Applied Engineering Research, 12*(11), 2731–2737.

Stojkoska, B. L. R., & Trivodaliev, K. V. (2017). A review of Internet of Things for smart home: Challenges and solutions. *Journal of Cleaner Production, 140*, 1454–1464. doi:10.1016/j.jclepro.2016.10.006

Suryadevara, N. K., Kelly, S., & Mukhopadhyay, S. C. (2014). Ambient Assisted Living Environment Towards Internet of Things Using Multifarious Sensors Integrated with XBee Platform. In S. C. Mukhopadhyay (Ed.), *Internet of Things: Challenges and Opportunities* (pp. 217–231). Cham: Springer International Publishing. doi:10.1007/978-3-319-04223-7_9

Swan, M. (2012). Sensor mania! the internet of things, wearable computing, objective metrics, and the quantified self 2.0. *Journal of Sensor and Actuator Networks, 1*(3), 217–253. doi:10.3390/jsan1030217

Toschi, G. M., Campos, L. B., & Cugnasca, C. E. (2017). Home automation networks: A survey. *Computer Standards & Interfaces, 50*, 42–54. doi:10.1016/j.csi.2016.08.008

Tudose, D. Ş., Voinescu, A., Petrăreanu, M.-T., Bucur, A., Loghin, D., Bostan, A., & Ţăpuş, N. (2011). *Home automation design using 6LoWPAN wireless sensor networks.* Paper presented at the Distributed Computing in Sensor Systems and Workshops (DCOSS), 2011 International Conference on. 10.1109/DCOSS.2011.5982181

Vikram, N., Harish, K., Nihaal, M., Umesh, R., Shetty, A., & Kumar, A. (2017). *A low cost home automation system using wi-fi based wireless sensor network incorporating Internet of Things (IoT).* Paper presented at the Advance Computing Conference (IACC), 2017 IEEE 7th International.

Weiser, M. (1991). The computer for the 21st century. *Scientific American, 265*(3), 94–104. doi:10.1038cientificamerican0991-94 PMID:1675486

Wilson, C., Hargreaves, T., & Hauxwell-Baldwin, R. (2017). Benefits and risks of smart home technologies. *Energy Policy, 103*, 72–83. doi:10.1016/j.enpol.2016.12.047

Withanage, C., Ashok, R., Yuen, C., & Otto, K. (2014). *A comparison of the popular home automation technologies.* Paper presented at the Innovative Smart Grid Technologies-Asia (ISGT Asia), 2014 IEEE. 10.1109/ISGT-Asia.2014.6873860

Ye, X., & Huang, J. (2011). *A framework for cloud-based smart home.* Paper presented at the Computer Science and Network Technology (ICCSNT), 2011 International Conference on.

Younis, S. A., Ijaz, U., Randhawa, I. A., & Ijaz, A. (2018). Speech Recognition Based Home Automation System using Raspberry Pi and Zigbee. *NFC IEFR Journal of Engineering and Scientific Research, 5.*

Zhou, B., Li, W., Chan, K. W., Cao, Y., Kuang, Y., Liu, X., & Wang, X. (2016). Smart home energy management systems: Concept, configurations, and scheduling strategies. *Renewable & Sustainable Energy Reviews*, *61*, 30–40. doi:10.1016/j.rser.2016.03.047

ADDITIONAL READING

Apthorpe, N., Reisman, D., Sundaresan, S., Narayanan, A., & Feamster, N. (2017). Spying on the smart home: Privacy attacks and defenses on encrypted iot traffic. *arXiv preprint arXiv:1708.05044*.

Bojanova, I., Hurlburt, G., & Voas, J. (2014). Imagineering an internet of anything. *Computer*, *47*(6), 72–77. doi:10.1109/MC.2014.150

Do, H. M., Pham, M., Sheng, W., Yang, D., & Liu, M. (2018). RiSH: A robot-integrated smart home for elderly care. *Robotics and Autonomous Systems*, *101*, 74–92. doi:10.1016/j.robot.2017.12.008

Dorri, A., Kanhere, S. S., Jurdak, R., & Gauravaram, P. (2017). *Blockchain for IoT security and privacy: The case study of a smart home*. Paper presented at the Pervasive Computing and Communications Workshops (PerCom Workshops), 2017 IEEE International Conference on. 10.1109/PERCOMW.2017.7917634

García-Pereira, I., Gimeno, J., Pérez, M., Portalés, C., & Casas, S. (2018). *MIME: A Mixed-Space Collaborative System with Three Levels of Immersion and Multiple Users*. Paper presented at the IEEE and ACM International Symposium for Mixed and Augmented Reality 2018 (ISMAR 2018).

Gill, K., Yang, S.-H., Yao, F., & Lu, X. (2009). A zigbee-based home automation system. *IEEE Transactions on Consumer Electronics*, *55*(2), 422–430. doi:10.1109/TCE.2009.5174403

Herrero, S. T., Nicholls, L., & Strengers, Y. (2018). Smart home technologies in everyday life: Do they address key energy challenges in households? *Current Opinion in Environmental Sustainability*, *31*, 65–70. doi:10.1016/j.cosust.2017.12.001

Jain, S., Vaibhav, A., & Goyal, L. (2014). *Raspberry Pi based interactive home automation system through E-mail*. Paper presented at the Optimization, Reliabilty, and Information Technology (ICROIT), 2014 International Conference on. 10.1109/ICROIT.2014.6798330

Miraz, M. H., Ali, M., Excell, P. S., & Picking, R. (2015). *A review on Internet of Things (IoT), Internet of everything (IoE) and Internet of nano things (IoNT)*. Paper presented at the 2015 Internet Technologies and Applications (ITA). 10.1109/ITechA.2015.7317398

Pavithra, D., & Balakrishnan, R. (2015). *IoT based monitoring and control system for home automation*. Paper presented at the Communication Technologies (GCCT), 2015 Global Conference on. 10.1109/GCCT.2015.7342646

Strengers, Y., & Nicholls, L. (2017). Convenience and energy consumption in the smart home of the future: Industry visions from australia and beyond. *Energy Research & Social Science*, *32*, 86–93. doi:10.1016/j.erss.2017.02.008

Vujović, V., & Maksimović, M. (2015). Raspberry Pi as a Sensor Web node for home automation. *Computers & Electrical Engineering*, *44*, 153–171. doi:10.1016/j.compeleceng.2015.01.019

Yeo, K. S., Chian, M. C., & Ng, T. C. W. (2014). *Internet of Things: Trends, challenges and applications.* Paper presented at the Integrated Circuits (ISIC), 2014 14th International Symposium on. 10.1109/ISICIR.2014.7029523

KEY TERMS AND DEFINITIONS

Automation: The technique of making an apparatus, process, device, or system operate automatically.

Internet of Everything (IoE): The intelligent connection of people, process, data, and things. The IoE builds on the foundation of the IoT by adding network intelligence that allows convergence, orchestration, and visibility across previously disparate systems.

Internet of Things (IoT): The interconnection via Internet of computing devices embedded in everyday objects, enabling them to send and receive data.

Interoperability: The ability of a system or device to work with or use the parts or equipment of another system.

Open-Source: A decentralized collaborative software-development paradigm based on peer-production. The code is accessible and available for the general public. Therefore, everyone can use and modify it without licensing restrictions.

openHAB: A vendor and technology agnostic open-source automation software for the home. It is a platform for integrating different home automation systems and technologies into one single solution that allows overarching automation rules and offers uniform user interfaces.

Smart Home: A home that incorporates automation systems to provide its inhabitants with remote control and sophisticated monitoring over the building.

This research was previously published in Harnessing the Internet of Everything (IoE) for Accelerated Innovation Opportunities; pages 148-174, copyright year 2019 by Engineering Science Reference (an imprint of IGI Global).

APPENDIX: OPENHAB FILES FOR THE INTEROPERABILITY EXAMPLE

File *knx.cfg:*
```
# KNX gateway IP address
ip=192.168.1.2
# KNX IP connection type. Could be either TUNNEL or ROUTER
type=TUNNEL
# KNX gateway port
port=3671
# Timeout in milliseconds to wait for a response from the KNX bus
timeout=2000
# Use NAT (Network Address Translation)
useNAT=true
```
File *ntp.things:*
```
Thing ntp:ntp:TimeES [hostname="hora.roa.es", refreshInterval=60, refreshNtp=30
]
```
File *samsungtv.things:*
```
Thing samsungtv:tv:myTv [hostName="192.168.1.4", port=55000, refreshInter-
val=1000]
```
File *example.rules:*
```
rule Thermostat
when
    Item nbTemp changed or
    Item nbSetPointTemp changed
then
    var float temp = (nbTemp.state as DecimalType).floatValue()
    var float setPointTemp = (nbSetPointTemp.state as DecimalType).floatVal-
ue()
    if (setPointTemp > nbTemp)
        swHeater.sendCommand(ON)
    else
        swHeater.sendCommand(OFF)
end
rule LightsOff
when
    Item ctMotion changed or
    Item nbLight changed
```

```
then
    var float lum = (nbLight.state as DecimalType).floatValue()
    if ((ctMotion.state == CLOSED) || (lum > 100))
        swLights.sendCommand(OFF)
end
rule TvOff
when
    Time cron "0 0 0 * * ?"
then
    swTvPower.sendCommand(OFF)
end
```

Chapter 31
Enhancing Information Retrieval System Using Change-Prone Classes

Deepa Bura

Manav Rachna International Institute of Research and Studies, India

Amit Choudhary

Maharaja Surajmal Institute, India

ABSTRACT

In today's competitive world, each company is required to change software to meet changing customer requirements. At the same time, an efficient information retrieval system is required as changes made to software in different versions can lead to complicated retrieval systems. This research aims to find the association between changes and object-oriented metrics using different versions of open source software. Earlier researchers have used various techniques such as statistical methods for the prediction of change-prone classes. This research uses execution time, frequency, run time information, popularity, and class dependency in prediction of change-prone classes. For evaluating the performance of the prediction model, sensitivity, specificity, and ROC curve are used. Higher values of AUC indicate the prediction model gives accurate results. Results are validated in two phases: Experimental Analysis I validates results using OpenClinic software and OpenHospital software and Experimental Analysis II validates result using Neuroph 2.9.2 and Neuroph 2.6.

INTRODUCTION

The unending growing complexity and dependency has led to a rise in demand of high quality software that can be maintained at cheaper costs. Finding software change proneness is a significant and essential activity for improving software feature and reducing maintenance effort formerly the software is installed in real world. Koru & Liu (2007) proved change prone classes as a significant peripheral quality attribute that signifies degree of alterations in a class through various versions of software. Software industry

DOI: 10.4018/978-1-7998-9158-1.ch031

is expanding manifolds day by day. Software changes to incorporate new features or to remove errors. This rapidly changing software demand has resulted in significant increase of effort from development to testing phase in software life cycle. Developing and maintaining software requires resources such as development time, cost to build and effort required. But all these resources are limited. Research has also been carried out to find the association between fault prone classes and object oriented metrics. Weak classes of any software can be predicted using these quality attributes. Changes if predicted during earlier stages of life cycle, can help a developer in efficiently allocating project's resources by properly allocating the appropriate resources to weaker change prone class, so that such type of classes can be maintained properly and tested rigorously. Predicting such changes can be useful as such evaluations can be utilized to forecast changes from one release to next.

Maintenance phase is considered as one of the costly and significant phases of software. Malhotra & Khanna (2013) identified maintenance cost incurs 40-70% of entire cost of software. Estimation of change in classes i.e. probability with which class will modify or not needs to be evaluated as it can help in reducing maintenance cost and testing. As the software evolves it demands more rigorous testing so that good quality software can be developed with less changes and defects. By focusing on weak change prone classes utilization of resources can be done in a better way. Detection of such classes earlier in life cycle model of software can reduce maintenance costs as because if an error is detected early in a product, it would require lesser amount of resources to correct that error. Else in a later stage the cost of correcting an error increases exponentially in every unnoticed phase. Quality problems related to design can be identified in software before implementing codes, if developers are able to identify change prone classes early in life cycle of the software. Similarly, existing design can be customized or alternate designs can be selected easily. These types of prediction models give high return on investment. As a result, change proneness prediction model contributes in improving quality of the software and reduces development cost also. Thus change prediction model serves to deliver high quality software at optimal costs, as lesser changes and faults are carried forward in later stages of software life cycle.

Various object oriented metrics are used throughout the software process. It is not possible to use a single metric to quantify various aspects of OO application. Various different metrics are required to completely analyse software. To predict change prone classes, various researchers have used various object oriented metrics like size, cohesion, coupling, inheritance, etc. This research summarizes different object oriented features which can be utilized to predict amount of change in classes. This will benefit researchers to get through various metrics elaborated here. In addition to that, it will help the researchers to predict more parameters for estimating changes in a class.

Researchers and Practitioners have used various Object-Oriented metrics throughout the software process. But it is not feasible to use a single metric for quantifying various aspects of Object-Oriented application. Several different metrics and methods are needed for completely analyzing the software. Things that need to be considered before developing an efficient change proneness prediction model: (1) it is required to review the effectiveness of several methods as various methods may give different outcomes with different types of data sets. (2) Secondly it becomes essential to test whether the prediction model provides good results on another data set or not.

This study aims to build an efficient change prone prediction model that will predict change prone classes. The study includes the following objectives:

1. It aims to explore the association amongst different Object-Oriented metrics and change prone classes.

2.   To propose some new dynamic metrics that can help in predicting degree of change in class.

RELATED WORK

Change proneness gives the degree of change across various versions of software. These change prone prediction model can help developers in efficient resource allocation, developing improved quality software and reduced maintenance costs. In the last two decades' researchers and practitioners have made a lot of effort for finding the association amongst change prone classes and object oriented metrics. Research gives a strong correlation amongst object oriented features and change prone class.

Godara and Singh (2015) proposed a model in which dynamic features were used to evaluate the frequency of change in a particular class. Further to minimize the rules and to improve the accuracy, Artificial Bee Colony (ABC) algorithm was used. Using ABC algorithm most significant rules ere extracted to define change prone classes of a software. Catolina et al. (2018) stated that number of developers working on a project also affects change proneness feature of a class. Results concluded that considering this feature improves effectiveness of the change prone model. Malhotra and Khanna (2018) analyzed evolution metrics if considered along with object oriented metrics results in better prediction of change prone classes.

Bansal and Jajoria (2019) conducted various experiments using meta heuristic algorithms on intra and cross projects. Research predicted that hybrid algorithms give better accuracy. Bansal et al. (2019) compared six machine learning algorithms and stated that resampling leads to more accurate model.

Godara and Singh (2017) explored various types of dependencies in a software. Research stated that if such dependencies can be predicted earlier in software development life cycle using UML 2.0 class diagrams it would result in a better-quality product and would minimize testing and maintenance efforts.

Bura et al. (2017) studied various metrics used for finding change prone classes and evaluated all the metrics on two open source software OpenClininc and OpenHospital. Researchers investigated that if object-oriented features are used for change proneness prediction model it would give better results. Previous researchers used static object-oriented metrics for prediction of change prone classes. But they failed to incorporate dynamic metrics for prediction of degree of change proneness of any class. Our research tries to incorporate dynamic metrics for predicting change prone classes. Lu et al. (2012) investigated various object-oriented metrics for predicting change proneness of a class. Overall, Researchers concluded that object-oriented features can predict degree of change in a class. All these researchers used existing static object-oriented metrics for prediction of change prone classes.

Han et al (2008) calculated how one class depends on other using behavioral dependency. They measured change proneness in terms of behavioral dependency. If BDM (Behavior Dependency Measurement) of a class is higher than other, it is more likely to change. Using UML2.0 (Unified Modeling Language 2.0) Sequence diagrams and class diagrams they evaluated the feature of behavioral dependency. Their research proved behavioral dependency can be effectively used for finding possibility of change in a class. However, their research ignored other factors which affects change proneness of a class.

Lu et al (2012) used AUC technique (the area under relative operating characteristic) for evaluating predictive effectiveness of OO metrics. The steps followed were: (1) Compute Area under a relative characteristic and corresponding variance for each object oriented metrics. (2) For computing the average AUC random effect model is employed. (3) Sensitivity analysis is performed for investigating whether the result of AUC technique is applicable vigorously to the data selection. Results show that size metrics can moderately differentiate between a likely to change and non-likely to change class whereas cohesion and coupling metrics have low predictive capability of finding change prone classes. Inheritance feature have very reduced predicting capability as compared to size, cohesion and coupling metrics. Their research work just considered three metrics size, cohesion and coupling for finding change prone classes. However, other factors were ignored in the research. Elish and Zouri (2014) constructed logistic regression models for finding change-prone classes. Research analyzed statistical correlation between change prone classes and coupling metrics. The results show that a prediction model made with coupling feature gives more accurate results than a model built with cohesion feature. Wherein, a prediction model made with import coupling metrics is more accurate than a model built with export coupling metrics. Research mainly focussed on two attributes i.e. coupling and cohesion. Their research just determined which one is better attribute for finding change proneness of a class. In this research we have incorporated dependency feature for finding the association between the classes and other factors such as frequency and Implementation Period are also considered.

Romano and Pinzger (2011) empirically studied the orrelation between object oriented features and changes in interfaces of source code. They evaluated ten Java open-source systems for predicting the results. Furthermore, they evaluated the metrics to find degree of change in Java interfaces. Results revealed strongest association between cohesion metric of external interface and changes in source code.

Zhou and Leung (2009) based on Eclipse analyzed 1) Effect of class size (whichever metrics of size is taken) on change proneness. 2) Their research analyzed size metrics lead to an overestimation of association between object oriented features and change proneness. Zhu et al (2013) validated Pareto's law. Using classification methods, they identified change prone classes. They used open source software product, Datacrow for static metrics collection and change in class. Pareto's Law states that 80% of changes in software can be found in 20% of the classes. Experimental results show that results can be used for finding change prone classes and for enhancing developer's efficiency. Researchers tried to find out the relation amongst object oriented features and change in interface of source code. But they didn't analyze other factors which contribute in affecting change proneness of a class.

Cetolino and Ferrucci (2019) conducted a detailed study to check whether ensemble techniques can lead to improved prediction models.

Khomh et al (2009) tested the assumption i.e. if a class with code smell is more change prone than the classes without code smell. They analyzed various versions of Azerus (9 releases) Eclipse (13 releases), in which they found 29 code smells. Their research studied relationship between code smell and change proneness. Their results revealed classes have a high probability of change with code smells. Eski and Buzluca (2011) studied association of object oriented features and change proneness. Experimental outcomes of the research indicated that the portions of the software which have a low level quality, change often during the software life cycle development process. Janes et al (2006) used arithmetical models for exploring the relationship between OO features and defect prone classes. The results of the models were evaluated via correlations, dispersion coefficients and Alberg diagrams. Abdi et al (2009) used probabilistic model using Bayesian nets to predict change impact in object-oriented systems. By assigning probabilities to network nodes a model was built. For studying the relation of software attributes and impact of change, data of a real system was used. By executing various scenarios, research analyzed coupling as a good predictor of change. Researchers used various complex technologies and models for prediction of change prone classes. All these models required a lot of time for evaluation of change prone classes. Compared to this our prediction model is simpler and requires less time for prediction.

Wilkie and Kitchenham (2000) determined number of classes involved in a change-ripple. Research also analyzed the effect of CBO values and public function. Results show that high CBO values and high public function count values exhibit more ripple effects. Classes with large public and private member functions participate more often in change ripples. Bacchelli et al (2010) used the tool infusion, to extract FAMIX-compliant object-oriented models. Using this model, they computed a catalog of object oriented features proposed by Chidamber and Kemerer. Code development was analyzed using change metrics. For using the change metrics in the experiments, source code was linked with entities, i.e., classes. Bergenti and Poggi (2000) developed an approach wherein, UML diagrams were analyzed to suggest changes to the software design which would cause design patterns to occur. Their research included automated finding of design patterns. Input to the tool used was UML design (class and collaboration) diagrams in XMI (XML Metadata Interchange) format. Researcher's analyzed association amongst object-oriented metrics and change prone classes. But, outcomes for software in real world was not presented in their research.

Malhotra and Khanna (2018) proposed to use metrics based on evolution along with metrics evaluated from object- oriented concepts. Finding change prone classes based upon these two factors would lead to improved results. The study was analyzed using two android software Contacts & Gallery2. Khiaty et al. (2017) proposed to use group based method, evolution metrics and object-oriented metrics to find change prone classes. The research suggested that an improvement of 10% increases in accuracy using above mentioned methods.

Godara et al. (2018) used machine learning techniques to evaluate the performance of change prediction model. Various dynamic measures were evaluated to find the change prone classes. Proposed model was evaluated on open source software to check the accuracy of the model.

Kyriakakis et al. (2019) defines the uses of PHP, author states that various flexible program can be made using dynamic features of PHP. And it provides several patterns, programs built using such patterns provide additional benefit that these are less prone to changes.

Overall, all the previous research is focused mainly on application of static object-oriented attributes. However, dynamic features are ignored. If dynamic features are used in the change prediction model it can lead to more efficient model. Our research tries to fill all the above mentioned gaps, and incorporates both static and dynamic features (class dependency and frequency) for prediction of change prone classes in an object oriented software. Our proposed prediction method is simpler and can be applied in real world for building efficient object oriented software. Further, it can be used for effectively allocating the manpower resources such that change prone classes are more focused and can lead to reduction in maintenance and testing efforts.

RELATIONSHIP BETWEEN CHANGE PRONENESS AND OBJECT ORIENTED METRICS

This section, presents association between object oriented features and change prone classes. To explore this relationship dependent and independent variables are defined in this study.

Independent Variables

Various aspects of a software process can be enumerated using object oriented metrics. Malhotra and Chug (2013) stated a single metric is not sufficient to study all the aspects of software. A number of metrics or their combination is required to completely understand the software. Various object oriented metrics (i.e. independent variables) are summarized here in Table 1.

Table 1. Object Oriented metrics for change proneness prediction

S.No	Metrics	Definition	Dimension
1.	LOC (Line of code) • No: of Lines • SLOC (Source line of code) • BLOC (Blank line of code) • Comment line • LDC (Lines with Declarative Code) • LEC(Lines with Executable Code) • Statement Count	• count of all lines • count of lines with source code • count of blank lines • count of lines with Comment • count of lines with declarative source code • count of lines that will be executed • count of total declarative and executable code	Size
2.	Methods • No: of Methods • No: of local methods • No: of private methods • No: of public methods • No: of instance method	• count of methods in a class • count of methods not inherited • count of local/not inherited methods • count of public methods • object created using class. It contains instance method	Size
3.	No: of children	count of immediate subclasses	Inheritance
4.	No: of attributes per class	count of total no: of variables of a class	Size
5.	No: of instance variable	count of variables contained by object	Inheritance
6.	Response for class	It shows interaction of class methods with other methods	Coupling
7.	Coupling between objects	Represents the no: of other types of classes a class is coupled to	Coupling
8.	DIP(Depth of Inheritance)	Count of nodes from parent node to root node.	Inheritance
9.	Lack of Cohesion	Percentage of methods in the class using a particular data field.	Cohesion
10.	WMC(Weighted methods per class)	Count of complexities of all methods.	Size
11.	Interface ■ No: of methods ■ Arguments(i) ■ No: of instance method ■ APP(i)	■ count of methods declared in interface. ■ count of arguments of declared methods in interface(i) ■ No: of instance method ■ Measure of mean size of method declared. App(i)=Arguments/No: of methods(i)	Size
12.	Coupling between Methods (CBM)	It is a measure of new/redefined methods to which all the inherited methods are coupled.	Coupling
13.	Number of Object/Memory Allocation (NOMA)	It is a measure of the total number of statements that allocate new objects or memories in a class.	Size
14.	Average Method Complexity(AMC)	It is average method size of each class. It does not count virtual and inherited methods.	Size

Various characteristics of software that are included in Table 1 comprises of coupling, inheritance, size, cohesion, etc. For calculating all these metrics Understand for Java (UFJ) software is used.

Apart from all these metrics other metrics such as Implementation Period for class, class dependency, log information, frequency and popularity are also proposed in this research for finding change prone classes.

Dependent Variables

With the increase in utility of software, software requires many modifications and upgradations. Finding change prone classes lead to better enhancements in any software with a minimal cost. This research aims to explore the association amongst different object oriented features and change prone attributes. Possibility of occurrence of change in software is mentioned as change proneness. Change can be in relation to addition, deletion or modification of source line of code (SLOC). Change proneness is used as dependent variable in this study.

EMPIRICAL DATA COLLECTION

This section explains the data collection methods and sources that are used in this study. Two open source software (developed using Java language) from warehouse (www.sourceforge.net) are analyzed. Changes in software are analyzed by calculating the number of changes in different versions of same software.

Firstly, Open clinic software is analyzed, which is open source incorporating management of hospital enclosing management of organization, financial, medical lab etc. The two stable versions of open clinic software analyzed in this study are v3 and v4. Version 3 was released on September 17, 2010 and consists of 237 classes and version 4 was released on May 28, 2011 and consists of 254 classes. Another software that is analyzed is open hospital software, which supports management and hospital activities. Its two stable versions that were evaluated are v1.7.2 and v1.7.3. Version 1.7.2 was released on May 21, 2013 and consists of 349 classes and version 1.7.3 was released on September 13, 2014 and consists of 363 classes. Table 2 exhibits the details of software used in this study such as various version, language used, total LOC, total no. of common classes, total classes in which change encountered, and the classes without change.

Table 2 exhibits the details of software used in this study such as various version, language used, total LOC, total no. of common classes, total classes in which change encountered, and the classes without change.

Table 2. Data set used

Name	Version1	Version2	P/L used	Total LOC	Total classes	Classes with change	Classes without change
Open Clinic Software	3	4	Java	44,211	248	107	141
Open Hospital Software	1.7.2	1.7.3	Java	59,575	356	20	336

Object oriented metrics were collected between different versions of software using following steps:

Object Oriented Metrics Collection

With the help of http://sourceforge.net source code is collected for both versions of software. All the object oriented metrics stated above in table I are collected using Understand for Java(UFJ)tool for previous version of software (Open Clinic Software v3, Open Hospital Software1.7.2). It is static code analysis tool. As the research is predicting change in object oriented classes, accordingly metrics for only these classes are considered. In this research, metrics for classes are generated using UFJ tool, although metrics for methods and files can also be generated with the help of this tool. As we are predicting change prone classes we have taken metrics for classes only.

Common Classes' Collection

Here, common classes from both versions (previous and new) are collected. Changes in these classes were taken into consideration for both the versions of the software. Similar approach is used by (Zhou and Leung, 2009) also.

Classes' Comparison

After step 2, common classes that were collected are compared line by line using DiffMerge Software. It has been developed by a software company named SourceGear. By comparing, each class is categorized as a change prone class and non-change prone class. Change in a class is considered if:

- There is addition, deletion, or modification in SLOC of class in the newer version of software.
- Addition, deletion or modification in comment is not considered as change.
- Addition or deletion of blank line does not affect change.
- Reordering of lines does not affect the change.
- Change in class definition affects the change.

Data Point Collection

Step 3 and step 1 were used to generate data points. In Open Clinic Software 248 classes are present in both the versions. Out of total, 107 classes exhibited change (which constitutes 43% of total classes) and 141 classes did not change. In Open Hospital Software, 152 classes exhibited change (which constitutes almost 42% of total classes) and 204 classes did not change.

Using source code of both the versions obtained from http://sourceforge.net_data statistics for both the OpenClinic software and OpenHospital software are analyzed as shown in Table 3 and Table 4.

Using various statistics given in Table 3 and Table 4 data set characteristics for OpenClinic software and OpenHospital software were analyzed. The statistics evaluated in this study include minimum, maximum, mean, median, and standard deviation for every object oriented metrics. All these statistics are related to metrics present in classes. Minimum values relate to the class having minimum value of a particular metrics. And maximum relates to the class having maximum value of a particular metrics. Observations show software systems that have less number of children (NOC) and least value of inheritance results in low values of NOC metric and DIT metric. For example, mean value for NOC metric for (OpenClinic Software is 0.49 and OpenHospital software is 0.43) and the DIT metric is (OpenClinic,

3.03 and OpenHospital, 2.01). LCOM measure is high for the software systems. It counts for method invocation within a class. Its higher value suggests larger number of methods are invoked in a class. Similar approach is followed in Briand et al. (2000) and Cartwright & Shepperd (2000).

Table 3. Statistics for OpenClinic software

Metrics	Min.	Max.	Mean	Mid.	SD
NL	4	2032	233.97	52	2007.54
SLOC	4	4928	227.3	110	310.5
BLOC	0	178	23.32	7	232.7
LC	0	257	28.81	4	257.5
LDC	2	245	25.73	9	249.6
LEC	0	989	82.72	18	632.79
SC	2	1,109	110.38	28	931.91
NOM	0	18	.87	0	16.62
NLM	0	75	14.21	3	117.23
NPRM	0	12	0.68	0	15.9
NPM	0	62	10.9	3	99.97
NIM	0	68	11.89	3	105.78
NOC	0	10	0.49	0	15.59
NOA	0	22	1.98	1	21.48
NIV	0	115	8.25	2	71.09
RFC	0	117	23.2	5	185.68
CBO	0	27	6.82	2	57.8
DIT	1	4	3.03	2	30.03
LCOM	0	102	89.9	49.8	728.23
WMC	0	155	25.69	6	211.65
CBM	0	19	4.8	2	48.9

Table 4. Statistics for OpenHospital software

Metrics	Min.	Max.	Mean	Mid.	SD
NL	2	2050	203.97	52	2027.54
SLOC	4	6759	177.5	98	564.3
BLOC	0	213	33.12	8	256.7
LC	0	263	32.11	6	265.5
LDC	1	273	35.73	9	252.6
LEC	0	1081	87.12	34	752.79
SC	1	1,217	119.88	56	987.91
NOM	0	54	.67	0	19.82
NLM	0	85	11.61	4	127.53
NPRM	0	22	0.78	0	18.8
NPM	0	69	8.5	3	102.80
NIM	0	69	11.99	3	106.18
NOC	0	7	0.43	0	12.09
NOA	0	42	0.88	1	18.28
NIV	0	119	8.25	2	72.10
RFC	2	186	17.4	3	179.08
CBO	0	20	5.02	1	43.8
DIT	1	3	2.01	2	50.03
LCOM	0	100	79.3	51.2	778.23
WMC	1	215	15.69	5	232.65
CBM	0	2	5.8	2	54.9

Apart from these metrics we propose some other metrics such as Implementation Period, run time information (i.e. log information), class dependency, frequency and popularity are also proposed in this research work, which can be utilized effectively in predicting change prone classes.

- **Implementation Period:** Implementation Period of a class is directly related to size of the class. The research proposes to use this feature for predicting change prone classes.

For calculating the Implementation Period, Eclipse Test and Performance Tools Platform (TPTP) profiling tool is used. Research uses Eclipse SDK version 3.6.2. Size can be estimated from the Implementation Period of product, it can be in relation to classes, methods etc. Using TPTP the Implementation Period can be generated, it creates an XML report of the time. TPTP gives three types of Implementation Period:

Base Time: It is the total time taken by methods to execute. Implementation Period of other methods called from this method is excluded from base time.

$$T_{bt} = T_{me} - T_{oe} \tag{1}$$

where, T_{bt} =Implementation Period of message in seconds and T_{oe} = time taken by other methods to execute

Average base time: It is the average base time needed for execution of method once. It is denoted as T_{abt}.

Cumulative base time: It is the time required by methods to execute. However, it also takes into account Implementation Period of methods that are called from this method.

$$T_{cbt} = T_{me} - T_{oe} \tag{2}$$

Calls: It can be defined as the count of times a method is invoked.

The Implementation Period analysis tool records all data that is related to the count of method calls and their Implementation Period. The gathered data can be viewed in several different ways:

Execution Statistics: These statistics provide information about the Implementation Period of each method that has been called as well as the number of calls. Additionally, it also shows the method invocation details, i.e. which method is invoked by other methods and how often it is invoked.

Execution Flow: It visualize the thread based execution flow of the observed application. This view contains a time scale diagram.

UML Interactions: This view shows an UML based view of the execution flow and method invocations. The UML diagram can either be based on class or thread interactions.

Table 5. Implementation Period

Classes	Implementation Period
a11	0.008
a12	0.001
a13	0.001
a20	0.0
Eight	0.001
Fifth	0.01

Implementation Period for some of the classes is given in Table 5, evaluated using eclipse TPTP tool. Higher value of Implementation Period indicates higher probability of change proneness of a class.

Log Information

Software metrics can be categorized as static and dynamic. Metrics which are applied to source code are static metrics and metrics which are obtained during run time are dynamic metrics. Earlier Researchers and Practitioners have focused significantly on static metrics; however dynamic metrics have been ignored up to a significant level. But this metrics needs more concentration as it gives the actual information because it is collected during run time. In this research we emphasize on the concept whether a method which is executed imports or exports other object's method.

Table 6. Log information

Classes	Log information
a11	3
a12	5
a13	7
a20	5
Eight	3
Fifth	11

At runtime, within considered scope we can count the total number of messages which are sent and received by objects. For evaluating log information we consider which methods are executed during runtime and the count of times each method is run. Table 6 gives log information for our application.

Class Dependency

Class Dependency can be used as one of the significant attributes for predicting the change proneness in software. If a class is affected by change, it will affect another class also. This can be evaluated by finding dependencies between classes. UML2.0 class diagrams (CD) and sequence diagrams (SD) are used for evaluating class dependency. Similar approach has been used in research by Han et al. (2008).

For measuring the class dependency from the source code, UML class diagrams and sequence diagrams are generated from the code. Class dependency can be measured using the below stated approach:

- Build separate object dependency model
- Build complete system dependency model
- Create Class Route table
- Find weighted sum of routes
- Evaluate the Dependency for each class

Build Separate Object Dependency Model

Using SD and CD of Unified Modeling Language 2.0, separate Object Dependency model can be constructed.

For a SD, an Object Dependency model consists of 2-tuple (O,M), where,

O- denotes every object in SD.

M- denotes message passed amongst objects.

Message $m \in M$ consists of below mentioned attributes:

$m_D \in O$ - Message dispatched by source object

$m_A \in O$ - Message arrived at Receiver object where $m_D \neq m_A$

m_T - Message title

$m_p \in M$ - Parent message if present where, $m_p \neq M$. If parent message is not applicable, then it is the originating message and is represented as "-"

$m_{LR} \in O$- Likelihood rate of execution of message in SD such that $0 \leq m_{LR} \leq 1$.

$m_{PR} \in O$- Projected rate of execution of message in SD such that $0 \leq m_{PR} \leq 1$.

Build Complete System Dependency Model

For finding the class dependency for the complete system, dependency values of objects are combined into a single system dependency model.

Create Class Route Table (CRT)

For creating the class route table, the paths between source and destination object are traversed. These paths become input to CRT. Route is evaluated from the traversed path of incoming message of destination to outgoing message of source. Messages encountered during traversal are added to CRT. In case there is a direct dependency between source and destination, at that time the title of message incoming to destination is same as the message departing from source. In other words, in direct class dependency only a single message is counted in CRT. However, in case of indirect dependency outgoing message of source can be traversed with the help of parent message from the destination to source traversed in backward direction.

Find Weighted Amount of Routes

Weighted amount of routes for every pair of source class C_S and destination class C_D can be evaluated from CRT using below mentioned equation (3).

$$Weighted\,amount\,of\,routes(C_S, C_D) = \sum \frac{1}{N} \times F_{LR} \times F_{PR} \qquad (3)$$

where,

N - count of messages in CRT

F_{LR} - Likelihood rate of execution of message in CRT

F_{PR} - Projected rate of execution of first message in CRT

Calculate Class Dependency

The value of class dependency for any class, for instance C_i can be evaluated by summing the pair of corresponding classes (C_i, C_j) as shown in equation 4.

$$CD(C_i) = \sum_{1 \le i,j \le n} Weighted \quad sum \quad of \quad Routes(C_i, C_j) \tag{4}$$

Table 7 shows class dependency values of some of the classes using above method. Higher values of dependency indicate higher probability of changes in a class.

Table 7. Class Dependency values

Classes	Class Dependency
a11	2.690476
a12	0.896825
a13	2.690476
a20	0.309523
Eight	0.246031
Fifth	0.198412

Frequency

For evaluating the frequency feature, frequent item set mining method is used in this research. Frequency can be defined as the number of times a method is called by another method. A software consists of *n* number of functions, which can be called by other functions. Since a class has many methods, it is likely to happen some methods are frequently called by others, while others are not called. Because of this frequency attribute can be used as one of the main attribute for predicting change prone classes. For finding this attribute of how frequently a method is called, rules for method calls are generated.

In data mining, frequent sets play a vital role. It can be used to find patterns from databases such as association rules. The most important problem that can be tackled using frequent item set is the mining of association rules. Various item sets, and their characteristics can be identified using frequent item set mining. In data mining, transaction can be defined as set of instances, wherein each class is referred to as item in each method call. In this research, calling of methods by various classes is referred to as instance. And every class is referred to as item.

Frequent item set mining algorithm finds common classes for a method called. Classes which have minimum support are selected. Minimum support states the minimum no: of intervals the calling of method occurs in the common set of classes. Further classes are categorized as {1-term grouping, 2-term grouping... (n-1)-term grouping} based on method call. For example, if classes are {m, n, o}, then 1-term groupings are {m}, {n}, {o} and the 2-term groupings is {m, n}, {n, o}, {m, o} obtained from common set. Similarly, based upon the size of the classes set, the groupings are used accordingly by frequent item set mining algorithm. Table 8 shows rules generated using frequent item set mining algorithm.

Association rules are generated after finding frequent item sets. Association rules are conditional statements such as if/then statements which can be used to uncover relationships between disparate data.

Data found in item is known as antecedent. Item found in combination with antecedent is known as consequent. For identifying significant relationships association rules are created using if/ then patterns. Support can be defined as number of times an item appears in database. Confidence can be defined as count of times if/then statements have been found to be true.

After the identification of a set of frequent item sets, association rules are produced. Association rules are conditional statements such as if/then statements which can be used to uncover relationships between disparate data and information repository. An association rule consists of two parts, i.e. Antecedent and consequent. Data found in item is known as antecedent. Item found in combination with antecedent is known as consequent. For identifying significant relationships association rules are created using if/ then patterns. Support can be defined number of times an item appears in database. Confidence can be defined as number of times if/then statements have been found to be true.

Table 8. Rules generated for the method calls using frequent item set mining algorithm.

Classes	Two Length Combination	Two length Rule above threshold value	Three length rule above threshold value
a112 a111 a113 thirddisp print1 fourthdisplay	[a112, a111] [a112, a113] [a111, a113] [a112, print1] [a112, fourthdisplay] [a111, thirddisp] [thirddisp, print1] [thirddisp, fourthdisplay]	[a112, a111] [a112, a113] [a111, a113] [thirddisp, print1] [thirddisp, fourthdisplay]	[a112, a111, a113] [a112, a113, a111] [a111, a113, a112]

Till now all the change prediction models have considered the metrics explained in Table 1. This chapter contributes some more attributes (time, class dependency, frequency) which can be used to predict change prone classes. However, in order to develop an effective prediction model, there is a need to minimize the dimensions of input set. This was done by finding a subset of independent variables that were significant in predicting the dependent variable and change prone classes. Artificial Bee Colony algorithm (ABC) as shown in Figure1 is used for reducing the number of input variables.

Table 9. Optimized Rules using ABC

Optimized Rules
[thirddisp, print1] [print1, thirddisp] [thirddisp, fourthdisplay] [fourthdisplay, thirddisp] [a112, a111, a113] [a111, a113, a112] [a113, a112, a111] [a112, a113, a111] [a113, a111, a112]

Figure 1. Flowchart for ABC Algorithm

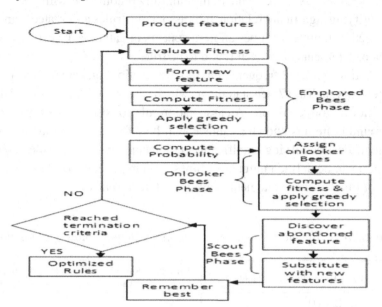

Table 9 gives a set of optimized rules which have been generated using ABC algorithm. Using these optimized rules, frequency of how many times a method is called is evaluated. Higher value of frequency attributes indicates higher chances of change to occur. Frequency, is:

$$F = \frac{No:of \ times \ method \ occurs \ in \ input}{Number \ of \ values} \tag{5}$$

Using the above equation 5, values of frequency attribute can be obtained which was optimized using ABC algorithm. Table 10 gives the generated values for this metric.

Table 10. Frequency

Classes	Frequency
a11	7.631578
a12	5.000000
a13	7.631578
a20	2.631578
Eight	0.315789
Fifth	0.105263

Popularity

This metrics is obtained from the frequency metrics, it indicates how popular a method is in terms of calling and being called. It can be evaluated with the help of equation 6.

$$Popularity = F_1 + F_2 \tag{6}$$

where,

$$F_2 = \frac{\left(M_1\right) \cdot \left(M_2\right)}{Total\ Number\ of\ methods}$$

M_1- count of intervals a method is called be various methods
M_2- count of intervals a method calls various methods

EXPERIMENTAL FRAMEWORK

In this section firstly we describe the values obtained for various metrics and secondly we briefly describe the methods and techniques used for evaluating our change prediction model.

For effectively predicting change prone class, apart from existing change object oriented features other features such as Implementation Period, class dependency and frequency are also evaluated in this chapter.

For calculating the Implementation Period, Eclipse TPTP tool is used wherein, Eclipse SDK version 3.6.2 is used. Values generated for methods is given in Figure 2.

Figure 2. Implementation Period generated using Eclipse TPTP profile tool

Package	<	Base Time (seconds)	Average Base Time (seconds)	Cumulative Time (seco...	Calls
⊿ ⊕ code	◇	9.990104	0.014933	10.189101	669
▷ ⊖ Newfirst	◇	6.091768	3.045884	6.091768	2
▷ ⊖ OBDM	◇	2.239859	0.003441	2.393795	651
▷ ⊖ ExeTime	◇	1.088570	1.088570	1.088570	1
▷ ⊖ First	◇	0.349820	0.058303	10.189101	6
▷ ⊖ Table	◇	0.153935	0.051312	0.153935	3
▷ ⊖ Frequent	◇	0.033917	0.011306	6.125685	3
▷ ⊖ Findifvalue	◇	0.032234	0.010745	0.032234	3
⊿ ⊕ Test	◇	0.198998	0.000287	10.142756	694
▷ ⊖ Fourth	◇	0.041822	0.001307	0.048686	32
▷ ⊖ Third	◇	0.039354	0.004919	0.046445	8
▷ ⊖ First1	◇	0.030868	0.003087	10.142756	10
▷ ⊖ Second	◇	0.021149	0.021149	0.169005	1
▷ ⊖ a17	◇	0.011022	0.003674	0.013611	3
▷ ⊖ a16	◇	0.010882	0.003627	0.024553	3
▷ ⊖ Writer	◇	0.010811	0.000031	0.010811	347
▷ ⊖ a14	◇	0.006255	0.002085	0.034157	3
▷ ⊖ a13	◇	0.005041	0.001680	0.039251	3
▷ ⊖ a12	◇	0.003724	0.001241	0.043021	3

Using UML2.0 sequence and class diagrams, class dependency values are generated as shown in Figure 3. Dependency indicates if a class is affected by change how it will affect other class.

Count of times how frequently a method is called by other method is defined as frequency. Frequency values are generated as shown in Figure 4.

Figure 3. Dependency values generated using Sequence and class diagrams

Figure 4. Frequency values evaluated using optimized rules

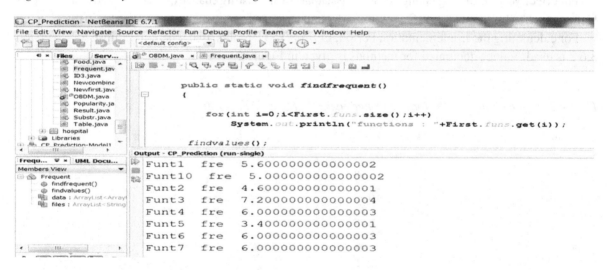

For evaluating and comparing the proposed change prediction model we have used the multivariate logistic regression method.

Statistical Logistic Regression Method

This method is used when combination of independent variables contributes in prediction of dependent variable. Complete description is given by Hosmer & Lemeshow (2004) Menard (2002). Logistic regression analysis is classified into: univariate and multivariate logistic regression analysis. Univariate predicts association amongst the two variables i.e. dependent and independent and discovers the importance of their relationship. Conversely, multivariate regression is used for building prediction model for the identification of change prone class. This type of analysis results in finding important metrics. For identifying significant metrics two types of selection methods are used:(i) Forward selection: In this type of selection, a single metric is analyzed at every step. (ii) Backward selection: In this type all the metrics are taken initially and eliminated one after the other till stopping condition is not met.

Mathematically it can be expressed as:

$$prob\left(X_1, X_2, X_3, \ldots\ldots X_N\right) = \frac{exp^{f(x)}}{1 + exp^{f(x)}} \tag{7}$$

where,

$$f(x) = C_0 + C_1 X_1 + C_2 X_2 + \ldots + C_N X_N$$

where the variable X denotes the independent variables and prob is the probability of change proneness of a class.

Odds ratio (OR): It defines the ratio of the likelihood that the event will be caused to the probability event will not be caused. Event here refers to the occurrence of change in the latest version Hosmer & Lemeshow (2004). It is represented by exp (C_i).

Maximum Likelihood Estimation: Statistical method predicts model's coefficients. It predicts the coefficients which support the possibility functions and contribute in making the log value as high as possible. Larger value indicates the improved effect of the independent variable on the expected result variable.

Statistical significance(Sig.): All (C_i) i.e. coefficients have significant level. Higher value of this attribute indicates, independent metrics have lesser impact in estimating change prone classes. We have considered threshold value of 0.7.

Model Development Procedures

For data classification, implementation of Artificial Bee Colony algorithm was done using Java language with WEKA tool and LibSVM. We have used WEKA tool for the validation of our prediction model. This tool is used with association rules, machine learning techniques, classification and for preprocessing of data.

For evaluating the classification process's precision and correctness, we have used a tenfold cross validation. Here we have divided the data set into 10 equally partitions (folds), wherein one partition is consumed for testing part and rest all others are used for training purposes. The process was repeated 10 times, such that every time one of the part became test data. Average of 10 results produced an accuracy of estimation.

For evaluating the performance of the prediction model we have used following methods:

1. **Sensitivity & Specificity:** For characterizing the accuracy of the prediction model we have used sensitivity and specificity. Sensitivity is defined as the accuracy by which the percentage of classes are correctly identified to be change prone class amongst all the classes which are actually change

prone. And specificity is defined as the accuracy by which the percentage of non-change prone classes are correctly identified.

2. **Receiver Operating Characteristics (ROC) Curve:** It is an essential tool for analytic test evaluation. Here sensitivity i.e. (true positive rate) is plotted against specificity i.e. (false positive rate) at different cut off points. Accuracy of prediction model is achieved by selecting cut off point that has higher sensitivity and specificity as suggested by Emam et al. (1999)

RESULT ANALYSIS

This section shows validation results for our model using Open Clinic Software and Open Hospital Software. Using tenfold cross validation, we have illustrated the results. The results can be compared with other prediction models developed using various techniques given by Malhotra and Jangra (2015) which reveals the proposed model gives better results.

Table 11. Statistics for LR multivariate analysis of OpenClinic software

Metrics	B	SE	Sig.	OR
B.D.	0.021	0.21	0.001	1.212
Freq.	0.351	0.25	0.000	1.311
Pop.	0.121	0.11	0.003	0.501
Exec. Time	0.011	0.05	0.025	0.312
T.E.	0.001	0.15	0.031	0.112

Table 12. Statistics for LR multivariate analysis of OpenHospital software

Metrics	B	SE	Sig.	OR
B.D.	0.052	0.31	0.000	1.321
Freq.	0.231	0.021	0.000	1.512
Pop.	0.122	0.032	0.000	1.311
Exec. Time	0.001	0.254	0.010	0.517
T.E.	-0.02	0.212	0.010	0.252

Table 11 and Table 12 shows results for statistics obtained from OpenClinic Software and OpenHospital software using LR multivariate technique. We have obtained the statistics B(coefficient), SE (Standard error), Sig. (Significance) and OR (Odds ratio) for our metrics which are B.D. (Behavioral Dependency), Freq.(Frequency), Pop.(Popularity), Exec. Time(Implementation Period), T.E.(Log information) using LR multivariate technique. Values of B, SE, Sig. and OR indicates behavioral dependency and frequency have a significant effect in predicting change.

Table 13. Validation results for OpenClinic software

Method	Specificity	Sensitivity	Cut Off Point	AUC
LR proposed model	69.7	70.7	0.012	0.750
	80.2	82.4	0.545	0.925

Table 14. Validation results for OpenHospital software

Method	Specificity	Sensitivity	Cut Off Point	AUC
LR proposed model	68.2	68.2	0.245	0.725
	79.8	81.2	0.564	0.915

Table 13 and Table 14 shows validation results obtained using LR technique and our proposed model which is based on ID3 and ABC (Artificial Bee Colony Algorithm). Values of specificity (69.7) and sensitivity (70.7) for LR technique of OpenClinic software has AUC (0.750) which is less than AUC (0.925) obtained by our prediction model. Similarly, AUC obtained for OpenHospital Software using LR method is 0.725 and AUC obtained by our prediction model is 0.915. The above values indicate that proposed prediction model gives better values as compared to LR multivariate technique.

EXPERIMENTAL ANALYSIS II

This section shows the Experimental Analysis using the proposed approach. Open source software Neuroph2.9.2 and Neuroph2.6 is used to find the accuracy of change prediction model. K-Means clustering,

K-Means Clustering

K-Means clustering is applied for clustering data sets. The data set is split into k disjoint clusters, where the value of k is constant. The algorithm has two steps. In the first step, k centroids are defined one for each cluster. And in the second step, the data points are linked to the nearest centroid.

K-Means Clustering for Neuroph2.9.2 and Neuroph2.6

The process of k-Means clustering system applied to dataset of Neuroph2.9.2 and Neuroph2.6 is given as follows: SimpleKMeans is performed with initial value set as 0, maximum candidates is 100 and number of iterations considered as 2. Sum of squared errors within cluster is 0.0. Neuroph2.9.2 and Neuroph2.6 are selected as two clusters wherein, number of instances is 2 and number of attributes considered are 30 Object-Oriented metrics (CBO, NOCH, NOA, NIV, DIT, NOMMIN, NOMMAX, NIM, NLM, RFC, NOSM, NPRM, NPROM, NPM, LCOM, NC, NLSC, NOI, NCM, RCM, NMI, NIMI, NEMI, NCCM, NCMI, NCI, NOC, TI, ITI, ETI). Test mode is evaluation on training data and clustering model is full training set.

Cluster 0: Neuroph2.9.2 366, 114, 4928, 341, 17, 1, 97, 2148, 3818, 559, 233, 167, 69, 1679, 91, 366, 42295, 2540, 2864, 17, 2864, 236, 1912, 175, 116, 480, 266, 2864, 236, 1912
Cluster 1: Neuroph2.6 197, 94, 1934, 188, 15, 1, 72, 1157, 1736, 310, 110, 57, 58, 932, 10, 187, 21430, 1435, 1302, 15, 1302, 115, 1042, 83, 55, 291, 161, 1302, 115, 1042

The missing values in the data set are globally replaced with Mean/mode. Final cluster centroids output is given in table.

The values of metrics of two versions of Neuroph software is given in Table 15. The mean of cluster 1 and 0 for all metrics are provided. For example, after clustering the mean of the value for NOC metric is 213.5 ((266+ 161)/2).

Table 15. Clustering output of Neuroph software

Attribute	full data	cluster 0	cluster 1
	2	1	1
Software	Neuroph2.9.2	Neuroph2.6	Neuroph2.6
CBO	281.5	366	197
NOCH	104	114	94
NOA	3431	4928	1934
NIV	264.5	341	188
DIT	16	17	15
NOMMIN	1	1	1
NOMMAX	84.5	97	72
NIM	1652.5	2148	1157
NLM	2777	3818	1736
RFC	434.5	559	310
NOSM	171.5	233	110
NPRM	112	167	57
NPROM	63.5	69	58
NPM	1305.5	1679	932
LCOM	50.5	91	10
NC	276.5	366	187
NLSC	31862.5	42295	21430
NOI	1987.5	2540	1435
NCM	2083	2864	1302
RCM	16	17	15
NMI	2083	2864	1302
NIMI	175.5	236	115
NEMI	1477	1912	1042
NCCM	129	175	83
NCMI	85.5	116	55
NCI	385.5	480	291
NOC	213.5	266	161
TI	2083	2864	1302
ITI	175.5	236	115
ETI	1477	1912	1042

Naïve Bayes

This is a well-established Bayesian method that is mainly expressed for executing classification tasks. When the independent variables are assumed as statistically independent, Naïve Bayes model provides more effective classification tools which are easy for usage and interpretation. Naïve Bayes is mostly suitable for large number of independent variables. Due to these reasons, Naïve Bayes performs better than other sophisticated classification techniques. Results of Naïve Bayes classification for all the three software's is evaluated in this section.

Table 16. Naïve Bayes classifier for Neuroph2.6 and Neuroph2.9.2

Metrics	Mean		Standard Deviation		Weighted Sum		Precision	
Software	Neuroph 2.6	Neuroph 2.9.2	Neuroph 2.6	Neuroph 2.9.2	Neuroph 2.6	Neuroph 2.9.2	Neuroph 2.6	Neuroph 2.9.2
CBO	169	338	28.1667	28.1667	1	1	169	169
NOCH	100	120	3.3333	3.3333	1	1	20	20
NOA	2994	5988	499	499	1	1	2994	2994
NIV	153	306	25.5	25.5	1	1	153	153
DIT	16	16	0.3333	0.3333	1	1	2	2
NOMMIN	1	1	0.0017	0.0017	1	1	0.01	0.01
NOMMAX	75	100	4.1667	4.1667	1	1	25	25
NIM	991	1982	165.1667	165.1667	1	1	991	991
NLM	2082	4164	347	347	1	1	2082	2082
RFC	249	498	41.5	41.5	1	1	249	249
NOSM	123	246	20.5	20.5	1	1	123	123
NPRM	110	220	18.3333	18.3333	1	1	110	110
NPROM	55	66	1.8333	1.8333	1	1	11	11
NPM	747	1494	124.5	124.5	1	1	747	747
LCOM	0	81	13.5	13.5	1	1	81	81
NC	179	358	29.8333	29.8333	1	1	179	179
NLSC	20865	41730	3477.5	3477.5	1	1	20865	20865
NOI	1105	2210	184.1667	184.1667	1	1	1105	1105
NCM	1562	3124	260.3333	260.3333	1	1	1562	1562
RCM	16	16	0.3333	0.3333	1	1	2	2
NMI	1562	3124	260.3333	260.3333	1	1	1562	1562
NIMI	121	242	20.1667	20.1667	1	1	121	121
NEMI	870	1740	145	145	1	1	870	870
NCCM	92	184	15.3333	15.3333	1	1	92	92
NCMI	61	122	10.1667	10.1667	1	1	61	61
NCI	378	567	31.5	31.5	1	1	189	189
NOC	210	315	17.5	17.5	1	1	105	105
TI	1562	3124	260.3333	260.3333	1	1	1562	1562
ITI	121	242	20.1667	20.1667	1	1	121	121
ETI	870	1740	145	145	1	1	870	870

Naïve Bayes Classifier Output for Neuroph2.6 and Neuroph2.9.2

The proposed system used Naïve Bayes classifier with the number of Instances equal to 2 and the attributes considered as 30.

The Mean, standard deviation, weight sum and precision of 30 attributes of Neuroph2.6 and Neuroph2.9.2 are given in Table 16. Confusion Matrix is given as follows:

a b is classified as
1 0 | a = Neuroph2.6
0 1 | b = Neuroph2.9.2
Following values are obtained from the confusion matrix:

TP is 1, TN is 1, FP is 0 and FN is 0.

Table 17. Naïve Bayes classifier output for Neuroph2.6 and Neuroph2.9.2

		Value	Percentage
Correctly Classified Instances		2	100%
Incorrectly Classified Instances		0	0%
Kappa statistic		1	
Mean absolute error		0	
Root Mean squared error		0	
Relative absolute error			0.00%
Root relative squared error			0.00%
Total Number of Instances		2	

TP Rate	FP Rate	Precision	Recall	F-Measure	MCC	ROC Area	Area class
1	0	1	1	1	1	1	Neuroph2.6
1	0	1	1	1	1	1	Neuroph2.9.2

After clustering, classification is done for evaluating the data sets. Here the Naïve Bayesian classifier is applied for classification of software chosen as data sets. The metrics after classification procedure is given in Table 17 for the two versions of Neuroph software. The TP Rate, FP rate, precision, recall F-measure, MCC, ROC area and PRC area are found to be 1,0, 1,1, 1,1 for Neuroph software.

Sensitivity = $TP/(TP+FN) = 1/(1+0) = 1$
Specificity = $TN/(TN+FP) = 1/(1+0) = 1$
Accuracy = $(TP+TN)/(TP+TN+FP+FN) = (1+1)/(1+1+0+0) = 1$
Precision = $TP/TP+FP = 1/(1+0) = 1$
Recall = $TP/(TP+FN) = 1/(1+0) = 1$
F-Measure = $2*precision*recall/(precision+recall) = 2*1*1/(1+1) = 1$.

From the above results, it is found that the sensitivity, specificity, recall, precision, accuracy and F-Measure of classification process are found to be 1 which reveals the accuracy of the proposed system.

Table 18. Logistic regression output for Neuroph2.6 and Neuroph2.9.2

Parameter	Even ratios	Odd ratios
CBO	0.9941	-0.0059
NOCH	0.9512	-0.05
NOA	0.9997	-0.0003
NIV	0.9935	-0.0065
DIT	0.6065	-0.5
NOMMAX	0.9608	-0.04
NIM	0.999	-0.001
NLM	0.9995	-0.0005
RFC	0.996	-0.004
NOSM	0.9919	-0.0081
NPRM	0.9131	-0.0091
NPROM	0.9987	-0.0909
NPM	0.9877	-0.0013
LCOM	0.9944	-0.0123
NC	1	-0.0056
NLSC	0.9991	0
NOI	0.9994	-0.0009
NCM	0.6065	-0.0006
RCM	0.9994	-0.5
NMI	0.9918	-0.0006
NIMI	0.9989	-0.0083
NEMI	0.9892	-0.0011
NCCM	0.9837	-0.0109
NCMI	0.9947	-0.0164
NCI	0.9905	-0.0053
NOC	0.9994	-0.0095
TI	0.9918	-0.0006
ITI	0.9989	-0.0083
ETI	0.9989	-0.0011
Intercept		66.4671

Logistic Regression Analysis

Logistic regression processes the relationship between the dependent variable and independent variables by approximating likelihoods by a logistic function, which is the accumulative logistic distribution. Logistic regression is a special type of the general linear model and thus equivalent to linear regression.

Logistic regression is evaluated for all the Object-Oriented metrics to predict the accuracy of their values in two versions of software.

Logistic Regression Value for Neuroph2.6 and Neuroph2.9.2

The Logistic regression value for Neuroph2.6 and Neuroph2.9.2 is given in Table 18.

Table 19. Logistic regression value for Neuroph2.6 and Neuroph2.9.2

					Value			Percentage
Correctly Classified Instances					2			100%
Incorrectly Classified Instances					0			0%
Kappa statistic					1			
Mean absolute error					0			
Root Mean squared error					0			
Relative absolute error								0.001%
Root relative squared error								0.001%
Total Number of Instances								2
	TP Rate	FP Rate	Precision	Recall	F-Measure	MCC	ROC Area	Area class
Weighted average	1	0	1	1	1	1	1	Neuroph2.6
	1	0	1	1	1	1	1	Neuroph2.9.2
	1	0	1	1	1	1	1	

The instances taken hereare the two versions Neuroph 2.6 and Neuroph 2.9.2. From the Table 19, the correctly classified instances are 2 which implies that the classification is performed correctly. The values of incorrect classified instances, mean absolute error, Root Mean squared error are zero. The Relative absolute error and Root relative squared error are found to be 0.001%. The TP Rate, FP Rate, Precision, Recall, F-Measure, MCC, ROC Area are 1, 0, 1, 1, 1, 1 and 1. The weighted average of TP Rate, FP Rate, Precision, Recall, F-Measure, MCC, and ROC Area are 1, 0, 1, 1, 1, 1 and 1. Values obtained of TP Rate, FP Rate, Precision, Recall, F-Measure, MCC, and ROC Area for all the three open source software shows the accuracy of proposed model in terms of Object- Oriented metrics, as all the above used metrics has been evaluated using code analyzer and trace events feature of prediction model

Table 20. Change prone prediction of Neuroph software

S.No	Change prone class	Execution time	Frequency	Popularity
1	BackPropagation	Faster	2	7
2	BenchmarkTask	Faster	1	8
3	Connection	Faster	1	8
4	DelayedNeuron	Faster	1	8
5	Hashtable	Faster	1	8
6	ImageRecognitionHelper	Faster	1	8
7	InputFunction	Faster	1	8
8	InputStreamAdapter	Faster	2	7
9	IterativeLearning	Faster	2	7
10	LMS	Faster	3	6
11	Layer	Faster	2	7
12	LearningRule	Faster	3	6
13	MomentumBackpropagation	Faster	1	8
14	NeuralNetwork	Slow	15	1
15	Neuron	Faster	5	5
16	NeurophException	Faster	3	6
17	Observable	Faster	2	7
18	OutputStreamAdapter	Faster	2	7
19	PerceptronLearning	Faster	1	8
20	PluginBase	Faster	3	6
21	Properties	Faster	1	8
22	RangeRandomizer	Faster	1	8
23	RuntimeException	Faster	1	8
24	SigmoidDeltaRule	Faster	1	8
25	SummingFunction	Medium	8	3
26	SupervisedLearning	Faster	3	6
27	TrainingElement	Faster	1	8
28	TrainingElement	Faster	1	8
29	TrainingSetImport	Faster	1	8
30	TransferFunction	Medium	10	2
31	UnsupervisedHebbianLearning	Medium	6	4
32	UnsupervisedLearning	Faster	2	7
33	Weight	Faster	1	8
34	WeightsFunction	Faster	2	7
35	WeightsRandomizer	Faster	3	6

Change Prone Prediction of Neuroph Software

The change prone class, its execution time, frequency and popularity of two different versions of Neuroph are given in Table 20.

Total number of classes in Neuroph 2.9.2 and Neuroph 2.6 software are 366 and 187. Using the behavioral dependency approach number of classes that are predicted to be behaviorally dependent are 35. After evaluating dependent class, execution time and frequency of each dependent class is evaluated as depicted in Table 20. Further, popularity feature is evaluated which specifies the degree of change proneness of a class.

From the above table, the frequency, execution time and popularity of each dependent class of Neuroph software are obtained. Depending on popularity rank, the change proneness is predicted. For example, the class NeuralNetwork exhibit *slow* execution time and frequency of the methods called in class is 15. So, NeuralNetwork is ranked with popularity 1. It indicates the most sensitive class which is to be given more attention in next release of software. Thus, such type of information is significant to software developers as the NC metrics is significantly reduced to behavioral dependent classes and popularity values provides the rank to change prone classes.

CONCLUSION AND FUTURE WORK

The chapter examines association amongst change prone classes and object oriented features. In addition to existing object oriented attributes the research proposes some new attributes such as Implementation Period of class, run time information of methods, frequency of method call, class dependency and popularity. Higher values of proposed metrics indicate higher is the probability of a class to be changed. For calculating the Implementation Period, Eclipse TPTP profiling tool is used, wherein Eclipse SDK version 3.6.2 is used. Runtime information of methods is used to evaluate the values of log information which is a dynamic metric and gives the accurate values of imported and exported methods. For evaluating the frequency attribute, frequent item set mining algorithm is used. For finding this feature of how frequently a method is called, rules for method calls are generated using association rules. For effectively building the prediction model, dimensions of the input set are reduced using, Artificial Bee Colony algorithm (ABC), which optimizes the rules for finding change prone classes. Further, using source code of Open Hospital application values for proposed metrics were generated. Research evaluated higher values of proposed metrics indicates, higher probability of degree of change prone class. The results were validated using various versions of open source software. For evaluating the performance of the prediction model we used Sensitivity, Specificity and ROC Curve. Higher values of AUC indicate the prediction model gives significant accurate results. And the proposed metrics contribute to predict accurate change prone classes.

For effectively evaluating change proneness in object oriented software, following future directions can be utilized by practitioners and researchers in their research work and studies. As the research is focused on real life software, the usage of commercial data should be increased up to a considerable extent so that real time results can be obtained more effectively. For validating the results, inter project validation can be used in which training set of one project can be used for testing in other similar projects. This would lead to better planning of scarce resources and would help in generating a good quality software. Several studies in literature have used machine learning technique, more machine learning methods can be used for analyzing the performance of change prediction model. A limited work is done using threshold methodology of metrics, the work can be extended by identifying threshold values of all the metrics for change proneness prediction.

REFERENCES

Abdi, M. K., Lounis, H., & Sahraoui, H. (2009, July). Predicting change impact in object-oriented applications with bayesian networks. In *Computer Software and Applications Conference, 2009. COMPSAC'09. 33rd Annual IEEE International* (Vol. 1, pp. 234-239). IEEE. 10.1109/COMPSAC.2009.38

Al-Khiaty, M., Abdel-Aal, R., & Elish, M. O. (2017). Abductive network ensembles for improved prediction of future change-prone classes in object-oriented software. *The International Arab Journal of Information Technology*, *14*(6), 803–811.

Bacchelli, A., D'Ambros, M., & Lanza, M. (2010). Are popular classes more defect prone? In *Fundamental Approaches to Software Engineering* (pp. 59–73). Springer Berlin Heidelberg. doi:10.1007/978-3-642-12029-9_5

Bansal, A., & Jajoria, S. (2019). Cross-Project Change Prediction Using Meta-Heuristic Techniques. *International Journal of Applied Metaheuristic Computing*, *10*(1), 43–61. doi:10.4018/IJAMC.2019010103

Bansal, A., Modi, K., & Jain, R. (2019). Analysis of the Performance of Learners for Change Prediction Using Imbalanced Data. In *Applications of Artificial Intelligence Techniques in Engineering* (pp. 345–359). Singapore: Springer. doi:10.1007/978-981-13-1819-1_33

Bergenti, F., & Poggi, A. (2000, July). Improving UML designs using automatic design pattern detection. In *12th International Conference on Software Engineering and Knowledge Engineering (SEKE)* (pp. 336-343). Academic Press.

Bura, D., Choudhary, A., & Singh, R. K. (2017). A Novel UML Based Approach for Early Detection of Change Prone Classes. *International Journal of Open Source Software and Processes*, *8*(3), 1–23. doi:10.4018/IJOSSP.2017070101

Catolino, G., & Ferrucci, F. (n.d.). An extensive evaluation of ensemble techniques for software change prediction. Journal of Software: Evolution and Process, e2156.

Catolino, G., Palomba, F., De Lucia, A., Ferrucci, F., & Zaidman, A. (2018). Enhancing change prediction models using developer-related factors. *Journal of Systems and Software*, *143*, 14–28. doi:10.1016/j.jss.2018.05.003

Elish, M. O., & Al-Zouri, A. A. (2014, January). Effectiveness of Coupling Metrics in Identifying Change-Prone Object-Oriented Classes. In *Proceedings of the International Conference on Software Engineering Research and Practice (SERP)* (p. 1). The Steering Committee of The World Congress in Computer Science, Computer Engineering and Applied Computing (WorldComp).

Emam, K., Benlarbi, S., Goel, N., & Rai, S. (1999). *A validation of object-oriented metrics*. Technical Report ERB-1063, National Research Council of Canada.

Eski, S., & Buzluca, F. (2011, March). An empirical study on object-oriented metrics and software evolution in order to reduce testing costs by predicting change-prone classes. In *Software Testing, Verification and Validation Workshops (ICSTW), 2011 IEEE Fourth International Conference on* (pp. 566-571). IEEE. 10.1109/ICSTW.2011.43

Godara, D., Choudhary, A., & Singh, R. K. (2018). Predicting Change Prone Classes in Open Source Software. *International Journal of Information Retrieval Research*, 8(4), 1–23. doi:10.4018/IJIRR.2018100101

Godara, D., & Singh, R. K. (2015). Enhancing Frequency Based Change Proneness Prediction Method Using Artificial Bee Colony Algorithm. In *Advances in Intelligent Informatics* (pp. 535–543). Cham: Springer. doi:10.1007/978-3-319-11218-3_48

Godara, D., & Singh, R. K. (2017). Exploring the relationships between design measures and change proneness in object-oriented systems. *International Journal of Software Engineering, Technology and Applications*, 2(1), 64–80.

Han, A. R., Jeon, S. U., Bae, D. H., & Hong, J. E. (2008, July). Behavioral dependency measurement for change-proneness prediction in UML 2.0 design models. In Computer Software and Applications, 2008. COMPSAC'08. 32nd Annual IEEE International (pp. 76-83). IEEE.

Hosmer, D. W. Jr, & Lemeshow, S. (2004). *Applied logistic regression*. John Wiley & Sons.

Janes, A., Scotto, M., Pedrycz, W., Russo, B., Stefanovic, M., & Succi, G. (2006). Identification of defect-prone classes in telecommunication software systems using design metrics. *Information Sciences*, 176(24), 3711–3734. doi:10.1016/j.ins.2005.12.002

Khomh, F., Penta, M. D., & Gueheneuc, Y. G. (2009, October). An exploratory study of the impact of code smells on software change-proneness. In *Reverse Engineering, 2009. WCRE'09. 16th Working Conference on* (pp. 75-84). IEEE. 10.1109/WCRE.2009.28

Koru, A. G., & Liu, H. (2007). Identifying and characterizing change-prone classes in two large-scale open-source products. *Journal of Systems and Software*, 80(1), 63–73. doi:10.1016/j.jss.2006.05.017

Kyriakakis, P., Chatzigeorgiou, A., Ampatzoglou, A., & Xinogalos, S. (2019). Exploring the frequency and change proneness of dynamic feature pattern instances in PHP applications. *Science of Computer Programming*, 171, 1–20. doi:10.1016/j.scico.2018.10.004

Lu, H., Zhou, Y., Xu, B., Leung, H., & Chen, L. (2012). The ability of object-oriented metrics to predict change-proneness: A meta-analysis. *Empirical Software Engineering*, 17(3), 200–242. doi:10.100710664-011-9170-z

Malhotra, R., & Chug, A. (2013). An empirical study to redefine the relationship between software design metrics and maintainability in high data intensive applications. In *Proceedings of the World Congress on Engineering and Computer Science* (*Vol. 1*). Academic Press.

Malhotra, R., & Jangra, R. (2015). Prediction & Assessment of Change Prone Classes Using Statistical & Machine Learning Techniques. Journal of Information Processing Systems, 1-26.

Malhotra, R., & Khanna, M. (2013). Investigation of relationship between object-oriented metrics and change proneness. *International Journal of Machine Learning and Cybernetics*, 4(4), 273–286. doi:10.100713042-012-0095-7

Malhotra, R., & Khanna, M. (2018). Prediction of change prone classes using evolution-based and object-oriented metrics. *Journal of Intelligent & Fuzzy Systems*, 34(3), 1755–1766. doi:10.3233/JIFS-169468

Menard, S. (2002). *Applied logistic regression analysis* (Vol. 106). Sage. doi:10.4135/9781412983433

Pritam, N., Khari, M., Kumar, R., Jha, S., Priyadarshini, I., Abdel-Basset, M., & Long, H. V. (2019). Assessment of Code Smell for Predicting Class Change Proneness using Machine Learning. *IEEE Access: Practical Innovations, Open Solutions*, 7, 37414–37425. doi:10.1109/ACCESS.2019.2905133

Romano, D., & Pinzger, M. (2011, September). Using source code metrics to predict change-prone java interfaces. In *Software Maintenance (ICSM), 2011 27th IEEE International Conference on* (pp. 303-312). IEEE. 10.1109/ICSM.2011.6080797

Wilkie, F. G., & Kitchenham, B. A. (2000). Coupling measures and change ripples in C++ application software. *Journal of Systems and Software*, 52(2), 157–164. doi:10.1016/S0164-1212(99)00142-9

Zhou, Y., Leung, H., & Xu, B. (2009). Examining the potentially confounding effect of class size on the associations between object-oriented metrics and change-proneness. *Software Engineering. IEEE Transactions on*, 35(5), 607–623.

Zhu, X., Song, Q., & Sun, Z. (2013). Automated identification of change-prone classes in open source software projects. *Journal of Software*, 8(2), 361–366. doi:10.4304/jsw.8.2.361-366

This research was previously published in Critical Approaches to Information Retrieval Research; pages 40-68, copyright year 2020 by Information Science Reference (an imprint of IGI Global).

Chapter 32
Optimized Test Case Generation for Object Oriented Systems Using Weka Open Source Software

Rajvir Singh

Deenbandhu Chhotu Ram University of Science and Technology, Haryana, India

Anita Singhrova

Deenbandhu chhotu Ram University of Science and Technology, Haryana, India

Rajesh Bhatia

PEC University of Technology, Chandigarh, India

ABSTRACT

Detection of fault proneness classes helps software testers to generate effective class level test cases. In this article, a novel technique is presented for an optimized test case generation for ant-1.7 open source software. Class level object oriented (OO) metrics are considered as effective means to find fault proneness classes. The open source software ant-1.7 is considered for the evaluation of proposed techniques as a case study. The proposed mathematical model is the first of its kind generated using Weka open source software to select effective OO metrics. Effective and ineffective OO metrics are identified using feature selection techniques for generating test cases to cover fault proneness classes. In this methodology, only effective metrics are considered for assigning weights to test paths. The results indicate that the proposed methodology is effective and efficient as the average fault exposition potential of generated test cases is 90.16% and test cases execution time saving is 45.11%.

DOI: 10.4018/978-1-7998-9158-1.ch032

1. INTRODUCTION

According to IEEE glossary definition, software testing is executing any software with an intent to find errors. Every system is prone to hidden faults which causes the system failure, if executed. So, the effective test cases are generated to discover maximum unrevealed faults from the software. For this purpose, the test cases are generated considering the factors which help in revealing maximum faults during software testing. A good number of researchers are working in the area of generating optimized test cases. In their methods, the researchers' select test cases based on specified criteria e.g. execution time, fault exposing potential of test cases.

Test cases play the decisive role in testing of software systems. Today's epoch is the era of generating selected test cases for testing software systems to save time and resources. Software testing is performed to reveal maximum faults by running selected test cases. Further these fault-prone classes are identified using effective object oriented (OO) metrics.

Machine learning techniques are helpful in delivering software systems to the user with maximum accuracy. In this paper, linear regression methods and feature selection techniques such as Boruta, Regsubset, Fselector, e.g., random forest, linear correlation, rank correlation, and information gain) are used for categorizing OO metrics in two categories namely effective and ineffective metrics for finding fault-prone classes.

Waikato environment for knowledge analysis (Weka) developed at university of Waikato, New Zealand is written in Java. It is open source software which contains powerful machine learning techniques for data cleaning, classification, clustering, regression, rules mining for association and visualization of data (Weka, 2018). This tool is used for implementation of proposed methodology because of the following salient features (1) easy to use due to user friendly interface, (2) freely available in public domain, (3) comprising of powerful built-in machine learning algorithms for mathematical modeling, (4) easily applicable to deep learning and big data analysis i.e. supports large volume of data cleaning, (5) easy to build mathematical model.

Weka's main user interfaces are the explorer and component-based knowledge flow interface which also supports command line. Experimenter enables the user to conduct systematic comparison of prophetical performance of machine learning algorithms. The explorer interface features several panels enabling the user to interact easily with the components of workbench. These panels are (i) Preprocess panel that provides facility to import database, coma separated values (CSV) file, etc., and preprocessing filtering algorithms used to transform data, for example, converting numeric attributes into discrete ones, (ii) Classify panel provides classification and regression algorithms, accuracy of resulting predictive mathematical model. (iii) Associate panel enables association rule learners to identify all important inter-relationships between attributes in the data. (iv) Cluster panel provides access to clustering techniques of Weka. (v) Select attributes panel provides access to select effective attributes in dataset. (vi) Visualize panel shows visual plots of data to be visualize.

Each of the developed software has to undergo testing before it could be put to use which is important phase of software development life cycle. Test case generation is time consuming and important step in software testing. To reduce the time a good number of researchers are currently working on the optimized test case generation techniques so as to achieve optimizing time, improved efficiency and effectiveness. Further, machine learning can also be used in optimized test case generation by using Weka tool. This gives the motivation to explore the possibilities in this area.

This paper presents a novel methodology for generating optimized test cases for OO systems and analyzes the results for their effectiveness in terms of fault exposition potential. In the proposed methodology, the novelty is due to the introduction of mathematical model generated using Weka open source software tool considering only effective metrics for assigning weights to test paths.

The rest of the paper is organized as follows: Sections 2 presents the related work. Section 3 discusses the proposed methodology, followed by simulation environment in section 4. Section 5 is about the results and discussions, and finally section 6 concludes the paper.

2. RELATED WORK

This section presents the existing work related to test case generation for OO systems.

(Arar & Ayan, 2016) advocated for effective maximum values of the OO metrics exposing defined risk types for module. Firstly, authors defined three different risk types (1) non-fault-prone (0fp), (2) fault-prone (1+fp), (3) three-or-more-fault-prone (3+fp) and used two case studies for evaluation of the proposed methodology.

(Bashir & Nadeem, 2017) advocated the improved genetic algorithm considering the cost of mutation testing. The ten programs were used to evaluate the methodology and compared the results with the results of evosuite tool (Evosuite, 2017) and subsequently mutation score of 80.6% was achieved. (Boucher & Badri, 2017) adapted existing HySOM to predict fault-prone classes using four OO source code metrics namely loc, cbo, rfc and wmc at class level, as unit test cases are generally written at class level by the testing team. The twelve open source datasets were used in their study.

(Boucher & Badri, 2016) compared two threshold metric values calculation methods namely (1) ROC curves and (2) alves rankings, for different source code metric for achieving fault-proneness prediction.

(Bansal & Agrawal,2014) presented analysis of OO Metrics in software development which did not included Lorenz and Kidd metric suite, because criticism by various researchers. For quality and complexity measurement they have suggested four metrics as effective namely noc, wmc, rfc and cbo and advocated that lcom and dit are insignificant for OO Systems.

(Carvalho et. al., 2008) advocated multi-objective PSO algorithm for finding fault proneness classes considering cbo, dit, lcom, noc, rfc and wmc metrics and suggested that wmc and rfc are most effective metrics. (Elish & Elish, 2008) presented the method for predicting fault-prone modules using Support Vector Machine (SVM) and concluded that SVM is generally better or at least performs equally good. NASA dataset and nine prediction models were used for evaluating the proposed method. (Gao et. al., 2011) advocated that software metrics play vital role in software quality assurance in software development, and further suggested that the selection of metrics before building and training machine learning model plays an important role in developing quality software.

(Goel et al., 2017) presented the list of different classifier models used in machine learning, and emphasized on wide heterogeneity in predicting cross projects fault proneness of classes. (Gyimothy et al., 2008) presented an empirical validation of OO metrics for fault prediction on open source software. Automatic method for calculation of OO metrics for C++ has been presented and authors suggested that cbo metric is the best metric for predicting fault-proneness of C++ classes. (Halim, 2013) showed revealing of 70% of faults prone classes for OO software. (Hosseini et al., 2017) advocated cross project defect prediction (CPDP) studies. (Hussain et al., 2016) presented a study on selection of effective OO software metrics for finding fault-prone classes and dit, npm, lcom were considered as effective metrics for fault-proneness of classes.

(Jeevarathinam & Thanamani, 2010) presented mutation-based fault classification to generate test cases for OO systems and the average Fault Exposition Potential (FEP) of ten case studies as 82.31%. (Khosrowjerdi et al., 2018) presented an automatic fault injection-based test case generation (TCG) methodology for safety critical systems.

(Kursa & Rudnicki,2010) presented feature selection method using the Boruta Package for selecting effective variables. (Larsen et. al.,2017) presented mutation based TCG using Ecdar tool for finite automata model-based testing. (Liaw & Wiener, 2002) advocated the classification and regression using random forest method. (Malhotra &Bansal, 2015) suggested to calculate firstly the threshold values for OO metrics and secondly, validate the model for effectiveness of methodology. (Menzies, 2013) discusses how to collect training data for model learning from projects and generate rules to minimize the effort or number of defects during software development. (Mishra & Shukla,2011) discussed advantages of selecting attributes for prediction of defect proneness classes in OO Software.

(Morozov et al., 2017) presented fault propagation and activation analysis for OO systems for model-based regression testing. (Nugroho et al., 2010) investigated empirically the importance of UML design metrics for classes fault-proneness. The results showed that (1) message detailedness and, (2) import coupling are effective predictors of class fault-proneness. (Osuna et al., 1997) presented method to train support vector machine (SVM). (Paradkar, 2006) presented a review on software fault model based TCG techniques.

Puranik et al. (2016) presented a novel strategy by selection of metrics for bug counts. (Radjenović et al., 2013) found the noticeable differences between OO metrics with respect to software fault prediction. The traditional software complexity metrics were found suitable for size measures. (Rahm & Do, 2000) presented data cleaning methods and their associated problems.

(Rana et. al., 2015) presented the formulae for calculation of Root Mean Squared Error (RMSE), correlation (r), coefficient of determination (R^2) and accuracy. These formulae have been used in various machine learning algorithms.

(Romanski & Kotthoff, 2016) presented PackageFSelector used to select the effective variables (or metrics). (Saha & Kanewala, 2018) empirically evaluated effectiveness of testing in terms of FEP for four TCG techniques namely MT: line, branch, weak mutation and random. For requirements modeling (Schlick et al., 2011) advocated a model-based TCG for mutation testing using UML-state diagrams.

(Selvaraj & Thangaraj, 2013) presented SVM based method for software defect prediction for early fault detection in software testing whereas (Song & Lu, 2015) showed the usage of decision tree for handling datasets with missing or error values. Oversensitivity was the main limitation of decision tree against noisy datasets.

(Subramanyam & Krishnan,2013) presented empirical literature on CK metrics for OO design complexity. The OO metrics, e.g. dit, wmc, cbo on defects were different across Java and C++ case studies. (Suffian & Ibrahim, 2012) applied statistical regression model to formulate prediction model for revealing system testing defects.

(Tay & Cao, 2001) advocated the SVM's sensitivity to parameters and regression approximation using SVMs. (Zhang et al., 2017) used 255 open source modules and explored aggregation methods and their impact on performance of defect prediction models.

Table 1. Optimized Test case generation techniques using OO metrics

S. No.	Reference	Technique used	Advantages	Limitations
1.	(Basir & Nadeem, 2016)	Improved genetic algorithm for mutation testing	Test coverage in less number of epochs is achieved	AFEP can be improved
2.	(Boucher & Badri,2017)	Adapted HySOM algorithm	Used loc, cbo, rfc and wmc metrics for fault proneness classes as effective metrics.	Not included npm, lcom effective OO metrics.
3.	(Boucher & Badri, 2016)	ROC curves and Alves Rankings techniques	Compared very efficiently the two techniques namely ROC curves & Ranking technique.	Presented comparison of two techniques only.
4.	(Goel et. al., 2017)	Comparative study	Compared study on different cross projects defects prediction (CPDP) models.	Not discussed effect of OO metrics like lcom, cbo, rfc, npm, wmc.
5.	(Hussain et. al., 2016)	Logistic regression technique	Threshold values has been calculated for OO metrics.	Effective and in effective metrics are not categorized.
6.	(Larsen et. al., 2016)	Mutation testing technique	Test case generation is presented using Ecdar tool. Improved quality w.r.t. adaptiveness.	Test case generation time is high which can further be minimized.
7.	(Malhotra & Bansal, 2015)	Machine learning techniques	Successfully categorized different OO metrics for their effectiveness.	Used univariate logistic regression. Multivariate logistic regression can be used to improve the effectiveness.
8.	(Morozov et. al., 2017)	Regression test case prioritization for model-based testing	Successfully, test cases are prioritized using Simulink model. AFEP is 67.50.	AFEP can be increased & method is not evaluated on large application.
9.	(Puranik et. al., 2016)	Comparative analysis of fault prediction models	Good comparative analysis.	Only models are discussed but not the OO metrics.
10.	(Saha & Kanewala, 2018)	Metamorphic testing technique (MT).	Presented empirical analysis of fault effectiveness of test case generation methods for MT: line, branch, weak mutation and random.	Further analysis can be carried out for larger open source applications.

(Zhou & Leung, 2006) studied OO design metrics to identify the fault-proneness of classes when the severity of faults was taken into account. The wmc, rfc, cbo, and lcom have been identified as effective metrics for finding severe fault prone-classes.

(Suresh et. al., 2012) suggested that traditional and OO metrics provided priceless information to testers for finding fault prone classes. (Takagi & Beyazıt, 2015) presented a formal model called an operational profile with fault-proneness information (OPFPI) and a novel technique for optimized TCG from the OPFPI.

In light of the above discussion, it is inferred that the categorization of OO metrics in two categories namely effective metrics and ineffective metrics for fault proneness of classes is still an open area of research. Moreover, the OO metrics serve the key role in finding fault prone classes. The machine learning algorithms play important role in statistical model design using selected OO metrics. Hence, OO metrics-based test case generation is still open research area.

3. PROPOSED METHODOLOGY

The block diagram for the proposed methodology is given in Figure 1.

Figure 1. Proposed test case generation method for OO systems

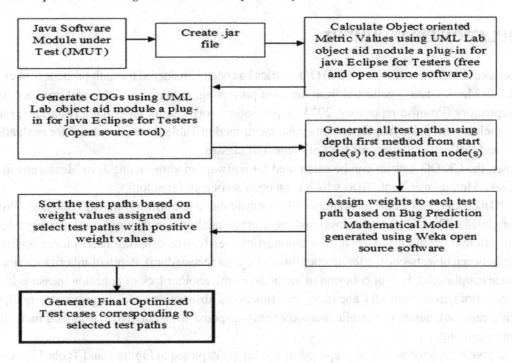

The steps of proposed methodology given in Figure 1 are given in Table 2.

Table 2. Proposed novel methodology for optimized test case generation

Proposed Methodology	
Step 1.	Select the effective and ineffective object-oriented metrics for fault proneness of classes of selected OO case study using machine learning tools.
Step 2.	Generate class level interaction diagrams i.e. class dependency graphs (CDGs) using free and open source UML Lab object aid module a plug-in for Java Eclipse for Testers version Neon.3 Release 4.6.3. Also, generate test paths from CDGs using depth first traversal method from start node(s) to destination node(s).
Step 3.	Select test paths based on the bug prediction value using mathematical model generated using Weka tool.
Step 4.	Generate final optimized class level test cases corresponding to selected test paths.

The proposed methodology is first of its kind that uses mathematical model at step 3 generated using Weka open source software tool. In mathematical model only effective metrics are used for calculating and assigning weights to test paths. The effective and ineffective metrics are classified using machine learning techniques e.g. Boruta, Regsubset, FSelector(RandomForest), FSelector(InformationGain), FSelector(LinearCorrelation), FSelector(RankCorrelation).

The proposed methodology given in Figure 1 and Table 1 is implemented using Weka. This study is evaluated using an open source software ant-1.7. The source code for this module is accessible from apache websites.

4. SIMULATION ENVIRONMENT

The class level Chidamber Kemerer (CK) OO metrics has been considered for fault proneness of classes. The CK OO Metrics data is collected from the most promising, publicly available and open access scientific repository (Promise repository, 2014). Open source software modules namely ant, ivy, tomcat, berek, camel, lucene, poi, synapse, velocity, also mentioned in Table 2 are considered for evaluation of effective and ineffective metrics for fault proneness of classes.

Further, the CK OO metrics can be calculated for software modules using Java Measurement Tool V.0.90 (Java Measuremet Tool,2018) which is an open source and free tool.

The OO metrics values for the software modules are available at scientific promising repository (Promise repository,2014). The OO metrics considered are average method complexity (amc), average McCabe (avg_cc), afferent couplings(ca), cohesion amongst classes (cam), coupling between methods(cbm), coupling between objects(cbo), efferent couplings(ce), data access(dam), depth of inheritance tree(dit), inheritance coupling(ic), lack of cohesion in methods(lcom), another lack of cohesion measure(lcom3), lines of code(loc), maximum McCabe (max_cc), functional abstraction (mfa), aggregation(moa), number of children(noc), number of public methods(npm), response for a class(rfc), weighted methods per class(wmc) and bugs.

The stepwise implementation of proposed methodology depicted in Figure 1 and Table 3 is as under:

Table 3. Software Modules used as subject systems available as open source and free

Software modules	Ant-1.7	Break-1.0	Camel-1.6	Ivy-2.0	Lucene-2.4	Poi-3.0	Synapse-1.2	Tomcat-6.0	Velocity-1.6
No. of variables	21	21	21	21	21	21	21	21	21
No. of classes	745	44	965	352	340	442	256	858	229

Step 1. Selection of effective and ineffective OO Metrics for fault proneness of classes: The different techniques are used for selection of efficient metrics are shown in Figures 2 to 11.

Effective metrics selected using Boruta are wmc, rfc, loc, lcom and npm as these metrics have higher values on y-axis for software modules, as visible in Fig.2.

Effective metrics selected using Regsubset are wmc, rfc, loc, lcom and npm as they have higher y-axis values for software modules. The values are shown in Figure 3.

Effective metrics using FSelector(RandomForest) are wmc, rfc, npm, loc and amc because values on y-axis corresponding to these metrics for software modules are higher in Figure 4.

Figure 2. OO Metrics selection using Boruta

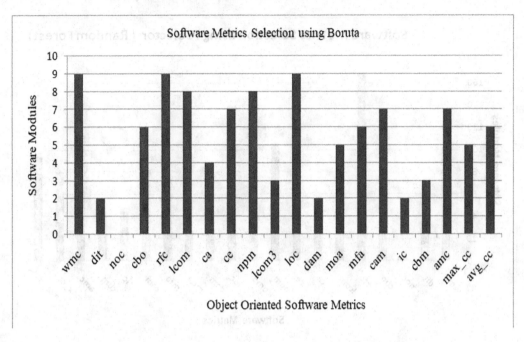

Figure 3. OO Metrics selection using Regsubset

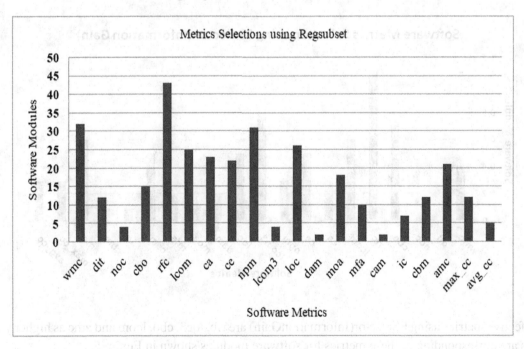

Figure 4. OO Metrics selection using FSelector(Random Forest)

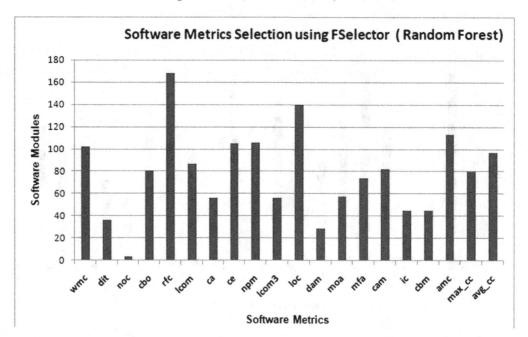

Figure 5. OO Metrics selection using FSelector(Information Gain)

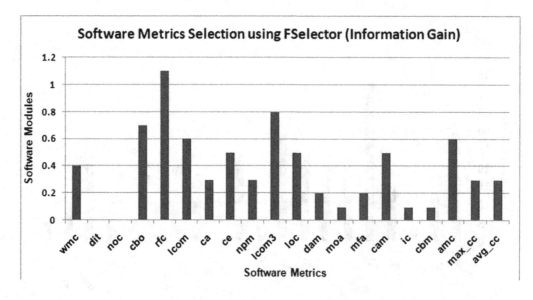

Effective metrics using FSelector(InformationGain) are rfc, loc3, cbo, lcom and amc as higher y-axis values are corresponding to these metrics for software modules shown in Figure 5.

Using FSelector(Linear Correlation) effective selected metrics are rfc, loc, wmc, ce, and cbo shown in Figure 6.

Using FSelector(RankCorrelation), the selected metrics are rfc, loc, wmc, cbo and ce shown in Figure 7.

Figure 6. OO Metrics selection using FSelector(Linear Correlation)

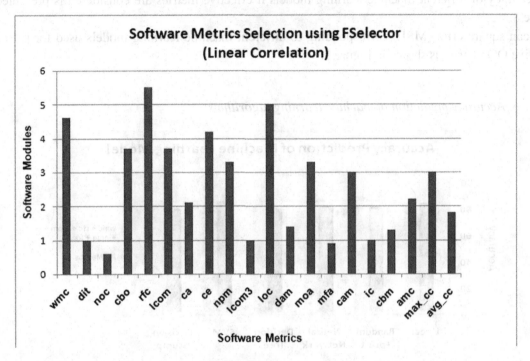

Figure 7. OO Metrics selection using FSelector(Rank Correlation)

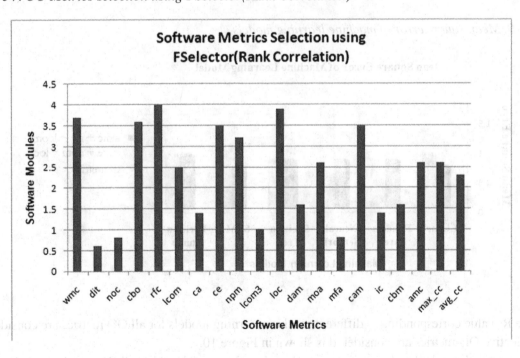

Accuracy of different machine learning models if effective metrics are considered is presented in Figure 8.

Mean square error (MSE) corresponding to different machine learning models used for selecting effective OO metrics is shown in Figure 9.

Figure 8. Accuracy prediction of machine learning algorithms

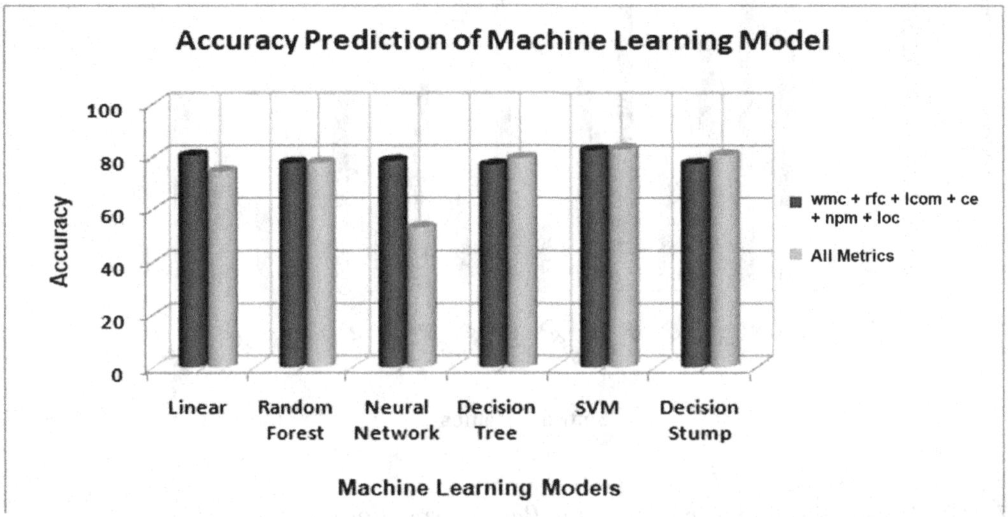

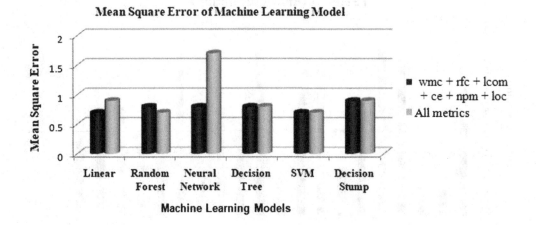

Figure 9. Mean square error of machine learning models

The R^2 value corresponding to different machine learning models for all OO metrics are considered and effective OO metrics are considered is shown in Figure 10.

The correlation calculated on different machine learning models taking all OO metrics and effective OO metrics is shown in Figure 11.

Figure 10. R^2 calculated on machine learning models

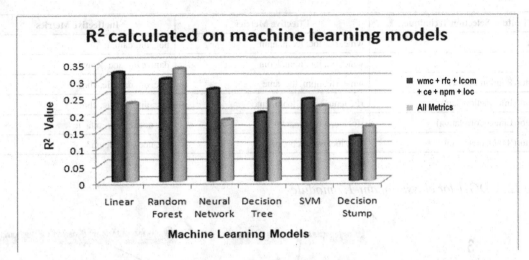

Figure 11. Correlation calculated on machine learning models

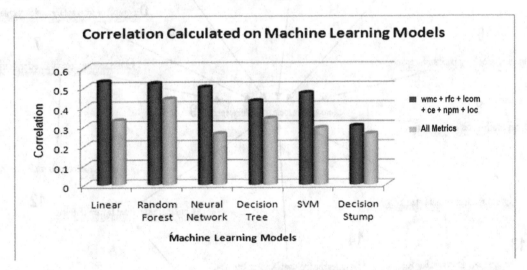

The above analysis for categorization of the effective and ineffective OO metrics for finding fault proneness of classes is summarized in Table 4.

Step 2. Generating class level CDGs and test paths: The test paths are generated from class dependency graph (CDG) or class relationship diagrams (CRD). CDG-1 is generated using open source and free tool namely UML Lab object aid which is a plug-in for java Eclipse for Testers version Neon.3 Release 4.6.3. For the apache ant-1.7.0, the CDG diagram is shown below:

From the Class dependency graph (CDG-1) in Figure 12 the class level test cases are generated using depth first search method. The test scenarios generated are given below:

These generated test paths are listed in Table 5:

Table 4. Categories of OO metrics

Feature Selection Technique	Effective Metrics	Ineffective Metrics
Boruta	wmc, rfc, loc, lcom, npm	noc, dit, dam, ic
Regsubset	wmc, rfc, loc, npm, lcom	dam, cam, noc, lcom3
FSelector(RandomForest)	wmc, rfc, npm, loc, amc	noc, dit, dam, ic, cbm
FSelector(InformationGain)	rfc, lcom3, cbo, lcom, amc	noc, dit, moa, ic, cbm
FSelector(LinearCorrelation)	rfc, loc, wmc, ce, cbo	dit, noc, lcom3, mfa, ic
FSelector(RankCorrelation)	Rfc, loc, wmc, cbo, ce	dit, noc, mfa, lcom3

Figure 12. CDG-1 for classes of ant-1.7 module

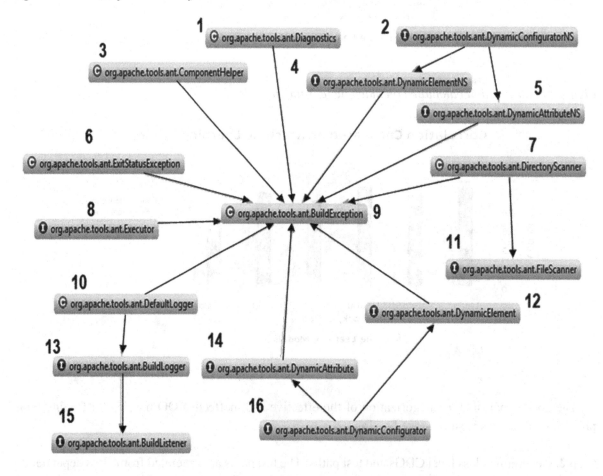

Step 3. Selecting Test paths using mathematical formula (1) generated using Weka open source software: The test cases are selected based on weight assigned to individual test cases. The weights are assigned to individual test cases using bug prediction linear regression model (1) i.e. weight values are calculated by using fault proneness mathematical model generated for apache ant-1.7 open source software using Weka tool as shown in Figure 14.

Figure 13. Test Paths generated from CDG-1 using depth first search

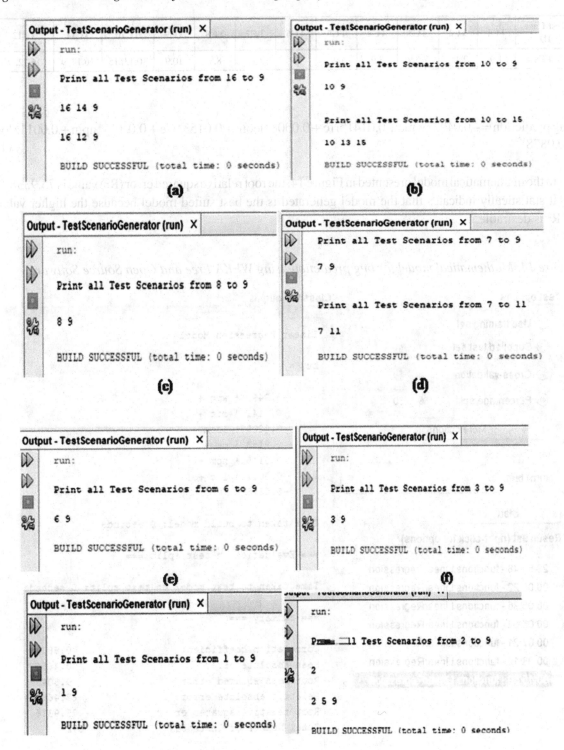

Table 5. Test paths from CDG-1

Test Case ID	TC1	TC2	TC3	TC4	TC5	TC6	TC7	TC8	TC9	TC10	TC11	TC12
Test Case	1,9	2,4,9	2,5,9	3,9	6,9	7,9	7,11	8,9	10,9	10,13, 15	16,14, 9	16,12, 9

Bug prediction $= -0.0492*$wmc$+0.0141*$rfc$+0.0008*$lcom$+0.0153*$Ce$+0.0.145*$npm$+0.0011*$loc -0.0878 (1)

In the mathematical model presented in Figure 14, the root relative squared error (R^2) value is 73.9336%. It statistically indicates that the model generated is the best suited model because the higher value of R^2 is desirable.

Figure 14. Mathematical model for bug prediction using WEKA Free and Open Source Software

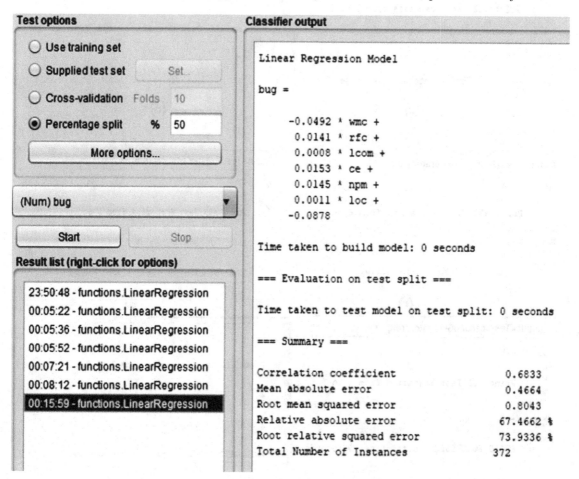

In Table 6, the test paths are assigned the weights based on mathematical model, represented by Equation (1) generated using Weka open source and free tool.

The sorted test paths in decreasing order of the weights as assigned to individual test paths are shown in Table 6. The sorting of test paths helps in selecting the optimum test paths.

Step 4. Generation of selected class level test cases: The final class level test cases are generated corresponding to the selected test paths. For the case study of ant 1.7, the Table 8 shows the selected test paths based on the weights assigned to each test path.

Table 6. Weights assigned to test cases

Test Case ID	Weight
TC1	1.5961
TC2	-0.6727
TC3	-0.6657
TC4	3.0262
TC5	-0.0674
TC6	3.2595
TC7	2.9732
TC8	-0.0971
TC9	0.3802
TC10	0.0440
TC11	-0.1509
TC12	-0.1509

Table 7. Ordered test cases

Test Case ID	Weight
TC6	3.2595
TC4	3.0262
TC7	2.9732
TC1	1.5961
TC9	0.3802
TC10	0.0440
TC5	-0.0674
TC8	-0.0971
TC11	-0.1509
TC12	-0.1509
TC3	-0.6657
TC2	-0.6727

Table 8. Selected test paths

Test Case ID	Test Case	Selected TC
TC1	1,9	
TC2	2,4,9	
TC3	2,5,9	
TC4	3,9	
TC5	6,9	
TC6	7,9	
TC7	7,11	TC6, TC4, TC7, TC1, TC9, TC10
TC8	8,9	
TC9	10,9	
TC10	10,13,15	
TC11	16,14,9	
TC12	16,12,9	

The test cases generated corresponding to the selected test scenarios based on Figure 12 are listed in Table 9.

Table 9. Final test case generated

Test case ID	Test case	Class level test case
TC6	7,9	Org.apache.tools.ant.DirectoryScanner → Org.apache.tools.ant.BuildException
TC4	3,9	Org.apache.tools.ant.ComponentHelper → Org.apache.tools.ant.BuildException
TC7	7,11	Org.apache.tools.ant.DirectoryScanner → Org.apache.tools.ant.FileScanner
TC1	1,9	Org.apache.tools.ant.Diagnostics → Org.apache.tools.ant.BuildException
TC9	10,9	Org.apache.tools.ant.DefaultLogger → Org.apache.tools.ant.BuildException
TC10	10,13,15	Org.apache.tools.ant.DefaultLogger → Org.apache.tools.ant.BuildLogger → Org.apache.tools.ant.BuildListener

5. RESULTS AND DISCUSSIONS

The analysis of results obtained using open source software namely Weka and UML Lab object aid module in the proposed methodology are discussed below:

- Total faults revealed by all the twelve test cases = 16.
- Total number of faults revealed by selected six test cases = 16.
- Fault Exposition Potential (FEP) of selected test cases = 100%.
- Ten different Class Dependency Graphs (CDGs) were generated to cover maximum number of classes of ant 1.7 open source software system.

For the generated ten CDGs the FEP is given as presented in Table 10.

Graphically, the percentage fault exposing potential (FEP) of selected test cases is shown in Figure 15 and Figure 16:

As visible in Figure 15 and Figure 16, the proposed methodology has increased fault exposing potential (FEP) of selected test cases. This effect of increased FEP has been shown on other quality parameters namely efficiency, effectiveness and execution time.

1. **Efficiency:** The average percentage of fault exposing potential (AFEP) of selected test cases by using proposed methodology is 90.16% as mentioned in Table 10. This shows that the proposed methodology is an efficient methodology.
2. **Effectiveness:** The faults revealed by the selected test cases are 192 out of 216 (corresponding to all test cases) faults injected. It means the 88.89% faults are revealed by the proposed methodology. Hence the proposed methodology is effective methodology.
3. **The execution time:** The execution time is reduced because the number of test cases selected is less than the total test cases. If per unit time (i.e. one second) is assumed as the execution time for each test case, then the time saving is 235-129 = 106s i.e. 45.11% time saving.

Table 10. Analysis of results

CDG No.	#Total Test Cases	#Selected Test Cases using proposed methodology	#Total Faults revealed by all test cases	#Total faults revealed by selected test cases using proposed methodology	%FEP of selected Test cases
1	12	6	16	16	100
2	18	8	20	18	90
3	26	17	30	25	83
4	20	10	20	17	85
5	25	12	20	18	90
6	30	18	26	21	80.77
7	26	10	17	17	100
8	33	20	25	20	80
9	35	22	28	26	92.86
10	10	6	14	14	100
Sum	235	129	216	192	90.16%

Figure 15. Faults revealed

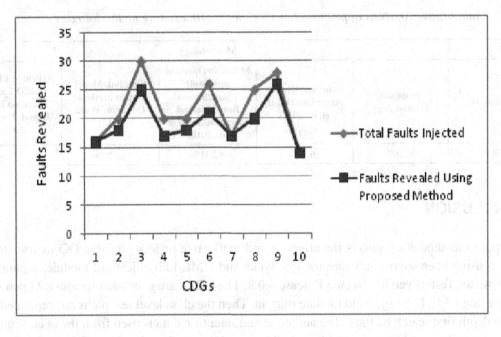

The AFEP for various existing methodologies are summarized in Table 11.

Figure 16. Percentage of faults revealed

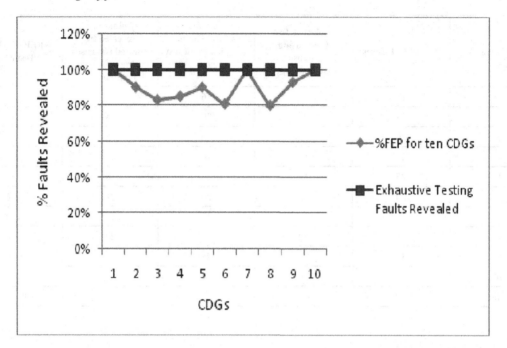

Table 11. Comparative Analysis of proposed methodology with existing methodologies

Parameters	Methodology				
	Proposed Methodology	Improved Genetic Algorithm (Basir et. al, 2017)	Mutation Operator and Fault Classification Based Method (Jeevarathinam et al., 2010)	Simulink Model Based Method (Morozov et al., 2017)	Hybrid of EFSMS, BZ-TT and Mutation Based Method (Paradkar, 2006)
AFEP	90.16%	86.20%	82.31%	67.50%	77.17%

6. CONCLUSION

The proposed methodology selects the effective and ineffective or less effective OO metrics for bug prediction using open source software namely Weka and UML Lab object aid module, a plug-in for java Eclipse for Testers version Neon.3 Release 4.6.3. The CDGs are generated for ant-1.7 open source software using UML Lab object aid module plug-in. Then the class level test paths are generated using modified depth first search method. The authentic and scientific data is used from the open source and free repository (Promise repository,2014) for building mathematical model using Weka to assign weights to each test path generated from ten different CDGs for ant-1.7 open source software. Finally, optimized test cases are generated corresponding to these selected test paths. The finally generated test cases are having AFEP = 90.16% and execution time saving is 45.11%. Hence, the proposed methodology is effective and efficient methodology in terms of FEP and execution time.

REFERENCES

Arar, O. F., & Ayan, K. (2016, November). Deriving Thresholds of Software Metrics to Predict Faults on Open Source Software: Replicated Case Studies. *Expert Systems with Applications*, *61*, 106–121. doi:10.1016/j.eswa.2016.05.018

Bansal, M., & Agrawal, C. P. (2014). Critical analysis of object oriented metrics in software development. In *Fourth International Conference on Advanced Computing & Communication Technologies*, Rohtak (pp. 197-201).

Bashir, M. B., & Nadeem, A. (2017). Improved Genetic Algorithm to Reduce Mutation Testing Cost. *IEEE Access: Practical Innovations, Open Solutions*, *5*, 3657–3674. doi:10.1109/ACCESS.2017.2678200

Boucher, A., & Badri, M. (2016). Using software metrics thresholds to predict fault-prone classes in object-oriented software. In *4th International Conference on Applied Computing and Information Technology*, Las Vegas, NV (pp. 169-176).

Boucher, A., & Badri, M. (2017). Predicting fault-prone classes in object-oriented software: an adaptation of an unsupervised hybrid SOM algorithm. In *IEEE International Conference on Software Quality, Reliability and Security*, Prague (pp. 306-317). 10.1109/QRS.2017.41

Carvalho, A. B. d., Pozo, A., Vergilio, S., & Lenz, A. (2008). Predicting fault proneness of classes through a multiobjective particle swarm optimization algorithm. In *20th IEEE International Conference on Tools with Artificial Intelligence*, Dayton, OH (pp. 387-394). 10.1109/ICTAI.2008.76

Elish, K. O., & Elish, M. O. (2008, May). Predicting defect-prone software modules using support vector machines. *Journal of Systems and Software*, *81*(5), 649–660. doi:10.1016/j.jss.2007.07.040

Evosuite, open source and free tool, downloaded on 23rd January, 2017 and available at: www.evosuite.org

Gao, K., Khoshgoftaar, T. M., Wang, H., & Seliya, N. (2011, April). Choosing software metrics for defect prediction: An investigation on feature selection techniques. *Software, Practice & Experience*, *41*(5), 579–606. doi:10.1002pe.1043

Goel, L., Damodaran, D., Khatri, S. K., & Sharma, M. (2017). A literature review on cross project defect prediction. In *4th IEEE International Conference on Electrical, Computer and Electronics*, Mathura, India, (pp.680-685).

Gyimothy, T., Ferenc, R., & Siket, I. (2008, October). Empirical validation of object-oriented metrics on open source software for fault prediction. *IEEE Transactions on Software Engineering*, *31*(10), 897–910. doi:10.1109/TSE.2005.112

Halim, A. (2013). Predict fault-prone classes using the complexity of UML class diagram. In *International Conference on Computer, Control, Informatics and Its Applications*, Jakarta (pp. 289-294).

Hosseini, S., Turhan, B., & Gunarathna, D. (2017). A Systematic Literature Review and Meta-Analysis on Cross Project Defect Prediction. *IEEE Transactions on Software Engineering*, *99*, 1–40. doi:10.1109/TSE.2017.2770124

Hussain, S., Keung, J., Khan, A. A., & Bennin, K. E. (2016). Detection of Fault-Prone Classes Using Logistic Regression Based Object-Oriented Metrics Thresholds. In *IEEE International Conference on Software Quality, Reliability and Security Companion*, Vienna, Austria (pp. 93-100).

Java Measurement Tool V. 0.90, open source and free tool. (n.d.). Retrieved from http://jmt.stage.tigris.org/

Jeevarathinam, R., & Thanamani, A. S. (2010). Test Case Generation using Mutation Operators and Fault Classification. *International Journal of Computer Science and Information Security*, 7(1), 190–195.

Khosrowjerdi, H., Meinke, K., & Rasmusson, A. (2018). Virtualized-fault injection testing: A machine learning approach. In *IEEE 11th International Conference on Software Testing, Verification and Validation*, Vasteras (pp. 297-308).

Kursa, M., & Rudnicki, W. (2010). Feature Selection with the Boruta Package. *Journal of Statistical Software*, 36(11), 1–13. doi:10.18637/jss.v036.i11

Larsen, K. G., Lorber, F., Nielsen, B., & Nyman, U. M. (2017). Mutation-based test-case generation with Ecdar. In *IEEE International Conference on Software Testing, Verification and Validation Workshops*, Tokyo, Japan (pp. 319-328).

Liaw, A., & Wiener, M. (2002, December). Classification and regression by random Forest. *R News*, 2(3), 18–22.

Malhotra, R., & Bansal, A. J. (2015). Fault prediction considering threshold effects of object-oriented metrics. *Expert Systems: International Journal of Knowledge Engineering and Neural Networks*, 32(2), 203–219. doi:10.1111/exsy.12078

Menzies, T., Butcher, A., Cok, D., Marcus, A., Layman, L., Shull, F., ... Zimmermann, T. (2013, June). Local versus Global Lessons for Defect Prediction and Effort Estimation. *IEEE Transactions on Software Engineering*, 39(6), 822–834. doi:10.1109/TSE.2012.83

Mishra, B., & Shukla, K. K. (2011). Impact of attribute selection on defect proneness prediction in OO software. In *2nd International Conference on Computer and Communication Technology*, Allahabad, (pp. 367-372).

Morozov, A., Ding, K., Chen, T., & Janschek, K. (2017). Test Suite Prioritization for Efficient Regression Testing of Model-Based Automotive Software. In *IEEE International Conference on Software Analysis, Testing and Evolution*, Harbin (pp. 20-29).

Nugroho, A., Chaudron, M. R. V., & Arisholm, E. (2010). Assessing UML design metrics for predicting fault-prone classes in a Java system. In *7th IEEE Working Conference on Mining Software Repositories.*, Cape Town (pp. 21-30).

Osuna, E., Freund, R., & Girosit, F. (1997). Training support vector machines: an application to face detection. In *IEEE Computer Society Conference on Computer Vision and Pattern Recognition*, San Juan (pp. 130-136). 10.1109/CVPR.1997.609310

Paradkar, A. (2006). A quest for appropriate software fault models: Case studies on fault detection effectiveness of model-based test generation techniques. *Information and Software Technology*, 48(10), 969–979. doi:10.1016/j.infsof.2006.03.003

Promise repository. (2014). Retrieved from http://openscience.us/repo/defect/ck/

Puranik, S., Deshpande, P., & Chandrasekaran, K. (2016). A Novel Machine Learning Approach for Bug Prediction. *Procedia Computer Science*, *93*, 924–930. doi:10.1016/j.procs.2016.07.271

Radjenović, D., Heričko, M., Torkar, R., & Živkovič, A. (2013, August). Software fault prediction metrics: A systematic literature review. *Information and Software Technology*, *55*(8), 1397–1418. doi:10.1016/j.infsof.2013.02.009

Rahm, E., & Do, H. H. (2000, December). Data cleaning: Problems and current approaches. *IEEE Bulletin on Data Engineering*, *23*(4), 3–13.

Rana, P. S., Sharma, H., Bhattacharya, M., & Shukla, A. (2015, April). Quality assessment of modeled protein structure using physicochemical properties. *Journal of Bioinformatics and Computational Biology*, *13*(2), 1–15. doi:10.1142/S0219720015500055 PMID:25524475

Romanski, P., & Kotthoff, L. (August, 2016). *Package FSelector*. Retrieved from https://cran.r-project.org/web/packages/FSelector/FSelector.pdf

Saha, P., & Kanewala, U. (2018). Fault detection effectiveness of source test case generation strategies for metamorphic testing. In *ACM 3rd International Workshop on Metamorphic Testing*, New York (pp. 2-9).

Schlick, R., Herzner, W., & Jöbstl, E. (2011). Fault-based generation of test cases from UML-Models – Approach and some experiences. *Computer Safety, Reliability, and Security*, *6894*, 270–283.

Selvaraj, P. A., & Thangaraj, P. (2013). Support Vector Machine for Software Defect Prediction. *International Journal of Engineering & Technology Research*, *1*(2), 68–76.

Song, Y., & Lu, Y. (2015). Decision tree methods: applications for classification and prediction. Shanghai Archives of Psychiatry, 27(2), 130-135.

Subramanyam, R., & Krishnan, M. S. (2013, April). Empirical analysis of CK metrics for object-oriented design complexity: Implications for software defects. *IEEE Transactions on Software Engineering*, *29*(4), 297–310. doi:10.1109/TSE.2003.1191795

Suffian, M. D. M., & Ibrahim, S. (2012). A prediction model for system testing defects using regression analysis. *International Journal of Soft Computing and Software Engineering*, *2*(7), 55–68. doi:10.7321/jscse.v2.n7.6

Suresh, Y., Pati, J., & Rath, S. K. (2012). Effectiveness of software metrics for object-oriented system. *Procedia Technology*, *6*, 420–427. doi:10.1016/j.protcy.2012.10.050

Takagi, T., & Beyazıt, M. (2015). Optimized test case generation based on operational profiles with fault-proneness information. *Software Engineering Research. Management and Applications*, *578*, 15–25.

Tay, F. E. H., & Cao, L. (2001, August). Application of support vector machines in financial time series forecasting. *Omega*, *29*(4), 309–317. doi:10.1016/S0305-0483(01)00026-3

Waikato. (2018). Weka ver. 3.8.3 (stable) software. Retrieved from https://www.cs.waikato.ac.nz/ml/weka/

Zhang, F., Hassan, A. E., McIntosh, S., & Zou, Y. (2017, May). The use of summation to aggregate software metrics hinders the performance of defect prediction models. *IEEE Transactions on Software Engineering*, *43*(5), 476–491. doi:10.1109/TSE.2016.2599161

Zhou, Y., & Leung, H. (2006, October). Empirical analysis of object-oriented design metrics for predicting high and low severity faults. *IEEE Transactions on Software Engineering*, *32*(10), 771–789. doi:10.1109/TSE.2006.102

This research was previously published in the International Journal of Open Source Software and Processes (IJOSSP), 9(3); pages 15-35, copyright year 2018 by IGI Publishing (an imprint of IGI Global).

Section 3
Prediction Models, Big Data, and Statistics

Chapter 33
Demography of Open Source Software Prediction Models and Techniques

Kaniz Fatema
American International University, Bangladesh

M. M. Mahbubul Syeed
American International University, Bangladesh

Imed Hammouda
South Mediterranean University, Tunisia

ABSTRACT

Open source software (OSS) is currently a widely adopted approach to developing and distributing software. Many commercial companies are using OSS components as part of their product development. For instance, more than 58% of web servers are using an OSS web server, Apache. For effective adoption of OSS, fundamental knowledge of project development is needed. This often calls for reliable prediction models to simulate project evolution and to envision project future. These models provide help in supporting preventive maintenance and building quality software. This chapter reports on a systematic literature survey aimed at the identification and structuring of research that offers prediction models and techniques in analysing OSS projects. The study outcome provides insight into what constitutes the main contributions of the field, identifies gaps and opportunities, and distils several important future research directions. This chapter extends the authors' earlier journal article and offers the following improvements: broader study period, enhanced discussion, and synthesis of reported results.

DOI: 10.4018/978-1-7998-9158-1.ch033

INTRODUCTION

The use of Open Source Software (OSS) is increasingly becoming part of the development strategy and business portfolio of more and more IT organizations. This is, for example, demonstrated by the growing numbers of downloads of OSS code by companies (Samoladas;Angelis;& Stamelos, 2010). The primary motivation is that OSS can offer huge benefits to an organization, with minimal development costs while taking advantage of free access to code and high quality driven by the power of distributed peer review (Capiluppi & Adams, Reassessing brooks law for the free software community, 2009). Successful OSS projects, such as Eclipse have reached thousands of downloads per day (Eclipse, 2013). However, such projects are typically complex, both from the point of view of the code base, and the community. They may consist of a wide range of components, and come with a large number of versions reflecting their development and evolution history.

In order to adopt an OSS component effectively, an organization often needs fundamental knowledge of the project development, composition, and the possible risks associated with its use. This is because OSS code is primarily developed outside the company by an ultra-wide distributed community (Thy;Ferenc;& Siket, 2005) (Samoladas;Angelis;& Stamelos, 2010). In particular, organizations might need to understand how an OSS project may evolve, as this may impact the future of the organization itself. Additionally, the concern of the quality and reliability of OSS components should be addressed adequately. From a proactive perspective, foreseeing the evolution of an OSS component may provide the organization with useful information including the kind of maintenance practices, resources, and strategic decisions need to be allocated and adopted in supporting their development strategies.

Accordingly, a wide range of prediction models have been proposed by the research community for the purpose of simulating the evolution and approximating the future of OSS projects, with regard to various aspects. For instance, a number of methods supporting error prediction have been developed to provide valuable information for preventive maintenance, and for building quality software. An example prediction scenario has been to foresee potential error prone segments of the code base for tracing down the modules that would most likely require future maintenance tasks (Thy;Ferenc;& Siket, 2005) (Yuming & Baowen, 2008). Despite the variety and volume of OSS prediction studies, it has been argued that the efforts for analysing the evolutionary behaviour of OSS systems still lag behind the high adoption levels of OSS. Furthermore, the focus of OSS prediction studies in general has been restricted to a small number of projects, which limits the generalizability of the methods and results. Such claims thus need empirical evidence (Russo;Mulazzani;Russo;& Steff, 2011).

This chapter is an enhanced version of the literature review that is aimed to provide an in-depth analysis of the prediction research work targeted to analysing OSS projects (Syeed, Hammouda, & Systa, 2014). To carry out this review a review protocol was developed following the guidelines presented in (Kitchenham, Procedures for performing systematic reviews, 2004), a detail discussion of which is resented in the following sections.

The outcome of this review would benefit the readers in following capacities: first, it offers a single point reference to the state-of-the-art studies on the topic; second, it offers a detail break down of what constitute the prediction study concerning OSS projects (e.g., which facets of prediction studies are mostly explored, what data sources are used, what methods and metrics are used along with others), and third, it distils the gaps and opportunities to formulate future research directions. This chapter reflects the following enhancement: (1) a broader study period with enhanced list of articles (65 peer reviewed articles), (2) enhanced discussion on the research question highlighting the results taken from current publications, (3) synthesis on the reported results, and (3) a more elaborated discussion.

This chapter is structured as follows. In REVIEW METHODOLOGY the research questions and the review protocol are discussed. Answers to the research questions, and a synthesis on the reported results are presented in sections REVIEW RESULT and SYNTHESIS respectively. A discussion on open areas in the field of OSS and prediction are presented in section AVENUE TO FUTURE WORK. Section THREATS TO VALIDITY throws light on the validity issues related to the review protocol. Finally, concluding remarks are presented in the CONCLUSION section. Additionally, a complete list of reviewed articles can be found in section REFERENCES section and the data collection table can be downloaded from the following link (OSS prediction studies: Data collection Table, 2017).

REVIEW METHODOLOGY

Evidence-based Software Engineering (EBSE) relies on aggregating the best available evidence to address engineering questions posed by researchers. A recommended methodology for such studies is Systematic Literature Review (SLR) (Kitchenham, ym., 2010). Performing an SLR involves several discrete tasks, which are defined and described by Kitchenham (Kitchenham, Procedures for performing systematic reviews, 2004). As a starting point, SLR recommends to pre-define a review protocol to reduce the possibility of researcher bias (Kitchenham, Procedures for performing systematic reviews, 2004). Along those guidelines and following the review process described in (Cornelissen;Zaidman; Deursen;Moonen;& Koschke, 2009), Figure 1 shows the tasks involved in this review protocol. These tasks are discussed in the subsequent subsections.

It has to be noted that the following procedure is replicated to select and analyse the latest 13 articles which published between 2012 and March 2017. Therefore, this chapter reviewed a total of 65 articles (of which 52 articles are taken from the journal).

Research Questions

The research questions defined for this study fall within the context of OSS projects and prediction strategies. In total, we have formulated 9 questions, as presented in Table 1. These questions are proposed to portray the holistic view of OSS prediction studies, covering aspects, for instance, the focus of the study, methodological detail, case study projects, prediction methods, metric suites, OSS data sets and validation process. A subset of these questions is typical for SLR conducted for prediction studies (Catal & Diri, A systematic review of software fault prediction studies, 2009).

Article Selection

This section describes the article selection process (phase (b) in Figure 1) that includes defining the inclusion criteria for article selection, an automated keyword search process to search digital libraries, a manual selection from the initial set of articles, and the reference checking of the listed articles.

- **Inclusion/Exclusion Criteria:** Along the research questions shown in Table 1, we have defined a set of selection criteria in advance that should be satisfied by the reviewed articles. Articles that fail to pass either of these criteria are excluded from the review. The criteria set for the article selection are as follows:

- Subject area of the articles must unveil strong focus on prediction. Authors must explicitly state the type of prediction performed (e.g., fault, quality, security, effort, survivability, success prediction) and provide detailed evidence of metrics, methods, and data sets exploited.

- Articles must exhibit a profound relation to OSS projects and take into consideration those aspects that are particularly attributed to the OSS community and projects. Articles using OSS as a case study are taken into account if they satisfy the above criterion.

- Articles published in referred journals and conferences are included for the review. Books are not considered in this study.

The suitability of the articles was determined against the above mentioned selection criteria through a manual analysis (discussed later in this section) of title, keywords, abstract. In case of doubt conclusions are checked (Brereton; Kitchenham; Budgen; Turner; & Khalil, 2007).

Figure 1. Systematic literature review process (adopted from (Cornelissen;Zaidman;Deursen;Moonen;& Koschke, 2009))

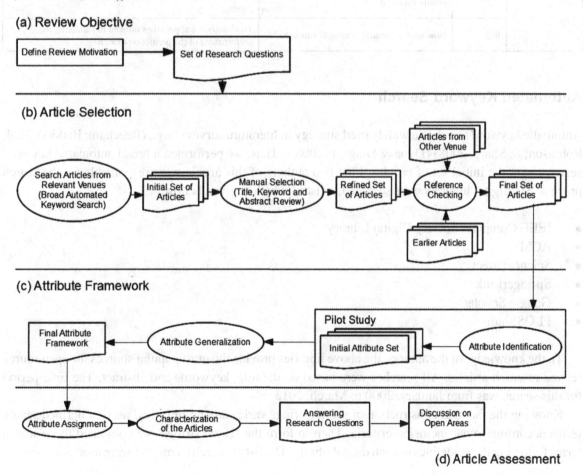

(a) Review Objective

(b) Article Selection

(c) Attribute Framework

(d) Article Assessment

Table 1. Research Questions

Category	Sl. No.	Research Question	Main Motivation
Target	RQ1	Which facets of prediction approaches were explored, and how many articles were published under each facet?	To identify the focus area of the prediction work (e.g., fault or defect prediction) and to decompose the articles according to their study focus.
	RQ2	Does the interest on "OSS prediction study" follow an increasing trend?	To identify the beginning and growth of research interest in the field OSS project prediction.
Target Group	RQ3	What is the portfolio of projects analyzed for prediction studies and what are the domains of the projects?	To determine the mode of prediction studies (e.g., horizontal or vertical) by statistically measuring the studied OSS projects and their domains.
Approach and Results	RQ4	What are the research approaches followed in the studies?	To identify the general trend of research methodology used in research.
	RQ5	What datasets or data sources of OSS projects are mostly exploited?	To identify the data sources of OSS projects those are used for prediction.
	RQ6	What metric suites are evaluated and what tools are used for metric data collection?	To explore the metric suites used for the prediction study and frequently used tools for data extraction.
	RQ7	What are the methods used in prediction models?	To explore the prediction methods used in OSS.
	RQ8	How are the research methodology and results validated?	To identify the approaches employed to evaluate the research approaches in mitigating associated validity threats.
	RQ9	How are the prediction models validated?	To identify the approaches utilized in validating the performance of the prediction models.

Automated Keyword Search

Automatic keyword search is a widely used strategy in literature surveys (e.g., (Beecham; Baddoo; Hall; Robinson; & Sharp, 2008) (Dyba & Dingsyr, 2008)). Thus, we performed a broad automated keyword search to get the initial set of articles. First two authors of this article were responsible for the search process. Six digital libraries were searched, a list of which is given bellow:

- IEEE Computer Society Digital Library
- ACM
- ScienceDirect
- SpringerLink
- Google Scholar
- FLOSShub

To the knowledge of the authors, the above libraries provide the most popular sources for open source related research articles. All searches were based on the title, keywords and abstract. The time period for this search was from January, 2000 to March, 2013.

Knowing the fact that construction of search strings varies among libraries, we first defined search terms according to our inclusion criteria. Then to form the search strings, we combined these search terms following the guidelines of each digital library. The list of search terms that were used is as follows.

Terms representing OSS: "Open source" or OSS or "Open Source Software" or "Open Source Software projects" or FLOSS or "Libre Software" or "F/OSS".

Terms representing prediction: "Prediction" or "Prediction model" or "Fault prediction" or "Defect prediction" or "Test effort prediction" or "Correction cost prediction" or "Reusability prediction" or "Security prediction" or "Effort prediction" or "Quality prediction".

The automated keyword search resulted in 1047 articles. From this list of articles, we excluded those that were obviously false positives. False positives include results, e.g., from other fields than software engineering and computer science. The first two authors reviewed the results of each search independently looking at the title, and the venue of the articles. The output of this step was the common selection of 84 articles consisting of 24 journal articles and 60 conference articles.

Manual Selection

Recent studies (Brereton;Kitchenham;Budgen;Turner;& Khalil, 2007) (Cornelissen;Zaidman;Deursen;Moonen;& Koschke, 2009) pointed out that (a) current digital libraries on software engineering do not provide good support for automated keyword search due to lack of consistent set of keywords, and (b) the abstracts of software engineering articles are relatively poor in comparison to other disciplines. Thus, it is possible that the 84 articles identified in the earlier step might contain irrelevant ones and some relevant might be missing. Due to this, the first two authors performed a manual selection of these articles by reviewing the title, keywords and abstract (and in case of doubt, checking the conclusion (Brereton;Kitchenham;Budgen;Turner;& Khalil, 2007)). To reduce the researcher bias in this selection process, the domain expert (third author) examined the selected articles against the selection criterion. Any disagreement was resolved through discussion. This process ended up with 50 articles consisting of 16 journal articles and 34 conference articles.

- **Reference Checking:** To ensure the inclusion of other relevant but missing articles (as mentioned above), the first two authors independently performed a non-recursive search through the references of the 50 selected articles. This process identified 2 additional conference articles.
- **Final Set of Articles:** The article selection process finally ended up with 52 articles (16 journal and 36 conference articles). A complete list of these articles is presented in section LIST OF REVIEWED ARTICLES.

Attribute Framework

The next step in the review protocol was the construction of an attribute framework (phase (c) in Figure 1). This framework was used to characterize the selected articles and to answer the research questions. Following is a brief description of this process.

- **Attribute Identification:** The attribute set was derived based on two criteria: (a) The domain of the review (i.e., prediction of OSS projects) and (b) the research questions. A pilot study was run for this step, as shown in phase (c) of Figure 1. This phase consists of a number of activities:

First, we performed an exploratory study on the structure of 5 randomly selected articles (from the pool of 52 articles). This study led to a set of seven general attributes that can be used to describe the articles and to answer the research questions. This attribute list is shown in the Attribute column of Table 2.

Second, this list of attributes was refined further into a number of specific sub-attributes to get a precise description of each of the general attributes and fine tune the findings on the research questions. To do this, we made a thorough study of the same set of articles and wrote down words of interest that could be relevant for a particular attribute (e.g., "fault prediction", or "effort prediction" for the Study Target attribute). The result after reading all articles was a (large) set of initial sub attributes. This data extraction task was performed by the first two authors of this survey.

- **Attribute Generalization and Final Attribute Framework:** We further generalized the attributes and sub-attributes to increase their reusability (Cornelissen;Zaidman;Deursen;Moonen;& Koschke, 2009). For example, sub-attributes "mailing list archive" or "chat history" are intuitively generalized to Communication.

To reduce the change of researcher bias in this stage, two step validations were done. First, the attributes and associated sub-attributes were identified and then generalized independently by the first two authors. Then they were merged to a single set of attributes through discussion. Second, the final attribute list selected by the first two authors was examined and validated by the domain expert (third author), who did not have any connection with the attribute identification process. Table 2 shows the final set of attributes and their connection to the research questions in answering them.

Table 2. Attribute Framework

Attribute	Sub Attribute	Brief Description	RQ Addressed
General		Publication Type, Year of Publication.	RQ2
Study Type		Empirical, comparative, case study, tool implementation.	RQ4
Study Target		Study facets (e.g., fault prediction).	RQ1
Case Study	OSS projects studied	List of OSS Projects studied.	RQ3
	Programming language	Target programming languages of OSS projects.	
	Project Domain	Application domain of the OSS projects covered.	
Data Source	Source code	Code base, CVS/SVN.	RQ5
	Contribution	Change log, bug tracking systems.	
	Communication	Mailing list archive, chat history.	
	External sources	Sourceforge, github, ohloh.	
Methodology	Method	Implication or application of prediction methods.	RQ6 and RQ7
	Metric	Implication or application of metrics / features / attributes for prediction.	
	Tool implementation	Implementation of a tool to automate prediction.	
	Tool used	Existing tools, algorithms used for study.	
Validation	Validation of the study	Validation process of the research methodology.	RQ8 and RQ9
	Validation of the prediction model	Validation process of the accuracy and applicability of a prediction model.	

Article Assessment

The article assessment step consists of four distinct activities as shown in phase (d) of Figure 1. In this section, we focus on the first two steps.

- **Attribute Assignment:** Using the attribute framework from the previous section, we processed all articles and assigned the appropriate attribute sets to each of the articles. These attributes effectively capture the essence of the articles in terms of the research questions and allow for a clear distinction between (and comparison of) the articles under study.

The assignment process was performed independently by the first two authors of this survey. During this process, authors claim of contribution is assessed against the results presented in the articles. For example, to validate the claim on the target of the study (e.g., fault/defect prediction), we assessed what relevant data sources are explored, what metrics and methods are used, and the duration and process of the data collection. Also, we did not draw any conclusions from what was presented in an article if it was not explicitly mentioned. For example, we left the attribute field study type empty if it was not mentioned in the article.

- **Characterization of the Reviewed Articles:** Since the attribute assignment process is subject to different interpretations, different reviewers may predict different attribute subsets for the same article (Cornelissen; Zaidman; Deursen; Moonen; & Koschke, 2009). Thus to ensure the quality of the assignment and to reduce the reviewer bias (Cornelissen; Zaidman; Deursen; Moonen; & Koschke, 2009) following measures were taken: (a) attributes assigned to an article by the two authors were cross-checked, and any conflicts and disagreements were resolved through discussion, and (b) the domain expert assessed the final attribute assignment table against the reviewed articles. This table can be downloaded here (OSS prediction studies: Data collection Table, 2017).

Next, the results of this review have been presented by answering the research questions and discussing future research agenda.

REVIEW RESULT

Given the article selection and attribute assignment, the next step is to present and interpret the study findings. We start with discussing answers to the research questions based on the study outcome.

RQ1: Which facets of the prediction approaches were explored, and how many articles were published under each facet?

An in-depth study of the selected articles led us to decompose the OSS prediction articles into a number of facets. Figure 2 presents the complete listing of these facets along with article count under each facet. According to this figure, articles are highly skewed towards fault prediction and reliability prediction facets. Traditionally, software fault prediction approaches use software metrics and fault data from previous releases to predict fault-prone modules for the next release. Research under reliability prediction studies the stability, volatility, vulnerability and residual defects within OSS projects, among others. Alongside a recent trend is devoted to explore the OSS specific properties in prediction. This includes for instance, predicting the popularity of repositories, predicting future forks of a project based of past trend, and trustworthiness.

Figure 2. Focus area of the prediction studies

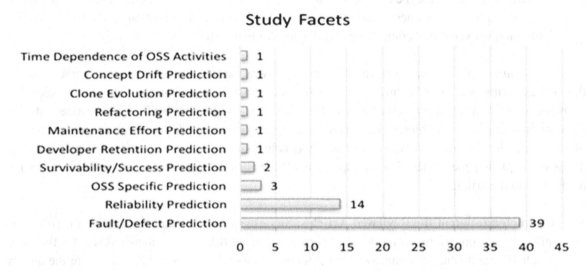

Among the Facets, Software Fault/Defect Prediction Is Studied Extensively

RQ2: Does the interest on "oss prediction study" follow an increasing trend?

Although our study period started from the beginning of the year 2000, we got the first article published in year 2005 (according to the article selection criteria). Figure 3 is a line curve which plots publication year on the x-axis and the number of articles published in that year on the y-axis for the articles under review. Exposition of the curve reveals that research on this domain is recent (the first article in year 2005), and follows a growing trend in terms of number of publications till the year 2012. However, a sharp decline since then has been noted.

Research in the Domain of OSS Project Prediction Is One of the Key Interest for the Researchers

RQ3: What is the portfolio of projects analysed for prediction studies and what are the domains of the projects?

The realm of open source consists of thousands of projects. These projects have diverse characteristics including different application domain, community size, evolution pattern, and success history. Our review identified that prediction studies mostly used data from the flagship OSS projects that are large in size with a large user and developer community, and that belong to popular application domains.

Findings suggest that Development Platform, Application Software and Application Suite are the most popular application domains (Figure 4). Projects within those domains, such as Eclipse, NetBeans, Mozilla, Apache, Office suites got the highest attention in the reviewed studies. Most of these projects enjoy more than 5 years of development and evolution history. Figure 5 presents the list of OSS projects that were studied at least in two articles.

Figure 3. Year-wise distribution of the prediction studies

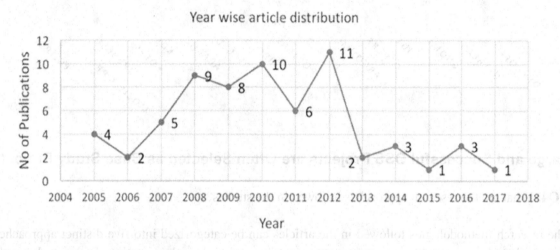

This finding supports the fact that research to date is mostly vertical (Capiluppi, Models for the evolution of os projects, 2003) taking only the flagship projects into account. However, vast majority of projects do not belong to the domain of large and successful one (Boldyreff;Beecher;& Capiluppi, 2009). Therefore, reported results cannot be extended to broader population of OSS projects.

Figure 4. Application Domain of the OSS projects

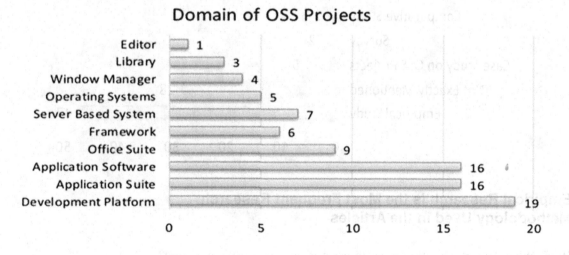

Figure 5. List of OSS projects studied

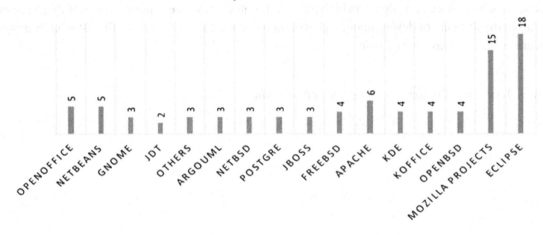

Large and Successful OSS Projects are Often Selected as Case Study Projects

RQ4: What are the research approaches followed in the studies?

The research methodologies followed in the articles can be categorized into five distinct approaches: empirical study, case study, comparative study, survey, and tool implementation. Figure 6 shows the count of published articles according to this classification. As can be seen from the figure, 72% of the studies (47 articles out of 65) followed an empirical research approach.

Figure 6. Main focus of the prediction studies

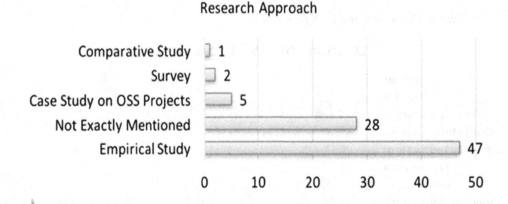

Empirical Research Is the Most Frequent Research Methodology Used in the Articles

RQ5: What datasets or data sources of oss projects are mostly exploited?

One of the most important aspects of prediction studies is the usage of project datasets. These datasets of OSS projects are termed as repositories which contain a plethora of information on the underlying software and its development processes (Cook;Votta;& Wolf, 1998) (Atkins;Ball;Graves;& Mockus, 1999). These data sources offer several benefits: the approach is cost effective, requires no additional instrumentation, and does not depend on or influence the software process under consideration (Cook;Votta;& Wolf, 1998). Sources for such data can be divided into two broad categories, e.g., project sources and external sources, as shown in Figure 7. Project sources are managed and maintained by the respective project with the aid of data management tools, e.g., source code version control systems (e.g., CVS, SVN, GIT), bug tracking systems (e.g., Bugzilla), mailing list archives and others. However, many third-party hosting sites offer facilities in hosting and maintaining project data, e.g., Sourceforge, and Ohloh. In this study, these sources are categorized as external sources. Utilization count of the sources under these two categories is summarized in Figure 7.

Figure 7. Data Sources for OSS Prediction Studies

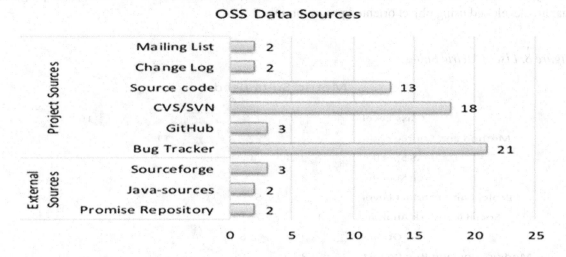

As shown in this figure, repositories maintained by the respective projects have a clear popularity over the external sources. Among the project sources, bug tracking systems and the source code version management systems were mostly explored. This is reasonable as majority of the reviewed articles are skewed towards fault/defect prediction of the software (as discussed in RQ1), and the sources listed above are the primary candidate for that. Among the external sources, SourceForge (Schilling;Laumer;& Weitzel, 2012) is one of the most popular repository hosting thousands of OSS projects and having over four million downloads per day (Schilling;Laumer;& Weitzel, 2012).

Repositories Maintaining Source Code (e.g., SVN/CVS) and Bug Reports (e.g., Bugzilla, Jira, Email Archives) Are Mostly Explored in the Prediction Studies

RQ6: What metric suites are evaluated and what tools are used for metric data collection?

Distributions of metric suites in the articles are shown in Figure 8. A good sample of the reviewed articles (16 out of 65) used class-level metrics, followed by method and source-code level (11 articles) metrics. When class-level metrics are used instead of method-level/ source-code level metrics, predicted fault-prone modules are the classes instead of methods. Yet, more specific parts of source code that are fault-prone can be identified with method/source code level metrics. Both categories of metrics fit well within OSS projects as the majority of projects studied in the reported articles are implemented using object oriented languages (Figure 9). As a side not, the use of such languages is limited to only three languages, namely, JAVA, C++ and C. Even though these languages are the most popular ones, yet the studies left a side many other contemporary languages. This affects the completeness of fault prediction studies, a discussion on which is made in the AVENUE TO FUTURE WORK section.

Among the class-level metrics, the CK (Chidamber & Kemerer metrics) suite, proposed in 1994, is the most popular one. It is being used by several software tool vendors and researchers working on fault prediction (Catal & Diri, A systematic review of software fault prediction studies, 2009). Apart from this, other popular metric suites are MOOD (metrics for object-oriented design), QMOOD (quality metrics for object-oriented design), and L&K (Lorenz and Kidd's metrics). These metrics are used for programs that are developed using object oriented programming.

Figure 8. List of Metric Suites

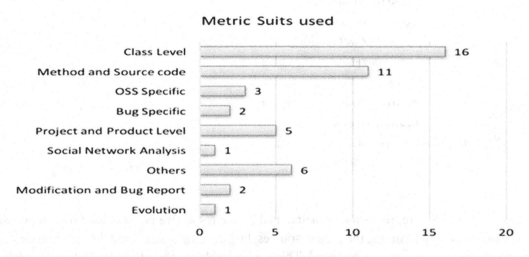

Figure 9. Programming language distribution among the studied OSS projects

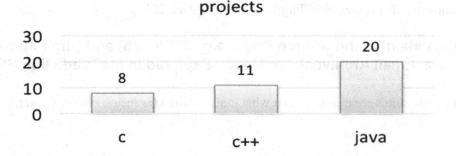

Within method/source code level metrics, Halstead (proposed in 1977) and McCabe (proposed in 1976) metrics have been the most popular ones. Method-level metrics can be collected for programs developed with structured programming or object-oriented programming paradigms. Because source code developed with these paradigms include methods.

A summary of the analysis of the metrics reported in the reviewed articles from the point of view of performance can be found in Table 3. In this table, statistical significance of the metrics (based on prediction accuracy) is classified into three categories, e.g., significant (or best), satisfactory (or good), and bad predictors, keeping alignment to the classification used in the reviewed articles. Additionally, metrics are classified in the category contradictory if they are identified as significant/satisfactory predictors, as well as, bad predictors in the reviewed articles.

Amongst the metric suites, class level metrics, e.g., CK metrics show strong predictive capability (P.M. & Duraiswamy, 2011) in general, although few of the metrics performance are inconclusive. For instance, DIT (Depth of Inheritance Tree) is noted as a satisfactory predictor in (Wahyudin;Schatten; Winkler;Tjoa;& Biffl, 2008) (Subramanyan & Krishnan, Empirical analysis of ck metrics for object-oriented design complexity- Implications for software defects, 2003), but classified as a bad predictor in (Thy;Ferenc;& Siket, 2005) (Shatnawi & Li, 2008). Similar results exist for LOC (Lines Of Code) metric. Within individual studies, the LOC is reported as a significant predictor for fault prediction (Catala;Sevima;& Diri, 2011) (Li;Herbsleb;& Shaw, 2005) (Thy;Ferenc;& Siket, 2005). According to these studies, the LOC metric alone performs better (or similar) compared to the CK metrics. Within other individual studies, LOC is reported to have poor predictive power (Knab;Pinzger;& Bernstein, 2006). Results analogous to this also exist in literature beyond the context of OSS (Fenton & Ohlsson, 2000) (Bell;Ostrand;& Weyuker, 2006).

Apart from fault prediction metrics, the use of SNA (Social Network Analysis) metrics shows a considerable decrease in false positives rates without compromising the detection rates (Gerger;Basar;& aglayan, 2011). Recently, a different trend of prediction work has been carried out in (Schilling;Laumer;& Weitzel, 2012), where prediction of developer retention in OSS projects has been studied. For doing this, actual Person-Job and Person-Team Fit parameters were used as metrics. Reported results have identified that the level of developer retention is positively related to facts like participant's level of relevant development experience and familiarity with the coordination practices within the team. Further, the level of retention has been found to be negatively associated with the level of academic qualification and underrating the contributions of a developer. In other words, developers who are undervalued, or having high academic degrees are inclined to leave projects.

Recent studies also explore OSS project specific metrics to predict several aspects of the projects. For instance, predicting future forking trend of a project based on the fork history, or determining the trustworthiness of a project.

Data collection for metrics is traditionally supported by a wide range of data collection and analysis tools. We, thereby, bring together the tools used in each reviewed article, the list of which is presented in Figure 10, along with their usage count. As can be seen from the figure, Weka is the most popular among the used tools. The reason might be that Weka provides a comprehensive collection of machine learning algorithms both for data mining and for generating prediction models that distinguish between the class of files "No bug" and the class "One or more bug". Most of the other tools used are third party software. Thus, the quality of the data is limited to the accuracy of such tools.

Table 3. Metric performance evaluation

Metric Category and Example	Statistical Significance
Class level metrics (E.g. CK, MOOD, QMOOD, L&K)	- Pareto's law holds which implies that the majority of faults is rooted in a small proportion of classes. - Significant metrics are CBO, RFC, LOC, WMC, RFC, LCOM, LCOMN, CTA, CTM, OCMEC, LCOM3, and OSAVG. - Satisfactory metrics include NOC, DIT, NOOM, NOAM, NOA, NOO, LCOM, CSA, CSO, NPAVGC, SDIT, SNOC, POF, and PDIT. - Bad predictors are NOC and DIT. - Metrics that resulted in contradictory performance include NOC and DIT. - Compared to other metrics, CK metrics showed consistent fault prediction capability for OSS object oriented software. - Also, an Eclipse plug-in based tool implementing the Naive Bayes algorithm with class level metrics resulted in the same performance as with WEKA tools Naive Bayes implementation. **Reference:** (English;Exton;Rigon;& Cleary, 2009), (Yuming & Baowen, 2008), (Thy;Ferenc;& Siket, 2005), (P.M. & Duraiswamy, 2011), (Shatnawi & Li, 2008), (Korua & Liu, 2007), (Catala;Sevima;& Diri, 2011), (Johari & Kaur, 2012), (Singh & Verma, 2012), (Okutan & Yildiz, 2012), (Zimmermann;Premraj;& Zeller, Predicting Defects for Eclipse, 2006)
Method and Source code level metrics (E.g., Halstead, McCabe, Cyclomatic complexity)	- Significant source code metrics are size, if statements, Nested routine declarations, Include files, switch and case usage, Data type declarations, and Accumulated McCabe complexity. - Significant method level metrics are Number of method calls and Number of methods. - Metrics (or Predictors) obtained from one project can be applied to (a) different projects with a reasonable accuracy and (b) projects within the same domain with higher accuracy. **Reference:** (Zimmermann;Premraj;& Zeller, Predicting Defects for Eclipse, 2006), (Phadke & Allen, 2005), (Ferzund;Ahsan;& Wotawa, 2008), (Zimmermann;Nagappan;Gal;Giger;& Murphy, 2009)
Evolution metrics (E.g. linesChangePer-Change, linesActivityRate, coChangedFiles, linesChange.)	- High quality prediction models can be built using evolution metrics. These models can identify refactoring prone/non refactoring prone classes very accurately. Additionally, an increase in refactoring has a significant positive impact on the quality of the software. - Prediction accuracy of the metrics varies among projects. - Significant metrics in this category include coChangedNew, linesActivityRate, coChangedFiles, linesChangePerChange, linesActivityRate, coChangedFiles, changeFrequencyBefore, and coChangedNew. **Reference:** (Ratzinger;Sigmund;Vorburger;& Gall, 2007), (J. Ratzinger, 2008), (Lee;Lee;& Baik, 2011), (Kenmei;Antoniol;& Penta, 2008)
SNA metrics (E.g., Betweenness Centrality, Closeness Centrality, Barycenter Centrality.)	- Considerably decreases high false alarm rates without compromising the defect detection rates. - Considerably increases low prediction rates without compromising low false alarm rates compared to churn metrics. - Information flow within the developer communication network has significant effect on code quality. **Reference:** (Biçer;Basar;& Çaglayan, 2011)
Project and Product metrics (E.g., RDD, RCD, Software Documentation Completeness.)	- Significant metrics are Resolved Defects/Reported Defects (RDD), Closed Defects/Reported Defects (RCD), Changes by peripheral developers/total changes (CBD), Class Data Abstraction Coupling (CDA), and TechMailing. - Models proposed based on this metric class resulted high prediction accuracy for the studied projects. **Reference:** (Wahyudin;Schatten;Winkler;Tjoa;& Biffl, 2008), (Lee;Lee;& Baik, 2011), (English;Exton;Rigon;& Cleary, 2009)
Modification and Bug report metrics (E.g., sharedMRs, nrPRs, reporter(bug).)	- Bug report metrics having significant performance are assignee, reporter, and monthOpened (in which month the bug is reported). - Modification and Bug report metrics with satisfactory performance includes nrMRs (checkins of a *.cpp file), sharedMRs (the number of times a file was checked in together with other files), and nrPRs (the number of reported problems). - Between 60% and 70% of incoming bug reports can be correctly classified into fast and slowly fixed. **Reference:** (Giger;Pinzger;& Gall, 2010), (Knab;Pinzger;& Bernstein, 2006)
Other metrics	- Heuristic metrics: Significant predictors are MFM (Most Frequently Modified) and MFF (Most Frequently Fixed). Bad predictors are MRM (Most Recently Modified) and MRF (Most Recently Fixed). - Historical metrics: Significant predictors are files age, DA (number of distinct authors), and FC (frequency of change). Additionally, old unstable or old fluctuating files are the most fault-prone ones. The number of defects found in the previous release of a file does not correlate with its current defect count. **Reference:** (Hassan & Holt, The Top Ten List: Dynamic Fault Prediction, 2005), (Illes-Seifert & Paech, 2010)

Figure 10. Tools used for metric data collection and modelling

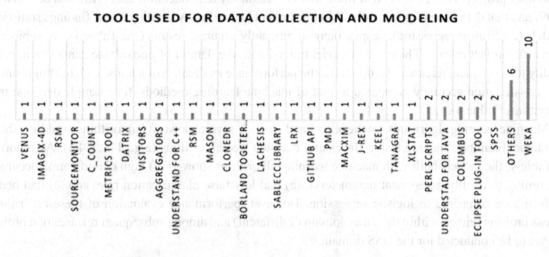

RQ7: What are the methods used in prediction models?

Methods and algorithms that are used to build fault/defect prediction models, primarily fall into two categories: statistical methods and machine learning algorithms. As can be seen from Figure 11, 46% (30 out of 65) of the articles exploited statistical methods whereas 29% (19 out of 65) used machine learning algorithms. We summarize in Table 4, the key performance evaluation of these models extracted from the reviewed articles.

Figure 11. Methods for Prediction

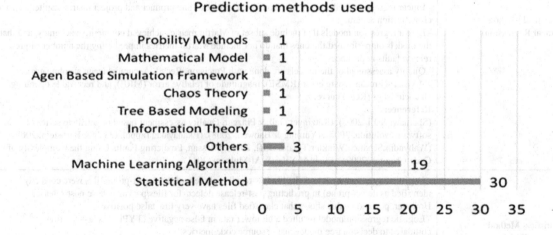

Researchers apply statistical methods, such as univariate or multivariate linear regression, logistic regression, or cox regression to predict faults. However, statistical models are considered black box solutions because the relationship between input and response cannot be seen easily (Almeida & Matwin, 1999). Also, a model that has been validated with a specific project's data is not convenient to be used in another project. The reason is that these models are highly dependent on data (Almeida & Matwin, 1999) and that data varies significantly from one project to another. According to our findings statistical models (e.g., linear regression), despite their significantly accurate results (see Table 4), are subject to a specific project release. Therefore, a model trained with the dataset of one release cannot be applied readily to subsequent releases. Additionally, the performance evaluation of a logistic algorithm resulted low classification accuracy compared to that of machine learning methods, for example decision tree algorithms (Table 4).

Machine learning algorithms, on the other hand, provide several powerful algorithms to address these problems. Examples include Naive Bayes and decision tree algorithms (e.g., J48, C4.5). As reported in Table 4, the models built with machine learning algorithms showed (a) high classification accuracy (according to quality assessment parameters), (b) had low false classification rate, and (c) had better performance compared to logistic regression. However, performance evaluation of these algorithms across projects (either, within the same domain or different) and among subsequent releases of a project are yet to be conducted for the OSS domain.

Table 4. Performance evaluation of Prediction models

Prediction Model and Example	Model Performance
Statistical Method (Linear Regression)	- Linear regression can be used to build accurate prediction models using evolution metrics. - Univariate linear regression analysis showed that many class level metrics are strongly related to maintainability. Whereas, multivariate linear regression demonstrates reasonable prediction accuracy. - According to ROC measure, MMLR model showed better performance in predicting severity levels of faulty classes, than the multivariate logistic regression (MLR) model. Additionally, these models identify more severe errors slightly better than they can do to less severe errors. However, a prediction model used in one release cannot be used in subsequent releases without training it with that release data. - Linear regression model using evolution metrics resulted in good performance according to mean absolute error (MAE), and root mean square error (RMSE) measure. - Linear regression model using both source code metrics and product and project metric resulted in good classification accuracy. - Linear regression models that include subset of Martin metrics achieved competitive accuracy, and that the models outperformed the ones that do not include Martin metrics in predicting the number of pre-release faults in packages. - Quality assessment of the models are done with Precision, Recall, Accuracy, mean absolute error (MAE), root mean square error (RMSE), magnitude of relative error (MRE), and receivable operating characteristics (ROC) curve. **Reference:** (Shatnawi & Li, 2008), (Ratzinger;Gall;& Pinzger, Quality assessment based on attribute series of software evolution, 2007), (Yuming & Baowen, 2008), (Ekanayake;Tappolet;Gall;& Bernstein, 2009), (Wahyudin;Schatten;Winkler;Tjoa;& Biffl, 2008), (Hassan, Predicting Faults Using the Complexity of Code Changes, 2009), (Elish;Al-Yafei;& Al-Mulhem, 2011)
Statistical Method (Regression Analysis, Correlation)	- Logistic regression model resulted in low recall (only few of the defect-prone files were correctly identified as defect-prone) in predicting post-release defects for files/packages have post-release. However, precision value shows that classified files have very low false positives. - Logistic regression model resulted a bit lower rate in false negative (TYPE II) classification as compared to decision tree models using source code metrics. - Cox proportional hazards modeling with recurrent events identified significant relationship between the logarithmic transformation of class size and defect-proneness. - Quality assessment of the models is done with Precision, Recall, and Accuracy. **Reference:** (Koru;Zhang;& Liu), (Zimmermann;Premraj;& Zeller, Predicting Defects for Eclipse, 2006), (Phadke & Allen, 2005)

continues on following page

Table 4. Continued

Prediction Model and Example	Model Performance
Machine Learning Algorithms (Decision Tree, e.g., J48, C4.5, LMT, Random Forest)	- Decision tree models with initial and post-submission bug report data showed adequate performance when compared to random classification. Between 60% and 70% of incoming bug reports can be correctly classified into fast and slowly fixed. The best performing prediction models were obtained with 14-days or 30-days of post-submission data. However, implementation of a fully automated system based on these models is questionable. - A Decision tree learner (J48) can predict defect densities at source code/class level with acceptable accuracies. J48 along with other prediction models identifies refactoring prone classes with high accuracy and recall. - Decision tree model (C4.5) performs better than logistic regression model with significantly low false negative (TYPE II) classification. - Random Forest algorithm classifies fault prone classes with high accuracy, recall, F-measure, and AUC. - The classification accuracy (using Weka tool) varies between 68% and 92% for different releases of the projects. - Quality assessment of the models is done with Precision, Recall, F-measure, Accuracy, and AUC. **Reference:** (Gerger;Basar;& aglayan, 2011), (Knab;Pinzger;& Bernstein, 2006), (Phadke & Allen, 2005), (Zimmermann;Nagappan;Gal;Giger;& Murphy, 2009), (Ferzund;Ahsan;& Wotawa, 2008)
Machine Learning Algorithms (Naive Bayes)	- Naive Bayes has performed better than J48 according to ROC, Precision, Recall, F-measure, Accuracy and Mean absolute error measures. - Model built with Naive Bayes algorithm and using SNA metrics either (a) considerably decreases high false alarm rates without compromising the detection rates, or (b) considerably increases low prediction rates without compromising low false alarm rates. - Quality assessment of the models are done with Precision, Recall, F-measure, Accuracy, ROC curve, Mean absolute error, Probability of detection(pd), and Probability of false alarms(pf). **Reference:** (P. Singh, 2012), (Catala;Sevima;& Diri, 2011), (Biçer;Basar;& Çaglayan, 2011)
Machine Learning Algorithms (Neural network, KStar, Adtree)	- Univariate models built with Neural Network, KStar, and Adtree do not offer improved fault-proneness discrimination ability compared to using the complexity metrics directly. - The neural network model resulted in the weakest model (according to precision and completeness) compared to logistic regression and decision tree models. **Reference:** (Y. Zhoua, 2010), (Thy;Ferenc;& Siket, 2005)

Statistical Methods Are Mostly Used to Build Fault/Defect Prediction Models

RQ8: How are the research methodology and results validated?

Threats to validity in experimental studies can be classified into three broader categories. They are, external, internal, and construct validities (Subramanyan & Krishnan, Empirical analysis of ck metrics for object-oriented design complexity: Implications for software defects, 2003). External validity refers to the extent to which reported results can be generalized to the whole population (or outside the study settings). Internal validity means that changes in the dependent variables can be safely attributed to changes in the independent variables. Construct validity means that the independent and dependent variables accurately model the abstract hypotheses.

Our review results concerning these validity issues reveal that 52% (27 out of 52) of the articles reported one or more of the validity threats concerning the underlying research methodology and research results. These articles either reported quantifiable measure to minimize one or more of the validity threats or admitted the threat as a delinquent to the study. Figure 12 presents the number of articles that discuss the validity threats concerting the study. As can be seen from the figure, 20 articles out of 65 addresses internal validity threat, whereas, only 13 studies cited external validity. This implies that a large part of the studies (52 out of 65) needs to be extended to a broader domain of OSS projects for generalizability of the reported results. Many of these studies also recommend further replication of the approach across other OSS projects to gain confidence on reported results (English;Exton;Rigon;& Cleary, 2009) (Shatnawi & Li, 2008). Relating to this, in (Turhan;Menzies;Bener;& Stefano, 2009) it is reported that for defect prediction models there exists very little evidence on their cross-project applicability.

Figure 12. Validation of the research methodology

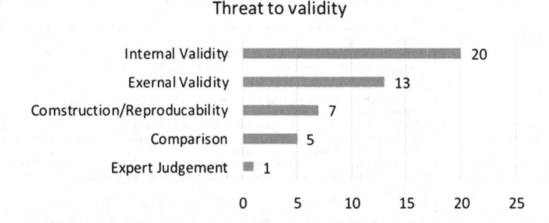

Majority of the Studies Suffer From External Validity Threats and Thus Fall Short in Generalizing the Results to the Population of OSS Projects

RQ9: How are the prediction models validated?

There are many ways in which the performance of a prediction model can be measured. Indeed, many different categorical and continuous performance measures are used in the articles. A list of such measures is presented in Figure 13. There is no one best way to measure the performance of a model. This depends on factors like class distribution of the training data, how the model has been built, and how the model will be used. In assessing the performance of a classification model, the evaluation measures applied most are (a) precision/ correctness (the ratio of the number of classes correctly predicted as fault prone to the number of classes predicted as fault-prone), (b) recall/ sensitivity (the ratio of the number of classes correctly predicted as fault prone to the total number of classes that are actually fault prone), and (c) accuracy (the ratio of number of classes correctly predicted to the total number of classes) (Kaur & Malhotra, 2008).

It should be noted that cross comparison of studies is sometimes difficult if uniform performance measures are not reported. Current literature (Kitchenham, ym., 2010) in this regard reports that the ROC (Receivable Operating Characteristics) curves, AUC (Area Under the Concentration-time curve), and ARE (Average Relative Error) are effective when comparing the ability of modelling techniques. They are particularly useful to cope with different datasets and for continuous studies.

Figure 13. Validation of the prediction model

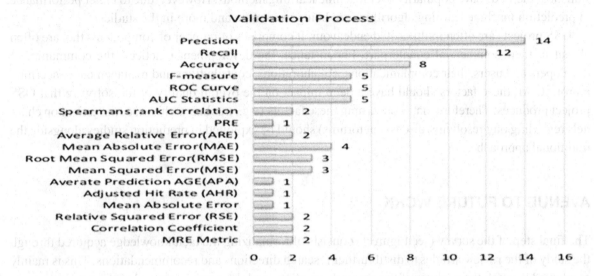

SYNTHESIS

This chapter is dedicated in pursuing a systematic literature review on the topic- prediction methods and techniques for OSS projects. Under the hood, 65 research articles published in peer reviewed journals and conferences are reviewed systematically to answer 9 key queries related to the topic.

According to the recorded response of the review, it is noted that OSS prediction studies have largely focused on Fault/Defect prediction and Reliability prediction. Many methods, models, metrics and data sources are presented, explored and analysed for predicting defects of OSS projects. Such interest in research is reasonable since dealing with software faults is a vital and foremost important task in software development (Santosh & Kumar, 2016). Presence of faults is always detrimental to the quality and reliability of the software, and has a negative impact on the development and maintenance cost of the software (Menzies, et al., 2010). Therefore, locating fault prone segments within a software should help improving its quality and reliability.

As cited in (Gupta & Saxena, 2017), prediction of software defect can only be possible either based on historical data accumulated during implementation of similar or same software projects or it can be developed using design metrics collected during design phase of software development. In this regard, this review reported extensive use of source code version control (e.g., CVS, SVN, GIT) and bug reporting systems (e.g., Bugzilla, Jira) for extracting historical data on both development and error tracking and resolution.

Contemporary software development utilizes Object-oriented (OO) approach as a de-facto standard for implementing software (Gupta & Saxena, 2017). In line to this observation, this review reported that majority of the projects studied for prediction are implemented using OO languages (e.g., JAVA and C++). Consequently, use of OO metrics (e.g, class level and method level metrics) are predominantly used in prediction studies.

In identifying defects, two main categories of prediction methods are predominantly used by the studies. They are, statistical methods and machine learning methods. According to the review outcome, statistical methods have popularity over machine learning methods. However, due to better performance in prediction machine learning algorithms are being used more and more in the studies.

OSS projects are often multifaceted endeavour. It comprises of number of components that are often absent in their commercial counterpart. For instance, the development practices, the community of developers and users, their communications, collaborations, contributions and management concerning a project. All these factors should have a deep impact on the overall quality of the software that OSS project produces. Therefore, data concerning these factors (e.g., mailing archives, communication channels regarding bug resolving, discussion forums) should be exploited in prediction studies alongside the traditional approaches.

AVENUE TO FUTURE WORK

The final step of the survey (see Figure 1) consists of formalizing the tacit knowledge acquired through the study of the review articles to distil further research directions and recommendations. This is mainly conducted through the analysis of the research questions and the results reported in the articles.

On Data Sources and Data Quality

The quality of the data used for metrics in prediction (especially in fault prediction) has significant potential to undermine the efficacy of a model. Data quality is complex and many aspects of the data are important to ensure reliable predictions (Hall;Beecham;Bowes;Gray;& Counsell, 2012). Yet, collecting good quality data in OSS projects is very hard due to their use of different data management systems (Figure 7), tools, and techniques for managing historical data. This makes it difficult to ensure availability and quality of the data required for metric suites, which may hinder the comparability of the results (Askari & Holt, 2006). Also collected data is usually noisy and often needs to be cleaned (Caglayan;Bener;& Koch, 2009) for reliable fault prediction (Jiang;Lin;Cukic;& Menzies, 2009). None-the-less the size of training and test dataset has an impact on the accuracy of the prediction (Jiang;Lin;Cukic;& Menzies, 2009). Yet, without good quality and clearly reported data, it is difficult to gain confidence in the predictive results. Taking these issues in consideration, future studies may focus on the followings.

- Proposing standard approaches to assess the quality and quantity of the data required to build reliable prediction models.
- Proposing and adopting standard approaches for data collection, considering different available data sources. Data cleaning mechanisms should be explicitly addressed. This will make the reported results more cohesive and comparable.
- Addressing the issue of confidence on the tool performance to gain overall confidence on the data quality and results.

On the Methods

Prediction research in OSS projects is skewed towards fault/defect prediction, as shown in Figure 3. Consequently, fault prediction models are mostly used, which can be broadly classified into statistical methods and machine learning algorithms (Figure 11). Our review identified the dominance of statistical methods over machine learning algorithms in the articles (as shown in Figure 11). However, statistical methods have their limiting factors, and thus the following recommendations could be considered.

- Exploring the potential of machine learning methods for prediction. We argue that machine learning algorithms have better features than statistical methods (Catal & Diri, A systematic review of software fault prediction studies, 2009).
- Using simpler models as they have relatively better prediction performance. For instance, Naive Bayes and Logistic regression, in particular, seem to be the techniques used in models that are performing relatively well (Hall;Beecham;Bowes;Gray;& Counsell, 2012).

On Predictive Performance of the Methods

Performance comparison across studies is only possible if studies report a set of uniform measures (Hall;Beecham;Bowes;Gray;& Counsell, 2012). Additionally, any uniform set of measures should give a full picture of correct and incorrect classification. Prediction studies utilize a number of measuring techniques (as listed in Figure 13 in the Appendix), namely precision, recall, accuracy, ROC curve, and AUC. According to our findings, 63% of the reviewed articles (33 out of 52 articles) did not report performance measure of the model. Thus, future works may focus on the followings areas to increase confidence on the prediction models and their comparability.

- Using uniform measures such as ROC curves, AUC, and Average Relative Error (ARE) to improve the comparing ability of modelling techniques. These are particularly useful to cope with different datasets and for continuous studies.
- Exploring the potential of cost and/or effort aware measurement for prediction models. This takes into account the cost/effort of falsely identifying modules and has been increasingly reported as useful (Lessmann;Baesens;Mues;& Pietsch, 2008) (Zimmermann;Herzig;Nagappan;Zeller;& Murphy, 2010).
- Developing heuristics and recommendations for reliable measure selection. Inappropriate measures can present a misleading picture of predictive performance and can undermine the reliability of predictions (Catala;Sevima;& Diri, 2011).

On the Metrics

Class level metrics and source code metrics are used predominantly in the studied literature (as reported in Figure 8). Overall these metrics have good prediction accuracy. Yet, conflicting results among studies exist concerning the performance of some metrics, as discussed in RQ6. Thus the following need to be considered in future works.

- Identifying factors that can influence performance inconsistency. This may include, among other factors, the diverse nature of OSS data sources, unavailability of required data, and hindering the metric accuracy while applying to certain prediction models.
- Developing heuristics and best practices to minimize the factors that lead to inconsistency of the metric performance and to provide reliable results.

Traditionally defect prediction models rely on metrics that represent the state of the software system at a specific moment in time. These metrics are used to capture a particular snapshot or release of a project to predict the next one. But metrics capturing changes over time in projects also play a significant role in prediction. For example, metrics presenting software evolution were used to predict the need of refactoring (Y. Zhoua, 2010) and quality of OSS projects (Lee;Lee;& Baik, 2011) with significant accuracy. Though such results are encouraging, these metrics are not mature enough to gain prediction confidence. Thus, future study can consider the following recommendations.

- Deriving an empirically validated set of evolution metrics for fault prediction.
- Performing exploratory studies to verify whether it can complement the existing metric suites to experience better prediction results.

Additionally, metrics modelling the community dynamics of OSS projects can play a pivotal role in predicting the future of the project, including fault prediction. Current research (as discussed in RQ6) gives affirmative indication towards this direction.

On OSS Community and Prediction

What sets open source development apart from the traditional proprietary setting is the developer community driving the project. Hence it seemed natural to include the community aspect as one of the questions. However, although the structure, social connections and internal communication of OSS communities have gained significant interest, research effort devoted to studying the community in relation to prediction appears quite the opposite (as shown in Figure 2). For instance, such topic has been studied in (Bettenburg & Hassan, 2010) where the authors investigated the impact of social structures between developers and end-users on software quality. Their results give support to thinking that social structures in the community do hold prediction power in addition to the source code centric approaches. It is also suggested that combining metrics focusing on code and social aspects work as a better prediction model than either alone. On a similar note, development communities and their communication have been studied from the prediction point of view (Wolf;Schroter;Damian;& Nguyen, 2009) outside the scope of OSS giving prediction power to communication structure measures in build failures. A similar result is reported in (Bird;Nagappan;Gall;Murphy;& Devanbu, 2009) in which developer information is used as an element within a socio-technical network of variables, which offered better predictive performance. This suggest the following questions could be studied in future works.

- How can community structures be used as a predictive instrument?
- Can metric suites and models be community-oriented? Would this complement traditional approaches to achieve improved prediction accuracy?

On the Generalizability Issue

Decisions made under the selected research methodology lead to the generalizability concern of the reported results. One major concern is that the population of case study OSS projects is skewed towards the flagship ones (Figure 4 and Figure 5), having a long history of project evolution with large user and developer community. Thus, the reported results fall short in representing the wider population of OSS projects [many projects are small and not successful].

Moreover, prediction models applied in one project may not be applicable to others. The reason is that these models are highly dependent on data (Almeida & Matwin, 1999) and that data varies significantly from one project to another. Also, statistical models are strongly tied to a specific release of a project, and therefore, a model trained with one snapshot of a project cannot be applied to subsequent releases. Additionally, data collection process for metrics should have traceability to increase confidence on the metric performance. All these issues contributed to the validity of the reported results, especially the generalizability dimension (Figure 12). The following points could be taken care in future studies to address external validity.

- Approaches and techniques for data selection, collection and processing should be made explicit to increase the confidence on metric performance.
- Metric and method selection should be justified with uniform measurement techniques.
- Case study projects should be selected in order to increase the generalizability of the reported results.

On the Programming Languages

For fault prediction studies, it is important to include programming language as one of the criterion for predicting numbers of faults. According to the study results in (Ostrand;Weyuker;& Bell, 2003), it has been noted that Makefiles, SQL, shell, HTML, and "other" files had significantly higher fault rates than java files when holding all else constant, while c files had significantly lower rates. There might be several factors contributed to this fact, e.g., different languages may be designed for different tasks and functionalities, and given the same functionality, different language may require diverse amount of codes lines to achieve the functionality (Ostrand;Weyuker;& Bell, 2003). However, the exact impact of programming languages on fault prediction are yet inconclusive (Ostrand;Weyuker;& Bell, 2003). This observation, however, raises a validity threat towards the fault prediction results reported to date for OSS, as only 3 of the most popular programming languages (Ranking, 2014) (Figure 9) are considered in the studies. Keeping this in mind, future studies should carefully pick divertive languages and incorporate them within the prediction model.

THREATS TO VALIDITY

Carrying out a literature review is mostly a manual task. Thus, most threats to validity relate to the possibility of researcher bias (Cornelissen;Zaidman;Deursen;Moonen;& Koschke, 2009). To minimize this, we adopted guidelines on conducting SLR suggested by Kitchenham (Kitchenham, Procedures for performing systematic reviews, 2004). In particular, we documented and reviewed all steps we made in advance, including selection criteria and attribute definitions.

In what follows, description related to validity threats pertaining to article selection, attribute framework, and article characterization.

Article Selection

Following the advice of Kitchenham (Kitchenham, Procedures for performing systematic reviews, 2004), the inclusion criteria is defined based on the research questions and during the definition of the review protocol, which may reduce the likelihood of bias. Only articles satisfying this selection criterion have been considered in this study. For collecting relevant articles, we first performed automated keyword search and then performed manual selection. The first step condenses the selection bias whereas the later ensures the relevance of the selected articles. Finally, a non-recursive search through the references of the selected articles is performed. This increases the representativeness and completeness of our selection. To minimize the selection bias and reviewer bias further, a domain expert (third author) verified the relevance of the selected articles against the selection criterion.

Attribute Framework

The construction of the attribute framework may be the most subjective step (Cornelissen; Zaidman; Deursen; Moonen; & Koschke, 2009). Thus we took a two-step validation measure to minimize bias. First, the attribute set is derived based on the research questions and domain of study. A pilot study was run by the first two authors in which five articles were randomly selected to derive these attributes. The resultant attribute sets from both the authors were then merged through discussion to get the final set of attributes. Second, the representativeness of this attribute framework is then examined by the domain expert (third author).

Article Assessment

Similar to the construction of the attribute framework, the process of assigning the attributes to the research articles is subjective and may be difficult to reproduce (Cornelissen; Zaidman; Deursen; Moonen; & Koschke, 2009). We address this validation threat through a two-step evaluation process as discussed in section REVIEW METHODOLOGY.

CONCLUSION

In this chapter, we have reported a systematic literature review (SLR) on the prediction studies of open source software projects. To carry out this review we adopted a review protocol following the guidelines presented in (Kitchenham, Procedures for performing systematic reviews, 2004) and (Cornelissen; Zaidman; Deursen; Moonen; & Koschke, 2009). A set of 65 articles were reviewed in the study, which is the result of a systematic article selection process defined in the protocol. Through a detailed reading of a subset of the selected articles, we derived an attribute framework that was consequently used to characterize the articles in a structured fashion. We also posed a set of research questions in advance that are investigated and answered throughout the study. The attribute framework was sufficiently specific to characterize the articles in answering the research questions. None-the-less, an elaborated discussion on the validity of the review process is also presented.

The characterization of the reviewed articles will help researchers to investigate previous prediction studies from the perspective of metrics, methods, datasets, tool sets, and performance evaluation and validation techniques in an effective and efficient manner. We also put an elaborated discussion on the most significant research results. In summary, this article provides a single point reference on the state-of-the-art of OSS prediction studies which could benefit the research community to establish future research in the field.

To the best of our knowledge this is the first study that provides a systematic review on prediction studies of OSS projects. However, systematic literature review in the field of software fault prediction was first conducted in (Catal & Diri, A systematic review of software fault prediction studies, 2009). Focus area of this review was the articles on software fault prediction with a specific focus on metrics, methods and datasets. Later on, this work was extended in (Catal, Software fault prediction: A literature review and current trends, 2011) incorporating more articles and presenting current trends on the field of fault prediction. But these reviews concerned fault prediction studies only and were not targeting open source projects.

Yet in comparing our results concerning fault prediction with these studies, we noted contradictions. For instance, the dominance of statistical methods in OSS fault prediction contradicts with the findings reported in (Catal & Diri, A systematic review of software fault prediction studies, 2009). This study pointed out that machine learning algorithms are gaining more interest (they increased from 18% to 66%) over statistical methods (they decreased from 59% to 14%) for prediction. This difference in findings might be for two reasons, (a) the survey in (Catal & Diri, A systematic review of software fault prediction studies, 2009) focused only on fault prediction studies of in-house software, whereas our survey covers the entire domain of prediction studies on OSS projects, and (b) prediction studies are relatively new (as discussed in RQ2) in OSS. However, it will be promising to see that researchers explore the potential of machine learning methods in OSS prediction studies which is also suggested in (Catal & Diri, A systematic review of software fault prediction studies, 2009).

ACKNOWLEDGMENT

We would like express our sincere gratitude to Late Prof. Tarja Systä, Department of Pervasive Computing, Tampere University of Technology, Finland, for her invaluable contributions to the journal version of this chapter.

REFERENCES

Almeida, M. D., & Matwin, S. (1999). Machine learning method for software quality model building. *International symposium on methodologies for intelligent systems*, 565-573.

Askari, M., & Holt, R. (2006). Information theoretic evaluation of change prediction models for large-scale software. *International workshop on Mining software repositories*, 126–132. 10.1145/1137983.1138013

Atkins, D., Ball, T., Graves, T., & Mockus, A. (1999). Using version control data to evaluate the impact of software tools. *International Conference on Software Engineering*, 324-333. 10.1145/302405.302649

Beecham, S., Baddoo, N., Hall, T., Robinson, H., & Sharp, H. (2008). Motivation in software engineering: A systematic literature review. *Information and Software Technology, 50*(9-10), 860–878. doi:10.1016/j.infsof.2007.09.004

Bell, R., Ostrand, T., & Weyuker, E. (2006). Looking for bugs in all the right places. Intl Symp. Software Testing and Analysis, 61–72.

Bettenburg, N., & Hassan, A. (2010). Studying the impact of social structures on software quality. *International Conference on Program Comprehension*, 124–133. 10.1109/ICPC.2010.46

Biçer, S., Basar, A., & Çaglayan, B. (2011). Defect prediction using social network analysis on issue repositories. *International Conference on Software and Systems Process*, 63-71.

Bird, C., Nagappan, N., Gall, H., Murphy, B., & Devanbu, P. (2009). *Putting it all together: Using socio-technical networks to predict failures*. Intl Symp. Software Reliability Eng.

Boldyreff, C., Beecher, K., & Capiluppi, A. (2009). Identifying exogenous drivers and evolutionary stages in Floss projects. *Journal of Systems and Software, 82*(5), 739–750.

Brereton, P., Kitchenham, B. A., Budgen, D., Turner, M., & Khalil, M. (2007). Lessons from applying the systematic literature review process within the software engineering domain. *Journal of Systems and Software, 80*(4), 571–583. doi:10.1016/j.jss.2006.07.009

Caglayan, B., Bener, A., & Koch, S. (2009). Merits of using repository metrics in defect prediction for open source projects. *CSE Workshop Emerging Trends in Free/Libre/Open Source Software Research and Development*, 31–36. 10.1109/FLOSS.2009.5071357

Capiluppi, A. (2003). *Models for the evolution of os projects*. ICSM. doi:10.1109/ICSM.2003.1235407

Capiluppi, A., & Adams, P. J. (2009). Reassessing brooks law for the free software community. *IFIP Advances in Information and Communication Technology, 299*, 274–283. doi:10.1007/978-3-642-02032-2_24

Catal, C. (2011). Software fault prediction: A literature review and current trends. *Expert Systems with Applications, 38*(4), 4626–4636. doi:10.1016/j.eswa.2010.10.024

Catal, C., & Diri, B. (2009). A systematic review of software fault prediction studies. *Expert Systems with Applications, 36*(4), 7346–7354. doi:10.1016/j.eswa.2008.10.027

Catala, C., Sevima, U., & Diri, B. (2011). Practical development of an Eclipse-based software fault prediction tool using Naive Bayes algorithm. *Expert Systems with Applications, 38*(3), 2347–2353. doi:10.1016/j.eswa.2010.08.022

Cook, J., Votta, L., & Wolf, A. (1998). Cost-effective analysis of in-place software processes. *IEEE Transactions on Software Engineering, 24*(8), 650–663. doi:10.1109/32.707700

Cornelissen, B., Zaidman, A., Deursen, A., Moonen, L., & Koschke, R. (2009). A systematic survey of program comprehension through dynamic analysis. *IEEE Transactions on Software Engineering, 35*(5), 684–702. doi:10.1109/TSE.2009.28

Dyba, T., & Dingsyr, T. (2008). Empirical studies of agile software development: A systematic review. *Information and Software Technology, 50*(9-10), 833–859. doi:10.1016/j.infsof.2008.01.006

Eclipse. (2013). Retrieved from Eclipse: http://www.eclipse.org/proposals/packaging/

Ekanayake, J., Tappolet, J., Gall, H., & Bernstein, A. (2009). *Tracking Concept Drift of Software Projects Using Defect Prediction Quality*. MSR. doi:10.1109/MSR.2009.5069480

Elish, M., Al-Yafei, A., & Al-Mulhem, M. (2011). Empirical comparison of three metrics suites for fault prediction in packages of object-oriented systems: A case study of Eclipse. *Advances in Engineering Software, 42*(10), 852-859.

English, M., Exton, C., Rigon, I., & Cleary, B. (2009). *Fault detection and prediction in an open-source software project*. PROMISE. doi:10.1145/1540438.1540462

Fenton, N. E., & Ohlsson, N. (2000). Quantitative analysis of faults and failures in a complex software system. *IEEE Transactions on Software Engineering, 26*(8), 797–814. doi:10.1109/32.879815

Ferzund, J., Ahsan, S., & Wotawa, F. (2008). Analysing Bug Prediction Capabilities of Static Code Metrics in Open Source Software. *International Conferences IWSM*, 331-343.

Gerger, S. B., Basar, A., & Aglayan, B. (2011). Defect prediction using social network analysis on issue repositories. *ICSSP*, 63–71.

Giger, E., Pinzger, M., & Gall, H. (2010). *Predicting the fix time of bugs*. RSSE.

Hall, T., Beecham, S., Bowes, D., Gray, D., & Counsell, S. (2012). A systematic literature review on fault prediction performance in software engineering. *IEEE Transactions on Software Engineering, 38*(6), 1276–1304. doi:10.1109/TSE.2011.103

Hassan, A. (2009). *Predicting Faults Using the Complexity of Code Changes*. ICSE. doi:10.1109/ICSE.2009.5070510

Hassan, A., & Holt, R. (2005). *The Top Ten List: Dynamic Fault Prediction*. ICSM.

Illes-Seifert, T., & Paech, B. (2010). Exploring the relationship of a files history and its fault-proneness: An empirical method and its application to open source programs. *Information and Software Technology, 52*(5), 539–558. doi:10.1016/j.infsof.2009.11.010

Jiang, Y., Lin, J., Cukic, B., & Menzies, T. (2009). *Variance analysis in software fault prediction models*. Intl Symp. Software Reliability Eng. doi:10.1109/ISSRE.2009.13

Johari, K., & Kaur, A. (2012). Validation of object oriented metrics using open source software system: An empirical study. *Software Engineering Notes, 37*(1), 1–4. doi:10.1145/2088883.2088893

Kaur, A., & Malhotra, R. (2008). Application of random forest in predicting fault-prone classes. *International Conference on Advanced Computer Theory and Engineering*, 37–43. 10.1109/ICACTE.2008.204

Kenmei, B., Antoniol, G., & Penta, M. D. (2008). *Trend Analysis and Issue Prediction in Large-Scale Open Source Systems*. CSMR. doi:10.1109/CSMR.2008.4493302

Kitchenham, B. (2004). *Procedures for performing systematic reviews*. Technical Report TR/SE-0401, Keele University, and Technical Report 0400011T.1, National ICT Australia.

Kitchenham, B., Pretorius, R., Budgen, D., Brereton, O. P., Turner, M., Niazi, M., & Linkman, S. (2010). Systematic literature reviews in software engineering- a tertiary study. *Information and Software Technology, 52*(8), 792–805. doi:10.1016/j.infsof.2010.03.006

Knab, P., Pinzger, M., & Bernstein, A. (2006). *Predicting defect densities in source code? les with decision tree learners.* MSR.

Koru, A. G., Zhang, D., & Liu, H. (2007). Modeling the effect of size on defect proneness for open-source software. *Third International Workshop on Predictor Models in Software Engineering.*

Korua, A., & Liu, H. (2007). Identifying and Characterizing change-prone classes in two large-scale open-source products. *Journal of Systems and Software, 80*(1), 63–73. doi:10.1016/j.jss.2006.05.017

Lee, W., Lee, J., & Baik, J. (2011). *Software reliability prediction for open source software adoption systems based on early lifecycle measurements.* COMPSAC. doi:10.1109/COMPSAC.2011.55

Lessmann, S., Baesens, B., Mues, C., & Pietsch, S. (2008). enchmarking classi?cation models for software defect prediction: A proposed framework and novel findings. *IEEE Transactions on Software Engineering, 34*(4), 485–496. doi:10.1109/TSE.2008.35

Li, P. L., Herbsleb, J., & Shaw, M. (2005). Finding predictors of? eld defects for open source software systems in commonly available data sources: a case study of openbsd. *International Software Metrics Symposium (METRICS).* 10.1109/METRICS.2005.26

Okutan, A., & Yildiz, O. (2012). *Software defect prediction using Bayesian networks.* Journal Empirical Software Engineering.

OSS prediction studies: Data collection Table. (2013). Retrieved from OSS prediction studies: Data collection Table: http://literature-review.weebly.com/

Ostrand, T., Weyuker, E., & Bell, R. (2003). Predicting the Location and Number of Faults in Large Software Systems. *IEEE Transactions on Software Engineering.*

Perry, D., Porter, A., & Votta, L. (2000). Empirical studies of software engineering: A roadmap. *The Future of Software Engineering.*

Phadke, A., & Allen, E. (2005). *Predicting Risky Modules in Open-Source Software for High-Performance Computing.* SE-HPCS. doi:10.1145/1145319.1145337

P.M., S., & Duraiswamy, K. (2011). An Empirical Validation of Software Quality Metric Suites on Open Source Software for Fault-Proneness Prediction in Object Oriented Systems. *European Journal of Scientific Research, 52*(2).

Ranking, S. (2014). *Top 10 Programming Languages.* Retrieved from Top 10 Programming Languages: http://spectrum.ieee.org/computing/software/top-10-programming-languages

Ratzinger, J. T. S. (2008). On the Relation of Refactoring and Software Defects. MSR, 35-38.

Ratzinger, J., Gall, H., & Pinzger, M. (2007). Quality assessment based on attribute series of software evolution. *Working Conference on Reverse Engineering,* 80–89. 10.1109/WCRE.2007.39

Ratzinger, J., Sigmund, T., Vorburger, P., & Gall, H. (2007). Mining software evolution to predict refactoring. *International Symposium on Empirical Software Engineering and Measurement*, 354–363. 10.1109/ESEM.2007.9

Russo, B., Mulazzani, F., Russo, B., & Steff, M. (2011). Building knowledge in open source software research in six years of conferences. *IFIP Advances in Information and Communication Technology*, *365*, 123–141. doi:10.1007/978-3-642-24418-6_9

Samoladas, I., Angelis, L., & Stamelos, I. (2010). Survival analysis on the duration of open source projects. *Information and Software Technology*, *52*(9), 902–922. doi:10.1016/j.infsof.2010.05.001

Schilling, A., Laumer, S., & Weitzel, T. (2012). Who Will Remain? An Evaluation of Actual Person-Job and Person-Team Fit to Predict Developer Retention in FLOSS Projects. *Hawaii International Conference on System Sciences*, 3446–3455.

Shatnawi, R., & Li, W. (2008). The effectiveness of software metrics in identifying error-prone classes in post-release software evolution process. *Journal of Systems and Software*, *81*(11), 1868–1882. doi:10.1016/j.jss.2007.12.794

Singh, P. S. V. (2012). Empirical Investigation of Fault prediction capability of object oriented metrics of open source software. JCSSE, 323 – 327.

Singh, P., & Verma, S. (2012). *Empirical Investigation of Fault prediction capability of object oriented metrics of open source software*. JCSSE.

Subramanyan, R., & Krishnan, M. (2003). Empirical analysis of ck metrics for object-oriented design complexity- Implications for software defects. *IEEE Transactions on Software Engineering*, *29*(4), 297–310. doi:10.1109/TSE.2003.1191795

Syeed, M., Kilamo, T., Hammouda, I., & Systä, T. (2012). Open Source Prediction Methods: a systematic literature review. In *IFIP International Conference of Open Source Systems* (pp. 280-285). Springer. 10.1007/978-3-642-33442-9_22

Thy, T., Ferenc, R., & Siket, I. (2005). Empirical validation of object-oriented metrics on open source software for fault prediction. *IEEE Transactions on Software Engineering*, *31*(10), 897–910. doi:10.1109/TSE.2005.112

Turhan, B., Menzies, T., Bener, A. B., & Stefano, J. D. (2009). On the relative value of cross-company and within-company data for defect prediction. *International Symposium on Empirical Software Engineering and Measurement2009*, *14*(5), 540–578. 10.100710664-008-9103-7

Wahyudin, D., Schatten, A., Winkler, D., Tjoa, A. M., & Biffl, S. (2008). *Defect prediction using combined product and project metrics a case study from the open source apache. myfaces project family*. Euromicro Conference Software Engineering and Advanced Applications. doi:10.1109/SEAA.2008.36

Wolf, T., Schroter, A., Damian, D., & Nguyen, T. (2009). Predicting build failures using social network analysis on developer communication. *International Conference on Software Engineering*, 1-11. 10.1109/ICSE.2009.5070503

Yuming, Z., & Baowen, X. (2008). *Predicting the maintainability of open source software using design metrics.* Academic Press.

Zhoua, Y. (2010). On the ability of complexity metrics to predict fault-prone classes in object-oriented systems. *Journal of Systems and Software, 83*(4), 660–674. doi:10.1016/j.jss.2009.11.704

Zimmermann, T., Herzig, K., Nagappan, N., Zeller, A., & Murphy, B. (2010). *Change bursts as defect predictors.* Intl Symp. Software Reliability Eng.

Zimmermann, T., Nagappan, N., Gal, H., Giger, E., & Murphy, B. (2009). *Cross-project Defect Prediction- A Large Scale Experiment on Data vs. Domain vs. Process.* ESEC/FSE.

Zimmermann, T., Premraj, R., & Zeller, A. (2006). Predicting Defects for Eclipse. *Third International Workshop on Predictor Models in Software Engineering.*

ADDITIONAL READING

Badri, M., Badri, L., Flageol, W., & Toure, F. (2016). Source code size prediction using use case metrics: An empirical comparison with use case points. *Innovations in Systems and Software Engineering,* 1–17.

Borges, H., Hora, A., & Valente, M. T. 2016. Predicting the Popularity of GitHub Repositories, *International Conference on Predictive Models and Data Analytics in Software Engineering, Article no.* 9.

Bouktif, S., Sahraoui, H., & Ahmed, F. (2014). Predicting Stability of Open-Source Software Systems Using Combination of Bayesian Classifiers [. *ACM Transactions on Management Information Systems, 5*(1), 3. doi:10.1145/2555596

Braunschweig, B., Dhage, N., Viera, M. J., Seaman, C., Sampath, S., & Koru, A. G. 2012. Studying Volatility Predictors in Open Source Software, *International Symposium on Empirical Software Engineering and Measurement (ESEM),* Pages 181-190. 10.1145/2372251.2372286

Bucholz, R., & Laplante, P. A. (2009). A dynamic capture model for software defect prediction. *Innovations in Systems and Software Engineering, 5*(4), 265–270. doi:10.100711334-009-0099-y

Catala, C., Sevima, U., & Diri, B. (2011). Practical development of an Eclipse-based software fault prediction tool using Naive Bayes algorithm. *Expert Systems with Applications, 38*(3), 2347–2353. doi:10.1016/j.eswa.2010.08.022

Chen, F., Li, L., Jiang, J., & Zhang, L. 2014. Predicting the Number of Forks for Open Source Software Project, *International Workshop on Evidential Assessment of Software Technologies,* Pages 40-47. 10.1145/2627508.2627515

Ekanayake, J., Tappolet, J., Gall, H. C., & Bernstein, A. (2012). Time variance and defect prediction in software projects. *Empirical Software Engineering, 17*(4), 348–389. doi:10.100710664-011-9180-x

Ekanayake, J., Tappolet, J., Gall, H. C., & Bernstein, A. (2012). Time variance and defect prediction in software projects. *Journal Empirical Software Engineering, 17*(4-5), 348–389. doi:10.100710664-011-9180-x

English, M., Exton, C., Rigon, I., & Cleary, B. 2009. Fault Detection and Prediction in an Open-Source Software Project. *Proceedings of the 5th International Conference on Predictor Models in Software Engineering (PROMISE)*. 10.1145/1540438.1540462

Ferzund, J., Ahsan, S. N., & Wotawa, F. (2008). Analysing Bug Prediction Capabilities of Static Code Metrics in Open Source Software, Software Process and Product Measurement. *Lecture Notes in Computer Science, 5338*, 331–343. doi:10.1007/978-3-540-89403-2_27

Garcia, H. V., & Shihab, E. 2014. Characterizing and Predicting Blocking Bugs in Open Source Projects, *11th Working Conference on Mining Software Repositories (MSR)*, Pages 76-81.

Giger, E., Pinzger, M., & Gall, H. 2010. Predicting the Fix Time of Bugs, *Proceedings of the 2nd International Workshop on Recommendation Systems for Software Engineering*. 10.1145/1808920.1808933

Gitzel, R., Krug, S., & Brhel, M. (2010). *Towards A Software Failure Cost Impact Model for the Customer: An Analysis of an Open Source Product*. PROMISE. doi:10.1145/1868328.1868354

Gyimothy, T., Ferenc, R., & Siket, I. (2005). Empirical Validation of Object-Oriented Metrics on Open Source Software for Fault Prediction. *IEEE Transactions on Software Engineering, 31*(10), 897–910. doi:10.1109/TSE.2005.112

Illes-Seifert, T., & Paech, B. (2010). Exploring the relationship of a files history and its fault-proneness: An empirical method and its application to open source programs. *Information and Software Technology, 52*(5), 539–558. doi:10.1016/j.infsof.2009.11.010

Koru, A. G., Zhang, D., & Liu, H. (2007). Modeling the Effect of Size on Defect Proneness for Open-Source Software. *ICSE, 2007*, 115–124.

Korua, A. G., & Liu, H. (2007). Identifying and Characterizing change-prone classes in two large-scale open-source products. *Journal of Systems and Software, 80*(1), 63–73. doi:10.1016/j.jss.2006.05.017

Lavazza, L., Morasca, S., Taibi, D., & Tosi, D. 2010. Predicting OSS Trustworthiness on the Basis of Elementary Code Assessment, *ACM-IEEE International Symposium on Empirical Software Engineering and Measurement, Article no.* 36. 10.1145/1852786.1852834

Luo Li, P., Shaw, M., & Herbsleb, J. (2005). Finding Predictors of Field Defects for Open Source Software Systems in Commonly Available Data Sources: A Case Study of OpenBSD. *METRICS, 05*, 32.

Malhotra, R., & Khanna, M. (2016). An exploratory study for software change prediction in object-oriented systems using hybridized techniques. *Automated Software Engineering, 24*(87), 1–45.

Okutan, A., & Yildiz, O. T. (2012). *Software defect prediction using Bayesian networks*. Journal Empirical Software Engineering.

Phadke, A. A., & Allen, E. B. (2005). Predicting Risky Modules in Open-Source Software for High-Performance Computing. *Proceedings of SE-HPCS, 05*, 60–64. doi:10.1145/1145319.1145337

Samoladas, I., Angelis, L., & Stamelos, I. (2010). Survival analysis on the duration of open source projects. *Information and Software Technology, 52*(9), 902–922. doi:10.1016/j.infsof.2010.05.001

Shanthi, P. M., & Duraiswamy, K. (2011). An Empirical Validation of Software Quality Metric Suites on Open Source Software for Fault-Proneness Prediction in Object Oriented Systems. *European Journal of Scientific Research, 51*(2).

Shatnawia, R., & Li, W. (2008). The effectiveness of software metrics in identifying error-prone classes in post-release software evolution process. *Journal of Systems and Software, 81*(11), 1868–1882. doi:10.1016/j.jss.2007.12.794

Shihab, E., Ihara, A., Kamei, Y., Ibrahim, W. M., Ohira, M., Adams, B., ... Matsumoto, K. (2013). Studying re-opened bugs in open source software. *Empirical Software Engineering, 18*(5), 1005–1042. doi:10.100710664-012-9228-6

Ullah, N. (2015). A method for predicting open source software residual defects. *Journal of Software Quality, 23*(1), 55–76. doi:10.100711219-014-9229-3

Yu, L. (2006). Indirectly predicting the maintenance effort of open-source software. *Journal of Software Maintenance and Evolution: Research and Practice., 18*(5), 311–332. doi:10.1002mr.335

Zanetti, M. S., Scholtes, I., Tessone, C. J., & Schweitzer, F. 2013. Categorizing Bugs with Social Networks: A Case Study on Four Open Source Software Communities, *International Conference on Software Engineering*, Pages 1032-1041. 10.1109/ICSE.2013.6606653

Zhou, Y., & Xu, B. (2008). Predicting the Maintainability of Open Source Software Using Design Metrics. *Wuhan University Journal of Natural Sciences, 13*(1), 14–20. doi:10.100711859-008-0104-6

Zhoua, Y., Xua, B., & Leung, H. (2010). On the ability of complexity metrics to predict fault-prone classes in object-oriented systems. *Journal of Systems and Software, 83*(4), 660–674. doi:10.1016/j.jss.2009.11.704

Zimmermann, T., Premraj, R., & Zeller, A. 2006. Predicting Defects for Eclipse. *Proceedings of the Third International Workshop on Predictor Models in Software Engineering*.

This research was previously published in Optimizing Contemporary Application and Processes in Open Source Software; pages 24-56, copyright year 2018 by Engineering Science Reference (an imprint of IGI Global).

Chapter 34
Predicting Change Prone Classes in Open Source Software

Deepa Godara
Uttarakhand Technical University, Sudhowala, India

Amit Choudhary
Maharaja Surajmal Institute, Delhi, India

Rakesh Kumar Singh
Uttarakhand Technical University, Sudhowala, India

ABSTRACT

In today's world, the heart of modern technology is software. In order to compete with pace of new technology, changes in software are inevitable. This article aims at the association between changes and object-oriented metrics using different versions of open source software. Change prediction models can detect the probability of change in a class earlier in the software life cycle which would result in better effort allocation, more rigorous testing and easier maintenance of any software. Earlier, researchers have used various techniques such as statistical methods for the prediction of change-prone classes. In this article, some new metrics such as execution time, frequency, run time information, popularity and class dependency are proposed which can help in prediction of change prone classes. For evaluating the performance of the prediction model, the authors used Sensitivity, Specificity, and ROC Curve. Higher values of AUC indicate the prediction model gives significant accurate results. The proposed metrics contribute to the accurate prediction of change-prone classes.

DOI: 10.4018/978-1-7998-9158-1.ch034

INTRODUCTION

The unending growing complexity and dependency has led to a rise in demand of high quality software that can be maintained at cheaper costs. Finding software change proneness is a significant and essential activity for improving software feature and reducing maintenance effort formerly the software is installed in real world. Koru and Liu (2007) proved change prone classes as a significant peripheral quality attribute that signifies degree of alterations in a class through various versions of software. Software industry is expanding manifolds day by day. Software changes to incorporate new features or to remove errors. This rapidly changing software demand has resulted in significant increase of effort from development to testing phase in software life cycle. Developing and maintaining software requires resources such as development time, cost to build and effort required. But all these resources are limited. Research has also been carried out to find the association between fault prone classes and object-oriented metrics. Weak classes of any software can be predicted using these quality attributes. Changes if predicted during earlier stages of life cycle, can help a developer in efficiently allocating project's resources by properly allocating the appropriate resources to weaker change prone class, so that such type of classes can be maintained properly and tested rigorously. Predicting such changes can be useful as such evaluations can be utilized to forecast changes from one release to next.

Maintenance phase is considered as one of the costly and significant phases of software. Malhotra and Khanna (2013) identified maintenance cost incurs 40-70% of entire cost of software. Estimation of change in classes i.e. probability with which class will modify or not needs to be evaluated as it can help in reducing maintenance cost and testing. As the software evolves it demands more rigorous testing so that good quality software can be developed with less changes and defects. By focusing on weak change prone classes utilization of resources can be done in a better way. Detection of such classes earlier in life cycle model of software can reduce maintenance costs as because if an error is detected early in a product, it would require lesser amount of resources to correct that error. Else in a later stage the cost of correcting an error increases exponentially in every unnoticed phase. Quality problems related to design can be identified in software before implementing codes, if developers are able to identify change prone classes early in life cycle of the software. Similarly, existing design can be customized, or alternate designs can be selected easily. These types of prediction models give high return on investment. As a result, change proneness prediction model contributes in improving quality of the software and reduces development cost also. Thus, change prediction model serves to deliver high quality software at optimal costs, as lesser changes and faults are carried forward in later stages of software life cycle.

Various object-oriented metrics are used throughout the software process. It is not possible to use a single metric to quantify various aspects of OO application. Various different metrics are required to completely analyse software. To predict change prone classes, various researchers have used various object-oriented metrics like size, cohesion, coupling, inheritance, etc. This research summarizes different object-oriented features which can be utilized to predict amount of change in classes. This will benefit researchers to get through various metrics elaborated here. In addition to that, it will help the researchers to predict more parameters for estimating changes in a class.

Researchers and Practitioners have used various object-oriented metrics throughout the software process. But it is not feasible to use a single metric for quantifying various aspects of Object Oriented application. Several different metrics and methods are needed for completely analyzing the software. Things that need to be considered before developing an efficient change proneness prediction model: (1) it is required to review the effectiveness of several methods as various methods may give different outcomes with different types of data sets. (2) Secondly it becomes essential to test whether the prediction model provides good results on another data set or not.

This study aims to build an efficient change prone prediction model that will predict change prone classes. The study includes the following objectives:

1. It aims to explore the association amongst different object-oriented metrics and change prone classes;
2. To propose some new dynamic metrics that can help in predicting degree of change in class.

RELATED WORK

Change proneness gives the degree of change across various versions of software. This change prone prediction model can help developers in efficient resource allocation, developing improved quality software and reduced maintenance costs. In the last two decades' researchers and practitioners have made a lot of effort for finding the association amongst change prone classes and object-oriented metrics. Research gives a strong correlation amongst object oriented features and change prone class.

Researchers investigated that if object oriented features are used for change proneness prediction model it would give better results. Previous researchers used static object-oriented metrics for prediction of change prone classes. But they failed to incorporate dynamic metrics for prediction of degree of change proneness of any class. Our research tries to incorporate dynamic metrics for predicting change prone classes. Lu et al. (2012) investigated various object-oriented metrics for predicting change proneness of a class. Aggarwal et al. (2009) empirically analyzed the relationship between object oriented metrics and fault proneness of a class. Arisholm et al. (2004) investigated dynamic coupling feature as major signs of change prone classes. Koru and Tian (2005) used measurement values such as scope, coupling, cohesion and inheritance metrics for calculating change in classes. Based on these results they analyzed the effect of big size, closely coupled, little cohesion and large inheritance on classes i.e. whether a class having all these measurement values is more likely to change or not. Their research evaluated highly change prone class does not necessarily have highest dimension but change prone classes followed such classes having highest value of measurement. Overall, Researchers concluded that object oriented features can predict degree of change in a class. All these researchers used existing static object-oriented metrics for prediction of change prone classes.

Han et al. (2008) calculated how one class depends on other using behavioral dependency. They measured change proneness in terms of behavioral dependency. If BDM (Behavior Dependency Measurement) of a class is higher than other, it is more likely to change. Using UML2.0 (Unified Modeling Language 2.0) Sequence diagrams and class diagrams they evaluated the feature of behavioral dependency. Their research proved behavioral dependency can be effectively used for finding possibility of change in a class. However, their research ignored other factors which affects change proneness of a class.

Tsantalis et al. (2005) studied the result of addition or the update of a class on degree of change proneness. To elaborate their work, they categorized their work in three axes i.e. dependency, inheritance and reference. They worked on two multi version software projects (JFlex and JMol). They extracted probabilities from these open source projects for evaluating the design stability over various successive versions of software. The process was completely automated by a program written in Java language, and statistical study illustrated ameliorated relationship amongst the extracted possibilities and genuine changes made in classes as compared to a prediction model which is built on previous facts. Their results proved that their analysis was better than the prediction which relied on past data. But they didn't analyzed changes early in software life cycle. Our research predicts metrics such as execution time, class dependency and frequency, which if predicted earlier can help in early finding of change prone classes. Chaumum et al. (1999) used C language to define a change impact model. Effect of changes made to classes were also studied. Change prediction model developed by them depends on two main factors i.e. types and links such as association, aggregation and inheritance. Their research was focused on telecommunication system for proving the results. Result of the paper stated that software design plays an important role to received changes and selected design features can be used for measuring change. However, their research didn't consider the fact how one class affects other classes. Our research tries to find solutions to these shortcomings by considering class dependency, which finds out how much a class is dependent on other.

Lu et al. (2012) used AUC technique (the area under relative operating characteristic) for evaluating predictive effectiveness of OO metrics. The steps followed were: (1) Compute Area under a relative characteristic and corresponding variance for each object-oriented metrics. (2) For computing the average AUC random effect model is employed. (3) Sensitivity analysis is performed for investigating whether the result of AUC technique is applicable vigorously to the data selection. Results show that size metrics can moderately differentiate between a likely to change and non-likely to change class whereas cohesion and coupling metrics have low predictive capability of finding change prone classes. Inheritance feature have very reduced predicting capability as compared to size, cohesion and coupling metrics. Their research work just considered three metrics sizes, cohesion, and coupling for finding change prone classes. However, other factors were ignored in the research. Elish and Zouri (2014) constructed logistic regression models for finding change-prone classes. Research analyzed statistical correlation between change prone classes and coupling metrics. The results show that a prediction model made with coupling feature gives more accurate results than a model built with cohesion feature. Wherein, a prediction model made with import coupling metrics is more accurate than a model built with export coupling metrics. Research mainly focused on two attributes i.e. coupling and cohesion. Their research just determined which one is better attribute for finding change proneness of a class. In this research we have incorporated dependency feature for finding the association between the classes and other factors such as frequency and execution time are also considered.

Romano and Pinzger (2011) empirically studied the correlation between object oriented features and changes in interfaces of source code. They evaluated ten Java open-source systems for predicting the results. Furthermore, they evaluated the metrics to find degree of change in Java interfaces. Results revealed strongest association between cohesion metric of external interface and changes in source code. Zhou and Leung (2009) based on Eclipse analyzed 1) Effect of class size (whichever metrics of size is taken) on change proneness. 2) Their research analyzed size metrics lead to an overestimation of association between object oriented features and change proneness. Zhu et al. (2013) validated Pareto's law. Using classification methods, they identified change prone classes. They used open source software product, Datacrow for static metrics collection and change in class. Pareto's Law states that 80% of changes in software can be found in 20% of the classes. Experimental results show that results can be used for finding change prone classes and for enhancing developer's efficiency. Researchers tried to find out the relation amongst object oriented features and change in interface of source code. But, they didn't analyze other factors which contribute in affecting change proneness of a class

Khomh et al. (2009) tested the assumption i.e. if a class with code smell is more change prone than the classes without code smell. They analyzed various versions of Azerus (9 releases) Eclipse (13 releases), in which they found 29 code smells. Their research studied relationship between code smell and change proneness. Their results revealed classes have a high probability of change with code smells. Eski and Buzluca (2011) studied association of object oriented features and change proneness. Experimental outcomes of the research indicated that the portions of the software which have a low-level quality, change often during the software life cycle development process. Janes et al. (2006) used arithmetical models for exploring the relationship between OO features and defect prone classes. The results of the models were evaluated via correlations, dispersion coefficients and Alberg diagrams. Abdi et al. (2009) used probabilistic model using Bayesian nets to predict change impact in object-oriented systems. By assigning probabilities to network nodes a model was built. For studying the relation of software attributes and impact of change, data of a real system was used. By executing various scenarios, research analyzed coupling as a good predictor of change. Researchers used various complex technologies and models for prediction of change prone classes. All these models required a lot of time for evaluation of change prone classes. Compared to this our prediction model is simpler and requires less time for prediction.

Wilkie and Kitchenham (2000) determined number of classes involved in a change-ripple. Research also analyzed the effect of CBO values and public function. Results show that high CBO values and high public function count values exhibit more ripple effects. Classes with large public and private member functions participate more often in change ripples. Bacchelli et al. (2010) used the tool infusion, to extract FAMIX-compliant object-oriented models. Using this model, they computed a catalog of object oriented features proposed by Chidamber and Kemerer. Code development was analyzed using change metrics. For using the change metrics in the experiments, source code was linked with entities, i.e., classes. Bergenti and Poggi (2000) developed an approach wherein, UML diagrams were analyzed to suggest changes to the software design which would cause design patterns to occur. Their research included automated finding of design patterns. Input to the tool used was UML design (class and collaboration) diagrams in XMI (XML Metadata Interchange) format. Researcher's analyzed association amongst object oriented metrics and change prone classes. But, outcomes for software in real world was not presented in their research.

Overall, all the previous research is focused mainly on application of static object-oriented attributes. However, dynamic features are ignored. If dynamic features are used in the change prediction model it can lead to more efficient model. Our research tries to fill all the above mentioned gaps, and incorporates both static and dynamic features (class dependency and frequency) for prediction of change prone classes in an object-oriented software. Our proposed prediction method is simpler and can be applied in real world for building efficient object-oriented software. Further, it can be used for effectively allocating the manpower resources such that change prone classes are more focused and can lead to reduction in maintenance and testing efforts.

RELATIONSHIP BETWEEN CHANGE PRONENESS AND OBJECT-ORIENTED METRICS

This section, presents association between object oriented features and change prone classes. To explore this, relationship dependent and independent variables are defined in this study.

Independent Variables

Various aspects of a software process can be enumerated using object oriented metrics. Malhotra and Chug (2013) stated a single metric is not sufficient to study all the aspects of software. A number of metrics or their combination is required to completely understand the software. Various object-oriented metrics (i.e. independent variables) are summarized here in Table 1.

Table 1. Object Oriented metrics for change proneness prediction

S.No	Metrics	Definition	Dimension
1.	LOC (Line of code) • No: of Lines • SLOC (Source line of code) • BLOC (Blank line of code) • Comment line • LDC (Lines with Declarative Code) • LEC(Lines with Executable Code) • Statement Count	• count of all lines • count of lines with source code • count of blank lines • count of lines with Comment • count of lines with declarative source code • count of lines that will be executed • count of total declarative and executable code	Size
2.	Methods • No: of Methods • No: of local methods • No: of private methods • No: of public methods • No: of instance method	• count of methods in a class • count of methods not inherited • count of local/not inherited methods • count of public methods • object created using class. It contains instance method	Size
3.	No: of children	count of immediate subclasses	Inheritance
4.	No: of attributes per class	count of total no: of variables of a class	Size
5.	No: of instance variable	count of variables contained by object	Inheritance
6.	Response for class	It shows interaction of class methods with other methods	Coupling
7.	Coupling between objects	Represents the no: of other types of classes a class is coupled to	Coupling
8.	DIP (Depth of Inheritance)	Count of nodes from parent node to root node.	Inheritance
9.	Lack of Cohesion	Percentage of methods in the class using a particular data field.	Cohesion
10.	WMC (Weighted methods per class)	Count of complexities of all methods.	Size
11.	Interface § No: of methods § Arguments(i) § No: of instance method § APP(i)	§ count of methods declared in interface. § count of arguments of declared methods in interface(i) § No: of instance method § Measure of mean size of method declared. App(i) = Arguments/No: of methods(i)	Size
12.	Coupling between Methods (CBM)	It is a measure of new/redefined methods to which all the inherited methods are coupled.	Coupling
13.	Number of Object/Memory Allocation (NOMA)	It is a measure of the total number of statements that allocate new objects or memories in a class.	Size
14.	Average Method Complexity(AMC)	It is average method size of each class. It does not count virtual and inherited methods.	Size

Various characteristics of software that are included in Table 1 comprises of coupling, inheritance, size, cohesion, etc. For calculating all these metrics Understand for Java (UFJ) software is used.

Apart from all these metrics other metrics such as execution time for class, class dependency, trace events, frequency and popularity are also proposed in this research for finding change prone classes.

Dependent Variables

With the increase in utility of software, software requires many modifications and upgradations. Finding change prone classes lead to better enhancements in any software with a minimal cost. This research aims to explore the association amongst different object-oriented features and change prone attributes. Possibility of occurrence of change in software is mentioned as change proneness. Change can be in relation to addition, deletion or modification of source line of code (SLOC). Change proneness is used as dependent variable in this study.

EMPIRICAL DATA COLLECTION

This section explains the data collection methods and sources that are used in this study. Two open source software (developed using Java language) from warehouse (www.sourceforge.net) are analyzed. Changes in software are analyzed by calculating the number of changes in different versions of same software.

Firstly, Open clinic software is analyzed, which is open source incorporating management of hospital enclosing management of organization, financial, medical lab etc. The two stable versions of open clinic software analyzed in this study are v3 and v4. Version 3 was released on September 17, 2010 and consists of 237 classes and version 4 was released on May 28, 2011 and consists of 254 classes. Another software that is analyzed is open hospital software, which supports management and hospital activities. Its two stable versions that were evaluated are v1.7.2 and v1.7.3. Version 1.7.2 was released on May 21, 2013 and consists of 349 classes and version 1.7.3 was released on September 13, 2014 and consists of 363 classes. Table 2 exhibits the details of software used in this study such as various version, language used, total LOC, total no. of common classes, total classes in which change encountered, and the classes without change.

Table 2 exhibits the details of software used in this study such as various version, language used, total LOC, total no. of common classes, total classes in which change encountered, and the classes without change.

Table 2. Data set used

Name	Version 1	Version2	P/L Used	Total LOC	Total Classes	Classes With Change	Classes Without Change
Open Clinic Software	3	4	Java	44,211	248	107	141
Open Hospital Software	1.7.2	1.7.3	Java	59,575	356	20	336

Object oriented metrics were collected between different versions of software using following steps.

Object Oriented Metrics Collection

With the help of http://sourceforge.net source code is collected for both versions of software. All the object-oriented metrics stated above in table I are collected using Understand for Java(UFJ)tool for previous version of software (Open Clinic Software v3, Open Hospital Software1.7.2). It is static code analysis tool. As the research is predicting change in object oriented classes, accordingly metrics for only these classes are considered. In this research, metrics for classes are generated using UFJ tool, although metrics for methods and files can also be generated with the help of this tool. As we are predicting change prone classes we have taken metrics for classes only.

Common Classes' Collection

Here, common classes from both versions (previous and new) are collected. Changes in these classes were taken into consideration for both the versions of the software. Similar approach is used by (Zhou & Leung, 2009) also.

Classes' Comparison

After step 2, common classes that were collected are compared line by line using DiffMerge Software. It has been developed by a software company named SourceGear. By comparing, each class is categorized as a change prone class and non-change prone class. Change in a class is considered if:

- There is addition, deletion, or modification in SLOC of class in the newer version of software;
- Addition, deletion or modification in comment is not considered as change;
- Addition or deletion of blank line does not affect change;
- Reordering of lines does not affect the change;
- Change in class definition affects the change.

Data Point Collection

Step 3 and step 1 were used to generate data points. In Open Clinic Software 248 classes are present in both the versions. Out of total, 107 classes exhibited change (which constitutes 43% of total classes) and 141 classes did not change. In Open Hospital Software, 152 classes exhibited change (which constitutes almost 42% of total classes) and 204 classes did not change.

Using source code of both the versions obtained from http://sourceforge.net data statistics for both the OpenClinic software and OpenHospital software are analyzed as shown in Table 3 and Table 4.

Using various statistics given in Table 3 and Table 4 data set characteristics for OpenClinic software and OpenHospital software were analyzed. The statistics evaluated in this study include minimum, maximum, mean, median, and standard deviation for every object-oriented metrics. All these statistics are related to metrics present in classes. Minimum values relate to the class having minimum value of a particular metrics. And maximum relates to the class having maximum value of a particular metrics. Observations show software systems that have less number of children (NOC) and least value of inheritance results in low values of NOC metric and DIT metric. For example, mean value for NOC metric for (OpenClinic Software is 0.49 and OpenHospital software is 0.43) and the DIT metric is (OpenClinic,

3.03 and OpenHospital, 2.01). LCOM measure is high for the software systems. It counts for method invocation within a class. Its higher value suggests larger number of methods are invoked in a class. Similar approach is followed in Briand et al. (2000) and Cartwright and Shepperd (2000).

Apart from these metrics we propose some other metrics such as execution time, run time information (i.e. trace events), class dependency, frequency and popularity are also proposed in this research work, which can be utilized effectively in predicting change prone classes.

Table 3. Statistics for OpenClinic software

Metrics	Min.	Max	Mean	Mid.	SD
NL	4	2032	233.97	52	2007.54
SLOC	4	4928	227.3	110	310.5
BLOC	0	178	23.32	7	232.7
LC	0	257	28.81	4	257.5
LDC	2	245	25.73	9	249.6
LEC	0	989	82.72	18	632.79
SC	2	1,109	110.38	28	931.91
NOM	0	18	.87	0	16.62
NLM	0	75	14.21	3	117.23
NPRM	0	12	0.68	0	15.9
NPM	0	62	10.9	3	99.97
NIM	0	68	11.89	3	105.78
NOC	0	10	0.49	0	15.59
NOA	0	22	1.98	1	21.48
NIV	0	115	8.25	2	71.09
RFC	0	117	23.2	5	185.68
CBO	0	27	6.82	2	57.8
DIT	1	4	3.03	2	30.03
LCOM	0	102	89.9	49.8	728.23
WMC	0	155	25.69	6	211.65
CBM	0	19	4.8	2	48.9

Execution Time

Execution time of a class is directly related to size of the class. The research proposes to use this feature for predicting change prone classes.

For calculating the execution time, Eclipse Test and Performance Tools Platform (TPTP) profiling tool is used. Research uses Eclipse SDK version 3.6.2. Size can be estimated from the execution time of product, it can be in relation to classes, methods etc. Using TPTP the execution time can be generated, it creates an XML report of the time. TPTP gives three types of execution time.

Base Time

It is the total time taken by methods to execute. Execution time of other methods called from this method is excluded from base time:

$$T_{bt} = T_{me} - T_{oe} \tag{1}$$

where:

T_{bt} =execution time of message in seconds

T_{oe} = time taken by other methods to execute

Average Base Time

It is the average base time needed for execution of method once. It is denoted as T_{abt}.

Cumulative Base Time

It is the time required by methods to execute. However, it also takes into account execution time of methods that are called from this method:

$$T_{cbt} = T_{me} - T_{oe} \tag{2}$$

Calls

It can be defined as the count of times a method is invoked. The execution time analysis tool records all data that is related to the count of method calls and their execution time. The gathered data can be viewed in several different ways.

Execution Statistics

These statistics provide information about the execution time of each method that has been called as well as the number of calls. Additionally, it also shows the method invocation details, i.e. which method is invoked by other methods and how often it is invoked.

Execution Flow

It visualizes the thread based execution flow of the observed application. This view contains a time scale diagram.

UML Interactions

This view shows an UML based view of the execution flow and method invocations. The UML diagram can either be based on class or thread interactions.

Table 4. Statistics for OpenHospital software

Metrics	Min.	Max	Mean	Mid.	SD
NL	2	2050	203.97	52	2027.54
SLOC	4	6759	177.5	98	564.3
BLOC	0	213	33.12	8	256.7
LC	0	263	32.11	6	265.5
LDC	1	273	35.73	9	252.6
LEC	0	1081	87.12	34	752.79
SC	1	1,217	119.88	56	987.91
NOM	0	54	.67	0	19.82
NLM	0	85	11.61	4	127.53
NPRM	0	22	0.78	0	18.8
NPM	0	69	8.5	3	102.80
NIM	0	69	11.99	3	106.18
NOC	0	7	0.43	0	12.09
NOA	0	42	0.88	1	18.28
NIV	0	119	8.25	2	72.10
RFC	2	186	17.4	3	179.08
CBO	0	20	5.02	1	43.8
DIT	1	3	2.01	2	50.03
LCOM	0	100	79.3	51.2	778.23
WMC	1	215	15.69	5	232.65
CBM	0	2	5.8	2	54.9

Execution time for some of the classes is given in Table 5, evaluated using eclipse TPTP tool. Higher value of execution time indicates higher probability of change proneness of a class.

Trace Events

Software metrics can be categorized as static and dynamic. Metrics which are applied to source code are static metrics and metrics which are obtained during run time are dynamic metrics. Earlier Researchers and Practitioners have focused significantly on static metrics; however dynamic metrics have been ignored up to a significant level. But this metrics needs more concentration as it gives the actual information because it is collected during run time. In this research we emphasize on the concept whether a method which is executed imports or exports other object's method.

Table 5. Execution time

Classes	Execution Time
a11	0.008
a12	0.001
a13	0.001
a20	0.0
Eight	0.001
Fifth	0.01

Table 6. Trace events

Classes	Trace Events
a11	3
a12	5
a13	7
a20	5
Eight	3
Fifth	11

At runtime, within considered scope we can count the total number of messages which are sent and received by objects. For evaluating trace events we consider which methods are executed during runtime and the count of times each method is run. Table 6 gives trace events for our application.

Class Dependency

Class Dependency can be used as one of the significant attributes for predicting the change proneness in software. If a class is affected by change, it will affect another class also. This can be evaluated by finding dependencies between classes. UML2.0 class diagrams (CD) and sequence diagrams (SD) are used for evaluating class dependency. Similar approach has been used in research by Han et al. (2008).

For measuring the class dependency from the source code, UML class diagrams and sequence diagrams are generated from the code. Class dependency can be measured using the below stated approach:

- Build separate object dependency model;
- Build complete system dependency model;
- Create Class Route table;
- Find weighted sum of routes;
- Evaluate the Dependency for each class.

Build Separate Object Dependency Model

Using SD and CD of Unified Modeling Language 2.0, separate Object Dependency model can be constructed.

For a SD, an Object Dependency model consists of 2-tuple (O,M) where:

O - denotes every object in SD.
M- denotes message passed amongst objects.

Message $m \in M$ consists of below mentioned attributes:

$m_D \in O$ - Message dispatched by source object
$m_A \in O$ - Message arrived at Receiver object where $m_D \neq m_A$
m_T - Message title

$m_p \in M$ - Parent message if present where, $m_p \neq m$. If parent message is not applicable, then it is the originating message and is represented as "-"

$m_{LR} \in P$ - Likelihood rate of execution of message in SD such that $0 \leq m_{LR} \leq 1$.

$m_{PR} \in O$ - Projected rate of execution of message in SD such that $0 \leq m_{PR} \leq 1$.

Build Complete System Dependency Model

For finding the class dependency for the complete system, dependency values of objects are combined into a single system dependency model.

Create Class Route Table (CRT)

For creating the class route table, the paths between source and destination object are traversed. These paths become input to CRT. Route is evaluated from the traversed path of incoming message of destination to outgoing message of source. Messages encountered during traversal are added to CRT. In case there is a direct dependency between source and destination, at that time the title of message incoming to destination is same as the message departing from source. In other words, in direct class dependency only a single message is counted in CRT. However, in case of indirect dependency outgoing message of source can be traversed with the help of parent message from the destination to source traversed in backward direction.

Find Weighted Amount of Routes

Weighted amount of routes for every pair of source class C_S and destination class C_D can be evaluated from CRT using below mentioned equation (3):

$$Weighted \; amount \; of \; routes(C_S, C_D) = \sum \frac{1}{N} \times F_{LR} \times F_{PR} \tag{3}$$

where:

N - count of messages in CRT.

F_{LR} - Likelihood rate of execution of message in CRT.

F_{PR} - Projected rate of execution of first message in CRT.

Calculate Class Dependency

The value of class dependency for any class, for instance C_i can be evaluated by summing the pair of corresponding classes (C_i, C_j) as shown in equation 4:

$$CD(C_i) = \sum_{1 \leq i, j \leq n} Weighted \; sum \; of \; Routes(C_i, C_j) \tag{4}$$

Table 7 shows class dependency values of some of the classes using above method. Higher values of dependency indicate higher probability of changes in a class.

Table 7. Class dependency values

Classes	Class Dependency
a11	2.690476
a12	0.896825
a13	2.690476
a20	0.309523
Eight	0.246031
Fifth	0.198412

Frequency

For evaluating the frequency feature, frequent item set mining method is used in this research. Frequency can be defined as the number of times a method is called by another method. A software consists of n number of functions, which can be called by other functions. Since a class has many methods, it is likely to happen some methods are frequently called by others, while others are not called. Because of this frequency attribute can be used as one of the main attribute for predicting change prone classes. For finding this attribute of how frequently a method is called, rules for method calls are generated.

In data mining, frequent sets play a vital role. It can be used to find patterns from databases such as association rules. The most important problem that can be tackled using frequent item set is the mining of association rules. Various item sets, and their characteristics can be identified using frequent item set mining. In data mining, transaction can be defined as set of instances, wherein each class is referred to as item in each method call. In this research, calling of methods by various classes is referred to as instance. And every class is referred to as item.

Frequent item set mining algorithm finds common classes for a method called. Classes which have minimum support are selected. Minimum support states the minimum no: of intervals the calling of method occurs in the common set of classes. Further classes are categorized as {1-term grouping, 2-term grouping… (n-1)-term grouping} based on method call. For example, if classes are {m, n, o}, then 1-term groupings are {m}, {n}, {o} and the 2-term groupings is {m, n}, {n, o}, {m, o} obtained from common set. Similarly, based upon the size of the classes set, the groupings are used accordingly by frequent item set mining algorithm. Table 8 shows rules generated using frequent item set mining algorithm.

Association rules are generated after finding frequent item sets. Association rules are conditional statements such as if/then statements which can be used to uncover relationships between disparate data. Data found in item is known as antecedent. Item found in combination with antecedent is known as consequent. For identifying significant relationships association rules are created using if/ then patterns. Support can be defined as number of times an item appears in database. Confidence can be defined as count of times if/then statements have been found to be true.

After the identification of a set of frequent item sets, association rules are produced. Association rules are conditional statements such as if/then statements which can be used to uncover relationships between disparate data and information repository. An association rule consists of two parts, i.e. Antecedent and consequent. Data found in item is known as antecedent. Item found in combination with antecedent is known as consequent. For identifying significant relationships association rules are created using if/then patterns. Support can be defined number of times an item appears in database. Confidence can be defined as number of times if/then statements have been found to be true.

Table 8. Rules generated for the method calls using frequent item set mining algorithm

Classes	Two Length Combination	Two Length Rule Above Threshold Value	Three Length Rule Above Threshold Value
a112 a111 a113 thirddisp print1 fourthdisplay	[a112, a111] [a112, a113] [a111, a113] [a112, print1] [a112, fourthdisplay] [a111, thirddisp] [thirddisp, print1] [thirddisp, fourthdisplay]	[a112, a111] [a112, a113] [a111, a113] [thirddisp, print1] [thirddisp, fourthdisplay]	[a112, a111, a113] [a112, a113, a111] [a111, a113, a112]

Till now all the change prediction models have considered the metrics explained in Table 1. The research paper contributes some more attributes (time, class dependency, frequency) which can be used to predict change prone classes. However, in order to develop an effective prediction model, there is a need to minimize the dimensions of input set. This was done by finding a subset of independent variables that were significant in predicting the dependent variable and change prone classes. Artificial Bee Colony algorithm (ABC) as shown in Figure 1 is used for reducing the number of input variables.

Figure 1. Flowchart for ABC Algorithm

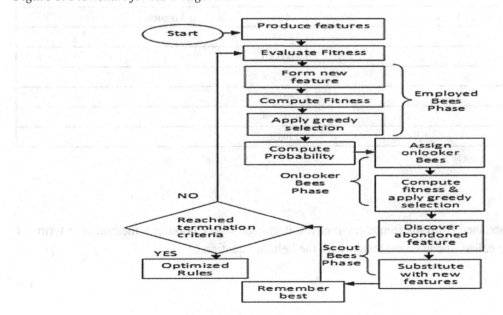

Table 9 gives a set of optimized rules which have been generated using ABC algorithm. Using these optimized rules, frequency of how many times a method is called is evaluated. Higher value of frequency attributes indicates higher chances of change to occur.

Table 9. Optimized Rules using ABC

Optimized Rules
[thirddisp, print1]
[print1, thirddisp]
[thirddisp, fourthdisplay]
[fourthdisplay, thirddisp]
[a112, a111, a113]
[a111, a113, a112]
[a113, a112, a111]
[a112, a113, a111]
[a113, a111, a112]

Frequency, is:

$$F = \frac{No. \ of \ times \ method \ occurs \ in \ input}{Number \ of \ values} \tag{5}$$

Using the above equation 5, values of frequency attribute can be obtained which was optimized using ABC algorithm. Table 10 gives the generated values for this metric.

Table 10. Frequency

Classes	Frequency
a11	7.631578
a12	5.000000
a13	7.631578
a20	2.631578
Eight	0.315789
Fifth	0.105263

Popularity

This metrics is obtained from the frequency metrics, it indicates how popular a method is in terms of calling and being called. It can be evaluated with the help of equation 6:

$$Popularity = F_1 + F_2 \tag{6}$$

where:

$$F_2 = \frac{(M_1)\cdot(M_2)}{Total\ Number\ of\ methods}$$

M_1 - count of intervals a method is called be various methods.
M_2 - count of intervals a method calls various methods.

EXPERIMENTAL FRAMEWORK

In this section firstly, we describe the values obtained for various metrics and secondly, we briefly describe the methods and techniques used for evaluating our change prediction model.

For effectively predicting change prone class, apart from existing change object oriented features other features such as execution time, class dependency and frequency are also evaluated in this research paper.

For calculating the execution time, Eclipse TPTP tool is used wherein, Eclipse SDK version 3.6.2 is used. Values generated for methods is given in Figure 2.

Figure 2. Execution time generated using Eclipse TPTP profile tool

Package	<	Base Time (seconds)	Average Base Time (seconds)	Cumulative Time (seco...	Calls
⊿ ⊕ code	◇	9.990104	0.014933	10.189101	669
▷ ⊖ Newfirst	◇	6.091768	3.045884	6.091768	2
▷ ⊖ OBDM	◇	2.239859	0.003441	2.393795	651
▷ ⊖ ExeTime	◇	1.088570	1.088570	1.088570	1
▷ ⊖ First	◇	0.349820	0.058303	10.189101	6
▷ ⊖ Table	◇	0.153935	0.051312	0.153935	3
▷ ⊖ Frequent	◇	0.033917	0.011306	6.125685	3
▷ ⊖ Findifvalue	◇	0.032234	0.010745	0.032234	3
⊿ ⊕ Test	◇	0.198998	0.000287	10.142756	694
▷ ⊖ Fourth	◇	0.041822	0.001307	0.048686	32
▷ ⊖ Third	◇	0.039354	0.004919	0.046445	8
▷ ⊖ First1	◇	0.030868	0.003087	10.142756	10
▷ ⊖ Second	◇	0.021149	0.021149	0.169005	1
▷ ⊖ a17	◇	0.011022	0.003674	0.013611	3
▷ ⊖ a16	◇	0.010882	0.003627	0.024553	3
▷ ⊖ Writer	◇	0.010811	0.000031	0.010811	347
▷ ⊖ a14	◇	0.006255	0.002085	0.034157	3
▷ ⊖ a13	◇	0.005041	0.001680	0.039251	3
▷ ⊖ a12	◇	0.003724	0.001241	0.043021	3

Using UML2.0 sequence and class diagrams, class dependency values are generated as shown in Figure 3. Dependency indicates if a class is affected by change how it will affect other class.

Count of times how frequently a method is called by other method is defined as frequency. Frequency values are generated as shown in Figure 4.

For evaluating and comparing the proposed change prediction model we have used the multivariate logistic regression method.

Figure 3. Dependency values generated using Sequence and class diagrams

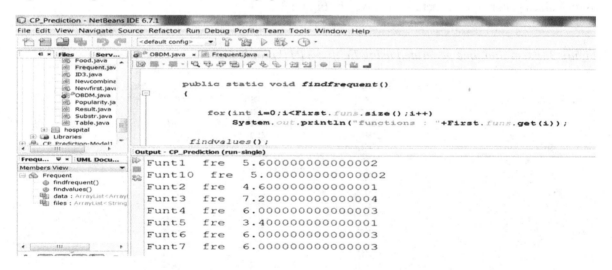

Figure 4. Frequency values evaluated using optimized rules

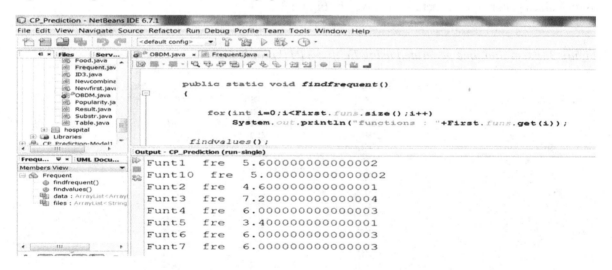

Statistical Logistic Regression Method

This method is used when combination of independent variables contributes in prediction of dependent variable. Complete description is given by Hosmer and Lemeshow (2004) Menard (2002). Logistic regression analysis is classified into: univariate and multivariate logistic regression analysis. Univariate predicts association amongst the two variables i.e. dependent and independent and discovers the importance of their relationship. Conversely, multivariate regression is used for building prediction model for the identification of change prone class. This type of analysis results in finding important metrics. For identifying significant metrics two types of selection methods are used:(i) Forward selection: In this type of selection, a single metric is analyzed at every step. (ii) Backward selection: In this type all the metrics are taken initially and eliminated one after the other till stopping condition is not met.

Mathematically it can be expressed as:

$$prob\left(X_1, X_2, X_3, \ldots\ldots X_N\right) = \frac{exp^{f(x)}}{1 + exp^{f(x)}} \tag{7}$$

where:

$$f(x) = C_0 + C_1 X_1 + C_2 X_2 + \ldots + C_N X_N$$

where the variable X denotes the independent variables and prob is the probability of change proneness of a class:

Odds ratio (OR): It defines the ratio of the likelihood that the event will be caused to the probability event will not be caused. Event here refers to the occurrence of change in the latest version Hosmer and Lemeshow (2004). It is represented by exp (C_i);

  ○   **Maximum Likelihood Estimation:** Statistical method predicts model's coefficients. It predicts the coefficients which support the possibility functions and contribute in making the log value as high as possible. Larger value indicates the improved effect of the independent variable on the expected result variable;

Statistical significance(Sig.): All (C_i) i.e. coefficients have significant level. Higher value of this attribute indicates, independent metrics have lesser impact in estimating change prone classes. We have considered threshold value of 0.7.

Model Development Procedures

For data classification, implementation of Artificial Bee Colony algorithm was done using Java language with WEKA tool and LibSVM. We have used WEKA tool for the validation of our prediction model. This tool is used with association rules, machine learning techniques, classification and for pre-processing of data.

For evaluating the classification process's precision and correctness, we have used a tenfold cross validation. Here we have divided the data set into 10 equally partitions(folds), wherein one partition is consumed for testing part and rest all others are used for training purposes. The process was repeated 10 times, such that every time one of the part became test data. Average of 10 results produced an accuracy of estimation.

For evaluating the performance of the prediction model we have used following methods:

1.   **Sensitivity and Specificity:** For characterizing the accuracy of the prediction model we have used sensitivity and specificity. Sensitivity is defined as the accuracy by which the percentage of classes are correctly identified to be change prone class amongst all the classes which are actually change prone. And specificity is defined as the accuracy by which the percentage of non-change prone classes are correctly identified;

2. **Receiver Operating Characteristics (ROC) Curve:** It is an essential tool for analytic test evaluation. Here sensitivity i.e. (true positive rate) is plotted against specificity i.e. (false positive rate) at different cut off points. Accuracy of prediction model is achieved by selecting cut off point that has higher sensitivity and specificity as suggested by Emam et al. (1999).

RESULT ANALYSIS

This section shows validation results for our model using Open Clinic Software and Open Hospital Software. Using tenfold cross validation, we have illustrated the results. The results can be compared with other prediction models developed using various techniques given by Malhotra and Jangra (2015) which reveals the proposed model gives better results.

Table 11. Statistics for LR multivariate analysis of OpenClinic software

Metrics	B	SE	Sig.	OR
B.D.	0.021	0.21	0.001	1.212
Freq.	0.351	0.25	0.000	1.311
Pop.	0.121	0.11	0.003	0.501
Exec. Time	0.011	0.05	0.025	0.312
T.E.	0.001	0.15	0.031	0.112

Table 12. Statistics for LR multivariate analysis of OpenHospital software

Metrics	B	SE	Sig.	OR
B.D.	0.052	0.31	0.000	1.321
Freq.	0.231	0.021	0.000	1.512
Pop.	0.122	0.032	0.000	1.311
Exec. Time	0.001	0.254	0.010	0.517
T.E.	-0.02	0.212	0.010	0.252

Table 11 and Table 12 shows results for statistics obtained from OpenClinic Software and Open-Hospital software using LR multivariate technique. We have obtained the statistics B (coefficient), SE (Standard Error), Sig. (Significance) and OR (Odds Ratio) for our metrics which are B.D. (Behavioral Dependency), Freq. (Frequency), Pop. (Popularity), Exec. Time (Execution Time), T.E. (Trace Events) using LR multivariate technique. Values of B, SE, Sig. and OR indicates behavioral dependency and frequency have a significant effect in predicting change.

Table 13. Validation results for OpenClinic software

Method	Specificity	Sensitivity	Cut Off Point	AUC
LR	69.7	70.7	0.012	0.750
proposed model	80.2	82.4	0.545	0.925

Table 14. Validation results for OpenHospital software

Method	Specificity	Sensitivity	Cut Off Point	AUC
LR	68.2	68.2	0.245	0.725
proposed model	79.8	81.2	0.564	0.915

Table 13 and Table 14 shows validation results obtained using LR technique and our proposed model which is based on ID3 and ABC (Artificial Bee Colony Algorithm). Values of specificity (69.7) and sensitivity (70.7) for LR technique of OpenClinic software has AUC (0.750) which is less than AUC (0.925) obtained by our prediction model. Similarly, AUC obtained for OpenHospital Software using LR method is 0.725 and AUC obtained by our prediction model is 0.915. The above values indicate that proposed prediction model gives better values as compared to LR multivariate technique.

CONCLUSION

The research paper examines association amongst change prone classes and object-oriented features. In addition to existing object-oriented attributes the research proposes some new attributes such as execution time of class, run time information of methods, frequency of method call, class dependency and popularity. Higher values of proposed metrics indicate higher is the probability of a class to be changed. For calculating the execution time, Eclipse TPTP profiling tool is used, wherein Eclipse SDK version 3.6.2 is used. Runtime information of methods is used to evaluate the values of trace events which is a dynamic metric and gives the accurate values of imported and exported methods. For evaluating the frequency attribute, frequent item set mining algorithm is used. For finding this feature of how frequently a method is called, rules for method calls are generated using association rules. For effectively building the prediction model, dimensions of the input set are reduced using, Artificial Bee Colony algorithm (ABC), which optimizes the rules for finding change prone classes. Further, using source code of Open Hospital application values for proposed metrics were generated. Research evaluated higher values of proposed metrics indicates, higher probability of degree of change prone class. The results were validated using various versions of open source software. For evaluating the performance of the prediction model, we used Sensitivity, Specificity and ROC Curve. Higher values of AUC indicate the prediction model gives significant accurate results. And the proposed metrics contribute to predict accurate change prone classes.

Future Work

For effectively evaluating change proneness in object oriented software, following future directions can be utilized by practitioners and researchers in their research work and studies. As the research is focused on real life software, the usage of commercial data should be increased up to a considerable extent so that real time results can be obtained more effectively. For validating the results, inter project validation can be used in which training set of one project can be used for testing in other similar projects. This would lead to better planning of scarce resources and would help in generating a good quality software. Several studies in literature have used machine learning technique, more machine learning methods can be used for analyzing the performance of change prediction model. A limited work is done using threshold methodology of metrics, the work can be extended by identifying threshold values of all the metrics for change proneness prediction.

REFERENCES

Abdi, M. K., Lounis, H., & Sahraoui, H. (2009, July). Predicting change impact in object-oriented applications with bayesian networks. In *Proceedings of the 33rd Annual IEEE International Computer Software and Applications Conference COMPSAC'09* (Vol. 1, pp. 234-239). IEEE. 10.1109/COMPSAC.2009.38

Aggarwal, K. K., Singh, Y., Kaur, A., & Malhotra, R. (2009). Empirical analysis for investigating the effect of object-oriented metrics on fault proneness: A replicated case study. *Software Process Improvement and Practice, 14*(1), 39–62. doi:10.1002pip.389

Arisholm, E., Briand, L. C., & Foyen, A. (2004). Dynamic coupling measurement for object-oriented software. *IEEE Transactions on* Software Engineering, *30*(8), 491–506.

Bacchelli, A., D'Ambros, M., & Lanza, M. (2010). Are popular classes more defect prone? In *Fundamental Approaches to Software Engineering* (pp. 59–73). Springer Berlin Heidelberg. doi:10.1007/978-3-642-12029-9_5

Bergenti, F., & Poggi, A. (2000, July). Improving UML designs using automatic design pattern detection. In *Proceedings of the 12th International Conference on Software Engineering and Knowledge Engineering (SEKE)* (pp. 336-343).

Chaumun, M. A., Kabaili, H., Keller, R. K., & Lustman, F. (1999). A change impact model for changeability assessment in object-oriented software systems. In *Proceedings of the Third European Conference on Software Maintenance and Reengineering* (pp. 130-138). IEEE. 10.1109/CSMR.1999.756690

Elish, M. O., & Al-Zouri, A. A. (2014, January). Effectiveness of Coupling Metrics in Identifying Change-Prone Object-Oriented Classes. In *Proceedings of the International Conference on Software Engineering Research and Practice (SERP)*. The Steering Committee of The World Congress in Computer Science, Computer Engineering and Applied Computing (WorldComp).

Emam, K., Benlarbi, S., Goel, N., & Rai, S. (1999). A validation of object-oriented metrics (Technical Report ERB-1063). National Research Council of Canada.

Eski, S., & Buzluca, F. (2011, March). An empirical study on object-oriented metrics and software evolution in order to reduce testing costs by predicting change-prone classes. In *Proceedings of the 2011 IEEE Fourth International Conference on Software Testing, Verification and Validation Workshops (ICSTW)* (pp. 566-571). IEEE. 10.1109/ICSTW.2011.43

Han, A. R., Jeon, S. U., Bae, D. H., & Hong, J. E. (2008, July). Behavioral dependency measurement for change-proneness prediction in UML 2.0 design models. In Proceedings of the 32nd Annual IEEE International Computer Software and Applications COMPSAC'08 (pp. 76-83). IEEE.

Hosmer, D. W. Jr, & Lemeshow, S. (2004). *Applied logistic regression*. John Wiley & Sons.

Janes, A., Scotto, M., Pedrycz, W., Russo, B., Stefanovic, M., & Succi, G. (2006). Identification of defect-prone classes in telecommunication software systems using design metrics. *Information Sciences, 176*(24), 3711–3734. doi:10.1016/j.ins.2005.12.002

Khomh, F., Penta, M. D., & Gueheneuc, Y. G. (2009, October). An exploratory study of the impact of code smells on software change-proneness. In *Proceedings of the 16th Working Conference on Reverse Engineering WCRE'09* (pp. 75-84). IEEE. 10.1109/WCRE.2009.28

Koru, A. G., & Liu, H. (2007). Identifying and characterizing change-prone classes in two large-scale open-source products. *Journal of Systems and Software, 80*(1), 63–73. doi:10.1016/j.jss.2006.05.017

Koru, A. G., & Tian, J. (2005). Comparing high-change modules and modules with the highest measurement values in two large-scale open-source products. *Software Engineering. IEEE Transactions on, 31*(8), 625–642.

Lu, H., Zhou, Y., Xu, B., Leung, H., & Chen, L. (2012). The ability of object-oriented metrics to predict change-proneness: A meta-analysis. *Empirical Software Engineering, 17*(3), 200–242. doi:10.100710664-011-9170-z

Malhotra, R., & Chug, A. (2013). An empirical study to redefine the relationship between software design metrics and maintainability in high data intensive applications. In *Proceedings of the World Congress on Engineering and Computer Science* (Vol. 1).

Malhotra, R., & Jangra, R. (2015). Prediction & Assessment of Change Prone Classes Using Statistical & Machine Learning Techniques. *Journal of Information Processing Systems.*

Malhotra, R., & Khanna, M. (2013). Investigation of relationship between object-oriented metrics and change proneness. *International Journal of Machine Learning and Cybernetics, 4*(4), 273–286. doi:10.100713042-012-0095-7

Menard, S. (2002). *Applied logistic regression analysis* (Vol. 106). Sage. doi:10.4135/9781412983433

Romano, D., & Pinzger, M. (2011, September). Using source code metrics to predict change-prone java interfaces. In *Software Maintenance (ICSM), 2011 27th IEEE International Conference on* (pp. 303-312). IEEE. 10.1109/ICSM.2011.6080797

Tsantalis, N., Chatzigeorgiou, A., & Stephanides, G. (2005). Predicting the probability of change in object-oriented systems. *IEEE Transactions on* Software Engineering, *31*(7), 601–614.

Wilkie, F. G., & Kitchenham, B. A. (2000). Coupling measures and change ripples in C++ application software. *Journal of Systems and Software, 52*(2), 157–164. doi:10.1016/S0164-1212(99)00142-9

Zhou, Y., Leung, H., & Xu, B. (2009). Examining the potentially confounding effect of class size on the associations between object-oriented metrics and change-proneness. *Software Engineering. IEEE Transactions on, 35*(5), 607–623.

Zhu, X., Song, Q., & Sun, Z. (2013). Automated identification of change-prone classes in open source software projects. *Journal of Software, 8*(2), 361–366. doi:10.4304/jsw.8.2.361-366

This research was previously published in the International Journal of Information Retrieval Research (IJIRR), 8(4); pages 1-23, copyright year 2018 by IGI Publishing (an imprint of IGI Global).

Chapter 35
Predicting the Severity of Open Source Bug Reports Using Unsupervised and Supervised Techniques

Pushpalatha M N
Ramaiah Institute of Technology, Bengaluru, India

Mrunalini M
Ramaiah Institute of Technology, Bengaluru, India

ABSTRACT

The severity of the bug report helps for the bug triagers to prioritize the handling of bug reports for giving more importance to high critical bugs than less critical bugs, since the inexperienced developers and new users can make mistakes while assigning the severity. The manual labeling of severity is labor-intensive and time-consuming. In this article, both unsupervised and supervised learning algorithms are used to automate the prediction of bug report severity. Because the data was unlabeled, the Gaussian Mixture Model is used to group similar kinds of bug reports. The result is labeled data with the severity level given for each bug reports. Then, the training of classifiers is performed to predict the severity of new bug reports submitted by the user using Multinomial Naïve Bayes Classifier, Logistic Regression Classifier and Stochastic Gradient Descent Classifier. Using these methods, around 85% accuracy is obtained. More accurate predictions can be done using the authors approach.

1. INTRODUCTION

Open source projects such as Firefox, Mozilla, Android, Bugzilla, etc., receives lot of bug reports from all over the world by user and developers, which are stored in the Bugzilla bug Repositories; on average of 29 bug reports per day (Anvik et al., 2006). If assume that the triager takes 5 minutes to examine and handle the bug report, then the traiger has to spend around two hour per day on bug reports. If the

DOI: 10.4018/978-1-7998-9158-1.ch035

large number of bug reports are present in the repositories only fractions of bugs will get chance for fixing. Before fixing any bugs, it needs to be prioritized according to its severity. Severity field helps to identify how urgent the bug needs to be fixed. Prioritizing the bug reports based on the severity helps for the bug triager to assigns the high severe bug report to appropriate developer in order to speed up the fixing process.

New users and inexperienced developers make a mistake in identifying the correct severity label while reporting the bug reports. (Lamkanfi et al., 2010; Pushpalatha et al., 2016) authors not considered the normal severity for severity prediction, because it is default option. In (Lamkanfi et al., 2010) authors suspected that submitters did not assess the severity of bug report consciously. They confirmed this with manual sampling. (Yuan et al., 2016) done research on checking the reliability of the bug report severity labels. Duplicate bug reports refer to the same problem, each duplicate bug report contains different severity label, even though they refer the same problem. There is inconsistency in assigning the severity label. Manual checking and assigning the correct severity will take lot of time and resources, because of lots of bug reports in the bug repository.

In (Lamkanfi et al., 2010; Lamkanfi et al., 2011; Pushpalatha et al., 2016) used Naïve Bayes, Naïve Bayes multinomial, Support vector machine, K-nearest neighbor, J48 and bagging classifiers for predicting the severity of new bug reports using already labeled historical bug reports. (Nachai et al., 2014) authors used the Expectation Maximization (EM) and X-means clustering algorithm for grouping the similar kind of bug reports based on the similarity and done experimentation on Jira bug reports. (Guo, Chen & Li, 2017) Android bug reports severity is predicted using Naïve bayes. Model is built using the labeled data of Eclipse and Mozilla bug reports and built model is tested on the unlabeled bug reports of Android software.

In this work, Gaussian mixture model is used grouping similar kind of bug reports and experimentation is done on the Firefox bug reports taken from the Bugzilla Bug repository. Using this model, a bug triager can use the bugs reported by their users and developer, group them into clusters. After assigning the label to each cluster, labeled data is used for predicting the label of unlabelled bug reports for that used different supervised algorithms such as Naïve Bayes, logistic regression and Stochastic Gradient Descent on the labeled data. This will help to save time and resources.

Contribution of this work:

- Grouped the similar kind bug reports and predicted the labels of bug reports using unsupervised learning;
- Using labeled data Predicted the severity of bug reports using supervised learning such as Logistic Regression, Multinomial Naïve Bayes and Stochastic Gradient descent.

Organization of the paper is as follow, section 2 discusses about the Framework of proposed approach, section 3 gives background information, result and discussion in section 4, section 5 explains about the related work. Finally, in section 6, we conclude and discuss future enhancements of our work.

2. FRAMEWORK FOR PROPOSED WORK

Figure 1 shows the Framework for the proposed model, each step of the Framework is explained in the following sections.

Figure 1. Framework of the proposed model

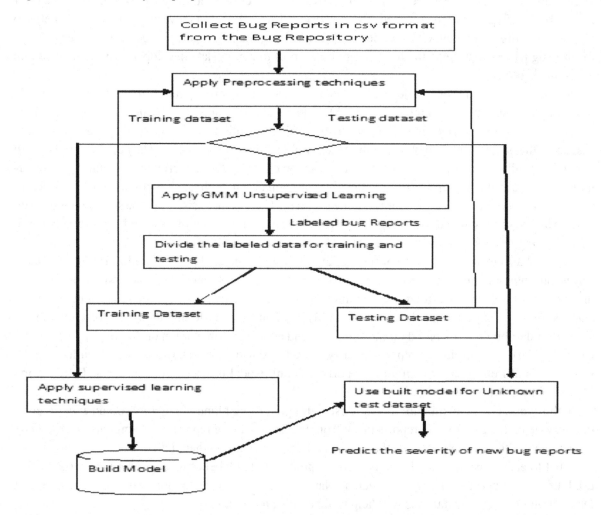

2.1. Collect Bug Reports in CSV Format From the Bug Repository

Collected bug reports for Firefox for desktop and android bug reports in Comma Separated Value (CSV) format from Bugzilla open source bug repository which contains bug reports of different open source software such as Bugzilla, Firefox, etc.

2.2. Apply Preprocessing Techniques

Different preprocessing steps are applied on the collected bug reports such as Tokenization, Stop word removal, Stemming, weighted tf-idf calculation and dimensionality reduction using Singular value decomposition.

Pre-Processing phase is the first step before building the classification model for text document. The pre-processing phase helps in converting the original input into pre-processed structure where the most important text features are retrieved. An efficient pre-processed document helps in improving classification accuracy. The main aim of the pre-processing is to obtain the most relevant terms from the documents. Bug description is given as input to the pre-processing module. The Figure 2 illustrates the overall process of the pre-processing module.

Figure 2. Preprocessing techniques used in our model

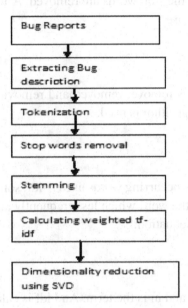

Bug Reports: Taken Firefox for both desktop and android bug reports
Extracting Bug Description: Extracted only bug description from the bug reports

2.2.1. Tokenization

Involves methods of breaking down the input document D into tokens of words w. Then camel case conversion is applied where all the upper-case characters are converted into lower case characters. Then the document is subjected to removal of special characters and numbers. URL check is done on the bug description to check if any URL is present and if present it is removed. Now the document is processed document is given as input to the next phase.

2.2.2. Stop Words Removal

Stop words are words which carries less importance during text classification process. Most of the documents or bug descriptions contain 60-70% of stop words. Stop words removal is applied to obtain most relevant results. Some examples of stop words are "always," "as," "before," etc.

stopwords.txt document is created which contains a list of stop words. Following steps are involved in removing stop words:

Step 1: The input document is broken down into words during tokenization and stored in a separate array.

Step 2: Now single stop word is read from stopwords.txt file and is compared with tokenized document using sequential search technique.

Step 3: If matched, the corresponding word is removed from the array and the process is continued.

Step 4: After comparison with the first stop word then Step 2 is repeated for all the stop words.

The process is repeated until all the stop words are removed. After stop word removal the document is then given as input to the next phase.

2.2.3. Stemming

If the bug report contains the words remove, removed and removing, then it is stemmed to the word remove for that porter stemming algorithm is used.

2.2.4. Tf-Idf Weight

Instead of just using most frequently occurring words used tf-idf, sometimes the word which occur more frequently is less informative than the word which less frequently and scaling down the impact of that. tf-idf is calculated using the below equation:

tf-idf(v, m) = tf(m) *idf(v, m)

where v is the particular document and m is the term. And idf is calculated using the below equation:

$$idf(v,m)=\log \left[\frac{n}{df\left(v, m\right)} +1 \right]$$

Total number of bug reports is n and df(v,m) is number of documents v contain the word m called document frequency.

2.2.5. Dimensionality Reduction

After processing the data and obtaining the numerical attributes, the next step is to reduce the dimension of the input data. Since the data was in text format, converting them into tokens of attributes made thousands of attributes which is very huge. Dimensions are reduced using truncated singular value decomposition (TrucatedSVD). Using the dimensionality reduction, dimensions are reduced to 100. Now, data is ready to feed into Unsupervised Learning Algorithm i.e. Gaussian Mixture Model (GMM).

2.3. Apply GMM Unsupervised Learning

Now that the data is pre-processed and its dimension is reduced, it is ready to be passed as input to Unsupervised Learning algorithm. Unsupervised Learning is one of the categories of Machine Learning Algorithm that draws the conclusions from the dataset consisting of the input data that doesn't have labeled responses. That means it is most suitable algorithm for those problems that doesn't have any labeled data. Recently, due to the increase in the big data, Unsupervised Learning is gaining more popularity. One popular example where it is used is Google News page. The method implemented here is called Document Clustering which makes the clusters of similar documents without having any prior knowledge of which articles are to be shown in which document. In similar way, in this work, we make clusters of similar bug reports.

Since the data fed to the unsupervised learning algorithm are completely unlabeled, the accuracy of the algorithm over the given data cannot be calculated. However, there are some internal methods to calculate the performance of the algorithm, but this is not simple as in supervised learning. This separates Unsupervised Learning algorithm from Supervised and reinforcement learning methods. The most common unsupervised learning method is Cluster Analysis, which is used for exploratory data analysis to find the hidden patterns and relationships between the data. Also, it is used to group the data according to the relationship between the data. Cluster Analysis is also known as clustering and it is the task of grouping a set of objects in such a way that the objects that fall under same group called clusters are more similar to each other than those objects that fall under different clusters.

Clustering can be achieved by various algorithms that are available today. All those algorithms differ significantly in their notion of what constitutes a cluster. Some algorithms use distance metrics to form a cluster whereas some use density metric to form a cluster. All algorithms might not work effectively on all the dataset. The efficiency of the algorithm depends on the type of dataset and what problem we want to solve.

For labeling Gaussian Mixture Model is used. A Gaussian mixture model is a probabilistic model that assumes all the data points are generated from a mixture of a finite number of Gaussian distributions with unknown parameters. One can think of mixture models as generalizing k-means clustering to incorporate information about the covariance structure of the data as well as the centers of the latent Gaussians. This algorithm is directly available in Scikit-learn library of Python. Scikit-learn implements different classes to estimate Gaussian mixture models that correspond to different estimation strategies detailed below.

2.3.1. Gaussian Mixture

The expectation-maximization (EM) algorithm was implemented by the Gaussian Mixture object for fitting mixture-of-Gaussian models. It can also draw confidence ellipsoids for multivariate models, and compute the Bayesian Information Criterion to assess the number of clusters in the data. Gaussian Mixture Model for train data is learned through GaussianMixture.fit method. For test data, the Gaussian Mixture predicts method is used to assign each bug report the Gaussian it most probably belongs. The Gaussian Mixture comes with different options to constrain the covariance of the difference classes estimated: spherical, diagonal, tied or full covariance.

2.3.2 Different Categories of Gaussian Mixture

The main difficulty in learning Gaussian mixture models from unlabeled data is that it is one usually doesn't know which points came from which latent component (if one has access to this information it gets very easy to fit a separate Gaussian distribution to each set of points). For solving above difficulty Expectation-maximization is used it is an iterative process. First one assumes random components (randomly centered on data points, learned from k-means, or even just normally distributed around the origin) and computes for each point a probability of being generated by each component of the model. Then, one tweaks the parameters to maximize the likelihood of the data given those assignments. Repeating this process is guaranteed to always converge to a local optimum.

Splitting Data: Divided the enter dataset into two parts. 80% are used for training and 20% are used for testing.

2.4. Apply Supervised Learning Techniques

Supervised Learning is one of the categories of Machine Learning algorithm which learns a function that maps an input to an output based on the example feature-label pairs. It infers a function from labeled training data consisting of a set of training dataset. The training data consist of a set of training examples. In supervised learning, each of the examples is the pair of feature and label. A supervised learning algorithm analyzes the training data and produces and inferred function, which can be used later for mapping new examples. An optimal scenario will allow for the algorithm to correctly determine the class of the unseen instances. This requires the learning algorithm to generalize from the training data to unseen situations in a "reasonable" way. There are tens and hundreds of machine learning algorithms available today. Each has its own strength and weaknesses. Each algorithm performs differently on the same dataset as its working is different. So, there is no single supervised algorithm that works best on all the problems. Some examples of Supervised Learning algorithms are Naïve Bayes classifier, Decision Trees, Random Forest, Artificial Neural Networks, K nearest neighbour, Support Vector Machines and so on. Each has different working and approaches differently towards a problem.

In this work, labeled data from the previous step is taken for classification which contains bug description along with label. The model is built using Multinomial Naïve Bayes, Logistic regression and Stochastic Gradient Descent classifiers. Multinomial Naïve Bayes (MNB) is used in our work, because in (Ahmed et al., 2011) compared MNB with Naïve Bayes, k-nearest neighbor and Support vector machines for severity prediction. In that authors concluded that MNB gives good accuracy over other three and also concluded that it is fastest of four and needs small set of datasets. In the earlier work, severity of bug report prediction is not done using Logistic regression and Stochastic Gradient Descent classifiers. That's why, in this work, those classifiers are used and compared with MNB.

2.4.1 Multinomial Naïve Bayes

Multinomial Naïve Bayes (MNB) classifier is used because our data contains the textual information. Multinomial Naïve Bayes is a specialized version of Naïve Bayes that is designed more for text documents. Whether the particular is word is present or not is considered in the simple naïve byes, but in MNB models the frequency of word counts i.e., integer word counts or tf-idf weight which gives the fractional counts.

Naïve Bayes works on the principles of Bayes theorem. The strong assumption is that the value of the particular dimension is independent of the value of other dimension while predicting the class for the given record. Bayes theorem is used for calculating the probability of each class. The class which has highest probability will be considered as output.

2.4.2 Logistic Regression

Binomial logistic regression is used for binary outcome where we will have only two possible outcomes whether yes (1) or no (0), for our work, suppose if we consider only two classes such as severe or non-severe [1], then binary logistic regression would be good classifier, but in this work, we considered multiple classes, that's why used multinomial logistic regression. Logistic regression is one of statistical technique used for classification where result or outcome is categorical unless linear regression where outcome is numeric prediction. Dependent variable or outcome depends on the one or more independent variables. Logistic function is also known as sigmoid function is used in the logistic regression. Using logistic function all the values will be mapped in between 0 and 1 limit.

2.4.3 Stochastic Gradient Descent (SGD)

SGD classification algorithm supports multi-class classification, where it combines multiple binary classifiers. For each N classes, a binary classifier is trained for distinguish between that class and all other N-1 classes. The confidence score (signed distance to hyper plan) for each classifier will be computed at testing time and the confidence which is highest will be chosen. Main benefits of using SGD are, it works on huge dataset and dimensions and it is easy to implement using Python.

2.5. Use Built Model for Unknown Test Dataset

Once the model built using trained dataset, the built model is used to test the working using the testing dataset. Using class that the model predicted and the true class of the testing data, a confusion matrix is created and analyzed the accuracy of the classifier. After the model is trained and tested, it is ready to work for all the unseen bug reports submitted by the user.

3. EXPERIMENTATION

The proposed approach is applied on a sample data set and experimented. The Experimentation is done using Python v3.5 on Jupyter notebook. The experiment is demonstrated below.

3.1. Collect Bug Reports in CSV Format From the Bug Repository

Bugzilla is the bug tracking tool used by many open source software as well as proprietary software. The dataset obtained from was parsed from the Bugzilla open source repository. Parsed around 7000 entries for the product "Firefox" for both desktop and android. The dataset contained 4 columns initially which included *Bug ID*, *Product*, *Product Component* and *Bug Description*. Table 1 explains about the severity levels present for Open source Bugzilla Bug reports taken from (Pushpalatha et al., 2016).

The sample data collected for experimentation is shown in Figure 3.

Figure 3. Sample bug dataset

	Bug ID	Product	Component	Summary
1	Bug ID	Product	Component	Summary
2	1249318	Firefox for Android	Web Apps	Galaxy s8 apps crash since updating to oreo
3	1285858	Firefox for Android	Web Apps	Pixel 2 XL proximity sensor not working properly
4	1337345	Firefox for Android	Web Apps	Battery reading goes from 37% to 1%, then shuts off
5	1399279	Firefox for Android	Web Apps	Android 8.1 max audio volume significantly lower
6	1411068	Firefox for Android	Web Apps	Messages not being marked as read
7	1411777	Firefox for Android	Web Apps	Headphones not detected in my Pixel phone
8	1413589	Firefox for Android	Web Apps	With the 6.0 update from yesterday MTP doesn't work on 2 of my devices
9	1427611	Firefox for Android	Web Apps	There is "SD card-Not inserted" after format the SD card as portable storage
10	1428969	Firefox for Android	Web Apps	Cannot import PKCS12 Certificate and Private Key on Marshmallow
11	1432140	Firefox for Android	Web Apps	"Allow USB debugging" "Always allow" not retained
12	1434269	Firefox for Android	Web Apps	Nexus 5 switches off more often after update
13	1435420	Firefox for Android	Web Apps	cannot move files on sd-cards using DocumentFile API
14	1440661	Firefox for Android	Web Apps	Media Store doesn't detect audio's artist ID3 field capital letter changes
15	1410343	Firefox for Android	Web Apps	The Bluetooth app hard closes randomly when connect to this Bluetooth stereo
16	1413952	Firefox for Android	Web Apps	Phone unlocks when plugged in to charge
17	1391271	Firefox for Android	Web Apps	Audio glitch on sony XPERIA devices
18	1338561	Firefox for Android	Activity Stream	An incomplete preview context menu is displayed when the keyboard is triggered
19	1340541	Firefox for Android	Activity Stream	Add toast when user chooses to Copy Address from Top sites or Highlights
20	1350886	Firefox for Android	Activity Stream	Remove MOZ_ANDROID_ACTIVITY_STREAM build flag

3.2. Apply Preprocessed Techniques

The only useful data for our research was Bug description so discarded all the other columns so that can work with Bug Descriptions only. Since the data that needed for our research are in text format.

For converting the text to numerical attribute, first, CountVectorizer is used which converts the collection of bug reports description to a matrix of token counts. It produces the lot of entries in matrix to be 0. That is why TfidfTransformer was used instead of CountVectorizer. Here, tf means term-frequency whereas tf-idf means term-frequency time's inverse-document frequency. These have been found good to use in the text classification. Next dimensions are reduced using TruncatedSVD. It performs linear dimensionality reduction by means of truncated singular value decomposition (SVD). Using the dimensionality reduction, the dimensions of the data are reduced to 100 attributes.

Table 1. Explanation about the severity levels

Block	Testing or/and development work blocks.
Critical	Stops all application from working
Major	For many applications, Major functionality loss.
Minor	Minor functionality loss.
Trivial	Some UI enhancements
Enhancement	Feature enhancement request.

3.3. Applying Unsupervised Algorithm

Unlabeled data is labeled using the Gaussian Mixture Model (GMM). Before using GMM, we tried with other clustering algorithms such as MeanShift, Spectral clustering, Ward and Birch on our datasets, but those clustering algorithms groups all the bug reports into only one cluster. Using GMM, we could able to group all the bug reports into five clusters.

The best number of clusters are found out using GridSearchCV for 2 clusters it gives good Silhouette scores In this work, 5 clusters are needed, So, selected clusters size as 5. The implementation of GridSearchCV is shown in Figure 4.

Figure 4. Using GridsearchCV to calculate the best number of clusters

```
#Using GridSearchCV to find out the best number of n_components
from sklearn.model_selection import GridSearchCV
params = {'n_components':range(1,6)}
grid = GridSearchCV(GMM(), params)
grid.fit(t_tfidf)
print(grid)
print("Grid Best Score: {}, Grid Best n_component: {}".format(grid.best_score_,grid.best_estimator_.n_components))

GridSearchCV(cv=None, error_score='raise',
       estimator=GaussianMixture(covariance_type='full', init_params='kmeans', max_iter=100,
          means_init=None, n_components=1, n_init=1, precisions_init=None,
          random_state=None, reg_covar=1e-06, tol=0.001, verbose=0,
          verbose_interval=10, warm_start=False, weights_init=None),
       fit_params=None, iid=True, n_jobs=1,
       param_grid={'n_components': range(1, 6)}, pre_dispatch='2*n_jobs',
       refit=True, return_train_score='warn', scoring=None, verbose=0)
Grid Best Score: 105.79790537265593, Grid Best n_component: 5
```

Also, the bar plot of the Gaussian Mixture Model is shown Figure 5.

In this work, a huge amount of time was taken by Gaussian mixture model to create the clusters of data. After tuning some parameters, the time taken decreased a bit and also it increased accuracy. It took around 15 seconds to create the clusters. System memory consumption was more for unsupervised learning and it had to put more pressure on the cores whereas it was negligible for supervised learning. The amount of storage consumed depended upon the size of the data, more the data more the storage.

The result obtained from Unsupervised Learning algorithm is then analyzed carefully. The bug reports grouped under each cluster are analyzed thoroughly and came up with the name for each cluster. For example, in this project, Cluster number 3 contained all those data that were most severe such as *"Error at Java.lang.NullPointerException, application crashed"* so the cluster was given a name *"Critical"*. Similarly, all the other clusters were analyzed and given the name accordingly. The five clusters made were *Blocker, Critical, Major, Minor and Trivial.* After this step, labeled data which contains the label, in this case is one of the five severity level and bug description is given as input to the supervised learning algorithms such as Multinomial Naïve Bayes, Stochastic Gradient Descent and Logistic Regression.

After unsupervised learning, the data was grouped into 5 different clusters. The sample data after clustering is shown in Figure 6.

Figure 5. Bar plot of the number of clusters vs. their silhouette scores

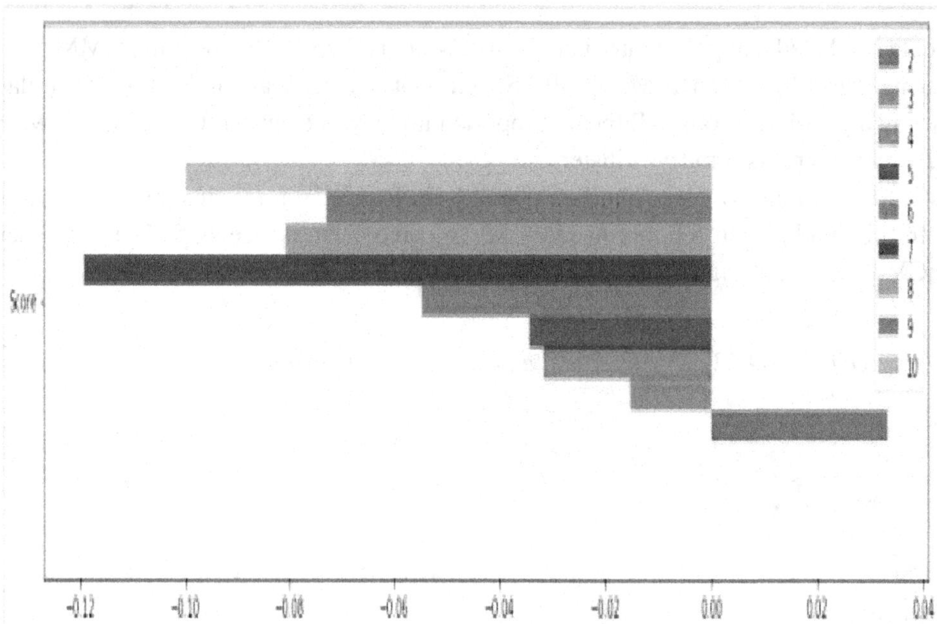

Figure 6. Labeled data after implementing Gaussian Mixture Model

	BugID	Description	label	label_name
0	1249318	Galaxy s8 apps crash since updating to oreo	3	Critical
1	1285858	Pixel 2 XL proximity sensor not working properly	2	Major
2	1337345	Battery reading goes from 37% to 1%, then shuts off	3	Critical
3	1399279	Android 8.1 max audio volume significantly lower	1	Minor
4	1411068	Messages not being marked as read	1	Minor
5	1411777	Headphones not detected in my Pixel phone	1	Minor
6	1413589	With the 6.0 update from yesterday MTP doesn't work on 2 of my devices	2	Major
7	1427611	There is "SD card-Not inserted" after format the SD card as portable storage	0	Blocker
8	1428969	Cannot import PKCS12 Certificate and Private Key on Marshmallow	3	Critical
9	1432140	"Allow USB debugging" "Always allow" not retained	4	Trivial
10	1434269	Nexus 5 switches off more often after update	1	Minor
11	1435420	cannot move files on sd-cards using DocumentFile API	3	Critical
12	1440661	Media Store doesn't detect audio's artist ID3 field capital letter changes	2	Major
13	1410343	The Bluetooth app hard closes randomly when connect to this Bluetooth stereo	2	Major
14	1413952	Phone unlocks when plugged in to charge	1	Minor
15	1391271	Audio glitch on sony XPERIA devices	3	Critical

The label name was assigned after clusters were analyzed. Here 0 is Blocker group, 1 is Minor, 2 is Major, 3 is Critical and 4 is Trivial. Evaluated the accuracy of clustering using Purity measure. Proposed approach gave 79% purity.

To perform the evaluation determined the purity of the cluster. This purity helps us to determine whether all bug reports are grouped into respective cluster or not. We determine the purity using the following formula 1:

$$Purity = \frac{1}{N} \sum_{k=1}^{n} \max_{c} \left| y_i \cap z_c \right|$$

where N is the number of bug reports, n is the number of clusters, y_i is cluster in y and z_c is the maximum number of bug reports correctly classified for that cluster y_i. Purity gives the accuracy of clustering algorithm. It sums ups the correctly classified class per cluster over the total number of bug reports.

3.4. Splitting Labeled Data Set Into Training and Testing

Data set is divided into two splits i.e., 80-20 split is used. 80% of the data is considered for training the classification model and remaining 20% is used for testing the model.

3.5. Applying Supervised Techniques

In this project, after getting the labeled data using Gaussian Mixture Model (GMM), different supervised learning algorithms are used to train the function according to the data. In this work, Multinomial Naïve Bayes, Logistic Regression and Stochastic Gradient Descent Classifiers are used for building the model. The training data is given as input to the classifier so that it can learn a function that maps the input to the output.

For supervised learning, the time taken is quite less compared to unsupervised learning. The time taken by our system to train the Naïve Bayes classifier was 2 milliseconds which is blazing fast. Similarly, it took around 79 milliseconds for Logistic Regression to train and 121 milliseconds for Stochastic Gradient Descent to train. This is checked by using the IPython time command. Naïve Bayes didn't depend on the size of the data. It could train all the data on almost same time. However, Gaussian Mixture Model took more time when the size of the data was more.

Now that the data is labeled, next supervised learning such as Naïve Bayes, Logistic regression and Stochastic Gradient Descent applied on the labeled data.

3.6. Use Built Model for Unknown Test Dataset

Once the model built using trained dataset, the built model is used to test the working using the testing dataset. Using class that the model predicted and the true class of the testing data, a confusion matrix is created and analyzed the accuracy of the classifier. Now the model is trained and tested, it is ready to work for all the unseen bug reports submitted by the user.

Using supervised learning, got the accuracy of 83% for Multinomial Naïve Bayes, 85% for Logistic Regression and 80% for Stochastic Gradient Descent. Precision and Recall varies between 0.67 to 0.90

and 0.77 to 0.90 respectively using Naïve Bayes given in Table 2. Similarly, precision and recall varies between 0.73 to 0.93 and 0.66 to 0.93 respectively using Logistic Regression classifier given in Table 3 and precision and recall varies between 0.62 to 0.91 and 0.72 to 0.89, respectively, using Stochastic Gradient Descent classifier given in Table 4. We got improved Precision and Recall over (Lamkanfi et al., 2010).

Severity Class of Bug report is S:

$$\text{Precision} = \frac{\text{Number of severity of bug reports correctly predicted as S}}{\text{Number of severity of bug reports predicted as S}}$$

$$\text{Recall} = \frac{\text{Number of Severity of bug reports correctly predicted as S}}{\text{Number of severity of bug reports S}}$$

$$\text{Accuracy} = \frac{\text{Total number of bug reports correctly predicted}}{\text{Total Number of Prediction}}$$

Table 2. Precision and recall for multinomial naïve Bayes classifier

Class Label	Precision	Recall
Blocker	0.699	0.81
Minor	0.67	0.90
Major	0.90	0.77
Critical	0.77	0.82
Trivial	0.85	0.86

Table 3. Precision and recall for logistic regression classifier

Class Label	Precision	Recall
Blocker	0.84	0.78
Minor	0.93	0.77
Major	0.91	0.79
Critical	0.86	0.66
Trivial	0.73	0.93

Table 4. Precision and recall for stochastic gradient descent classifier

Class Label	Precision	Recall
Blocker	0.86	0.72
Minor	0.91	0.81
Major	0.90	0.76
Critical	0.65	0.82
Trivial	0.62	0.89

From the Figure 7, for Minor, Major and Critical labels Logistic regression is given the good Precision. For Blocker label Stochastic Gradient descent and Trivial label Naïve Bayes is given the good precision.

From the Figure 8, observe that for Blocker, Minor and Critical Naïve Bayes is given good recall compared to other two and for Major and Trivial logistic regression is given good recall compared to other two.

Figure 7. Precision comparison of three classifiers

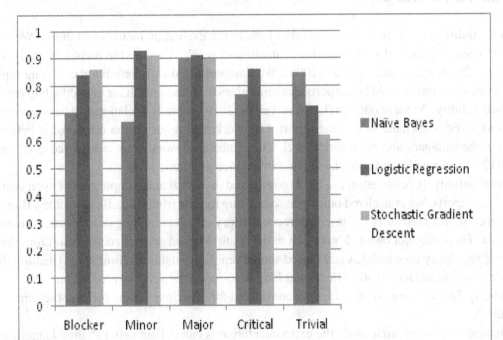

Figure 8. Recall comparison of three classifiers

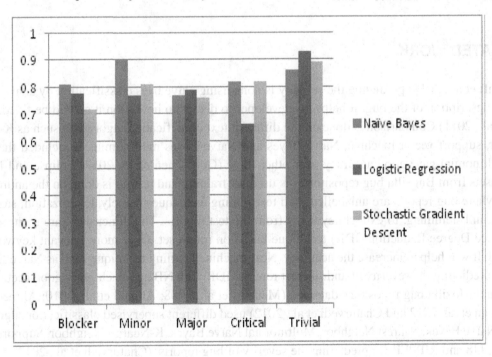

4. THREATS TO VALIDITY

Construct validity: Threats to construct validity refer to the evaluation metrics suitability. We used accuracy, precision, recall and F-measure for evaluation of result. This are the metrics already used by (Yuan et al., 2012) and (Menzies et al., 2008). We have collected sufficient number of bug reports of Firefox for desktop and android bug reports that minimizes the biased result for a specific bug repository.

Internal validity: As mentioned in (Lamkanfi et al., 2010), there is a relationship between attributes contents to severity attribute in the bug report. Our work also relies on the relationship between the contents of the summary and the severity level. Class imbalance work is not considered in (Chaturvedi et al., 2012). Even we also not considered class imbalance problem.

External validity: (Chaturvedi et al., 2012) considered the individual components of open source and NASA's bug reports. We considered only open source bug reports from Bugzilla repository. Bug reports of other open source repository or closed source repository also contain long description, summary and other fields. There may not be much variation in the result. We can generalize this result for other open source bug repository such as JIRA and closed source repository datasets. Similar to (Chaturvedi et al., 2012), we also not considered other fields and long description for severity prediction.

Reliability: Normal severity labels are not considered for experimentation, because they are assigned by default.

Limitation: In this research work, the experimentation is carried out using Python language on the Bugzilla bug reports. It is one of the increased tools used for machine learning and data science community. This confirms the reliability of the tool. For other bug trackers bug reports and programming languages it may not be representative.

5. RELATED WORK

(Lamkanfi et al., 2010*)* predicting the severity is done using naïve byes classification by analyzing the one line description of the bug. It helps for developer to decide to how soon it should be fixed. (Lamkanfi et al., 2011) Comparison is done on the different text classification algorithms such as K-nearest neighbor, support vector machine, Naïve Bayes and Naïve Bayes multinomial. Concluded that naïve byes multinomial gave good accuracy over other three (Guo, Chen & Li, 2017) Eclipse and Mozilla bug datasets from Bugzilla bug repositories is used for training and testing is done on the android bug reports where bug reports are unlabelled used text mining techniques namely, tokenization, stop-word removal, and stemming, to extract keywords from the test reports. The dimensions are reduced using Importance Degree Reduction (IDR) technique based on rough set. Only more relevant keywords are extracted. It will help to increase the accuracy. Next machine learning technique such as Naïve Bayes is used for predicting the severity of android test reports. IDR with NB approach gives good accuracy for eclipse and Mozilla bug repository datasets. (Menzies et al., 2008; Ahmed et al., 2010; Ahmed et al., 2011; Yuan et .al, 2012 and Chaturvedi et al., 2012) used different supervised classification algorithms such as Naïve Bayes, Nearest Neighbor, Multinomial Naïve Bayes, K-Nearest Neighbor, Support vector machine, J48 and RIPPER for predicting the severity of bug reports. (Chaturvedi et al., 2012) done experimentation on of both open source and closed source datasets using different classification algorithms such as support Vector Machine, J48, Naïve Bayes, RIPPER and Random Forest. (Pushpalatha et al., 2016) used the bagging ensemble method for more accurate prediction of severity. In this work, supervised learning algorithms such as multinomial Naïve Bayes, Logistic regression and Stochastic Gradient Descent is tested on the labeled data. In a similar way, automatic bug assignment to developer is done using different classification algorithms. (Anvik et al., 2006) used text information in the bug report for assigning the bug report to appropriate developer using different classification algorithm such as SVM, C4.8 and Naïve Bayes. (Pushpalatha et al., 2015) used bagging and Naïve Bayes algorithm for assigning the bug report to developer. If bug report is assigned incorrectly to developer for fixing then it need to be assigned to correct developer the process is called as bug tossing. Tossing increases the time to fix the bug. (Gaeul et al., 2009) suggested the graph model based on Markov chains that helps for finding the suitable developer for the fixing the bug. Similar to automatic severity and developer prediction using textual information, duplicate bug detection is also done using natural language (Runeson et al., 2007).

6. CONCLUSION AND SCOPE FOR FURTHER ENHANCEMENT

Lot of different versions of same open source software is developing quickly in open source software development. The number of bug reports received in the open source repositories such as Bugzilla and Jira are very large. User submits the bug report whenever they come across the bug; new users and inexperienced developer make a mistake while assigning the correct severity label. Normal is default option; however, using unsupervised techniques it can be labeled correctly. This helps to save time and resources with correct labeling and more importance can be given to high severity bug for fixing first. In this work, automatic labeling of Firefox android bug reports is done using Gaussian Mixture Model clustering algorithm. After labeling the unlabeled bug reports, different classification algorithms are used for predicting the class label of unknown bug reports. For supervised learning, the experiment has given the accuracy of 83% for Multinomial Naïve Bayes, 85% for Logistic Regression and 80% for Stochastic Gradient Descent.

The proposed model can be taken a step further and provide an alert to the appropriate developer whenever a severe bug is reported. Further it can be extended by taking bug reports from the different repositories and different techniques can be used on large datasets.

REFERENCES

Anvik, J., Hiew, L., & Murphy, G. C. (2006). Who should fix this bug? In *Proceedings of the 28th international conference on Software engineering* (pp. 361–370).

Bettenburg, N., Just, S., & Schröter, A. (2010). What Makes a Good Bug Report? *IEEE Transactions on Software Engineering, 36*(5), 618–643. doi:10.1109/TSE.2010.63

Chaturvedi, K. K., & Singh, V. B. (2012). Determining bug severity using machine learning techniques. In *CSI-IEEE International Conference on Software Engineering (CONSEG)* (pp. 378–387). 10.1109/CONSEG.2012.6349519

Chaturvedi, K. K., & Singh, V. B. (2012). An empirical comparison of machine learning techniques in predicting the bug severity of open and close source projects. *International Journal of Open Source Software and Processes, 4*(2), 32–59. doi:10.4018/jossp.2012040103

Cubranic, D., & Murphy, G. C. (2004). Automatic bug triage using text categorization. In *Proceedings of the Sixteenth International Conference on Software Engineering & Knowledge Engineering* (pp. 92-97).

Gaeul, J., Sunghun, K., & Zimmermann, T. (2009). Improving bug triage with bug tossing graphs. In *Proceedings of the European Software Engineering Conference* (pp. 111–120).

Guo, S., Chen, R., & Li, H. (2017). Using Knowledge Transfer and Rough Set to Predict the Severity of Android Test Reports via Text Mining. *Symmetry*, *9*(8), 161. doi:10.3390ym9080161

Lamkanfi, A., Demeyer, S., Giger, E., & Goethals, B. (2010). Predicting the severity of a reported bug. In *7th Working Conference on Mining Software Repositories*, Cape Town, South Africa (pp. 1-10) 10.1109/MSR.2010.5463284

Lamkanfi, A., Demeyer, S., Soetens, Q. D., & Verdonck, T. (2011). Comparing Mining Algorithms for Predicting the Severity of a Reported Bug. In *15th European Conference on Software Maintenance and Reengineering* (pp. 249–258). IEEE. 10.1109/CSMR.2011.31

Limsettho, N., Hata, H., Monden, A., & Matsumoto, K. (2014). Automatic Unsupervised Bug Report Categorization. In *6th International Workshop on Empirical Software Engineering in Practice* (pp 7–12)

Menzies, T., & Marcus, A. (2008). Automated severity assessment of software defect reports. In *IEEE International Conference on Software Maintenance* (pp. 346–355). 10.1109/ICSM.2008.4658083

Pushpalatha, M. N., & Dr. Mrunalini, M. (2015). Automatic Bug Assignment using Bagging Ensemble method. *International Journal of Advanced Information Science and Technology*, *40*(40), 98–103.

Pushpalatha, M. N., & Mrunalini, M. (2016). Predicting the severity of bug reports using classification algorithms. In *International Conference on Circuits, Controls, Communications and Computing (I4C)* (pp. 1-4). 10.1109/CIMCA.2016.8053276

Runeson, P., Alexandersson, M., & Nyholm, O. (2007). Detection of duplicate defect reports using natural language processing. In *Proceedings of the 29th international conference on Software Engineering* (pp. 499–510) 10.1109/ICSE.2007.32

Tian, Y., Ali, N., Lo, D., & Hassan, A. E. (2016). On the unreliability of bug severity data. *Empirical Software Engineering*, *21*(6), 2298–2323. doi:10.100710664-015-9409-1

Tian, Y., Lo, D., & Sun, C. (2012). Information Retrieval Based Nearest Neighbor Classification for Fine-Grained Bug Severity Prediction. In *19th Working Conference on Reverse Engineering* (pp. 215–224). 10.1109/WCRE.2012.31

This research was previously published in the International Journal of Open Source Software and Processes (IJOSSP), 10(1); pages 1-15, copyright year 2019 by IGI Publishing (an imprint of IGI Global).

Chapter 36
Ensemble Techniques–Based Software Fault Prediction in an Open–Source Project

Wasiur Rhmann
Babasaheb Bhimrao Ambedkar University, Amethi, India

Gufran Ahmad Ansari
B. S. Abdur Rehman Crescent Institute of Science and Technology, India

ABSTRACT

Software engineering repositories have been attracted by researchers to mine useful information about the different quality attributes of the software. These repositories have been helpful to software professionals to efficiently allocate various resources in the life cycle of software development. Software fault prediction is a quality assurance activity. In fault prediction, software faults are predicted before actual software testing. As exhaustive software testing is impossible, the use of software fault prediction models can help the proper allocation of testing resources. Various machine learning techniques have been applied to create software fault prediction models. In this study, ensemble models are used for software fault prediction. Change metrics-based data are collected for an open-source android project from GIT repository and code-based metrics data are obtained from PROMISE data repository and datasets kc1, kc2, cm1, and pc1 are used for experimental purpose. Results showed that ensemble models performed better compared to machine learning and hybrid search-based algorithms. Bagging ensemble was found to be more effective in the prediction of faults in comparison to soft and hard voting.

1. INTRODUCTION

Data available in software repositories can help to improve various activities of the software development cycle. Mining software repository may be helpful for bug prediction, software testing, and maintenance (Xie et al., 2007). Software quality heavily depends on software testing. Software testing aims to find bugs in software. The identification of bugs earlier in the software development life cycle can reduce the total development cost of software (Lim & Goel, 2008).

DOI: 10.4018/978-1-7998-9158-1.ch036

Software fault prediction models are created with the historical data of the software projects and help to identify faulty modules before actual testing of the products. Identification of faulty modules can help to properly allocate resources for testing and maintenance. The quality of the software heavily depends on software testing, which is an integral part of software development. Software testing consumes around 40-50% of the cost and time of software development. Identification of faulty modules early in the development cycle can be very helpful to effectively allocate testing resources. Software fault prediction studies aim to predict faulty modules using historical data related to software projects. Software fault prediction uses various characteristics of software and the characteristics of software are measured using software metrics to predict fault-prone software modules. Different software metrics were proposed and used for software defect prediction (He et al., 2015). Various studies have been done to obtain a suitable subset of efficient software metrics for software bug prediction (Malhotra et al., 2010; Emam et al., 2001; Gyimothy et al., 2005). Software metrics are used to measure the characteristics of the software project, product, and process. Different types of software metrics have been used to predict different quality attributes of the software like change proneness, defectiveness. In recent years, metrics related to developers, organizations, and networks were used in software fault prediction (Caglayan et al., 2015). Software fault prediction studies have used Object-oriented metrics more than source code metrics or process metrics (Radjenovic et al., 2013).

Various machine learning techniques named Random forest, Support vector machine, Decision tree, Neural Network, etc., have been explored to predict fault-prone modules (Malhotra, 2015). Ensemble techniques combine more than one machine learning techniques and have been applied in various fields like spam detection (Singh & Batra, 2018), accident risk assessment (Kaeeni et al., 2018), bankruptcy prediction (Verikas et al., 2010), breast cancer classification (Nagarajan et al., 2017), etc., to obtain better accuracy. The novelty of this study is that change metrics obtained from open source android projects are used for software fault prediction using ensemble techniques and compared our fault prediction performance with the available static code metrics based fault prediction and hybrid search-based algorithm based fault prediction. The motivation behind the selection of change metrics for fault prediction is that they can be easily computed from different versions of the software obtained from Git repository while computation of static code metrics is difficult. No works have been reported to compare the performance of ensemble techniques based models with Hybrid Search-based algorithms (HSBA) for software fault prediction.

The present work addresses the followings research questions:

RQ1: How Ensemble models perform in software fault prediction using change-metrics?
RQ2: Are change-metrics based ensemble-models are better compared to the change metrics based ML model for fault prediction?
RQ3: Which method is better in predicting faulty modules? Hybrid Search-based algorithms or Ensemble-based models?

The main contributions of the present work are:

1. Assessing the predictive performances of Ensemble-based techniques in the prediction of faulty modules of the software;

2. Comparing the predictive performance of change metrics based ensemble models in the identification of faulty modules with the available change metrics based fault prediction study (Choudhary, et al., 2018);

3. Comparing the performances of ensemble model-based fault prediction models with the Hybrid search-based algorithms (Rhmann, 2018a).

The present work is divided into nine sections. Section 1 is the introduction, section 2 describes the previous works on software fault prediction, section 3 describes ensemble models used in the study, in section 4 different datasets, various software metrics used in the study and workflow of the software fault prediction have been described, section 5 describes various metrics to measure predictive performance, section 6 contains results and implementation details, section 7 contains the comparison with the related work, threats to the validity of the study and conclusion of the work are discussed in section 8 and 9 respectively.

2. RELATED WORK

In this section work related to software fault prediction is described. It was observed that most of the software fault prediction studies have used product based software metrics compared to the process-based metrics. The computation of product-based software metrics is easy and they can be obtained from mining software repositories. Choudhary et al. (2018) have used software change metrics for the prediction of faults using machine learning techniques. They proposed some new change metrics for fault prediction. They used Git repository and performed experiments on eclipse projects. Moser et al. (2008) have used to code and change metrics for the prediction of faulty modules of software for eclipse data. They observed that change metrics performed better in comparison to code metrics. Zhou & Leung (2006) have used Object-Oriented (OO) metrics from the NASA datasets and observed that Software metrics named CBO, WMC, RFC, and LCOM are suitable while DIT is not appropriate for fault prediction. Low severity faults can be predicted efficiently with software design metrics. Subramanyam and Krishnan (2003) have used object-oriented metrics for fault prediction. They have used only WMC, CBO, and DIT metrics for the prediction of faulty modules in the software. They observed that the predictive power of OO design metrics in fault prediction varies with the programming language. Nagappan et al. (2010) have used change bursts for the prediction of faulty software modules. Change burst is measured from consecutive changes in the system during a period. For experimental purposes, Windows Vita datasets are used and change burst was found to be the best fault prediction. Precision and recall values were found around 90%. Rhmann (2018a) has used hybrid algorithms for the prediction of defective classes using static software metrics. The defect prediction capabilities of different algorithms have been compared. Datasets KC1, KC2, CM1 are obtained from the Promise data repository. It was found that GFS-logitboost-c has shown better performance in comparison to other hybrid algorithms. Rhmann (2018b) has used hybrid search-based algorithms for cross-project defect prediction and compared the defect prediction capability within defect prediction. Hybrid search based algorithms are a combination of search-based algorithms and machine learning techniques. Geng (2018) has used Deep Neural Network method for the prediction of faulty software modules. The proposed method is based on BPSO (Bound Particle swarm Optimization). 21 Software metrics are used as independent variables for software fault prediction. BPSO is used to reduce dimensions then deep neural network is used to predict faulty modules. NASA software projects have been used for experimental purpose. Datasets of PC1; JM1 projects are based on C and KC1, KC3 projects are written in C++ and Java. Erturk and Seze (2016) have used Artificial Neural Network (ANN) and Adaptive Neuro-Fuzzy Inference System(ANFIS) for software fault prediction. They proposed an iterative model. Experiments were performed on datasets obtained from the PROMISE repository and they are evaluated in terms of ROC (Receiver Operator Characteristic) and AUC (Area under the curve). They implemented a technique in e\Eclipse plug-in. Juneja (2019) has presented a software fault prediction based on a weighted neuro-fuzzy framework. They applied fuzzy rules to obtain relevant features. Promise, Eclipse, PDE datasets were used for experimental purposes. Obtained results are evaluated using accuracy, RMSE, MAE, AUC metrics. Jin and Jin (2015) presented an approach to predict software fault using a hybrid artificial neural network and Quantum particle swarm optimization. ANN is used for the classification of faulty modules while QPSO is used for obtaining a subset of features. Abaei et al. (2015) have used a semi-supervised hybrid self-organizing map (HySOM) for software fault prediction. The proposed technique reduces the need of an expert to identify faulty classes. Obtained results improved the false-negative rate and overall error rate. Rathore and Kumar (2017a) have used heterogeneous and homogeneous ensembles for software fault number prediction. Two linear and two non-linear rules were used to combine base learners. The experiments were performed on inter release and intra release scenarios and on publicly available datasets. Rathore and Kumar(2017b) have used the ensemble of various techniques for prediction of the number of faults in a software module. A heterogeneous ensemble based on the linear and non-linear rule is used for prediction of the number of software faults on different publicly available datasets.

3. ENSEMBLE MODELS

Ensemble models are created by combining multiple models of the same types or different types to obtain better prediction results. In the study, bagging and Vote classifications are used to create Software fault prediction models (Swamynathan, 2017).

3.1 Bagging Classifier

Bagging or Bootstrap aggregation is an ensemble technique that helps to reduce model variance. Training data is used to generate different samples of the same size as the original data with a replacement called bootstrap samples. Each bootstrap contains ¾ of the original values. For each bootstrap, an independent model is used and then majority voting is used to classify. Bagging classifier based prediction is given in Figure 1.

The algorithm of ensemble bagging which is used in the study is given below:

```
Step1: Input Dataset(D),Base learning algorithm(L), Number of base learner(N)
where D={(x₁,y₁),(x₂,y₂),(x₃,y₃).....(xₙ, yₙ)}
Step2: for n=1 to N
            hₙ=L(D,D_bs)  where D_bs is bootstrap distribution
Step3: H(x)=arg maxå I(hₙ(x)=y)
```

Figure 1. Bagging classifier

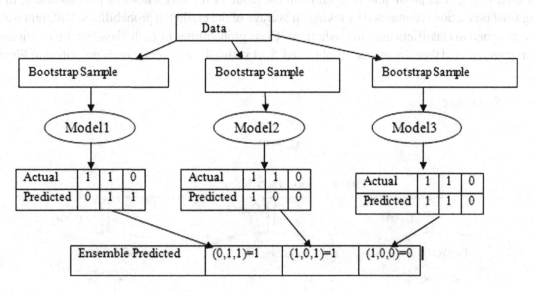

3.2 Voting Classifier

It combines multiples machine learning algorithms using majority voting. In this classification, multiple standalone models are created from the training dataset. Different models are wrapped into one to make a better prediction. Prediction for new data is made by averaging the predictions of sub-models.

3.2.1 Hard Voting vs. Soft Voting

These are used to predict the outcome from an ensemble of the set of classifiers. Hard voting is also termed as majority voting. Hard voting based prediction is described in Figure 2.

Figure 2. Hard voting

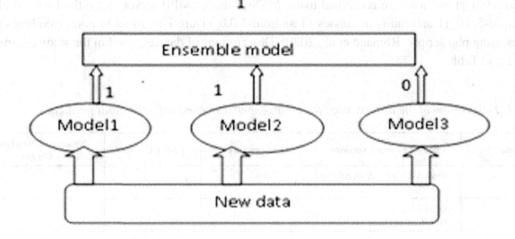

In hard voting final prediction is taken from the mode of the predictions of the classifiers. In Soft voting final prediction is computed by taking an average of the predicted probabilities. Different weights can be assigned to classifiers used in predictions. Class probabilities of each classifier are multiplied by classifier weight and then the average is obtained. Soft voting-based prediction is described in Figure 3.

Figure 3. Soft voting

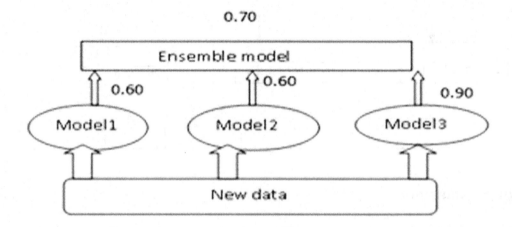

4. DATASETS AND SOFTWARE METRICS FOR FAULT PREDICTION

In this section different datasets, software metrics and workflow that are used in the study are described.

4.1 Datasets

Software fault prediction datasets (kc1, kc2, cm1,pc1) are collected from PROMISE repository (Shirabad and Menzies, 2005). These datasets are based on static code metrics. In addition to that change metrics based fault datasets are extracted from GIT repository. For the collection of datasets, Git repository is used. Change metrics between version android-4.0.1_r1 and android-5.0.0_r1, android-2.0.1_r1 and android-5.0.0_r1 versions are computed using MYSQL in XAMPP server. Then the faults in classes of android-5.0.0_r1 and faults in classes of android-5.0.0_r1 are integrated to corresponding change metrics using php scripts (Rhmann et al., 2020). Descriptions of datasets used in the study are given in Table 1 and Table 2.

Table 1. Description of the dataset used for change metrics based software fault prediction

Dataset	Changes Between Versions	No. of Instances	Faulty Classes	Number of Non-Faulty Classes
v4-v5	android-4.0.1_r1 android-5.0.0_r1	170	62	108
v2-v5	android-2.0.1_r1 -android-5.0.0_r1	324	62	262

Table 2. Description of the datasets used for static code metrics based software fault prediction

Dataset	Programming Language Used	No. of Instances	Non-Faulty	Faulty
kc1	C++	2109	1783	326
kc2	C++	520	415	105
cm1	C	498	449	49
pc1	C	1109	77	1032

4.2 Independent and Dependent Variables

In the study two types of datasets are used: Static code based metrics and change metrics. Table 3 describes the software change metrics which are used as independent variables. Change metrics (Krishnan et al., 2011; Bell et al., 2011) measure the change during the life cycle of software development. They are collected from multiple releases of the software. Table 3 contains 9 change metrics. Table 4 contains static code based metrics. Static code metrics are directly related to code and they can be derived from Software code. 21 metrics are static code metrics which are independent variables while a defect is a dependent variable.

Table 3. Software change metrics used in the prediction for software fault

No.	Metrics	Description
1	LOC-ADDED	Number of lines of code added to the file
2	LOC-DELETED	Number of lines of code deleted from the file
3	LOC-CHANGED	Number of lines of code changed from the file
4	MAX-LOC-ADDED	Maximum number of lines of code deleted for all commits
5	MAX_LOC-CHANGED	Maximum number of lines of code added to the file
6	MAX_LOC_DELETED	Maximum number of lines of code deleted to the file
7	Code churn:	Sum total of (the difference between added lines of code and deleted lines of code) for a file considering all of its revisions in the repository
8	Max Code Churn:	It is defined as the maximum of (the difference between added lines of code and deleted lines of code)) for a file considering all of its revisions in the repository
9	Average Code Churn:	It is defined as the average of (the difference between added lines of code and deleted lines of code)) for a file considering all of its revisions in the repository

4.3 Workflow of the Proposed Technique

Figure 4 shows the workflow used to obtain different performance measures using ensemble techniques and Hybrid search-based algorithms. First change metrics datasets obtained using Git repository or static code metrics datasets from promise software engineering repository are obtained and preprocessed. Then datasets are divided into training and testing sets and they are trained using ensemble techniques or an HSBA and the results of performances are obtained in terms of accuracy, precision, recall, and g-mean.

Table 4. Static code metrics used for Software fault prediction

S.N.	Metrics	Description
1	Loc	McCabe's line count of code
2	v(g)	McCabe cyclomatic complexity
3	ev(g)	McCabe essential complexity
4	iv(g)	McCabe design complexity
5	N	Halstead total operators + operands
6	V	Halstead volume
7	L	Halstead program length
8	D	Halstead difficulty
9	I	Halstead intelligence
10	E	Halstead effort
11	B	Halstead
12	t	Halstead's time estimator
13	lOCode	Halstead's line count
14	lOComent	Halstead's count of lines of comments
15	lOBlank	Halstead's count of blank lines
16	lOCodeAndComment	Numeric
17	uniq_Op	unique operators
18	uniq_Opnd	unique operands
19	total_Op	total operators
20	total_Opnd	total operands
21	branchCount	% of the flow graph
22	defects	{no, yes}

5. PERFORMANCE EVALUATION MEASURES

In this study classes with faults are positive cases while classes without faults are negative cases. Predictive models created are binary classifiers that classify the classes into faulty or non-faulty classes. Accuracy, precision, recall, and g-means are used to measure the performance of the models (Malhotra, 2016). TP (True Positive), TN (True Negative), FP (False Positive) and FN (False Negative) are the basic terms used in the measure of different performance metrics are calculated using the formulas given by equion1, 2, 3 and 4.

TP (True Positive): It is the number of correctly predicted faulty classes.
TN (True Negative): It is the number of correctly predicted non-faulty classes.
FP (False Positive): It is the number of non-faulty classes wrongly classified as faulty.
FN (False Negative): It is the number of faulty classes wrongly classified as non-faulty.

$$\text{Accuracy} = \frac{TP + TN}{TP + FP + FN + TN} \times 100 \qquad (1)$$

$$\text{Precision} = TP/(TP+FP) \qquad (2)$$

$$\text{Recall} = TP/(TP+FN) \qquad (3)$$

G-mean is useful for class imbalance problem. It is defined as G-mean1=Ö(Precision*Recall) (4)

Figure 4. workflow of the proposed model

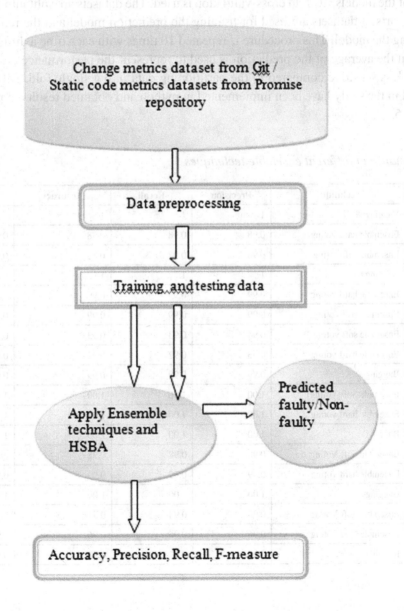

Values of recall and precision lie between 0 and 1. The best model will have values of recall and precision equal to 1. When the number of faulty and non-faulty classes is unequal in each dataset used in the study, datasets are skewed and precision, recall, and g-means will be more appropriate for the measure of performance. Precision and recall have been used by various researchers (Kim & Whitehead, 2008; Nam, Pan & Kim, 2013) in software fault prediction. High precision is required as low precision means more effort in testing. The high recall is also required as low recall means some faulty classes have been left and these faulty classes can lead to failure of the software.

6. IMPLEMENTATION AND RESULTS

For validation of the models, 10-fold cross-validation is used. The datasets are split into 10 parts without replacement. 9 parts of datasets are used for training the prediction model and the remaining one part is used for testing the model. This procedure is repeated 10 times with each time a different part is used for testing. Then the average of the prediction is used to represent the performance estimate. Obtained performance is less sensitive compared to the partitioning data into a single fold. Different ensemble techniques used in the study have been implemented in python and obtained results of performance are shown in Table 5.

Table 5. Performance of different ensemble techniques

Dataset	Technique	Precision	Recall	Accuracy	g-Mean
v4-v5	Bagging	1	1	1	1
v4-v5	Ensemble hard voting	0.98	0.98	0.98	0.97
v4-v5	Ensemble soft voting	0.98	0.98	0.98	0.97
v2-v5	Bagging	1	1	1	1
v2-v5	Ensemble hard voting	0.99	0.99	0.99	0.98
v2-v5	Ensemble soft voting	0.99	0.99	0.99	0.98
kc1	Ensemble soft voting	0.94	0.93	0.93	0.90
	Ensemble hard voting	0.93	0.92	0.92	0.88
	Bagging	0.99	0.99	0.99	0.98
cm1	Ensemble Soft Voting]	1.00	1.00	1.00	1
	Ensemble hard voting	1.00	1.00	1.00	1
	Bagging	1.00	1.00	1.00	1
pc1	Ensemble Soft Voting	0.98	0.98	0.98	.97
	Ensemble hard voting	0.99	0.99	0.99	0.98
	Bagging	1.00	1.00	1.00	1
kc2	Ensemble Soft Voting	0.95	0.94	0.94	0.91
	Ensemble hard voting	0.96	0.96	0.96	0.94
	Bagging	0.98	0.97	0.97	0.96

Figure 5 and Figure 6 represent the performances of ensemble techniques on different datasets using precision and recall respectively. Bagging has shown best precision and recall values for all datasets.

Figure 5. Precision values of different techniques

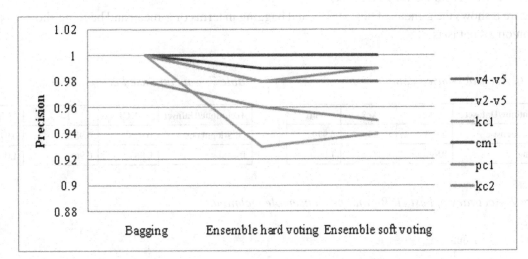

Figure 6. Recall values of different techniques

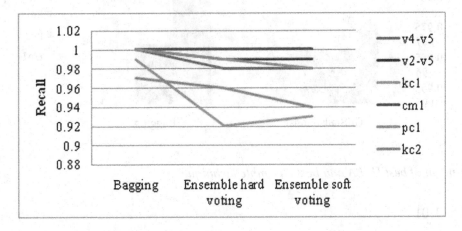

7. COMPARISON WITH PREVIOUS WORK

From Table 5, it is clear that the bagging technique has better precision, recall, accuracy, and g-mean compared to the Ensemble Soft Voting and Ensemble hard voting. Hybrid search algorithms combine the SBAs with non-SBAs into a single algorithm. In the study by (Rhmann, (2018a) algorithms Fuzzy Adaboost (GFS-AB), Fuzzy Logitboost (GFS-LB), Logitboost with Single Winner Inference (GFS-MaxLB), Hierarchical decision rules (HIDER), Particle Swarm Optimization - Linear Discriminant Analysis (PSOLDA) were used for fault prediction. Hybrid search-based algorithms have been applied on dataset kc1, kc2, cm1, and highest accuracy and g-mean are obtained by GFS-adaboost-c and GFS-logitboost and given in Table 6 and Table 7. For change metrics based fault prediction in (Choudhary, et al., 2018) best performance obtained by Random Forest and KNN recall values which are 0.717 and 0.488 respectively while in our approach Precision and recall is 1, 1.

Figure 7 shows the accuracy of best HSBA and bagging and performance of bagging is better compared to HSBA technique on all datasets.

Figure 8 shows the g-mean of best HSBA and bagging in terms of g-mean and bagging showed batter g-mean on all datasets.

Table 6. Accuracy-based comparison

Technique/Dataset	kc1	kc2	cm1
GFS-adaboost-c	0.979	0.969	0.979
Bagging	0.99	0.97	1.0

Table 7. g-mean based comparison

Technique/Dataset	KC1	KC2	CM1
GFS-logitboost	0.929	0.98302	0.9754
Bagging	0.98	0.96	1.0

Figure 7. Accuracy of best HSBA and best ensemble technique

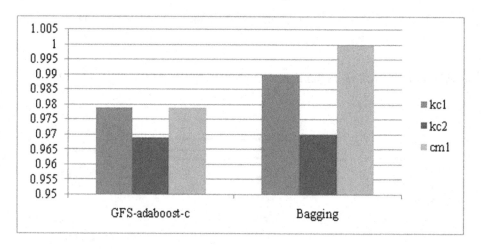

Figure 8. g-mean of best HSBA and best ensemble technique

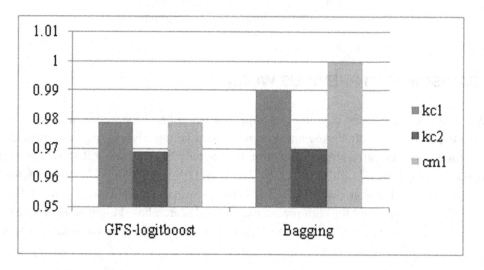

7.1 Answer to Various Research Questions

The answers to various research questions are discussed below:

RQ1: What is the predictive performance of change metrics for fault prediction using Ensemble models?
Answer 1: Bagging technique is better in comparison to Ensemble Soft Voting and Ensemble hard voting.
RQ2: Are change-metrics based ensemble-models are better compared to the change metrics based ML model for fault prediction?
Answer 2: Ensemble techniques based fault prediction models are better compared to ML technique based models.
RQ3: Which method is better for software fault prediction? Hybrid Search-based algorithms or Ensemble-based models?
Answer 3: Ensemble techniques used in the study are better compared to Hybrid search-based algorithms.

8. THREATS TO THE VALIDITY

The following are various threats to the study.

8.1 Internal Validity

If there is something that may affect the independent and dependent variables, then there is a threat of internal validity (Wright et al., 2010). Software size can affect the fault proneness of class i.e. larger the class more chances of being faulty.

8.2 External Validity

When the results of the study can be generalized then there is no external validity threat (Briand et al., 2001). As change metrics are collected for an android project based on java, there is a threat to generalize results for other programming languages for change metrics based defect prediction. While as code metrics are collected for C, C++ there is a threat to generalize the results for other programming languages. However, our experiments can be repeated and replicated.

8.3 Construct Validity

If the variables used in the study don't refer to the same things as they were supposed to measure then there is a threat of construct validity (Zhou et al., 2009). In the study change metrics based dataset and code metrics based datasets are used. Change metrics based dataset is obtained from GIT repository and metrics are calculated using MYSQL and these metrics are well known. There is no threat of construct validity, but code metrics based datasets are obtained from NASA datasets kc1, kc2, and cm1, pc1. As there is no information about how they are calculated, their accuracy cannot be assured. So there is a possibility of construct validity.

9. CONCLUSION AND FUTURE SCOPE

Obtained results showed that Ensemble techniques: bagging, hard voting, soft voting, which have been used for fault prediction based on change metrics and code-based metrics have shown remarkable performance. Bagging technique performed better in comparison to hard voting and soft voting. As precision and recall values obtained by bagging technique are almost 1 for each dataset i.e. there is the efficient allocation of testing resources and the chances of latent defects in software are zero. Ensemble techniques applied on kc1, kc2, cm1, and pc1 outperformed the Hybrid search-based algorithm GFS-logitboost-c. The performance of software fault prediction models built on change metrics outperformed the change metrics-based model available in the literature. For the generalization of results based on change metrics, there is a need to perform experiments with other programming languages. In the future, more experiments can be performed with industrial projects and new ensemble techniques may be developed to predict faulty classes with better accuracy.

REFERENCES

Abaei, G., Selamat, A., & Fujita, H. (2015). An empirical study based on semi-supervised hybrid self-organizing map for software fault prediction. *Knowledge-Based Systems*, *74*, 28–39. doi:10.1016/j.knosys.2014.10.017

Bell, R. M., Ostrand, T. J., & Weyuker, E. J. (2011). Does measuring code change improve fault prediction? *Proceedings of the 7th international conference on predictive models in software engineering,* 1–8. 10.1145/2020390.2020392

Briand, L., Wust, J., & Lounis, H. (2001). Replicated case studies for investigating quality factors in object oriented designs. *Empirical Software Engineering Journal*, *6*(1), 11–58. doi:10.1023/A:1009815306478

Caglayan, B., Turhan, B., Bener, A., Habayeb, M., Miransky, A., & Cialini, E. (2015). Merits of organizational metrics in defect prediction: an industrial replication. *2015 IEEE/ACM 37th IEEE international conference on software engineering IEEE,* 89–98. 10.1109/ICSE.2015.138

Choudhary, G. R., Kumar, S., Kumar, K., Mishra, A., & Catal, C. (2018). Empirical analysis of change metrics for software fault prediction. *Computers & Electrical Engineering*, *67*, 15–24. doi:10.1016/j.compeleceng.2018.02.043

Emam, K. E., Melo, W., & Machado, J. C. (2001). The prediction of faulty classes using object-oriented design metrics. *Journal of Systems and Software*, *56*(1), 63–75. doi:10.1016/S0164-1212(00)00086-8

Erturk, E., & Seze, E. A. (2016). Iterative software fault prediction with a hybrid approach. *Applied Soft Computing*, *49*, 1020–1033. doi:10.1016/j.asoc.2016.08.025

Geng, A. (2018). Cognitive Deep Neural Networks prediction method for software fault tendency module based on Bound Particle Swarm Optimization. *Cognitive Systems Research*, *5*(2), 12–20. doi:10.1016/j.cogsys.2018.06.001

Gyimothy, T., Ference, R., & Siket, I. (2005). Empirical validation of object-oriented metrics on open source software for fault prediction. *IEEE Transactions on Software Engineering, 31*(10), 897–910. doi:10.1109/TSE.2005.112

He, P., Li, B., Liu, X., Chen, J., & Ma, Y. (2015). An empirical study on software defect prediction with a simplified metric set. *Information and Software Technology, 59*, 170–190. doi:10.1016/j.infsof.2014.11.006

Jin, C., & Jin, S. W. (2015). Prediction approach of software fault-proneness based on hybrid artificial neural network and quantum particle swarm optimization. *Applied Soft Computing, 35*, 717–725. doi:10.1016/j.asoc.2015.07.006

Juneja, K. (2019). A fuzzy-filtered neuro-fuzzy framework for software fault prediction for inter-version and inter-project evaluation. *Applied Soft Computing, 77*, 696–713. doi:10.1016/j.asoc.2019.02.008

Kaeeni, S., Khalilian, M., & Mohammadzadeh, J. (2018). Derailment accident risk assessment based on ensemble classification method. *Safety Science, 110*, 3–10. doi:10.1016/j.ssci.2017.11.006

Kim, S., Whitehead, E. J., & Zhang, Y. (2008). Classifying software changes: Clean or buggy. *IEEE Transactions on Software Engineering, 4*(2), 181–196. doi:10.1109/TSE.2007.70773

Krishnan, S., Strasburg, C., Lutz, R. R., & Popstojanova, K. G. (2011). Are change metrics good predictors for an evolving software product line? *Proceedings of the 7th international conference on predictive models in software engineering,* 1–10. 10.1145/2020390.2020397

Lim, H., & Goel, A. L. (2008). Software Effort Prediction. *Wiley Encyclopedia of Computer Science and Engineering.* doi:10.1002/9780470050118.ecse706

Malhotra, R. (2015). A Systematic review of Machine learning techniques for Software fault Prediction. *Applied Soft Computing, 27*(15), 504–518. doi:10.1016/j.asoc.2014.11.023

Malhotra, R. (2016). *Empirical Research in Software Engineering.* CRC Press, Taylor and Francis Group.

Malhotra, R., Kaur, A., & Sigh, Y. (2010). Empirical validation of object-oriented metrics for predicting fault proneness at different severity levels using support vector machines. *International Journal of System Assurance Engineering and Management., 1*(3), 269–281. doi:10.100713198-011-0048-7

Moser, R., Pedrycz, W., & Succi, G. (2008). A comparative analysis of the efficiency of change metrics and static code attributes for defect prediction. *2008 ACM/IEEE 30th international conference on software engineering,* 181-190, 10.1145/1368088.1368114

Nagappan, N., Zeller, A., Zimmermann, T., Herzig, K., & Murphy, B. (2010). Change bursts as defect predictors. *2010 IEEE 21st international symposium on software reliability engineering,* 309–318, 10.1109/ISSRE.2010.25

Nagarajan, R. K., & Upret, M. (2017). An ensemble predictive modeling framework for breast cancer classification. *Methods (San Diego, Calif.), 131*(1), 128–134. doi:10.1016/j.ymeth.2017.07.011 PMID:28716511

Nam, J., Pan, S. J., & Kim, S. (2013). Transfer defect learning. Proc. Int'l Conf. on Software Engineering, (ICSE'13), 382–391. doi:10.1109/ICSE.2013.6606584

Radjenovic, D., Herič, M., Torkar, R., & Zivkovic, A. (2013). Software fault prediction metrics: A systematic literature review. *Information and Software Technology*, *55*(8), 1397–1418. doi:10.1016/j.infsof.2013.02.009

Rathore, S. S., & Kumar, S. (2017a). Linear and non-linear heterogeneous *ensemble* methods to predict the number of *faults* in software systems. *Knowledge-Based Systems*, *1191*, 232–256. doi:10.1016/j.knosys.2016.12.017

Rathore, S. S., & Kumar, S. (2017b). Towards an *ensemble* based system for predicting the number of software *faults*. *Expert Systems with Applications*, *821*, 357–382. doi:10.1016/j.eswa.2017.04.014

Rhmann, W. (2018a). Application of Hybrid Search Based Algorithms for Software defect Prediction. *I. J. Modern Education and Computer Science*, *4*, 51-62.

Rhmann, W. (2018b). Cross project defect prediction using hybrid search based algorithms. *International Journal of Information Technology*, *12*(2), 531–538. doi:10.100741870-018-0244-7

Rhmann, W., Pandey, B., Ansari, G., & Pandey, D. K. (2020). Software fault prediction based on change metrics using hybrid algorithms: An empirical study. *Journal of King Saud University - Computer and Information Sciences, 32*(4), 419-424.

Shirabad, J. S., & Menzies, T. J. (2005). *The PROMISE Repository of Software Engineering Databases*. School of Information Technology and Engineering, University of Ottawa. http://promise.site.uottoawa.ca/SERepository

Singh, A., & Batra, S. (2018). Ensemble based spam detection in social IoT using probabilistic data structures. *Future Generation Computer Systems*, *8*, 359–371. doi:10.1016/j.future.2017.09.072

Subramanya, R., & Krishnan, M. S. (2003). Empirical analysis of ck metrics for object-oriented design complexity: Implications for software defects. *IEEE Transactions on Software Engineering*, *29*(4), 297–310. doi:10.1109/TSE.2003.1191795

Swamynathan, M. (2017). *Mastering Machine Learning with Python in six Steps*. Apress.

Verikas, A., Kalsyte, Z., & Bacauskiene, M. (2010). Hybrid and ensemble based soft computing techniques in bankruptcy prediction: a survey. *Soft Computing-A Fusion of Foundations, Methodologies and Applications*, *14*(9), 995-1010.

Wright, H. K., Kim, M., & Perry, D. E. (2010). Validity concerns in software engineering research. *Proceedings of the FSE/SDP Workshop on Future of Software Engineering Research*, 411–414. 10.1145/1882362.1882446

Xie, T., Pei, J., & Hassan, A. E. (2007). Mining Software engineering data. *29th International Conference on Software Engineering Companion, ICSE20007*, 172-173.

Zhou, Y., & Leung, H. (2006). Empirical analysis of object-oriented design metrics for predicting high and low severity faults. *IEEE Transactions on Software Engineering, 32*(10), 771–789. doi:10.1109/TSE.2006.102

This research was previously published in the International Journal of Open Source Software and Processes (IJOSSP), 11(2); pages 33-48, copyright year 2020 by IGI Publishing (an imprint of IGI Global).

710

Chapter 37
Generalized Multi-Release Framework for Fault Prediction in Open Source Software

Shozab Khurshid
University of Kashmir, Srinagar, India

A.K. Shrivastava
 https://orcid.org/0000-0001-7794-7129
International Management Institute, Kolkata, West Bengal, India

Javaid Iqbal
University of Kashmir, Srinagar, India

ABSTRACT

Software developing communities are shifting to open source software (OSS) because of the reason that software development takes place in successive releases, thereby improving its quality and reliability. Multi-release development of OSS can provide an opportunity to inculcate the dynamic needs of the user in a very short span of time to survive in the market. In spite of having these benefits, numerous challenges can be faced during the multi-release OSS development. Some of the challenges can be the generation of errors during the addition of new features. To address the changing fault detection process, a change point phenomenon is considered so as to give more practicality to the model. In this article, we present a general framework for multi-release OSS modelling incorporating imperfect debugging and change points. Parameter estimation and model validation is done on the three releases of Apache, an open source software project.

DOI: 10.4018/978-1-7998-9158-1.ch037

INTRODUCTION

In recent years, a rapid shift from closed source software to open source has been noticed. Reasons being availability of the source code, cutting of cost, development of skill, support from outside which in turn leads to more mature and reliable software product. A large number of users participate in testing the code and design of the OSS during its development process. Initially, OSS is developed by an individual or a small group of software developers for their own purpose. As OSS gains popularity, its volunteers increase tremendously and get involved in modifying the code and reporting the bugs in the software. The communities that are involved in the OSS development are moving towards multi up-gradation of the software so as to release the software early in the market, to meet the changing demands of the user and to correct the bugs reported by the users. Although this approach promotes feature addition of the software but there can be an increase in the fault content with the up-gradations. Thus, multi-release development approach should be embraced only if it provides better reliability.

Since multi up-gradation strategy provides benefits to the users as well as the software firms but it is considered as the most challenging task. When the software is being updated, an increase in the failure rate is being observed. This is because of the increase in the fault content due to the addition of the new functionality, the faults left in the previous release and also the bug reports from the users. Nevertheless, during the debugging process the failure rate tends to decrease gradually. A number of multi-version OSS projects are available namely Apache, Genome, Mozilla Firefox and R.

LITERATURE REVIEW

In the field of information technology, reliable software has become the most important concern. Software reliability is defined as "the probability of error free operation of the software for a given time period within some specified environment" (Kapur et al., 2011; Pham, 2006). Software Reliability Growth Models are used to quantitatively estimate the reliability of the software during the testing phase. A mathematical relationship between the testing time and total number of faults is given by SRGMs. Although a number of reliability models have been proposed so far, but all these are based on some limitations (Musa, 2004; Kapur et al., 2011).

Tremendous work has been done to assess the reliability and also to find a suitable model for Open Source Software. The phases that are involved in the development process of OSS was given by (Jorgensen, 2001). A comparative study between open and closed software was done by (Ven et al., 2008). In their study, comparison between the two was carried with respect to the development, cost, number of users and software design. Due to the limitations in the time and the resources, it becomes impossible for the developers to deliver a software product meeting the desired level of reliability within a single Software Development Life Cycle. Successive release is planned by the software developers which provides a number of benefits over a single release policy. The benefits that are provided by successive release policy has been studied by (Garmabaki et al., 2012). Kapur et al. (2014) proposed a multi up-gradation model for closed software that considers the issues related to the generation of faults when new functionality is added in the software. The SRGM proposed by them has the capability to capture the faults that are generated due to the add-ons along with the faults from the previous release that have been left undetected.

Although a lot of research pertaining to multi-release modelling has been put forth by a number of researchers but only a little work has been done considering multi-release modelling for Open Source Software. The research on the optimal time for the up-gradation of the version based on the maintenance effort of the software was done by Tamura and Yamada (2007). Li et al. (2011) proposed an optimization problem based on multi attribute utility for determining the time that is optimal to release Open Source Software's next version. A multi-release Open Source Software reliability framework based on fault detection and correction process has been provided by Yang et al. (2016) in which the debugging is taken as a delayed fault removal process. Very few studies considering factors such as perfect or imperfect debugging (Goel, 1985), change point (Zhao, 1993) that help in assessing the reliability accurately under multi-release strategy for OSS projects have been done. Under perfect debugging assumptions, a multi-release model for OSS was proposed by Garmabaki et al. (2015). Singh et al. (2010) incorporated change point to assess the reliability growth for OSS based on the instructions executed so as to cater the diverse user profile.

In the present investigation, multi-release modelling for OSS considering the imperfect debugging assumptions and change point concept is studied on real life data set. In OSS, the debugging is carried out by a number of users which are connected through the internet across the world. The users take part in testing of OSS in its operational phase and report the bugs in the software which in turn helps to increase the reliability of the product. When the first release is being developed no reported bugs from the volunteers are there to improve the software quality. It is after the first release that bug reporting and new functionalities as per the market demand are incorporated to improve the quality of the next version. Addition of functionalities increases the fault content and the associated risk. In the current study, error generation and imperfect debugging are incorporated to address the issue of the bugs introduced due to the add-ons in the next release and to detect some of the leftover faults from the just previous release.

Sudden changes during the fault removal process of each version is observed which may be due to the changing testing strategies. The changes at some time point in the fault removal rate can be observed by kinks or jumps in the failure dataset plot and are known as change points. There can be a single or multiple change points in the failure dataset. A software known as change point analyser is also used to identify the change points. Change point based SRGMs give more practicality to the model as they represent the testing environment in a true sense wherein the fault removal process undergoes a considerable change. A vast literature considering change point phenomenon with the perfect or imperfect debugging assumptions for single release or multi release is available (Nijhawan and Aggarwal, 2015; Kapur et al., 2010).

In this study, a generalized framework to model multi up-gradations for OSS incorporating the change point concept under the error generation and imperfect debugging assumption is proposed. The error generation is because of the introduction of faults during new additions in the next release and imperfect debugging is to consider the leftover faults from the just previous release in the successive release. The content of this paper is divided in the following sections. Section III focuses on the proposed model along with some notations and underlying model assumptions. In Section IV, model validation and performance analysis on multi-release of Apache dataset is carried out and parameter estimates are presented. The weighted criteria ranking approach is discussed in section V and the SRGMs are ranked for all the releases. Section VI discusses the conclusion and the future work.

PROPOSED MODEL

Notations

$\omega(t)$: Time varying initial fault content in the software
$\Lambda(t)$: Total faults detected or corrected by time t
I: Perfect debugging probability
e: The rate at which the faults get introduced during the debugging process
τ: Change point
$r(t)$: Fault removal/correction rate varying with time
$D(t)$: Distribution functions for fault removal/correction times
$d(t)$: Density functions for fault removal/correction times
$s(t)$: Hazard rate function
θ: Learning parameter in logistic function

Model Assumptions

The proposed model is formulated by considering the underlying assumptions:

1. Software testing is done to find the faults lying in the software which in turn results in failures. A failure is said to occur if there is a deviation in the output obtained from the desired/actual output on the given input data;
2. The fault removal at any instant of time is proportional to the number of remaining software faults;
3. There is a mutual independence between all the faults which are responsible for software failures;
4. Non-homogenous Poisson process is used to model the phenomenon of fault removal process;
5. The removal of faults is taken to be a single step process in which the detected faults are corrected immediately;
6. Initially, there are some finite number of faults present in the software i.e. before the testing process starts;
7. During the debugging process, new faults creep in with a constant rate e;
8. The detection/correction rate of faults might change at some instance of time and is known as change point;
9. During fault repairing, the fault content is reduced by 1 with probability I and with probability 1-I, the fault content remains unchanged;
10. The faults that have been left unaddressed in the ith release are passed on to the $(i+1)^{th}$ release.

Model Development

In this section, a general multi release framework is proposed that covers the dimensions of imperfect debugging and change point. By using different distribution functions in the generalized framework, several different SRGMs have been obtained. The fundamental equation that is used to model software reliability growth models that are based on NHPP is given below:

$$\frac{d\Lambda(t)}{dt} = r(t)\big(\bar{\omega} - \Lambda(t)\big) \tag{1}$$

In the proposed model, '$r(t)$' which denotes the time varying fault detection/removal rate is considered as hazard rate, '$s(t)$'. Also, the error introduction rate 'e' is assumed to be linear and a function of time and thus the equation for initial fault content, '$\bar{\omega}$' will become as follows:

$$\omega(t) = \bar{\omega} + e\Lambda(t)$$

On embedding imperfect debugging along with error generation, the Equation (1) becomes:

$$\frac{d\Lambda(t)}{dt} = s(t)\,I\big(\bar{\omega} + e\Lambda(t) - \Lambda(t)\big) \tag{2}$$

'I' denoting the probability of perfect debugging and '$s(t)$' the hazard rate function. On incorporating the change point phenomenon, the hazard rate function, '$s(t)$' and the fault content, '$\omega(t)$' becomes as follows:

$$s(t) = \begin{cases} \dfrac{d_1(t)}{1 - D_1(t)} & for\ t \leq \tau \\[3mm] \dfrac{d_2(t)}{1 - D_2(t)} & for\ t > \tau \end{cases} \tag{3}$$

$$\omega(t) = \begin{cases} \bar{\omega} + e_1\Lambda(t) & for\ t \leq \tau \\[2mm] \bar{\omega} + e_1\Lambda(\tau) + e_2\big(\Lambda(t) - \Lambda(\tau)\big) & for\ t > \tau \end{cases} \tag{4}$$

Using Equation (3) and (4) in Equation (2), we get the following:

$$\frac{d}{dt}\Lambda(t) = \begin{cases} \dfrac{d_1(t)}{1 - D_1(t)}\,I_1\big(\bar{\omega} + e_1\Lambda(t) - \Lambda(t)\big) & for\ t \leq \tau \\[3mm] \dfrac{d_2(t)}{1 - D_2(t)}\,I_2\big(\bar{\omega} + e_1\Lambda(\tau) + e_2\big(\Lambda(t) - \Lambda(\tau)\big) - \Lambda(t)\big) & for\ t > \tau \end{cases} \tag{5}$$

where 'I_1' and 'I_2' is the probability of perfect debugging before and after change point. On solving Equation (5), under initial conditions, $\Lambda(0)=0$ & $\Lambda(t=\tau)=\Lambda(\tau)$, we get:

$$\Lambda(t) = \begin{cases} \dfrac{\bar{\omega}}{1-e_1}\left[1-\left(1-D_1\left(t\right)\right)^{I_1(1-e_1)}\right] & for\ t \le \tau \\[4mm] \dfrac{\bar{\omega}}{1-e_2}\left[1-\left(1-D_1\left(\tau\right)\right)^{I_1(1-e_1)}\left(\dfrac{1-D_2\left(t\right)}{1-D_2\left(\tau\right)}\right)^{I_2(1-e_2)}\right] + \left(\dfrac{\left(e_1-e_2\right)}{\left(1-e_2\right)}\right)\Lambda\left(\tau\right) & for\ t > \tau \end{cases} \tag{6}$$

In Equation (6), after using different distribution functions from Table 1, we will be able to obtain several different SRGMs.

Multi-Release Modeling Framework for OSS With Imperfect Debugging and Change Point

The competitive and dynamic nature of the market urges the need of software up-gradations. Due to time and resource constraint, it becomes difficult to develop highly reliable software in a single cycle. Thus, software is developed in multiple versions but software up-gradation is considered to be a challenging task. This is because during up-gradation there is an increase in the failure rate because of the additional faults that are present in the newly developed code and the undetected faults from the just previous release. This newly developed code contains enhanced functionalities for customer satisfaction so as to survive in the market. The failure rate then decreases eventually when testing process is carried out.

The first version of the OSS is thoroughly tested before releasing it in the market. The aim of the testing team is to detect/correct maximum number of faults before it can be introduced to its customers. Since it becomes impossible to correct all the faults, so only a finite number of faults are detected which fulfils the need of releasing the software in market. The following equation is used for representing the total number of faults that are removed in the first release:

$$\Lambda_1(t) = \begin{cases} \bar{\omega}_{11}^*\left[1-\left(1-D_{11}\left(t\right)\right)^{I_{11}\left(1-e_{11}\right)}\right] & for\ t \le \tau_1 \\[4mm] \bar{\omega}_{12}^*\left[1-\left(1-D_{11}\left(\tau_1\right)\right)^{I_{11}\left(1-e_{11}\right)}\left(\dfrac{1-D_{12}\left(t\right)}{1-D_{12}\left(\tau_1\right)}\right)^{I_{12}\left(1-e_{12}\right)}\right] + \left(\dfrac{\left(e_{11}-e_{12}\right)}{\left(1-e_{12}\right)}\right)\Lambda\left(\tau_1\right) & for\ t > \tau_1 \end{cases} \tag{7}$$

where, $\bar{\omega}_{11}^* = \dfrac{\bar{\omega}_1}{1-e_{11}}$ and $\bar{\omega}_{12}^* = \dfrac{\bar{\omega}_1}{1-e_{12}}$. The bugs that are reported in OSS from the just previous release by the millions of volunteers helps in improving its quality in the subsequent releases. In multi-release framework, the software developers make new versions having enhanced functionalities available to their clients. The bugs that are reported by the users immediately after the software is released in the market and the bugs that are discovered due to the addition of new code in the next release are removed during the testing process of the next release. The following equation is used to represent the total number of faults removed in the next subsequent releases:

$$
\Lambda_i(t) = \begin{cases}
\dfrac{\bar{\omega}_i + \left(\bar{\omega}^*_{(i-1)2} - \Lambda(t_{i-1})\right)}{1 - e_{i1}}\left[1 - \left(1 - D_{i1}(t)\right)^{I_{i1}(1-e_{i1})}\right] & for\ t \le \tau_i \\[4mm]
\dfrac{\bar{\omega}_i + \left(\bar{\omega}^*_{(i-1)2} - \Lambda(t_{i-1})\right)}{1 - e_{i2}}\left[1 - \left(1 - D_{i1}(\tau_i)\right)^{I_{i1}(1-e_{i1})}\left(\dfrac{1 - D_{i2}(t)}{1 - D_{i2}(\tau_i)}\right)^{I_{i2}(1-e_{i2})}\right] \\[4mm]
\quad + \left[\dfrac{(e_{i1} - e_{i2})}{(1 - e_{i2})}\right]\Lambda(\tau_i) & for\ t > \tau_i
\end{cases}
$$

Software Reliability Growth Models Based on Different Distributions

Table 1 shows different distributions which we will use to obtain different SRGMs before and after change point. In our study, we have derived first release of all SRGMs. Further, we have derived second and third release of SRGM1. In the same manner, by using the generalized framework for subsequent releases we can derive mean value function for next releases of other SRGMs.

Table 1. Distribution functions

Models	$D_1(t),\ t<\tau$	$D_2(t),\ t>\tau$
SRGM-1(Logistic)	$\dfrac{\left(1 - e^{-r_1 t}\right)}{\left(1 + \theta_1 e^{-r_1 t}\right)}$	$\dfrac{\left(1 - e^{-r_2 t}\right)}{\left(1 + \theta_2 e^{-r_2 t}\right)}$
SRGM-2(Delayed S-shaped)	$\left(1 - \left(1 + r_1 t\right)e^{-r_1 t}\right)$	$\left(1 - \left(1 + r_2 t\right)e^{-r_2 t}\right)$
SRGM-3(Exponential)	$\left(1 - e^{-r_1 t}\right)$	$\left(1 - e^{-r_2 t}\right)$
SRGM-4(Weibull)	$\left(1 - e^{-r_1 t^k}\right)$	$\left(1 - e^{-r_2 t^k}\right)$
SRGM-7(Normal) (s,q) are mean and standard deviation	$\varphi(t;\ s1,\ q1)$	$\varphi(t;\ s2,\ q2)$
SRGM-8(Gamma) (l,δ) are shape and scale parameters.	$\Gamma(t;\ l_1, \delta1)$	$\Gamma(t;\ l_2, \delta2)$

1. SRGM1:

$$
\Lambda_1(t) = \begin{cases}
\dfrac{\bar{\omega}_1}{(1-e_{11})} \left[1 - \left(\dfrac{(1+\theta_{11})}{(1+\theta_{11}\exp(-r_{11}t))} \right)^{I_{11}(1-e_{11})} \exp\left(-r_{11}I_{11}(1-e_{11})t\right) \right] & \text{for } 0 \le t \le \tau_1 \\[4ex]
\dfrac{\bar{\omega}_1}{(1-e_{12})} \left[1 - \left(\dfrac{(1+\theta_{11})}{(1+\theta_{11}\exp(-r_{11}\tau_1))} \right)^{I_{11}(1-e_{11})} \left(\dfrac{(1+\theta_{12}\exp(-r_{12}\tau_1))}{(1+\theta_{12}\exp(-r_{12}t))} \right)^{I_{12}(1-e_{12})} \right. & \\
\left. {}* \exp\left(-r_{11}I_{11}(1-e_{11})\tau_1 - r_{12}I_{12}(1-e_{12})(t-\tau_1)\right) \right] & \text{for } t > \tau_1 \\[4ex]
{}+ \left(\dfrac{(e_{11}-e_{12})}{(1-e_{12})} \right) \Lambda(\tau_1) &
\end{cases}
$$

2nd **Release:**

$$
\Lambda_2(t) = \begin{cases}
\dfrac{\bar{\omega}_2 + \left(\bar{\omega}_{12}^{\;*} - \Lambda(t_1)\right)}{(1-e_{21})} \left[1 - \left(\dfrac{(1+\theta_{21})}{(1+\theta_{21}\exp(-r_{21}t))} \right)^{I_{21}(1-e_{21})} \exp\left(-r_{21}I_{21}(1-e_{21})t\right) \right] & \text{for } 0 \le t \le \tau_2 \\[4ex]
\dfrac{\bar{\omega}_2 + \left(\bar{\omega}_{12}^{\;*} - \Lambda(t_1)\right)}{(1-e_{22})} \left[1 - \left(\dfrac{(1+\theta_{21})}{(1+\theta_{21}\exp(-r_{21}\tau_2))} \right)^{I_{21}(1-e_{21})} \left(\dfrac{(1+\theta_{22}\exp(-r_{22}\tau_2))}{(1+\theta_{22}\exp(-r_{22}t))} \right)^{I_{22}(1-e_{22})} \right. & \\
\left. {}* \exp\left(-r_{21}I_{21}(1-e_{21})\tau_2 - r_{22}I_{22}(1-e_{22})(t-\tau_2)\right) \right] & \text{for } t > \tau_2 \\[4ex]
{}+ \left(\dfrac{(e_{21}-e_{22})}{(1-e_{22})} \right) \Lambda(\tau_2) &
\end{cases}
$$

Next release:

$$\Lambda_i(t) = \begin{cases} \dfrac{\overline{\omega}_i + \begin{pmatrix} \overline{\omega}_{(i-1)2}^{*} \\ -\Lambda\left(t_{(i-1)}\right)\end{pmatrix}}{\left(1-e_{i1}\right)} \begin{bmatrix} 1 - \left(\dfrac{\left(1+\theta_{i1}\right)}{\left(1+\theta_{i1}\exp\left(-r_{i1}t\right)\right)}\right)^{I_{i1}\left(1-e_{i1}\right)} \\ \exp\left(-r_{i1}I_{i1}\left(1-e_{i1}\right)t\right) \end{bmatrix} & \text{for } 0 \le t \le \tau_i \\[40pt] \dfrac{\overline{\omega}_i + \begin{pmatrix} \overline{\omega}_{(i-1)2}^{*} \\ -\Lambda\left(t_{(i-1)}\right)\end{pmatrix}}{\left(1-e_{i2}\right)} \begin{bmatrix} 1 - \left(\dfrac{\left(1+\theta_{i1}\right)}{\left(1+\theta_{i1}\exp\left(-r_{i1}\tau_i\right)\right)}\right)^{I_{i1}\left(1-e_{i1}\right)} \\ \left(\dfrac{\left(1+\theta_{i2}\exp\left(-r_{i2}\tau_i\right)\right)}{\left(1+\theta_{i2}\exp\left(-r_{i2}t\right)\right)}\right)^{I_{i2}\left(1-e_{i2}\right)} \\ *\exp\begin{pmatrix}-r_{i1}I_{i1}\left(1-e_{i1}\right)\tau_i \\ -r_{i2}I_{i2}\left(1-e_{i2}\right)\left(t-\tau_i\right)\end{pmatrix} \end{bmatrix} + \left[\dfrac{\left(e_{i1}-e_{i2}\right)}{\left(1-e_{i2}\right)}\right]\Lambda\left(\tau_i\right) & \text{for } t > \tau_i \end{cases}$$

2. SRGM2:

$$\Lambda_1(t) = \begin{cases} \dfrac{\overline{\omega}_1}{\left(1-e_{11}\right)}\left[1 - \left(\left(1+r_{11}t\right)\exp\left(-r_{11}t\right)\right)^{I_{11}\left(1-e_{11}\right)}\right] & \text{for } t \le \tau_1 \\[30pt] \dfrac{\overline{\omega}_1}{\left(1-e_{12}\right)}\begin{bmatrix} 1 - \left(1+r_{11}\tau_1\right)^{I_{11}\left(1-e_{11}\right)}\left(\dfrac{\left(1+r_{12}t\right)}{\left(1+r_{12}\tau_1\right)}\right)^{I_{12}\left(1-e_{12}\right)} \\ *\exp\begin{pmatrix}-r_{11}I_{11}\left(1-e_{11}\right)\tau_1 \\ -r_{12}I_{12}\left(1-e_{12}\right)\left(t-\tau_1\right)\end{pmatrix}\end{bmatrix} + \left[\dfrac{\left(e_{11}-e_{12}\right)}{\left(1-e_{12}\right)}\right]\Lambda\left(\tau_1\right) & \text{for } t > \tau_1 \end{cases}$$

3. SRGM3:

$$\Lambda_1(t) = \begin{cases} \dfrac{\overline{\omega}_1}{1-e_{11}}\left[1 - \exp\left(-r_{11}I_{11}\left(1-e_{11}\right)t\right)\right] & \text{for } t \le \tau_1 \\[20pt] \dfrac{\overline{\omega}_1}{1-e_{12}}\left[1 - \exp\left(-r_{11}I_{11}\left(1-e_{11}\right)\tau_1\right) - r_{12}I_{12}\left(1-e_{12}\right)\left(t-\tau_1\right)\right] \\ + \left[\dfrac{\left(e_{11}-e_{12}\right)}{\left(1-e_{12}\right)}\right]\Lambda\left(\tau_1\right) & \text{for } t > \tau_1 \end{cases}$$

4. SRGM4:

$$\Lambda_1\left(t\right)=\begin{cases}\dfrac{\overline{\omega}_1}{\left(1-e_{11}\right)}\left[1-\left(1-\left(1-\exp\left(-r_{11}t^{k_{11}}\right)\right)\right)^{I_{11}\left(1-e_{11}\right)}\right] & for\ t\leq\tau_1\\[4mm]\dfrac{\overline{\omega}_1}{\left(1-e_{12}\right)}\left[1-\left(1-\left(1-\exp\left(-r_{12}t^{k_{12}}\right)\right)\right)^{I_{11}\left(1-e_{11}\right)}\left(\dfrac{\left(1-\left(1-\exp\left(-r_{12}t^{k_{12}}\right)\right)\right)}{\left(\left(1-\left(1-\exp\left(-r_{12}\tau_{12}^{\ k_{12}}\right)\right)\right)\right)}\right)^{I_{12}\left(1-e_{12}\right)}\right]+\left(\dfrac{\left(e_{11}-e_{12}\right)}{\left(1-e_{12}\right)}\right)\Lambda\left(\tau_1\right) & for\ t>\tau_1\end{cases}$$

5. SRGM5:

$$\Lambda_1\left(t\right)=\begin{cases}\dfrac{\overline{\omega}_1}{\left(1-e_{11}\right)}\left[1-\left(1-\varphi\left(t,s_{11},q_{11}\right)\right)^{I_{11}\left(1-e_{11}\right)}\right] & for\ t\leq\tau_1\\[4mm]\dfrac{\overline{\omega}_1}{\left(1-e_{12}\right)}\left[1-\left(1-\varphi\left(\tau_1,s_{11},q_{11}\right)\right)^{I_{11}\left(1-e_{11}\right)}\left(\dfrac{\left(1-\varphi\left(t,s_{12},q_{12}\right)\right)}{\left(1-\varphi\left(\tau_1,s_{12},q_{12}\right)\right)}\right)^{I_{12}\left(1-e_{12}\right)}\right]\\[4mm]+\left(\dfrac{\left(e_{11}-e_{12}\right)}{\left(1-e_{12}\right)}\right)\Lambda\left(\tau_1\right) & for\ t>\tau_1\end{cases}$$

6. SRGM6:

$$\Lambda_1\left(t\right)=\begin{cases}\dfrac{\overline{\omega}_1}{\left(1-e_{11}\right)}\left[1-\left(1-\Gamma\left(t,l_{11},\delta_{11}\right)\right)^{I_{11}\left(1-e_{11}\right)}\right] & for\ t\leq\tau_1\\[4mm]\dfrac{\overline{\omega}_1}{\left(1-e_{12}\right)}\left[1-\left(1-\Gamma\left(\tau_1,l_{11},\delta_{11}\right)\right)^{I_{11}\left(1-e_{11}\right)}\left(\dfrac{\left(1-\Gamma\left(t,l_{12},\delta_{12}\right)\right)}{\left(1-\Gamma\left(\tau_1,l_{12},\delta_{12}\right)\right)}\right)^{I_{12}\left(1-e_{12}\right)}\right]\\[4mm]+\left(\dfrac{\left(e_{11}-e_{12}\right)}{\left(1-e_{12}\right)}\right)\Lambda\left(\tau_1\right) & for\ t>\tau_1\end{cases}$$

NUMERICAL ILLUSTRATION

For the validation of the proposed model, we have taken OSS datasets from the three versions of Apache project. The datasets are available on (http://softeng.polito.it/najeeb/confdata/DS1.pdf). The testing for the first release of Apache (Apache 2.0.35) is carried for 43 days in which the number of faults detected were 74. In case of second release (Apache 2.0.36), testing was performed for 103 days and faults detected were 50. For third release (Apache 2.0.39), 58 faults were detected during 164 days of testing.

The change points for the three releases has been observed with the change point analyser software. For the first release, the change point has been observed at the 10th day of testing. For the second and third release, change point is observed at the 9th and 14th day respectively. Although, it has been observed that multiple change points are present but we will consider only a single change point in our proposed model.

The estimation of the unknown parameters is done with the help of SPSS 20.0 and for the purpose of simplification, it has been assumed that the perfect debugging probability 'I' and the error introduction rate 'e' remains same before and after change point.

Comparison Criteria

A number of approaches are available for evaluating the performance of the SRGMs and selecting the one that fits the data well. For quantitative analysis of SRGMs, some comparison criteria are used. In our study, we have used twelve different criteria that have been identified in the literature (Pham 2006; Kapur et al. 2011). These are stated as follows:

1. **The Mean Square Fitting Error (MSE):** The deviation that is present between the observed values and the values that are predicted from the model is measured through MSE, and is shown as:

$$MSE = \frac{\sum_{i=1}^{m} \left(a_i - p\left(t_i\right)\right)^2}{x}$$

where a_i denotes the actual values, $p(t_i)$ denotes the predicted values and x the number of entries in the dataset.

2. **Bias:** To calculate bias, we need to first calculate the prediction error (PE). PE is given by the difference between the estimated value and the actual data at any time instant. On taking the average of the prediction errors, we get the measure of bias:

$$Bias = \frac{\sum_{i=1}^{m} \left(p\left(t_i\right) - a_i\right)}{x}$$

3. **The mean absolute error (MAE):** Unlike MSE, MAE makes use of absolute values to measure the deviation and is given as (Chiu et al., 2008):

$$MAE = \frac{\sum_{i=1}^{m} \left(a_i - p\left(t_i\right)\right)}{x - y}$$

where y denotes the unknown parameters in the model.

4. **The mean error of prediction (MEOP):** MEOP is given by (Zhao and Xie, 1992):

$$MEOP = \frac{\sum_{i=1}^{m} \left(a_i - p\left(t_i \right) \right)}{x - y + 1}$$

Lesser the value of the measure, better is the prediction capability of the model.

5. **The predictive ratio risk (PRR):** The deviation of the model estimates from the observed data with respect to the estimated values is given by PRR. Mathematically, it can be written as:

$$PRR = \sum_{i=1}^{m} \frac{\left(p\left(t_i \right) - a_i \right)}{p\left(t_i \right)}$$

6. **The Variance:** The variance is defined as the prediction error's standard deviation:

$$Variance = \sqrt{\frac{\sum_{i=1}^{m} \left(PE - BIAS \right)^2}{x - 1}}$$

7. **The Root Mean Square Prediction Error (RMSPE):** How close the model is in estimating the actual data is given by this measure:

$$RMSPE = \sqrt{Variance^2 + Bias^2}$$

8. **The sum of squared error (SSE):** SSE is mathematically written as (Zhang et al., 2003):

$$SSE = \sum_{i=1}^{m} \left(a_i - p\left(t_i \right) \right)^2$$

9. **The Thiel Statistic (TS):** This measure is given in terms of percentage and is defined as the average deviation with regard to the observed values. The closer this measure approaches to zero, the better is the goodness of fit. Mathematically, it is given as:

$$TS = \sqrt{\frac{\sum_{i=1}^{m} \left[a_i - p\left(t_i \right) \right]^2}{\sum_{i=1}^{m} \left(a_i \right)^2}} \times 100\%$$

10. **The coefficient of multiple determination (R^2)**: The variation of the data with regard to the fitted curve is given by this measure (Chiu et al., 2008). It is given by:

$$R^2 = 1 - \frac{\sum_{i=1}^{m} \left(a_i - p\left(t_i\right) \right)^2}{\sum_{i=1}^{m} \left[a_i - \frac{1}{m} \sum_{j=1}^{m} a_j \right]^2}$$

Adjusted R^2: This measure is a modification of R^2 and is given by:

$$AdjR^2 = 1 - \left(1 - R^2\right) \frac{x - 1}{x - y - 1}$$

11. **Akaikes Information Criterion (AIC):** It is related to SSE and the unknown model parameters:

$$AIC = 2*y + x*LN(SSE)$$

All the comparison criteria except R^2 and Adjusted R^2 that are mentioned above are lower value-based criteria which means lower the value of the criteria, better is the data fitting. However, R^2 and adjusted R^2 are higher value-based criterion.

DATA ANALYSIS

The parameter estimates for the three releases of Apache project are demonstrated in Tables 2, 3 and 4 respectively for different SRGMs that have been derived from the proposed generalized framework. From the parameter estimation tables for all the three releases, it may be observed that the values that are estimated for the initial number of faults in the software and the actual/observed values are quite same. Considering the multi release modelling framework, the remaining faults left undetected in the immediate previous release are passed on to the next release. For e.g. in SRGM-1, the estimated value of $\bar{\omega}$ in release 1 comes out to be 75 whereas the actual number of faults is 74. So, 1 fault remains undetected which is passed on to second release for correction and so on. In the same manner, remaining faults are calculated and passed on to the next release in other SRGMs. The error generation rate is found to be low in all the models which is taken into consideration because of the faults generated due to the addition of new functionalities. The value of 'Γ' is found to be high in case of SRGM1, SRGM3 and SRGM 4 in release1. For release 3, the value of 'Γ' is again found to be high for the same SRGMs. Further in case of SRGM1, the learning parameter θ increases after change point for all the releases. Also, it is observed that in most of the models the detection rate increases after change point.

For comparison criteria, we have used 12 different criteria including both low value based and high value based criteria (MSE, Bias, PRR, RMSPE, R^2, etc.). The results that are obtained from the comparison criteria are demonstrated for individual releases in Tables 5, 6, and 7 for Apache 2.0.35, 2.0.36 and 2.0.39. The goodness of fit curves for the SRGMs are graphically shown in Figure 1, Figure 2 and Figure 3 for the three releases.

Table 2. Parameter estimates (release 1)

Distribution	Parameter Estimates
1. Logistic	$\bar{\omega} = 5.329$, $r_1 = .119$, $r_2 = .244$, $\theta_1 = .003$, $\theta_2 = .714$, $I = .494$, $e = .030E\text{-}12$
2. Yamada Delayed S-shaped	$\bar{\omega} = 73.187$, $r_1 = .534$, $r_2 = .568$, $e = .056$, $I = .177$
3. Exponential Model	$\bar{\omega} = 1.091$, $r_1 = .113$, $r_2 = .185$, $e = .077$, $I = .533$
4. Weibull	$\bar{\omega} = 75.688$, $r_1 = .145$, $r_2 = .263$, $e = .022$, $I = .369$, $k = .980$
5. Normal	$\bar{\omega} = 68.581$, $e = .055$, $s_1 = .001$, $q_1 = 2.834$, $I = .069$, $s_2 = 4.663$, $q_2 = 2.814$
6. Gamma	$\bar{\omega} = 71.126$, $e = .023$, $l_1 = .981$, $\delta_1 = .750$, $I = .073$, $l_2 = 4.322$, $\delta_2 = 1.661$

Table 3. Parameter estimates (release 2)

Distribution	Parameter Estimates
1. Logistic	$\bar{\omega} = .1$, $r_1 = .372$, $r_2 = .379$, $\theta_1 = .515$, $\theta_2 = 7.787$, $I = .126$, $e = .716E\text{-}018$
2. Yamada Delayed S-shaped	$\bar{\omega} = .50$, $r_1 = .228$, $r_2 = .181$, $e = .804E\text{-}020$, $I = .327$
3. Exponential Model	$\bar{\omega} = .9$, $r_1 = .255$, $r_2 = .393$, $e = .015$, $I = .122$
4. Weibull	$\bar{\omega} = .49$, $r_1 = .170$, $r_2 = .455$, $e = .025$, $I = .181$, $k = .853$
5. Normal	$\bar{\omega} = 43.131$, $e = .101$, $s_1 = .006$, $q_1 = 1.653$, $I = .016$, $s_2 = 7.943$, $q_2 = 2.696$
6. Gamma	$\bar{\omega} = 46.311$, $e = .035$, $l_1 = 3.465$, $\delta_1 = .037$, $I = .015$, $l_2 = .466$, $\delta_2 = .489$

Table 4. Parameter estimates (release 3)

Distribution	Parameter Estimates
1. Logistic	$\bar{\omega} = 6.850$, $r_1 = .084$, $r_2 = .120$, $\theta_1 = .647$, $\theta_2 = 2.548$, $I = .575$, $e = .004$
2. Yamada Delayed S-shaped	$\bar{\omega} = 56.367$, $r_1 = .340$, $r_2 = .349$, $e = .021$, $I = .146$
3. Exponential Model	$\bar{\omega} = 6.644$, $r_1 = .069$, $r_2 = .115$, $e = .016$, $I = .416$
4. Weibull	$\bar{\omega} = 52.641$, $r_1 = .012$, $r_2 = .010$, $e = .078$, $I = .397$, $k = 1.598$
5. Normal	$\bar{\omega} = 56.525$, $e = .006$, $s_1 = 3.357$, $q_1 = 7.601$, $I = .180$, $s_2 = 1.759$, $q_2 = 10.671$
6. Gamma	$\bar{\omega} = 56.297$, $e = .011$, $l_1 = .786$, $\delta_1 = .282$, $I = .093$, $l_2 = 0.200$, $\delta_2 = .854$

Table 5. Comparison criteria (release 1)

SRGM Criteria	1	2	3	4	5	6
MSE	2.2369	4.7191	2.4599	2.3020	2.1070	2.5961
BIAS	-0.0528	-0.3944	-0.0684	0.04256	0.02698	-0.2179
VARIATION	1.5124	2.1615	1.5854	1.5346	1.4685	1.6153
PRR	-0.3743	-5.0899	-0.5372	0.0401	0.2586	-0.2025
SSE	96.185	202.92	105.77	98.99	90.60	111.63
AIC	210.35	238.45	210.44	209.58	207.78	216.75
RMSPE	1.513	2.197	1.587	1.5352	1.4687	1.6299
R^2	0.995	0.99	0.995	0.995	0.995	0.994
ADJ R^2	0.994	0.9887	0.994	0.9942	0.994	0.993
TS	2.5979	3.7735	2.7244	2.6356	2.5215	2.7988
MAE	1.4081	1.8821	1.4768	1.4592	1.2978	1.5214
MEOP	1.37	1.8339	1.4389	1.4208	1.2627	1.4803

Table 6. Comparison criteria (release 2)

SRGM Criteria	1	2	3	4	5	6
MSE	7.4499	7.4892	7.7857	8.7244	6.4322	6.6575
BIAS	0.0739	-0.1077	-0.0866	-0.4413	0.0163	0.01097
VARIATION	2.7418	2.7479	2.8026	2.9348	2.5485	2.5928
PRR	-4.796	-12.527	-3.4719	-3.656	0.3668	-0.292
SSE	767.34	771.38	801.9	898.6	662.5	685.7
AIC	698.2	694.76	698.76	712.49	683.09	686.6
RMSPE	2.743	2.7499	2.804	2.9678	2.5486	2.593
R^2	0.96	0.96	0.958	0.953	0.966	0.964
ADJ R^2	0.9571	0.9579	0.9558	0.9501	0.9635	0.9614
TS	6.4899	6.5070	6.6346	7.0232	6.0304	6.1351
MAE	2.3517	2.2683	2.3108	2.517	1.673	1.7139
MEOP	2.327	2.2454	2.2875	2.4909	1.655	1.6962

Table 7. Comparison criteria (release 3)

SRGM Criteria	1	2	3	4	5	6
MSE	0.7473	1.3125	0.7829	0.8231	0.7886	0.4417
BIAS	-0.0203	-0.1545	-0.0392	-0.0556	0.0109	0.0065
VARIATI ON	0.8669	1.1386	0.8867	0.9083	0.8907	0.6666
PRR	0.10661	-7.1088	-0.9268	-0.4339	0.7963	0.7975
SSE	122.56	215.25	128.40	134.99	129.34	72.4
AIC	802.61	890.97	806.25	816.45	811.44	716.35
RMSPE	0.867	1.1491	0.888	0.9100	0.8908	0.6666
R^2	0.996	0.993	0.996	0.996	0.996	0.998
ADJ R^2	0.9958	0.9928	0.9959	0.9959	0.9958	0.998
TS	1.7036	2.2577	1.7438	1.7879	1.7501	1.3097
MAE	0.4936	0.7958	0.6848	0.5241	0.5815	0.4270
MEOP	0.4904	0.7908	0.6806	0.5208	0.5779	0.4243

Figure 1. Goodness of fit (release 1)

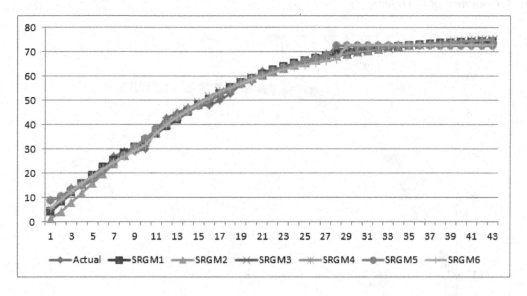

Figure 2. Goodness of fit (release 2)

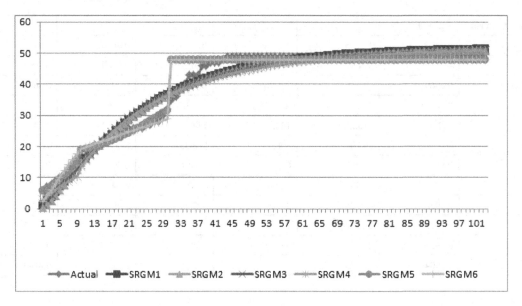

Figure 3. Goodness of fit (release 3)

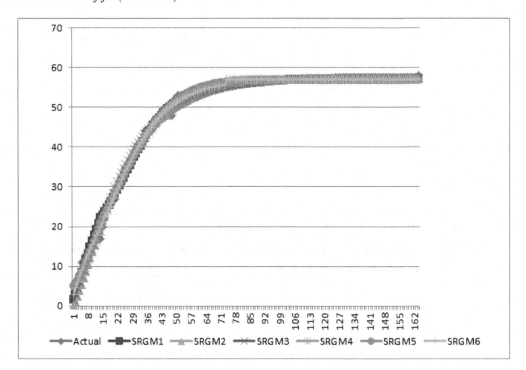

RANKING METHODOLOGY

Several different comparison criteria are available in the literature for the purpose of evaluating the best SRGM among all the available SRGM. Each comparison criterion has some advantages and disadvantages over the other. Therefore, it becomes difficult to judge which SRGM is having good prediction capability when different comparison criteria are taken into consideration. The aim of ranking methodology is to obtain a normalized mathematical measure in which there is an equal participation of every criteria. In our paper, we have used weighted criteria method (Anjum et al., 2013) for the purpose of ranking. The following steps are involved in this ranking methodology:

1. **Measurement of the comparison** n criteria: Let there be n SRGMs each having p criteria. We need a matrix of dimension $(n+2)*p$ to store all the criteria measurements. The matrix is shown below:

$$\text{Criteria matrix} = \begin{bmatrix} a_{11} & a_{12} & \cdots & a_{1p} \\ a_{21} & a_{22} & \cdots & a_{2p} \\ \vdots & \vdots & \ddots & \vdots \\ a_{n1} & a_{n2} & \cdots & a_{np} \\ \left(Amin()_1\right) & \left(Amin()_2\right) & \cdots & \left(Amin()_p\right) \\ \left(Amax()_1\right) & \left(Amax()_2\right) & \cdots & \left(Amax()_p\right) \end{bmatrix}$$

where each element in the matrix represented as a_{ij} shows the criteria value of the ith model and j^{th} criteria. $(Amax()_j)$ stores the maximum value of the jth criteria and vice versa.

2. **Rating of criteria:** The main purpose behind this rating is to normalize all the criteria so that they help in obtaining a uniform measurement. Two cases can be formed in this regard:
    Case-I: When smaller value of the comparison criteria is considered as best i.e. indicates a better fitting to the observed data, then:

$$\text{Rating} = \frac{\max criteriavalue - criteriavalue}{\max criteriavalue - \min criteriavalue}$$

    Case-II: When larger value of the comparison criteria is considered to be the best i.e. a better curve fitting, then:

$$\text{Rating} = \frac{criteriavalue - \min criteriavalue}{\max criteriavalue - \min criteriavalue}$$

3. **Weight of the criteria:** After calculating the rating of each criteria value in the matrix, the next step is to find the weight corresponding to each criteria rating. Let us suppose R_{ij} represents the rating for i^{th} model and j^{th} criteria and X_{ij} represents the weight. The weight can then be calculated as follows:

$$X_{ij} = 1 - R_{ij}$$

where:

$$R_{ij} = \frac{\left(\left(Amax()_{jij}\right)()\right)}{\left(\left(Amax()_{j}\left(Amin()_{j}\right)\right)\right)}$$

or:

$$R_{ij} = \frac{\left(a_{ij} - \left(Amin()_{j}\right)()\right)}{\left(\left(Amax()_{j}\left(Amin()_{j}\right)\right)\right)}$$

The values calculated are then stored in a weight matrix represented as:

$$\text{Weight Matrix, } X_{ij} = \begin{bmatrix} X_{11} & X_{12} & \cdots & X_{1p} \\ X_{21} & X_{22} & \cdots & X_{2p} \\ \vdots & \vdots & \ddots & \vdots \\ X_{n1} & X_{n2} & \cdots & X_{np} \end{bmatrix}$$

4. **Weighted Value of the Criterion:** Let W_{ij} denote the weighted value of the criterion. To calculate this measure, we simply multiply the weight value X_{ij} with the criteria value a_{ij}, $W_{ij} = X_{ij} * a_{ij}$. Thus, the weighted criterion matrix is represented as follows:

$$W_{ij} = \begin{bmatrix} W_{11} & W_{12} & \cdots & W_{1p} \\ W_{21} & W_{22} & \cdots & W_{2p} \\ \vdots & \vdots & \ddots & \vdots \\ W_{n1} & W_{n2} & \cdots & W_{np} \end{bmatrix}$$

5. **Permanent model value:** The weighted mean of all the comparison criteria that are taken for goodness of fit measure is the permanent value of the model. The formula for the permanent model value is:

$$Modelvalue = \frac{\sum_{j=1}^{p} W_{ij}}{\sum_{j=1}^{p} X_{ij}}$$

The value of $i=1,2,\ldots,n$.

Based on the permanent values, ranking is performed. Lower the permanent value, higher is the rank and vice versa. For release 1 and release 2, it is observed that SRGM 5 grabs the first rank among all the other models. It is evident from the weighted criteria value that SRGM5 should take the first rank as the weighted criteria values are lower than the other SRGMs. Similarly, for release 3. rank 1 is grabbed by SRGM6 followed by SRGM3 and SRGM5.

Table 8. Weighted criteria value (release 1)

SRGM Criteria	1	2	3	4	5	6
MSE	0.1112	4.7191	0.3323	0.1718	0	0.4861
BIAS	-0.041	0	-0.051	0.0426	0.0260	-0.088
VARIATION	0.0958	2.1615	0.2676	0.1464	0	0.3423
PRR	-0.3299	0	-0.4573	0.0385	0.2586	-0.1851
SSE	4.7801	202.92	14.287	7.3882	0	20.901
AIC	17.6297	238.45	18.229	12.335	0	63.425
RMSPE	0.0926	2.197	0.2574	0.1400	0	0.3607
R^2	0	0.99	0	0	0	0.199
ADJ R^2	0.0568	0.9887	0	0.0275	0.0568	0.2666
TS	0.1588	3.7735	0.4416	0.2401	0	0.6200
MAE	0.2657	1.8821	0.4526	0.4031	0	0.5822
MEOP	0.2574	1.8339	0.4441	0.3933	0	0.5639

Table 9. Weighted criteria value (release 2)

SRGM Criteria	1	2	3	4	5	6
MSE	3.3074	3.453	4.5971	8.7244	0	0.6543
BIAS	0.0739	-0.0697	-0.0596	0	0.01449	0.0096
VARIATION	1.3716	1.4180	1.84298	2.9348	0	0.2972
PRR	-2.8757	0	-2.4382	-2.5152	0.3668	-0.2774
SSE	340.66	355.69	473.50	898.61	0	67.395
AIC	359.34	275.83	372.48	712.49	0	82.826
RMSPE	1.2705	1.3211	1.7076	2.9678	0	0.2736
R^2	0.4431	0.4431	0.5895	0.953	0	0.1483
ADJ R^2	0.4590	0.3963	0.5451	0.9501	0	0.1537
TS	3.00396	3.12396	4.0376	7.0232	0	0.64699
MAE	1.8922	1.6009	1.7475	2.51659	0	0.08397
MEOP	1.8721	1.5855	1.73059	2.49092	0	0.0831

Table 10. Weighted criteria value (release 3)

SRGM Criteria	1	2	3	4	5	6
MSE	0.26229	1.3125	0.3069	0.3605	0.3142	0
BIAS	-0.0165	0	-0.0273	-0.0332	0.01098	0.00629
VARIATION	0.36782	1.13865	0.41342	0.46513	0.42288	0
PRR	0.097297	0	-0.7246	-0.3663	0.7962	0.7975
SSE	43.017	215.25	50.32	59.127	51.535	0
AIC	396.46	890.97	415.07	468.01	441.84	0
RMSPE	0.360	1.1491	0.406	0.4591	0.4139	0
R^2	0.398	0.993	0.3984	0.3984	0.3984	0
ADJ R^2	0.4054	0.9928	0.3953	0.4003	0.4054	0
TS	0.7079	2.2577	0.7985	0.9019	0.8130	0
MAE	0.0891	0.7958	0.4788	0.1380	0.2437	0
MEOP	0.0885	0.7908	0.4758	0.1372	0.2421	0

Table 11. Permanent value and ranking (release 1)

SRGM	Sum of Weight	Sum of Weighted Value	Permanent Value	Rank
1	2.46595	23.077	9.3582	3
2	10	459.92	45.992	6
3	3.0623	34.203	11.169	4
4	3.026	21.326	7.0485	2
5	2.021	0.3413	0.1689	1
6	3.8717	87.47	22.593	5

Table 12. Permanent value and ranking (release 2)

SRGM	Sum of Weight	Sum of Weighted Value	Permanent Value	Rank
1	6.9785	710.82	101.86	3
2	5.7304	644.79	112.52	5
3	7.6782	860.28	112.04	4
4	10.688	1637.1	153.18	6
5	1.8881	0.381	0.2019	1
6	2.8811	152.295	52.8597	2

Table 13. Permanent value and ranking (release 3)

SRGM	Sum of Weight	Sum of Weighted Value	Permanent Value	Rank
1	5.3429	442.23	82.770	4
2	10	1115.65	111.57	6
3	6.3545	468.31	73.697	2
4	5.7410	529.99	92.317	5
5	6.3902	497.44	77.844	3
6	1.9727	0.8038	0.4075	1

CONCLUSION

In order to meet the dynamic needs of the customer, industries involved in the development of OSS are shifting towards the paradigm of multi release modelling. Keeping in view the time and resource constraint, multi release modelling plays a significant role but at the same time it becomes challenging too. The increase in the failure detection rate in the next releases due to the addition of new functionalities and the remaining faults from the previous releases, demands to incorporate the imperfect debugging and error generation concept. In view of above-mentioned issues, we propose a generalized framework from which different SRGMs are derived incorporating imperfect debugging and change point. The three releases of Apache project are used for the evaluation of unknown model parameters and comparison criteria. In our study, Weighted Criteria method has been used for ranking the models in order to select the appropriate model based on their predictive capabilities. Further, fault detection and correction are taken as a single stage process. In the future, we will try to separate the fault detection and correction process. These models can also be extended for effort-based modelling incorporating multiple change points.

REFERENCES

Anjum, M., Haque, M. A., & Ahmad, N. (2013). Analysis and ranking of software reliability models based on weighted criteria value. *International Journal of Information Technology and Computer Science*, *2*(1), 1–14. doi:10.5815/ijitcs.2013.02.01

Chiu, K. C., Huang, Y. S., & Lee, T. Z. (2008). A study of software reliability growth from the perspective of learning effects. *Reliability Engineering & System Safety*, *93*(10), 1410–1421. doi:10.1016/j.ress.2007.11.004

Garmabaki, A. H. S., Aggarwal, A. G., Kapur, P. K., & Yadavali, V. S. S. (2012). Modeling two-dimensional software multi-upgradation and related release problem (a multi-attribute utility approach). *International Journal of Reliability Quality and Safety Engineering*, *19*(3), 1250012. doi:10.1142/S021853931250012X

Garmabaki, A. S. H., Barabadi, A., Yuan, F., Lu, J., & Ayele, Y. Z. (2015). Reliability Modeling of Successive Release of Software using NHPP. In *IEEE International Conference on Industrial Engineering and Engineering Management (IEEM)* (pp. 761-766). IEEE. 10.1109/IEEM.2015.7385750

Goel, A. L. (1985). Software Reliability Models: Assumptions, Limitations and Applicability. *IEEE Transactions on Software Engineering*, *11*(12), 1411–1423. doi:10.1109/TSE.1985.232177

Jorgensen, N. (2001). Putting it all in the trunk: Incremental software development in the Free BSD open source project. *Information Systems Journal*, *11*(4), 321–336. doi:10.1046/j.1365-2575.2001.00113.x

Kapur, P. K., Aggarwal, A. G., & Nijhawan, N. (2014). A Discrete SRGM for Multi-Release software system. *International Journal of Industrial and Systems Engineering*, *16*(2), 143–155. doi:10.1504/IJISE.2014.058833

Kapur, P. K., Anand, S., & Singh, V. B. (2009). Distribution Based Change-Point Problem with Two Types of Imperfect Debugging in Software Reliability. *International Journal of Information Technology*, *1*(2), 29–34.

Kapur, P. K., Pham, H., Gupta, A., & Jha, P. C. (2011). *Software reliability assessment with OR applications*. UK: Springer. doi:10.1007/978-0-85729-204-9

Kapur, P.K., Singh, O., Garmabaki, A.S. and Singh, J.(2010). Multi Up-gradation software reliability model with imperfect debugging. *International Journal of System Assurance Engineering and management, 1*(4), 299-306.

Li, X., Li, Y. F., Xie, M., & Ng, S. H. (2011). Reliability Analysis and Optimal Version-Updating for Open Source Software. *International Journal of Information and Software Technology, 53*(9), 929–936. doi:10.1016/j.infsof.2011.04.005

Musa, J. D. (2004). *Software Reliability Engineering: More Reliable Software Faster and Cheaper*. Authorhouse.

Nijhawan, N., & Aggarwal, A. G. (2015). On Development of Change Point Based Generalized SRGM for Software with Multiple Releases. In *Proceedings of IEEE 4th International Conference on Reliability, Infocom Technologies and Optimization (ICRITO)*, Amity University, India. 10.1109/ICRITO.2015.7359362

Pham, H. (2006). *System software reliability*. London: Springer. doi:10.1007/1-84628-295-0

Singh, V. B., Kapur, P. K., & Basirzadeh, M. (2010). Instructions Executed Dependent Software Reliability Growth Modeling For Open Source Software By Considering Change – Point. In *Proceedings of the 4th National Conference; INDIACom Computing For Nation Development*.

Tamura, Y., & Yamada, S. (2007). Software Reliability Assessment and Optimal Version-Upgrade Problem for Open Source Software. In *Proceedings of IEEE International Conference on Systems, Man, and Cybernetics*, Montreal, Canada (pp. 1333-1338).

Ven, K., Verelst, J., & Mannaert, H. (2008). Should you adopt open source software? *IEEE Software, 25*(3), 54–59. doi:10.1109/MS.2008.73

Yang, J., Liu, Y., Xie, M., & Zhao, M. (2016). Modeling and Analysis of Reliability of Multi-Release Open Source Software Incorporating Both Fault Detection and Correction Processes. *Journal of Systems and Software, 115*(May), 102–110. doi:10.1016/j.jss.2016.01.025

Zhang, X., Teng, X., & Pham, H. (2003). Considering Fault Removal Efficiency in Software Reliability Assessment. *IEEE Trans. on Systems, Man and Cybernetics- Part A Systems and Humans, 33*(1), 114–120. doi:10.1109/TSMCA.2003.812597

Zhao, M. (1993). Change-Point Problems In Software And Hardware Reliability. *Communications in Statistics. Theory and Methods, 22*(3), 757–768. doi:10.1080/03610929308831053

Zhao, M., & Xie, M. (1992). On the log-power NHPP software reliability model. In *Proceedings of the Third IEEE International Symposium on Softw. Reliability Engineering* (pp. 14-22). IEEE. 10.1109/ISSRE.1992.285862

This research was previously published in the International Journal of Software Innovation (IJSI), 7(1); pages 86-107, copyright year 2019 by IGI Publishing (an imprint of IGI Global).

Chapter 38
Logging Analysis and Prediction in Open Source Java Project

Sangeeta Lal
Jaypee Institute of Information Technology, India

Neetu Sardana
Jaypee Institute of Information Technology, India

Ashish Sureka
Ashoka University, India

ABSTRACT

Log statements present in source code provide important information to the software developers because they are useful in various software development activities such as debugging, anomaly detection, and remote issue resolution. Most of the previous studies on logging analysis and prediction provide insights and results after analyzing only a few code constructs. In this chapter, the authors perform an in-depth, focused, and large-scale analysis of logging code constructs at two levels: the file level and catch-blocks level. They answer several research questions related to statistical and content analysis. Statistical and content analysis reveals the presence of differentiating properties among logged and nonlogged code constructs. Based on these findings, the authors propose a machine-learning-based model for catch-blocks logging prediction. The machine-learning-based model is found to be effective in catch-blocks logging prediction.

INTRODUCTION

Logging is an important software development practice that is used to record important program execution points in the source code. The recorded log generated from program execution provides important information to the software developers at the time of debugging. Fu et al. (2014) conducted a survey of Microsoft developers, asking them their opinion on source code logging. Results of the survey showed that 96 percent of the developers consider logging statements the primary source of information for prob-

DOI: 10.4018/978-1-7998-9158-1.ch038

lem diagnosis. In many scenarios, logging is the only information available to the software developers for debugging because the same execution environment is unavailable (which makes bug regeneration difficult) or the same user input is unavailable (because of security and privacy concerns) (Yuan et al., 2012). Yuan et al. (2012) showed in their characterization study that the bug reports consisting of logging statements get fixed 2.2 times faster compared to the bug reports not consisting of any logging statements. Logging statements are not only useful in debugging, but they are also useful in many other applications, such as anomaly detection (Fu et al., 2009), performance problem diagnosis (Nagaraj et al., 2012), and workload modeling (Sharma et al., 2011).

Logging statements are important, but they have an inherent cost and benefit tradeoff (Fu et al., 2014). A large number of logging statements can affect system performance because logging is an I/O-intensive activity. An experiment by Ding et al. (2015) and Sigelman et al. (2010) reveal that in the case of search engines, logging can increase average execution time of requests by of 16.3%. Similar to excess logging, less logging is also problematic. An insufficient number of logging statements can miss important debugging information and can lessen the benefits of logging. Hence, developers need to avoid both excessive and insufficient logging. However, previous research and studies show that developers often face difficulty in optimal logging, that is, identifying which code construct to log in the source code (Fu et al., 2014; Zhu et al., 2015). It happens because of lack of training and the domain experience required for optimal logging. For example, Shang et al. (2015) reported an incident of a user from a Hadoop project complaining about less logging of catch-blocks. Recently the software engineering research community has conducted studies to understand the logging practices of software developers in order to build tools and techniques to help with automated logging. The current studies provide limited characterization study or conduct analysis on fewer code constructs. There are gaps in previous studies, as they do not analyze all the code constructs in detail, which this study aims to fill.

The work presented in this chapter is the first large-scale, in-depth, and focused study of logged and nonlogged code constructs at multiple levels. High-level (source code files) and low-level (catch-blocks) analysis were conducted to identify relationships between code constructs and logging characteristics. Based on the finding of this multilevel analysis authors proposed a machine leanirng based model for log statement prediction for catch-blocks. . A case study was performed on three large, open-source Java projects: Apache Tomcat (Apache Tomcat, n.d.), CloudStack (Apache CloudStack, n.d.), and Hadoop (Page, n.d.). Empirical analysis reveals several interesting insights about logged and nonlogged code constructs at both the levels. The machine learning based model give encouraging results for catch-blocks logging prediction on Java projects.

RELATED WORK

This section presents the closely related work and the novel research contributions of the study presented in this chapter in context to existing work. The authors categorize the related work in three dimensions: 1) improving source code logging, 2) uses of logging statements in other applications, and 3) applications of LDA in topic identification.

Improving Source Code Logging

Yuan et al. (2012) analyze source code and propose *ErrorLog* tool that logs all the generic exception patterns. However, logging all the generic exception can cause excess of log statements in the source code. Fu et al. (2014) empirically analyzed logging practices of software developers on two industrial systems. They addressed three research questions in their study: first, finding code snippets that were logged frequently; second, identifying the distinguishing characteristics of logged and nonlogged code constructs; and third, building a tool for logging prediction. They analyzed 100 randomly chosen logging statements and identified the most frequently logged code construct types. They performed detailed analysis of return value check and exception snippets. They computed the logging ratio of each unique exception type and reported that the majority of the exception types falls in the range of a medium logging ratio (i.e., 10 percent to 90 percent). They analyzed 70 nonlogged catch-blocks and identified the main reasons for not inserting a logging statement in the catch-block. They reported the correlations among the presence of some specific keywords that affect the logging decision such as "delete," "remove," "get," etc. The machine learning–based tool proposed by Fu et al., which used contextual information from the code, gave an F-score of 80 percent to 90 percent. This shows that contextual information can be an important factor when making logging decisions. This study extends the characterization study performed by Fu et al. on many dimensions. First, the study performed by Fu et al. presents results on the basis of manual analysis of only a few code constructs, whereas in this work the authors present their analysis using much larger code constructs. Second, the authors extended their study by answering many more research questions at two levels. Third, the authors analyzed open-source Java project, whereas they analyzed closed-source C# projects. Hence, the results in this chapter can be reproduced by the software engineering research community. Zhu et al. (2015) extended the study performed by Fu et al. by using more features for building the logging prediction. However, their study also lack comprehensive analysis of the features used for building the logging prediction model.

Yuan et al.'s (2012b) work involved empirically analyzing modifications to log messages. They reported many interesting findings from their empirical analysis performed on four large open-source projects. Yuan et al. (2012b) reported that 18 percent of all the committed revisions modify logging code, and 26 percent of the time developers modify the verbosity level of the logging code as an afterthought. Forty-five percent and 27 percent of the time developers modify the text and variable of the log messages, respectively, to incorporate changes in the execution information. Based on these findings, they proposed a simple code clone-based technique to find inconsistent verbosity levels in the source code. In another study, Yuan et al. (2012c) propose model for enhancing the content of log statements. Chen et al. (2016) replicated the study performed by Yuan et al. (2012b) for Java projects and reported several differences in results as compared to the results reported by Yuan et al. (2012b). Kabinna et al.'s (2016) work on predicting the stability of logging statements using features from three different domains: context, developer, and content. In another study, Kabinna et al.'s (2016b) work on empirically analyzing migration of log libraraies in Java projects. Li et al. (2016) worked on predicting verbosity level of log statement. In another study, Li et al. (2016b) worked on predicting just in time log changes. In contrast to these studies, our work focuses on finding distinguishing features of logged and non-logged code constructs and to predict logged code constructs. This book chapter is based on our previous published work (Lal et al., 2015, Lal & Sureka, 2016; Lal et al., 2016b). This work is found to be useful and has been extended for if-blocks logging prediction (Lal et al., 2016) and cross-project catch-blocks and if-blocks logging prediction (Lal et al., 2017a; Lal et al., 2017b).

Uses of Logging Statements in Other Applications

Logging statements have been found useful in various software development tasks (Mariani & Pastore, 2008; Nagaraj et al., 2012; Shang et al., 2015; Xu et al., 2009; Yuan et al., 2010). Shang et al. (2015) used logging statements present in a file to predict defects. Shang et al. (2015) proposed various product and process metrics using logging statements to predict post-release defects in software. Nagaraj et al. (2012) used good and bad logs of the system to detect performance issues. Nagaraj et al. (2012) also developed a tool, DISTALYZER, that helps developers find components responsible for poor system performance. Xu et al.'s (2009) work involved mining console logs from distributed systems at Google. They used logging information to find anomalies in the system. The authors verified anomalies were detected at the time when the system raised performance-related issues. They reported that performance issues are raised at the same time when anomalies are detected in system. Yuan et al. (2010) proposed a technique for finding the root cause of the failures by using logging information. They developed a tool, SherLog, that can use logs to find information about failed runs. SherLog can find important information about failures without requiring any re-execution of the code. All these studies focused on using log information in other applications such as finding root causes and performance issue detection. In contrast to these studies, the work described in this chapter focuses on the comparison between logged and nonlogged code constructs at two levels.

LDA Applications in Topic Identification

LDA is a popular topic modeling technique (Blei et al., 2003). It has been utilized widely in various software engineering applications to discover meaningful topics (Barua et al., 2012; Pagano & Maalej, 2013; Thomas et al., 2014;Tian et al., 2009). Tian et al. (2009) used LDA for software categorization. They proposed a system that can learn topic models from the identifier and comments present in the source code and can categorize software into one of the 43 programming languages such as C, C++, Java, PHP, Perl, etc. Thomas et al. (2014) used LDA topic models for software evolution analysis. Results reported by them show that topic models are effective in discovering actual code changes. Pagano et al. (2013) used LDA to study blogging behavior of committers and noncommitters. Results showed that committers' blogs consist of topics related to features and domain concepts, and 15 percent of the time blogs consist of topics related to source code. In contrast, blogs of noncommitters consist of topics related to conferences, events, configuration and deployment. Barua et al. (2012) used LDA on a StackOverflow questions and answers dataset in order to discover the most popular topics among the developer community. Results showed that a wide variety of topics are present in the developer discussions. They also showed that topics related to Web and mobile application development are gaining popularity compared to other topics. All these previous studies show the effectiveness of LDA topic models in the software engineering applications, and hence the authors of this chapter choose LDA for topic analysis. However, in contrast to these studies, the authors used LDA for topic identification in logging and nonlogging code constructs. To the best of their knowledge, LDA has never been used for topic modeling in this context.

Table 1. Details of individual research questions addressed in each research dimension

Research Dimension	Research Questions
Statistical analysis of high-level code constructs (source code files)	1. Is distribution of the logged files skewed? 2. Do logged files have greater complexity compared to that of nonlogged files? 3. Is there a positive correlation between file complexity and log statement count?
Statistical analysis of low-level code constructs (catch-blocks)	4. Do try-blocks associated with logged catch-blocks have greater complexity compared to that of nonlogged catch-blocks? 5. What is the logging ratio of different exception types? 6. Is the exception type contribution the same in total catch-blocks as well as in total logged catch-blocks? 7. Are the top20 exception types and their respective logging ratios the same in all three projects? 8. Can logged and nonlogged catch-blocks co-exist?
Content-based analysis of low-level code constructs (catch-blocks)	9. Do try-blocks associated with logged and nonlogged catch-blocks have different topics?
Logging prediction model for low-level code constructs (catch-blocks)	10. Can we predict logged catch-blocks using machine learning based model?

RESEARCH DIMENSIONS AND RESEARCH QUESTIONS

Table 1 shows four main research dimensions (RDs) and respective research questions (RQs) considered in this work. Following is a brief description of each RD and respective RQs:

- **RD1 - Statistical Analysis of Source Code Files:** In RD1, the authors answer three main research questions related to the statistical properties of logged and nonlogged files. Statistical analysis is important because it provides insights about the logged and nonlogged code constructs without looking at the semantics of the code. The first and second RQs compute the percentage of logged files and their average SLOCs. The third RQ computes the correlation between file SLOC and respective logging count.

- **RD2 - Statistical Analysis of Catch-Blocks:** In RD2, the authors answer five research questions related to the statistical properties of logged and nonlogged catch-blocks. The fourth research question compares the complexities of the try-blocks associated with logged and nonlogged catch-blocks to investigate whether complexities of try-blocks have any effect on the corresponding catch-block logging decision or not. The fifth and seventh RQs compute the logging ratio of all the exception types and the top 20 exception types in all three projects. The sixth RQ computes the contribution of an exception type in total catch-blocks and total logged exception types. The eighth RQ investigates whether logged and nonlogged catch-blocks can co-exist.

- **RD3 - Content-Based Analysis of Catch-Blocks:** In RD3, the authors use an LDA-based topic modeling technique on the contextual information present in the try-blocks associated with logged and nonlogged catch-blocks. They hypothesize that the contextual information present in the try-blocks can reveal important information for the corresponding catch-block logging.

- **RD4 - Logging Prediction Model for Catch-Blocks:** In RD4, the authors use finding of this empirical study and propose machine learning based model for logged catch-blocks prediction.

Figure 1. Research method followed in this study

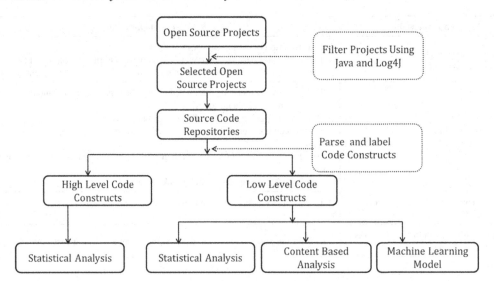

RESEARCH METHOD AND EXPERIMENTAL DATASET

This section presents the research methodology and experimental dataset details (refer to Figure 1). The research method consists of two phases: dataset selection and dataset preparation.

Dataset Selection Phase

In this phase, the authors selected open-source projects on which to conduct their experiments. Following are the list of properties and essential criteria which were taken into account while selecting the three open-source projects for the analysis:

1. **Type: Open Source:** The authors conducted their study on open-source software projects so that the work can be replicated and used for benchmarking and comparison.
2. **Programing Language: Java:** The authors selected a Java-based project for the study because Java is one of the most used programing languages (Kim, 2016;Krill, 2016).
3. **Logging Framework: Log4J:** The authors used Java projects utilizing the Log4J (Goers, n.d.) framework for logging. They targeted projects using the Log4J framework only because this is one of the widely used frameworks for Java logging.
4. **Number of Java Files: More Than 1,000:** The authors set this threshold so that they can draw statistically significant conclusions.
5. **Number of Catch-Blocks: More Than 1,000:** The authors set this threshold so that they can draw statistically significant conclusions.

Experimental Dataset Details

The authors selected three projects for their empirical study based on the criteria defined for the dataset selection phase: Apache Tomcat, CloudStack, and Hadoop. All three projects are long-lived Java projects with a development history of ≈7 to 17 years. Table 2 shows the SLOC of all three projects. SLOC are computed using the LocMetrics tool (LocMetrics, n.d.). Apache Tomcat, CloudStack and Hadoop have been previously used by the research community for logging and other studies (Kabinna et al., 2016; Lal & Sureka, 2016; Lal et al., 2016; Shang et al., 2015; Zimmermann et al.,2009). Following are the details of each project.

- **Apache Tomcat:** Apache Tomcat is open-source software developed under the umbrella of the Apache Software Foundation (Apache Tomcat, n.d). It is a Web server that implements many Java EE specifications like Java Servlet, Java EL, Java Sever Pages, and WebSocket. Logging is important in Apache Tomcat Web server; it has its own LogManager implementation; and it also supports private per-application logging configurations (Crossley, n.d.;Team, n.d.).
- **CloudStack:** CloudStack is open-source software developed by the Apache Software Foundation (Apache CloudStack, n.d). It provides public, private, and hybrid cloud solutions. It also provides a highly available and scalable Infrastructure as a Service (IaaS) cloud computing platform for deployment and management of networks of virtual machines. It provides support for many hypervisors such as VMware, KVM and Xen Cloud Platform (XCP). CloudStack provides large amounts of log entries, and for a CloudStack administrator investigating errors in the logs is an inevitable task (Kosinski, 2013).
- **Hadoop:** Hadoop is also developed by the Apache Software Foundation (Page, n.d). It is a framework that enables distributed processing of large datasets. It is scalable from a single server to multiple machines. The Apache Hadoop library is designed to detect and handle application-layer failures. Hadoop is one of the most widely used software platforms, and various tools have been developed to monitor the status of the Hadoop using generated logs (Shang et al., 2015; Rabkin & Katz, 2010).

Dataset Preparation Phase

In this step, the authors extract logging statements and target code constructs from the source code. Following are the details of the data preparation.

- **Files:** The authors extracted all the high-level (source code files) code constructs from the source code. They focused only on Java files in this work and removed other types of files such as CSS and XML. Table 2 shows statistics on the number of Java files extracted from each of the projects. For example, the Apache Tomcat project consists of 2,037 Java files, whereas the CloudStack project consists of 5,351 Java files. The authors extracted logging statements from each file (refer to Table 3). They marked a file as "logged" if it consisted of at least one logging statement; otherwise, it was marked as "non-logged."
- **Catch-Blocks:** Next the authors extract all the catch-blocks from the source code. They extracted all the catch-blocks from the Java files using the Eclipse Java source code parsing library (Beaton, n.d). However, a single try-block can have multiple catch-blocks. In such cases the authors con-

sidered all catch-blocks belonging to a single try-block as a separate instance. Figure 2 shows an illustrative example of separate instance creation. The authors marked a catch-block as "logged" if it consisted of at least one logging statement. Table 2 shows that the experimental dataset consists of 3,325, 12,591, and 7,947 catch-blocks in Apache Tomcat, CloudStack, and Hadoop, respectively. It also shows that 27 percent, 26.15 percent, and 22 percent of the catch-blocks are logged in Apache Tomcat, Hadoop, and CloudStack, respectively.

Figure 2. Catch-block instance creation from try-blocks

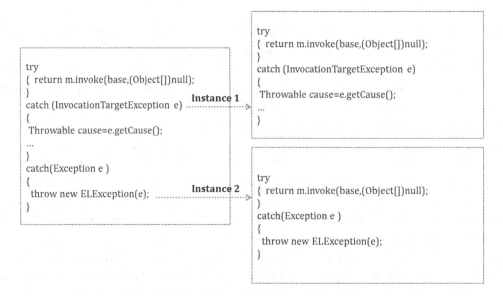

- **Logging Lines:** All three projects used in the empirical study are Java and Log4J based projects. However, the authors observed several inconsistencies in logging statement formats and hence created 26 regular expressions to extract all the logging statements. The authors observed two semantically different types of logging: first, in which the logging level is explicitly mentioned (for example, Type 1 and Type 2 logging statements in Listing 1) and second, in which the logging level is not mentioned explicitly (for example, Type 4 and Type 5 in Listing 1). The authors also observed several inconsistencies in the uses of the log levels. For example, Listing 1 shows three different ways in which the log level "warn'" is used in different datasets (refer to Type 1, Type 2, and Type 3 in Listing 1).

STATISTICAL ANALYSIS ON HIGH-LEVEL CODE CONSTRUCTS

The following subsections present the work on characterizing high-level code constructs (source code files). The authors answer research questions related to the distribution and complexity of logged files. They also analyze correlations between the logging count of a file and it's SLOC.

RQ 1: Is the distribution of the logged files skewed?

Listing 1. Example of logging statements taken from the dataset

```
/*------------------Type 1: (Taken from Hadoop)----------------*/
LOG.warn(AuthenticationToken ignored: + ex.getMessage());
/*------------------Type 2: (Taken from Hadoop)--------------*/
logWarningWhenAuxServiceThrowExceptions(service, AuxServicesEventType.APPLICATION_INIT, th);
/*------------------Type 3: (Taken from Apache Tomcat)--------*/
Logger.getLogger(getLoggerName(getHost(),url)).log(Level.WARNING,""Unable to determine web application context.xml "" +
docBase,e);
/*-------------Type 4: (Taken from Apache Tomcat)---------*/
log("Error closing redirector: " + ioe.getMessage(),Project.MSG_ERR);
/*--------------Type 5: (Taken from Apache Tomcat)---------*/
project.log(wrong object reference + refId + - + pref.getClass());
```

Table 2. Experimental dataset details

Project	Apache Tomcat	CloudStack	Hadoop
Version	8.0.9	4.3.0	2.7.1
Logging Library	Log4J	Log4J	Log4J
Java File	2,037	5,351	6,332
SLOC	276,209	1,142,970	951,629
Log Line Count	2,703	10,428	10,108
Total Catch Blocks	3,325	12,591	7,947
Logged Catch Blocks	887 (27%)	2,790 (22.16%)	2,078 (26.15%)
Distinct Exception Types	120	163	265

The authors counted the number of files that consisted of at least one logging statement. Table 3 shows that only 17.9 percent, 14.9 percent, and 22.3 percent of files consisted of logging statements in Apache Tomcat, CloudStack, and Hadoop, respectively. This result shows that distribution of files containing logging statements is highly skewed, that is, less than 23 percent of files consist of logging statements. The authors believe that understanding the characteristics of source code for files that do not contain any logging statements can provide useful insights for logging prediction tools, as the tool does not need to predict logging in the files, given that there is no history of logging statements.

Table 3. The count (%) of logged files in the total files. It also shows the average SLOC of logged and nonlogged files. LFC: Logged File Count; AS: Average SLOC; LF: Logged Files; NLF: Nonlogged Files

Project	Total Files	LFC (%)	AS	
			LF	NLF
Apache Tomcat	2,037	365 (17.9%)	260.04	69.37
CloudStack	5,351	798 (14.9%)	290.81	159.87
Hadoop	6,332	1414 (22.3%)	254	75.51

The distribution of files containing and not containing log statements is skewed as only ≈14 percent to 22.3 percent of files contain logging statements.

RQ 2: Do logged files have greater complexity compared to nonlogged files?

This subsection presents a comparison of the complexity of the logged and nonlogged files. The authors measured the complexity of a file using its SLOC. To compute SLOC, they removed all the blank lines, package statements, import statements, and comments from the file. They also removed lines containing only '{' or '}'. Table 3 shows the values of average SLOC of logged and nonlogged files for all three projects. The table also shows that for the Apache Tomcat project, the average SLOC value of logged and nonlogged files is 260.04 and 69.37. Results show a similar trend for other two projects, that is, the average SLOC of logged files is higher than that of nonlogged files. Average values provide useful statistics, but they lack significant details about the actual distribution. Hence the authors drew a box-and-whisker plot for the SLOC of logged and nonlogged files. The graph in Figure 3 shows that the median SLOC values of logged files is higher that of nonlogged files for all three projects. For example, the median SLOC value for logged files in the CloudStack project is 114.5, whereas the median SLOC value for nonlogged files in the CloudStack project is 46.0. Figure 3 also shows a higher interquartile range for logged files, which shows a higher spread of SLOC values in logged files compared to that of nonlogged files. The results presented in this subsection lead to many more questions regarding the analysis of more complex metrics (such as object-oriented metrics; Thwin & Quah 2005) of files to get a deeper understanding about the relation between file complexity and logging.

Logged files have greater complexity and spread (measured using SLOC of a file) as compared to that of nonlogged files.

Figure 3. SLOC comparison of logged and nonlogged files

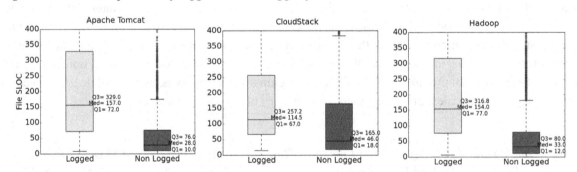

RQ 3: Is there a positive correlation between file complexity and log statement count?

The box-and-whiskers plot of the previous subsection shows that files with higher SLOC (i.e., higher complexity) are more likely to contain logging statements. Hence the authors hypothesize that there exists a positive correlation between file SLOC and its log statement count, that is, the higher the SLOC, the higher the log statement count of the file. To test this hypothesis the authors created a scatter plot between file SLOC and the respective log statement count. Scatter plots are one of the simplest yet powerful methods to visualize correlations between two variables. The authors created two scatter plots: the first scatter plot was between the SLOC of all the files in the database and respective log statement count, and the second scatter plot was between the SLOC only of logged files and respective log statement counts. The authors also computed the Pearson correlation between file SLOC and log statement count (Welcome to Statistics, n.d.). They obtained correlation values of 0.58, 0.76, and 0.67 for Apache Tomcat, CloudStack, and Hadoop, respectively, which shows that a positive correlation exists between SLOC and log statement count of a file (refer to Figure 5). However, it is interesting to observe the correlation value between file SLOC and logging count decreases after the addition of nonlogged files (refer to Figure 4). The authors observed the presence of three (one in each project) very large, nonlogged files in all three projects. Figure 4 shows these three files, marked using a red circle. Manual analysis reveals that these three files are tool-generated files and hence do not consist of any log statements. Table 4 gives details about the files and the tool used to generate these files. The experimental results presented in this subsection show a positive correlation between file SLOC and log statement count. The authors believe that these findings can be utilized by logging prediction tools to predict logging in the files if they exceed some project-specific threshold of file SLOC.

Figure 4. Scatter plot showing correlation between SLOC of the files and respective logging counts

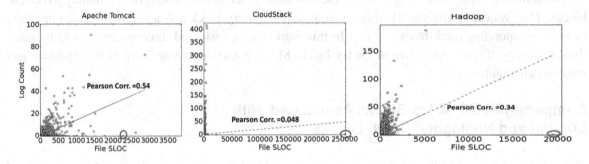

Figure 5. Scatter plot showing correlation between SLOC of only logged files and respective logging counts

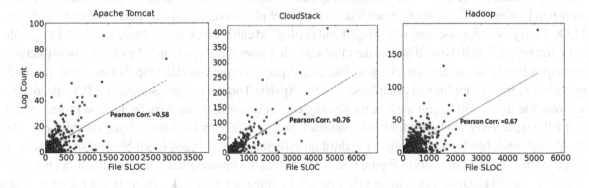

A positive correlation exists between the SLOC of logged files and the logging count.

Table 4. Details of the three large nonlogged files

Project	File Name	File SLOC	Log Count	Analysis
Apache Tomcat	ELParser.java	2,272	0	Auto-generated using JJTree and JavaCC
CloudStack	AmazonEC2 Stub.java	250,323	0	Auto-generated using WSDL
Hadoop	Hamlet.java	19,431	0	Auto-generated using HamletGen

STATISTICAL ANALYSIS ON LOW-LEVEL CODE CONSTRUCTS

The following subsections work on characterizing low-level code constructs (catch-blocks). The authors answer research questions related to complexity, logging ratio distribution, and whether logged and nonlogged catch-blocks can exist together.

RQ4: Is the complexity of try-blocks associated with logged catch-blocks greater than that of nonlogged catch-blocks?

The authors compared the complexity of the try-blocks associated with logged and nonlogged catch-blocks. They wanted to analyze whether the complexity of a try-block acts a parameter when deciding to log corresponding catch-blocks or not. In this work, they considered three parameters to measure the complexity of a try-block: size of the try-block (SLOC count), operator count of the try-block and method call count.

Comparing SLOC of Try-Blocks Associated With Logged and Nonlogged Catch-Blocks

The authors computed SLOC of the corresponding try-blocks associated with logged and nonlogged catch-blocks. They computed SLOC using the same method described in a previous section. Listing 2 shows an example of a try-block from the Apache Tomcat project. The SLOC value of the try-block shown in Listing 2 is 2. Figure 6 shows box-and-whisker plots revealing the dispersion and skewness in SLOC for try-blocks associated with logged and nonlogged catch-block across three projects. The graph in Figure 6 reveals that the median and the third-quartile values for logged catch-blocks are more than the corresponding values for nonlogged catch-blocks in Apache Tomcat and Hadoop. For example, the third quartile and median for logged catch-blocks in the Apache Tomcat project is 7.0 and 2.0, respectively, whereas the third quartile and median for nonlogged catch-blocks in the Apache Tomcat project is 2.0 and 1.0, respectively. However, for the CloudStack project, the authors observed that the third quartile for logged catch-blocks is higher than the third quartile for the nonlogged catch-blocks but the median value is smaller. The box plots in Figure 6 also reveal that the interquartile range (width of the box: Q3 – Q1) for logged catch-blocks is higher than those of nonlogged try-blocks, indicating a higher spread.

Listing 2. Example of a try-block taken from the Apache Tomcat project

```
try{
lc=new LoginContext(getLoginConfigName());
lc.login();
}catch(LoginException e)
{
log.error(sm.getString(spnegoAuthenticator.serviceLoginFail),e);
response.sendError(HttpServletResponse.SC_INTERNAL_SERVER_ERROR);
return false;
}
Try-LOC: 2
Operator Count: 7 (()()() =)
Method Call Count: 2 (getLoginConfigName, login)
Catch Exception: LoginException
```

Figure 6. Comparison of SLOC of try-blocks associated with logged and nonlogged catch-blocks

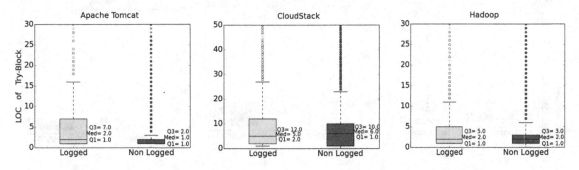

Figure 7. Comparison of operator count of try-blocks associated with logged and nonlogged catch-blocks

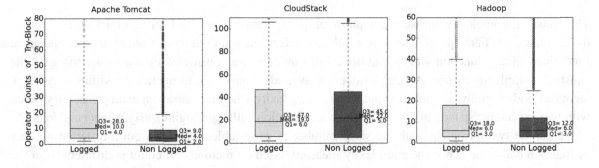

Comparing Operator Count of Try-Blocks Associated With Logged and Nonlogged Catch-Blocks

Counting the total number of operators in a program has been widely used as a metric to measure the complexity of given source code. The Halstead metric for computing program complexity is based on counting the total and distinct numbers of operators and operands in the source code (Virtual Machinery, n.d.). The authors created a list of 19 arithmetic operators (=, *, +, −, %, !, (,), [,], &, ?,:, >, <, |,

^, ~, /) that perform normal mathematical operations such as add, subtract, multiplication, division, and modulo. They counted the number of operators (from the list of 19) in the try-block linked to logged and nonlogged catch-blocks. The box plots in Figure 7 reveal that the third-quartile values for logged try-blocks (28, 47, and 18) are greater than the corresponding values (9, 45, and 12) for nonlogged try-blocks in Apache Tomcat, CloudStack, and Hadoop. The median values for Apache Tomcat indicate that logged try-blocks have greater complexity in terms of operator count. The authors observed that the median value for logged try-blocks and nonlogged try-blocks for the Hadoop project is the same. They believe that the lines-of-code metric is correlated to the number-of-operators metric, and hence they observe similar trends for both measures.

Figure 8. Comparison of method call count of try-blocks associated with logged and nonlogged catch-blocks

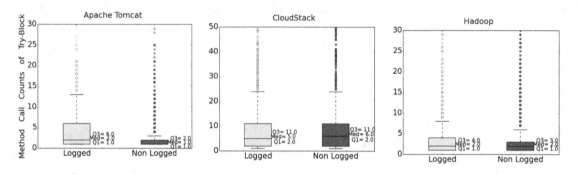

Comparing the Method Call Count of Try-Blocks Associated With Logged and Nonlogged Catch-Blocks

The Halstead complexity measure computes program complexity based on several factors, such as the number of distinct operators and operands, as well as the total number of operators and operands. Predefined library function and user-defined function calls are considered operators according to the Halstead complexity metric. A large number of methods (equivalent to operators) within a try-block increases both cognitive complexity and testing complexity. Listing 2 shows an example of a try-block with two executable statements, both of which are function calls (getLoginConfigName() and login()). There can be two try-blocks with the same number of executable statements but a different number of function calls, and hence the complexity measure based on method call count is different from the complexity measure based on lines of code, as well as the complexity measure based on total number of operators. The authors computed the number of function calls for every try-block in the source code dataset. Figure 8 shows the box plots for the number of methods for the three projects in the experimental dataset. It reveals that the third-quartile value for the logged try-block is higher than the corresponding values for the nonlogged try-block for the Apache Tomcat and Hadoop projects. For example, the median and third-quartile value for Apache Tomcat is 2.0 and 6.0, respectively, for the logged try-block, which is higher than the median and third-quartile value of 1.0 and 2.0, respectively, for the nonlogged try-block. The authors observed that for the CloudStack project, the third-quartile value is the same for both logged and nonlogged try-blocks. Results give an indication that complexity of try-blocks can be use as a parameters for catch-blocks logging prediction.

Try-blocks associated with logged catch-blocks have greater complexity than that of nonlogged catch-blocks for the Apache Tomcat and Hadoop projects.

RQ 5: What is the logging ratio trend of the various exception types?

This subsection statistically analyzes the logging ratio (LR_i) of distinct exception types in all three projects. The logging ratio of each exception type is computed using Equation 1 (refer to Table 5 for details about the acronyms used in this equation). The logging ratio metric is defined and used earlier by Fu et al. (2014) for analysis of exception types on C# projects. The logging ratio of an exception type shows the percentage of its logged catch-blocks ($TLCB_i$) to its total number of catch-blocks (TCB_i). For example, the "ChannelException" exception type in the Tomcat dataset has 25 catch-blocks, out of which 15 are logged. Hence, the logging ratio of ChannelException exception type i.e., $LR_{ChannelException}$, is 60 percent. Figure 9 shows the histogram of the logging ratio of distinct exception types for all three projects. In Figure 9, the x-axis shows the range of the logging ratio (with an interval of 10 percent) and the y-axis shows the percentage of the distinct exception types falling in that range. On top of each bar of the histogram, the distinct exception types falling in that logging ratio range are plotted and counted. For example, Figure 9a shows that 47 exception types in the Apache Tomcat project have a logging ratio between 0 percent and 10 percent. Fu et al. (2014) reported in their study that the majority of exception types belong to either a very high ($>=90\%$) or low ($<=10\%$) logging ratio range. Although they computed the results on C# projects and results of a Java project can differ, the authors observed results similar to Fu et al. (2014) with Java projects.

$$LR_i = \frac{|TLCB_i| * 100}{|TCB_i|} \tag{1}$$

Figure 9. Logging ratio of all three projects

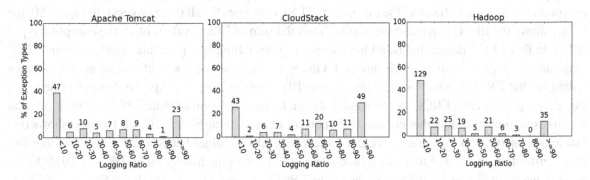

The majority of the exception types in the Java project belong to either a very high ($>=90\%$) or very low ($<=10\%$) logging ratio.

Table 5. Various acronyms used in Equation 1, Equation 2, and Equation 3

Variable Name	Acronym
Total Catch-Blocks in the Dataset	TCB_{DT}
Total Logged Catch-Blocks in the Dataset	$TLCB_{DT}$
Total Catch-Block of ith Exception Type	TCB_i
Total Logged Catch-Blocks of ith Exception Type	$TLCB_i$
Exception Type Ratio (Catch Count) of ith Exception Type	$ERCC_i$
Exception Type Ratio (Log Count) of ith Exception Type	$ERLC_i$
Logging Ratio of ith Exception Type	LR_i

RQ 6: Is the exception type contribution the same in total catch-blocks and in total logged catch-blocks?

This subsection measures the contribution of each exception type in total catch-blocks as well as in total logged catch-blocks. The authors define two metrics: Exception Type Ratio (Catch Count) [ERCC] and Exception Type Ratio (Log Count) [ERLC] for the same; refer to Equation 2 and Equation 3 for details (refer to Table 5 to get details on the acronyms used in these equations). ERCC defines the percentage of contribution of a particular exception type in total catch-blocks whereas ERLC defines it for logged catch blocks. ERCC computes the percentage of total catch-blocks of an exception type (TCB_i) to total catch-blocks in the dataset (TCB_{DT}), whereas the ERLC metric computes the percentage of total logged catch-blocks of an exception type ($TLCB_i$) to total logged catch-blocks in the dataset ($TLCB_{DT}$). For example, for the Apache Tomcat project we have TCB_{DT}= 3325 and $TLCB_{DT}$ =887. Now for 'ChannelException' exception type we have $TCB_{ChannelException}$=25 and $TLCB_{ChannelException}$=15. Hence, for ChannelException type we have value of ERCC=7.5 and ERLC=1.69. The motivation behind computing these two metrics is to find exception types that contribute a great deal to total catch-blocks and less to logged catch-blocks, or vice versa. For example, ChannelException type have comparatively less contribution in logged catch-blocks as compared to that in all catch-blocks because for it the value of ERCC metric is greater than ERLC metric. Early detection of such exception types can be beneficial to developers as well as logging prediction tools, because exception-specific rules can be created for such exception types. Figure 10 shows the histogram of ERCC metrics for all three projects. In Figure 10, the x-axis shows the ERCC range and the y-axis shows the sum of ERCC values of all the exception types falling in that ERCC range, that is, all the exception types falling in a particular group give an ERCC range and their ERCC value can be summed. On top of each bar is a count of unique exception types falling in that ERCC range. For example, Figure 10a shows that for the Apache Tomcat project 116 exception types have an ERCC metric value between 0 and 5 and sum of their ERCC values is 35, that is, 116 exception types together constitute 35 percent of total catch-blocks. Figure 10a also shows that two exception types in the Apache Tomcat project have ERCC values between 20 and 25 and together they constitute 42 percent of total catch-blocks. Figure 11 shows the histogram for ERLC metrics for all three projects. In Figure 11, the x-axis shows the ERCC range and the y-axis shows the sum of ERLC values of all the exception types falling in that ERCC range. The x-axis is the same in both graphs so the contribution of the same exception type in total catch-blocks (using the ERCC metric) and in total logged catch-blocks (using the ERLC metric) can be compared. Figure 11a shows that 116 exception types together constitute 38 percent of all logged catch-blocks, whereas these same 116 exception types constitute only 35 percent of total catch-blocks (refer to Figure 10a).

Figure 10b and Figure 11b show an interesting finding about four exception types (marked by arrows in the Figure) from the CloudStack project. These four exception types—ADBException, AxisFault, IllegalArgumentException, and XMLStreamException—have very large ERCC values (i.e., very large contribution in total catch-blocks), but very low ERLC values (i.e., much smaller contribution in the total logged catch-blocks). For example, the exception type "XMLStream" has 1,952 occurrences in the CloudStack project, but none of these occurrences are logged. Detection of such exception types can be beneficial for logging prediction tools, as the tool can learn the exception types that have such drastic differences in ERCC and ERLC values.

$$\text{ERCC}_i = \frac{\left|TCB_i\right| * 100}{\left|TCB_{DT}\right|} \tag{2}$$

$$\text{ERLC}_i = \frac{\left|TLCB_i\right| * 100}{\left|TLCB_{DT}\right|} \tag{3}$$

Figure 10. ERCC metric value for all three projects

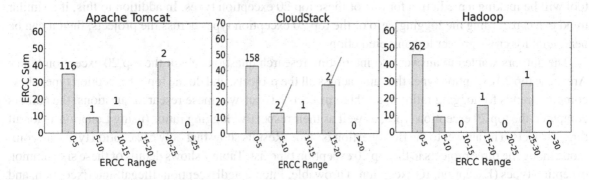

Figure 11. ERLC metric value for all three projects

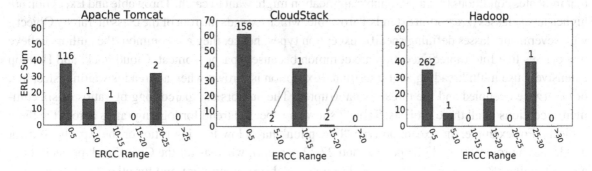

Table 6. Details of four exception types from the CloudStack project with very high ERCC but very low ERLC values. CCB: Count of Total Catch-Blocks; CLCB: Count of Total Logged Catch-Blocks; LR: Logging Ratio.

Exception Type	CCB	ERCC	CLCB	ERLC	LR
ADB Exception	960	0.0762	0	0	0
AxisFault	643	0.0511	0	0	0
IllegalArgumentException	1,971	0.1565	19	0.0068	0.0096
XMLStreamException	1,952	0.155	0	0	0

Some exception types in the CloudStack project have very high ERCC values (i.e., very large contribution in total catch-blocks) but very low ERLC values (i.e., much less contribution in the total logged catch-blocks).

RQ 7: Are the top 20 exception types and their respective logging ratios the same in all three projects?

This section presents an analysis of the logging ratio of the top 20 most frequent exception types in all three projects. The authors plotted a pie chart showing the contribution of the top 20 most frequent exception types in total catch-blocks. Figure 12 shows that the top 20 most frequent exception types contribute to ≈80 percent to 88 percent of the total catch-blocks for all three projects. Hence, analyzing the top 20 exception types can be crucial for the logging prediction tools, as ≈80 percent of the time the tool will be making a prediction for one of these top 20 exception types. In addition to this, if a similar trend exists regarding the logging ratio of the top 20 exception types across the projects, then it can be beneficial for cross-project logging prediction.

The authors wanted to answer two interesting research questions about the top 20 exception types: Are these top 20 exception types the same across all the projects, and do the top 20 exception types show common trends for logging ratios in all three projects? To answer these research questions, the authors computed the top 20 exception types, as well as their respective logging ratios (using Equation 1) for all three projects. The answer to the first question is "No." Results show that only 6 exception types are common among the three projects in the top 20 exception type list. Table 7 shows details of these six common exception types (Exception, IQException, Throwable, InterruptedException, IllegalStateException, and IllegalArgumentException) in all the three projects. The Throwable class is the superclass of all errors and exceptions in the Java language. The Exception class and its subclasses are a form of Throwable that indicates conditions that a reasonable application might want to catch. Throwable and Exception are higher-level classes (Exception extends Throwable, which extends the root of the class hierarchy Object), with several subclasses defining specific exception types; hence, they are common. the authors believe that classes like InterruptedException are common because Apache Tomcat, CloudStack, and Hadoop extensively use multithreading, and InterruptedException is thrown when a thread is waiting, sleeping, or otherwise occupied and the thread is interrupted. The authors compared logging ratios of six common exceptions in all three projects. Table 7 shows no specific trend for logging ratios across the three projects. For example, the exception type "Exception" has a low logging ratio for the Apache Tomcat and Hadoop projects (i.e., 37.25 percent and 27.72 percent), whereas for the CloudStack project, it has a high logging ratio (i.e., 66.81 percent). The authors observed similar trend for other exception types.

Thus, the answer to the second research question is also "No." This indicates that the logging ratio of an exception type is project specific, and hence a cross-project defect-prediction technique might need more sophisticated features than logging ratio.

Figure 12. Pie chart of top 20 exception types, showing percentage in total contribution

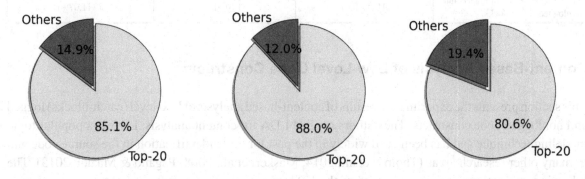

Table 7. Logging ratio details of 6 common exceptions in the top 20 exception type list of the three projects

Exception Type	Apache Tomcat	CloudStack	Hadoop
Exception	37.25%	66.81%	27.72%
IOException	27.41%	54.69%	36.69%
Throwable	45.66%	72.24%	53.05%
InterruptedException	6.12%	25.15%	23.28%
ClassNotFoundException	32.14%	4.48%	6.49%
IllegalArgumentException	23.19%	0.96%	16.67%

The most frequent exception types, as well as their respective logging ratios, are project specific.

RQ 8: Do logged and nonlogged catch-blocks coexist together?

The Java programing language allows associating multiple catch-blocks (each with a different exception type) to a single try-block. In this subsection, the authors' aim is to investigate whether a single try-block can have both logged and nonlogged catch-blocks or not. This research question is important to answer, as many times catch-block logging prediction tools use features from try-blocks. If the frequency of such try-blocks is very high, then it can affect the performance of such machine learning–based catch-block logging prediction tools. To answer this research question, the authors computed the count of try-blocks with both logged and nonlogged catch-blocks in all three projects. Table 8 shows that a very small percentage (i.e., ≈0.33 percent to 1.4 percent) of total try-blocks has both logged and nonlogged catch-blocks.

A very small percentage of try-blocks have both logged and nonlogged catch-blocks.

Table 8. Details of try-blocks with multiple catch-blocks

Project	Apache Tomcat	CloudStack	Hadoop
Unique try-blocks	2,914	9,899	7,171
Try-block with more than one catch-block	254	1,002	653
Try-block with mix of logged and nonlogged catch-blocks	41 (1.40%)	31 (0.31%)	77 (1.07%)

Content-Based Analysis of Low-Level Code Constructs

This section presents the experimental results of content-based analysis of low-level (catch-blocks) logged and nonlogged code constructs. The authors applied LDA for content analysis. LDA is a popular topic modeling technique and has been used widely in the past for topic identification in the source code and in many other research areas (Thomas et al., 2014; Maskeri et al., 2008; Pagano & Maalej, 2013). The following subsections describe the steps of the LDA model creation, results of LDA topic modeling, and the authors' observations from the obtained results.

Preprocessing Steps for LDA Analysis

The preprocessing steps for LDA model creation are as follows:

1. To identify the topics present in the logged and nonlogged catch-blocks, the authors analyzed the contents of the try-blocks associated with logged and nonlogged catch-blocks. They created corpus consisting of the content of try-blocks associated with logged and nonlogged catch-blocks.
2. The authors performed prepossessing and removed all the English stop words, special characters, and operators. They removed English stop words such as "is," "the," and "of" from the analysis because they were mainly interested in identifying the core functionality of the code constructs that leads to logging. The authors then applied stemming on the obtained corpus. Stemming is useful in reducing inflected words to the same root words and hence helps in reducing the corpus size. The authors used the Python NLTK library for stop word removal and stemming (Natural Language Toolkit, n.d.).
3. The authors believe that words that occur in almost all the documents or that occur in very few documents may not be helpful in retrieving useful topics. Hence they removed all the words that occurred in 80 percent of the documents and in less than 2 percent of the documents.
4. The authors performed LDA for 10,000 runs because LDA gives better results when the number of iterations is increased. Previous studies in software engineering research have also used the same threshold value for LDA (Thomas et al., 2014).
5. The authors set the number of topics parameter for the LDA algorithm as 10.
6. The authors used a default value of other LDA parameters in the Python LDA library (Gensim, n.d.).
    RQ 9: Do try-blocks associated with logged and nonlogged catch-blocks have different topics?

Table 9 shows the result obtained by LDA topic modeling on try-blocks associated with both logged and nonlogged catch-blocks. From this table, the authors observed that topics listed under try-blocks associated with logged and nonlogged catch-blocks are different. Hence they randomly picked some of the topics from the logged and nonlogged category and analyzed the differences in the associated code blocks. The authors drew the following interesting observations from this analysis:

1. They observed the "thread sleep" topic in the Apache Tomcat project. This topic is mentioned in the nonlogged catch-block category. The authors further analyzed occurrences of "thread sleep" in the Apache Tomcat project. They observed that in 84 occurrences of "thread sleep," it occurred 71 times in try-blocks associated with nonlogged catch-blocks.

Table 9. Topics discovered in try-blocks associated with logged and nonlogged catch-blocks

Project	Logged Catch-Block		Nonlogged Catch-Block	
	Topic	**Word**	**Topic**	**Word**
Apache Tomcat	1. channel file 2. method param 3. context log 4. **socket status**	1. channel, get, file, new, stream 2. method, get, param, valu, type 3. context, get, log, null, host 4. socket, statu, get, wrapper	1. **thread sleep** 2. channel read 3. **socket pool** 4. connect pool	1. results, thread, sleep, get 2. channel, close, read, buffer 3. socket, get, key, pool 4. get, connect, null, set, pool
CloudStack	1. byte key 2. response value 3. network 4. vm host	1. key, byte, new, pair, string 2. respons, valu, string, name, equal 3. network, ip, host, string, conn 4. vm, host, cmd, answer, state	1.**result stub** 2. pram om 3. java lang 4. stmt	1. result, stub, amazon, object, ec 2. om, factori, param, amazon, ec 3. class, java, lang, name, except 4. id, pstmt, string, set, long, rs
Hadoop	1. key id 2. assert 3. job conf 4. rm token	1. id, key, get, contain, info 2. request, fail, system, assert 3. job, get, name, map, conf, 4. token, rm, get, except, new	1. user token 2. key 3. get response 4. file path	1. token, user, arg, run, els 2. key, get, context, string 3. get, respons, job, request 4. file, path, fs, get, dir, statu

2. The authors observed the presence of a topic related to "socket" in both try-blocks associated with logged and nonlogged catch-blocks. They analyzed all 43 try-blocks consisting of socket and wrapper words and found that in try-blocks associated with logged catch-blocks, the socket wrapper is mostly used for close or error functions, whereas for try-blocks associated with nonlogged catch-blocks, the socket function is used for timeout operations. LDA is able to detect this difference, as shown in the Apache Tomcat project regarding topics 4 (logged catch-blocks) and 3 (nonlogged catch-blocks).

3.   The authors analyzed the "result stub (topic 1)" topic from the CloudStack project. They found 161 occurrences of try-blocks consisting of both words. They also noticed that catch-blocks associated with all 161 try-blocks are nonlogged. LDA is able to detect this because the "request stub" topic is not present in logged catch-blocks.

The contextual information present in the try-blocks provides important information for the associated catch-block logging.

LOGGING PREDICTION MODEL FOR CATCH-BLOCKS

Using finding from our empirical analysis we propose a machine learning based catch-blocks logging prediction model, *LogOpt* (Lal & Sureka, 2016; Lal et al., 2016b). Based on this study we extract 46 distinguishing features for catch-blocks logging prediction (refer to Table 10 for details). These features have three properties: *Type, Domain*, and *Class. Type* of a feature specifies whether a feature is: t*extual, numeric or Boolean. Textual* features can take any textual value. *Numeric* features can take any positive numeric value. *Boolean* features can take value either 0 or 1. *Domain* of the feature specifies part of the source code from where the feature is extracted. We identified three domains: *try/catch, method_bt,* and *other*. If a feature extracted from try/catch-block it will have domain '*try/catch*'. If a feature extracted from the first line of the containing methods to the previous line of try-block associated with target catch-block, it will have domain '*method_bt'*. If a feature extracted from some other part of source code, it will have domain '*other'*. Features can belong to *positive class* feature of *negative class*. *Positive* class features are beneficial in predicting logged catch-blocks whereas *negative* class features are beneficial in predicting nonlogged catch-blocks. We use total 46 features for catch-blocks logging prediction model building (refer to Table 10)

LogOpt Model Building

Using the 46 features, the authors propose *LogOpt* model for catch-blocks logging prediction. *LogOpt* is a machine learning based model. For *LogOpt* model training, the authors, first extract all the catch-blocks from the dataset and label them as 'logged' or 'nonlogged'. A catch-block is marked as logged if it consists of at least one log statement; otherwise, it is marked as 'nonlogged'. Second, the authors extract all the 46 features (textual, numeric, and Boolean) from the all the instances. Uses of textual features directly for machine learning model building can increase in model complexity. Hence, in the third step authors applied feature preprocessing techniques to clean the textual features. Authors applied camel case conversion, lower case, stop word removal, stemming, and tf-idf (Han et al., 2011) conversion. Fourth, author combine tf-idf representation of textual features with Boolean and numeric features and create final feature vector. Authors, then train machine learning algorithms such as Radom Forest (RF), J48, Support Vector Machine (SVM), on the final feature vector to create the *LogOpt* model. This model is then used for logging prediction on new instances.

Table 10. Features used for building catch-block logging prediction model. Class: Positive (P), Negative (N). Domain: Try/Catch (T), Method_bt (M), Other (O).

Type of Feature	Catch-Block Features (Class, Domain)	Explanation
Textual Features	1.Catch Exception Type (P,T) 2.Log Levels in Try Block (P,T) 3.Log Levels in Method_BT(P,M) 4.Operators in Try Block(P,T) 5.Operators in Method_BT(P,M) 6.Method Parameters (Type) (P,O) 7.Method Parameters (Name) (P,O) 8.Container Package Name (P,O) 9.Container Class Name (P, O) 10.Container Method Name (P,O) 11.Variable Declaration Name in Try Block(P,T) 12.Variable Declaration Name in Method_BT(P,M) 13.Method Call Name in Try Block(P,T) 14.Method Call Name in Method_BT(P,M)	1. Exception type of catch-block. 2. Verbosity level of the log statements present in the try-block. 3. Verbosity level of the log statements present in the method_bt section. 4. Arithmetic operators used in the try-block. 5. Arithmetic operators used in the method_bt section. 6. Type of parameters used in the containing method. 7. Name of the parameters used in the containing method. 8. Name of the containing package. 9. Name of containing class. 10. Name of the containing method. 11. Names of the variables declared in the try-block. 12. Name of the variables declared in the method_bt section. 13. Names of the methods called in try-block. 14. Names of the methods called in method_bt section.
Numerical Features	1.Size of Try Block [SLOC](P,T) 2.Size of Method_BT[SLOC](P,M) 3.Log Count Try Block(P,T) 4.Log Count in Method_BT(P,M) 5.Count of Operators in Try Block(P,T) 6.Count of Operators in Method_BT(P,M) 7.Variable Declaration Count in Try Block(P,T) 8.Variable Declaration Count in Method_BT(P,M) 9.Method Call Count in Try Block(P,T) 10.Method Call Count in Method_BT(P,M) 11.Method Parameter Count(P,O) 12.IF Count in Try Block(P,T) 13.IF Count in Method_BT(P,M)	1. SLOC of try-block. 2. SLOC of method_bt section. 3. Count of log statements in try-block. 4. Count of log statements in method_bt section. 5. Count of arithmetic operators in try-block. 6. Count of operators in method_bt section. 7. Count of variables declared in try-block. 8. Count of variables declared in method_bt section. 9. Count of methods called in try-block. 10. Count of methods called in method_bt section. 11. Count of parameters in containing method. 12. Count of if-statements in try-block. 13. Count of if-statements in method_bt section.
Boolean Features	1.Previous Catch Blocks(P,T) 2.Logged Previous Catch Blocks (P,T) 3.Method have Parameter (P, O) 4.Logged Try Block(P,T) 5.Logged Method_BT(P,M) 6.IF in Try(P,T) 7.IF in Method_BT(P,M) 8.Throw/Throws in Try Block(N,T) 9.Throw/Throws in Catch Block(N,T) 10.Throw/Throws in Method_BT(N,M) 11.Return in Try Block(N,T) 12.Return in Catch Block(N,T) 13.Return in Method_BT(N,M) 14.Assert in Try Block(N,T) 15.Assert in Catch Block(N,T) 16.Assert in Method_BT(N,M) 17.Thread.Sleep in Try Block(N,T) 18.Interrupted Exception Type(N,T) 19.Exception Object "Ignore" in Catch(N,T)	1. Previous catch-blocks are present. 2. Previous catch-blocks have any log statement. 3. Containing method has parameter. 4. Try-block has log statement. 5. Method_bt section has log statement. 6. Try-block has if-statement. 7. Method_bt section has if-statement. 8. Throw/throws statement present in the try-block. 9. Throw/Throws statement present in catch-block. 10. Throw/Throws statement present in the method_bt section. 11. 'Return' statement present in the try-block. 12. 'Return' statement present in the catch-block. 13. 'Return' statement present in the method_bt section. 14. 'Assert' statement present in try-block. 15. 'Assert' statement present in the catch-block. 16. 'Assert' statement present in the method_bt section. 17. 'thread.sleep' method called in try-block. 18. Catch-block exception types is 'InterruptedException'. 19. Exception class object name is 'ignore' in catch-block.
Total Features =	Textual (14) + Numeric (13)+ Boolean(19) =46 Feature	

LogOpt Model Evaluation

Authors evaluate performance of *LogOpt* model on all the three project (Apache Tomcat, CloudStack, and Hadoop). For testing the performance of *LogOpt* model, authors divided the dataset into two parts in a ratio of 70:30 using stratified random sampling (Han et al., 2011). 70% of the dataset is used for training and 30% of the dataset is used for testing. Since, dataset sampling can lead to biases in the result the authors created 10 such random samples and reported average results. Authors evaluated performance of the model using several machine learning classifiers (RF, SVM, J48). SVM classifier performs the best and give the highest F1-score of 76.79% (Apache Tomcat), 84.32% (CloudStack), and 67.16% (Hadoop) (Lal & Sureka, 2016; Lal et al., 2016b).

CONCLUSION AND FUTURE WORK

Source code logging is an important software development practice, and tools and techniques that can help software developers make optimal and strategic logging decisions can be beneficial. Analysis of logged and nonlogged code constructs can provide useful insights to improve current logging prediction tools. In this chapter, the authors performed statistical and content-based analysis of source code files and catch-blocks from three large open-source Java projects. They answered several research questions in this chapter. Following are the main research findings of this work:

- Fewer files consist of logging statements.
- Source code files with logging statements have a much larger average SLOC compared to those without logging statements.
- There is a positive correlation between the SLOC of logged files and their respective log statement counts.
- Try-blocks associated with logged catch-blocks have greater complexity than that of nonlogged catch-blocks for the Apache Tomcat and Hadoop projects.
- Some exception types contribute greatly to total catch-blocks, whereas there is little or no contribution in total logged catch-blocks.
- The logging ratio of an exception type is project specific.
- The LDA-based topic modeling technique is effective in discovering topics of logged and nonlogged code constructs.

Authors proposed a machine leaning based model proposed for catch-blocks logging prediction. Machine learning based model is found to be effective in catch-blocks logging prediction and give the highest F1-score of 84.32% on CloudStack project .

The authors think that this work provides a future direction for three lines of work: *statistical analysis,content-based analysis, and machine leanring based logging prediction model*. Statistical analysis provides the ability to explore more deeply the features of logged code constructs. In this work, the authors analyzed a complexity metric (SLOC, operator count, etc.) with respect to logged and nonlogged code constructs. However, many other source code metrics, such as inheritance depth, and object-oriented metrics need to be evaluated for deeper analysis of logged and nonlogged files. Content-based research needs more exploration in terms of the topics present in the logged and nonlogged code constructs. In this work, the authors used LDA for topic modeling, and the initial results are encouraging. However, deeper analysis of code constructs with respect to multiple semantic techniques such as LDA and Latent Semantic Indexing (LSI) is required for in-depth analysis of the topics present in logged and nonlogged code constructs. In this work, authors propose a machine learning model based on static features from the source code for catch-blocks logging prediction. The proposed model can be extended for other type of code constructs such as if-blocks, while-loop, switch-case.

THREATS TO VALIDITY

- **Number and Type of Project:** The authors selected Apache Tomcat, CloudStack, and Hadoop projects for the study. All three projects are open-source, Java-based projects. Other types of projects, such as closed source, or projects written in other languages (e.g., C#, Python) need to be evaluated. Overall, the authors cannot draw any general conclusion that is applicable to all software logging. They believe that this study provides insight about logging practices of open-source, Java-based projects.
- **Quality of Ground Truth:** The authors assumed that logging statements inserted by software developers of Apache Tomcat, CloudStack, and Hadoop project are optimal. There is the possibility of errors or nonoptimal logging in the code by the developers, which can affect the results of the study. However, all three projects are long lived and are actively maintained; hence it is safe to assume that most of the code constructs have good (if not optimal) logging. The authors used 26 regular expressions to extract the logging statements from the source code. Manual analysis reveals that all the logging statements were extracted (to the best of the authors' knowledge). However, there is still a possibility that the regular expressions missed some types of logging statements in the source code.
- **Machine Learning Model Evaluation:** At the time of evaluating the performance of *LogOpt* model, authors removed the three tool generated files from the dataset. Authors believe that using data from tool generated files for training as well as for prediction can cause bias in the performance of model.

REFERENCES

Apache Cloudstack. (n.d.). Retrieved March 18, 2016, from https://cloudstack.apache.org/downloads.html

Apache Tomcat. (n.d.). Retrieved March 16, 2016, from https://tomcat.apache.org/download-80.cgi

Barua, A., Thomas, S. W., & Hassan, A. E. (2014). What are developers talking about? an analysis of topics and trends in stack overflow. *Empirical Software Engineering*, *19*(3), 619–654. doi:10.100710664-012-9231-y

Beaton, W. (n.d.). *Eclipse Corner Article*. Retrieved March 12, 2016, from https://www.eclipse.org/articles/article.php?file=Article-JavaCodeManipulation

Blei, D. M., Ng, A. Y., & Jordan, M. I. (2003). Latent dirichlet allocation. *The Journal of Machine Learning Research, 3*, 993-1022.

Chen, B., & Jiang, Z. M. J. (2016). Characterizing logging practices in Java-based open source software projects–a replication study in Apache Software Foundation. *Empirical Software Engineering*, 1–45.

Crossley, A., & Shapira, Y. (n.d.). *Apache Tomcat 7*. Retrieved March 20, 2016, from https://tomcat. apache.org/tomcat-7.0-doc/logging.html

Ding, R., Zhou, H., Lou, J. G., Zhang, H., Lin, Q., Fu, Q., ... Xie, T. (2015, July). Log2: A Cost-Aware Logging Mechanism for Performance Diagnosis. *USENIX Annual Technical Conference*, 139-150.

Fu, Q., Lou, J. G., Wang, Y., & Li, J. (2009, December). Execution anomaly detection in distributed systems through unstructured log analysis. In *2009 ninth IEEE international conference on data mining* (pp. 149-158). IEEE. 10.1109/ICDM.2009.60

Fu, Q., Zhu, J., Hu, W., Lou, J. G., Ding, R., Lin, Q., . . . Xie, T. (2014, May). Where do developers log? an empirical study on logging practices in industry. In *Companion Proceedings of the 36th International Conference on Software Engineering* (pp. 24-33). ACM.

Gensim: Topic modelling for humans. (n.d.). Retrieved March 19, 2016, from https://radimrehurek.com/ gensim/models/ldamodel.html

Goers, R., Gregory, G., & Deboy, S. (n.d.). *Log4j – Log4j 2 Guide - Apache Log4j 2*. Retrieved October 23, 2015, from http://logging.apache.org/log4j/2.x/

Han, J., Pei, J., & Kamber, M. (2011). *Data mining: concepts and techniques*. Elsevier.

Kabinna, S., Bezemer, C. P., Hassan, A. E., & Shang, W. (2016, March). Examining the Stability of Logging Statements. *Proceedings of the 23rd IEEE International Conference on Software Analysis, Evolution, and Reengineering (SANER)*.

Kabinna, S., Bezemer, C. P., Shang, W., & Hassan, A. E. (2016b, May). Logging library migrations: a case study for the apache software foundation projects. In *Proceedings of the 13th International Conference on Mining Software Repositories* (pp. 154-164). ACM. 10.1145/2901739.2901769

Kim, L. (2015). *10 Most Popular Programming Languages Today*. Retrieved March 20, 2016, from http://www.inc.com/larry-kim/10-most-popular-programming-languages-today.htm

Kosinski, K. (2013, February). *Advanced CloudStack Troubleshooting using Log Analysis - a session at ApacheCon North America 2013*. Retrieved March 19, 2016, from http://lanyrd.com/2013/apachecon/ scbrfk/

Krill, P. (2015). *Java regains spot as most popular language in developer index*. Retrieved March 23, 2016, from http://www.infoworld.com/article/2909894/application-development/java-back-at-1-in-language-popularity-assessment.html

Lal, S., Sardana, N., & Sureka, A. (2015). Two Level Empirical Study of Logging Statements in Open Source Java Projects. *International Journal of Open Source Software and Processes*, 6(1), 49–73. doi:10.4018/IJOSSP.2015010104

Lal, S., & Sureka, A. (2016, February). LogOpt: Static Feature Extraction from Source Code for Automated Catch Block Logging Prediction. In *Proceedings of the 9th India Software Engineering Conference* (pp. 151-155). ACM. 10.1145/2856636.2856637

Lal, S., Sardana, N., & Sureka, A. (2016, June). LogOptPlus: Learning to Optimize Logging in Catch and If Programming Constructs. In *Proceedings of 40th Annual Computer Software and Applications Conference* (pp. 215-220). IEEE. 10.1109/COMPSAC.2016.149

Lal, S., Sardana, N., & Sureka, A. (2016b). Improving Logging Prediction on Imbalanced Datasets: A Case Study on Open Source Java Projects. *International Journal of Open Source Software and Processes*, *7*(2), 43–71. doi:10.4018/IJOSSP.2016040103

Lal, S., Sardana, N., & Sureka, A. (2017a). ECLogger: Cross-Project Catch-Block Logging Prediction Using Ensemble of Classifiers. *e-Informatica. Software Engineering Journal*, *11*(1), 9–40.

Lal, S., Sardana, N., & Sureka, A. (2017b). Three-level learning for improving cross-project logging prediction for if-blocks. *Journal of King Saud University-Computer and Information Sciences*. (in press)

Li, H., Shang, W., & Hassan, A. E. (2016). Which log level should developers choose for a new logging statement. *Empirical Software Engineering*, 1–33.

Li, H., Shang, W., Zou, Y., & Hassan, A. E. (2016b). Towards just-in-time suggestions for log changes. *Empirical Software Engineering*, 1–35.

LocMetrics. (n.d.). Retrieved March 19, 2016, from http://www.locmetrics.com/

Mariani, L., & Pastore, F. (2008, November). Automated identification of failure causes in system logs. In *Software Reliability Engineering, 2008. ISSRE 2008. 19th International Symposium on* (pp. 117-126). IEEE. 10.1109/ISSRE.2008.48

Maskeri, G., Sarkar, S., & Heafield, K. (2008, February). Mining business topics in source code using latent dirichlet allocation. In *Proceedings of the 1st India software engineering conference* (pp. 113-120). ACM. 10.1145/1342211.1342234

Nagaraj, K., Killian, C., & Neville, J. (2012). Structured comparative analysis of systems logs to diagnose performance problems. *9th USENIX Symposium on Networked Systems Design and Implementation (NSDI 12)*, 353-366.

Natural Language Toolkit. (n.d.). Retrieved March 19, 2016, from http://www.nltk.org/

Pagano, D., & Maalej, W. (2013). How do open source communities blog? *Empirical Software Engineering*, *18*(6), 1090–1124. doi:10.100710664-012-9211-2

Page, B. W. (n.d.). *Welcome to Apache Hadoop!* Retrieved March 18, 2016, from http://hadoop.apache.org/#DownloadHadoop

Rabkin, A., & Katz, R. H. (2010, November). Chukwa: A System for Reliable Large-Scale Log Collection. LISA, 10, 1-15.

Sharma, B., Chudnovsky, V., Hellerstein, J. L., Rifaat, R., & Das, C. R. (2011, October). Modeling and synthesizing task placement constraints in Google compute clusters. In *Proceedings of the 2nd ACM Symposium on Cloud Computing* (p. 3). ACM. 10.1145/2038916.2038919

Shang, W., Nagappan, M., & Hassan, A. E. (2015). Studying the relationship between logging characteristics and the code quality of platform software. *Empirical Software Engineering, 20*(1), 1–27. doi:10.100710664-013-9274-8

Sigelman, B. H., Barroso, L. A., Burrows, M., Stephenson, P., Plakal, M., Beaver, D., . . . Shanbhag, C. (2010). Dapper, a large-scale distributed systems tracing infrastructure. Technical report, Google, Inc.

Team, C. D. (n.d.). *Apache Commons Logging - Overview*. Retrieved March 18, 2016, from https://commons.apache.org/proper/commons-logging/

Thomas, S. W., Adams, B., Hassan, A. E., & Blostein, D. (2014). Studying software evolution using topic models. *Science of Computer Programming, 80*, 457–479. doi:10.1016/j.scico.2012.08.003

Thwin, M. M. T., & Quah, T. S. (2005). Application of neural networks for software quality prediction using object-oriented metrics. *Journal of Systems and Software, 76*(2), 147–156. doi:10.1016/j.jss.2004.05.001

Tian, K., Revelle, M., & Poshyvanyk, D. (2009, May). Using latent dirichlet allocation for automatic categorization of software. In *Mining Software Repositories, 2009. MSR'09. 6th IEEE International Working Conference on* (pp. 163-166). IEEE. 10.1109/MSR.2009.5069496

Virtual Machinery - Sidebar 2 - The Halstead Metrics. (n.d.). Retrieved March 19, 2016, from http://www.virtualmachinery.com/sidebar2.htm

Welcome to Statistics How To! (n.d.). Retrieved March 19, 2016, from http://www.statisticshowto.com/

Xu, W., Huang, L., Fox, A., Patterson, D., & Jordan, M. I. (2009, October). Detecting large-scale system problems by mining console logs. In *Proceedings of the ACM SIGOPS 22nd symposium on Operating systems principles* (pp. 117-132). ACM. 10.1145/1629575.1629587

Yuan, D., Mai, H., Xiong, W., Tan, L., Zhou, Y., & Pasupathy, S. (2010, March). SherLog: error diagnosis by connecting clues from run-time logs. In ACM SIGARCH computer architecture news (Vol. 38, No. 1, pp. 143-154). ACM. doi:10.1145/1736020.1736038

Yuan, D., Park, S., Huang, P., Liu, Y., Lee, M. M., Tang, X., ... Savage, S. (2012). Be conservative: enhancing failure diagnosis with proactive logging. *10th USENIX Symposium on Operating Systems Design and Implementation*, 293-306.

Yuan, D., Park, S., & Zhou, Y. (2012b, June). Characterizing logging practices in open-source software. In *Proceedings of the 34th International Conference on Software Engineering* (pp. 102-112). IEEE Press.

Yuan, D., Zheng, J., Park, S., Zhou, Y., & Savage, S. (2012c). Improving software diagnosability via log enhancement. *ACM Transactions on Computer Systems, 30*(1), 4. doi:10.1145/2110356.2110360

Zhu, J., He, P., Fu, Q., Zhang, H., Lyu, M. R., & Zhang, D. (2015, May). Learning to log: Helping developers make informed logging decisions. In *Software Engineering (ICSE), 2015 IEEE/ACM 37th IEEE International Conference on* (Vol. 1, pp. 415-425). IEEE.

Zimmermann, T., Nagappan, N., Gall, H., Giger, E., & Murphy, B. (2009, August). Cross-project defect prediction: a large scale experiment on data vs. domain vs. process. In *Proceedings of the the 7th joint meeting of the European software engineering conference and the ACM SIGSOFT symposium on The foundations of software engineering* (pp. 91-100). ACM. 10.1145/1595696.1595713

This research was previously published in Optimizing Contemporary Application and Processes in Open Source Software; pages 57-85, copyright year 2018 by Engineering Science Reference (an imprint of IGI Global).

Chapter 39
Using Design of Experiments to Analyze Open Source Software Metrics for Change Impact Estimation

Miloud Dahane
iD https://orcid.org/0000-0002-1754-6005
Université Oran1, Oran, Algeria

Mustapha Kamel Abdi
Université Oran1, Oran, Algeria

Mourad Bouneffa
Université du Littoral Côte d'Opale, Dunkirk, France

Adeel Ahmad
Laboratoire d'Informatique Signal et Image de la Côte d'Opale, Calais, France

Henri Basson
Université du Littoral Côte d'Opale, Dunkirk, France

ABSTRACT

Software evolution control mostly relies on the better structure of the inherent software artifacts and the evaluation of different qualitative factors like maintainability. The attributes of changeability are commonly used to measure the capability of the software to change with minimal side effects. This article describes the use of the design of experiments method to evaluate the influence of variations of software metrics on the change impact in developed software. The coupling metrics are considered to analyze their degree of contribution to cause a change impact. The data from participant software metrics are expressed in the form of mathematical models. These models are then validated on different versions of software to estimate the correlation of coupling metrics with the change impact. The proposed approach is evaluated with the help of a set of experiences which are conducted using statistical analysis tools. It may serve as a measurement tool to qualify the significant indicators that can be included in a Software Maintenance dashboard.

DOI: 10.4018/978-1-7998-9158-1.ch039

1. INTRODUCTION

The software maintenance or evolution is an essential step in the software life cycle. Several works have, for many years, highlighted the importance of maintenance and/or evolution of the software and have established several taxonomies (Gasmallah et al., 2016). The oldest have allowed to consider three kinds of maintenance (Swanson, 1976): corrective maintenance leading to remove the residual errors or faults; adaptive maintenance that consists of adapting the software to changes affecting both its technical or managerial environments like the evolution of the deployment infrastructures or the change of some regulation policies, etc. The perfective maintenance includes changes intended to improve the software by introducing new features or improving some quality criteria, etc. In (Chapin, 2000), the author introduces a new maintenance type called preventive maintenance as the changes leading to make the software more able to evolve and then to change. In other words, the changes induced by this last kind of maintenance makes it possible to improve the maintainability criterion of the software without affecting the functionalities or performance of such a software.

In this work, we do not intentionally make any difference between maintenance and evolution, although these two concepts have been subjects to numerous comparisons. Maintenance is often seen as an engineering process in which academic research has delineated and characterized the stages, the activities to be carried out, the actors and resources to be implemented, etc. In other words, the concept of maintenance is the result of a kind of morphism between the industrial world and the software development activity. The term software evolution is the result of works (Lehman & Ramil, 2002.) aimed at understanding the phenomenon of change affecting the software artifacts. For example, Lehmann's laws of evolution attempt to explain how the software evolves during many years until becoming obsolete. These laws are the result of empirical studies conducted over several years on software used on the real world. In the same way, Benett and Rajlich drew up (Benett & Rajlich, 2000) a software life cycle designed not as a means to develop the software but as an explanation of how software is produced, evolved, maintained, and eventually removed from the information system.

As far as we are concerned, we indifferently use the terms maintenance or evolution. What we are particularly interested in, is the notion of the software change and more specifically the Change Impact Analysis (Abdi et al., 2009; Sun et al., 2012). It is clear that one of the major concerns of the software development stakeholders is to best control the change process and then the software maintenance/evolution one. In fact, an uncontrolled change can quickly lead to a slippage in terms of project's cost and time. During more than four decades, many works have addressed this problem making the maintenance the most important cost factor of all the software development process (Folmer & Bosch, 2008; Gupta et al., 2008). In addition, according to ISO 250010 Model (ISO, 2011) (José et al., 2014), maintainability or scalability is one of the main components of the software quality.

In this work, we are interested in estimating the impact of the software change but from a quantitative point of view. In other words, we try to produce a model based on mathematical equations allowing us to estimate, in a way, the cost of the change of a given software. It reflects the impact of change in terms of the lines of code to be further modified, as an effort required to adapt the change. Indeed, a modification in a software development results in changes made in the source code in order to improve or correct its operation. These changes include any change affecting any element of the software (variable, method, or class). This can be, for example, deleting a variable, changing the scope of a method, or moving the link between a class and its super class, etc. A change can have dramatic and unexpected effects on the rest of the system. The danger of modifying a software element consists of the occurring of undesirable side effects. To avoid these situations, it would be interesting to estimate the change impact before making the change. The question that arises at this stage is the choice of the knowledge to be used to make this estimate. According to Chidamber and Kemerer (Santos et al., 2017), a code is characterized by a number of measures reflating its structure. This is an interesting base for estimating the effect of changes. For this, we propose in this work to study the feasibility of estimating the change impact through these metrics. In other words, we propose to model the relationship between the change impact and the so-called coupling metrics.

In the rest of the article, in section 2 we show the works concerning the change impact estimation approaches. The section 3 is dedicated to recall some facets to measure the coupling metric between classes. In section 4 we describe the research methodology we follow to quantify the change impact by considering the evolution of coupling measurements or metrics on several versions of the software. The experimentation of this method as well as the robustness test to which the proposed model was submitted are presented in sections 5 and 6. In section 7, an analysis of the factors influence is made while citing studies that converged to the same results. Later on, in section 8, we conclude this work by showing the limits of its use and outline its perspectives.

2. RELATED WORK

The change is a crucial and inevitable characteristic of the software during all its lifecycle. This is due to the necessary maintenance and/or evolution effort concerning the various software artefacts leading inevitably to perform change operations affecting them. Since more than four decades, many works have been devoted to this area of the software engineering resulting in many definitions and taxonomies (Lehman & Ramil, 2002). The work in this domain can be broadly categorized on different approaches regarding the artefacts concerned by the change; some data or metrics measures attributes of such artefacts, or some empirical studies mainly deal with the software historical data. Hereafter, we consider four approaches mainly based on the graph representation of the software; the use of software metrics; the use of models and the empirical approaches based on the use of historical data.

The approaches concerning the graph-based software representation consist of drawing a graph based on the software artifacts in order to illustrate the change impact propagation. In (Abdi & Dinedane, 2015) an extracting dependency graph from the input system is realized. The underlying idea is to measure the reachability of the different nodes of the graph. It involves the calculation of the transitive closures of the relations represented by the edges of the graph. Whereas, this closure determines the strength of the dependency among nodes as, related or strongly related components; hence, it may inform about the change impact propagation. It is often calculated using a widely applied algorithm called Warshall algorithm (Pieterse & Cleophas, 2017). In (Bouneffa & Ahmad, 2014) the software is represented by a model based on a graph rewriting system where software components are linked by meaningful relationships. In this background (Vincenzo et al., 2014) propose a generic model of software dependency graphs that synthesizes the graphs where degree distribution is close to the empirical ones observed in real software systems. This model gives novel insights on the potential fundamental rules of software evolution. In (Ahmad et al., 2017) the authors propose a global modeling approach to interrogate the structural and qualitative interdependencies in a software during the incorporation of several changes. In (Bhattacharya et al., 2012) the authors construct graphs that capture software structures and then exploit recent advances in analysis of graph topology to better understand software evolution. In (Abdeen et al., 2015) change-impact predictors are learned from past change impact graphs, extracted from the version history, along with their associations with different influencing factors of change propagation.

The metrics-based approaches generally deal with the object-oriented concepts and mainly concern metrics known as a well estimation of the maintenance effort. In (Saraiva et al., 2015) the analysis metrics values show a strong correlation between the so-called coupling metrics and the measureof the maintenance effort. In (Almugrin et al., 2016) the authors established that a lower number of package revisions (REVISIONS) and a smaller number of revised lines of codes (RLOC) during the package maintenance history indicate less package maintenance effort.

The Model-based approaches mainly aim to predict the change impact at the design level. In (Chaumun et al., 2002) the various links between the classes of a system are considered to compute or estimate the change impact. So, the impact is expressed as a combination of these links. In the same manner (Müller & Rumpe, 2014) propose an approach to the change impact analysis in which explicit impact rules capture the consequences of changing UML class diagrams on the other artefacts. The analyzed UML class diagrams typically describe two versions of the system under development, and the differences are identified automatically using model differencing. By explicitly formulating consequences of changes in impact rules, in order to be able to create a checklist with accurate hints concerning development steps that are (potentially) necessary to manage the evolution.

The empirical approaches aim to use the advantages of applying methods and techniques from other domains to software engineering and illustrates how, despite difficulties, software evolution can be empirically studied. In (Hegedűs et al., 2018) the authors divided the source code elements into a group containing the refactored elements and a group with non-refactored elements. The authors analyzed the elements' characteristics in these groups using correlation analysis, Mann–Whitney U test (Hegedűs et al., 2018) and effect size measures. In (Anwer et al., 2017) the authors study the impact of afferent coupling (Ca), efferent coupling (Ce) and coupling between object metrics (CBO) on fault prediction using bivariate correlation. The result of this study is a prediction model using these metrics to predict faults by using the statistical technique of multivariate logistic linear regression.

Some studies, such as (Vogel-Heuser et al., 2015) have investigated the relationship between design and maintenance effort by considering other aspects to study the effect of architecture on maintenance effort. Yet, it is delicate to identify the exact source of software change. Moreover, its encapsulation may require considering the particular software evolution phase and the development model.

This work is closely related to the fourth category which focuses on the use of change impact estimation as the main indicator of maintenance effort estimation by exploiting software metrics. We also consider more specifically object-oriented systems and apply the Design of Experiments (DOE)method, generally used in experimental sciences, in the purpose of quantifying the maintenance effort that would be a measure of the change impact, in the form of an equation whose parameters would be the values of these metrics.

3. COUPLING METRICS

Software metrics may provide a wide variety of information concerning a software application. The measures of different aspects of the software may help to ensure its success. In the context of current work, we prefer to use coupling metrics (Almugrin et al., 2016) to estimate the change impact in a developed software application. We cogently choose coupling metrics as these can be extracted directly from the source code. This may provide meaningful measures to attributes related to the change impact analysis (Elmidaoui et al., 2016; Nuez-varela et al., 2017).

Given that, coupling represents the measurement of the degree of dependency between two software artefacts (Tempero & Ralph, 2018). We consider this measurement between classes on the software source code level. If the degree of the coupling of a class C is higher with another class C', the class C is more sensitive to the changes affecting C'; hence, it can be inferred that the more closely coupled classes may have higher capacity to conduct the change impact among them. This attribute may qualify the dependency among classes and makes them more significant to be modified or debugged. It is therefore, important to carefully maintain such classes.

In the following we recall some facets to measure the coupling metric between classes, to better understand their role during the software maintenance:

1. **Coupling Between Object:** Coupling Between Object (CBO) signifies the measure (Tempero & Ralph, 2018) between two classes A and B such that A and B are coupled if the methods of the class A use the methods or attributes of theclass B. It can be observed that the change in strongly coupled classes is generally error prone. This observation can be shown as follows:

$$CBO(c) = |\{d \in C - \{c\}\} \text{ uses}(c,d) \text{ uses}(d,c)\}| \tag{1}$$

where c is a class and C is the set of all classes.

2. **Response For a Class:** Response For a Class (RFC) is the sum of the number of methods and the number of invoked methods in a given class (Tempero & Ralph, 2018). This measure reflects the potential of communication between classes. It may denote that the higher the RFC of a class, the more it is significant to changes, hence it may require more effort for the testability and debugging:

$$RFC(c) = Nbre\Big(M(c)\Big) + Nbre\Big(Inv\Big(M'(c)\Big)\Big) \tag{2}$$

where *Nbre(M(c))* represents the number of methods of a class c and *Nbre(Inv(M'(c)))* represents the number of invoked methods of a class c.

3. **Message Passing Coupling:** Message Passing Coupling (MPC) metric computes the number of method invocations in a class (Tempero & Ralph, 2018):

$$MPC(c) = \sum_{mM(c)} \sum_{m'M(c)} NSI(m, m') \tag{3}$$

where, *NSI (m, m')* is the number of static invocations of m' by m (the number of invocations of methods in a class c where m' is invoked for a static type object of the class c and m' belongs to $M(c)$).

4. RESEARCH METHODOLOGY

The Design of Experiments (DOE) (Heck & Thomas, 2015) is an experimental design method, widely used in applied statistics. The DOE makes it possible to understand and model complex processes that depend on a large number of variables that are difficult to adjust intuitively. It has been used, for more than two decades now, in areas such as biology, chemistry, or physics, where hypothesis control is usually done through experience. The DOE's principle is the search for a link between a value of interest or a response, and input variables. Its implementation is based on the realization of a series of experiments, each of which makes it possible to acquire new knowledge by varying one to several input variables to obtain results in order to build a model with a minimum of investment (Dagnelie, 2012).

We investigate the use of this method to build a mathematical model that allows, on the basis of the variation of metric values, to predict the volume of source code changes. In fact, for each scenario of maintenance we can know the values of the metrics which will be influential by these changes. For this study, we have assimilated an experience to a source code where the input factors of this experiment are a set of coupling metrics (CBO, RFC and MPC) and the output is the percentage of the source code to modify. The strength of the DOE method is the possibility of creating the mathematical model on the basis of a reduced number of experiments (Goupy, 2006). For this reason, we deal with a low number of versions (12 versions). This will demonstrate the utility of this approach in order to avoid useless investments.

4.1. The Context of the Study

We modeled the interaction of a set of metrics, particularly CBO, RFC, and MPC, to evaluate their overall contribution to the change impact analysis in a given set of classes. A well-performed experiment may answer the following questions in this context:

Q1: What is the influence of the different software metrics in estimating the change impact?
Q2: Among the most significant metrics to estimate the change impact, which one has the most weight?
Q3: Can we predict the change impact by varying these software metrics?

The DOE method fits response data to the mathematical models, in order to find the best answer of an asked question. It can predict the optimal response to a given combination of values. A repetitive approach may then help to gain more refined knowledge to optimize critical responses and find the fittest combination of values.

We begin by asking one or more questions (see Figure 1) and then iteratively apply the different variations of CBO, RFC, and MPC on change impact. Thereafter, this cause-and-effect relationship refines the data to yield the influence of the variation of software metrics on change impact.

Among others, the three critical steps of the knowledge acquisition process are iteratively performed, these are discussed as follows:

1. The DOE ensures the maximum efficiency with the minimum number of experiences. The choice of the experimentation method facilitates the progressive interpretation of the results;
2. The analysis of the results of experiences is facilitated by the initial choice of the experiences. The software tools of the DOE support the construction of the plans of experiences and their calcula-

tions. They may also support the analysis of results with the help of the graphical representations and improve the understanding of the phenomena;

3. Progressive acquisition of knowledge is composed of series of experiences. A first series of experiences leads to intermediate conclusions; according to these intermediate conclusions, we continue to a new trial series. The set of series of experiences can be then used to obtain a precise outline of the results of study. The analyst can accumulate the proficient results and he may continue until the achievement of satisfactory needs.

4.2. Modeling of Mathematical Equations

The DOE method works on the basis of mathematical modeling of participating factors, to illustrate their interaction to achieve an optimal result, as shown in Equation 4:

$$y = f(x_1, \ldots, x_n) \tag{4}$$

We formalize the mathematical function that may indicate the response to the interaction of involved factors. In this case the factors are the different software metrics and the response is the change impact estimation. For instance, it can be shown as follows:

$$EIC = f(CBO, RFC, MPC) \tag{5}$$

where, *EIC* denotes the estimation of the change impact. It results as a function of interaction of CBO, RFC, and MPC.

As discussed, earlier in section 4.1, the DOE supports the calculations of interacting factors. Equation 5 provides the general change impact estimation. The DOE operation can be carried out by various software tools like STATISTICA[1], SPSS[2], R[3], Minitab[4], etc. We have used STATISTICA during this study to calculate the values of the constants and coefficients of the Equation 5. It is often customary to opt for a limited Taylor-Mac Laurin development (an approximation) (Bulut, 2014). This leads to transform the model into a polynomial structure of more or less degree, to obtain more precise knowledge. It can be shown as follows:

$$y = \beta_0 + \sum \beta_i x_i + \sum \beta_{ii} x_i^2 + \sum \beta_{ij} x_i x_{ij} \tag{6}$$

where y is the dependent variable of the model (the response), β_0 is a constant; $\beta_i, \beta_{ii}, \beta_{ij}$ are the coefficients of the model, whereas the x_i, x_j are the variables depending on the field of the experience.

The coefficients correspond to the degree of influence of each factor on the dependent variable to be modeled. If we take the previous example, each variable in the field of experience (CBO, RFC, or MPC) has a degree of influence on estimation of the change impact. It can be further refined by performing the steps of the experimental design method.

5. EMPIRICAL VALIDATION OF RESEARCH METHODOLOGY

The main objective, during this study, has been to determine the influence of the variation of some software metrics for change impact analysis in different versions of software. So, we experimented our approach on the different versions of the open-source library "JFreeChart," written in Java. This library is mainly reused to generate graphs in Java applications. It is composed of 331 classes and 12 versions provide us a stable test base.

The DOE is used as a practical method, during this study, to model the estimation of change impact for the different values of the set of software metrics. This method has particular advantages, such as, it requires minimum number of experiences (The different versions of software, in the context of our study) to build an optimal model (Tinsson, 2010).

Figure 1. Experimentation plan

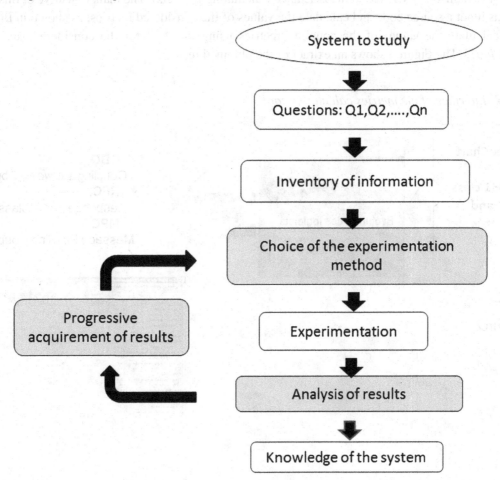

5.1. Experiments Plan

For this study, we collect data from the *JFreeChart* repository implemented in java. We dealt with data extracted from twelve versions of *JFreeChart* as shown in Table 1. As required by the DOE method; we implement a process consisting first to measure the software metrics and then the code change ratio by considering the twelve versions of *JFreeChart*. The different metric values (CBO, RFC and MPC) can be extracted directly from the code (Nuez-varela et al., 2017). We use the available source code of *JFreeChart* versions to measure the volume of software change. These are measured by comparing a given version to the following one, obtained after the software update (Silva et al., 2014).

5.2. The Prototype Tool

The values of the different software metrics are extracted from *JFreeChart* using a prototype tool developed in Java named "SACI" (System Assistance Calculating Impacts). The main objective of this tool is to take as input a source code and calculate the values of the considered metrics, as shown in Figure 2.

We calculate the values of the coupling metrics using this tool for the considered versions of "*JFreeChart*." The Figure3 shows an extract of the obtained results.

Figure 2. Interface of the metrics calculation tool

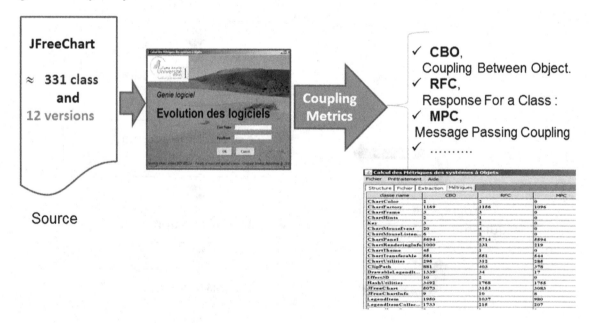

Figure 3. Extract from the extraction table of coupling metrics concerning the version of JFreeChart

classe name	CBO	RFC	MPC
ChartColor	2	2	0
ChartFactory	1169	1156	1096
ChartFrame	3	3	0
ChartHints	2	1	0
Key	3	2	0
ChartMouseEvent	20	4	0
ChartMouseListen...	6	2	0
ChartPanel	5694	5714	5594
ChartRenderingInfo	1000	231	219
ChartTheme	45	1	0
ChartTransferable	551	551	544
ChartUtilities	296	312	285
ClipPath	881	403	378
DrawableLegendIt...	1339	34	17
Effect3D	10	2	0

5.3. Adjustments of Parameters for DOE

The particularity of coupling metrics is that they concern each class of the software (Almugrin et al., 2016). We are required to define representative coupling metrics in order to study the whole software. So, we propose a particular technique to ensure a valid choice of the experimentation method. The proposed technique allows to determine the most prominent representative coupling metrics, for each type of metric, in the whole set of classes.

Consider a system denoted as S composed of *n* classes. This system can be represented as follows:

$$S = \{C_1, ..., C_i, ..., C_n\} \tag{7}$$

where, the qualitative measure of a given class C_i can be evaluated by a set of metrics, shown as follows:

$$C_1 = \left\{m_1^{C1},...,m_i^{C1},...,m_p^{C1}\right\} \tag{8}$$

where, m_p is a particular metric applied to a class C.

We propose a function *F(S)* that finds the optimal representation of the results from whole set of metrics; it can be shown as follows:

$$F(S) = \left\{ m_1^S, \ldots, m_i^S, \ldots, m_p^S \right\} \tag{9}$$

where, the measure of the metric m_i^S is the chosen metric (choice of the experimentation method) as required by the DOE method:

$$m_1^S = F\left(m_1^{c1}, \ldots, m_1^{ci}, \ldots, m_1^{cn} \right) \tag{10}$$

We describe, in below, the significance for the choice of the best parameter (function *F*) for each set of metrics:

- A higher value of the CBO metric by its nature represents the more required effort for the maintenance of a given class (Tiwari & Rathore, 2018). Hence, the prominent representation for the function F for the CBO metric is the maximum of all the CBOs of the considered classes. The MAX aggregation operator is chosen because it represents the worst situation in terms of the change impact. The increased CBO value means strong impact of change;
- The RFC metric reflects the degree of communication between classes in a given software system (Tiwari & Rathore, 2018). The most damaging case is to modify the class with the maximum value of the communication links, as this would cause modifications in all the classes related to this class. Therefore, the MAX aggregation that corresponds to the highest value of the RFC metric for a given system is the best representative of that type of metric;
- The MPC measures communication between objects in the class (Tiwari & Rathore, 2018). In the case where a class has a method that is invoked by a large number of objects, a change in this method will involve the modification of a maximum number of objects. Therefore, MAX aggregation, which is the highest number of method invocations, represents the highest dependency between a given class and the other classes. It is, then, the best representative of such metrics in the system.

On the basis of above given reasoning, we formulate the following choice of experimentation method:

$$CBO^S = \mathrm{Max}\left(CBO^{c_1}, \ldots, CBO^{c_i}, \ldots, CBO^{c_n} \right) \tag{11}$$

$$RFC^S = \mathrm{Max}\left(RFC^{c_1}, \ldots, RFC^{c_i}, \ldots, RFC^{c_n} \right) \tag{12}$$

$$MPC^S = \mathrm{Max}\left(MPC^{c_1}, \ldots, MPC^{c_i}, \ldots, MPC^{c_n} \right) \tag{13}$$

5.4. Application of the Adjusted DOE Parameters

The choice of experimentation method enables the eventual choice of a single value for each set of metrics representations. We apply this modeling, for each representation of coupling metric for all the classes in the version 1 of *JFreeChart*, as following:

$$CBO^{JFreeChart\_version1} = Max\left(CBO^{Chartcolor}, ..., CBO^{Chartrendering\,info}, ..., CBO^{Xycoordinatetype}\right) \tag{14}$$

$$RFC^{JFreeChart\_version1} = Max\left(RFC^{Chartcolor}, ..., RFC^{Chartrendering\,info}, ..., RFC^{Xycoordinatetype}\right) \tag{15}$$

$$MPC^{JFreeChart\_version1} = Max\left(MPC^{Chartcolor}, ..., MPC^{Chartrendering\,info}, ..., MPC^{Xycoordinatetype}\right) \tag{16}$$

We iteratively apply these measures on the 12 versions of *JFreeChart* to further develop the experimental protocol, as shown in Table 1.

The Table 2 gives the ratio of the modified lines for a given version. The entries given in Table 2 are obtained using the open source *WinMerge* tool[5], which compares two successive versions of the software source code to compute the modified lines of the code. The comparison considers only the executable lines of the source code i.e. it excludes the comments, spaces and empty lines. It compares the signature of methods from two different versions to compute the Levenshtein distance (Sudhish et al., 2016). The Levenstein distance between two words w1 and w2 is the minimum number of operations (insertions, deletions or substitutions) required to transform w1 into w2.

5.5. Execution of DOE Method

Conforming to the DOE method, we have a set of experiences i.e. the values of the CBO, RFC and MPC for each version of the *JFreeChart library* (Table 1) and the estimated change impact, expressed as a ratio (Table 2).

We calculate the values of the coefficients of the mathematical model, to be used in the polynomial Equation 6 as shown in Table3.

According the results in Table 3 where the p-values of the coefficients are up the recommended value (statistically significant values (below P-value = 0.05)), this has been caused by nature of applied design of experiments because the experimental results were obtained according to an Unconventional experimental design (Goupy, 2006) causing the experimental errors. The not signification of coefficients let impossible the construction of the mathematical model with three factors. In order to minimize the influence of the experimental errors generated by this kind of design of experiments (Goupy & Creighton, 2006) recommend minimizing the number of factors. In scope of this study the alternative was to combine the factors two by two, all combinations were tried only the combination of factors CBO, MPC gives interesting results.

By exploiting the results of the 12 versions (experiments) as shown in Table 1 and Table 2. (i.e., the conditions of DOE), we will have a two-factor plan and then we will apply the following mathematical equation:

Table 1. Experimental protocol

-	Version 1	Version 2	Version 3	Version 4	Version 5	Version 6	Version 7	Version 8	Version 9	Version 10	Version 11	Version 12
CBO	8348	8343	8300	7431	8348	8100	6278	8254	5998	8331	8312	8314
RFC	6602	6119	6502	6416	6341	5856	6245	6112	4990	6467	5876	5997
MPC	6372	6371	6245	6115	6243	5436	6224	6554	6345	5994	5973	6876
% Change Impact	0%	1%	3%	8%	5%	20%	7%	4%	30%	7%	6%	20%

Table 2. Observed responses

	Version 1	Version 2	Version 3	Version 4	Version 5	Version 6	Version 7	Version 8	Version 9	Version 10	Version 11	Version 12
% Change Impact	0%	1%	3%	8%	5%	20%	7%	4%	30%	7%	6%	20%

Table 3. Coefficients β_i of the change impact model

β_i	β_0	β_1	β_{11}	β_2	β_{22}	β_3	β_{33}	β_{12}	β_{13}	β_{23}
value	0,0704	-0,1847	0,2537	-0,1713	0,3215	-0,0422	0,0298	-0,5330	-0,0897	0,3008
P-value	0,4140	0,4727	0,5618	0,9151	0,1747	0,8785	0,9201	0,2405	0,7900	0,8722

$$y = \beta_0 + \beta_1 x_1 + \beta_2 x_2 + \beta_{11} x_1^2 + \beta_{22} x_2^2 + \beta_{12} x_1 x_2 \tag{17}$$

where, y denotes the change impact and x_i, x_j are the dependent variables in the domain of experience (coupling metrics in scale of model).

The different coefficients of the model β_i are obtained by matrix calculations which are shown in the Table 4:

Table 4. Coefficients β_i of the change impact model

β_i	β_0	β_1	β_2	β_{11}	β_{22}	β_{12}
Value	0,08864	1,50561	0,16427	0,44738	-0,29321	-1,70957
P-value	0,022994 *	0,004576 *	0,095781	0,000149 *	0,051806	0,003872 *

*=statistically significant values (below P-value = 0.05)

We obtain the following results after integrating the values on Equation 17:

$$y = 0,0886 + 1,5056 x_1 + 0,16427 x_2 + 0,4473 x_1^2 - 0,29321 x_2^2 - 1,7095 x_1 x_2 \tag{18}$$

Equation 19 gives the participant values of the significant effects (and ignores the less important values):

$$y = 0,0886 + 1,5056 x_1 + 0,4473 x_1^2 - 1,7095 x_1 x_2 \tag{19}$$

where, x_1 corresponds to MPC at generic scale of model and x_2 corresponds to CBO at generic scale of model.

In order to have the final model we realize a transformation from generic scale to the final scale, this transformation is obtained by the following Equation 20 (Goupy, 2006):

$$x = \frac{A - A_0}{pas} \tag{20}$$

where, A_0 is central value of the origin's units, A is Origin variable, and x isCoded variable.

The model of Change Impact Estimation (EIC) is then as under:

$$EIC = 0,0886 + 1,5056\left(\frac{MPC - 6165}{720}\right) + 0,4473\left(\frac{MPC - 6165}{720}\right)^2 - 1,7095\left(\frac{MPC - 6165}{720}\right)\left(\frac{CBO - 7173}{1175}\right)$$

$$(21)$$

We further improve the obtained model by performing a series of tests, as discussed in the next section.

6. MODEL ROBUSTNESS TEST

We study the model values at the experimental design points using techniques like randomization and repeatability (Watson & Petrie, 2010). Indeed, these plans tend to position the points at the edges of the domain to take into account the random variation and offer a more reliable tendency towards the answers in the presence of measurements errors. To do this, there are criteria to test the good match between observations and forecasts on the data used during the construction of the model. This is the role of the correlation coefficient R^2. The model is considered as robust when the value of this coefficient tends to 1 (Watson & Petrie, 2010).

In this case of experimentation, we obtain a correlation coefficient $R^2 = 0.94$. It may validate the correctness of the proposed model for estimating the change impact as it meets the robustness criteria, as shown in Figure 4.

7. DATA ANALYSIS

It can be inferred that the change impact estimation should be calculated on the combination of the metrics CBO and MPC. It may help the decision-maker to estimate concretely the percentage of the source code affected by each proposed scenario including metrics.

The change impact estimation model shows an influence of the quadratic effect of the MPC while the linear interaction effect of these two parameters (i.e. both the MPC and CBO).

The DOE method provides us with an opportunity to determine the most influential factors on the estimation of the change impact. This is possible by means of the technique called Surface Response Methodology (SRM) (Khoder, 2011).

On examining the response surface (Figure 5), we find influence of the MPC on the estimation of the change impact. This is consistent with the findings deduced by the model and expresses the quadratic effect of the MPC. This concentration (of color) in the MPC region is shown in Figure 5.

The same claims have yet been made by previous related works (Chaumun et al., 2002), (Abdi & Dinedane, 2015), (Abdeen et al., 2015). All these works have shown the importance of the coupling as the most accurate measure for the change impact estimation.

The proposed method emphasizes the fact that it ensures the construction of the model on the basis of a reduced number of experiments (versions). Finally, we achieve similar but better results with those obtained by the related literature with less effort in terms of the needed volume of data to analyze.

Another representation using the principle of iso response to visually detect the most influential, recognizable factors is shown in Figure 6 at color concentrations.

Figure 4. Graphical representation of the robustness test of the proposed model with $R^2 = 0.94$

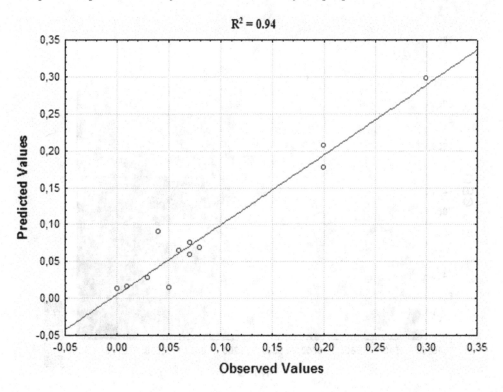

Figure 5. Three-dimensional representation of the influence of MPC and the CBO on the estimation of change impact

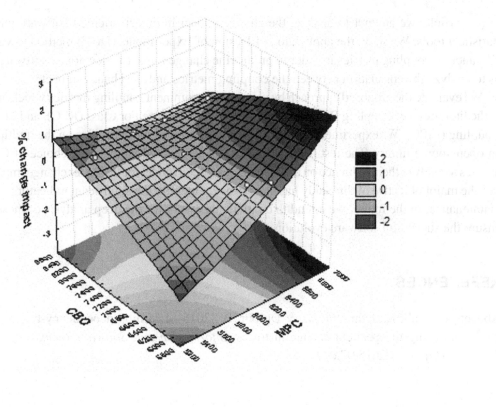

Figure 6. Isometric representation of the MPC influence and the CBO on the estimation of the change impact

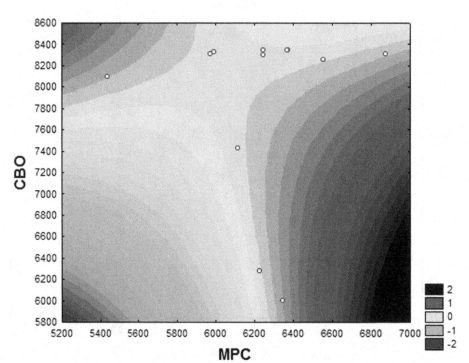

8. CONCLUSION

In this article, we attempt to analyze the change impact in object-oriented software with the help of statistical tools. We study the application of Design of Experiments (DOE) method to validate the significance of coupling metrics in order to predict the change impact in developed software. It may allow us to analyze the correlation between the coupling metrics and the change impact.

We evaluate the proposed approach by using three prominent coupling metrics which are widely used in the literature i.e. Coupling Between Objects (CBO), Response For Class (RFC), and Message Passing Coupling (MPC). We experimented the different variations of these metrics on the multiple versions of an open-source library. The test results using the DOE method validate the choice of CBO and MPC metrics to analyze their influence on the scale of developed model for the better change impact estimation.

The major objective of this study has been to better identify the significant indicators for the software maintenance. In the future, we intend to continue this work for the deep analysis of these indicators to ensure the successful software evolution.

REFERENCES

Abdeen, H., Bali, K., Sahraoui, H., & Dufour, B. (2015). Learning dependency-based change impact predictors using independent change histories. *Information and Software Technology*, *67*, 220–235. doi:10.1016/j.infsof.2015.07.007

Abdi, M.K. & Dinedane. M.Z. (2015). Change Impact Identification in Object-Oriented System: Dependence Graph Approach. *International Journal of Education and Management Engineering*, 1-8

Abdi, M.K, Lounis, H. & Sahraoui, H. (2009). Analyse et prédiction de l'impact de changements dans un système à objets: Approche probabiliste. *Revue des nouvelles technologies de l'information RNTI-L3*, 113-138.

Ahmad, A., Basson, H., & Bouneffa, M. (2017). Analyzing and modeling the structural and qualitative interdependencies of software evolution. *In Proceedings of 7th International Workshop on Computer Science and Engineering, (WCSE 2017), international Conference on Software Engineering (ICOSE)*, Beijing, China.

Almugrin, S., Albattah, W., & Melton, A. (2016). Using indirect coupling metrics to predict package maintainability and testability. *Journal of Systems and Software*, *121*, 298–310. doi:10.1016/j.jss.2016.02.024

Anwer, S., Adbellatif, A., Alshayeb, M., & Anjum, M. S. (2017). Effect of coupling on software faults: An empirical study. In *Proceedings of the International Conference on Communication, Computing and Digital Systems (C-CODE)*. Islamabad, Pakistan (pp. 211-215). 10.1109/C-CODE.2017.7918930

Benett, K. H., & Rajlich, V. T. (2000). Software Maintenance and Evolution: A Roadmap. In *Proceedings of the Conference on The Future of Software Engineering. ICSE'00*, Limerick, Ireland (pp. 73 –87). 10.1145/336512.336534

Bhattacharya, P., Iliofotou, M., Neamtiu, I., & Faloutsos, M. (2012). Graph-based analysis and prediction for software evolution. In *Proceedings of the 34th International Conference on Software Engineering (ICSE)*, Zurich, Switzerland (pp. 419-429). 10.1109/ICSE.2012.6227173

Bouneffa, M., & Ahmad, A. (2014). The Change Impact Analysis in BPM Based Software Applications: A Graph Rewriting and Ontology Based Approach. In S. Hammoudi, J. Cordeiro, L. Maciaszek, & J. Filipe (Eds.), *Enterprise Information Systems. ICEIS 2013*. Switzerland: Springer. doi:10.1007/978-3-319-09492-2_17

Bulut, S. (2014). Faber polynomial coefficient estimates for a comprehensive subclass of analytic bi-univalent functions. *Comptes Rendus Mathematique*, *352*(6), 479–484. doi:10.1016/j.crma.2014.04.004

Chapin, N. (2000). Do we know what preventive maintenance is? In *Proceedings of International Conference on Software Maintenance*, Los Alamitos, CA (pp. 15-17). 10.1109/ICSM.2000.882970

Chaumun, M. A., Kabaili, H., Keller, R. K., & Lustman, F. (2002). A change impact model for changeability assessment in object-oriented software systems. *Science of Computer Programming*, *45*(2), 155–174. doi:10.1016/S0167-6423(02)00058-8

Dagnelie, P. (2012). *Principes d'expérimentation (planification des expériences et analyse de leurs résultats)*. Gembloux, Belgique: les presses agronomiques de gembloux.

Elmidaoui, S., Cheikhi, L., & Idri, A. (2016). A survey of empirical studies in software product maintainability prediction models. In *Proceedings of the 11th International Conference on Intelligent Systems: Theories and Applications (SITA)*, Mohammedia, Morocco (pp. 1-6). 10.1109/SITA.2016.7772267

Folmer, E., & Bosch, J. (2008). Experiences with Software Architecture Analysis of Usability. *International Journal of Information Technology and Web Engineering*, *3*(4), 1–29. doi:10.4018/jitwe.2008100101

Gasmallah, N., Amirat, A., & Oussalah, M. (2016). Evolution Taxonomy for Software Architecture Evolution. In *Proceedings of the 11th International Conference on Evaluation of Novel Software Approaches to Software Engineering ENASE 2016*, Rome, Italy (pp. 124-131). 10.5220/0005775701240131

Goupy, J. (2006). Tutoriel les plans d'expériences. *Revue MODULAD*, *34*, 74–116.

Goupy, J., & Creighton, L. (2006). *Introduction au plan d'expériences*. Malakoff, France: DUNOD.

Gupta, N., Saini, D. K., & Saini, H. (2008). Class Level Test Case Generation in Object Oriented Software Testing. *International Journal of Information Technology and Web Engineering*, *3*(2), 18–26. doi:10.4018/jitwe.2008040102

Heck, R. H., & Thomas, S. L. (2015). *An introduction to multilevel modeling techniques: MLM and SEM approaches using Mplus* (3rd ed.). New York: Routledge. doi:10.4324/9781315746494

Hegedűs, P., Kádár, I., Ferenc, R., & Gyimóthy, T. (2018). Empirical evaluation of software maintainability based on a manually validated refactoring dataset. *Information and Software Technology*, *95*, 313–327. doi:10.1016/j.infsof.2017.11.012

José, P. M., Mauricio, D., & Rodríguez, G. (2014). A Review of Software Quality Models for the Evaluation of Software Products. *International Journal of Software Engineering and Its Applications*, *5*(6), 31–53. doi:10.5121/ijsea.2014.5603

Khoder, K. (2011). *Optimisation de composants hyperfréquences par la technique des plans à surfaces de réponses*. Retrieved from http://www.theses.fr/2011LIMO4039

Lehman, M. M., & Ramil, J. F. (2002). Software Evolution and Software Evolution Processes. *Annals of Software Engineering*, *14*(1), 275–309. doi:10.1023/A:1020557525901

Nuez-Varela, A. S., Prez-Gonzalez, H. G., Martnez-Perez, F. E., & Soubervielle-Montalvo, C. (2017). Source code metrics. *Journal of Systems and Software*, *128*(C), 164–197. doi:10.1016/j.jss.2017.03.044

Santos, L. D. C., Saraiva, R. M., Perkusich, M., Almeida, H. O., & Perkusich, A. (2017). An empirical study on the influence of context in computing thresholds for Chidamber and Kemerer metrics. In *Proceedings of The 29th International Conference on Software Engineering & Knowledge Engineering SEKE2017*, Pittsburgh, PA (pp. 357-362). 10.18293/SEKE2017-044

Silva, F. F., Borel, E., Lopes, E., & Murta, L. G. P. (2014). Towards a Difference Detection Algorithm Aware of Refactoring-Related Changes. In *Proceedings of the Brazilian Symposium on Software Engineering (SBES 2014)*, Maceio Alagoas, Brazil (pp. 111-120). 10.1109/SBES.2014.21

Sudhish, P. S., Jain, A. K., & Cao, K. (2016). Adaptive fusion of biometric and biographic information for identity de-duplication. *Pattern Recognition Letters*, *84*, 199–207. doi:10.1016/j.patrec.2016.10.011

Sun, X., Li, B., Li, B., & Wen, W. (2012). A comparative study of static CIA techniques. *In Proceedings of the Fourth Asia-Pacific Symposium on Internetware (Internetware 2012)*, Qing Dao, China (pp. 231-238).

Swanson, E. B. (1976). The Dimensions of Maintenance. In *Proceedings of the 2nd International Conference on Software Engineering (ICSE '76)*, San Francisco, CA (pp. 492-497).

Tempero, E., & Ralph, P. (in press). A framework for defining coup metrics. *Science of Computer Programming*.

Tinsson, W. (2010). *Plans d'expérience: constructions et analyses statistiques*. Springer.

Tiwari, S., & Rathore, S. S. (2018). Coupling and Cohesion Metrics for Object-Oriented Software: A Systematic Mapping Study. In *Proceedings of the 11th Innovations in Software Engineering Conference, ISEC 2018*, Hyderabad, India (pp. 1-8). 10.1145/3172871.3172878

Vincenzo, M., Martin, M., & Philippe, P. A. (2014). Generative Model of Software Dependency Graphs to Better Understand Software Evolution. Retrieved from http://arxiv.org/abs/1410.7921

Vogel-Heuser, B., Feldmann, S., Folmer, J., Rösch, S., Heinrich, R., Rostami, K., & Reussner, R. (2015, October). Architecture-Based Assessment and Planning of Software Changes in Information and Automated Production Systems State of the Art and Open Issues. *Paper presented at the IEEE International Conference on Systems, Man, and Cybernetics*, Hong Kong, China. 10.1109/SMC.2015.130

Watson, P. F., & Petrie, A. (2010). Method agreement analysis: A review of correct methodology. *Theriogenology*, *73*(9), 1167–1179. doi:10.1016/j.theriogenology.2010.01.003 PMID:20138353

ENDNOTES

[1]   http://www.statsoft.fr
[2]   https://www.ibm.com
[3]   https://www.r-project.org
[4]   http://www.minitab.com
[5]   Open source: http://winmerge.org

This research was previously published in the International Journal of Open Source Software and Processes (IJOSSP), 10(1); pages 16-33, copyright year 2019 by IGI Publishing (an imprint of IGI Global).

Chapter 40
Introduction to the Popular Open Source Statistical Software (OSSS)

Zhijian Wu
New York University, USA

Zichen Zhao
Yale University, USA

Gao Niu
Bryant University, USA

ABSTRACT

This chapter first introduces the two most popular Open Source Statistical Software (OSSS), R and Python, along with their Integrated Development Environment (IDE) and Graphical User Interface (GUI). Secondly, additional OSSS, such as JASP, PSPP, GRETL, SOFA Statistics, Octave, KNIME, and Scilab, will also be introduced in this chapter with function descriptions and modeling examples. The chapter intends to create a reference for readers to make proper selection of the Open Source Software when a statistical analysis task is in demand. The chapter describes software explicitly in words. In addition, working platform and selective numerical, descriptive, and analysis examples are provided for each software. Readers could have a direct and in-depth understanding of each software and its functional highlights.

INTRODUCTION

In this chapter, the authors discuss the most popular Open Source Statistical Software (OSSS) with its creation history, target practitioners, and statistical usage examples. Although Programming languages such as Java, C++ can also perform statistical analysis with intensive coding, the authors limit discussion to the software specifically designed for statistical analysis.

DOI: 10.4018/978-1-7998-9158-1.ch040

The objective of this chapter is to create a reference for the readers and guide them to make proper selection of Open Source Software (OSS) when a statistical analysis task is in demand. The discussion includes the background information, research areas that the software designed for, and the overview of how to use the software. R and Python are the two most important and popular software, their applications are discussed in detail throughout chapter four to seven in this book. The authors focus on creating an overview of all open source statistical software in this chapter.

BACKGROUND

Open Source Software (OSS) is a type of computer software that had its code released to the public. St. Laurent (2008) indicated that users have the right to study, change and redistribute the software under the copyright granted by the software license holder. Closed source or proprietary software can only be modified and maintained by the people, teams and organizations who own the software. Microsoft Office and Adobe Photoshop are well-known proprietary software.

Open Source Software is popular to statistical analysis practitioners, not only because it is free, but also because it is more adaptive to the current rapidly developing academic research advancement environment.

This chapter first introduces the two most popular Open Source Statistical Software (OSSS) R and Python along with its Integrated Development Environment (IDE) and Graphical User Interface (GUI). Then, additional OSSS, like JASP, PSPP, GRETL, SOFA Statistics, Octave, KNIME and Scilab, are introduced with description of their functions and modeling examples. Figure 1 lists all of the popular open source statistical software and IDEs that are introduced in this Chapter.

Figure 2 and 3 demonstrate the popularity development within last five years of the Open Source Statistical Software discussed in this chapter. The value represents the Google search interest. A value of 100 is the peak popularity which happens on the third week of 2019 for Python, a value of 50 represents the software is half as popular. The data is extracted on 12/19/2019 from trends.google.com under the category of "Science" and "Web Search". Since R and Python dominate the popularity charts, two figures are created in order to better presents the relationship between all of the software. Figure 2 demonstrates R and Python popularity. Figure 3 shows other Open Source Statistical Software (OSSS).

R

R is arguably the most popular Open Source Statistical Software. It has a strong statistical analysis capability and graphical visualization functionality. This section provides an overview of the software R by introducing most used packages, its popular IDEs and its functionalities. Following two chapters will introduce R with syntax examples and application. R was initially written by Ross Ihaka and Robert Gentleman from the University of Auckland, New Zealand (Contributors, 2019). R is licensed under GNU General Public License. As of June 2019, the most current version is 3.6.0, it was released on April, 26th, 2019. The official website of the software is https://www.r-project.org/.

As of July 18th, 2019, there are 14,580 CRAN packages (Contributed Packages, 2019). The authors select a few popular packages, categorize them by functionality, and list in table 1 based on Awesome R (2019).

Figure 1. Logos of popular open source statistical software and its IDEs (Designed by Niu, 2019)

R	Rstudio	Architect	Jamovi
Python	PyCharm	Spyder	Jupyter
JASP	PSPP	GRETL	SOFA
Octave	KNIME	Scilab	

Table 2 lists out popular R IDEs. Among them, RStudio, Jamovi and architect are further discussed with more details.

Figure 2. Python and R popularity 2014-2019 (Designed by Niu, 2019)

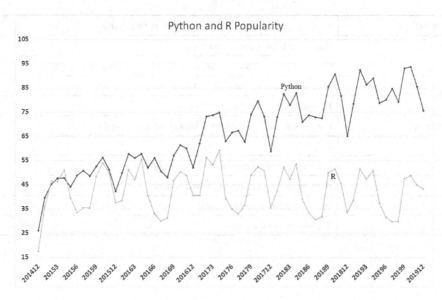

Figure 3. Stacked Area Graph for Open Source Statistical Software Popularity (Designed by Niu, 2019)

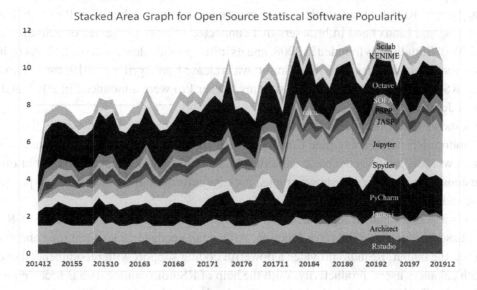

Table 1. Selected popular R packages by category

R Package Function Area	Package Names
Data Manipulation	dplyr, Data.table, readr, rlist, vroom, DataExplorer
Visualization	ggplot2, ggfortify, lattice, gganimate, plot3D
Database	RODBC, DBI, odbc, RMySQL, ROracle, RSQLite, RHive
Statistical Analysis and Machine Learning	Bigrf, C50, forecast, prophet, gbm, glmnet, kernlab, lasso2, maptree, randomForest, tree, mcmc, coda, igraph, network, ggmap, Remap, spacetime, spatstat, tigris
Finance	PerformanceAnalytics, fAssets, tseries, scorecard

Table 2. Selected popular R IDEs

R IDE	Short Description
RStudio	One of the most popular R user interface
Jamovi	GUI similar to SPSS and focuses on Bayesian and Frequentist analysis
Architect	IDE that focuses on the need of data scientist
StatET	Eclipse based IDE for R
Revolution R Enterprise	Free to academics, commercial software focus on big data.
R Commander	GUI
Deducer	Friendly user interface with direct data editing function
Radiant	Browser based user interface based on Shiny
Bio7	Focuses on ecological modeling
RTVs	R tools for visual studio

RStudio

RStudio is one of the most popular IDEs. The working platform includes a console, syntax-highlighting editor that supports direct code execution, as well as tools for plotting, history, debugging and workspace management. RStudio is available in open source and commercial edition. It runs on the desktop (Windows, Mac and Linux) and in browsers that connected to RStudio Server or RStudio Server Pro (RStudio, 2019). RStudio was founded in 2008, and its initial public release was in 2011. As of July 2019, the most current desktop version of the RStudio was released on April 8th, 2019, the version number is 1.2.1335. RStudio Server Pro and RStudio Shiny Server Pro were announced in 2013, and RStudio Connect was delivered in 2016.

Figure 4 shows the working user interface of RStudio. The top left window shows the syntax of R code. The bottom left window is called Console, which shows the syntax execution status and results. The top right window provides the basic variable and data information, such as number of observation and dimensions. The bottom right shows graphs, package information etc. The size and position of the windows are adjustable.

RStudio is a popular and strong IDE which improves significantly user experience of R. Original R software has almost no user interface function. All syntax needs to be programmed and executed in order to reach the output. RStudio provides a powerful coding support with recommended codes, error check which enhances users' productivity. With the help of RStudio, source data is accessed more visually and directly. The IDE is also linked with online databases. Users could utilize its automated package lookup, download and install functions instead of searching and downloading packages manually. RStudio supports more interactive graphics with RShinny. RStudio is well-received by researchers and practitioners from many areas, such as statistics, biostatistics, mathematics, actuarial science, finance, engineer, business and etc.

Figure 4. RStudio working user interface (Designed by Niu, 2019)

Architect

Architect is an Eclipse-based cross-platform IDE for R. Architect is a fully open source software. It is available on Windows, Mac and Linux. As of July 2019, the most current version of Architect is 0.9.11. The official website is https://www.getarchitect.io/

Architect provides a user-friendly interface that supports all data science tasks from statistical analysis to report generation. The working plate platform includes integrated R console, object browser, data viewer, graphing tools, package development, workspace management, and debugging tools. Architect is fully embedded in the Eclipse ecosystem (IDE for Data Science, 2019), and it can be used to work in multiple programming languages such as R, Python, Julia, Scala, C++ etc. It can also connect to NoSQL database which makes big data analysis easier. Figure 5 shows the working user interface of Architect.

Jamovi

Jamovi is a free open source GUI for R. It improves the functionality of R in two aspects. On one hand, the GUI component of Jamovi makes programming easier, especially for users who are not familiar with R syntax. Muenchen (2018) indicated that jamovi added functions and methods of programming that other software has, such as SPSS and SAS. Lakens (2017) wrote that Jamovi was developed by a group of developers who used to work on JASP, thus the user interface and functionality have a lot of similarities. It can be operated on Windows, MacOS, Linux and ChromeOS. The official website is https://www.jamovi.org/. As of June 2019, the most current version of the software was published on May 24th, 2019, the version number is 1.0.0. Jamovi's official website (2019) mentioned that it intends to be a free open source version of the costly statistical products.

Jamovi is adaptive to various data formats. SPSS, SAS and Stata files can be imported to Jamovi directly. The user interface of Jamovi has live data management, users could edit and modify data directly without syntax. Edelsbrunner (2017) indicated that, in Jamovi, data is dynamically linked with its analysis, and test results are automatically updated after the data has been edited or modified. The

Figure 5. Architect working user interface (Designed by Wu, 2019)

analytical results are edited such that tables, results can be easily copied and pasted into other editing software, such as LaTex, Word, Powerpoint and etc.

Figure 6 shows the working user interface of Jamovi. On the top part of data tab, there are functions, such as copy, paste, transform, add and delete for columns and rows. The left shows the imported data. Each data cell can be modified directly, such as changing numbers, deleting rows and adding columns. This graphical user interface made data manipulation easier compare to core calculation engine R, which requires data manipulation through syntax. On the right side of the interface, the software shows multiple statistical results, and they are all dynamically linked with the data on the right. The results are updated instantaneously with data modification.

Table 3 lists out the statistical analysis functions predefined in Jamovi. On top of the user interface, six major analysis options are available. Following table lists all of the statistical functions preprogramed in Jamovi.

On the left side of the Analyses tab, the user interface provides all options for each statistical function. The following figure provides an example of One-Way ANOVA analysis. Users could make selections of Variance, Missing Values, Additional Statistics, and Assumptions to generate results directly on the right-hand window. References of the analysis are also provided underneath the results. The results generated from Jamovi are preprogramed such that it can be used directly in text editing files such as LaTex, Word or Powerpoint. Figure 7 shows an example of statistical analysis in Jamovi.

Figure 6. Jamovi working user interface (Designed by Wu, 2019)

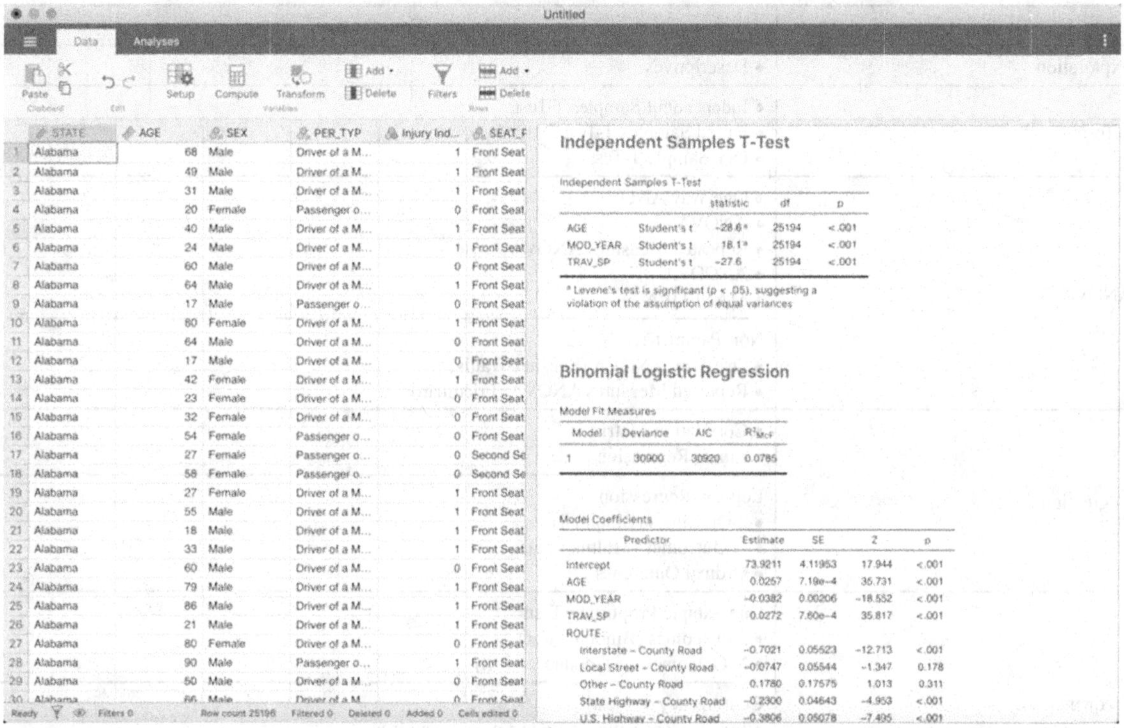

PYTHON

Python is one of the most popular open source programming software used for automation, artificial intelligence, application, websites as well as statistical analysis for big data. This section provides a brief overview of the software and several popular IDEs, such as Python IDEs, PyCharm, Spyder and Jupyter. Chapter 6 Introduction to Python and its Statistical Applications and Chapter 7 A Comparison of Machine Learning Models for Time Series Forecasting in Python will have a more detailed discussion and its applications. Python was created by Guido van Rossum in the early 1990s from Stichting Mathematisch Centrum in Netherlands (History and License, 2019). Python is licensed under General Public License (GPL)-compatible. The difference is that GPL compatible makes it possible to combine Python with other software that are released under the GPL. As of July 2019, the most current version of Python is 3.7.4. The official website of the software is https://www.python.org/.

PyCharm

PyCharm is one of the most popular Python IDEs. According to Taft (2010), PyCharm was developed by the Czech company JetBrains. It runs on Windows, Mac and Linux. As of July 2019, the most current version of PyCharm is 2019.1.3 and it was released on May 29th, 2019.

The basic text editor for Python is called IDLE (Integrated DeveLopment Environment) which provides limited support in code editing. PyCharm organizes files by projects and provides a user interface that can be modified with high flexibility. Figure 8 shows the working user interface of PyCharm. The

Table 3. Preprogramed statistical functions in Jamovi (Version 1.0.0)

Toolbar Options	Functions
Exploration	• Descriptives
T-Tests	• Independent Samples T-Test • Paired Samples T-Test • One Sample T-Test
ANOVA	• One-Way ANOVA • ANOVA • Repeated Measures ANOVA • ANCOVA • MANCOVA
	Non-Parametric: • One-Way ANOVA (Kruskal-Wallis) • Repeated Measures ANOVA (Friedman)
Regression	• Correlation Matrix • Linear Regression
	Logistic Regression: • 2 Outcomes (Binomial) • N Outcomes (Multinomial) • Ordinal Outcomes
Frequencies	One Sample Proportion Tests: • 2 Outcomes (Binomial test) • N Outcomes (χ^2 Goodness of fit)
	Contingency Tables: • Independent Samples (χ^2 test of association) • Paired Samples (McNemar test)
	• Log-Linear Regression
Factor	Scale Analysis: • Reliability Analysis
	Data Reduction: • Principal Component Analysis • Exploratory Factor Analysis • Confirmatory Factor Analysis

default user interface theme is called Darcula and it has dark background. Author changed the theme to IntelliJ, which has a bright background, to enhance contrast.

Spyder

Spyder is a Python IDE that designed for researchers, scholars, data analyst, engineers and etc. It provides a strong support for data analysis tasks with its built-in integration of many popular scientific packages, such as NumPy, SciPy, Pandas, IPython and more. Spyder runs on Windows, Mac and Linux. Spyder is included in Anaconda, and it is pre-installed in Anaconda Navigator. Anaconda is not an IDE, but a python distribution. Figure 9 shows the Anaconda Navigator that has linked multiple applications, including JupyterLab, Jupyter Notebook, Qt Console, Spyder, Glueviz, Orange 3, RStudio, VS Code and more.

Figure 7. Example of Jamovi statistical analysis (Designed by Wu, 2019)

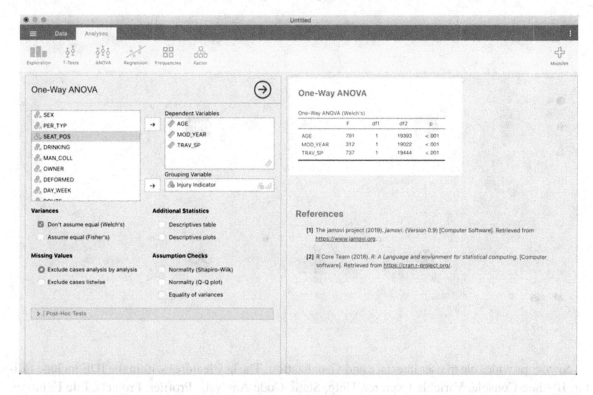

Figure 8. PyCharm working user interface (Designed by Niu, 2019)

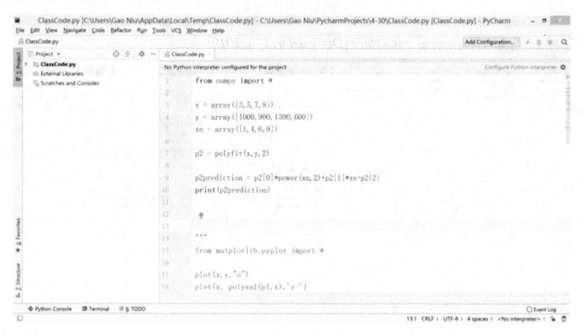

Figure 9. Anaconda working user interface (Designed by Niu, 2019)

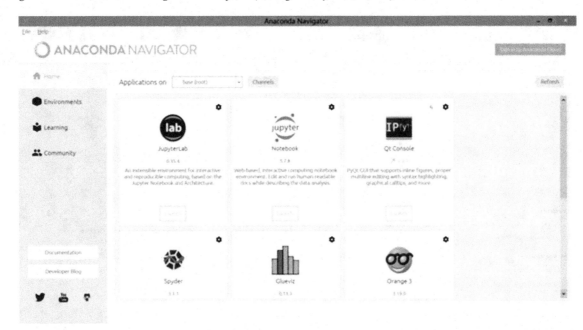

Spyder provides clean user interface and visualization. The key features within the IDE include Editor, IPython Console, Variable Explorer, Help, Static Code Analysis, Profiler, Projects, File Explorer, Find in Files, Online Help, History Log, Internal Console and etc. Figure 10 shows the working user interface of Spyder.

Figure 10. Spyder working user interface (Designed by Niu, 2019)

Jupyter

Project Jupyter is a non-profit organization that "exists to develop open-source software, open standard, and services for interactive computing across dozens of programming languages." (Jupyter, 2019). The two main platforms JupyterLab and Jupyter Notebook are both web-based applications. Jupyter Notebook was evolved from IPython, and was created by Perez (2014).

Figure 11 shows the Jupyter Notebook sample code runs on Google Chrome. Codes are executed and graphs are demonstrated underneath the code.

Figure 11. Example of Jupyter notebook (Designed by Niu, 2019)

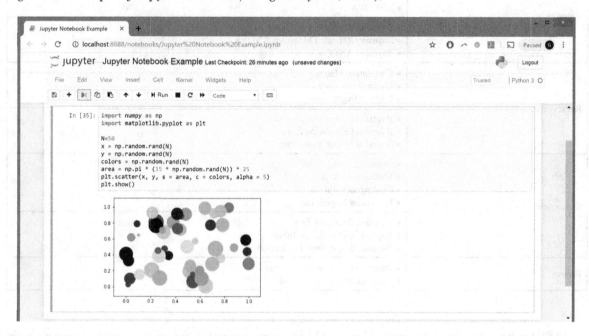

JASP

JASP is free and open source statistical analysis, image process software. The most recent version of JASP is 0.9.2 published on December 10th, 2018. It can be operated on Windows, MacOS X, and Linux. The programming languages used to develop this software are C++, R, and JavaScript. It can be considered as an open source version of SPSS. It is user friendly, and can be used interchangeably with SPSS. In the welcome page, JASP claims that it "aims to be a complete and full featured alternative to SPSS". The license is GNU Affero General Public License. JASP is developed and funded by several universities and research funds. The office website is https://jasp-stats.org/

JASP specializes and supports Bayesian statistical analysis and frequencies inference. For the Bayesian analysis, the software uses prior observations to estimate the posterior estimations and make inferences. The software has user-friendly Bayesian t-tests, Bayesian correlation analysis, Bayesian Linear Regression and more. The software produces APA format graphs, which can be used widely in academic publications. Table 4 lists out the preprogrammed functions when JASP is installed.

Table 4. Preprogramed statistical functions in JASP (Version 0.9.2)

Toolbar Options	Functions
Descriptives	• Descriptive Statistics • Reliability Analysis
T-Tests	• Independent Samples T-Test • Paired Samples T-Test • One Sample T-Test
	• Bayesian Independent Samples T-Test • Bayesian Paired Samples T-Test • Bayesian One Sample T-Test
ANOVA	• ANOVA • Repeated Measures ANOVA • ANCOVA
	• Bayesian ANOVA • Bayesian Repeated Measures ANOVA • Bayesian ANCOVA
Regression	• Correlation Matrix • Linear Regression • Logistic Regression
	• Bayesian Correlation Matrix • Bayesian Correlation Pairs • Bayesian Linear Regression
Frequencies	• Binomial Test • Multinomial Test • Contingency Tables • Log-linear Regression
	• Bayesian Binomial Test • Bayesian Contingency Tables • Bayesian Log-Linear Regression
Factors	• Principal Component Analysis • Exploratory Factor Analysis

JASP has a balanced user interface. Users could perform descriptive, frequency, and Bayesian analysis directly by selecting statistical assumptions, as mentioned by Wagenmakers, et al., (2018) and Love, et al., (2015). The results will be calculated and displayed on the right-hand side window automatically. Figure 12 is a screenshot after importing data to JASP.

As an example, figure 13 shows the operating platform of a Bayesian Correlation Matrix calculation from regression tab.

PSPP

PSPP was published in 1998, and was written in C. As of June 2019, the most current version of the software was published on October 6th, 2018, the version number is 1.2.0. It is also a replacement software for SPSS. One important advantage of selecting PSPP is that the free version of the software already includes variety of advanced statistical packages. The official website of the software is https://www.gnu.org/software/pspp/

Figure 12. JASP working user interface (Designed by Zhao, 2019)

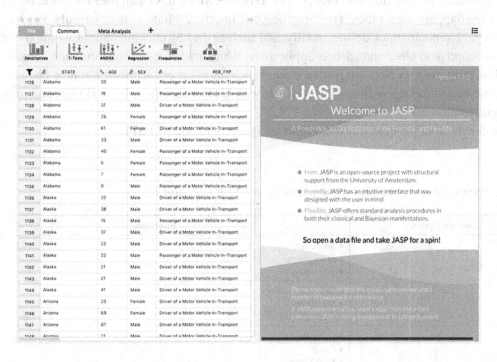

Figure 13. Example of JASP statistical analysis (Designed by Zhao, 2019)

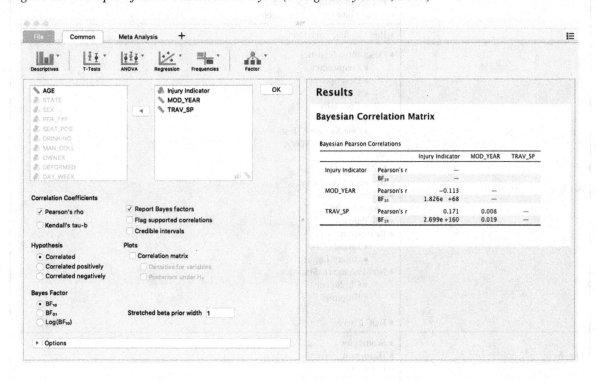

The software has three different modes. The Terminal Mode has clean user interface, no additional windows overlapping each other. The Graphic User Interface Mode is user-friendly and has limited syntax usage. Users can input, define, modify, and analyze data by clicking options within the interface. Also, it is adaptive to other spreadsheet applications which makes data transformation across software easily. The third mode is Non-Interactive mode which allows users access the source code directly. It has flexible output format, such as Unicode Text with UTF-8 encoding, PDF, HTML and more (GNU PSPP Screenshots, 2018).

Table 5 lists all of the core statistical functions preprogramed by PSPP.

Table 5. Preprogramed core statistical functions in PSPP (Version 1.2.0)

Toolbar Option	Functions
Data	• Sort Cases • Transpose • Aggregate
	• Split File • Select Cases • Weight Cases
Transform	• Compute • Count • Rank Cases • Automatic Recode
	• Recode into Same Variables • Recode into Different Variables
	• Run Pending Transforms

Analyze	• Descriptive Statistics
	  • Frequencies
	  • Descriptive
	  • Explore
	  • Crosstabs
	• Compare Means
	  • One Sample T Test
	  • One Way ANOVA
	  …
	• Univariate Analysis
	• Bivariate Correlation
	• K-Means Cluster
	• Factor Analysis
	• Reliability
	• Regression
	  • Linear
	  • Binary Logistic
	• Non-Parametric Statistics
	  • Chi Square
	  • Binomial
	  …
	• ROC Curve

Graphs	• Scatterplot • Histogram • Barchart
Utilities	• Variables • Data File Comments

PSPP user interface includes traditional options, such as file, edit, view, window, and help, which provide practitioners commonly used functions to input, output data and modify platform appearances. In addition, PSPP also has data, transform, analyze, graphs, and utilities as its core data analysis functions. Data function allows users to modify data and data file directly, such as sort cases and split files. Transform function allows user perform calculation and modification on the data in various levels. For example, the compute function under transform allows users to calculate the sum of two variables. Analyze function includes the core preprogramed statistical analysis, such as descriptive analysis, cluster analysis, regression etc. Current version of preprogramed SPSS also produces limited but high-quality graphs, such as Scatterplot, Histogram, and Barchart. Figure 14 and Figure 15 show sample descriptive statistical analysis and graphs in PSPP.

Figure 14. PSPP Sample descriptive statistical analysis (Designed by Wu, 2019)

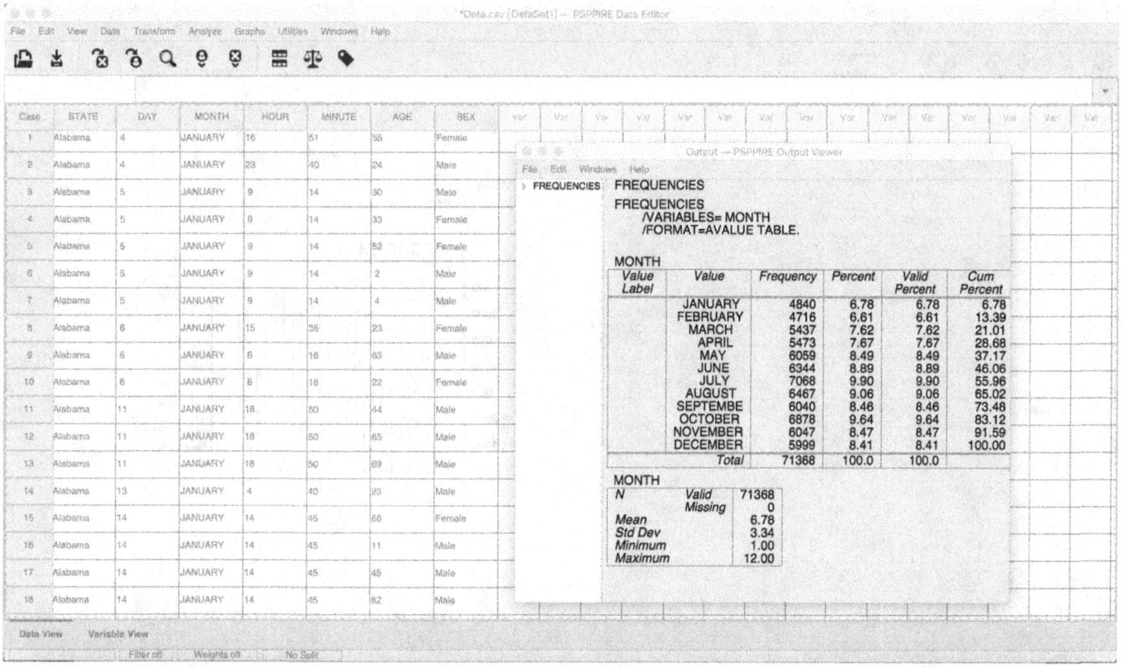

GRETL (GNU REGRESSION, ECONOMETRICS, AND TIME-SERIES LIBRARY)

GRETL is short for GNU Regression, Econometrics and Time-series Library. It is an open source statistical resource package and mainly serves the field of econometrics. GRETL has been reviewed multiple times by Journal of Applied Econometrics, such as Baiocchi and Distaso (2003), Yalta and Yalta (2007) and Mixon and Smith (2006). The earliest version of the software was published on January 31st, 2000. As of June 2019, the most current version is 2019b, which was published on May 21st, 2019. It was written in C language. GRETL has GUI (graphical user interface) and command-line interface. It is adaptive to multiple operating systems, such as Windows, MacOS, and Linux. There are multiple language environments available, such as English, Chinese, French, German and etc. GRETL's GNU license is GPLv3. The office website: gretl.sourceforge.net

GRETL's native scripting language is hansi. Its add-ons (packages) also needs to be written by hansi. However, the software is adaptive and able to work together with other statistical software including R, Python, Stata, and Julia.

In addition to GRETL's own data format XML, own binary databases (allowing mixed data frequencies and series lengths). It also supports the most popular data format, such as CSV, Excel, Stata. dta files, SPSS.sav files and etc. GRETL is adaptive and able to exchange data and results with other popular statistical software, such as R, Octave, Python and Stata. GRETL's output is in the format of LaTex (GNU Regression, Econometrics and Time-series Library, 2019).

Figure 15. PSPP sample graphs (Designed by Wu, 2019)

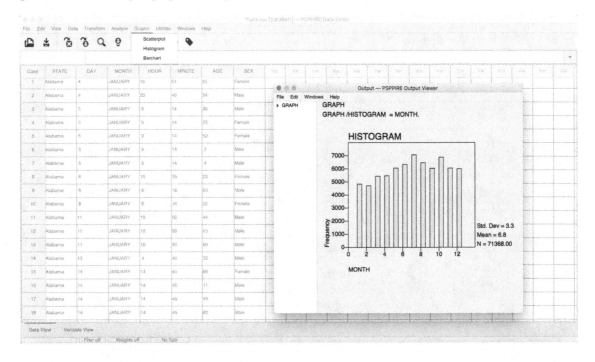

Figure 16 shows the working environment of GRETL. The left window is the working platform. Authors demonstrates an Ordinary least Squared (OLS) model on the right. The upright window is the graphical user interface allows variable selection. Bottom-right window is the output in LaTex format. For the OLS model, the output includes statistical summary as well as various residual plots, fitted plots, actual plots, and residual Q-Q plots.

GRETL user interface includes traditional options including file, data, view, and help. In addition, GRETL has Tools, Sample, Variable and Models as its core data analysis functions selected from its top tool bar. Table 6 lists out predefined functions which include popular and powerful quick statistical options, such as calculator, function packages, X-Y graph, OLS model, database and etc.

Figure 16. GRETL working user interface (Designed by Zhao, 2019)

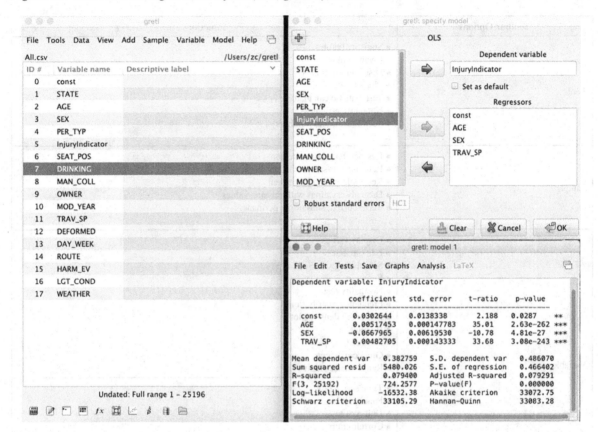

SOFA (STATISTICS OPEN FOR ALL) STATISTICS

SOFA statistics is an Open Source Statistical Software. It is short for Statistics Open for All. SOFA can produce many well-designed graphs for presentation. It can also perform basic statistical analysis and used on multiple operating systems including Windows, MacOS, and Linux. As of June 2019, the most current version of the software was published on May 19th, 2019, the version number is 1.5.1. The major feature of SOFA statistics is its user-friendly interface, which could connect to the commonly used database directly, such as MySQL, MS Access (mdb), Microsoft SQL Server etc (SOFA Statistics, 2019). It also has several other easy-to-use features, such as direct data entry, spreadsheet management, and graph share functions. The office website of the software is https://www.sofastatistics.com/home.php

Figure 17 shows the working user interface of SOFA.

The statistical analysis is limited in SOFA. They are under the tab of Statistics from the bottom left main user interface. Table 7 lists out all the core statistical functions predefined in SOFA.

Figure 18 shows the screenshot of graphic design user interface under the tab of Charts from the second to the bottom left main user interface.

Table 6. Preprogramed core statistical functions in GRETL (Version 2019b)

Toolbar Options	Functions
Tools	• Statistical tables • P-value finder • Distribution graphs • Plot a curve • Test statistic calculator • Nonparametric tests • Seed for random numbers …
Sample	• Restrict, based on criterion • Random sub-sample • Resample with replacement • Drop observations with missing values • Make current subsample permanent …
Variable	• Display values • Edit attributes • Set missing value code • Summary statistics • Normality test • Frequency distribution • Estimated density plot • Boxplot • Normal Q-Q plot • Gini coefficient • Range-mean graph
	• Time series plot • Panel plot • Unit root tests • Correlogram • Periodogram • Filter • X-12-ARIMA analysis • TRAMO analysis • Hurst exponent
Models	• Ordinary Least Squares • Instrumental variables • Other linear models • Limited dependent variable • Time series • Panel • Robust estimation • Nonlinear Least Squares • Maximum likelihood • GMM • Simultaneous equations

SOFA statistics preprograms eight types of charts. Its Graphical User Interface makes the graphical design process user-friendly. The graphs are featured by its professional design and color choice. It is adaptive to most presentation platforms and can be directly and easily implemented. Table 8 lists out all of the predesigned charts in SOFA. Figure 19 to Figure 26 show eight graphical examples generated from SOFA.

Figure 17. SOFA working user interface (Designed by Wu, 2019)

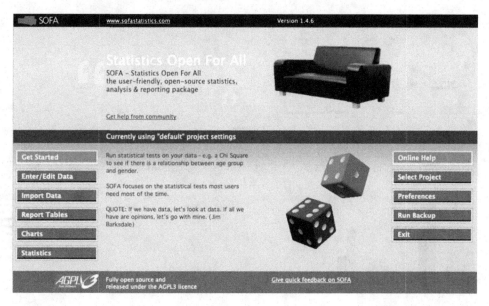

Table 7. Preprogramed core statistical functions in SOFA (Version 1.4.6)

ANOVA
Chi Square
Correlation – Pearson's
Correlation –Spearman's
Kruskal – Wallis H
Mann-Whitney U
t-test – independent
t-test – paired
Wilcoxon Signed Ranks

OCTAVE

Octave is a Free and Open Source Software (FOSS), which is designed for intensive numerical computation. It is used to model linear and nonlinear data. Octave has efficient matrix calculation algorithm (GNU Octave, 2019). Miao (2017) discussed that Octave is widely used in engineer and academic researches. For example, NASA used Octave to develop the flying object connecting system. Octave is very flexible in numerical programming and provides user-friendly visualization solutions. Octave was first published in 1988. As of June 2019, the most current version of the software was published on February 23rd, 2019, the version number is 5.1. Octave was written in C programming language, C++ and Fortran. It is adaptive to Windows, MacOS, Linux, and BSD (GNU Octave, 2019). The Octave's GNU license is GPLv3. There are multiple language environments available, such as English, Spanish, Chinese, French and etc. The official website of Octave is https://www.gnu.org/software/octave/.

Figure 18. SOFA graphic design user interface (Designed by Wu, 2019)

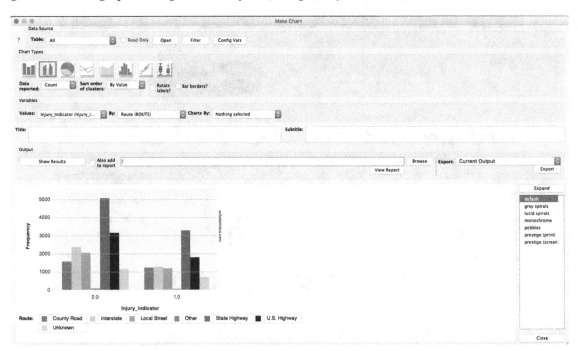

Table 8. Predesigned charts in SOFA (Version 1.4.6)

Bar Chart
Clustered Bar Chart
Pie Chart
Area Chart
Histogram
Scatterplot
Box and Whisker Plot
Line Chart

Octave can be considered as an open source version of MATLAB, many functions available in MATLAB can also be executed directly in Octave. However, there are some subtle syntax between Octave and MATLAB. Octave also has ample free packages can be downloaded from Octave Forge. Octave has community packages and external packages. Community packages are designed and maintained by Octave Forge and Octave Developers. External packages are developed by a third party which fulfill the requirements for hosting at Octave (Octave Forge, 2019). Table 9 lists out the community and external Octave packages.

Octave is a programming statistical software which does not have a graphical user interface. Figure 27 shows a screenshot of the working interface of Octave.

Figure 19. Bar chart example from SOFA (Designed by Wu, 2019)

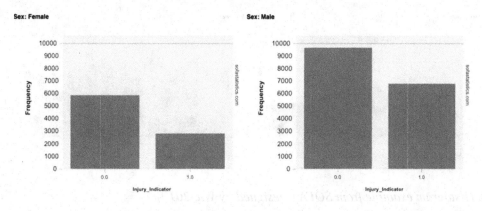

Figure 20. Clustered bar chart example from SOFA (Designed by Wu, 2019)

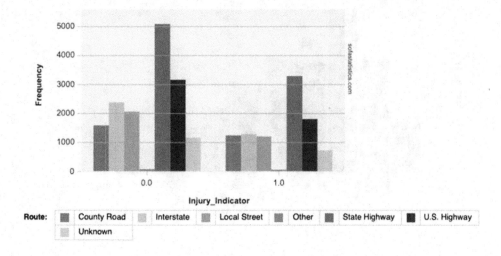

Figure 21. Pie chart example from SOFA (Designed by Wu, 2019)

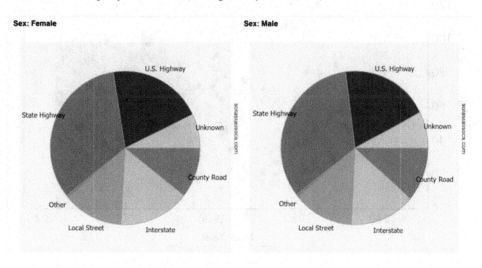

Figure 22. Area chart example from SOFA (Designed by Wu, 2019)

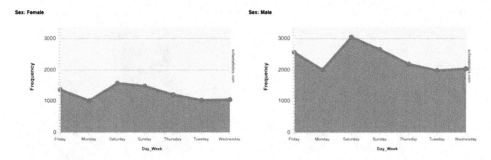

Figure 23. Histogram example from SOFA (Designed by Wu, 2019)

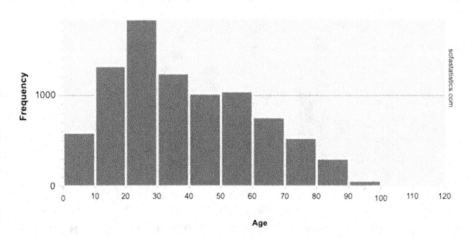

Figure 24. Scatterplot Example from SOFA (Designed by Wu, 2019)

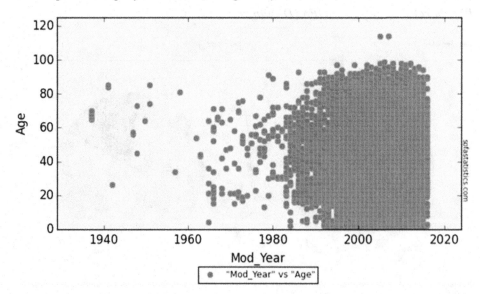

Figure 25. Box and Whisker Plot Example from SOFA (Designed by Wu, 2019)

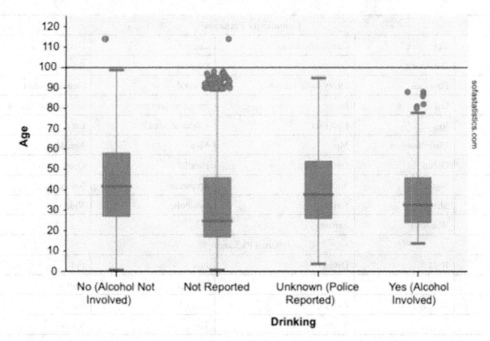

Figure 26. Line Chart Example from SOFA (Designed by Wu, 2019)

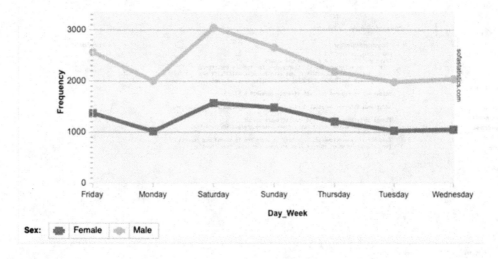

Octave has multiple features. Basic mathematical operators, including sin, cos, tan, exp, log, and floor, can be performed. Octave is an interpreted programming language. Similar to C++ and Java, Octave can be used to define and redefine variables. Traditional mathematical algorithms such as inverse, transpose can be operated on arrays, vectors and matrixes. Although Octave focuses on data operation, it can also be connected to graphing software, for example, GUNPLOT, to generate graphs in multiple dimensions and make comparisons for variable sensitivity tests.

Table 9. Community and external Octave packages

Community Packages				
Arduino	Cgi	Communications	Control	Data-smoothing
Database	Dataframe	Dicom	Doctest	Econometrics
Fem-fenics	Financial	Fuzzy-logic-toolkit	General	Generate_html
Geometry	Gsl	Image	Image-acquisition	Instrument-control
Interval	Io	Level-set	Linear-algebra	Lssa
Mapping	Miscellaneous	Mpi	Mvn	Netcdf
Optics	Optim	Optiminterp	Parallel	Quaternion
Queueing	Signal	Sockets	Sparsersb	Splines
Statistics	Strings	Struct	Symbolic	Video
Vrml	Windows	Zeromq		
External Packages				
Bim	Bsltl	Divand	Fits	Fpl
Ltfat	Msh	Nan	Ncarray	Nurbs
Ocs	Octclip	Octproj	Secs1d	Secs2d
Secs3d	Stk	Tisean	Tsa	Vibes

Figure 27. Octave working user interface (Designed by Zhao, 2019)

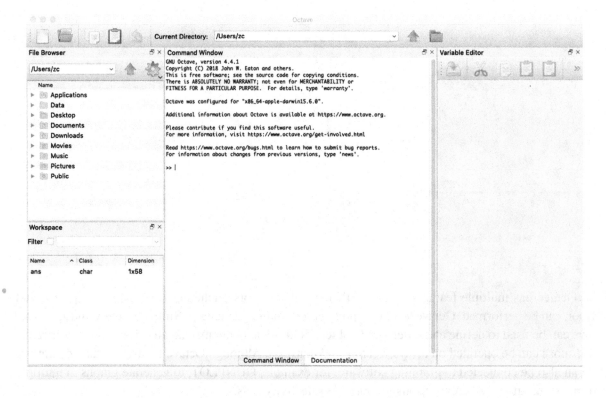

KNIME (KONSTANZ INFORMATION MINER)

KNIME, also called Konstanz Information Miner (Berthold, et al., 2008), is a free open source software for data processing, statistical analysis, and report generation. It was developed by a team of engineers from the University of Konstanz (German) in 2004 (End to End Data Science, 2019). As of June 2019, the most current version is 3.7.2, which was published on April 18th, 2019. The software was written in Java, and it can be operated on Windows, MacOS, and Linux. KNIME is licensed under GNU General Public License. Its official website is https://www.knime.com/.

Tiwari & Sekhar (2007) indicated in 2006, KNIME was introduced to the pharmaceutical research, and it also started rapidly gaining its popularity in business and financial area. Sieb, Meinl, & Berthold (2007) noted that KNIME's data mining and machine learning process are through data pipelining. Users can explicitly make variable selection, executive specific analysis, and validate the results. The software has a well-designed Graphical User Interface, which allows for direct data input, variable transformation, graphical design selection and statistical analysis. The software includes more than 2000 modules, which is called "nodes" in KNIME, for workflow construction. KNIME is considered as the open source version of its proprietary counterpart SAS.

KNIME's GUI allows users to select data source, process data through nodes (modules) and then get the result directly. The adaptive input and output data format include xls, csv, doc, ppt, and pdf.

Figure 28 shows a screenshot of KNIME's user interface once the software has been downloaded and installed. The left bottom window is called Node Repository, which has most of its core data input, process and statistical analysis functions. The bottom right window is the console, which describes the working process of the project.

Figure 28. KNIME working user interface (Designed by Zhao, 2019)

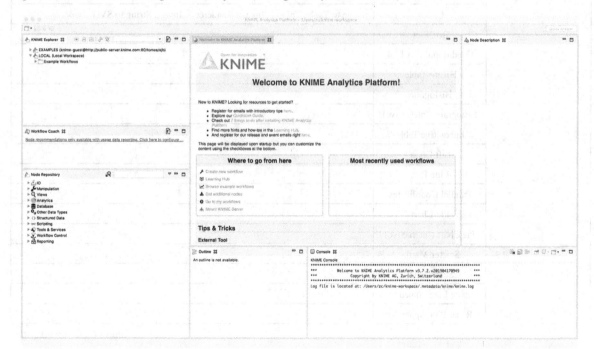

Table 10 lists out detailed functions within node repository in KNIME.

Table 10. Functions within node repository in KNIME (Version 3.7.2)

Major Categories	Subcategories	Nodes
IO	Read	Excel, File, ARFF, CSV, Line, Table, PMML, Model, Fixed Width File, List, Excel Sheet Names, Image, Explorer Brower
	Write	CSV, ARFF, Table, PMML, Model, Image Port, Image Column, Excel Sheet Appender, Excel Writer, Explorer Writer
	Other	Table Creator, Data Generator, Create Table Structure, Create Temp Dir, Send Email, Extract System Properties, Extract Context Properties
	File Handling	Binary Objects, Remote, URI, Zip, Copy/Move Files, File Meta Info, Find MME-Type, List MME-Types
	Cache	
Manipulation	Column	Binning, Covert & Replace, Filter, Split & Combine, Transform, Interactive HiLite Collector, Table Validator, Table Validator (Reference)
	Row	Filter, Transform, Other
	Table	Extract Table Dimension, Extract Table Spec, Transpose
	PMML	Column Filter, Denormalizer, Many to One, Normalizer, Normalizer Apply, Number to String, Numeric Binner, One to Many, Ruleset Editor, Ruleset Predictor, Ruleset to Table, String to Number, XML to PMML, Cell to PMML, PMML to Cell
Views	JavaScript	Table View, Scatter Plot, Line Plot, Lift Chart, ROC Curve, Decision Tree View, Generic JavaScript View, CSS Editor, Tag Cloud, Bar Chart, Box Plot, Conditional Box Plot, Histogram, Parallel Coordinates Plot, Pie/Donut Chart, Stacked Area Chart, Sunburst Chart
	Property	Color Manager, Size Manager, Shaper Manager, Color Appender, Size Appender, Shape Appender, Extract Color
	Utility	Image to Table, Table to Image, Renderer to Image, String to SVG
	Box Plot	
	Conditional Box Plot	
	HiLite Table	
	Histogram	
	Histogram (Interactive)	
	Interactive Table	
	Lift Chart	
	Line Plot	
	Parallel Coordinates	
	Pie Chart	
	Pie Chart (Interactive)	
	Scatter Matrix	
	Scatter Plot	
	Spark Line Appender	
	Radar Plot Appender	

continues on following page

Table 10. Continued

Major Categories	Subcategories		Nodes
Analytics	Mining	Bayes	Naïve Bayes Learner, Naïve Bayes Predictor
		Clustering	Cluster Assigner, DBSCAN, Naïve Bayes Predictor, Fuzzy c-Means, Hierarchical Clustering, SOTA Learner, SOTA Predictor, k-Means, k-Medoids, Hierarchical Clustering (DistMatrix), Hierarchical Cluster View, Hierarchical Cluster Assigner
		Rule Induction	Fuzzy Rules
		Neural Network	MLP, PNN
		Decision Tree	Decision Tree Learner, Decision Tree Predictor, Decision Tree to Image, Decision Tree to Ruleset, PMML Simple Regression Tree Predictor, Simple Regression Tree Learner, Simple Regression Tree Predictor, Simple Regression Tree to PMML
		Decision Tree Ensemble	Gradient Boosting, Random Forest
		Misc Classifiers	K Nearest Neighbor, K Nearest Neighbor (Distance Function)
		Ensemble Learning	PMML, Meta Nodes, Boosting Learner Loop End, Boosting Learner Loop Start, Boosting Predictor Loop End, Boosting Predictor Loop Start, Call to Model, Model Loop End, Model Loop Start, Model to Cell, Prediction Fusion, Voting Loop End
		Item Sets/ Association Rules	Association Rule Learner, Create Bit Vector, Subset Matcher
		Linear/Polynomial Regression	Linear Regression Learner, Polynomial Regression Learner, Regression Predictor
		Logistic Regression	Logistic Regression Learner, Logistic Regression Predictor
		MDS	MDS, MDS (DisMatrix), MDS Prediction, MDS Prediction (DisMatrix)
		PCA	PCA, PCA Compute, PCA Apply, PCA Inversion
		PMML	PMML Predictor
		SVM	SVM Learner, SVM Predictor
		Feature Selection	Meta Nodes, Feature Selection Loop Start (1:1), Feature Selection Loop Start (2:2), Feature Selection Loop End, Feature Selection Filter, Linear Correlation, Correlation Filter, Low Variance Filter
		Scoring	Cross Validation, Meta Nodes, Scorer, Numeric Scorer, Entropy Scorer, ROC Curve, Enrichment Plotter
	Statistics		Hypothesis Testing, Cronbach Alpha, Standardized Cronbach Alpha, Rank Correlation, Statistics, Crosstab, Value Counter, Linear Correlation, Numeric Outliers, Numeric Outliers (Apply)
	Distance Calculation		Distance Functions, Distance Matrix

continues on following page

Table 10. Continued

Major Categories	Subcategories	Nodes
Database	Read/Write	Database Reader, Database Table Connector, Database Connection Table Reader, Database Connection Table Writer, Database Looping, Parameterized Database Query, Database Table Selector, Database Writer, Database Update, Database Delete
	Connector	Database Connector, H2 Connector, Microsoft SQL Server Connector, MySQL Connector, PostgreSQL Connector, SQLite Connector, Vertica Connector
	Manipulation	Database Apply-Binner, Database Auto-Binner, Database Column Rename, Database Numeric-Binner, Database Pivot, Database Row Filter, Database Query, Database Column Filter, Databse Sorter, Database GroupBy, database Joiner, Database Table Creator, Database Sampling
	Utility	Database Drop Table, Database SQL Executor, SQL Extract, SQL Inject
Other Data Types	Time Series	Manipulate, Transform, Smoothing, Meta Nodes, Time Series (legacy)
Structured Data	JSON	Container Input (JSON), Container Output (JSON), JSON Reader, JSON Writer, String to JSON, Table to JSON, JSON to Table, Columns to JSON, XML to JSON, JSON to XML, JSON Path, JSON Path (Dictionary), JSON Column Combiner, JSON Row Combiner, JSON Row Combiner and Writer, JSON Transformer, JSON Schema Validator, JSON Diff
	XML	XML Reader, XML Writer, String To XML, XPath, XSLT, Column To XML, XML Column Combiner, XML Row Combiner, XML Row Combine and Write
Scripting	Java	Java Snippet, Java Snippet (Simple), Java Snippet Row Filter, Java Snippet Row Splitter
Tools & Services	Rest Web Services	GET Request, POST Request, PUT Request, DELETE Request
Workflow Control	Automation	Call Local Workflow (Row Based), Call Remote Workflow (Row Based), Call Workflow (Table Based), Container Input (Credentials), Container Input (Table), Container Input (Variable), Container Output (Table), Wait…, Save Workflow, Timer Info, Global Timer Info
	Quick Forms	Input, Selection, Filter, Output
	Variables	Create File Name, Inject Variables (Data), Inject Variables (Database), Extract Variables (Data), Extract Variables (Database), Table Column to Variable, Table Row to Variable, Variable to Table Column, Variable to Table Row, Java Edit Variable, Java Edit Variable (Simple), Math Formula (Variable), Merge Variables, Rule Engine Variable, Rule Engine Variable (Dictionary), String Manipulation (Variable)
	Loop Support	Breakpoint, Counting Loop Start, Chunk Loop Start, Column List Loop Start, Generic Loop Start, Table Row To Variable Loop Start, Loop End, Variable Condition Loop End, Group Loop Start, Interval Loop Start, Loop End (2 ports), Loop End (Column Append), Recursive Loop End, Recursive Loop End (2 ports), Recursive Loop Start, Recursive Loop Start (2 ports), Variable Loop End
	Switch	If Switch, End IF, CASE Switch Data (Start), CASE Switch Data (End), CASE Switch Model (Start), CASE Switch Model (End), CASE Switch Variable (Start), CASE Switch Variable (End), Empty Table Switch, Java IF (Table)
	Error Handling	Catch Errors (DB Ports), Catch Errors (Data Ports), Catch Errors (Generic Ports), Catch Errors (Var Ports), Try (Data Ports), Try (Variable Ports), Active Branch Inverter
	Meta Nodes	Variables Loop (Data), Variables Loop (database), Iterate List of Files, Loop x-times
Reporting	Data to Report	
	Image to Report	

Users need to make selections within the node repository to manage the project. The selection can be simply executed by clicking the corresponding node and dragging the node into the middle top window to create a workflow structure. Figure 29 shows screenshot of a workflow structure example from a csv format dataset to four notes. The nodes are Box Plot, Scatter Plot, Rank Correlation and Linear Correlation. The three circles underneath each node represent the execution status. The first red circle represents that the node has not been executed. The second yellow circle represents that the node has been reset after execution. The third green circle represents that the node has been successfully executed.

Figure 29. Example of KNIME workflow structure (Designed by Zhao, 2019)

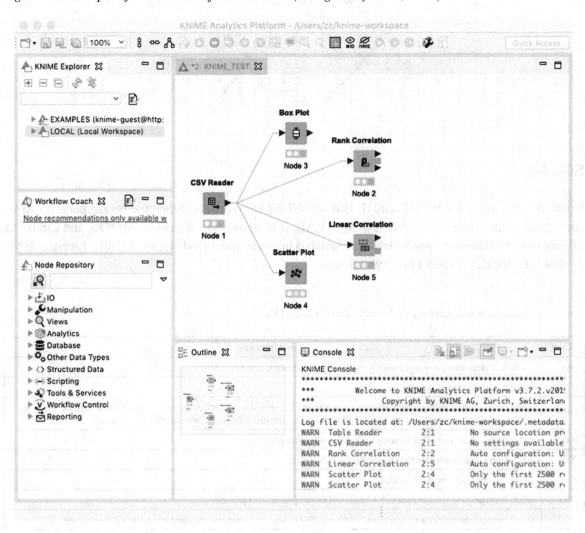

Upon successful execution of the workflow structure. Results could be generated on a separate window. Figure 30 shows a screenshot example that demonstrates the graphical output. The result includes a Box Plot, a Scatter Plot, and two correlation coefficient matrices.

Figure 30. Example of KNIME graphical output (Designed by Zhao, 2019)

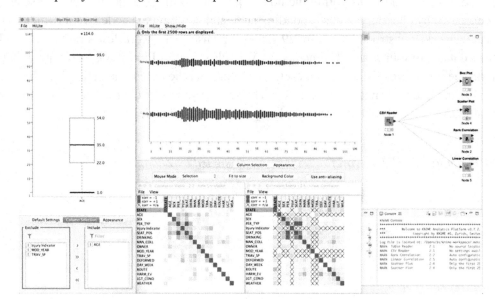

SCILAB

Scilab is a free open source software. It is designed for engineer and academic researchers. It can be considered as an open source version of MATLAB. It is adaptive to Windows, MacOS, and Linux. Its official website is https://www.Scilab.org/. Scilab is licensed under GNU General Public License. Table 11 describes the development history of Scilab.

Table 11. Development history of Scilab (History, 2019)

Time	Development
1980	Blaise was created and developed mainly by Francois Delebecque and Serge Steer.
1984	Blaise became Basile, distributed by Simlog
1990	Simlog stopped distributing Basile. Basile's name became Scilab and was then developed by Inria (French National Institute for Research in Computer Science and Control) startup. The updated software is freely distributed online
2003	Scilab Consortium: supported by companies and academic organizations
2008	Scilab Consortium integrates the Digiteo Research Network
2010	Scilab Enterprises Company Founded
2012	Scilab Enterprises in Charge of Scilab Edition and Development, also provides
2017	Scilab Enterprises operational team joins ESI Group, ESI Group is a world leading provider in Virtual Prototyping

The software has more than 1500 mathematical functions provided by math and simulation features (Scilab, 2019). Continuous and discrete mathematical optimization calculations can be executed through its advanced algorithms efficiently. Scilab also has strong statistical analysis and modeling capability. Scilab is featured by its 2-dimension and 3-dimension visualization functions.

Figure 31. Scilab working user interface (Designed by Wu, 2019)

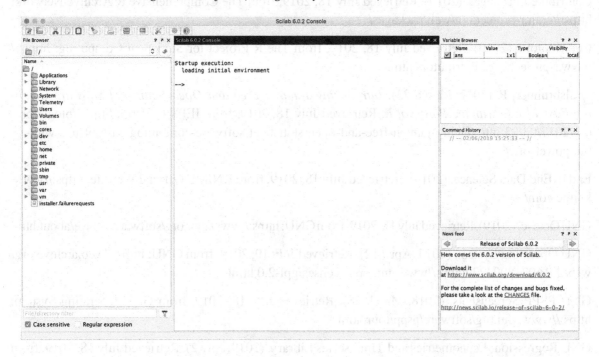

Scilab is driven by syntax, and most of its statistical and modeling work are processed through sophisticated codes. Figure 31 shows the Scilab user interface. Folder management window is on the left. The window in the middle is the console where the code is displayed and executed. And windows on the right show the variables information and command history.

CONCLUSION

This chapter introduces a list of popular Open Source Statistical Software with their functionalities, working user interfaces and selected practical data visualization examples. The software selected are up-to-date popular choices for programmers, statisticians, researchers and practitioners. It is served as a reference for readers to make open source software selections.

REFERENCES

Awesome R. (2019). Retrieved July 18, 2019, from Awesome R: https://awesome-r.com/

Baiocchi, G., & Distaso, W. (2003). GRETL: Econometric Software for the GNU Generation. *Journal of Applied Econometrics*, *18*(1), 105–110. doi:10.1002/jae.704

Berthold, M. R., Cebron, N., Dill, F., Gabriel, T. R., Kotter, T., Meinl, T., & Wiswedel, B. (2008). *KNIME: The Konstanz Information Miner. In Data Analysis, Machine Learning and Applications* (pp. 319–326). Freiburg: Springer. doi:10.1007/978-3-540-78246-9_38

Contributed Packages. (2019). Retrieved July 18, 2019, from The Comprehensive R Archive Network: https://cran.r-project.org/web/packages/

Contributors. (2019). Retrieved July 18, 2019, from The R Project for Statistical Computing: https://www.r-project.org/contributors.html

Edelsbrunner, P. (2017, March 23). *Introducing Jamovi: Free and Open Statistical Software Combing Ease of Use with the Power of R.* Retrieved July 18, 2019, from JEPS Bulletin: https://blog.efpsa.org/2017/03/23/introducing-jamovi-free-and-open-statistical-software-combining-ease-of-use-with-the-power-of-r/

End to End Data Science. (2019). Retrieved July 18, 2019, from KNIME Official Website: https://www.knime.com/

GNU Octave. (2019). Retrieved July 18, 2019, from GNU: https://www.gnu.org/software/octave/about.html

GNU Operating System. (2014, April 12). Retrieved July 19, 2019, from GNU: https://web.archive.org/web/20160718094739/http://www.gnu.org/licenses/gpl-2.0.html

GNU PSPP Screenshots. (2018, March 28). Retrieved July 18, 2019, from GNU Operating System: https://www.gnu.org/software/pspp/tour.html

GNU Regression, Econometrics and Time-series Library. (2019, July 2). Retrieved July 18, 2019, from GRETL Official Website: http://gretl.sourceforge.net/

History. (2019). Retrieved July 18, 2019, from Scilab Official Website: https://www.scilab.org/about/company/history

History and License. (2019). Retrieved July 18, 2019, from Python Official Website: https://docs.python.org/3/license.html

IDE for Data Science. (2019). Retrieved July 18, 2019, from Get Architect: https://www.getarchitect.io/

Jamovi. (2019). Retrieved July 18, 2019, from Jamovi Official Website: https://www.jamovi.org/

Jupyter. (2019). Retrieved July 18, 2019, from Jupyter Official Website: https://jupyter.org/

Lakens, D. (2017, March 14). *Equivalence testing in jamovi.* Retrieved July 18, 2019, from The 20% Statistician: http://daniellakens.blogspot.com/2017/03/equivalence-testing-in-jamovi.html

Love, J., Selker, R., Verhagen, J., Marsman, M., Gronau, Q. F., Jamil, T., . . . Rouder, J. N. (2015, March). Software to Sharpen Your Stats. *Association for Psychological Science Observer, 28*(3). Retrieved 7 18, 2019, from https://www.psychologicalscience.org/observer/bayes-or-bust-with-new-softwares

Miao, B. (2017, April 26). *Octave Introduction and Study.* Retrieved July 18, 2019, from CSDN: https://blog.csdn.net/imbenben/article/details/70768980

Mixon, J. W. Jr, & Smith, R. J. (2006). Teaching undergraduate econometrics with GRETL. *Journal of Applied Econometrics, 21*(7), 1103–1107. doi:10.1002/jae.927

Muenchen, B. (2018, February 13). *Jamovi for R: Easy but Controversial.* Retrieved July 18, 2019, from r4stats: https://r4stats.com/2018/02/13/jamovi-for-r-easy-but-controversial/

Octave Forge. (2019). Retrieved July 18, 2019, from Source Forge: https://octave.sourceforge.io/

Perez, F. (2014, July 8). *Project Jupyter*. Retrieved July 18, 2019, from Speakerdeck: https://speakerdeck.com/fperez/project-jupyter

RStudio. (2019). Retrieved July 18, 2019, from RStudio Official Website: https://www.rstudio.com/products/rstudio/

Scilab. (2019). Retrieved July 18, 2019, from Predictive Analytics Today: https://www.predictiveanalyticstoday.com/scilab/

Sieb, C., Meinl, T., & Berthold, M. R. (2007). Parallel and Distributed Data Pipelining with KNIME. *The Mediterranean Journal of Computers and Networks*, *3*(2), 43–51.

SOFA Statistics. (2019). Retrieved July 18, 2019, from Predictive Analytics Today: https://www.predictiveanalyticstoday.com/sofa-statistics/

St. Laurent, A. M. (2008). *Understanding Open Source and Free Software Licensing*. Sebastopol, CA: O'Reilly Media.

Taft, D. (2010, October 14). *JetBrains Strikes Python Developers with PyCharm 1.0 IDE*. Retrieved July 18, 2019, from eWeek: https://www.eweek.com/development/jetbrains-strikes-python-developers-with-pycharm-1.0-ide

Tiwari, A., & Sekhar, A. K. (2007, October). Workflow based framework for life science informatics. *Computational Biology and Chemistry*, *31*(5-6), 305–319. doi:10.1016/j.compbiolchem.2007.08.009 PMID:17931570

Wagenmakers, E.-J., Love, J., Marsman, M., Jamil, T., Ly, A., Verhagen, J., ... Morey, R. (2018, February). Bayesian inference for psychology. Part II: Example applications with JASP. *Psychonomic Bulletin & Review*, *25*(1), 58–76. doi:10.375813423-017-1323-7 PMID:28685272

What does JASP stand for? (2019). Retrieved July 20, 2019, from JASP Official Website: https://jasp-stats.org/faq/what-does-jasp-stand-for/

What is open source? (2019). Retrieved July 19, 2019, from Open Source: https://opensource.com/resources/what-open-source

Yalta, A., & Yalta, A. (2007). GRETL 1.6.0 and its numerical accuracy. *Journal of Applied Econometrics*, *22*(4), 849–854. doi:10.1002/jae.946

KEY TERMS AND DEFINITIONS

General Public License: A license that intended to provide freedom to share, study, modify software and guarantee the freedom for all its users (GNU Operating System, 2014).

Graphical User Interface (GUI): A user interface that allows users visually interact with computer through items such as window, buttons, menus.

GRETL: A cross-platform software package for econometric analysis, written in the C programming language. GRETL is short for GNU Regression, Econometrics and Time-series Library (GNU Regression, Econometrics, and Time-Series Library, 2019).

Integrated Development Environment (IDE): IDE a software application that supports programmers for software development.

KNIME: KNIME is short for Konstanz Information Miner (Berthold et al., 2008). It is a free open source software for data processing, statistical analysis, and report generation.

JASP: JASP is free and open source statistical software, image process software. JASP is considered as an open source version of SPSS. The software name stands for Jeffreys's Amazing Statistics Program (What does JASP stand for?, 2019).

Octave: Octave is a free and open source software, which is designed for intensive numerical computation. It is widely used in the field of engineer and academic research. Octave is considered as an open source version of MATLAB.

Open Source Software (OSS): Open source software is software that any users could share, study, inspect, modify and enhance (What is open source?, 2019).

PSPP: PSPP is a free and open source statistical software that includes various advanced statistical packages. PSPP is adaptive to many other spreadsheet applications which makes data transformation across software easily.

Python: Python is a programming language. It was created by Guido van Rossum and released in 1911. Python could be used for web development, software development, system scripting, statistical analysis and many others purposes.

R: R is a programming language and open source statistical software. It has a strong statistical analysis capability and graphical visualization functionality.

Scilab: Scilab is a free open source software. It is designed for engineer and academic researchers. Scilab is considered as an open source version of MATLAB.

SOFA Statistics: SOFA statistics is an open source statistical software. It is short for Statistics Open for All. SOFA can produce many well-designed graphs for presentation.

This research was previously published in Open Source Software for Statistical Analysis of Big Data; pages 73-110, copyright year 2020 by Engineering Science Reference (an imprint of IGI Global).

Chapter 41
What Is Open Source Software (OSS) and What Is Big Data?

Richard S. Segall
Arkansas State University, USA

ABSTRACT

This chapter discusses what Open Source Software is and its relationship to Big Data and how it differs from other types of software and its software development cycle. Open source software (OSS) is a type of computer software in which source code is released under a license in which the copyright holder grants users the rights to study, change, and distribute the software to anyone and for any purpose. Big Data are data sets that are so voluminous and complex that traditional data processing application software are inadequate to deal with them. Big data can be discrete or a continuous stream data and is accessible using many types of computing devices ranging from supercomputers and personal workstations to mobile devices and tablets. It is discussed how fog computing can be performed with cloud computing for visualization of Big Data. This chapter also presents a summary of additional web-based Big Data visualization software.

INTRODUCTION: HOW OPEN SOURCE SOFTWARE, FREE SOFTWARE, AND FREEWARE DIFFER

Open Source Software (OSS)

Open-Source Software (OSS) is a type of computer software in which source code is released under a license in which the copyright holder grants users the rights to study, change, and distribute the software to anyone and for any purpose. (Wikipedia (2019a))

For software to be considered "Open Source", it must meet ten conditions as defined by the Open Source Initiative (OSI). Of these ten conditions, it's the first three that are really at the core of Open Source and differentiates it from other software. These three conditions are according to the Open Source Initiative (2007):

DOI: 10.4018/978-1-7998-9158-1.ch041

1. **Free Redistribution**: The software can be freely given away or sold.
2. **Source Code**: The source code must either be included or freely obtainable.
3. **Derived Works**: Redistribution of modifications must be allowed.

The other conditions are: (Open Source Initiative (2007))

4. **Integrity of The Author's Source Code**: Licenses may require that modifications are redistributed only as patches.
5. **No Discrimination against Persons or Groups**: no one can be locked out.
6. **No Discrimination against Fields of Endeavor**: commercial users cannot be excluded.
7. **Distribution of License**: The rights attached to the program must apply to all to whom the program is redistributed without the need for execution of an additional license by those parties.
8. **License Must Not Be Specific to a Product**: the program cannot be licensed only as part of a larger distribution.
9. **License Must Not Restrict Other Software**: the license cannot insist that any other software it is distributed with must also be open source.
10. **License Must Be Technology**:Neutral: no click-wrap licenses or other medium-specific ways of accepting the license must be required.

Macaulay (2017) discussed benefits of open source software that are summarized in Figure 1 below.

Figure 1. Benefits of Open Source Software (OSS) (Derived from Macaulay (2017))

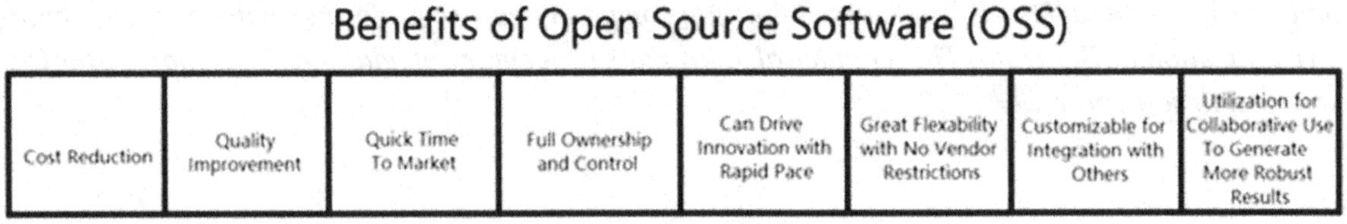

Benefits of Open Source Software (OSS)

Cost Reduction	Quality Improvement	Quick Time To Market	Full Ownership and Control	Can Drive Innovation with Rapid Pace	Great Flexability with No Vendor Restrictions	Customizable for Integration with Others	Utilization for Collaborative Use To Generate More Robust Results

Open Source License

According to Wikipedia (2019f) an open source license is a type of license for computer software and other products that allows the source code, blueprint or design to be used, modified and/or shared under defined terms and conditions. This allows end users and commercial companies to review and modify the source code, blueprint or design for their own customization, curiosity or troubleshooting needs.

Open-source licensed software is mostly available free of charge, though this does not necessarily have to be the case.

Licenses that only permit non-commercial redistribution or modification of the source code for personal use only are not considered generally as open source licenses.

Free Software or Freeware

Unlike the Open Source term, Free Software only has 4 "Freedoms" with its definition and are numbered 0-3 as created by the Free Software Foundation (FSF) (2019a) as follows:

The freedom to run the program for any purpose (Freedom 0)
The freedom to study how the program works and adapt it to your needs (Freedom 1)
The freedom of redistribution of software (Freedom 2)
The freedom to improve the program and release your improvements to the public to benefit the while community. (Freedom 3)

Although not explicitly outlined as a freedom, access to source code is implied with Freedoms 1 and 3. You need to have the source code in order to study or modify it. Figure 2 illustrates the relationship and overlap of these properties of Free Software with Open Source Software and was drawn using Drake (2019) discussion of the difference between free and open source software.

Figure 2. Comparisons of features of Open Source Software (OSS) versus Free Software

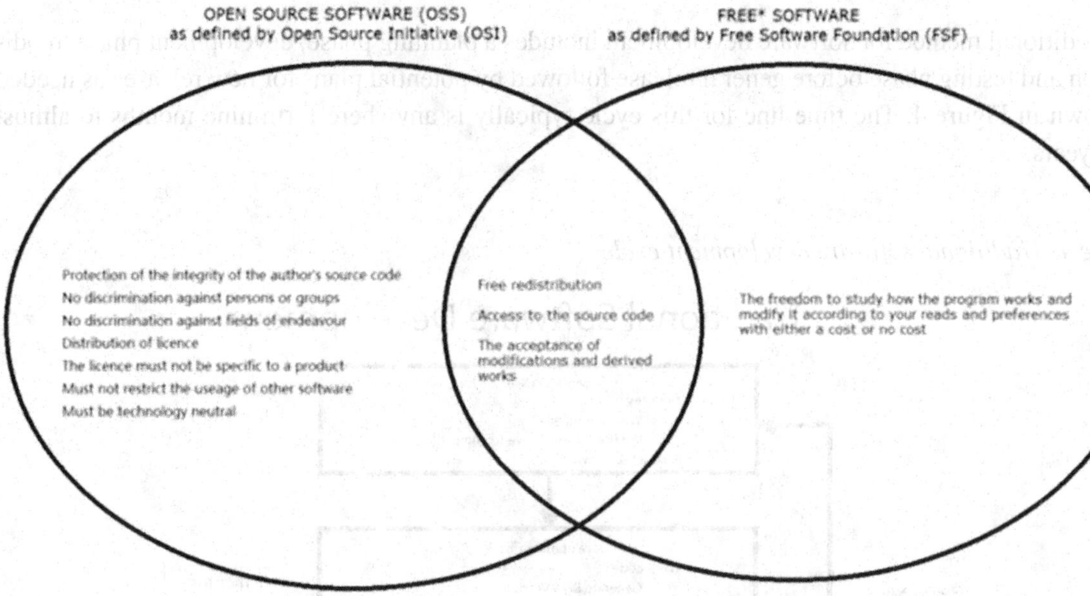

Figure 3 compares the features of freeware versus shareware that illustrates the later has fewer features than the former freeware.

Free Open Source Software (FOSS)

Not all software is free and Free Open Source Software (FOSS) is both free and open. The Free Software Foundation (FSS) (2019b) provides a searchable directory of over 15,000 free software packages.

Figure 3. Comparison of the features of Freeware and Shareware

Features of Freeware and Shareware	
Freeware	**Shareware**
No cost to acquire	Limited Free Trial Period
Normally shared with no source code	
Unable to modify	Probably Limited Features of Full Version
Not Proprietary Protected	

Free and open-source software (FOSS) is software that can be classified as both free software and open-source software. That is, anyone is freely licensed to use, copy, study, and change the software in any way, and the source code is openly shared so that people are encouraged to voluntarily improve the design of the software. This is in contrast to proprietary software, where the software is under restrictive copyright licensing and the source code is usually hidden from the users. (The Free Software Foundation (FSS) (2019b))

Open Source Software Development Versus Traditional Software Development

The traditional method for software development includes a planning phase, development phase, modification and testing phase before general release followed by potential plans for new releases as needed as shown in Figure 4. The time line for this cycle typically is anywhere form nine months to almost three years.

Figure 4. Traditional software development cycle

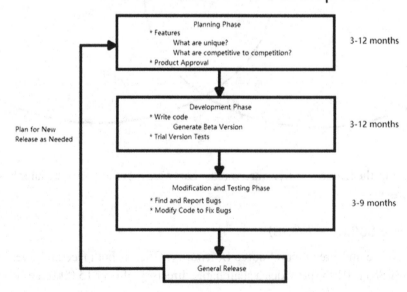

Saini & Kaur (2014) performed an extensive review of open source software development life cycle models, and Mandal et al. (2011) preformed open incremental model for an Open Source Software Development Life Cycle Model 'OSDLC'.

The Open Source Development Life Cycle (OSDLC) as discussed by Linux Foundation (2011), Haddan (2008), and Goldman & Gabriel (2005) entails multiple internal users/developers who each provide improvements to the Open Source Software (OSS) prior to its release to worldwide users/developers. These external users then subsequently provide an additionally enhanced source code for a new release version for potentially additionally improved source code upon feedback from both internal and external users. Figure 5 below illustrates the Open Source Development Cycle.

Figure 5. Open Source Software development cycle

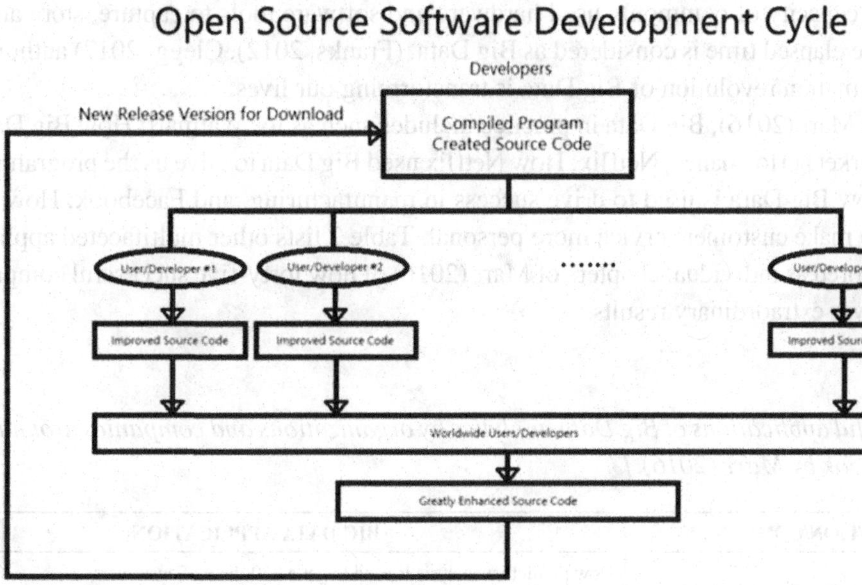

Freeman et al. (2018) discussed several of the best open source software for software development from which the following Table 1 was derived.

Table 1. Open Source Software for software development

Open Source Software Name	Features
Tuffle Framework	Suite of tools to help develop. test, and deploy smart contracts to the Ethereum blockchain.
Blockstack	Set of application development tools for building blockchain-based decentralized applications (dapps) on the Bitcoin blockchain.
Julia	High performance dynamic programming language for numerical computing.
Taucharts	Data-focused JavaScript charting library

INTRODUCTION: WHAT IS BIG DATA?

Big Data is defined as the collections of datasets whose volume, velocity or variety is so large that it is difficult to store, manage, process, and analyze the data using traditional databases and data processing tools. (Bahga & Madisetti, 2016) According to an estimate by IBM, 2.5 quintillion bytes of data is created every day, and that 90% of the data in the world today has been created in the last two years alone. (IBM, 2017)

In 2012, United States (US) government committed $200 million in "Big Data" research and development investment. (The White House, 2012) Big Data application is estimated worth $300 billion dollars for the US health care industry, and $250 billion euros for the Europe's public section administration. (Manyika, Chui, Brown, Bughin, Dobbs, & Roxburgh, 2011) So what is Big Data? The numerical definition of Big Data is evolving with the development of the technology. A dynamic definition is that data that exceeds the capacity of commonly used hardware and software tools to capture, store and analyze within a tolerable elapsed time is considered as Big Data. (Franks, 2012). Clegg (2017) authored a book on how the information revolution of Big Data is transforming our lives.

According to Marr (2016), Big Data in practice includes such as for Walmart: How Big Data is used to drive supermarket performance, Netflix: How Netflix used Big Data to Give us the programs we want, Rolls-Royce: How Big Data is used to drive success in manufacturing, and Facebook: How Facebook uses Big Data to make customer service more personal. Table 2 lists other multifaceted applications of Big Data as authored as individual chapters of Marr (2016) of how forty-five successful companies used Big Data to deliver extraordinary results.

Table 2. Successful applications of Big Data analytics by organizations and companies around the world [Derived from book by Marr (2016).]

ORGANIZATION/COMPANY	BIG DATA APPLICATION
Amazon	How predictive analysis is used to get a 360-view of customers
Caesar's	Big Data at the Casino
Dickey's Barbecue Pit	How Big Data is used to gain performance insights into one of America's most successful restaurant chains
Experian	Using Big Data to make lending decisions and to crack down on identify fraud.
Fitbit	Big Data in the fitness arena
John Deere	How Big Data can be applied on farms
LinkedIn	How Big Data is used to fuel social media success
Ralph Lauren	Big Data in the fashion industry
Tera Seismic	Using Big Data to predict earthquakes
Transport for London	How Big Data is used to improve and manage public transportation in London, UK.
Twitter	How Twitter is used and IBM deliver customer insights from Big Data
Uber	How Big Data is at the center of Uber's Transportation Business
US Olympic Women's Cycling Team	How Big Data Analytics is used to optimize athletes performance
Walt Disney Parks and Resorts	How Big Data is Transforming our Family Holidays
ZSL and London Zoo	Big Data in the zoo and to protect animals

Le (2016) discussed Big Data with machine learning algorithms such as those used by Netflix's to make movie suggestions based on movies you have watched in the past or Amazon's algorithms that recommend books based on books you have bought before. Opportunities and challenges of using machine learning algorithms for Big Data were studied by Zhou et al. (2017).

Previous research in Big Data was presented in Segall & Cook (2018), Segall (2016a) and in the context of supercomputing in Segall (2013), Segall & Cook (2014), Segall, Cook, & Zhang (2015), Segall & Gupta (2015), and Segall (2016b).

CHARACTERISTICS OF BIG DATA

The Big Data concept is formed due to the rapid development of computer technology. There is tremendous amount of data being generated and analyzed every day. The concept describes how this large amount data has been utilized to benefit the society. It is not just large amount data, instead, it is an ad-hoc definition of how the data is being collected, processed and distributed. There are some commonly accepted characteristics of Big Data, such as volume, velocity and variety. (Russom, 2011).

- Volume represents the size of the data. For example, number of observations, number of variables, number of files etc. Because most personal and working computers equipped with hard drives have memories with gigabyte (GB) level or terabyte (TB) capacity, the TB is considered as the minimum threshold of Big Data volume as of 2019. However, "big" as of today will not be "big" as of tomorrow as in Figure 6 due to the rapid growth of the data storage and processing technology.
- Velocity represents the speed or frequency of the data that has been generated and streamed into the database. Big Data often involves high velocity. For example, Facebook has more than 10 million photos uploaded every hour. (Mayer-Schönberger & Cukier, 2013)
- Variety represents the data coming from various sources and in various formats. Data is not collected by handwritten notebook anymore, it comes from social network, smart phones, trading platforms, machines and others. Browsing Facebook or driving a car that records driving behavior, contributes to the current generation of the Big Data. The data is also in different format such as continuous or discrete, longitudinal or time series, and different computer science or communication languages. The data could also be structured or unstructured. If the data is stored in various format such as dates, numbers and texts and has no predefined format, it is considered as unstructured data.

3V of Big Data is then extended into a 5V characteristics which includes value and veracity as shown in Figure 7 and discussed. (Ishwarappa & Anuradha, 2015).

- Value represents the data needing to have potential useful information for future study. It cost human and technology resources for companies and institutions to maintain a Big Data database. It cannot be considered as Big Data unless there is potential value from it.
- Veracity represents the accuracy of the data. It is almost impossible for all of the data to be 100% accurate when dealing with Big Data, but the accuracy level is still a critical aspect to check with. A data sources full with incorrect information will only mislead the conclusions drawn from the study.

Figure 6. Big data characteristics (Designed by Niu, November, 2017)

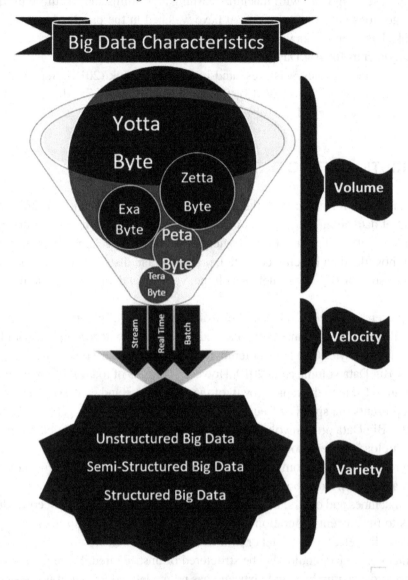

Streaming vs Real Time vs Batch

Streaming data is generated and delivered continuously, such as financial trading information, social network and geospatial service (GPS signals). Real time data has tight deadlines that result are guaranteed, such as TV signals are requested, processed and transmitted within time interval such as a minute. Batch data is collected and processed, then transmitted as a package to the client, it has higher latency tolerance.

Streaming and real time data processing consist of individual or micro batches of data with continues and high frequency of transmission between end-points and central data processor. But batch data transmission involves with large portfolio of data and normally involves with latencies in minutes or hours. Figure 8 illustrates a comparison of the generation of streaming, real time, and batch data.

Figure 7. 5V of Characteristics (Designed by Niu, November, 2017)

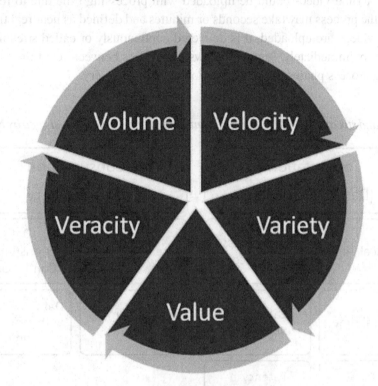

Figure 8. Streaming, real time and batch data comparison (Designed by Niu, March, 2018)

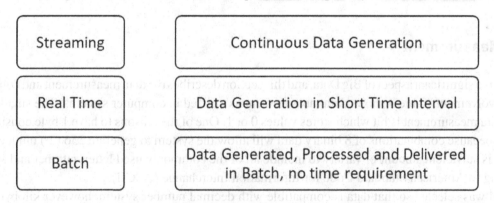

A more thorough description of streaming data is achieved by splitting the Big Data analysis into computation and consumption phases (Psaltis, 2017). The computation phase includes data collection and processing. And consumption phase includes data delivery to users such as clients, smart phone application or clouds. In data computation phase, data collection could be hard real-time systems (i.e. with absolute deadlines that must be met), soft real-time systems (i.e. need not meet absolute deadlines at all times) or near real-time systems (i.e. meeting deadlines within a time window). In consumption phase, data delivery could be streaming or non-streaming.

For example, YouTube videos could be uploaded with processing time due to regulation compliance process time, the process may take seconds or minutes and defined as near real time computation. However, once the videos are uploaded, it is delivered continuously or called streaming data, since it is delivered to viewers immediately. Figure 9 shows differences between real time and streaming data under different data process phases of data collection and data delivery.

Figure 9. Real time and streaming data under different data process phase (Designed by Niu, March, 2018)

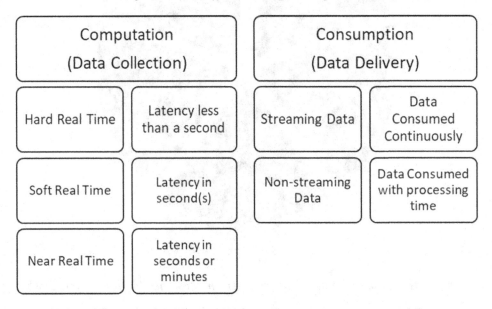

Data Measurement

Volume is a significant aspect of Big Data, and this section describes the data measurement and computing power evolvement. Table 3 shows data measurement as utilized in computer systems. The smallest unit of the data measurement is bit which stores values 0 or 1. One of the reasons to have 1 byte consisting of 8 bits is because combinations of 8 binary data will allow the system to generate 256 (2^8) unique values and this is sufficient amount of variety to include all of the commonly used letter, number and symbols according to American Standard Code for Information Interchange (ASCII).

1,024 was selected so that data is compatible with decimal number system, however kilobyte is not exactly 1,000 bytes due to the binary storage and data processing mechanism of computer. But, it is common to see the measurement equivalency represented by 1,000. For example, if "My computer" icon is clicked for a commercially made personal computer with hard drive labeled with 250GB storage, it would then show a maximum of 232.83GB free space. Because traditionally 250GB represents 250 * 1000 * 1000 * 1000 byte. But for computer, 250G represents 250 * 1024 * 1024 * 1024 byte. Therefore, if a hard drive labeled with 250GB, the computer will only recognize it as

$$232.83\text{GB} = \frac{250*1000*1000*1000}{1024*1024*1024}$$

Table 3. Data measurement (Designed by Niu, November 2017)

Category	Exact Measurement		Traditional Measurement
Bit	Binary Data (0 or 1)	Binary Data (0 or 1)	Binary Data (0 or 1)
Byte (B)	8 bits	8 bits or 1 B	8 bits or 1 B
Kilobyte (KB)	1,024 B	1,024	1,000
Megabyte (MB)	1,024 KB	1,048,576	1,000,000
Gigabyte (GB)	1,024 MB	1,073,741,824	1,000,000,000
Terabyte (TB)	1,024 GB	1,099,511,627,776	1,000,000,000,000
Petabyte (PB)	1,024 TB	1,125,899,906,842,620	1,000,000,000,000,000
Exabyte (EB)	1,024 PB	1,152,921,504,606,850,000	1,000,000,000,000,000,000
Zettabyte (ZB)	1,024 EB	1,180,591,620,717,410,000,000	1,000,000,000,000,000,000,000
Yottabyte (YB)	1,024 ZB	1,208,925,819,614,630,000,000,000	1,000,000,000,000,000,000,000,000

With the basic understanding of what is the data measurement, the following will establish how much information each of the data measurement unit stores:

- 1 Megabyte stores information equivalent to a medium sized novel; (Indiana University, 2013)
- 1 Terabyte stores information equivalent to all of the books in a large library; (Indiana University, 2013)
- 1 Petabyte stores information equivalent to 13.3 years of high-definition video, or all of the content in the U.S. library of congress. (Johnston, 2012)
- 2.5 Exabyte data is generated each day in 2012. There more data generated and stored each second across internet than 20 years ago. (McAfee & Brynjolfsson, 2012)
- 1.2 Zettabyte is the annual run rate for global Internet Protocol (IP) traffic in 2016. (Cisco, 2015)

Big Data concepts have been developing rapidly; it is dynamic, what was considered as Big Data 20 years ago is not anymore in today's computing power.

THE INTERFACE OF COMPONENTS OF BIG DATA STACK

Big Data can be utilized in batch analysis, real-time analysis, data storage, interactive querying and serving databases with NoSQL (Not Only Structured Query Language) or SLQ (Structured Query Language), and other methods. Figure 10 below illustrates the interface of these components in a stack of Big Data that is created from raw data that is accessed by many types of connectors such as queries and SQL. This chapter discusses the methods shown in Figure 10 for each of these Big Data stacks.

Figure 10. Big Data stack

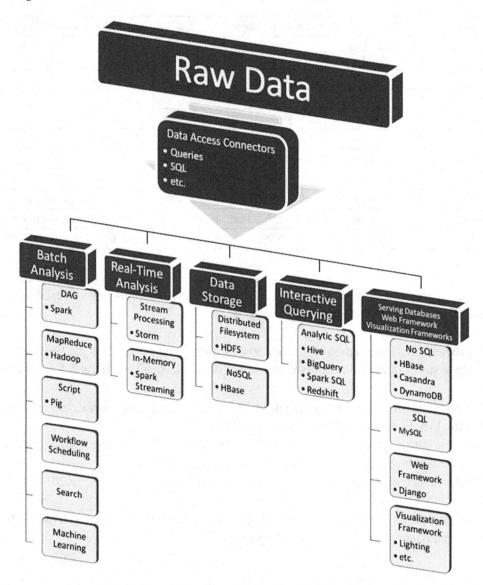

OPEN SOURCE SOFTWARE PLATFORMS FOR CLOUD AND FOG COMPUTING

This section describes the key characteristics of Cloud Computing and Fog Computing. Cloud Computing is a major computing technology currently used to store, process and analyze Big Data. Fog Computing is a supplement to Cloud Computing and it can be performed with Cloud Computing as a mechanism for visualization of Big Data.

What Is Cloud Computing?

Cloud computing happens when a task is distributed to the cloud server. The task is not transmitted to a specific one or one cluster of computers. Grid computing is when more than one computers are working simultaneously for one task. Normally the task is transmitted to a number of processing computers. The cloud server usually could be in a format of grid, but conversely not all grids are a cloud or part of cloud.

One of the benefits of cloud computing is the flexibility of task assignment for processing efficiency. Tasks with low processing requirement could be moved to processors with low computing power, and if the requirement ever increased, cloud server can maintain and distribute the task to one or a group of processors.

According to Gartner's 2017 Magic Quadrant for Cloud Infrastructure as a Service (IaaS) as discussed in Leong et al. (2017), the following Table 4 demonstrates the leading providers based on their ability to execute.

Table 4. Leading cloud infrastructure as a service (IaaS) (Designed by Niu, November 2017)

Rank	Cloud Provider		Recommended Usage						
			Cloud-native Application	E-Business Hosting	General Business Application	Enterprise Application	Development Environments	Batch Computing	Internet of Things Application
1	Amazon Web Services		x	x	x	x	x	x	x
2	Microsoft Azure		x		x		x	x	
3	Google Cloud Platform		x					x	
4	Alibaba Cloud		x				x	x	
5	Virtustream					x			
6	IBM Cloud			x	x			x	
7	Rackspace	Public Cloud	x	x			x		
		Private Cloud	x		x		x		

Source: Leong, L., Bala, R., Lowery, C., & Smith, D. (2017)

What Is Fog Computing?

Fog Computing is defined in detail in "The National Institute of Standards and Technology (NIST) Definition of Fog Computing" and is the title of NIST Special Publication 800-191 published in August 2017. This "Special Publication" not only includes definition and characteristics of Fog Computing, but also definitions of Fog Node, architectural service types and deployment method, and Mist Computing as "Lightweight Fog Layer". The "Fog Computing Conceptual Model" is the title of NIST Special Publication 500-325 published in March 2018.

The NIST (2017) definition of Fog Computing is the following:

"Fog computing is a horizontal, physical or virtual resource paradigm that resides between smart end devices and traditional cloud or data centers. This paradigm supports vertically-isolated, latency-sensitive applications by providing ubiquitous, scalable, layered, federated, and distributed computing, storage, and network connectivity."

Fog Computing is related with cloud computing. It is extension of the cloud that performs computing before serving the data to the cloud. Fog Computing could reduce cloud computing latency, because limited number of edge devices are communicating with the fog, then fog communicate computing to reduce traffic and latency on the cloud.

Fog Computing also could solve limited cloud bandwidth issue. Because of the layers of fog, data protection mechanism could be enhanced on each fog compared with overly broad protection on cloud. Lastly Fog Computing also could enhance internet connectivity due to its point-knot-source structure compared with point-source, where the point represents the edge device, the knot represents the fog, and the source presents the cloud

Fog is a middleware between Internet of Things (IoT) and cloud as shown by Aazam et al. (2018) within book "Fog Computing and Internet of Things" edited by Rahmani et al. (2018) that shows the range of applications benefiting by Fog Computing as health care, connected wind farms, smart grids, smart traffic light applications, smart homes and factories, and energy conservation.

Books on the subject of Fog Computing that have been recently published by IGI Global include those of Raj and Raman (2018) handbook of research on cloud and Fog Computing infrastructures, Srinivas, Lather and Siddesh (2018) on the rise of Fog Computing in the digital era, and Information Resources Management Association (2019) on breakthroughs in research and practice in Fog Computing.

Ahuja and Deval (2018) indicated that Fog Computing has been proposed by Cisco in early 2014 and that is otherwise known as Edge Computing is the integration of Cloud Computing and IoT. According to Ahuja and Deval (2018), Fog Computing meets the data processing needs of IoT devices that are resource constrained by bringing computation, communication, control and storage closed to the end users, and further indicates that one can think of IoT-Fog-Cloud as being part of a continuum.

Bhardwaj (2018) discussed novel taxonomy to select fog products and challenges faced in fog environments, and presented a review of academic literature work on Fog Computing. Dubey et al. (2015) studied fog computing for enhancing Telehealth Big Data using Fog Data. Yang (2017) studied IoT stream processing and analytics in the fog.

Barik et al. (2018) discussed the emergence of Fog Computing for mining analytics in Big Data from geospatial and medical health applications by proposing and developing a fog computing-based framework named FogLearn. The research of Barik et al. (2018) applied the FogLearn framework by utilizing machine learning for the analysis of pathological feature data that was obtained from smart watches worn by patients with diabetes with location indicated by geographical parameters of a geospatial database.

Fog computing and Edge Computing are similar and had been referred interchangeable. However, there are some difference between the mechanisms. The following section discusses the difference between two computing mechanisms.

What Is Fog Computing Versus Edge Computing?

The difference between Fog Computing and edge computing is where the processing intelligence is placed. Fog Computing's intelligence is placed at the local area network level, and edge computing's intelligence is placed at the end user's appliance level. Both Fog Computing and edge computing are measures of enhancing the efficiency of cloud computing by preprocess the data, instead of replacing the cloud computing. Figure 11 shows the Fog Computing mechanism and Figure 12 shows the edge computing mechanism.

Fog Computing collects endpoints or appliance's generated data in the local area network level. And once the data is collected and processed, then it will be transmitted to the cloud. This intermediate step significantly reduced the latency between the appliances and cloud, thus improved the efficiency. Fog Computing is scalable. Because of its layered processing mechanism, it is easier to down device and procedure with failure.

Edge computing had end gateway at the appliance level. End point generates or collects data, and then at the same time processed the data. For example, smart phone application collects and process health data and then sent the requested data to the cloud for further analysis. Edge gateway also improves cloud efficiency since it processes the information before communicating with cloud which improved the quality of data. It also reduces the points of failure compared with Fog Computing, because each edge gateway works independently.

Figure 11. Fog computing mechanism (Designed by Niu, March, 2018)

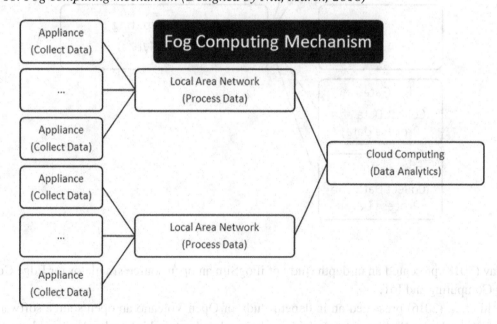

Open Source Software (OSS) for Fog and Cloud Computing

Huang et al. (2013) discussed evaluating open source cloud computing solutions for geosciences. Bellavista and Zanni (2017) studied the feasibility of fog computing deployment based on dcoker containerization over an embeeded microprocessor named RaspberryPi.

Bellavista and Zanni (2017) also extended an open-source framework for IoT application named Kura that is used for building IoT gateways for scalable fog computing.

Pan and McElhannon (2018) discuss the applications of open source platform Cloudlet in their study of future edge cloud and edge computing for IoT.

Barik et al. (2016) used open source compression techniques for reducing the transmission to the cloud in their study that developed a Fog Computing based framework named FogGIS for mining analytics from geospatial data.

Figure 12. Edge computing mechanism (Designed by Niu, March, 2018)

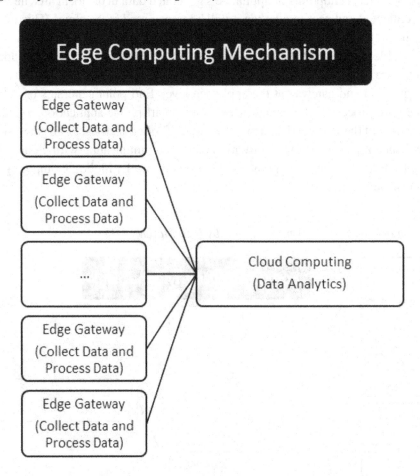

Gaurav (2018) presented an in-depth study of iFogSim an open source simulator for Edge Computing, Fog Computing and IoT.

Bruschi et al. (2016) presented an in depth study of Open Volcano an open source software platform for fog computing that provides scalable and virtualized networking technologies able to natively integrate cloud services.

Dianomic (2019) discusses their product FogLAMP that is an open source platform for the Internet of Things (IoT) as the most powerful platform to simplify data management in the fog that can distributed at the Edge to act together provide scalability, elasticity and resilience.

The following is a list and description for some current Fog Computing open source software and platforms:

OpenVolcano

OpenVolcano is an Open Source Software that supports mobile edge and Fog Computing services. StratoV and Caldera are the main control and data plan of architecture components. Data plan of architecture includes data collection, configuration and elaboration. The project was introduced by DROP project and is the lead by the CNIT S3ITI Laboratory. It is a major result of INPUT project. European Commission under the Horizon 2020 program funded the project. (INPUT - In-Network Programmability for next-generation personal cloud service support, 2018 & OpenVolcano, 2018)

FogLAMP

FogLAMP os an open source platform for the Internet of Things (IoT) that uses modular microservices architecture with forwarding to cloud-based services (Dianomic (2019)).

FOG Project

FOG Project is a free open source network computer cloning and management solution that can be used with various versions of Windows. It ties together a few open source tools with a PHP-based web interface. (FOG Project (2019))

iFogSim

IFogSim is an open source simulator for edge computing, fog computing and Internet of Things (IoT). iFogSim evaluates resource management and scheduling policies across edge and cloud resource under different scenarios. (Gaurav (2018))

BIG DATA ANALYTICS SOFTWARE AND PLATFORMS

Categories of Big Data Analytics software that can be used as interfaces for Fog Computing include the following: Data Ingestion, Hadoop Systems, Stream computing, Analytics/Machine Learning, Content Management, Integration, and Data Governance. (PredictiveAnalyticsToday (2018).)

The categories in Table 6 "Top 20 Big Data Analytics Software and Platforms" that provides each in ranked order with website of each. Descriptions of the features for each of the twenty Big Data software and platform follows Table 6.

Talend Open Studio

Software for Data Integration is free to download open-source license tool that fully supports all facets of Extract, Transform and Load (ETL) processes. It provides more than 800 built-in connects than any other ETL solution, thus making it easy to implement connections between diverse database types, file formats, and enterprise solutions. (Talend Open Studio, 2018)

Arcadia Data

Arcadia Data unifies data discovery, visual analytics and business intelligence in a single, integrated platform that runs on Hadoop clusters. (Arcadia Data, 2018)

Table 5. Categories of Big Data analytics software (Derived from PredictiveAnalyticsToday (2018).)

CATEGORY OF BIG DATA ANALYTICS SOFTWARE	DESCRIPTION
Data Integration, Data Management, ELT, and Warehouse	Provides features for effective Data Warehousing and Management for managing data as a valuable resource.
Hadoop System	Provides features for massive storage for any kinds of data with enormous processing power and ability to handle virtually limitless concurrent tasks or jobs.
Stream Computing	Features for pulling in streams of data and streaming it back as a single flow.
Analytics/Machine Learning	Features for advanced analytics and machine learning.
Content Management	Features for comprehensive content life cycle and document management.
Integration	Features for Big Data integration from any source with ease.
Data Governance	Comprehensive Security and Compliance solution to protect the data.

Informatica PowerCenter Big Data Edition

Is highly scalable, high performance enterprise data integration software that uses visual environment to build Extract, Transform and Load (ETL) data flows that run on Hadoop. The data flows can be reused and collaborate with other developers and analysts with a common integrated development environment. (Informatica PowerCenter Big Data Edition, 2018)

GoodData

The GoodData platform includes advanced distribution and product lifecycle management features to automate the process of maintaining one-to-many cloud deployments. (Good Data, 2018)

Actian Analytics Platform

Features include Vectorized Query Execution, maximizing CPU cache for execution, column-based storage, data compression, positional data trees (PDTs), and storage indices. Actian Analytics Platform runs complex queries against billions of records in just seconds. (Actian Analytics Platform, 2018)

Google Big Data

Google Big Data is a cloud platform that unifies batch and stream processing that is fully managed with serverless architecture that utilizes Spark and Hadoop. (Google Big Data, 2018)

Wavefront

Wavefront is a hosted platform for ingesting, storing, visualizing and alerting on metric data. It is based on a stream processing approach invented at Google that allows metric data to be manipulated with unparalleled power. (Wavefront, 2018)

Table 6. Top 20 Big Data analytics software and platforms ((PredictiveAnalyticsToday (2018).)

Name of Big Data Analytics Software / Platform	Category	Web URL
1. Talend Open Data	ETL Software	https://www.talend.com/?utm_source=PredictiveAnalyticsToday&utm_medium=Review&utm_campaign=PA2.
2. Arcadia Data	Business Intelligence Software	https://www.arcadiadata.com/
3. Informatica	Big Data Software	https://www.informatica.com/products/big-data.html?utm_source=PredictiveAnalyticsToday&utm_medium=Review&utm_campaign=PAT#fbid=2tuRknAh7K4
4. GoodData	Business Intelligence Software	https://www.gooddata.com/?utm_source=PredictiveAnalyticsToday&utm_medium=Review&utm_campaign=PAT
5. Actian Analytics Platform	Dig Data, Big Data Analytics, Predictive Analysis	https://www.actian.com/
6. Google BigData	Big Data Platform	https://cloud.google.com/solutions/big-data/
7. Wavefront	Big Data Software	https://www.predictiveanalyticstoday.com/wavefront/
8. IBM Big Data	Big Data Platform	https://www.ibm.com/analytics/hadoop/big-data-analytics
9. Attivio Active Intelligence Engine	Big Data Software	https://www.attivio.com/?utm_source=PredictiveAnalyticsToday&utm_medium=Review&utm_campaign=PAT
10. Datameer	Big Data Analytics Platform	https://www.datameer.com/?utm_source=PredictiveAnalyticsToday&utm_medium=Review&utm_campaign=PAT
11. Opera Solutions Signal Hubs	Big Data Software	https://www.operasolutions.com/?utm_source=PredictiveAnalyticsToday&utm_medium=Review&utm_campaign=PAT
12. Amazon Web Services	Big Data Platform	https://aws.amazon.com/products/#analytics-1
13. FICO Big Data Analyzer	Big Data Analytics Platform	http://www.fico.com/en/analytic-cloud
14. Cloudera Enterprise Big Data	Big Data Platform	https://www.cloudera.com/products.html
15. DataTorrent	Big Data Ingestion Software	https://www.datatorrent.com/?utm_source=PredictiveAnalyticsToday&utm_medium=Review&utm_campaign=PAT
16. Palantir Big Data	Big Data Platform	https://www.palantir.com/products/
17. Oracle Big Data Analytics	Big Data Platform	https://www.oracle.com/big-data/products.html
18. Qubole	Big Data Platform	https://www.predictiveanalyticstoday.com/qubole/
19. Syncsort	Big Data Ingestion Software	https://www.predictiveanalyticstoday.com/syncsort/
20. Amdocs Insight	Big Data Platform	https://www.amdocs.com/real-time-data-management

IBM Big Data

Features include Data Management & Warehouse, Hadoop System, Stream Computing, Content Management, and Information Integration & Governance. (IBM Big Data, 2018))

Attivio Active Intelligence Engine

Attivio Active Intelligence Engine is a unified information access platform that brings together structured and unstructured content by integrating and correlating all data and content with no advance data modeling. It provides advanced text analytics, intuitive, Google-like search for business intelligence (BI) and integration with BI and data visualization tools. (Attivio Active Intelligence Engin, 2018)

Datameer

Datameer is a SaaS Big Data analytics platform that is targeted for department special deployments. (Datameer, 2018)

Opera Solutions Signal Hubs

The signal hubs employs machine learning and are domain specific collections of signals along with the technology required to continually extract, store, and refresh, and present selected signals and recommended best actions. (Opera Solutions Signal Hubs, 2018)

Amazon Web Service

Features include computing using Amazon Cloud Front, Storage using Amazon S3, database using Amazon Aurora, migration using Database Migration Service, and Amazon Virtual Private Cloud. (Amazon Web Service, 2018)

FICO Big Data Analyzer

Big Data Analyzer empowers a broad range of users to collaborate, explore data and discover new insights from any type and size of data on Hadoop. (FICO Big Data Analyzer, 2018)

Cloudera Enterprise Big Data

Cloudera enterprise Big Data is powered by Apache Hadoop and features include Data Engineering, Analytical and Operational Database, secure without compromise, and easy to manage. (Cloudera Enterprise Big Data, 2018)

DataTorrent

DataTorrent RTS is proven in production environments to reduce time to market, development costs and operational expenditures for Fortune 100 and leading Internet companies. It provides connectors for technologies such as message busses, SQL and NoSQL databases, flat files, Kafka, Scoop, Flume, and Twitter. (DataTorrent, 2018)

Palantir Big Data

Features include Data Integration, Iteration and Collaboration, Custom Metric Development, Flexible Modeling, Privacy and Security Controls, and Algorithmic Processing. (Palantir Big Data, 2018)

Oracle Big Data Analytics

Features include SQL Cloud Service, Oracle Big data Discovery, Oracle R Advanced Analytics for Hadoop, Business Intelligence and Data Visualization Cloud Service. (Oracle Big Data Analytics, 2018)

Qubole Data Service

Qubole Data Service is a comprehensive autonomous bog data platform that self-optimizes, self-manages, and learns form usage through combinations of heuristics and machine learning. (Qubola, 2018)

Syncsort

Syncsort provides enterprise software that allows organizations to collect, integrate, sort and distribute more data in less time, with fewer resources and lower costs. Syncsort software provides specialized solutions spanning "Big Iron to Big Data," including next gen analytical platforms such as Hadoop, cloud, and Splunk. (Syncort, 2018)

Amdocs Insight

Features include Real-Time Analytics, Amdocs Logical Data Model, Modern Data Infrastructure Management, and Analytical Applications Ecosystems. (Amdocs Insight, 2018)

BIG DATA VISUALIZATION

Once data is transmitted by devices that may or not be connected directly to the cloud by using a fog environment, the problem arises as how to visualize Big Data and what techniques can be used. The following discusses data visualization techniques using Big Data that was extracted from Fatality Analysis Reporting System (FARS) managed by National Highway Traffic Safety Administration (NHTSA) of United States Department of Transportation (DoT). (National Highway Traffic Safety Administration, 2017)

Big Data visualization is different from traditional classical data visualization, because the data has a higher volume, larger variety of data format and high data processing speed. Unlike traditional graphs, Big Data visualization methods focus on high dimensional relationships. The following visualization methods provide better presentation to thoroughly understand the data.

Treemap method uses size and color to demonstrate the data. In Figure 13, size represents the population of the state, and the color represents the number of vehicle accident fatal injuries per person. Darker color corresponds to a higher number of fatal injuries per person.

Figure 13. Example of treemap graph (Designed by Niu, November 2017)

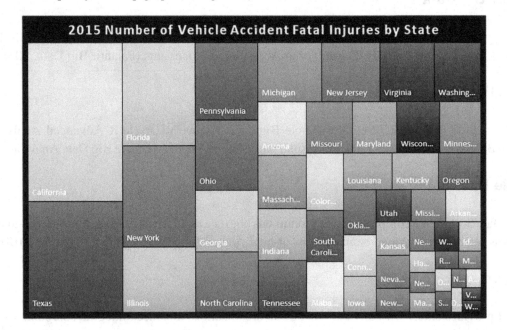

Sunburst graph is a ring chart, also known as a sunburst chart or a multilevel pie chart, is used to visualize hierarchical data, depicted by concentric circles. The circle in the centre represents the root node, with the hierarchy moving outward from the center. (Sunburst graph, 2017).

Sunburst method projects out the proportional relationship within each of the variables visually like a sun. In Figure 10, the inner circle has higher portion of male which represents the number of fatal injuries mostly happened to males. And within male fatalities, it most likely happened in the state highway. Within the categories of male together with State Highway fatalities in Figure 14, the highest proportion was for "Alcohol Not Involved".

Parallel coordinates method shows the relative relationship. In Figure 15, the highest fatal injuries categories (21-30 years old) on country road (1096 fatal injuries) and state highway (2121 fatal injuries) are different. But with the parallel coordinates, the relationship between different categories are demonstrated proportionally.

Circle packing method uses color and circle size to describe the dataset. In figure 16, the color represents the region and size represent the total number of fatal injuries in 2015.

Heat map demonstrates map with coloring algorithm. Figure 17 shows number of fatal injuries by state, color towards black represents higher total number of fatal injuries in 2015, and color towards grey represents lower total number of fatal injuries. Heat map could utilize more than two colors to demonstrate numerical value.

Streamgraph demonstrate time series data in a centered coordinate system. In Figure 18, four US (United States) regions total number of fatal injuries are aggregated into one wave according to time. And the proportional relationship between each region can be interpreted from this graph.

There are also numerous other types of visualization methods that could help with Big Data analysis, such as network analysis, circular network diagram. Method selection depends on data type and logical conclusions that the graph attempted to demonstrate.

Figure 14. Example of sunburst graph (Designed by Niu, November 2017)

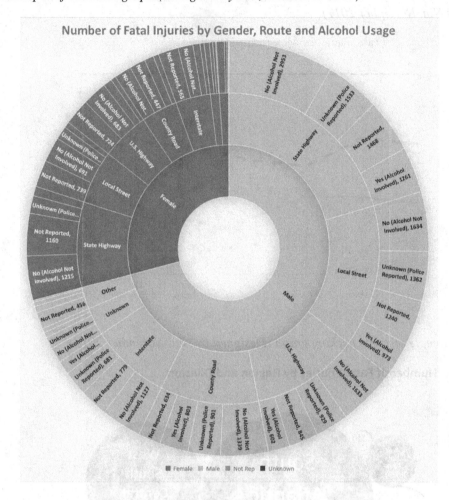

Various visualization techniques were designed and implemented to realize the visualization methods. Script based techniques are developed, such as Java, so that programmers and software engineers are able to add interactive charts into their websites or applications conveniently. Some of the techniques are developed with user friendly interface so that Big Data analytics can be performed without coding. The following table includes a list of popular Big Data visualization tools, it categorized the tool as JavaScript based and user interface based techniques.

BIG DATA VISUALIZATION SOFTWARE

Table 7 summarizes the most popular software for Big Data Visualization software in the categories of JavaScript Based and User Interface Based as designed by the authors, and followed by brief description and web page images. More complete information can be obtained from the web page URL addresses provided for each. Additional Web-Based Big Data Visualization Software with URLs and brief descriptions is provided by Table 8 in Appendix of this chapter.

Figure 15. Example of parallel coordinates graph: number of fatal injuries by age group and route (Designed by Niu, November 2017)

Figure 16. Example of circle packing graph (Designed by Niu, November 2017)

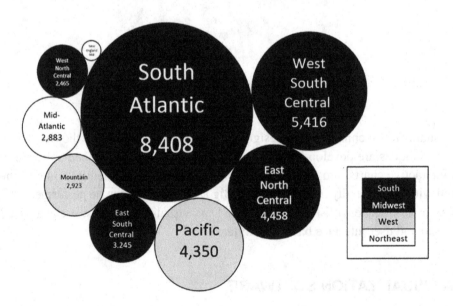

Figure 17. Example of heatmap graph (Designed by Niu, November 2017)

2015 Number of Fatal Injuries by State

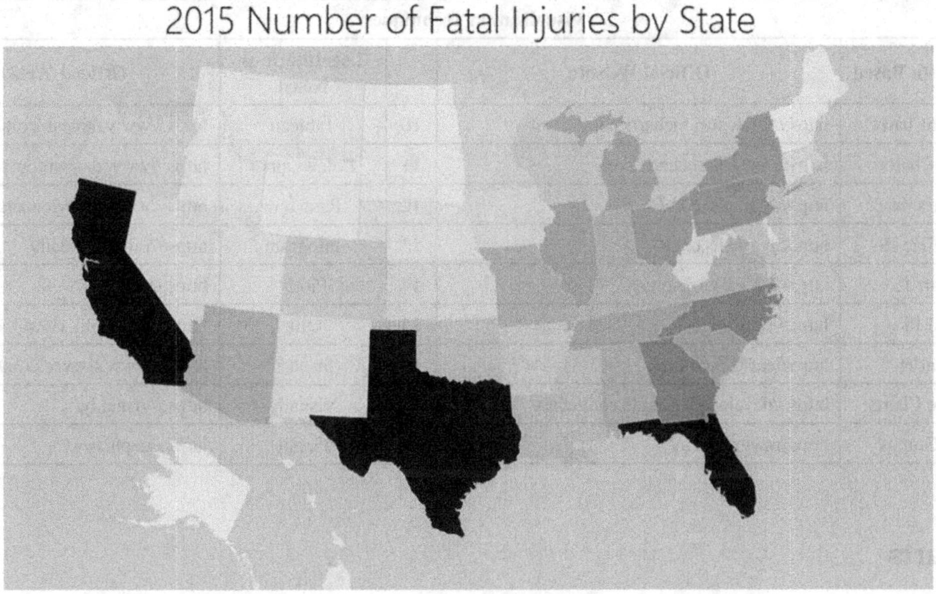

Figure 18. Example of streamgraph graph (Designed by Niu, November 2017)

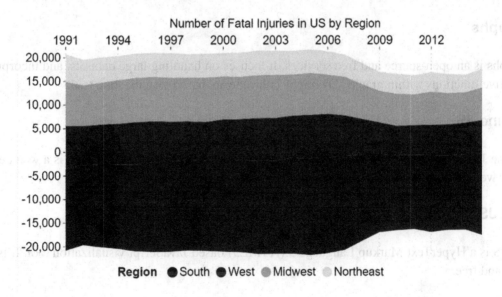

Number of Fatal Injuries in US by Region
1991
1994
1997
2000
2003
2006
2009
2012
20,000
15,000
10,000
5,000
0
-5,000
-10,000
-15,000
-20,000
Region
South
West
Midwest
Northeast

Fusion Charts

Fusion charts is a JavaScript based visualization service for web developers. It offers more than 90 chart types and 1400 maps. Service has been categorized as FusionCharts XT, FusionWidgets XT, Power-Charts XT and FusionMaps XT.

Table 7. Big Data Visualization Techniques (Designed by Niu, November 2017)

Visualization Techniques					
	JavaScript Based	**Official Website**		**UserInterface based**	**Official Website**
1	FusionCharts	https://www.fusioncharts.com/	10	Tableau	https://www.tableau.com/
2	HighCharts	https://www.highcharts.com/	11	Datawrapper	https://www.datawrapper.de/
3	Dygraphs	http://dygraphs.com/	12	Paraview	https://www.paraview.org/
4	Timeline JS	http://dygraphs.com/	13	Infogram	https://infogram.com/
5	Chart JS	http://www.chartjs.org/	14	Plotly	https://plot.ly/
6	D3 JS	https://d3js.org/	15	Qlik	https://www.qlik.com/
7	Leaflet	http://leafletjs.com	16	Sisense	https://www.sisense.com/
8	Google Charts	https://developers.google.com/chart/	17	Visually	https://visual.ly/
9	RawGraphs	http://rawgraphs.io/	18	Gephi	https://gephi.org/

HighCharts

HighCharts provides JavaScript services to help developers for their visualization needs. It focuses on interactive graphs.

Dygraphs

Dygraphs is an open-source and free services. It focuses on handling large datasets, and incorporating interactive functions within graphs. Dygraphs is JavaScript based visualization tool.

Timeline JS

Timeline JS is JavaScript free visualization tool that focuses on a timeline graph. It is a web designed tool for web developers to show the time line of a story.

Chart JS

Chart JS is a HyperText Markup Language 5 (HTML5) based JavaScript visualization tool. It is open-source and free.

D3 JS

D3 JS is a JavaScript library that provides visualization solutions. It focuses on the control of the final visual results and be able to provide innovative and interactive graphs.

Leaflet

Leaflet is an open-source and JavaScript based visualization tool. It focuses on mobile based interactive maps.

Google Charts

Google charts provides interactive visualization solutions by taking user supplied data. It will express the visualization in JavaScript for developer's further utilization.

RawGraphs

RawGraphs is an open-source software that allows users to generate graphs through the web. It can also generate JavaScript for additional use for developers. Users have generated various typical Big Data graphs such as streamgraph, customized treemap etc.

Tableau

Tableau is a visualization software that focuses on business intelligence. It is built with a user-friendly interface, so that users of the software only need to drag the variable names to generate graphs after inputing the data. It has a powerful geographical processing function. Segall (2017a, 2017b) discusses the use of Tableau Software for university teaching. Instructors' resources web pages for Tableau software are provided at Tableau (2017).

Datawrapper

Datawrapper is a user interface based visualization tool. The website generates charts and maps. It has a rich map library including various countries option for visualization.

Paraview

Paraview is an open-source user interface based visualization tool. The software has visualization functions specifically designed for structural analysis, fluid dynamics, astrophysics and climate science.

Infogram

Infogram is a user interface based visualization tool. The software focuses on business intelligence and is able to generate infographics and create business reports based on users' data.

Plotly

Plotly is an open-source visualization tool that allows users to create interactive data graphs and share via the web. It also provides consulting services.

Qlik

Qlik is a user interface data visualization software. Users only need to drag and click to explore and generate data after uploading. It is a business oriented instead of scientific research oriented Big Data visualization tool.

Sisense

Sisense is a user interface data visualization software. The software is designed for various types of business such as Healthcare, Finance, Marketing, Retail and Public Sector.

Visually

Visually is a web based data visualization and infographics technique. Data analysts and designers utilize the technology to provide services such as visualization animated videos.

Gephi

Gephi is an open-source and free software. It has a powerful network analysis function.

BIG DATA VISUALIZATION FOR STREAMING DATA

Big Data visualization for streaming data is inevitably involved with dynamic graph. Most of the commonly used data analytics software are designed to process batch data, such as SAS, R or Excel VBA. Updated versions of these software started to incorporated functions of visualizing dynamic data. However, collecting and processing data in real time is still a challenge for the traditional batch processing software.

The following Figure 19 is an example of visualization of streaming cyber-attack data created by NORSE. Cyber-attack incidents are captured, its origination location, targeting location, types of attack, IP address and other vital information are captured and visualized. The data is streamed out in less than a second, and demonstrates the attacks in a dynamic pattern.

Data stream management for processing high-speed data streams is discussed in depth in Garofalakis et al.(2016) for foundations and basic stream synopses, mining data streams, applications, and system architectures and languages such as the Stanford Data Stream Management System and Sensor network integration with streaming database systems.

Many of the primary software tools used to do large-scale data analysis required by applications such as Internet web search, teleconferencing, geo-location and map services were born in the cloud as discussed by Li & Qiu (2014) in their book titled "Cloud Computing for Data-Intensive Applications". Li & Qiu (2014) includes titled chapters pertaining to systems and applications of "Cloud Networking to Support Data Intensive Computing", programming models of "Executing Storm Surge Essential Ensembles on PAAS Cloud", and cloud storage "Supporting a Social Media observatory with Customizable Index Structures: Architecture and Performance".

Figure 19. Cyber-attack streaming data visualization example (NORSE, 2018)

Deshpande (2011) authored a text for data replication for Oracle Streams 11g for design and management for powerful data replication solution. Nabi (2016) authored a book on Pro Spark Streaming for real-time analytics that includes chapters on real-time ETL (Extract Transform Load) and corresponding analytics, discretized streams or DStreams for Real-Time Resilient Distributed Datasets (RDD). Gupta (2016) authored a book on real-time Big Data Analytics for design, process, and analysis of large data sets of complex data in real time. Chapters in Gupta (2016) include that devoted to programming with RDDs and analysis of streaming data using Spark steaming.

Ellis (2014) wrote book on real-time analytics with techniques to analyze and visualize streaming data that has chapters devoted to topics such as designing real-time streaming architectures, data-flow management in streaming analysis, processing streaming data, storing streaming data, delivering streaming metrics, and statistical approximation of streaming data.

Dunning & Friedman (2016) authored a book about streaming architecture for new designs using Apache Kafka and MapR streams. Dunning & Friedman (2016) explained how to recognize opportunities where streaming data may be useful and show how to design streaming architecture for best results in a multi-user system. They also explained why stream-based architectures are helpful to support microservices, and describe particular tools for messaging and streaming analytics that best fit the requirements of a strong stream-based design.

Basek et al. (2017) authored book on stream analytics with Microsoft Azure for real-time data processing for quick insights using Azure Stream Analytics that includes chapters on designing real-time streaming pipelines, developing real-time event processing with Azure streaming, and how to achieve seamless scalability with automation.

Bifet et al. (2017) authored book on machine learning (ML) for data stream with practical examples in Massive Online Analysis (MOA) that is an open-source software framework that allows users to build and run ML and data mining experiments on evolving data streams. Bifet et al. (2017) discusses Big Data stream mining and hands-on introduction to MOA and its Graphical user Interface (GUI).

BIG DATA VISUALIZATION SOFTWARE FOR MOBILE DEVICES AND TABLETS

Fog Computing utilizes mobile devices such as tablets that interface with data in the cloud.

Segall (2017a, 2017b) discusses SAS® Visual Analytics and SAS® Visual Statistics as new software that are designed to provide Big Data Analytics for mobile devices and tablets. Segall (2017a) presents actual classroom experiences using tablets and mobile devices for visual analytics of Big Data in bioinformatics, and Segall (2017b) for technologies for teaching Big Data analytics.

SAS® Visual Statistics is one of the modules built within SAS® Visual Analytics software. Bell, Hardin and Matthews (2017) and Ravenna, Truxillo and Wells (2017) authored two books of SAS® Notes from SAS® Institute for classroom teaching that utilizes Big Data of over 3 million rows of data that can be uploaded from the Teradata University Network (TUN). This Big Data set is for the Insight Toy Company as available from TUN for classroom teaching using mobile devices.

CONCLUSION

This chapter discusses what Open Source Software (OSS) is and what Big Data is and its key characteristics and components that can be used for its visualization using software and platforms. These software and platforms could be those not only created with the sole purpose for Fog Computing but also others for Big Data Visualization that can be implemented into Fog Computing with the Internet of Things (IoT).

This chapter also illustrates how Fog Computing can use Big Data in both its discrete and continuous forms such as data streaming. The chapter also discusses the differences between Fog Computing and Edge computing. Visualization of Big Data is an important issue because of the dimensionalities and velocity of the data that otherwise would be unknown, and the elements of Internet of Things (IoT) with Fog Computing make this possible using the software discussed each with their unique characteristics.

The opportunities for utilization of Open Source Software (OSS) for Big Data and Fog Computing are endless. The applications of Open Source Software to Big Data and its visualization to Fog Computing that connects with the Internet of Things (IoT) is the future for economic growth. Open Source Software is also the mechanism for efficiency and effectiveness of software dissemination to not only individual researchers and entrepreneurs, but also to businesses and large-scale organizations who want to use their software tools for not only personnel computers, but also with tablets and mobile devices.

ACKNOWLEDGMENT

Acknowledgements to Co-Editor Dr. Gao Niu are indicated in several figures of this chapter who converted hand-drawn figures created by the author into computer images as shown.

REFERENCES

Aazam, M., St-Hilaire, M., Lung, C.-H., Lambadaris, I., & Huh, E.-H. (2018). IoT resource estimation challenges and modeling in fog. In *Free and open source software in modern data science and business intelligence*. IGI Global.

Actian Analytics Platform. (2018). Retrieved on May 13, 2018 from https://www.predictiveanalyticsto-day.com/actian-analytics-platform/

Ahuja, S. P., & Deval, N. (2018). From Cloud Computing to Fog Computing: Platforms for the Internet of Things (IoT). *International Journal of Fog Computing*, *1*(1), 1–14. doi:10.4018/IJFC.2018010101

Amazon web Service. (2018). Retrieved on May 13, 2018 from https://www.predictiveanalyticstoday.com/amazon-web-service/

Arcadia Data. (2018). Retrieved on May 13, 2018 from https://www.predictiveanalyticstoday.com/arcadia-data/

Attivio Active Intelligence Engine. (2018). Retrieved on May 13, 2018 from https://www.predictiveana-lyticstoday.com/attivio-active-intelligence-engine/

Barik, R. K., Dubey, H., Samaddar, A. B., Gupta, R. D., & Ray, P. K. (2016). FogGIS: Fog computing for geospatial big data analytics. Proceedings of 2016 IEEE Uttar Pradesh Section International Conference on Electrical Computer and Electronic Engineering (UPCON). Retrieved May 16, 2019 from https://arxiv.org/ftp/arxiv/papers/1701/1701.02601.pdf

Basak, A., Venkataraman, K., Murphy, R., & Singh, M. (2017). *Stream Analytics with Microsoft Azure*. Birmingham, UK: Packt Publishing Ltd.

Belavista, P., & Zanni, A. (2017) Feasibility of fog computing deployment based on docker containerization over RaspberryPi. ICDCN '17 Proceedings of the 18th International Conference on Distributed Computing and Networking. Retrieved May 16, 2019 from http://delivery.acm.org/10.1145/3010000/3007777/a16-Bellavista.pdf?ip=147.97.138.188&id=3007777&acc=ACTIVE%20SERVICE&key=F82E6B883-64EF649%2EB319B24617D6E2C4%2E4D4702B0C3E38B35%2E4D4702B0C3E38B35&__acm__=1558043198_90653cd3b7954cf3a7cfa60797254435

Bell, R., Hardin, B., & Matthews, L. (2017). *SAS® Visual Analytics for SAS® 9: Getting Started Course Notes*. Cary, NC: SAS Institute, Inc.

Benjelloun, F. Z., Lahcen, A. A., & Belfkih, S. (2015, March). An overview of big data opportunities, applications and tools. In Intelligent Systems and Computer Vision (ISCV), 2015 (pp. 1-6). IEEE. doi:10.1109/ISACV.2015.7105553

Bhardwaj, A. (2018). Novel Taxonomy to Select Fog Products and Challenges Faced to Fog Environments. *International Journal of Fog Computing*, *1*(1), 35–49. doi:10.4018/IJFC.2018010103

Bifet, A., Gavadlda, R., Holmes, G., & Pfahringer, D. (2017). *Machine Learning for Data Streams with Practical Examples in MOA*. Cambridge, MA: The MIT Press.

Brown, J. P. (2017). *Open Source Software: Implementing a Successful OSS Management Practice*. SilverStream Consulting, LLC.

Bruschi, R., Lago, P., Lamanna, G., Lombardo, C., & Mangialardi, S. (2016). Open Volcano: An open-source software platform for fog computing. 2016 28th International Teletraffic Congress- The First International Conference in Networking & Practice, Wurzburg, Germany.

Capterra. (2017). Big Data Software. Retrieved November 25, 2017 from https://www.capterra.com/big-data-software/?utf8=%E2%9C%93&users=&feature%5B4%5D=39433&commit=Filter+Results&sort_options=

Circle Packing Graph. (2017). Retrieved on November 19, 2017 from https://en.wikipedia.org/wiki/Circle_packing

Cisco. (2017). The Zettabyte Era: Trends and Analysis. Retrieved November 23, 2107 from https://www.cisco.com/c/en/us/solutions/collateral/service-provider/visual-networking-index-vni/vni-hyper-connectivity-wp.html

Clegg, B. (2017). *Big Data: How the information revolution is transforming our lives*. London, UK: Icon Books, Ltd.

Cloudera Enterprise Big Data. (2018). Retrieved on May 13, 2018 from https://www.predictiveanalyticstoday.com/cloudera-enterprise-bigdata/

Daas, P. J., Puts, M. J., Buelens, B., & van den Hurk, P. A. (2015). Big data as a source for official statistics. *Journal of Official Statistics*, *31*(2), 249–262. doi:10.1515/jos-2015-0016

Datameer. (2018). Retrieved on May 13, 2018 from https://www.predictiveanalyticstoday.com/datameer/

DataTorrent. (2018). Retrieved on May 13, 2018 from https://www.predictiveanalyticstoday.com/datatorrent/

Deshpande, K. (2011). *Oracle Streams 11g Data Replication*. Oracle Press.

Dianomic. (2019). The most powerful platform to simply data management in the fog. Retrieved May 16, 2019 from http://dianomic.com/platform/

DiBina, C., Cooper, D., & Stone, M. (2006). *Open Source 2.0: The continuing revolution*. O'Reilly Media Inc.

Drake, M. (2017). The Difference between Free and Open-Source Software. Retrieved Mary 22, 2019 from https://www.digitalocean.com/community/tutorials/Free-vs-Open-Source-Software

Dubey, H., Yang, J., Constant, N., Amiri, A. M., Yang, Q., & Makodiva, K. (2015). Article. Proceedings of the ASE Big Data & Social Informatics (ASE BD&SI '15).

Dunning, T., & Friedman, E. (2016). *Streaming Architecture: New Designs using Apache Kafke and MapR Streams*. O'Reilly Media, Inc.

Ellis, B. (2014). *Real-Time Analytics: Techniques to Analyze and Visualize Streaming Data*. John Wiley & Sons, Inc.

Familiar, B., & Barnes, J. (2017). *Business in real-time using Azure IoT and Cortanna Intelligence Suite*. Apress.

FICO Big Data Analyzer. (2018). Retrieved on May 13, 2018 from https://www.predictiveanalyticstoday.com/fico-big-data-analyzer/

Findley, K. (2016). Open source won. So, now what? Wired. Retrieved May 12 from https://www.wired.com/2016/08/open-source-won-now/?GuidesLearnMore

Findley, K. (2019). The WIRED guide to open source software. Retrieved May 12, 2019 from https://www.wired.com/story/wired-guide-open-source-software/

Frampton, M. (2018). *Complete guide to open source big data stack*. Apress.

Franks, B. (2012). Taming the big data tidal wave: Finding opportunities in huge data streams with advanced analytics. Hoboken, NJ: John Wiley & Sons; doi:10.1002/9781119204275.

Free Software Foundation. (2019a). Retrieved May 22, 2019 from https://www.fsf.org/

Free Software Foundation. (2019b). Free Software Resources. Retrieved May 22, 2019 from https://www.fsf.org/resources/

Freeman, J., Heller, M., Wayner, P., & Yegulalp. (2018). The best open source software for software development. InfoWorld. Retrieved May 22, 2019 from https://www.infoworld.com/article/3306453/the-best-open-source-software-for-software-development.html

Garfinkel, S. L. (1993). Is Stallman stalled: One of the greatest programmers alive saw a future where all software was free. Then reality set in. Retrieved May 12, 2019 from https://www.wired.com/1993/01/stallman/?GuidesLearnMore

Garofalakis, M., Gehrke, J., & Rastogi, R. (Eds.). (2016). Data Stream Management: Processing High-Speed Data Streams. Springer-Verlag; doi:10.1007/978-3-540-28608-0.

Gaurav, K. (2018). iFogSim: An open source simulator for Edge Computing, Fog Computing and IoT. Retrieved May 16, 2019 from https://opensourceforu.com/2018/12/ifogsim-an-open-source-simulator-for-edge-computing-fog-computing-and-iot/

Goldman, R., & Gabriel, R. P. (2005). How to do Open-Source Development. Chapter 6 of Innovations Happens Elsewhere. Retrieved May 22, 2019 from https://www.dreamsongs.com/IHE/IHE-54.html#pgfId-956812

GoodData. (2018). Retrieved on May 13, 2018 from https://www.predictiveanalyticstoday.com/gooddata/

Google Big Data. (2018). Retrieved on May 13, 2018 from https://www.predictiveanalyticstoday.com/google-bigdata/

Gupta, S., & Saxena, S. (2016). *Real-Time Big Data Analytics*. Birmingham, UK: Packt Publishing.

Haddan, I. (2008). The Open Source Development Model: Overview, Benefits and Recommendations. Retrieved May 22, 2019 from http://aaaea.org/Al-muhandes/2008/February/open_src_dev_model.htm

Haff, G. (2018). *How open source ate software: Understanding the open source movement and so much more*. Apress.

Hahn, R. W. (2002). *Government policy toward open source software*. Brookings Institute Press.

Hassan, N. A., & Hijazi, R. (2018). *Open source intelligence methods and tools: A practical guide to online intelligence*. Academic Press.

Heatmap. (2017). Retrieved on November 19, 2017 from https://en.wikipedia.org/wiki/Heat_map

Huang, Q., Yang, C., Liu, K., Xia, J., Xu, C., Li, J., ... Li, Z. (2013). Evaluating open-source cloud computing solutions for geosciences. *Computers & Geosciences*, *§§§*, 5941–5952.

IBM. (2017). What is Big Data? Retrieved on November 20, 2017 from http://www-01.ibm.com/software/in/data/bigdata/

IBM Big Data. (2018). Retrieved on May 13, 2018 from https://www.predictiveanalyticstoday.com/ibm-big-data/

Indiana University. (2013, January 7). What are bits, bytes, and other units of measure for digital information? Retrieved October 30, 2017 from https://kb.iu.edu/d/ackw

Informatica PowerCenter Big Data Edition. (2018). Retrieved on May 13, 2018 from https://www.predictiveanalyticstoday.com/informatica-powercenter-big-data-edition/

INPUT - In-Network Programmability for next-generation personal cloud service support. (2018). Retrieved on March 27, 2018 from http://www.cloudwatchhub.eu/serviceoffers/input-network-programmability-next-generation-personal-cloud-service-support

Janert, P. K. (2011). *Data analysis with open source tools*. O'Reilly Media, Inc.

Johnston, L. (2012, April 25). A "Library of Congress" Worth of Data: It's All In How You Define It. Retrieved October 30, 2017, from https://blogs.loc.gov/thesignal/2012/04/a-library-of-congress-worth-of-data-its-all-in-how-you-define-it/

Koranne, S. (2011). Handbook of open source tools. Springer Science+Media Business, LLC. doi:10.1007/978-1-4419-7719-9

Layton, R., & Watters, P. A. (2016). *Automating open source intelligence: Algorithms for OSINT*. Waltham, MA: Elsevier.

Le, J. (2016, Aug 18). The 10 Algorithms Machine Learning Engineers Need to Know. Retrieved from https://www.kdnuggets.com/2016/08/10-algorithms-machine-learning-engineers.html

Leong, L., Bala, R., Lowery, C., & Smith, D. (2017). Magic Quadrant for Cloud Infrastructure as a Service, Worldwide. Retrieved on November 24, 2017 from https://www.gartner.com/doc/reprints?id=1-2G2O5FC&ct=150519

Li, X., & Qiu, J. (Eds.). (2014). Cloud Computing for Data-Intensive Applications. Springer Science+Business Media. doi:10.1007/978-1-4939-1905-5

Lindberg, V. (2008). *Intellectual property and open source: A practical guide to protecting code*. O'Reilly Media Inc.

Linux. (2011). Understanding the Linux Open Source Development Model. Retrieved May 22, 2019 from http://www.ibrahimatlinux.com/uploads/6/3/9/7/6397792/00.pdf

Liu, X., Dastjerdi, A. V., & Buyya, R. (2016). Stream processing in IoT: Foundations, state-of-the-art, and future directions. In *Internet of Things: Principles and Paradigms*. Morgan Kaufmann.

Mandal, S., Kandar, S., & Ray, P. (2011). Open Incremental Model: A Open Source Software Development Life Cycle Model 'OSDLC'. *International Journal of Computers and Applications, 212*(1), 2473–3327.

Manyika, J., Chui, M., Brown, B., Bughin, J., Dobbs, R., & Roxburgh, C. (2011). *Big data: The next frontier for innovation, competition, and productivity*. Washington, DC: McKinsey Global Institute.

Marr, B. (2016). Big data in practice: How 45 successful companies used big data analytics to deliver extraordinary results. John Wiley & Sons, Ltd. doi:10.1002/9781119278825

Mayer-Schönberger, V., & Cukier, K. (2013). *Big data: A revolution that will transform how we live, work, and think*. Boston: Houghton Mifflin Harcourt.

McAfee, A., & Brynjolfsson, E. (2012). Big data: The management revolution. *Harvard Business Review, 90*(10), 61–68. PubMed

Metz, C. (2015). Google just open sourced the artificial intelligence engine at the heart of its online empire. Retrieved May 13, 2019 from https://www.wired.com/2015/11/google-open-sources-its-artificial-intelligence-engine/?GuidesLearnMore

Nabi, Z. (2016). Pro Spark Streaming: The Zen of Real-Time Analytics using Apache Spark. Apress. doi:10.1007/978-1-4842-1479-4

National Highway Traffic Safety Administration. (2017). NCSA Data Resource Website Fatality Analysis Reporting System (FARS) Encyclopedia. National Center for Statistics and Analysis (NCSA) Motor Vehicle Traffic Crash Data. U.S. Department of Transportation. Retrieved on November 20, 2017 from ftp://ftp.nhtsa.dot.gov/fars/

National Institute of Standards and Technology. (2017). *The Definition of Fog Computing NIST SP 800-191 Includes NIST SP-500-291*. U.S. Department of Commerce.

National Institute of Standards and Technology. (2018). Fog Computing Conceptual Model NIST SP 500-325 & 500-291. U.S. Department of Commerce. Retrieved from on April 8, 2018. doi:10.6028/NIST.SP.500-325

Superior Attack Intelligence, N. O. R. S. E. (n.d.). Retrieved (Screenshot) on March 19, 2018 from http://map.norsecorp.com/#/helps

Open Source Initiative. (2007). The Open Source Definition. Retrieved on May 22, 2019 from https://opensource.org/osd

Opera Solutions Signal Hubs. (2018). Retrieved on May 13, 2018 from https://www.predictiveanalyticstoday.com/opera-solutions-signal-hubs/

Oracle Big Data Analytics. (2018). Retrieved on May 13, 2018 from https://www.predictiveanalyticstoday.com/oracle-bigdata-analytics/

Palantir Big Data. (2018). Retrieved on May 13, 2018 from https://www.predictiveanalyticstoday.com/palantir-bigdata/

Pan, J., & McElhannon, J. (2018). Future edge cloud and edge computing for Internet of Things applications. IEEE Internet of Things Journal., 5(1), 438–449. doi:10.1109/JIOT.2017.2767608

Predictive Analytics Today. (2018). Top 50 Big Data Platforms and Big Data Analytics Software. Retrieved on May 11, 2018 from https://www.predictiveanalyticstoday.com/bigdata-platforms-bigdata-analytics-software/

Psaltis, A. (2017). *Streaming Data*. Shelter Island, NY: Manning Publications Co.

Qubole. (2018). Retrieved on May 13, 2018 from https://www.predictiveanalyticstoday.com/qubole/

Quora. (2017). What are the Apache Spark concepts around its DAG (Directed Acyclic Graph) execution engine, and its overall architecture? Retrieved on May 10, 2018 from https://www.quora.com/What-are-the-Apache-Spark-concepts-around-its-DAG-Directed-Acyclic-Graph-execution-engine-and-its-overall-architecture

Rahmani, A. M. Liljeberg, Preden, J-S., & Jantsch, A. (Eds.). (2018). Fog Computing in the Internet of Things: Intelligence at the Edge. Springer Nature.

Raj, P., & Raman, A. (2018). Handbook of Research on Cloud and Fog Computing Infrastructures for Data Science. Hershey, PA: IGI Global; doi:10.4018/978-1-5225-5972-6.

Ravenna, A., Truxilla, C., & Wells, C. (2017). *SAS® Visual Statistics: Interactive Model Building Course Notes*. Cary, NC: SAS Institute, Inc.

Russom, P. (2011). Big data analytics. *TDWI Best Practices Report*, *19*, 40.

Sani, M., & Kaur, K. (2014). A review of open source software development life cycle models. *International Journal of Software Engineering and Its Applications*, *8*(3), 417–434. Retrieved from https://www.researchgate.net/publication/289328296_A_review_of_open_source_software_development_life_cycle_models

Segall, R. S. (2013). Computational Dimensionalities of Global Supercomputing. *Journal of Systemics, Cybernetics and Informatics*, *11*(9), 75–86. Retrieved from http://www.iiisci.org/journal/sci/FullText.asp?var=&id=iSA625MW

Segall, R. S. (2016a). Invited Plenary Address at International Institute of Informatics and Systemics (IIIS) Conference titled "Big Data: A Treasure Chest for Interdisciplinary Research". 20th Multi-conference on Systemics, Cybernetics, and Informatics (WMSCI 2016), Orlando, FL. Retrieved on December 26, 2016 from http://www.iiis.org/ViewVideo2016.asp?id=14

Segall, R. S. (2016b). High Performance Computing and Data Mining in Bioinformatics. FedEx Institute of Technology. Presentation at 13th Annual Meeting of MidSouth Computational Biology and Bioinformatics Society (MCBIOS), Memphis, TN. Retrieved on June 19, 2017 from http://www.memphis.edu/bioinformatics/announcements/pdfs/mcbios2016.pdf

Segall, R. S. (2017a). Using Tablets and Mobile Devices for Visual Analytics of Big Data in Bioinformatics. Presentation at 14th Annual Meeting of MidSouth Computational Biology and Bioinformatics Society (MCBIOS), Little Rock, AR. Retrieved on June 19, 2017 from https://mcbios.org/sites/mcbios.org/files/MCBIOS2017_Program_Book_Final_1_0.pdf

Segall, R. S. (2017b). Technologies for Teaching Big Data Analytics. Proceedings of 48th Meeting of Southwest Decision Sciences (SWDSI). Retrieved on June 19, 2017 from http://www.swdsi.org/swdsi2017/SWDSI_2017_CONFERENCE_PROGRAM4.pdf

Segall, R. S., & Cook, J. S. (2014). Data Visualization and Information Quality by Supercomputing. In Proceedings of the Forty-Fifth Meeting of Southwest Decision Sciences Institute (SWDSI). Dallas, TX: Academic Press. Retrieved on June 19, 2017 from http://www.swdsi.org/swdsi2014/2014_SWDSI_CFP_MARCH_2014_v7.pdf

Segall, R. S., & Cook, J. S. (2018). Handbook of Big Data Storage and Visualization Techniques. IGI Global. Retrieved June 2, 2019 from https://www.igi-global.com/book/handbook-research-big-data-storage/179829

Segall, R. S., Cook, J. S., & Niu, G. (2019). Overview of Big Data-Intensive Storage and its Technologies for Cloud and Fog Computing. *International Journal of Fog Computing*, 2(1), 74–119. doi:10.4018/IJFC.2019010104

Segall, R. S., Cook, J. S., & Zhang, Q. (2015). Research and Applications in Global Supercomputing. Hershey, PA: IGI Global Inc. Retrieved on May 19, 2017 from http://www.igi-global.com/book/research-applications-global-supercomputing/118093

Segall, R. S., & Gupta, N. (2015). Overview of Global Supercomputing. In Research and Applications in Global Supercomputing (pp. 1-32). Hershey, PA: IGI Global Inc. Retrieved on May 19, 2017 from http://www.igi-global.com/chapter/overview-of-global-supercomputing/124335

Segall, R. S., & Niu, G. (2018). Big Data and Its Visualization with Fog Computing. *International Journal of Fog Computing*, 1(2), 51–82. doi:10.4018/IJFC.2018070102

Srinivasas, K. G., Lathar, P., & Siddesh, G. M. (2018). *The Rise of Fog Computing in the Digital Era.* Hershey, PA: IGI Global.

Sunburst Graph. (2017). Retrieved on November 19, 2017 from https://en.wikipedia.org/wiki/Pie_chart#Ring_chart_.2F_Sunburst_chart_.2F_Multilevel_pie_chart

Syncsort. (2018). Retrieved on May 13, 2018 from https://www.predictiveanalyticstoday.com/syncsort/

Tableau Software. (2017). Tableau Community Instructor's Resource Page. Retrieved on May 31, 2017 from https://community.tableau.com/community/teachers/overview

Talend Open Studio. (2018). Retrieved on May 13, 2018 from https://www.predictiveanalyticstoday.com/talend-open-studio-for-data-integration/

The Apache Software Foundation. (n.d.). Retrieved October 30, 2017, from http://hadoop.apache.org/

The White House. (2012, March 29). Obama Administration Unveils "Big Data" Initiative: Announces $200 Million in New R&D Investments. Retrieved October 30, 2017, from https://obamawhitehouse.archives.gov/the-press-office/2015/11/19/release-obama-administration-unveils-big-data-initiative-announces-200

ThinkSys. (2017). The Benefits and Challenges of Open Source Software. Retrieved May 22, 2019 from https://www.thinksys.com/development/benefits-and-challenges-open-source-software/

Tibco. (2017). Parallel Coordinates Plot. Retrieved on November 19, 2017 from https://docs.tibco.com/pub/spotfire/6.5.2/doc/html/para/para_what_is_a_parallel_coordinate_plot.htm

Tole, A. A. (2013). Big data challenges. *Database Systems Journal*, *4*(3), 31–40.

Tozzi, C. (2018). *For Fun and Profit: A History of the Free and Open Source Software Revolution*. Cambridge, MA: The MIT Press.

Treemap. (2017). Retrieved on November 19, 2017 from https://en.wikipedia.org/wiki/Treemapping

Wavefront. (2018). Retrieved on May 13, 2018 from https://www.predictiveanalyticstoday.com/wavefront/

Wikipedia. (2017). Streamgraph. Retrieved on November 19, 2017 from https://en.wikipedia.org/wiki/Streamgraph

Wikipedia. (2019a). Free and open source software. Retrieved from https://en.wikipedia.org/wiki/Free_and_open-source_software

Wikipedia. (2019b). Freeware. Retrieved from https://en.wikipedia.org/wiki/Freeware

Wikipedia. (2019c). Open Source Software. Retrieved from https://en.wikipedia.org/wiki/Open-source_software

Yang, E. (2015). Chuckwa. Hadoop Wiki. Retrieved on November 20, 2017 from https://wiki.apache.org/hadoop/Chukwa

Yang, S. (2017). IoT stream processing and analytics in the fog. *IEEE Communications Magazine*, *55*(8), 21–27.

Yottabyte. (2017). Retrieved on November 21, 2017 from https://en.wikipedia.org/wiki/Yottabyte

Young, M. (2019). *Software licensing agreement: What you need to know about software licensees*. Internet Attorneys Association, LLC.

Zhou, L., Pan, S., Wang, J., & Vasilakos, A. V. (2017). Machine learning on big data: Opportunities and challenges. *Neurocomputing*, *237*, 350–361. doi:10.1016/j.neucom.2017.01.026

KEY TERMS AND DEFINITIONS

Big Data: Data that exceeds the capacity of commonly used hardware and software tools to capture, store and analyze within a tolerable elapsed time is considered as big data. The three main characteristics of big data are volume, variety, and velocity.

Circle Packing Graph: Circle packing is the study of the arrangement of circles (of equal or varying sizes) on a given surface such that no overlapping occurs and so that all circles touch one another (Circle Packing Graph, 2017).

Data Measurement: Unit measurement to indicate the volume of data in modern computer storage devices.

Free and Open Source Software (FOSS): Software that can be classified as both free software and open source software (Wikipedia, 2019a).

Freeware: Software, most often proprietary, that is distributed at no monetary cost to the end user (Wikipedia, 2019b).

Heatmap: A heat map (or heatmap) is a graphical representation of data where the individual values contained in a matrix are represented as colors (Heatmap, 2017).

Machine Learning: A process that gives machine the ability to learn without being explicitly programmed.

Open Source Software (OSS): A type of computer software in which source code is released under a license in which the copyright holder grants users the rights to study, change, and distribute the software to anyone and for any purpose (Wikipedia, 2019c).

Parallel Coordinate Plot: A parallel coordinate plot maps each row in the data table as a line, or profile. Each attribute of a row is represented by a point on the line. This makes parallel coordinate plots similar in appearance to line charts, but the way data is translated into a plot is substantially different (Tibco, 2017).

Schema on Read: Data analysis strategy that new data is transferred to a plan or schema without a predefined format.

Schema on Write: Data analysis strategy that new data is transferred to a structured predefined format.

Streaming Data: Data that has been originated, collected, processed or delivered time-wise continuously is considered as streaming data.

Streammap: A streamgraph, or stream graph, is a type of stacked area graph, which is displaced around a central axis, resulting in a flowing, organic shape (Streammap, 2017).

Sunburst Chart: A ring chart, also known as a sunburst chart or a multilevel pie chart, is used to visualize hierarchical data, depicted by concentric circles. The circle in the centre represents the root node, with the hierarchy moving outward from the center (Sunburst Graph, 2017).

Treemap: Treemaps display hierarchical (tree-structured) data as a set of nested rectangles. Each branch of the tree is given a rectangle, which is then tiled with smaller rectangles representing sub-branches (Treemap, 2017).

Yottabyte: The yottabyte is a multiple of the unit byte for digital information. The prefix yotta indicates multiplication by the eighth power of 1000 or 1024 in the International System of Units (SI), and therefore one yottabyte is one septillion (one long scale quadrillion) bytes. The unit symbol for the yottabyte is YB. 1 YB = 10008bytes = 1024bytes = 1000000000000000000000000bytes = 1000zettabytes = 1 trillionterabytes (Yottabyte, 2017).

APPENDIX

Table 8. Additional web-based Big Data visualization software (Created by Jeffrey S. Cook, Co-Editor of Handbook of Big Data Storage and Visualization Techniques, IGI Global, 2018 using (Capterra, 2017).)

Name of Web-Based Big Data Visualization Software	Web URL	Description
1010data	https://1010data.com/	1010data is a leading business intelligence provider (Forrester & Gartner), trusted by over 850 of the world's largest companies.
Alooma	https://www.alooma.com/	Alooma brings all data sources together into BigQuery, Redshift, Snowflake and more.
AnswerMiner	https://www.answerminer.com/	An amazing and fast data exploration tool with many unique features like relation maps and decision trees.
Arimo	https://arimo.com/	Machine learning algorithms and a powerful big-compute platform, Big Apps multiply the value of organization's data and people.
Axibase Time Series Database	https://axibase.com/products/axibase-time-series-database/	ATSD is a distributed NoSQL database designed from the ground up to store and analyze time-series data at scale.
BI on Big Data	http://www.kyvosinsights.com/	Kyvos is revolutionizing analytics with its breakthrough OLAP on Big Data technology.
BillRun	https://billrun.com/	Open-source billing solution, designed for Big Data. On-prem and SaaS, pre- and post-pay.
Cloudera Enterprise	https://www.cloudera.com/products.html	Cloudera delivers the modern platform for machine learning and analytics optimized for the cloud.
Cogniteev	http://www.cogniteev.com/	Cogniteev is a data access automation platform that enables companies to access and analyze complex data sets.
Datadog Cloud Monitoring	https://www.datadoghq.com/	Datadog is the essential monitoring service for hybrid cloud environments. The platform assists organizations in improving agility, increasing efficiency and providing end-to-end visibility across dynamic or high-scale infrastructures.
DataLux	http://www.vivorbis.com/	Big Data Platform solution with state of the art analytics, data lake, aggregation capabilities, and more.
Datameer	https://www.datameer.com/	Empowers organizations to embark on a data journey that answers a wide range of new, deeper business questions.
DataPlay	https://dataplay.us/	Integrated suite of applications that fully meets analysis, visualization, and presentation needs in market research.
Domo	https://www.domo.com/	Domo is cloud -based business management platform, and first solution that brings together five products into one elegant platform enabling users to connect, prepare, visualize, engage and optimize their business around data.
Graph DB	https://ontotext.com/	A semantic repository, a NoSQL database system used for storage, querying, and management of structured data.

continues on following page

Table 8. Continued

Name of Web-Based Big Data Visualization Software	Web URL	Description
Ideata Analytics	https://ideata-analytics.com/	Self-service analytics platform to source, clean, analyze, and visualize Big Data at scale using Apache Spark.
IQLECT	http://www.iqlect.com/	Actionable insights with real-time Big Data analytics. Fully converged platform and solutions for organizations of any size.
Looker	https://looker.com/	Looker works the way the web does: browser-based, its unique modeling language lets any employee leverage the work of the best data analysts. Operating 100% in-database, Looker capitalizes on the newest, fastest analytic databases to get real results, in real time. Lookers lightweight open architecture make it easy for developers to quickly and flexibly build, deploy, and iterate custom on data applications.
MicroStrategy Enterprise Analytics	https://www.microstrategy.com/us	A comprehensive enterprise analytics and mobility platform that delivers a full range of analytical and reporting capabilities.
MongoDB	https://www.mongodb.com/	From startups to enterprises, for the modern and the mission-critical
Periscope	https://www.periscopedata.com/	Periscope connects directly to the database and lets users run, visualize, and share analyses on billions of rows of data in seconds.
Phocas Software	https://www.phocassoftware.com/	Phocas Software is an award-winning Business Intelligence software used by companies across numerous industries and around the globe.
Salesforce Analytics Cloud	https://www.salesforce.com/products/einstein-analytics/overview/	For every business user. Explore any combination of data, get answers instantly, and share with others. From any device, anywhere, faster than ever before. For analysts. Deliver new insights to business users however, wherever, and whenever they want them.
SEQUEL	http://sequel.jeremyevans.net/	SEQUEL provides easy-to-use data access solutions for IBM and empowers users with quality insight to make key business decisions.
Sisense	https://www.sisense.com/	Sisense provides an end-to-end solution for tackling growing data sets from multiple sources that comes out-of-the-box with the ability to crunch terabytes of data and support thousands of users--all on a single commodity server.

Chapter 42
Open Source Software (OSS) for Big Data

Richard S. Segall
Arkansas State University, USA

ABSTRACT

This chapter discusses Open Source Software and associated technologies for the processing of Big Data. This includes discussions of Hadoop-related projects, the current top open source data tools and frameworks such as SMACK that is acronym for open source technologies Spark, Mesos, Akka, Cassandra, and Kafka that together compose the ingestion, aggregation, analysis, and storage layers for Big Data processing. Tabular summaries and categories for 38 Open Source Statistical Software (OSSS) are provided that include for each listing of features and URLs for free downloads. The current challenges of Big Data and Open Source Software are also discussed.

OPEN SOURCE SOFTWARE AND TECHNOLOGY FOR BIG DATA

In the past, companies had been writing big checks to database corporations such as Oracle, Microsoft and IBM. After 2000, Google started to encounter a problem that the data they collected were so large that no single database vender will be able to store and process their data anymore, and hence the need for Big Data technology evolved as well as Big Data Analytics.

Balihausen (2019) indicated that the percentage of FOSS (Free and Open Source Software) in the average application exceeds the amount of proprietarily applications exceeds the amount of proprietarily licensed code. According to 2019 Open Source Security and Risk Analysis (OSSRA) report published by Synopsys Cybersecurity Research Center (2019), open source represented 60% of the code analyzed in 2018, up from 57% in 2017, and 64% Open Source Software (OSS) was used for financial services, Big Data, artificial intelligence, business intelligence machine learning.

An entire book on the technology of hands-on approaches to Big Data has been published by Bahga and Madisetti (2016). The following are a few of the tools and frameworks for "batch processing" of Big Data.

DOI: 10.4018/978-1-7998-9158-1.ch042

Several studies have been completed with the "best" Open Source Software for Big Data in specific categories. These include those of Freeman, Garza et al. (2018) that discussed the best Open Source Software for cloud computing, Heller et al. (2018) the best Open Source Software for data storage analytics, Heller and Pointer (2018) the best Open Source Software (OSS) for machine learning, and Freeman, Heller et al. (2018) the best open software for software development.

Riehle (2019) discussed that the needs of open source processes have led to two major tool investigations that have since become an important part of corporate software development: Software forges and distributed version control. A software forge is a website that allow the creation of new projects and provides developers with all of the tools needed for software development. According to Riehle (2019), distributed version control is version control in which one copies the original repository for Big Data and work with your copy that does not need commit rights or permission to start work. Git and Mercurial are the two best-known examples of such software for Big Data.

Harvey (2017b) provides a detailed study of the top 35 open source companies that use Big Data and play a major role in developing and maintaining the Open Source Software that powers today's businesses.

Frampton (2018) published a complete guide to open source Big Data stack that includes components for visualization, resource management, framework queueing, processing, storage monitoring, and resource management that interact with Apache CloudStack. The following Table 1 provides representative Open Source Software for Big Data for each of these components of Big Data Stack as presented by Frampton (2018) with many of which are discussed in more depth below Table 1 and elsewhere in the following part of this chapter.

Table 1. Representative Open Source Software (OSS) for Big Data stack

Big Data Stack Component	Representative Open Source Software (OSS)
1. Visualization	Zeppelin
2. Resource Management	Mesos
3. Frameworks	Akka Spring
4. Queueing	Apache Kafka
5. Processing	Apache Spark
6. Storage	Hadoop Distributed File System (HDFS) Riak Apache Cassandra
7. Monitoring	Brooklyn Mesos
8. Release Management	Brooklyn Mesos

[Derived using Frampton (2018)]

Apache Brooklyn

Apache Brooklyn is an open-source framework for modeling, deploying and managing distributed applications defined using declarative YAML blueprints. (Wikipedia, 2019a)

Apache Riak

Riak (pronounced "ree-ack") is a distributed NoSQL key-value data store that offers high availability, fault tolerance, operational simplicity, and scalability. In addition to the open source version, it comes in a supported enterprise version and a cloud storage version as discussed both in Wikipedia (2019b) and Harvey (2014) that presents in context of 60 Open Source Apps that you can use in the cloud.

Apache Spring

The Spring Framework is an application framework and inversion of control container for the Java platform. Although the framework does not impose any specific programming model, it has become popular in the Java community as an addition to, or even replacement for the Enterprise JavaBeans (EJB) model. The Spring Framework is open source. (Wikipedia, 2019c)

The Big Data stack was also discussed by Bui (2018) for powering data lakes, data warehouses and beyond.

The following Table 2 shows the significant highlights and differences for the top 10 open source data tools for Big Data for data scientists in 2019 as derived from Verma (2018), Sharma (2019), and Some (2019).

Hadoop was developed in 2005 several years after the introduction of MapReduce in 1995. The following paragraphs discusses both tools in more depth.

Table 2. Top 10 open source data tools in 2019

Open Source Software	Distinguishing Features
1. Hadoop	Most prominent and used tool in Big Data industry. Can be run on cloud infrastructure. Consists of Hadoop Distributed File System, MapReduce, YARN and libraries.
2. Apache Spark	Can handle both batch data and real-time data. Flexible to work with HDFS and Apache Cassandra. Can run jobs 100 faster than Hadoop Map Reduce.
3. Apache Storm	Distributed real-time processing system for processing unbounded data streams. Supports any programming language. Massive scalability. Supports direct acrylic graph (DAG) topology. (Jain (2017))
4. Apache Cassandra	Manages large sets of structured data across servers. Can handle numerous concurrent uses across data centers.
5. RapidMiner	Software platform for data science for machine learning, predictive analytics, and deep learning.
6. MongoDB	Open source NoSQL database that is cross-platform compatible and easily partitions data across servers in a cloud structure and uses dynamic schemas.
7. R Programming Tool	Most widely used Big Data tool for statistical analysis of data. Has its own public library CRAN (Comprehensive R Archive Network) that consists of more than 9000 modules and algorithms for statistical analyses.
8. Neo4j	Widely used for large volumes of network data or graphs. Supports query language for graphs called Cypher.
9. Apache SAMOA	One of most well-known Big Data tools for distributed streaming algorithms for Big Data mining. Existing infrastructure is reusable to avoid implementing cycles.
10. HPCC (High-Performance Computing Cluster)	Open source distributed data computing platform under Apache 2.0 license. Supports end-to-end Big Data workflow management. Comes with binary packages supported for Linux distributions.

MapReduce

MapReduce is an open source parallel processing model and programming concept that was initially developed by Google to solve the Big Data issue. Its implementation is designed to process and generate large data sets. (Dean & Ghemawat, 2008) It divides the dataset into smaller clusters, maps the clusters into different computers or servers for processing, and then aggregates the information for the results. MapReduce is a programming model that specifies the computation so that the computation can take advantage of utlizing lots of machines or computers. MapReduce based algorithm could be more computational efficient than other traditional algorithm such as frequent-sequence-pattern-mining algorithm. (Li, Yu & Ryu, 2014).

There are three phases for MapReduce, map, shuffle and reduce. Map phase breaks down the calculation by different elements of the document such as different format of data, or different dimension of the calculation. Shuffle phase reassigns all of the elements into different computing machine according to the characteristics. Then Reduce phase collects the calculations and aggregates them for resulting. The example provided next is an overly simplified illustration. How to divide the data into different groups or clusters with effective and efficient computation is a scientific subject. (Li, Yu & Ryu, 2014).

Figure 1. MapReduce mechanism example (Designed by Niu, November 2017)

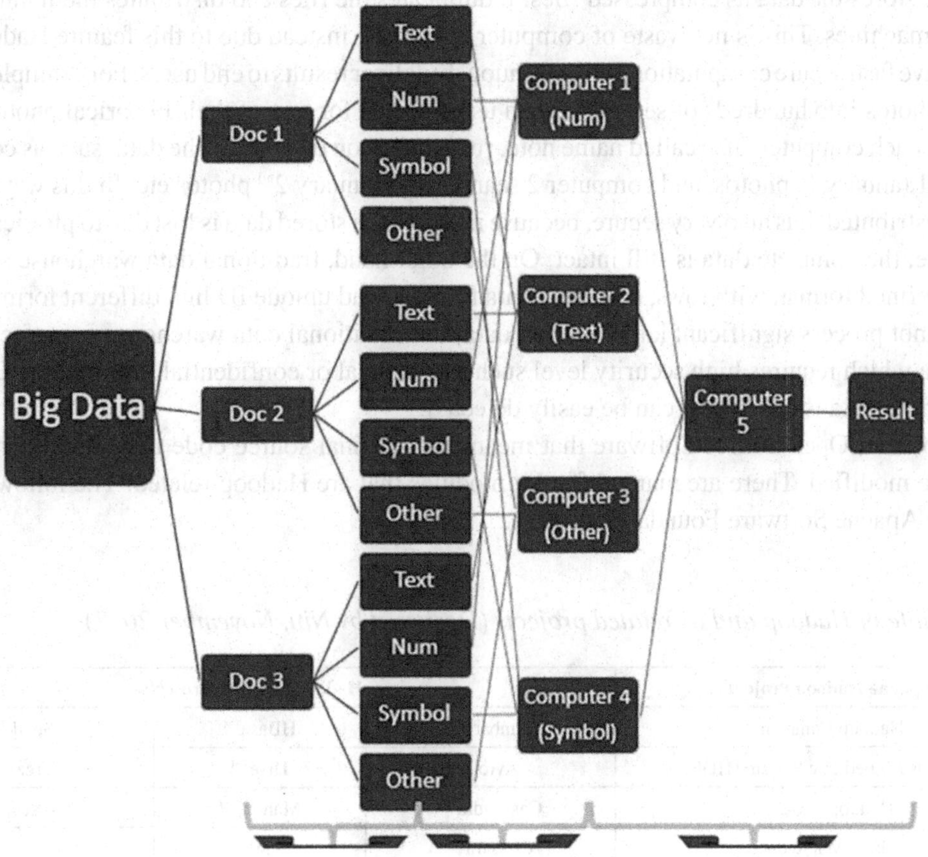

Hadoop

Hadoop is an Open Source Software framework for the storage and distributed batch processing of large datasets on a cluster of machines. (Ishwarappa & Anuradha, 2015). It is a leading Big Data technology with Hadoop YARN (Yet Another Resource Negotiator) as the next generation architecture of Hadoop. Hadoop was designed and developed by Doug Cutting and Mike Cafarella in 2005. It is widely used technology, for example, LinkedIn's Hadoop-based analytics predicts "People You May Know" for its over 200 million members. (Sumbaly, Kreps, & Shah, 2013). And Hadoop-based distributed sensor node management system will provide efficient ways to collect sensor data and managing multiple sensor nodes. (Jung, Kim, Han & Jeong, 2014)

Hadoop has a "Schema-on-read" mechanism when it collects and stores the data. "Schema- on -ead" means when transferring data from one location (file) to another, users do not have to specify the data format that needs to be transferred, but when accessing the data, users have to specify the format through extraction code. However, other traditional programming mechanism such as SQL utilizes a concept of Schema of write, which means when transferring, converting or saving the data into a different location, users have to preconfigure the data ahead of time, such as date should be for example MM/DD/YYYY or MM-DD-YYYY. When extracting the data, users only need to call on the name of the data. Schema on read feature allows the system to process data much more efficiently and be able to process a large amount of data and leave the processing work until later on.

Hadoop stores the data as compressed files. It duplicates the files and distributes them into multiple servers or machines. This is not waste of computer resources, instead due to this feature Hadoop could afford to have fast, secure computation and continuously deliver results to end users. For example, Hadoop stores all photos into hundreds of servers. When users search for one of their historical photo, Hadoop commands each computer, also called name note, run a query on one day of the data, such as computer 1 searches all January 1st photos, and computer 2 searches all January 2nd photos etc. In this way, the work has been distributed. It is also very secure, because if one of the stored data is lost due to physical damage to hardware, the complete data is still intact. On the other hand, traditional data warehouse stores data in a well-defined format, with rows, columns, data formats, and unique ID link different format. Speed-wise it cannot process significant large amount data, but traditional data warehouse is perfectly fine to handle data which requires high security level such as financial or confidential information. Because if any part of the data is missing, it can be easily detected.

Hadoop is an Open Source Software that means the original source code is made freely available and may be modified. There are many different modules that are Hadoop related. The following listed a few (The Apache Software Foundation, 2017).

Table 3. Table of Hadoop and its related projects (Designed by Niu, November 2017)

Apache Hadoop Project	Hadoop-Related Projects		
Hadoop Common	Ambari™	HBase™	Spark™
Hadoop Distributed File System (HDFS™)	Avro™	Hive™	Tez™
Hadoop YARN	Cassandra™	Mahout™	ZooKeeper™
Hadoop MapReduce	Chukwa™	Pig™	

OPEN SOURCE HADOOP-RELATED PROJECTS

The following are concise descriptions of each of the Hadoop-Related Projects listed in above Table 3. The source of these statements except for those as cited otherwise are from Bahga & Madisetti (2016).

Ambari

Ambari is a software project of Apache. It is a completely open source management platform for provisioning, managing, monitoring and securing Apache Hadoop clusters. (Hortonworks, 2017)

Avro

Avro is an Apache project that provides data serialization services. It provides compact, fast binary data format and rich data structure. It is also a container file that stores persistent data. (Apache Avro, 2013)

Cassandra

Cassandra is an open source NoSQL database management system. It is a scalable, highly available, fault tolerant open-source non-relational database system.

Chukwa

Chukwa is an open source Hadoop subproject devoted to large-scale log collection and analysis. Chukwa is built on top of the Hadoop Distributed File System (HDFS) and MapReduce framework and inherits Hadoop's scalability and robustness. Chukwa also includes a flexible and powerful toolkit for displaying, monitoring and analyzing results, in order to make the best use of this collected data. (Yang, 2015)

HBase

Apache HBase is an open source non-relational distributed database, plus Phoenix that is a high-performance SQL layer for low latency applications.

Hive

Apache Hive is an open source data warehouse system for querying and analyzing large data sets that are principally stored in Hadoop files. Hive is a data warehouse system for ad-hoc queries and analyses of large datasets and table and storage management service.

Mahout

Apache Mahout is an open source project of the Apache Software Foundation that is used to construct scalable libraries of machine learning algorithms focused primarily in the areas of collaborative filtering, clustering and classification.

Pig

Pig is an open source volunteer project under the Apache Software Foundation and is scripting platform for analyzing large datasets.

Spark

Apache Spark is an open source distributed general-purpose cluster-computing framework that is a fast and general engine for large-scale data processing. Spark features an advanced Directed Acyclic Graph (DAG) engine supporting cyclic data flow. Each Spark job creates a DAG of task stages to be performed on the cluster. (Quora (2017)). According to Zaharia et al. (2016), this open source computing framework unifies streaming, batch, and interactive Big Data workloads to enable new applications and combine them. Apache Spark applications range from finance to scientific data processing and combines libraries for SQL, machine learning and graphs

Tez

Apache Tez is an open source framework designed to build data-flow driven processing runtimes. Tez is the next generation Hadoop Query Processing framework written on top of YARN (Yet Another Resource Negotiator). Saha et al. (2015) discussed use of Apache Tez for building data processing applications.

ZooKeeper

ZooKeeper is an open source Apache project that provides centralized infrastructure and services that enable synchronization across an Apache Hadoop cluster.

BIG DATA SMACK

SMACK stands for <u>S</u>park, <u>M</u>esos, <u>A</u>kka, <u>C</u>assandra and <u>K</u>afka and all of these are open source technologies and all are Apache software except for Akka.

Apache Spark is an open source component of SMACK and is not a replacement for Hadoop. Apache Spark is a computing engine, whereas Hadoop is a complete stack for storage, cluster management, and computing tools. Apache Hadoop is used to solve issues relating to data warehousing and batch processing. Apache Spark should be used however if the issues are the speed of response and if the speed is measured in speed units instead of data size units. (Estrada & Ruiz (2016))

The following Table 4 present characteristics of each of these open source technologies as derived from Estrada & Ruiz (2016).

MEMSQL (2019) provided a guide to pairing open-source software Apache Kafka with a real-time database that uses a real-time infrastructure data pipeline that consists of a datacenter of message queue, transform tier, datastore, and applications and analytics.

Table 4. The open source components of Big Data SMACK

Open Source Technology	Role	Description
Spark	The engine: Aggregation Layer & Analysis Layer	Consists of 5 components: 1. Spark Core 2. Spark SQL 3. Spark Streaming 4. Spark MLib 5. Spark GraphX
Mesos	The container: Ingestion Layer, Aggregation Layer, Analysis Layer & Storage Layers	Orchestrates components and manages resources. It is equivalent of Apache YARN in Hadoop.
Akka	The model: Aggregation Layer & Analysis Layers	Free and open-source toolkit and runtime simplifying the construction of concurrent and distributed applications on the Java Virtual Machine (JVM) platform. Akka supports multiple programming models for concurrency.
Cassandra	The storage: Storage Layer	Handles the stack's operational data and is a distributed database that is ideal for real-time ingestion.
Kafka	The message broker: Ingestion Layer	The data ingestion point, mainly on the application layer. Kafka is an open-source stream processing software written in Scala and Java. It takes data from applications and streams and processes then into the stack by partitioning and distributing across the cluster nodes.

Apache Spark of SMACK Versus MapReduce

Table 5 below provides some comparisons of the characteristics of Apache Spark that is part of SMACK with MapReduce. Table 4 was created with reference Estrada & Ruiz (2016).

Table 5. Comparisons of some characteristics of Apache Spark with MapReduce

CONCEPT	Apache Spark	MapReduce
Language of Code	Scala/Akka	Java
Languages Supported	Java, Scala, Python, and R	Java only
Data Streaming	Able to perform real-time streaming processing without additional add-ons.	Requires additional add-on such as Apache Storm to perform and thus increases complexity.
Source Code Size	Scala programs have dozens of lines of code.	Java programs have hundreds of lines of code.
Machine Learning	Spark ML contained within.	Needs to separately integrate Machine Learning module that requires self-learning of operation.
Graphs	Spark Graph X contained within.	Needs to separately integrate Graphical module or some other technology that may create compatibility issues.

Some Other Open Source Big Data Formats

Table 6 below provides some other Open Source Software for Big Data and their characteristics that were discussed by Maayan (2018).

Table 6. Some other Open Source Software technologies for Big Data

Software Name	Software Technology	Properties
Apache Beam	Programming model	Can be used to define and execute both batch and streaming data processing pipelines.
TensorFlow	Open Source Library	Uses machine learning models that can be applied to analyze customer interactions in real-time and help virtual agents better answer questions.
MongoDB	NoSQL database program	Facilitates the storage of large volumes of unstructured data.
Lumify	Analysis and visualization platform	Can create 2D and 3D graphs and works on AWS (Amazon Web Server) environments.

OPPORTUNITIES FOR BIG DATA AND OPEN SOURCE SOFTWARE

The use of Open Source Software (OSS) with Big Data presents tremendous potentials both financially and socially in the future. The value of Big Data has already been recognized by many industries and governments. (Benjelloun, Lahcen & Belfkih, 2015)

Retailers use Big Data for better marketing and customer services; financial industry analyzes Big Data of business and economic vitals for dynamic decision-making support; health care industry utilize Big Data of patients for more effective treatment and pandemics prediction; and social media is generating massive amount data from its digital material to improve effective communications. With Big Data, weather and climate could be better predicted to help farmers increase production. Energy conservation and resource management as well as other application areas are important opportunities for Big Data and Fog Computing.

STATISTICAL OPEN SOURCE SOFTWARE (OSS) FOR BIG DATA

Many studies have been completed about open source or free statistical software. These include PAT Research (2018) that provides a detailed comparative report of the top 52 free statistical software, StatisticalConsultantsLtd. (2019) that provides links for 269 free software that are not specified if for Big Data or not, Medeval.com (2019), and Wikipedia (2019d).

Table 7 was constructed to provide categories of statistical purpose for the 38 Open Source Statistical Software (OSSS) provided in Wikipedia (2019d) from which Table 8 was constructed that also includes URLs for home page & free downloads in addition to the features for each of the 38 open source statistical software.

Table 7. Statistical purposes of Open Source Software (OSS) described in Table 6

STATISTICAL PURPOSE	OPEN SOURCE SOFTWARE (OSS)
1. Bayesian	Bayesian Filtering Library
2. Econometrics	GRETI JMulti
3. Data Mining	AdaMSoft KNIME Root
4. Machine Learning	LIBSVM and LIBLINEAR Mlpack OpenNN (Open Neural Network Library) Shogun Torch (machine learning)
5. Visualization and Graphics	DAP GNU Octave Mondrian Orange Ploticus SimFit Statitical Lab (Statistiklabor) Weka
6. Biometrics	Intrinsic Noise Analyzer (iNA) Neurophysiological Biomaker Toolbar (NBT) OpenEpi
7. Data Manipulation	Pandas Perl Data Language (PDL)
8. Structural Equation Modeling	OpenMx
9. Alternatives to MATLAB	GNU Octave Scilab
10. Python coded	Salstat SciPy
11. C++ coded	ADBM Bayesian Filtering Library Mlpal OpenNN (Open Neural Networks Library) Shogun Stan
12. General Purpose	ELKI PSPP R Statistical Online Computational Resource (SCOR) SOFA (Statistics Open for All)

Table 8. Some available Open Source Statistical Software (OSS) for Big Data analytics

OPEN SOURCE SOFTWARE (OSS)	FEATURES	URL for Home Page & Free Downloads
AdaMSoft	Developed in Java and can run on any platform supporting Java; performs Data Management, Data and Web Mining, Statistical Analysis.	http://adamsoft.sourceforge.net/ http://adamsoft.sourceforge.net/download.html
ADBM	Non-linear statistical modeling; based in C++, "AD": Automatic Differentiation.	http://www.admb-project.org/ http://www.admb-project.org/downloads/
Bayesian Filtering Library	Open source (GNU LGPL) C++ library for recursive Bayesian estimation.	http://www.orocos.org/bfl http://www.orocos.org/bfl/download
DAP	A statistics and graphics program based on the C programming language that performs data management, analysis, and C-style graphical visualization tasks without requiring complex syntax.	https://www.gnu.org/software/dap/
ELKI (Environment for DeveLoping KDD-Applications Supported by Index-Structures)	Cluster Analysis, Anomaly detection, spatial index structures, Principle component analysis, multidimensional scaling.	https://elki-project.github.io/
GNU Octave	Free alternative to MATHLAB; built-in plotting and visualization tools.	https://www.gnu.org/software/octave/
GRETI (GNU Econometrics, Time-Series,	Gretl is an open-source statistical package, mainly for econometrics. The name is an acronym for GNU Regression, Econometrics and Time-series Library.	http://gretl.sourceforge.net/
intrinsic Noise Analyzer (iNA)	For studying reaction kinetics in living cells.[1] The software analyzes mathematical models of intracellular reaction kinetics such as gene expression, regulatory networks or signaling pathways to quantify concentration fluctuations due to the random nature.	http://www.ina.bio.ed.ac.uk/
JASP	Offers frequentist inference and Bayesian inference on the same statistical models. Frequentist inference uses p-values and confidence intervals to control error rates in the limit of infinite perfect replications. Bayesian inference uses credible intervals and Bayes factors to estimate credible parameter values and model evidence given the available data and prior knowledge.	https://jasp-stats.org/
Just Another Gibbs Sampler (JAGS)	Program for simulation from Bayesian hierarchical models using Markov chain Monte Carlo (MCMC).	http://mcmc-jags.sourceforge.net/
JMulTi	Interactive software for econometric analysis, specialized in univariate and multivariate time series analysis.	http://www.jmulti.com/
KNIME (Konstanz Information Miner)	Integrates various components for machine learning and data mining through its modular data pipelining concept.	https://www.knime.com/
LIBSVM and LIBLINEAR	Machine learning libraries, A Library for Support Vector Machines.	https://www.csie.ntu.edu.tw/~cjlin/libsvm/
mlpack	Machine learning software library for C++.	https://mlpack.org/
Mondrian	General-purpose statistical data-visualization system, for interactive data visualization.	http://www.theusrus.de/Mondrian/
Neurophysiological Biomarker Toolbox (NBT)	Open source MATLAB toolbox for the computation and integration of neurophysiological biomarkers.	https://www.nbtwiki.net/
OpenBUGS	Software application for the Bayesian analysis of complex statistical models using Markov chain Monte Carlo (MCMC) methods.	http://openbugs.net/w/FrontPage
OpenEpi	A web-based, open-source, operating-independent series of programs for use in epidemiology and statistics based on JavaScript and HTML.	http://www.openepi.com/Menu/OE_Menu.htm
OpenNN (Open Neural Networks Library)	A software library written in the programming language C++ which implements neural networks, a main area of deep learning research	http://www.opennn.net/
OpenMx	Open source program for extended structural equation modeling.	https://openmx.ssri.psu.edu//

continues on following page

Table 8. Continued

OPEN SOURCE SOFTWARE (OSS)	FEATURES	URL for Home Page & Free Downloads
Orange	Open source data visualization, machine learning and data mining toolkit.	https://orange.biolab.si/
pandas	Software library written for the Python programming language for data manipulation and analysis.	https://pandas.pydata.org/
Perl Data Language (PDL)	Set of free software array programming extensions to the Perl programming language. PDL extends the data structures built into Perl, to include large multidimensional arrays, and adds functionality to manipulate those arrays as vector objects. It also provides tools for image processing.	http://pdl.perl.org/
Ploticus	Free, open source (GPL) computer program for producing plots and charts from data. It runs under Unix, Solaris, Mac OS X, Linux and Win32 system.	http://ploticus.sourceforge.net/doc/welcome.html
PSPP	Free software application for analysis of sampled data, intended as a free alternative for IBM SPSS Statistics. It has a graphical user interface (GUI) and conventional command-line interface, has support for over 1 billion variables.	https://www.gnu.org/software/pspp/
R	Programming language and free software environment for statistical computing and graphics supported by the R Foundation for Statistical Computing.	https://www.r-project.org/
Root	Object-oriented program (OOP) and library developed by CERN. It was originally designed for particle physics data analysis and contains several features specific to this field, but it is also used in other applications such as astronomy and data mining.	https://root.cern.ch/
Salstat	Free software application for the statistical analysis of numeric data with an emphasis on ease-of-use, written in Phython.	https://www.salstat.com/
Scilab	Free and open source, cross-platform numerical computational package and a high-level, numerically oriented programming language, one of the two major open-source alternatives to MATLAB, the other one being GNU Octave.	https://www.scilab.org/
SciPy	Free and open source Python library used for scientific computing and technical computing.	https://scipy.org/scipylib/
Shogun	Free, open source machine learning software library written in C++. It offers numerous algorithms and data structures for machine learning problems. It offers interfaces for Octave, Python, R, Java, Lua, Ruby and C# using SWIG.	http://www.shogun.ml/
Simfit	Free open source Windows package for simulation, curve fitting, statistics, and plotting, using a library of models or user-defined equations.	http://www.simfit.org.uk/
Statistics Online Computational Resource (SOCR)	Online multi-institutional research and education organization. SOCR designs, validates and broadly shares a suite of online tools for statistical computing, and interactive materials for hands-on learning and teaching concepts in data science, statistical analysis and probability theory.	http://socr.umich.edu/
SOFA (Statistics Open For All)	Open source statistical package that can connect directly to MySQL, PostgreSQL, SQLite, MS Access (mdb), Microsoft SQL Server, and CUBRID.	http://www.sofastatistics.com/home.php
Stan	Probabilistic programming language for statistical inference written in C++.	https://mc-stan.org/
Statistical Lab (Statistiklabor)	Explorative and interactive toolbox for statistical analysis and visualization of data. It supports educational applications of statistics in business administration, economics, social sciences and humanities.	http://www.statistiklabor.de/en/

continues on following page

Table 8. Continued

OPEN SOURCE SOFTWARE (OSS)	FEATURES	URL for Home Page & Free Downloads
Torch (machine learning)	Open source machine learning library, a scientific computing framework, and a script language based on the Lua programming language. It provides a wide range of algorithms for deep learning, and uses the scripting language LuaJIT, and an underlying C implementation.	http://torch.ch/
Weka (Waikato Environment for Knowledge Analysis)	Suite of machine learning software written in Java, developed at the University of Waikato, New Zealand. It is free software licensed under the GNU General Public License. Weka contains a collection of visualization tools and algorithms for data analysis and predictive modeling, together with graphical user interfaces for easy access to these functions	https://www.cs.waikato.ac.nz/~ml/weka/

References used to construct above Table 8.1.) https://en.wikipedia.org/wiki/List_of_statistical_packages

CHALLENGES FOR BIG DATA AND OPEN SOURCE SOFTWARE (OSS)

Challenges for Big Data

Data Quality Challenge

There are many challenges when dealing with Big Data, and especially with streaming data and its implementation with Fog Computing. Typical issues are those of missing data, volatility, inconsistent data, and selectivity with Big Data analysis. (Daas, Puts, Buelens & van den Hurk, 2015) Volatility occurs when the data collection phase involves inconsistent process, such as portion of data collected daily, and others collected weekly. Selectivity occurs when data collected is biasedly selectively instead of representative. It will challenge the researchers to be able to conduct unbiased statistical analysis to support decision-making process.

Privacy Violation

The Internet generates tremendous amounts of data continuously without explicit permission of users. This raises the question if a Big Data processor has legal right to collect, analyze or distribute the data and data-related products? Social security numbers and birthdates are obvious examples that are related to privacy and security. But other types of data such as medical search records may easily categorize into a grey area and challenges Big Data users to properly comply with regulations.

Hardware and Software

Building a large database is challenging due to the high cost of hardware. The current personal (PC) or working computer are in the level of GB (gigabyte) to process data, but the amount of data generated every day are in TB (terabyte) and PB (petabyte) levels such as social media and financial records. Purchasing and maintaining hardware with sufficient capacity would cost significant amounts of financial and human resources.

Because hardware capacity constrains software installation (Tole, 2013), this is also a challenge in the Big Data era. Currently, Hadoop and its related projects are the leading software dealing with Big

Data. There will be many more software developed to improve the efficiency of Big Data analytics for various sectors of industries as well as for the various types of hardware such as mobile devices and tablets that compose the Internet of Things (IoT) in Fog Computing.

Challenges With Big Data in Fog Computing

Fog Computing entails the previously described challenges with Big Data and also others. These other challenges include that for stream processing of scalability and elasticity as the ability of dynamically scaling to the correct size on demand, robustness for real-time processing, Service Level Agreement (SLA) compliance, and load balancing. (Liu et al., 2016).

Challenges for Open Source Software (OSS)

Challenges for Open Source Software (OSS) have been addressed by many including that of The Linux Foundation (2017), Tozzi (2017), and Harvey (2017b).

The Linux Foundation (2017) provides six operational challenges to using Open Source Software that includes (1.) the fact that some organizations must deal with OSS from hundreds of sources that may be both commercial and non-commercial, (2.) higher volume of third-party software acquisition decisions, (3.) integration of a large number of third party components can create complexity, (4.) how an organization can obtain technical support and updates from all of the different open source components.

Tozzi (2017) indicates that the open source community has a new set of challenges that includes: (1.) cloud computing that denies users many of the freedoms they would otherwise gain by using Open Source Software, (2.) The Internet of Things (IoT) that lack interfaces to modify code of the incorporated open source technologies, (3.) Apple products are currently mainly not accessible to its open-source codes and remains predominately proprietary, (4.) higher degree of corporate control over open source code by paid contractors such as Red Hat and Intel.

Harvey (2017b) discuss ten open source challenges that includes security, updates, licensing issues, too many contributors, corporate sponsorship, and software as a service (SaaS) that allows users to get access to the latest version of an application from any device they choose for a low flat monthly fee.

CONCLUSION

This chapter provides an overview of Open Source Software and the associated technologies currently available for processing Big Data that is both in batch and streaming data formats. Apache Spark had more versatility in computer languages supported than MapReduce and data streaming processing capabilities without additional add-ons.

This chapter also presents many Open Source Software for statistical processing of Big Data that is the theme of the following chapters of this Research Insights book.

ACKNOWLEDGMENT

Acknowledgement needs to be made to Co-Editor Dr. Gao Niu for using computer software to construct Figures 1 and Table 3 of this chapter to whom related preliminary descriptive information and hand sketches were provided.

REFERENCES

Apache Avro. (2013). Retrieved May 17, 2018 from https://cwiki.apache.org/confluence/display/AVRO/Index

Apache Brooklyn. (2019). Retrieved July 8, 219 from https://en.wikipedia.org/wiki/Apache_Brooklyn

Bahga, A., & Madisetti, V. (2016). *Big data science & analytics: A hands-on approach*. Big-Data-Analytics Book Company. Retrieved from www.big-data.analytics.com

Balihausen, M. (2019). Free and open source software explained. *Computer, 52*(6), 82–86. doi:10.1109/MC.2019.2907766

Bui, A. (2018). *The big data stack: Powering data lakes, data warehouses and beyond*. Retrieved July 8, 2019 from https://blog.panoply.io/the-big-data-stack-powering-data-lakes-data-warehouses-and-beyond

Dean, J., & Ghemawat, S., (2008). MapReduce: Simplified Data Processing on Large Clusters, *Communications of the ACM, 51*(1), 107-113.

Estrada, R. & Ruiz, I. (2016). *Big Data SMACK: A Guide to Apache Spark, Mesos, Akka, Cassandra, and Kafka*. Apress.'

Frampton, M. (2018). *Complete Guide to Open Source Big Data Stack*. Apress.

Freeman, J., Heller, M., Wayner, & Yegulalp, S. (2018). *The best open source software for software development*. Retrieved May 26, 2019 from https://www.infoworld.com/article/3306453/the-best-open-source-software-for-software-development.html

Freeman, J., Garza, V.R., Oliver, A.C., Pointer, I., & Yegulalp. (2018). *The best open source software for cloud computing*. Retrieved May 26, 2019 from https://www.infoworld.com/article/3306455/the-best-open-source-software-for-cloud-computing.html

Harvey, C. (2014). 60 Open Source Apps You Can Use in the Cloud. *Datamation*. Retrieved July 8, 2019 from https://www.datamation.com/open-source/60-open-source-apps-you-can-use-in-the-cloud-2.html

Harvey, C. (2017a). 10 Open Source Challenges. *Datamation*. Retrieved May 27, 2019 from https://www.datamation.com/open-source/slideshows/10-open-source-challenges.html

Harvey, C. (2017b). Top 35 Open Source Companies. *Datamation*. Retrieved May 27, 2019 from https://www.datamation.com/open-source/35-top-open-source-companies-1.html

Heller, M., Oliver, A. C., & Pointer, I. (2018). *The best open source software for data storage and analytics*. Retrieved May 26, 2019 from https://www.infoworld.com/article/3306454/the-best-open-source-software-for-data-storage-and-analytics.html

Heller, M., & Pointer, I. (2018). *The best open source software for machine learning.* Retrieved May 26, 2019 from https://www.infoworld.com/article/3308398/the-best-open-source-software-for-machine-learning.html

Hortonworks. (2017). *Apache Ambari.* Retrieved on November 20, 2017 from https://hortonworks.com/apache/ambari/

Ishwarappa, D., & Anuradha, J. (2015). A brief introduction on big data 5Vs characteristics and Hadoop Technology. *Procedia Computer Science*, *48*, 319–324. doi:10.1016/j.procs.2015.04.188

Jain, A. (2017). *Mastering Apache Storm: Real-time big data streaming using Kafka, Hbase and Redis.* Birmingham, UK: Packt Publishing Ltd.

Jung, I., Kim, K., Han, B., & Jeong, C. (2014). Hadoop-Based Distributed Sensor Node Management System. *International Journal of Distributed Sensor Networks*, *2014*, 1–7.

Li, M., Yu, X., & Ryu, K. (2014). MapReduce-based web mining for prediction of web-user navigation. *Journal of Information Science*, *40*(5), 557–567. doi:10.1177/0165551514544096

Liu, X., Dastjerdi, A. V., & Buyya, R. (2016). Stream processing in IoT: Foundations, state-of-the-art, and future directions. In Internet of Things: Principles and Paradigms. Morgan Kaufmann.

Maayan, G. D. (2018). Out in the open: Where Big Data and Open Source Coincide. *Dataversity.* Retrieved May 26, 2019 from https://www.dataversity.net/open-big-data-open-source-coincide/

Medeval.com. (2019). *20+ Open-source Free Statistical, Data analysis and Notebook Projects for Data Scientists.* Retrieved May 27, 2019 from https://medevel.com/open-source-data-science-analysis/

MEMSQL. (2019). *Whitepaper: A guide to pairing Apache Kakfa with a real-time database.* Retrieved July 8, 2019 from https://img04.en25.com/Web/MemSQL/%7Bd56d8cb4-c828-4651-81be-cd9235119e26%7D_MemSQL-Pairing-Kafka-with-a-Real-Time-Database.pdf

Quora. (2017). *What are the Apache Spark concepts around its DAG (Directed Acyclic Graph) execution engine, and its overall architecture?* Retrieved on May 10, 2018 from https://www.quora.com/What-are-the-Apache-Spark-concepts-around-its-DAG-Directed-Acyclic-Graph-execution-engine-and-its-overall-architecture

Research, P. A. T. (2018). *Top 52 Free Statistical Software - Compare Reviews, Features, Pricing in 2019.* Retrieved May 27, 2019 from https://www.predictiveanalyticstoday.com/top-free-statistical-software/

Saha, B., Shah, H., Seth, S., Vijayaraghavan, G., Murthy, A., & Curimo, C. (2015). *Apache Tex: A unifying framework for modeling and building data processing applications.* In SIGMOD'15 Proceedings (pp. 1357–1369). Melbourne, Australia: ACM.

Sharma, N. (2019). Top 10 Open Source Big Data Tools of 2019. *Eletimes.com.* Retrieved July 7, 2019 from https://www.eletimes.com/top-10-open-source-big-data-tools-in-2019

Some, K. (2019). *Top 10 Open Source Big Data Tools for Data Scientists.* Retrieved July 7, 2019 from https://www.analyticsinsight.net/top-10-open-source-big-data-tools-for-data-scientists/

Splunk, Inc. (2019). *Splunk Enterprise Admin Manual.* Retrieved May 27, 2019 from https://docs.splunk.com/Documentation/Splunk/7.2.6/Admin/MoreaboutSplunkFree

Statistical Consultants Ltd. (2019). *List of Free Statistical Software.* Retrieved May 27, 2019 from http://l-lists.com/en/lists/dz3a5t.html

Sumbaly, R., Kreps, J., & Shah, S. (2013, June). The big data ecosystem at linkedin. In *Proceedings of the 2013 ACM SIGMOD International Conference on Management of Data* (pp. 1125-1134). ACM. 10.1145/2463676.2463707

Synopsys Cybersecurity Research Center. (2019). *2019 Open Source Security and Risk Analysis Report.* Retrieved July 7, 2019 from https://www.synopsys.com/content/dam/synopsys/sig-assets/reports/rep-ossra-19.pdf

The Apache Software Foundation. (n.d.). Retrieved October 30, 2017, from http://hadoop.apache.org/

The Linux Foundation. (2017). *6 Operational Challenges to Using Open Source Software.* Retrieved May 27, 2019 from https://www.linuxfoundation.org/blog/2017/03/6-operational-challenges-to-using-open-source-software/

Tozzi, C. (2017). *Open Source Software Top Five Challenges for 2017.* Retrieved May 27, 2019 from https://www.channelfutures.com/open-source/open-source-softwares-top-five-challenges-for-2017

Verma, A. (2018). *Top 10 Open Source Data Tools in 2019.* Retrieved May 26, 2019 from https://www.whizlabs.com/blog/big-data-tools/

Wikipedia. (2019a). *Apache Brooklyn.* Retrieved July 8, 2019 from https://en.wikipedia.org/wiki/Apache_Brooklyn

Wikipedia. (2019b). *Apache Riak.* Retrieved July 9, 2019 from https://en.wikipedia.org/wiki/Riak

Wikipedia. (2019c). *Spring Framework.* Retrieved July 9, 2019 from https://en.wikipedia.org/wiki/Spring_Framework

Wikipedia. (2019d). *List of statistical packages.* Retrieved May 27, 2019 from https://en.wikipedia.org/wiki/List_of_statistical_packages

Wikipedia. (2019e). *Apache Kakfa.* Retrieved July 8, 2019 from https://en.wikipedia.org/wiki/Apache_Kafka

Yang, E. (2015). *Chuckwa. Hadoop Wiki.* Retrieved on November 20, 2017 from https://wiki.apache.org/hadoop/Chukwa

Zaharia, M., Xin, R. S., Wendell, P., Das, T., Armburst, M., Dave, A., ... Stonica, I. (2016). Apache Spark: A unified engine for big data processing. *Communications of the ACM, 59*(11), 56–65.

KEY TERMS AND DEFINITIONS

Apache Cassandra: Open Source Software for managing large sets of structured data across servers.

Apache Kafka: Open-source stream-processing software platform developed by LinkedIn and donated to the Apache Software Foundation, written in Scala and Java. Kafka can also connect to external systems (for data import/export) via Kafka Connect and provides Kafka Streams, a Java stream processing library (Wikipedia, 2019e).

Apache Spark: Open Source Software that composes the aggregation and analysis layer of Apache SMACK.

Apache Storm: Open Source Software for distributed real-time processing system for processing unbounded data streams.

Big Data Stack: Composed of layers for presentation, application, operating system, virtualization, network, and physical infrastructure such as cloud.

Hadoop: Hadoop is an open-source software framework for the storage and processing of large datasets on a cluster of machines.

MapReduce: A programming algorithm that divide and map the elements of dataset, then shuffle and distribute to cluster of computing powers for Big Data processing.

SMACK: Acronym for open source technologies Spark, Mesos, Akka, Cassandra, and Kafka that together compose the ingestion, aggregation, analysis, and storage layers for Big Data processing.

Splunk: A software technology that provides the engine for monitoring, searching, analyzing, visualizing and acting on voluminous streams of real-time machine data. Its wide application and suitability make it a versatile technology (Splunk, 2019).

Splunk Free: The totally free version of Splunk software. The free license lets you index up to 500 MB per day and will never expire. The 500 MB limit refers to the amount of new data you can add (we call this indexing) per day (Splunk, 2019).

Chapter 43
Role of Open Source Software in Big Data Storage

Rupali Ahuja
University of Delhi, India

Jigyasa Malik
University of Delhi, India

Ronak Tyagi
University of Delhi, India

R. Brinda
University of Delhi, India

ABSTRACT

Today, the world is revolving around Big Data. Each organization is trying hard to explore ways for deriving value out of huge pile of data we are generating each moment. Open Source Software are widely being adopted by most academicians, researchers and industrialists to handle various Big Data needs because of their easy availability, flexibility, affordability and interoperability. As a result, several open source Big Data tools have been developed. This chapter discusses the role of Open Source Software in Big Data Storage and how various organizations have benefitted from its use. It provides an overview of popular Open Source Big Data Storage technologies existing today. Distributed File Systems and NoSQL databases meant for storing Big Data have been discussed with their features, applications and comparison.

INTRODUCTION

The emergence of data from new data sources such as the Internet of Things, Sensor Networks, Open Data on the Web, Data from Mobile Applications, Social Network data have made traditional database management systems inadequate to handle large volumes of data sets. Moreover, the size of data being

DOI: 10.4018/978-1-7998-9158-1.ch043

generated is expanding at speed of light increasing the need of new tools and technologies for handling Big Data.

Big Data technology provides the capability of capturing, analyzing and processing huge volumes of disparate data at the right speed and within the right time frame which allows real time analysis. For instance, BMW uses sensor data to inform its customers when their cars need to be serviced (Patten, 2015). The interest in Big Data in every field has risen across academicians, researchers and industry alike because of the value that may be generated by it.

Open Source Software is any software whose source code is publicly available for use, modification, sharing and re-distribution under a licensing policy (Wikipedia, 2016c). Open Source Software is the driving force behind the success of many Big Data applications because of their collaborative and knowledge sharing aspects. Many Open Source Software have been developed to cater to the needs of Big Data Storage, Processing, Handling, Analysis, Management and Visualization. Organizations are either using these software directly or customizing them according to their needs adding to the number of Open Source Software available today.

NoSQL databases and File Systems form the core component of Big Data Storage competency. A File System is a component of the Big Data stack which administers the Distributed Storage nodes for storing data into databases/data stores efficiently. Since data is distributed across networks, a file system is responsible for communication with requisite nodes and aggregating data from vast nodes to perform analysis and thereby generate the result. It also deals with Organization, Storage, Naming, Sharing and Protection of files. (Kune, Konugurthi, Agarwal, Chillarige & Buyya, 2016)

Big Data demands massive and specialized storage infrastructure due to its characteristics of high velocity, wide data variety and huge data volume. NoSQL databases are the physical storage house of large amounts of varied data coming from wide variety of sources and generated at a high velocity. NoSQL databases rein the Big Data Storage world. Depending on the type of data and velocity of data being generated by various types of sources, different types of NoSQL open source databases are available today.

This chapter focuses on the role of Open Source Software in Big Data Storage and various Open Source tools available for storing Big Data. Also, it lists some popular companies who have successfully exploited Open Source Big Data tools to establish, enhance and improve profitability of their business.

BACKGROUND

The amount of data generated each second is continuously growing at an exponential rate. Facebook, a social networking website, is home to 40 billion photos and more than 100 hours of videos are uploaded to YouTube every minute and these statistics are burgeoning at speed of light in almost every field increasing the interest and demand for Big Data Storage and management technologies. A new forecast from International Data Corporation (IDC) sees the Big Data technology and services market growing at a Compound Annual Growth Rate (CAGR) of 23.1% over the 2014-2019 forecast periods with annual spending reaching $48.6 billion in 2019 (IDC, 2016).

Open Source tools are playing prominent role in managing Big Data Storage issues. The most dominant technologies used in Big Data world, Hadoop and Apache Spark are Open Source tools. The most popular Big Data software distribution companies like Cloudera and HortonWorks have based their business around open source technologies. Open Source is the platform best suited for Big Data solutions.

Almost all Big Data solutions work on top of UNIX Operating System which is open source. Without open source tools, the Big Data world would not have grown so rapidly. According to Talend's CEO, Mike Tuchen, "the entire next-generation data platform will be open source". (Noyes, 2016)

Big Data Storage Management

The basic requirements of Big Data Storage Management System are that it must handle very large amounts of data and keep scaling to keep up with growth and that it must be in sync with analytics tools. The ideal Big Data Storage system has the following features (Cavanillas & Curry, 2016)

- Storage of virtually unlimited amounts of data.
- Copes with high rates of random write and read access.
- Handles different data models flexibly and efficiently.
- Supports both structured and unstructured data.
- Works only on encrypted data for privacy reasons.

Storage of Big Data is handled mainly by two components of Big Data Management: File Systems and NoSQL databases. Myriad tools are available for Big Data Storage. This chapter discusses a subset of major Open Source File Systems and NoSQL based tools which are prominent in the Big Data Storage world.

Open Source File Systems for Big Data

File Systems administer the distributed storage nodes for storing data into databases efficiently. It is also responsible for Organization, Storage, Naming, Sharing and Protection of files. Some popular Open Source File Systems for Big Data are discussed here.

1. Quantcast File System

Quantcast File System (QFS) is an open source, high performance, fault tolerant, distributed file system developed to support large scale processing systems like MapReduce (QFS, n. d.). It was designed as an alternative to the Apache Hadoop Distributed File System (HDFS), intended to deliver better performance and cost efficiency for large scale processing clusters. QFS evolved from Kosmos File System. QFS is written in the C++ programming language, operates within a fixed memory footprint and uses direct input and output (Wikipedia, 2016b).

QFS uses Reed-Solomon erasure coding which doubles effective Storage and improves performance (Zicari, 2013). In Reed–Solomon Encoding, the original data is striped and stored redundantly over six chunks plus three parity chunks. If any data is lost, the file can be reconstructed by applying Reed Solomon Encoding on any of the remaining six stripes. Therefore it can tolerate a loss of up to 3 stripes.

QFS architecture is based on cluster of commodity servers. *Chunk Servers* store and manage data in files in the form of chunks of 64MB. *Metaserver* stores Metadata about files, directories and their locations in memory to improve performance. It also monitors and manages Chunk Servers. It also handles client requests and provides them the location of chunk of data required.

Table 1. Key features of Quantcast File System (Adapted from (Zicari, 2013), (Ovsiannikov, Rus, Reeves, Sutter, Rao & Kelly, 2013), (Quantcast, 2017b))

Key Features of Quantcast File System
Supports "Atomic Append" i.e. simultaneous appends to files by concurrent users can be made easily which results in higher throughput.
Fault Tolerance: QFS uses Reed–Solomon Encoding in which the original data is striped and stored redundantly over six chunks plus three parity chunks. If any data is lost, the file can be reconstructed by applying Reed Solomon Encoding on any of the remaining six stripes. Therefore, it can tolerate a loss of up to 3 stripes. (Zicari, 2013).
Has a significantly faster NameNode than HDFS (Ovsiannikov et al., 2013)
To store one petabyte of data, QFS uses only 1.5 petabytes of raw storage, 50% less than HDFS, and therefore saves half the associated costs. (Ovsiannikov et al., 2013)
It doubles the capacity of an existing cluster and reduces the amount spent per petabyte to build a new one (Ovsiannikov et al., 2013).
Faster reads: QFS reads every block from six drives in parallel making its top theoretical read speed 300 MB/s. (Quantcast, 2017a)
QFS uses low level APIs that give it more control to ensure that disk access (I/O) stays optimal. (Quantcast, 2017a)
Reliable

Use Case of Quantcast

Advertising: Quantcast is mainly being used to efficiently deliver advertising solutions. Many online companies like American Diabetes Association, Hunter and The Land of Nod have effectively used Quantcast to increase their number of customers, improve their operations and take smarter campaigning decisions (Quantcast, 2017a).

2.   Hadoop Distributed File System (HDFS)

HDFS, written in Java programming language, is a highly fault tolerant file system primarily deployed and run on low cost commodity hardware. It is capable of handling complex applications that deal with large datasets (up to terabytes) and streaming access with high throughput and power to scale to hundreds of nodes in a single cluster. HDFS believes in the principle that "in case of an extremely large dataset, moving computation is cheaper than moving data". Moving the requested computation, (which is relatively much smaller than the data it is required to operate on) to execute near the data greatly minimizes network congestion and thus enhances the throughput of entire system. HDFS is not used as independent software; it comes as a component in Hadoop package. It forms the base file system of other Hadoop components like HBase. (Sharma, Tim, Wong & Shashi, 2014).

HDFS reliably stores large files across multiple machines in a typically large cluster. Each file is stored as a sequence of blocks which in turn are replicated across other machines for Fault Tolerance. Block Size, Replication Factor and number of replicas are configurable attributes. A typical HDFS cluster consists of a master server called *Namenode* and a number of slaves called *Datanodes*, placed in racks. *Namenode* stores the Metadata and helps clients to access the file system. It manages the file system namespace and provides operations to open, close and rename files and directories. It also provides and maintains mapping between blocks of file and *Datanodes*. *Datanodes* store the actual data within files and provide operations to read/write data. They provide a block report and heartbeat to *Namenode* at regular intervals. (Sharma, Tim, Wong & Shashi, 2014).

Table 2. Key features of Hadoop Distributed File System (HDFS) (Adapted from (Sharma, Tim, Wong & Shashi, 2014), (Tutorialspoint, 2016))

Key Features of Hadoop Distributed File System (HDFS)
Reliable
Easily portable to different platforms
Has master-slave architecture
Robust
Scalable and Fault Tolerant
Provides Streaming access to file system data
Provides file permissions and authentication

Some Use Cases of Hadoop (Hadoop Wiki, 2016)

a. **TubeMogul** use Apache Hadoop HDFS to manage over 300 TB of HDFS data across four Amazon EC2 Availability Zone
b. **Adobe** currently have about 30 nodes running HDFS
c. **Facebook** have developed a FUSE implementation over HDFS.

Table 3. Feature Comparison between Hadoop Distributed File System and Quantcast File System (Adapted from (Quantcast, 2016))

Hadoop Distributed File System (HDFS)	Quantcast File System (QFS)	Features
Java	C++	Language
Slow in comparison to QFS	Fast in comparison to HDFS	Read/Write
Slow as compared to QFS	Faster namenode creation	Metaserver Creation
Quantcast	Part of Apache Hadoop Project	Developed by ??? (Incomplete sentence)

3. Lustre

Lustre is a Distributed File System or Network File System available for Linux. It is an open source high-performance file system from Cluster File Systems, Inc. It has three main components the Metadata Server, Object Storage Server and Clients.

a. The *Metadata Server* (MDS) provides metadata services for a file system and manages a Metadata Target (MDT) that stores the file metadata.
b. The *Object Storage Server* (OSS) manages the Object Storage Targets (OST) that stores file data objects (Lustre, 2016a). Lustre nodes contain references to the Object Storage Target (OST) that stores the file data objects.
c. *Clients* are the nodes that run Lustre client software.

Table 4. Key features of Lustre (Adapted from (nasa.gov, 2016))

Key Features of Lustre
Shared File System for Linux Clusters
Highly Scalable
High Performance
Highly Secure
File Stripping

Some Use Cases of Lustre

a. Department of Energy National Laboratories including Lawrence Livermore, Sandia and Oak Ridge were some early adopters of Lustre. Recently, Los Alamos' Cielo supercomputer is supported by the Lustre file system. (Lustre, 2016b)

b. The Scalability offered by Lustre deployments has made them common in the oil and gas manufacturing, rich media, and finance sectors. Around 10,000 downloads of Lustre software occur every month (Sun Microsystems Inc., 2007). And 70% of the top 100 fastest supercomputers in the world rely on Lustre for their storage needs.

4. GlusterFS

GlusterFS is an Open Source distributed file system written in C language. GlusterFS has developer community as well as commercial version is provided by Red Hat Inc. GlusterFS does not use the concept of storing the metadata of files on the server, instead it has a client server design and it employs Elastic Hashing Algorithm to distribute data efficiently and implements a fully distributed architecture. There is no metadata server in GlusterFS. Brick is the basic unit of Storage in GlusterFS and volume is the collection of all bricks. (GlusterFS Developer, 2006)

Table 5. Key features of GlusterFS (Adapted from (Deshmukh, 2015), (Kumar, 2015))

Key Features of GlusterFS
Highly Scalable - It can scale out petabytes of data to store and can handle thousands of clients.
Flexible - It provides privilege to users to flexibly combine Storage resources (Physical, Virtual or Cloud) and other computer resources to attain level of high performance and well manageable resource pool so that data can be managed in a single global namespace.
Low Cost - GlusterFS incurs minimal cost as compared to the conventional solutions for having the combined resources.
Easy to install and use

Some Use Cases of GlusterFS

a.   Scale-out Storage Systems based on GlusterFS are suitable for unstructured data such as documents, images, audio and video files, and log files. Early adopters of GlusterFS are the major visual film companies "Cutting edge" and "Picture Marketing" ((Brooks, 2013),(Brockmeier, 2013))

b.   GlusterFS has found applications in Cloud Computing and streaming Media Services.

c.   GlusterFS is also used for Content Delivery Networks (such as storing data of media sites, domain of education sites and business domain, etc.) (Rouse, 2013b)

d.   "Aaron Toponce" has put their workstations into a GlusterFS cluster to test distributed replication. (Toponce, 2016)

Table 6. Feature Comparison between Hadoop Distributed File System, GlusterFS and Lustre (Adapted from (Depardon, Le Mahec & Seguin, 2016))

Hadoop Distributed File System (HDFS)	GlusterFS	Lustre	Feature/File System
Centralized	Decentralized	Centralized	Architecture
All faults taken care of automatically as it is fully connected	Detected but no correction is done	Manual	Fault Detection
No failover	High	Failover	System Availability
Replication	RAID-like	No	Data Availability
Asynchronous	Synchronous	RAID-like	Replication
Automatic	Manual	None	Load Balancing

Major Open Source NoSQL Databases for Big Data

Today, data is being generated from a wide variety of sources like mobiles, sensors, Internet of Things, web data, etc. These wide varieties of data types have given rise to different ways of storing and handling them. NoSQL databases are dominantly used to provide storage and retrieval of large amounts of varied data coming from wide variety of sources and generated at a high velocity. NoSQL databases allow any type of data to be stored which may not require fixed table schemas. They can be efficiently used in distributed environment, are highly scalable and provide high availability. Depending on the type of data to be stored, NoSQL databases have been categorized as Key Value Store, Document Store, Column Oriented Store and Graph Sstores.

Key-Value Store

A Key Value Store is a database based on associative array as the fundamental data model where each key is associated with a value (image, document or file). It has no query language. It uses simple get, put and delete commands to store, retrieve and update data. The simplicity of this model makes a Key Value Store fast, easy to use, scalable, portable and flexible. (Aerospike, 2017c)

Some of the examples of Open Source Key Value Stores are Redis, Riak, Voldemort, Aerospike, Tarantool and LevelDB.

Riak

Riak is an Open Source, distributed Key/Value database written in Erlang. Its design is based on Amazon Dynamo. The basic structure of a Riak request is setting a value, reading it and deleting it. The actions are related to HTTP methods (PUT, GET, POST and DELETE). It is less expensive to operate than other NoSQL databases as it requires less CPU.

Table 7. Key Features of Riak (Adapted from (Basho Technologies, 2016))

Key Features of Riak
Massive Scalability
Global Object Expiration - As data ages, it may no longer be needed. Object Expiration provides a solution by deleting large volumes of aging data thus leading to the development of efficient application.
Intelligent Replication - Riak makes three replicas of data on different nodes. If one node is unavailable due to server failures or network outages, then application can still read and write data.
Robust API's and Client libraries

Riak is built to handle a variety of challenges facing Big Data applications that include tracking user or session information, storing connected device data and replicating data across the globe. Currently, it is being used by a number of organizations and firms which includes Github, Comcast, Voxer, Disqus and others with the larger systems storing hundreds of TBs of data and handling several GBs per node daily. (Redmond, 2013)

Redis

Redis database is in-memory data store used as Cache, Data Store and Memory Broker. It is an Open Source BSD licensed written in ANSI C. It supports a wide range of data structures such as Strings, Hashes, Lists and Sets, Sorted Sets with range queries, Bitmaps and Geospatial Indexes with radius queries. (Rouse, 2013a)

Table 8. Key Features of Redis (Adapted from (High Scalability, 2011), (ObjectRocket, 2016))

Key Features of Redis
Session Cache - Redis is persistent and because of this feature it is preferred over other session stores.
Built-in Replication supporting Master/Slave architecture
Performs Atomic Operations
Full Page Cache (FPC) - Redis operates in easy FPC .With Disk Persistence, users don't encounter any difference in page load speed.
Queues - Redis has in-memory Storage engine for performing operations and this makes it a good choice for Message Queue. It can perform set of additional queue operations other than traditional queue functions.

Redis can be used in a number of use cases like Caching, Messaging Queues, short lived data in application like web application sessions, web page hit counts, etc (Gulati, 2011). There are many popular organizations that are using powerful Redis databases like Twitter, GitHub, Weibo, Snapchat, Digg, StackOverflow, Flickr, Craigslist, Pinterest. (Redis, 2016)

Aerospike

Aerospike is an Open Source, distributed in-memory Key Value NoSQL database written in C. It supports flexible data schemas and ACID transactions. Aerospike's in-memory performance leads to simpler Application Development and simpler deployment. (Penchikala, 2014) The name Aerospike is derived from a type of rocket nozzle that is able to maintain its output efficiency over a large range of altitudes and is intended to refer to the software's ability to scale up. (Wikipedia, 2017a)

The architecture of Aerospike consists of three layers: (Penchikala, 2014)

- **Client Layer:** This layer includes the Open Source client libraries with Aerospike APIs, track nodes in the cluster and is aware of where data resides in the Aerospike cluster.
- **Clustering and Data Distribution Layer:** This layer oversees Cluster Communications and automates capabilities like Fail Over, Replication and Cross Data Center Synchronization.
- **Data Storage Layer:** This layer is responsible for storing the data in DRAM and Flash.

Table 9. Key Features of Aerospike (Adapted from (Penchikala, 2014), (Mullins, 2015), (Aerospike, 2017b))

Key Features of Aerospike
Supports both RAM and Flash Storage
Ability to query using secondary indexes
Minimal up-front administration work
Superior uptime and availability
Strongly typed data model, in-database computation with user defined functions, rich list and map interfaces, geographic replication and a management console.
Provides open source libraries and packages in 10+ languages including Node.js, Java, C#, PHP, Go and more
Aerospike's aggregation system allows simple statistics and highly parallel map/reduce style computations.

Aerospike is successfully being used for storing user profiles, Fraud Detection and Real time billing. Organizations that are using this database are Snapdeal, Gree, Inmobi, Cazamba, etc. (Aerospike, 2017a)

Use Cases of Key Value Stores

- **Messaging Applications:** It is used in chat applications as it provides highly-available, low-latency data architecture. For example, General Electric uses Riak to enable Internal Messaging Systems connecting their employees with customers.

- **Session Data:** These databases were originally developed to serve as a highly scalable session store. For example, Virgin America and Flywheel uses Riak to store passenger information and session data.
- **Content and Documents:** These databases store JSON or XML or HTML files. They can also be used to store PDFs, images, articles or videos. For instance, bet365, Hibernum, Riot Games, Rovio all use Riak to store session data for gamers and players. (Basho, 2016)
- **User Profile Stores and Session Management:** Aerospike is used for these applications. (Penchikala, 2014)
- **Personalization of Advertising:** Aerospike is the database of choice for low latency applications such as optimization and personalization of advertising. (Penchikala, 2014)
- **Real Time Analysis:** Redis store is very easy to implement a Spam Filtering System or other real time tracking system. (information, 2016)
- **Gaming Experience:** Aerospike's low latency feature makes it a good candidate for gaming. (Penchikala, 2014)

Column Oriented Databases

Columnar databases store and process data by column instead of by row. Both rows and columns are split over multiple nodes to achieve scalability. The main inspiration for Column Oriented Databases is Google's Bigtable. Some popular Column Oriented databases are Cassandra, HBase and Druid.

Apache Cassandra

It is massively scalable Open Source NoSQL database. It is capable of managing large amounts of Structured, Semi-Structured and Unstructured data across multiple datacenters and the cloud. It is capable of handling thousands of concurrent users/operations per second. It is designed as a distributed database with peer-to-peer communication. It does not support Master-Slave Architecture. It was initially developed by Facebook and was later taken over by Apache. The core features of Cassandra have been extracted from Amazon's Dynamo and Google's Bigtable. The most basic way to interact with Cassandra is by using the CQL shell (cqlsh) or through a graphical tool called DevCenter.

The Cassandra installation includes the cqlsh utility, a Python based command line client for executing Cassandra Query Language (CQL) commands. The cqlsh command is used on Linux or Windows command line to start the cqlsh utility. (DataStax, 2017a)

DevCenter: DataStax DevCenter is an Integrated Development Environment (IDE) which facilitates creation and execution of Cassandra Query Language (CQL) statements for developers, administrators and others. Users can quickly add and create new connections, import previously saved queries and navigate database instances. Tabbed editors allow administrators to work on multiple database sessions at a time and compare results. DataStax DevCenter is a Java Application and requires at least JRE 6. (DataStax, 2017c)

Organizations using Cassandra are Walmart, Netflix, eBay, Comcast, etc. (DataStax Academy, 2016)

Table 10. Key Features of Apache Cassandra (Adapted from (DataStax, 2017b))

Key Features of Apache Cassandra
Continuous Availability
Automatic Data Distribution: Data is transparently partitioned across all nodes in a cluster.
No single point of failure
Flexible data model designed for fast response times
Built-in customizable Replication.
Linear Scalability: Cassandra supplies Linear Scalability, i.e. Capacity may be easily added simply by adding new nodes online. For example, if 2 nodes can handle 100,000 transactions per second, 4 nodes will support 200,000 transactions/sec and 8 nodes will tackle 400,000 transactions/sec. (DataStax, 2016)

APACHE HBASE

HBase is a high-performance, scalable, distributed non-relational data store built for Hadoop and modeled after Google's Bigtable. HBase scales linearly to handle huge data sets. It easily integrates data sources that uses a wide variety of different structures and schemas. HBase is natively integrated with Hadoop and works seamlessly alongside other data access engines through YARN. (Hortonworks, 2016)

Table 11. Key Features of Apache HBASE (Adapted from (Apache HBase, 2016), (Hortonworks, 2016))

Key Features of Apache HBASE
Linear and Modular Scalability
Provides random, low-latency, real time access to large datasets
Capable of high volume Query Optimization
Automatic Sharding and Load Balancing of tables
Supports consistent read and write operations
Supports MapReduce for parallel processing of large volumes of data
Flashback Queries Possible: Users can query HBase for a particular former time period/ point in time
HBase supports an easy to use Java API for programmatic access.
HBase supports Thrift and REST API for non-Java front-ends.
Operational Management: HBase provides build-in web pages for operational insight

HBase supports consistent read and write operations which makes it very suitable for tasks such as high speed counter aggregation. Some organizations using HBase are Mendeley, Twitter, Yahoo! etc. (Apache HBase, 2016)

Table 12. Comparison of HBase and Cassandra. (Adapted from (Gupta & Thomas, 2012))

HBase	Cassandra	Feature/Database
Ordered Partitioning	Random Partitioning	Partitioning
Can be done	Cannot be done	Row Key Range Scans
No Native Support but can be done through triggers	Supported	Secondary Indexes
Automatic	Not needed with Random Partitioning	Rebalancing
No	Yes	Static Columns
Strong	Eventual (Strong is optional)	Consistency

DRUID

Druid is an open-source analytics data store designed for Business Intelligence queries on event data. Druid is most commonly used to power user facing analytic applications. Druid is partially inspired by existing analytic data stores such as Google's BigQuery/Dremel, Google's PowerDrill and search infrastructure. Druid's native query language is JSON (Druid, 2016b) and accepts queries as POST requests. (Yang, Tschetter, Léauté & Nelso, 2016) Druid is designed to perform single table operations and does not currently support joins.

Table 13. Key Features of Druid (Adapted from (Druid, 2016a))

Key Features of Druid
Supports fast aggregations and sub-second OLAP queries.
Multidimensional-filtering: Druid's column data model and inverted indexes enable complex multi-dimensional filtering and scan only what is required for a query.
Highly Optimized Storage Format: Custom column format highly optimized for aggregations and filters.
Real-time Streaming Ingestion: Druid employs lock-free ingestion of append-heavy data sets that allows simultaneous ingestion and querying of 10,000+ events per second per node.
Powers Analytic Applications: Support Multi Tenancy and can handle thousands of concurrent users
Highly Available: Scales up or down without any data loss. Supports SaaS implementations which needs to be online all the time due to Druid's high availability
Supports rolling updates so that your data is available and query able during software updates.
Deploy anywhere: Druid runs on commodity hardware. It can be deployed in the cloud or on-premise and can be integrated with existing data systems such as Hadoop, Spark, Kafka, Storm, Flink and Samza.
No Single Point of failure

Druid is used to analyze Ad-Tech, Dev-Ops, Network Traffic, Cloud Security, Website Traffic, Finance and sensor data. Some organizations using Druid are eBay, inmobi, Airbnb, Alibaba, etc. (Druid, 2016b)

Use Cases of Column Oriented Databases

- **Online Web and Mobile Applications:** Apache Cassandra is a perfect database choice for online web and mobile applications (Sharma, S., S Tim, U., Wong, J. & Shashi, 2014)
- **Personalization:** AOL is an online brand providing- Content Generation, Content Value add (Geo-Tagging, Entity Tagging, Personalization) and Advertising. AOL uses Cassandra as an article index for several AOL technologies; including as a service layer that facilitates the storage and retrieval of many millions of articles. (DataStax Academy, 2016)
- **Stocks and Messaging:** BUX is a mobile application that makes the big-bucks world of stock trading accessible to everyone with the help of Apache Cassandra. Cassandra keeps track of user stock state and messaging. (DataStax Academy, 2016)
- **High Availability:** Coursera partners with universities worldwide to offer free massive open online courses to over 7 million users. Coursera is transitioning from MySQL to Cassandra to support their high availability demands. (DataStax Academy, 2016)
- **Large Storage:** Mendeley is creating a platform for researchers to collaborate and share their research online. HBase is being used to create the world's largest research paper collection and is being used to store all raw imported data. HBase with Pig is being used to do analytics and produce the article statistics shown on the web site. (Apache HBase, 2016)
- **Read/Write Backup:** Twitter runs HBase across its entire Hadoop cluster. HBase provides a distributed, read/write backup of all MySQL tables in Twitter's production backend. A number of applications including people search rely on HBase internally for data generation. Additionally, the operations team uses HBase as a time series database for cluster-wide monitoring/performance data. (Apache HBase, 2016)
- **Biometric Data Storage:** Yahoo! uses HBase to store document fingerprint for detecting near duplications. (Apache HBase, 2016)
- **Realtime Reporting and Analysis:** inmobi is a mobile advertising and discovery platform. They use Druid majorly for internal real time reporting and analysis. They also use Caravel backend by Druid which allows users to build interactive dashboards. Apart from that, they use Druid as a Datastore for faster ingestion of large amounts of data and to query this data at sub second latencies. (Druid, 2016)

Document Oriented Databases

Document Oriented Databases are basically Key Value stores with additional features. They store and retrieve data as documents. A document consists of multiple Key Value pairs and it offers flexible schema. Document databases provide high performance when working with complex datasets. It also supports indexing. Some popular Open Source Document Oriented databases are MongoDB, CouchDB, RaptorDB, Terrastore and RavenDB.

MONGODB

MongoDB is an open source database written in C++, which stores data as documents. A MongoDB server has multiple databases. A database is composed of a number of collections. A collection is a group of documents. Documents have dynamic schema which means that documents in the same collection do not need to have the same set of fields or structure. Every document has a unique id (12 bytes hexadecimal number, _id: ObjectId (4 bytes timestamp, 3 bytes machine id, 2 bytes process id, 3 bytes incrementer)). If we don't specify the _id parameter, then MongoDB itself assigns a unique ObjectId to the document. In MongoDB, there is no concept of relationship but still it retains some properties of MySQL.

Table 14. Key Features of MongoDB (Adapted from (Roy, 2014), (Tutorials Point, 2016))

Key Features of MONGODB
MongoDB supports Map/Reduce framework
Master-Slave Replication
Sharding: It supports horizontal scaling through Sharding.
MongoDB Management Service (MMS) is a powerful web tool that allows users to track databases and machines and take back up of their data
GridFs - It allows MongoDB to store large files. GridFs divides a file into chunks and stores each chunk of data in a separate document, each of maximum size 255k.

A large number of organizations and startups uses MongoDB to gain useful insight of their business. At a lecture in September 2015, DevIttycheria, MongoDB's Chief Executive Officer, stated that the project is designed as technology "for startups that want to be enterprises and enterprises that want to be startups" (Taft, 2015). One such startup is x.ai. The company's founder, Alex Poon told eWeek that the flexibility of MongoDB's schema and its simplicity has made it "fundamental to our success early on when we were changing the data model weekly and remains so today with our focus on continuous integration through weekly sprints." The developer of an Artificial Intelligence - powered personal assistant says it uses MongoDB to support its Natural Language Processing, Supervised Learning, Analytics and Email. Some users in the growing list of organizations using MongoDB includes The Weather Channel, City of Chicago, Bosch Software Innovations, eBay, Metlife, Chico's FAS, Inc., ShopStage and AHL Man Group.(Aloto, 2015)

COUCHDB

Apache CouchDB is an Open Source database storing data in the form of documents having unique names or ids. Each document has two kinds of fields, metafields and datafields, where metafields include information like id and revision number of the document and data fields are user defined fields. A revision number identifies how many times the document has been modified. (CouchDB Tutorial, 2016) CouchDB is written in Erlang and provides an API called RESTful HTTP API for reading and updating (add, edit and delete) database documents. It uses JSON format (field/value pairs), for storing data and giving responses. Its field values can be strings, numbers, dates or ordered lists.

Table 15. Key Features of CouchDB (CouchDocs, 2016)

Key Features of COUCHDB
MVCC (Multi Version Concurrency Control)
Multi - Master Replication
Fault Tolerant
Futon, a browser based GUI
Replication Filters

It is used in large and small organizations for a variety of applications where a traditional SQL database isn't the best solution for the problem at hand. Some popular adopters of CouchDB are The BBC (for its dynamic content platforms), npm (for their package registry) and Credit Suisse (for internal use at commodities department for their marketplace framework). (Wikipedia, 2016c)

Table 16. MongoDB vs CouchDB (Adapted from (DB-Engines, 2017b))

MongoDB	CouchDB
Database contains collections. Collection contains documents	Database contains documents
Written in C++	Written in Erlang
Master-Slave Replication	Master-Master Replication
Offers strong consistency of data	Offers high availability of database
Uses BSON to store data	Uses JSON to store data

RAVENDB

RavenDB is an open source document database for .NET. RavenDB is transactional and schema-less. A transactional database is a Database Management System (DBMS) that has the capability to roll back or undo a database transaction or operation if it is not completed appropriately. It also supports ACID (Atomicity, Consistency, Isolation and Durability) properties. It allows you to build high-performance, low-latency applications with ease and efficiency.

Table 17. Key Features of RavenDB (Adapted from (RavenDB, 2016a))

Key Features of RAVENDB
Multi -master replication
Sharding
Supports Triggers

A large and growing number of organizations are using RavenDB because of its performance, schema-less architecture and reliability. Some of these popular organizations are Octopus Deploy Ltd., Beatman Ltd., msnbc.com and WebstepFokus. (RavenDB, 2016b)

One of the startups using RavenDB includes Truth Vine. The founder of the startup chose RavenDB because it has Automatic Indexing, Replication Support available and active community contributing to the project. (Genesky, 2013)

Use Cases of Document Oriented Databases

- **Mobile:** Document Oriented databases can build mobile apps that can scale up to millions of users. For example: The Weather Channel uses MongoDB to handle 2 million requests per minute and provides real-time weather alerts for 40 million users by their mobile application. (MongoDB, 2016)
- **Content Management**: These databases can store and serve any type of content, build any feature, incorporate any kind of data in a single database. For instance, Forbes uses MongoDB to gain critical insights into social sharing of their articles, to capitalize on stories going viral in real-time. (MongoDB, 2016)
- **Personalization:** They can personalize the experience of millions of customers in real time. Expedia using MongoDB, to send special travel offers to its users in real time by tracking their searches and comparisons across its site, serves as a perfect example. (MongoDB, 2016)
- **E-Commerce**: These databases also contribute in trading products electronically. For example, RavenDB is used by Adlersoftware, Germany to model and partition data to solve their business needs. (RavenDB, 2016b)
- **Backend Store**: Document Oriented databases like RavenDB are used by many prominent high traffic websites including msnbc.com for Traffic Management. (RavenDB, 2016b)

GRAPH DATABASES

Today's world is no longer revolving around data merely; it's also being driven by the connections between them. Businesses now a days need real-time insights into how data is related to make strategic decisions. Data relationships drive today's intelligent applications and there is a need of storage tool that is capable of exploiting this connection and optimize the competitive advantage. Graph databases provide this solution. (Neo4j, 2016)

A Graph Database is amalgamation of nodes and edges. Each node represents an entity (such as a person or business) and each edge represents a connection/relationship between two nodes. Each node and edge can have properties in key/value form. Graph Databases are schema free and don't need data typing so inherently are very flexible. Traversal is lightning fast as it uses index free adjacency. It supports ACID transactions to ensure predictability of queries. (Hurwitz, Nugent, Halper & Kaufman, 2013)

It has one limitation that it cannot reference itself. The mantra of graph database enthusiasts is "If you can whiteboard it, you can graph it." (Rouse, 2016). Some well-known open-source graph databases include Neo4J graph database, OrientDB and Velocity Graph.

NEO4J DATABASE

Neo4j is first and world's leading graph database. It is used by thousands of organizations including 50+ of the Global 2000 organizations. It is most widely deployed (around 500,000+ downloads) and has largest ecosystem: active forums, code contributions, etc. (Neo4j, 2016)

Neo4j is built to harness the power of graphs for real-time, bottom-line insights. It is an open source project licensed under the GNU public license v3.0. Neo4j query language "Cypher" is very easy to learn and we can choose from APIs and drivers for all major languages. (Florescu, 2006)

Neo4j is the only enterprise-strength graph database that combines native graph storage with Native GPE (Graph Processing Engine). It has a scalable architecture optimized for speed.

Table 18. Key Features of Neo4J Database (Adapted from (Neo4j, 2016), (Hurwitz, Nugent, Halper & Kaufman, 2013))

Key Features of Neo4j Database
Robust and Flexible
Schema less
Scalable
Interactive User Interface
Self-referencing not allowed
Replicates entire graphs
High Performance
Embedded persistence engine for efficient management of semi structured and network oriented data.

Popular adapters of Neo4j are Walmart, eBay, Adidas, Cisco HMP, Musicmap Cognitive Technologies, wobi - a price comparison site, ICIJ- the International Consortium of Investigative Journalists, megree, gamesys, Glowbl, LinkedIn, classmates.com, Telenor, migRaven, Qualia.

ORIENT DATABASE

OrientDB is the first Multi-Model Open Source NoSQL DBMS that combines the flexibility of documents and strength of graph. It is licensed under Apache2 terms, which means that it's free for any usage, even commercial. OrientDB can be used as a pure Graph Database (using TinkerPop standard) or as a Multi-Model. It is developed in pure Java. It provides commendable level of user and record level security. It uses extended SQL to support graph functionality. (OrientDB, 2017a)

It can store documents similar to document database but unlike traditional document database it embraces relationships by using super-fast pointer as used in graph databases instead of using slow and heavy joins. For example, original record is bifurcated and they are joined by using some id by which one document references other document.

Table 19. Key Features of OrientDB (Adapted from (OrientDB, 2017c))

Key Features of OrientDB
Multi Master architecture
Sharding
Object Oriented
Schema-less, schema-full and schema-mix modes
Elastic Scalability with zero configuration (nodes can be added without complex configuration)

OrientDB's multi-model database is popular among startups and large enterprises due to its unmatched enhanced security, performance, reliability and swiftness and is impeccable for virtually any use case. (OrientDB, 2017c)

Organizations that are using OrientDB successfully are Comcast, Warner music group, sky, Ericsson, CenturyLink, VeriSign, Kyocera, Sonatype, Progress, UltraDNS, RTI IU, Diaku Axon, Massiv.io and many more.

Table 20. OrientDB vs Neo4j (Adapted from (DB-Engines, 2017a) & (Mosters, 2014))

OrientDB	Neo4j
Multi-model – having features of document database additional to graph database	Supports only graph database features
It supports multi-master feature and sharding architecture	It supports Master/slave architecture
Uses SQL language, thus reducing training span. Other access methods are Java API RESTful HTTP/JSON API, Tinkerpop technology stack with Blueprints, Gremlin, Pipes	Uses cypher query language, which need expertise. Other access methods are Java API and RESTful HTTP API
It supports only the "label" concept to group vertices and edges of the same type. It does not use concepts of inheritance, polymorphism or complex constraints, but only the uniqueness of values by using indexes.	OrientDB supports the creation of schemas around graphs. We can create subclasses of Vertex and edge using object oriented concepts of inheritance and polymorphism.
Does not use Multithreading and mapping	Uses Multithreading and mapping
Access rights for users and roles; record level security are configurable	Very less security features are supported
Community Edition is free and supports clustering, sharding, replication and fault tolerance	Community Edition is free with no clustering facility.

Use Cases of Graph Database

- **Real Time Recommendations:** Recommendation engines powered by graph databases help companies personalize products, content and services by exploiting the connections between data in real time. For example – Adidas, Walmart, Wazoku, Wanderu, InfoJobs, Musicmap cognitive technologies and Wobi are using Neo4j
- **Master Data Management:** Master data, such as organizational and product data, has deep hierarchies with top-down, lateral and diagonal connections. For example, Neo4j is the heart of Cisco

HMP - used for governance and single source of truth and a one-stop shop for all of Cisco's hierarchies (Lyon, 2016). Other companies using Neo4j are Adidas, Schleich, Candiolo Cancer Institute (performs molecular and biological tests on cancer samples), Pitney Bowes, Die Bayerische and WDS -Wine Data System.

- **Fraud Detection**: Graph Databases offer new methods of uncovering fraud rings and other scams with a high level of accuracy and are capable of stopping advanced fraud scenarios in real-time. (Sadowski & Rathle, 2016)
- **Graph Based Search**: Lufthansa uses Neo4j to manage the digital assets. Other organizations using Neo4j for search are Adidas, Schleich. Massiv.io, Diaku Axon.
- **Network and IT Operations:** Organizations like Billes, vivendi SFR (partnering with Vodafone) are using Neo4j for their network and IT operations (Marzi, 2014). HP uses Neo4j for network topology analysis for big telecom service providers.
- **Identity and Access Management**: Neo4j can be used to seamlessly track all identity and access relationships (who can access what) with substantial depth and real-time results. For example – Telenor, migRaven, Qualia are using Neo4j.
- **Social Network**: Graph Databases are used to harness declared social connections or infer relationships between them based on activity. For example, Facebook, Megree, Gamesys, Glowbl, LinkedIn, classmates.com use Neo4j. (Neo4j, 2016)
- **Effective Traffic Management:** OrientDB exploits and processes large amounts of traffic data to intuitively analyze and act upon real-time information to find alternate routes, predict movements and safely store information. Locomotive industry, location service and security industry also use OrientDB for different purposes. (OrientDB, 2017b)

Spatial Database

A Spatial Database is a database that is optimized to store and query data that represents objects defined in a geometric space. (Rouse, 2013) Spatial data is standardized through the efforts of OGC - Open Geospatial Consortium which establishes OpenGIS - Geographic Information System and a number of other standards for spatial data. In easy terms, spatial databases store data about 2-dimensional, 2.5-dimensional and 3-dimensional objects. 2.5D objects are a special type of spatial data. They are 2D objects with elevation as the extra "half" dimension. Most 2.5D spatial databases contain mapping information and are often referred to as Geographic Information Systems (GISs) (Hurwitz, Nugent, Halper & Kaufman, 2013). The most commonly used spatial database is PostGIS/OpenGEO suite.

PostGIS

PostGIS is a spatial database extender for PostgreSQL object-relational database. It adds support for geographic objects allowing location queries to be run in SQL and provides ACID transactions (PostGIS, 2016). It is licensed under the GNU General Public License. PostGIS is also supplied as part of the OpenGeo Suite Community Edition and is offered and supported by OpenGeo under an enterprise license.

Mostly, maps and locations involve use of spatial data. Other applications could be precise 3D modeling of the human body, buildings, the atmosphere, and so on, gathering and analysis of data from sensor networks and integration with historical data to examine 3D space/objects over time.

Table 21. Key Features of PostGIS (Adapted from (Techopedia, 2016), (Hurwitz, Nugent, Halper & Kaufman, 2013))

Key Features of PostGIS
Supports ACID transactions
Uses lightweight implementations and hence have commendable speed

Use Cases of Spatial Data

- GlobeXplorer is a division of Digital Globe devoted to pushing imagery out to consumers.
- North Dakota State Water Commission has allowed the IT folks to start to provide direct access to scientists who are extracting and analyzing data directly from the database using scripting languages (Refractions Research, n.d.).
- Adoption of Big Data tools across Industries/Start Ups
- Cloudera pioneered the Hadoop based Big Data space. Cloudera lets users query their structured and unstructured data to gain insights from the data. Its adopters: Experian, FICO, Western Union, Intel.
- Hortonworks provide an open-source Apache Hadoop based Big Data solution. Their customers include eBay, Bloomberg.
- Aerospike provide a hybrid-memory (DRAM and Flash) NoSQL database for mission critical, real-time Big Data driven apps. Customers include eBay, Acuity, Federated Media Publishing, x+1, The Trade Desk and madvertise.
- Couchbase provides NoSQL database technology to its customers like AOL, Cisco, Concur, LinkedIn, Orbitz, Salesforce.com, Zynga, Amadeus, McGraw-Hill Education and Nielsen.
- MapR Technologies provide a Hadoop distribution/NoSQL Big Data platform. Their customers include Aadhaar (The World's largest Biometric Identity System), Ancestry.com, Rubicon, HP and comScore (Mapr, 2016).
- Companies using Apache Spark – Baidu, Databricks, NASA JPL, Yahoo (Apache, 2016).
- MongoDB adopters – Genentech, Royal Bank of Scotland, BuzzFeed, Facebook etc., Expedia, cisco (MongoDB, 2016).
- Users of Druid – Airbnb, Alibaba, Hulu, Inmobi (Druid, 2016).
- Talend offers products based on Open Source software focused on Big Data, cloud and application integration. Its customers include GE, Citi, Lufthansa, Orange and Virgin Mobile. (Noyes, 2016).

FUTURE RESEARCH DIRECTIONS

The incredible growth experienced by Open Source programs in Big Data application world is the real proof that it is the future of Big Data. With the shortage of data scientists and skilled workers, companies and individuals will always find it easier to opt for readily available, reliable and up to date Open Source Software (Augur, 2016). As Big Data continues to grow in size and importance, the list of Open Source tools for working with it will certainly continue to grow alongside.

CONCLUSION

Open Source Softwares are the dominant force in Big Data development today. The development, deployment and usage of Big Data applications using Open Source Softwares has seen a tremendous growth because of collaborative features and low upfront cost requirement of Open Source Softwares. There are countless Open Source solutions for working with Big Data, many of them specialized to provide optimal features and performance for a specific niche or for specific hardware configurations. This chapter provided a list of some Open Source tools, their applications and their adoption by organizations dealing with various Big Data Storage applications.

REFERENCES

Aerospike Inc. (2017a). *Aerospike customers, Deployed, mission critical apps requiring speed, scale and stability*. Retrieved on January 10, 2017 from http://www.aerospike.com/customers/#

Aerospike Inc. (2017b). *Product Matrix*. Retrieved January 11, 2017 from http://www.aerospike.com/products/

Aerospike Inc. (2017c). *What is a Key-Value Store?* Retrieved May 3, 2017 from-http://www.aerospike.com/what-is-a-key-value-store/

Aloto, E. (2015). *Who's Using MongoDB and Why?* Retrieved October 26, 2016 https://www.datavail.com/blog/whos-using-mongodb-and-why/

Apache HBase. (2017). *Hbase Con2017. Welcome to Apache HBase*. Retrieved October 25, 2016 from http://hbase.apache.org/

Apache Spark. (2016). *Project and Product names using "Spark"*. The Apache Software Foundation. Retrieved October 10, 2016 from http://spark.apache.org/powered-by.html

Augur, H. (2016). *The Future of Big Data is Open Source*. Dataconomy Media GMBH. Retrieved September 30, 2016 from http://dataconomy.com/the-future-of-big-data-is-open-source/

Basho. (2016). *Riak KV*. Retrieved November 8, 2016 from http://basho.com/products/riak-kv/

Basho Technologies. (2011-2017). *Why Riak KV*. Retrieved December 8, 2016 from http://docs.basho.com/riak/kv/2.2.0/learn/why-riak-kv/

Brockmeier, J. (2013). *How Picture Marketing is Using and Extending GlusterFS*. Retrieved October 30, 2016, from http://blog.gluster.org/category/use-case

Brooks, J. (2013). *GlusterFS Keeps VFX Studio on the Cutting Edge*. Retrieved November 6, 2016 from http://blog.gluster.org/2013/12/glusterfs-keeps-vfx-studio-on-the-cutting-edge

Cavanillas, J. M., Curry, E., & Wahlster, W. (2016). *New Horizons for a Data-Driven Economy, A Roadmap for Usage and Exploitation of Big Data in Europe*. Berlin, Germany: Springer International Publishing. Retrieved November 8, 2016 from http://www.springer.com/in/book/9783319215686

CouchDocs. (2016). *Apache CouchDB Wiki*. Apache CouchDB. Retrieved November 8, 2016 from https://cwiki.apache.org/confluence/display/COUCHDB/Apache+CouchDB+Wiki

DataStax. (2017b). *Featured Customers*. Retrieved November 3, 2016 from http://www.datastax.com/customers

DataStax Academy. (2016). *Companies using NoSQL Apache Cassandra, Planet Cassandra*. Retrieved October 29, 2016 from http://www.planetcassandra.org/com

DataStax, Inc. (2017a). *DataStax Distribution of Apache Cassandra 3.x for Windows*. Retrieved January 12, 2017 from http://docs.datastax.com/en/cassandra_win/3.x/index.html

DataStax Inc. (2017c). *NoSQL-Cassandra-and-Hadoop, Hadoop vs. Cassandra, Contrasting Hadoop & Apache Cassandra*. Retrieved February 15, 2017 from http://www.datastax.com/nosql-databases/nosql-cassandra-and-hadoop

DB-Engines. (2017a). *System Properties Comparison Neo4j vs. OrientDB*. Retrieved April 11, 2017 from http://db-engines.com/en/system/Neo4j%3BOrientDB

DB-Engines. (2017b). System Properties Comparison Couchbase vs. CouchDB vs. MongoDB Comparison. Retrieved January 23, 2017 from http://db-engines.com/en/system/CouchDB%3BCouchbase%3BMongoDB

Depardon, B., Le Mahec, G., & Seguin, C. (2013). *Analysis of Six Distributed File Systems. HAL, 1-39*. Retrieved December 8, 2016, from https://hal.inria.fr/hal-00789086/file/a_survey_of_dfs.pdf

Deshmukh, S. C., & Deshmukh, S. S. (2015). Simple Application of GlusterFs: Distributed file system for Academics. *Proceedings of International Journal of Computer Science and Information Technologies, 6*(3), 2972–2974. Retrieved October 15, 2016 from http://ijcsit.com/docs/Volume%206/vol6issue03/ijcsit20150603218.pdf

Druid. (2016). *About Druid*. Retrieved October 25, 2016 from http://druid.io/druid.html

Druid. (2016). *Powered by Druid*. Retrieved October 25, 2016 from http://druid.io/druid-powered.html

Florescu, D. (2006). The Neo Database. *ACM Queue; Tomorrow's Computing Today, 3*(8). Retrieved October 17, 2016 from http://dist.neo4j.org/neo-technology-introduction.pdf

Genesky, E. (2013). Why I Chose RavenDB for My Startup. *Dzone*. Retrieved October 26, 2016 from https://dzone.com/articles/why-i-chose-ravendb-my-startup-0

Gluster, F. S. Developers. (2006). *Gluster File System 3.3.0 Administration Guide, Using Gluster File System*. Retrieved October 30, 2016 from https://www.gluster.org/wp-content/uploads/2012/05/Gluster_File_System-3.3.0- Administration_Guide-en- US.pdf

Gulati, S. (2011). Introduction to Redis - In Memory Key Value Datastore. *Dzone*. Retrieved October 28, 2016, from https://dzone.com/articles/introduction-to-redis-in-memory-key-value-datastore

Gupta, A., & Thomas, L. (2012). *HBase Vs Cassandra*. BigDataNoob. Retrieved November 3, 2016 from http://bigdatanoob.blogspot.in/2012/11/hbase-vs-cassandra.html

Hadoop Wiki. (2017). *Powered by Apache Hadoop*. Retrieved March 4, 2017 from https://wiki.apache.org/hadoop/PoweredBy

High Scalability. (2011). *11 Common Web Use Cases Solved In Redis*. Retrieved on October 28, 2016 from http://highscalability.com/blog/2011/7/6/11-common-web-use-cases-solved-in-redis.html

Hortonworks Inc. (2017). *Apache HBase*. Retrieved on April 15, 2017 from http://hortonworks.com/apache/hbase/#section_1

Hurwitz, J. S., Nugent, A., Halper, F., & Kaufman, M. (2013). *Big Data For Dummies*. Hoboken, NJ: John Wiley & Sons, Inc. Retrieved on October 25, 2016 from http://eecs.wsu.edu/~yinghui/mat/courses/fall%202015/resources/Big%20data%20for%20dummies.pdf

Kumar, M. (2015). *Characterizing The GlusterFS Distributed File System for Software Defined Networks Research*. The State University of New Jersey. Retrieved October 8, 2016 from https://rucore.libraries.rutgers.edu/rutgers-lib/46377/PDF/1/

Kune, R., Konugurthi, K. P., Agarwal, A., Chillarige, R. R., & Buyya, R. (2016*). The anatomy of big data computing. Journal of Software-Practices & Experience, 46(1),* 79-105. Retrieved October 8, 2016 from http://dl.acm.org/citation.cfm?id=2904654

LiNUXLiNKS. (2015). *6 Best File Systems for Big Data*. Retrieved October 7, 2016 from http://www.linuxlinks.com/article/20130411155608341/FileSystems.html

Lustre. (2016a). *Getting Started With Lustre*. Retrieved November 8, 2016 from http://lustre.org/getting-started-with-lustre/

Lustre. (2016b). *About the Lustre File System*. Retrieved November 8, 2016 from http://lustre.org/about/

Lyon, W. (2016). *Introduction to Neo4j and Graph Databases. Neo4j Webinar conducted in March 2016*. Retrieved November 22, 2016 from www.slideshare.net/neo4j/intro-to-neo4j-and-graph-databases

MapR Technologies, Inc. (2016). *MapR Customers, Audi*. Retrieved October 10, 2016 from https://googleweblight.com/?lite_url=https://www.mapr.com/customers/

Marzi, M.D. (2014). *Graph Databases Use Cases*. SlideShare. Retrieved October 17, 2016 from https://www.slideshare.net/maxdemarzi/graph-database-use-cases

MongoDB. (2017). *Use Cases, Giant Ideas Brought to Life*. Retrieved May 24, 2017 from https://www.mongodb.com/use-cases

Mosters, C. (2015). OrientDB vs Neo4j, Comparisons (querys and functionality). SlideShare. Retrieved November 8, 2016 from https://www.slideshare.net/kwoxer/orientdb-vs-neo4j-comparison-of-queryspeedfunctionality

Mullins, C. S. (2015). *Aerospike NoSQL DBMS overview*. Retrieved October 29, 2016 from http://searchdatamanagement.techtarget.com/feature/Aerospike-NoSQL-DBMS-overview

NASA nasa.gov. (2016). *Pleiades Lustre Filesystems*. Retrieved December 8, 2016 from https://www.nas.nasa.gov/hecc/support/kb/pdf-cat/102/

Neo4j. (2016). *Neo4j: The World's Leading Graph Database. Products.* Retrieved October 16, 2016 from https://neo4j.com/product/

Neo4j., Neo Technology, Inc. (2017). *Customer Interviews.* Retrieved January 26, 2017 from https://neo4j.com/customers/

Noyes, K. (2016). Why open source is the 'new normal' for big data. *InfoWorld.* Retrieved October 2, 2016 from http://www.infoworld.com/article/3025931/big-data/why-open-source-is-the-new-normal-for-big-data.html

ObjectRocket. (2015). *Top 5 Redis use cases.* Retrieved October 28, 2016 from http://objectrocket.com/blog/how-to/top-5-redis-use-cases

OrientDB Ltd. (2017). *OrientDB Version 3.0.* Retrieved October 15, 2016 from http://orientdb.com/

OrientDB Ltd. (2017). *Effective Traffic Management With OrientDB.* Traffic Management- White Paper. Retrieved April 21, 2017 from http://orientdb.com/traffic-management_white-paper/

OrientDB Ltd. (2017). *Why OrientDB? OrientDB, Multi-Model Database.* Retrieved October 15, 2016 from http://orientdb.com/why-orientdb/

Ovsiannikov, M., Rus, S., Reeves, D., Sutter, P., Rao, S., & Kelly, J. (2013). *The Quantcast File System.* In *Proceedings of the 39th International Conference on Very Large Data Bases. Proceedings of the VLDB Endowment International Conference on Very Large Data Bases, 6*(11). Retrieved October 7, 2016 from http://www.cs.utah.edu/~hari/teaching/bigdata/qfs-ovsiannikov.pdf

Patten, B. (2015). *How Startups Are Using Big Data Tech to Disrupt Markets.* Retrieved October 28, 2016 from https://www.datanami.com/2015/03/17/how-startups-are-using-big-data-tech-to-disrupt-markets/

Penchikala, S. (2014). Aerospike NoSQL Database Architecture. *Infoq.* Retrieved October 29, 2016 from https://www.infoq.com/articles/aerospike-qa

PostGIS. (2016). *PostGIS, Spatial and Geographic objects for PostgreSQL.* Retrieved October 15, 2016 from http://www.postgis.net/

QFS. (n. d.). *Quantcast File System.* Retrieved October 30, 2016 from https://quantcast.github.io/qfs/

Quantcast. (2017a). *Quantcast Advertise, Unique data, better advertising.* Retrieved October 30, 2016 from https://www.quantcast.com/advertise/

Quantcast. (2017b). *Quantcast File System, Bigger Data, Smaller Bills.* Retrieved October 30, 2016 from https://www.quantcast.com/about-us/quantcast-file-system/

RavenDB. (2016a). *RavenDB, Safe by Default, Optimized for Efficiency. The open source NoSQL database for. NET.* Retrieved December 7, 2016 from https://ravendb.net/features

RavenDB. (2016b). *Testimonials.* Retrieved November 8, 2016 from http://ravendb.net/testimonials

Redis. (2016). *Introduction to Redis, redislabs.* Retrieved October 28, 2016 from http://redis.io/

Redmond, E., & Daily, J. (2013). *A Little Riak Book.* Retrieved October 27, 2016 from http://docshare.tips/little-riak-book_58567376b6d87f725d8b60f3.html

Refractions Research. (n. d.). *PostGIS Introduction and Case Studies, What is it, who is using it, and why?* Retrieved October 27, 2016 from http://www.refractions.net/expertise/whitepapers/postgis-case-studies/postgis-case-studies.pdf

Rego, F. (2014). *Open Source Continues to Drive Big Data, But Challenges Remain.* Wellesley Information Services. Retrieved October 10, 2016 from http://data-informed.com/linux-open-source-continue-drive-big-data-challenges-remain/

IDC Research, Inc. (2015). *New IDC Forecast Sees Worldwide Big Data Technology and Services Market Growing to $48.6 Billion in 2019, Driven by Wide Adoption Across Industries.* Retrieved October 12, 2016 from http://www.idc.com/getdoc.jsp?containerId=prUS40560115

Rouse, M. (2013a). Spatial data. *TechTarget.* Retrieved on October 27, 2016 TechTarget: http://searchsqlserver.techtarget.com/definition/spatial-data

Rouse, M. (2013b). GlusterFS (Gluster File System)? - Definition from WhatIs.Com. *TechTarget.* Retrieved October 29, 2016 from http://searchstorage.techtarget.com/definition/GlusterFS-Gluster-File-System

Rouse, M. (2016). *Graph database. Techtarget.* Retrieved October 27, 2016 from http://whatis.techtarget.com/definition/graph-database

Rouse, M. (n.d.). Open Source Software (OSS). *Techtarget.* Retrieved October 3, 2016 from http://searchenterpriselinux.techtarget.com/definition/open-source-software

Roy, J. (2014). MongoDB: Characteristics and future. *MongoDB Spain.* Retrieved December 7, 2016 from http://www.mongodbspain.com/en/2014/08/17/mongodb-characteristics-future/

Sadowski, G., & Rathle, P. (2016). Why Modern Fraud Detection Needs Graph Database Technology. *Neo4j Blog.* Retrieved November 23, 2016 from https://neo4j.com/blog/fraud-detection-graph-database-technology/

Sharma, S., & Tim, S. U., Wong, J. & Shashi (2014). A Brief Review on Leading Big Data Models. *Data Science Journal, 13(4).* Retrieved October 29, 2016 from http://lib.dr.iastate.edu/cgi/viewcontent.cgi?article=2055&context=abe_eng_pubs

Sun Microsystems Inc. (2007). *LUSTRE™ FILE SYSTEM: High-Performance Storage Architecture and Scalable Cluster File System* (White Paper). Retrieved October 29, 2016 from http://www.csee.ogi.edu/~zak/cs506-pslc/lustrefilesystem.pdf

Taft, D. (2015). MongoDB Empowers 'Giant Ideas' for Innovators. *eWeek News.* Retrieved November 22, 2016 from http://www.eweek.com/database/mongodb-empowers-giant-ideas-for-innovators.html

Techopedia Inc. (2017). *Spatial Database,* Retrieved November 23, 2016 from https://www.techopedia.com/definition/17287/spatial-database

Toponce, A. (2017). *GlusterFS Linked List Topology,* Retrieved May 3, 2017 from https://pthree.org/2013/01/25/glusterfs-linked- list-topology/

Tutorials Point. (2017). *CouchDB Tutorial.* Tutorials point simply easy learning. Retrieved November 8, 2016 from https://www.tutorialspoint.com/couchdb/

Vance, J. (2014). Big Data 50-2017 Group 2 Vote. *Startup 50*. Retrieved November 8, 2016 from Startup50.com

w3ants. (2017). Get Instant Access To Actionable Big Data Ebooks – For Free Hands- On Data Analytics Education For Busy Working Professionals. Retrieved May 25, 2017 from http://w3ants.com/abc/get-instant-access-actionable-big-data-ebooks-free-hands-data-analytics-education-busy-working-professionals/

Wikipedia. (2017a). *Aerospike database*. Retrieved October 29, 2016 from https://en.wikipedia.org/wiki/Aerospike_database

Wikipedia. (2017b). *Quantcast File System*. Retrieved October 30, 2016 from https://en.wikipedia.org/wiki/Quantcast_File_System

Wikipedia. (2017c). *Open-source software*. Retrieved October 30, 2016 from https://en.wikipedia.org/wiki/Open-source_software

Yang, F., Tschetter, E., Léauté, X., Ray, N., Merlino, G., & Ganguli, D. (2016). Druid A Real-time Analytical Data Store. In *Proceedings of the 2014 ACM SIGMOD International Conference on Management of Data SIGMOD '14* (pp. 157-168). Retrieved October 25, 2016 from static.druid.io/docs/druid.pdf

Zicari, R. V. (2013). *Big Data: Improving Hadoop for Petascale Processing at Quantcast. ODBMS.org*. Retrieved October 30, 2016 from http://www.odbms.org/blog/2013/03/big-data-improving-hadoop-for-petascale-processing-at-quantcast/

ADDITIONAL READING

Bertozzi, M. (2013). How Scaling Really Works in Apache Hbase. *Cloudera Engineering Blog*. Retrieved from https://blog.cloudera.com/blog/2013/04/how-scaling-really-works-in-apache-hbase/

Buerli, M. (2012). The Current State of Graph Databases. *Semanticscholar*. Retrieved from https://pdfs.semanticscholar.org/5b5b/6b80badccd291e3437460222e24326c65979.pdf

Bushik, S. (2016). *A Vendor-independent Comparison of NoSQL Databases: Cassandra, HBase, Mongodb, Riak*. Retrieved from https://s3-eu-west-1.amazonaws.com/benstopford/nosql-comp.pdf

Cartoon, H. D. F. S. (2016). *Hadoop Distributed File System (HDFS)*. Retrieved from https://wiki.scc.kit.edu/gridkaschool/upload/1/18/Hdfs-cartoon.pdf

Finley, K. (2012). NoSQL: The Love Child of Google, Amazon and … Lotus Notes. *Wired*. Retrieved from https://www.wired.com/2012/12/couchdb/

Hanson, J. J. (2011). An introduction to the Hadoop Distributed File System Explore HDFS framework and subsystems. *IBM*. Retrieved from https://www.ibm.com/developerworks/library/wa-introhdfs/

Henricsson, R. (2011). *Document Oriented NoSQL Databases: A comparison of performance in MongoDB and CouchDB using a Python interface* [Bachelor Thesis]. Retrieved from https://www.diva-portal.org/smash/get/diva2:832580/FULLTEXT01.pdf

Issa, A., & Schiltz, F. (2015). *Document Oriented Databases*. Universite Libre de Bruxelles Retrieved from http://cs.ulb.ac.be/public/_media/teaching/infoh415/student_projects/couchdb.pdf

Kaur, J., Kaur, H., & Kaur, K. J. (2013). A Review on Document Oriented and Column Oriented Databases. *International Journal of Computer Trends and Technology, 4*(3), 338–344. Retrieved from http://ijcttjournal.org/Volume4/issue-3/IJCTT-V4I3P128.pdf

Khurana, A. (2012). *Introduction to HBase Schema Design*. Retrieved from http://0b4af6cdc2f0c5998459-c0245c5c937c5dedcca3f1764ecc9b2f.r43.cf2.rackcdn.com/9353-login1210_khurana.pdf

Kumar, M. (2015). *Characterizing The GlusterFS Distributed File System For Software Defined Networks Research*. Rutgers, The State University of New Jersey. Retrieved from https://rucore.libraries.rutgers.edu/rutgers-lib/46377/PDF/1/

Kumar, R. (2014). Apache Hadoop, NoSQL and NewSQL solutions of Big Data. *International Journal of Advance Foundation and Research in Science & Engineering, 1*(6), 28–36. Retrieved from www.ijafrse.org/Volume1/Vol_issue6/4.pdf

Miller, J. (2013). *Graph Database Applications and Concepts with Neo4j*. In *Proceedings of the Southern Association for Information Systems Conference, 24*, 141-147. Retrieved from http://aisel.aisnet.org/sais2013/24/

Mohr, R., Rossiter, J., Oral, S., Brim, M., Hill, J., Reed, J., & Imam, N. (2016). *Introduction to Lustre*. Oak Ridge National Laboratory. Retrieved from http://lustre.ornl.gov/lustre101-courses/content/C1/L1/LustreIntro.pdf

Moniruzzaman, A. B. M., & Hossain, S. A. (2013). NoSQL Database: New Era of Databases for Big Data Analytics- Classification, Characteristics and Comparison. *International Journal of Database Theory and Application, 6*(4), 1–14. Retrieved from https://arxiv.org/ftp/arxiv/papers/1307/1307.0191.pdf

Navelkar, S. (2016). *NoSQL: The future of data economy*. Retrieved from http://www.livemint.com/Opinion/ub2sqRtvuGDgDPDDTP7gtL/NoSQL-The-future-of-data-economy.html

Patil, S., Vaswani, G., & Bhatia, A. (2014). Graph Databases-An Overview. *International Journal of Computer Science and Information Technologies, 5*(1), 657–660. Retrieved from http://www.ijcsit.com/docs/Volume%205/vol5issue01/ijcsit20140501141.pdf

Pore, S. S., & Pawar, S. B. (2015). Comparative Study of SQL & NoSQL Databases. *International Journal of Advanced Research in Computer Engineering & Technology, 4*(5), 1747–1753. Retrieved from http://ijarcet.org/wp-content/uploads/IJARCET-VOL-4-ISSUE-5-1747-1753.pdf

Rigaux, P., Scholl, M., & Voisard, A. (2002). *Spatial Databases: With Application to GIS*. Burlington, MA; Morgan Kaufmann Publishers. Retrieved from http://bsolano.com/ecci/claroline/backends/download.php/TGlicm9zX2RlX3RleHRvL1NwYXRpYWxEQnNXaXRoQXBwbGljYXRpb25Ub0dJUy5wZGY%3D?cidReset=true&cidReq=CI1314

Rus, S. (2016). Quantcast File System (QFS) - Alternative to HDFS. Quantcast – Petabyte Storage at Half Price with QFS. *SlideShare*. Retrieved from http://www.slideshare.net/bigdatagurus_meetup/quantcast-file-system-qfs-alternative-to-hdfs-55057370

Seeger, M. (2009). *Key Value Stores: a practical overview.* Retrieved on December 6, 2016 from http://blog.marc-seeger.de/assets/papers/Ultra_Large_Sites_SS09-Seeger_Key_Value_Stores.pdf

Sharma, S., & Tim, S. U., Wong, J. & Shashi (2014*). A Brief Review on Leading Big Data Models. Data Science Journal, 13(4),* 138-157. Retrieved from http://lib.dr.iastate.edu/cgi/viewcontent.cgi?article=2055&context=abe_eng_pubs

Shekhar, S., Chawla, S., Ravada, S., Fetterer, A., Liu, X., & Lu, C. T. (1999). Spatial Databases: Accomplishments and Research Needs. *IEEE Transactions on Knowledge and Data Engineering, 11*(1), 45–55. Retrieved from http://citeseerx.ist.psu.edu/viewdoc/download?doi=10.1.1.40.8043&rep=rep1&type=pdf doi:10.1109/69.755614

Sliwa, B. (2013). *Early adopters see Red Hat Storage Server as SAN alternative.* Retrieved from http://searchstorage.techtarget.com/news/2240187440/Early-adopters-see-Red-Hat-Storage-Server-as-SAN-alternative

Strauch, C. (2009). *NoSQL Databases.* (pp. 1-120). Retrieved from http://www.christof-strauch.de/nosqldbs.pdf

Suter, R. (2012) *MongoDB: An Introduction and Performance Analysis* [Seminar Thesis]. Retrieved from http://wiki.hsr.ch/Datenbanken/files/MongoDB.pdf

Teddyma. (2016). *Learn Cassandra.* GitBook. Retrieved from https://teddyma.gitbooks.io/learncassandra/content/about/about_cassandra.html

Vicknair, S., Macias, M., Zhao, Z., Nan, X., Chen, Y., & Wilkins, D. (2010). A Comparison of a Graph Database and a Relational Database: A Data Provenance Perspective. In *Proceedings of the 48th Annual Southeast Regional Conference (ACMSE'10)* (pp. 42:1– 42:6). New York, NY: ACM. Retrieved from https://pdfs.semanticscholar.org/4a30/343f3230dddd96fd6f79547fef9407262dbf.pdf

KEY TERMS AND DEFINITIONS

Distributed File Systems (DFS): A File System in which files are distributed across multiple storage resources but appear to users as they exist on a single location.

Geographic Replication: A replication system in which data is replicated across servers which are geographically apart to improve network performance.

Inode: In UNIX, inode is a data structure used to represent a file system object. It stores the attributes and disk block location of the file system object's data.

Master Slave Replication: Master Slave Replication allows data to be stored by a group of computers but it can be updated by only one member, the "master" of the group. Master is in charge of the group while several other database servers (the "slaves") keep copies of all the data that's been written to the master and can be queried. Data cannot be written to slaves directly.

Multi-Master Replication: It is a method of database replication in which a group of computers store and update data. All members can handle client requests and are responsible for transmitting modifications to rest of its group members.

MVCC (Multi Version Concurrency Control): It is a Concurrency Control method which allows concurrent access to the database without using any locking mechanism and by maintaining different versions of the same data.

Sharding: Sharding is a Database Partitioning scheme in which datasets are distributed across nodes for Load Balancing and improving performance.

This research was previously published in the Handbook of Research on Big Data Storage and Visualization Techniques; pages 123-150, copyright year 2018 by Engineering Science Reference (an imprint of IGI Global).

Index

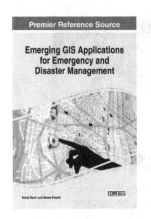

Printed in the United States
by Baker & Taylor Publisher Services

Printed in the United States
by Baker & Taylor Publisher Services